ECONOMIC DEVELOPMENT: THEORY AND PRACTICE FOR A DIVIDED WORLD

PRENTICE HALL SERIES IN ECONOMICS

Adams/Brock
The Structure of American Industry, Tenth Edition

Blanchard
Macroeconomics, Third Edition

Blau/Ferber/Winkler
The Economics of Women, Men, and Work,
Fourth Edition

Boardman/Greenberg/Vining/Weimer
Cost Benefit Analysis: Concepts and Practice,
Second Edition

Bogart
The Economics of Cities and Suburbs

Case/Fair
Principles of Economics, Sixth Edition

Case/Fair
Principles of Macroeconomics, Sixth Edition

Case/Fair
Principles of Microeconomics, Sixth Edition

Caves
American Industry: Structure, Conduct, Performance,
Seventh Edition

Colander/Gamber
Macroeconomics

Collinge/Ayers
Economics by Design: Principles and Issues,
Second Edition

Eaton/Eaton/Allen
Microeconomics, Fifth Edition

DiPasquale/Wheaton
Urban Economics and Real Estate Markets

Folland/Goodman/Stano
Economics of Health and Health Care, Third Edition

Fort
Sports Economics

Froyen
Macroeconomics: Theories and Policies, Seventh Edition

Greene
Econometric Analysis, Fifth Edition

Heilbroner/Milberg
The Making of Economic Society, Eleventh Edition

Hess
Using Mathematics in Economic Analysis

Heyne
The Economic Way of Thinking, Tenth Edition

Keat/Young
Managerial Economics, Third Edition

Lynn
*Economic Development: Theory and Practice for a Divided
World*

Mathis/Koscianski
Microeconomic Theory: An Integrated Approach

Milgrom/Roberts
Economics, Organization, and Management

O'Sullivan/Sheffrin
Economics: Principles and Tools, Third Edition

O'Sullivan/Sheffrin
Macroeconomics: Principles and Tools, Third Edition

O'Sullivan/Sheffrin
Microeconomics: Principles and Tools, Third Edition

O'Sullivan/Sheffrin
Survey of Economics: Principles and Tools

Petersen/Lewis
Managerial Economics, Fifth Edition

Pindyck/Rubinfeld
Microeconomics, Fifth Edition

Reynolds/Masters/Moser
Labor Economics and Labor Relations, Eleventh Edition

Roberts
The Choice: A Fable of Free Trade and Protectionism,
Revised

Schiller
The Economics of Poverty and Discrimination,
Eighth Edition

Singh
Electronic Commerce: Economics and Strategy

Weidenbaum
Business and Government in the Global Marketplace,
Sixth Edition

ECONOMIC DEVELOPMENT: THEORY AND PRACTICE FOR A DIVIDED WORLD

Stuart R. Lynn
Assumption College

Prentice Hall

UPPER SADDLE RIVER, NEW JERSEY 07458

Library of Congress Cataloging-in-Publication Data

Lynn, Stuart R.

   Economic development: theory and practice for a divided world / Stuart R. Lynn.
     p. cm.
   Includes bibliographical references and index.
   ISBN 0-13-014161-5
   1. Economic development.   2. Economic policy.   3. Economic development—
Case studies.   4. Economic policy—Case studies.   I. Title.
HD75.L96 2002
338.9—dc21

2001055179

Executive Editor: Rod Banister
Editor-in-Chief: P. J. Boardman
Assistant Editor: Marie McHale
Editorial Assistant: Lisa Amato
Senior Development Editor: Lena Buonanno
Executive Marketing Manager: Kathleen Mclellan
Marketing Assistant: Christopher Bath
Managing Editor (Production): John Roberts
Production Editor: Kelly Warsak
Permissions Coordinator: Suzanne Grappi
Associate Director, Manufacturing: Vincent Scelta
Production Manager: Arnold Vila
Manufacturing Buyer: Michelle Klein
Cover Designer: Bruce Kenselaar
Composition: UG / GGS Information Services, Inc.
Full-Service Project Management: UG / GGS Information Services, Inc.
Printer/Binder: Hamilton Printing Company
Cover Printer: Phoenix Color Corp.

Pearson Education LTD.
Pearson Education Australia PTY, Limited
Pearson Education Singapore, Pte. Ltd
Pearson Education North Asia Ltd
Pearson Education, Canada, Ltd
Pearson Educación de Mexico, S.A. de C.V.
Pearson Education–Japan
Pearson Education Malaysia, Pte. Ltd

10 9 8 7 6 5 4 3 2 1
ISBN 0-13-014161-5

To my father and to Susan
for their encouragement and support.

Brief Contents

Contents

Preface

APPROACH

Textbooks in economic development have a great deal in common. Still, each author brings a different style, approach, organization, and sense of what is important.

Economic Development: Theory and Practice for a Divided World has grown out of the economic development course that I have taught, off and on, for over 30 years. When I was introduced to economic development as a student, economic planning was given much more emphasis than it is today. Government responsibility was deemed essential in the absence of viable markets in many countries, and the serious deficiencies of many government solutions were not yet apparent. On the other hand, health, education, and environmental issues were not considered to be very important. As the concerns of economists have broadened over the last three decades, so has the coverage of courses in economic development.

My approach highlights three key ideas:

- **Divided World:** The title of the book includes the phrase "a divided world." This division has been manifested over the last four decades in the stages of development and the approaches to development policy. There are still wide gaps between rich and poor countries and between market-oriented and state-oriented approaches. Nevertheless, many countries are neither rich nor poor, and the line between market and state orientation is often blurred. I address the roles of market and government in each chapter.
- **Controversy:** One element I have often found muted in other texts is a sense of the controversy that has marked this field. Accepted answers change from one decade to the next, as do some of the key questions. It is important to understand how debates have led to current views in different areas of economic theory and policy, so I have included more background on these debates.
- **Theory and Practice:** Finally, I have combined theory and practice in a way that gives students a practical understanding of what the theoretical fuss is all about. Practical application is provided through numerous cases and Development Spotlight boxes in each chapter.

AUDIENCE

Economic Development: Theory and Practice for a Divided World is aimed at students taking a first course in economic development. It requires only a basic knowledge of economics—students need to have taken only introductory micro- and macroeconomics courses. Some concepts are introduced that go a bit beyond what is normally given at the introductory level. This approach allows, even encourages, students who may not be economics majors to become familiar with the subject. Students whose interest may be in political science, international studies, sociology, anthropology, and related areas will find the text interesting and accessible.

ORGANIZATION

The book is divided into five parts. Part I, "Introduction to Economic Development," consists of three chapters. Chapter 1, "The Idea of Economic Development," introduces students to the subject by raising questions of what we mean by development. Chapter 2, "Measuring Economic Development," describes problems of measuring the concept. Chapter 3, "The Evolution of Development Thought," shows how the economics profession has changed its approaches over the years. Because anthropologists, political scientists, and others have a great deal to say about these issues, it is important to stake out the realm of economics and to admit that the boundaries are often fuzzy.

Part II, "Resources for Development," discusses the "raw materials" of, or inputs into, economic development: capital, resources, and labor. Chapter 4, "Financial Resources for Development," discusses the role of saving and investment in economic development, while Chapter 5, "Natural Building Blocks of Development: Resources and the Environment," discusses natural resources and the environment. Chapter 6, "Population Growth and Migration," and Chapter 7, "Human Capital: Health and Education," address more specifically the human element: population growth and migration, and enhancing human capital through improved health and education.

Part III, "Productive Sectors and the State," first addresses the two main productive sectors in Chapter 8, "The Key Role of Agriculture in Development," and Chapter 9, "Industry, Technology, and Employment." Part III concludes with two chapters on the role of government. While governments, and their policies, are evident throughout the book, it is essential to provide a general framework for the debate over what government can do and how its performance can be improved. Chapter 10, "The Ambiguous Role of the State in Development," addresses these general questions, while Chapter 11, "Macroeconomic Policy, Inflation, and Stabilization," considers macroeconomic policy specifically.

Part IV, "The International Economics of Development," surveys the international economic environment of development. It begins with "Foreign Trade and Development Strategy," in Chapter 12, then "Foreign Aid and Direct Investment," in Chapter 13. Chapter 14, "Debt and Adjustment," addresses international debt and the problem of restructuring troubled economies, which bedeviled much of Latin America in the 1980s and weighs heavily on many African economies today. Chapter 15, "Global Capital Markets and the East Asian Development Model," follows up with the newer problem of adjusting to short-term capital flows, especially as it struck the East Asian economies in the late 1990s.

Part V, "Conclusions," consists of Chapter 16, "Lessons Learned and Open Questions." This final chapter takes stock of the changes in, and contributions of, economic development as a discipline and sums up the lessons of development policy, particularly as it relates to the role of government.

KEY FEATURES

Each chapter relies on a set of common features to bring the narrative into focus and to apply the concepts of the chapter.

- From one to five country-specific cases in each chapter help to provide real-world examples of important issues. A map located on the inside of the front and back covers guides the student to the location of each country.
- A series of "Development Spotlight" boxes brings additional illumination to key points.
- Graphs are presented as figures to clarify key theoretical issues.
- Crucial data about developing countries are presented in tables.
- Key terms appear in bold the first time they are used, are listed at the end of each chapter, and are compiled in a glossary at the end of the book.
- "Related Internet Resources" at the end of each chapter guide the student to additional information on the Web.
- A set of "Questions for Review" also appears at the end of each chapter and includes questions specifically aimed at the cases.
- Extensive endnotes lead students to further readings in many areas.

SUPPLEMENTAL PACKAGE

The *Instructor's Manual* provides the following key features for each chapter: chapter summary, key objectives, suggestions for lectures, assignments, and multiple choice and short essay exam questions. The Web site for the book, <www.prenhall.com/lynn>, contains a downloadable version of the *Instructor's Manual*, a full bibliography, and additional resources.

ACKNOWLEDGMENTS

Throughout the process of putting this book together, a number of people have been particularly helpful. Professor George Doyle of Assumption College read early drafts of all the chapters and provided extremely helpful comments and guidance. Also in the early stages, individual chapters were commented on by Al Field of the University of North Carolina (trade), Kooros Mahmoudi of Northern Arizona University (population and human capital), and Ed Karasek (introduction). My research efforts were aided by Cheryl Simmons of the U.S. Agency for International Development and by Jeanne Kasperson of the Marsh Library of Clark University. Students in my spring 1997 economic development course commented extensively on the manuscript. My thanks for their views go especially to Charlotte Ferland, Jen Shaw, and Amy Sullivan. Melissa Szydlow did an independent study with me and was merciless in her attempts to get me to show students what was important and why. The quotes that open all the chapters (with one exception) are taken from James Simon, *A Dictionary of Economic Quotations,* 2nd ed. (Totowa, NJ: Barnes and Noble Books, 1984). At Prentice Hall, Rod Banister shepherded the manuscript through the review process, and Lena Buonanno undertook the final, unenviable task of making the manuscript look like a textbook.

REVIEWERS

I extend my thanks to the reviewers who provided constructive feedback that made the book stronger:

Eliezer Ayal, University of Illinois at Chicago

Daniel Berkowitz, University of Pittsburgh

Jeff Bookwalter, University of Montana

Michael Cook, William Jewell College

Lloyd Dumas, University of Texas at Dallas

Constantine Glezakos, California State University, Long Beach

Katerine Huger, Charleston Southern University

Phil King, San Francisco State University

Sherri Kossoudji, University of Michigan

Jamie Ortiz, Florida Atlantic University

Denise Stanley, University of Tennessee

Shanti Tangri, Rutgers University

Mahmood Yousefi, University of Northern Iowa

ABOUT THE AUTHOR

Stuart R. Lynn is Associate Professor of Economics and Global Studies at Assumption College in Worcester, Massachusetts. He received his Ph.D. from the University of North Carolina in Chapel Hill (1971) and has taught Economic Development for 16 years, first at Indiana–Purdue University at Fort Wayne and since 1987 at Assumption College.

In addition to teaching, Professor Lynn spent 11 years in the U.S. Foreign Service. Four of those years were spent reporting on economic issues from the U.S. Embassies in Lagos, Nigeria, and Dar es Salaam, Tanzania. In Lagos, he reported on petroleum and macroeconomic issues. In Dar es Salaam, he reported on all economic issues, including Tanzania's negotiations with the International Monetary Fund. Professor Lynn also spent seven years at the State Department in Washington, D.C., working on issues of trade, investment, and petroleum in developing countries. His work included developing-country compliance with rules of the GATT (now WTO) and negotiation of Bilateral Investment Treaties. He also helped oversee economics training courses at the Foreign Service Institute.

CHAPTER

1

THE IDEA OF ECONOMIC DEVELOPMENT

No society can surely be flourishing
and happy, of which the far greater part
of the members are poor and miserable.
—ADAM SMITH (1723–1790)

INTRODUCTION

Your family's home is probably pretty comfortable. You wake up in your own room or maybe one shared with a sibling. Your home is warm in the winter and cool in the summer. After the alarm goes off, you get your breakfast from a pantry or a refrigerator or, if you are in a hurry, from a coffee and doughnut shop as you drive to class or work. If you are sick or injured, you will quickly get to a hospital. You talk to your friends and family on the phone, or you are part of a growing number of people who can turn on their computer and send an e-mail after checking the news, weather, and sports on the Internet. You buy most of what you need at the store (after first comparing prices on the Internet). Radio, cable television, and the Internet connect you to the world.

Unless you are one of the 2 or 3 billion people who have access to almost none of this. More likely you will wake up with the sun in a one-room house with a dirt floor, shared by a family of seven. Your only adaptation to the seasons is to put on or take off your clothing, which may consist of a shirt, a pair of pants or a skirt, and, unless you are among the poorest, one pair of shoes. You have a little breakfast—or none—before walking perhaps a mile or more to school or to work on dirt roads. If you are ill or injured, there may be a clinic in your village, but any serious problems will require the hospital many miles away. Getting there requires walking or finding someone with a truck heading in that direction. Conversation is with those you meet face-to-face. Local stores are few and sell only some basic commodities. Your interaction with the outside world comes, if at all, from one of a small number of radios or perhaps a television owned by only the wealthiest residents of the village or section of the city. Life is more difficult and more limited.[1]

In 1954, Indian novelist Kamala Markandaya described living conditions for the main character in her book *Nectar in a Sieve*.[2] Rukmani is wed at the age of 12 to a man she has never met. When they arrive at his home, she finds a mud hut: "two rooms, one a sort of storehouse for grain, the other for everything else." Roughly 30 years and seven children later, the land they have been renting for 30 years is sold and the couple must move. They have a few pots and pans and other cooking utensils, a few clothes, and almost no money: "two or three bundles" is what they have accumulated over that period.[3] Almost 50 years later, economist John Isbister describes some of the world's poor: "a family typically shares one room—and in rural areas, the room may provide shelter for farm animals as well. The family members do not have enough good food to eat."[4]

In urban areas things may be little better. Toward the end of *Nectar in a Sieve*, Rukmani and her husband—who is now very ill—have lost what few possessions they have. They have been driven to the city in search of a son who, it turns out, had left 2 years earlier without telling them. Trying to earn money for the trip home, the couple find work as stone breakers at a quarry: They use stones to break other stones that they pile up and turn in at the end of the day. Their city had some well-to-do families, but thousands slept in the streets or in temples and earned almost nothing during the day. At the beginning of a new century, cities of the developing world still have their rich, usually a larger middle class than before, and the poor. Many live in crowded conditions without water or electricity. In Callao, Peru, one author describes a large garbage dump where around 80 families live in filthy conditions, their health constantly at risk, making a living by sorting through the trash for anything that might be resold.[5]

THE RICH AND THE POOR

Disparities between rich and poor are considerable and, in some cases, are growing. In 1998, a typical baby born in Canada could expect to live to be 79. A baby born in Sierra Leone had a life expectancy of 37, lowest in the world. The typical child in the United States could expect 16 years of schooling. In Niger the typical boy would have 3 years and the typical girl 2 years. Throughout the 1990s, high-income countries routinely reported having 250 to 400 doctors per every 100,000 people; for the poorest countries, 20 doctors per 100,000 people was only a goal. Whereas the United States produced $29,000 worth of goods and services per person in 1998, the estimate for Mozambique was only $445. In 1997, the typical citizen of Burundi consumed about 1,685 calories per day, compared to about 3,194 in Sweden.

By one estimate, output per person in the rich countries was 49 times that in poor countries in 1998, up from 38 times in 1960 and only 9 times in 1870.[6] Another estimate, using a more realistic measuring device, puts the gap between average income in the 20 richest and 20 poorest countries at "only" 30 to 1 in 1998. However, that gap has doubled since 1960.[7] Economists compare countries in terms of the value of output or income produced per person, the **per capita income**. In 1998, the wealthier, industrialized countries such as Japan, Britain, and the United States comprised 15 percent of the world's population, but earned 78 percent of the world's income, with an average income per capita of over $25,000. The poorest countries, such as Haiti, Nigeria, and Bangladesh, with 60 percent of the population, earned only 6 percent of the income, or about $500 per person.

If the industrialized "North" is taken as the standard, the average citizen of the "South" lived 84 percent as long and ate 82 percent of the daily calories of their wealthier neighbors. Adult literacy is only 71 percent as great. For the poorest countries, life expectancy is 69 percent on 67 percent of the calories, with a literacy rate of only 50 percent.[8] Table 1–1 illustrates some of these gaps. Why are they so large? What can be done about them? How have some countries "made it" while others have not?

TABLE 1-1 Development Achievement—1999
(Ratios: Low Income = 1.0)

Income Group	Low Income	Lower Middle	Upper Middle	High Income
Per Capita GNI	1.0	2.85	11.60	62.95
Life Expectancy	1.0	1.17	1.17	1.32
Age 65 Survival: Male	1.0	1.25	1.20	1.47
Age 65 Survival: Female	1.0	1.30	1.33	1.52
Adult Literacy: Male*	1.0	1.28	1.28	1.39
Adult Literacy: Female*	1.0	1.50	1.71	1.90

*The source does not report data for the high-income group. The ratios have been calculated on the assumption that adult literacy in these countries is 99 percent.

Source: World Development Indicators 2001.

These gaps will not be narrowed significantly very soon. To understand them we need to consider the major social sciences—economics, anthropology, politics, sociology, geography, ecology, and psychology. Each course individually presents only a partial picture. A course in *economic development* focuses largely on the production and exchange of goods and services but also considers how the economy offers its citizens opportunities to live longer, be educated, and have a good job. And we incorporate, where possible, the impact of a country's cultural background and its political practices.

The idea of economic development is both a very old and a very new one in the economics profession. Eighteenth- and nineteenth-century economists wrote about the progress of mostly their own countries. Since the end of World War II, attention has shifted to "poor" countries; those that have not attained the economic levels of the industrialized countries of Europe, North America, and Japan. In this book we use the term "economic development" to refer to a process taking place in countries of Asia, Africa, Latin America, and some parts of Europe that have per capita income levels recognizably lower than those of the Western industrialized countries. We refer to the former as "developing" countries, and the latter, although there is some debate here, as "developed" or "industrialized."

The objectives of this chapter are to (1) present a usable definition of economic development and (2) present the major theme that flows through the book. We view the process of economic development in developing countries as beneficial for both the people of these countries and those in the developed countries. Economic development is not the only worthy objective of human activity, but it is an important one in which all people and all nations have a stake.

Growth vs. Development

For years, many economists used **economic growth**, the annual rate of growth of per capita income, to indicate economic **development**. Then some oil-exporting countries, such as Saudi Arabia, obtained tremendous wealth and income levels before changes took place in their economic structure that would allow broader participation of their people. In other countries, such as Brazil, structural change was achieved, but large portions of their population did not share this "progress." And in some countries, such as Ghana, economic progress was halted or even reversed. These apparent anomalies forced a more careful scrutiny of the concept of economic development as opposed to economic growth.

Every text in economic development has its own approach to defining economic development. All include economic growth but usually add the requirement that the structure of output—what sectors and industries exist—change as well. Some add improvement in individual choice and freedom. A useful definition that remains in the economic realm is that of Henry Bruton who sees development as

> creating an economy that is sufficiently flexible, diversified, and responsive that it can weather shocks, can respond to and indeed create opportunities for growth, and can, on its own, generate continually increasing welfare for its people.[9]

This definition probably places too much burden on an economy to accomplish such goals "on its own," given that even a large, diversified economy like the United States relies on interaction with other economies to assure its well-being. A better working definition might be the following:

> Economic development means sustained and sustainable growth in per capita income, accompanied by diversification of production, reduction of absolute poverty, and expanding economic opportunities for all citizens.

This definition requires economic growth, at a faster pace than the growth of population, but adds some qualifiers. *Sustainable* growth implies that the process can be maintained over a long period, which means that the nation's land and resources must not become so degraded that an environmental crisis is the result. Diversification of production means that the nation must increase the range of goods and services, not simply produce more of the same. Reduction of absolute poverty means that the poorest in the population must share the benefits of growth. And expanding opportunities for all implies greater freedom of choice in work, consumption, and leisure. The contrast between development and mere growth is illustrated by a comparison of Taiwan and Saudi Arabia in Case 1–1.

Economic Development and Development Economics

The title of the book contains the phrase "economic development." Yet it has become common to refer also to "development economics." To some extent this phrasing is just a matter of preference. However, there are also differences in approach. While an economist who studies development is certainly a development economist, our title suggests that we are applying economic analysis to the crucial issues of development. These include poverty, changes in the structure of production, and the extent to which economic activities take place in a **market economy**, a system in which resources are owned by individuals and allocated through a price mechanism. Development economics, on the other hand, attempts to fit the broad concerns of development into the analytical techniques favored by economists. We will consider this distinction in more detail at the end of our study when we review some of the major unsettled areas in the discipline.

DEVELOPMENT CONTRASTS: TAIWAN AND SAUDI ARABIA

FAST FACTS

Taiwan on the Map: East Asia

Population: 22 Million

Per Capita GNI and Rank: $14,216 (Not Ranked)

Life Expectancy: Male—72 Female—78

Adult Literacy Rate: Male—94% Female—90%

Saudi Arabia on the Map: West Asia

Population: 20 Million

Per Capita GNI and Rank: $6,900   (60)

Life Expectancy: Male—71 Female—74

Adult Literacy Rate: Male—83% Female—66%

Taiwan and Saudi Arabia represent contrasting attempts to develop. Taiwan is an island off China's east coast, just larger than Massachusetts and Connecticut combined. It has varied natural resources but was not well developed at mid-twentieth century. Saudi Arabia, in the Middle East, is about 60 times the size of Taiwan but is largely desert with less than 1 percent of its land cultivated. It does, however, have some of the world's largest oil reserves.

Taiwan is often cited as one of the "miracles" of modern economic development. The island was fairly isolated until the Chinese Nationalist government was driven from the mainland by the Communists in 1949. The Nationalists received considerable foreign aid and protection from the United States, but also embarked on a series of policies that resulted not only in growth but also structural transformation and considerable social improvement.

For successive five-year periods between 1965 and 1985, GNP per capita grew rapidly, between 5.4 and 8.6 percent per year. Between 1971 and 1988, more than 30 percent of GNP was saved, and anywhere between 20 and 30 percent of GNP was devoted to investment. Unemployment has been about 2 percent and inflation no more than 13.3 percent per year for any five-year period, often one-third of that rate.

Structural change—change in the sectoral origin of production and the sophistication of production methods—was significant. In the mid-1950s, agriculture produced one-third of the nation's output and employed over one-half of the labor force. By 1988, agriculture produced only 6 percent of output with 14 percent of the labor force. In 1966, one-half of manufacturing and employment was in basic industries (food, textiles) and only 14 percent in capital goods (machinery) and advanced products such as scientific instruments. Twenty years later basic products accounted for 30 percent of output and employment, while capital and advanced goods were 29 percent of output and 26 percent of employment. In 1970, Taiwan contributed one-half of 1 percent of the world's manufactured exports; by 1988, more than $2\frac{1}{2}$ percent.

Impressive social gains have been made. Income has become more equally distributed. Infant mortality has fallen to developed-country standards of 5.6 per thousand, and life expectancy has risen to 72 years for men and 78 for women. In 1964, 23 percent of the population was illiterate, and another 55 percent had completed only primary school: Only 3 percent were graduates of junior college, college, and graduate schools. By 1987, only

5 percent were illiterate, 14 percent had a junior college or better education, and only 33 percent finished their education with primary school.

The Taiwanese government has promoted both international trade and domestic production. It has spent considerable amounts on education and health, and has followed policies that permitted relative equality of income. On the other hand, until recently government was dictatorial, workers had few rights, and increasing environmental problems were largely ignored. Whether Taiwan's progress is "sustainable" may be open to question, but there is no doubt of the success of its policies over the last half century: as good a record as can be found.

The Saudi story has been much different from that of Taiwan. Its fortunes have fluctuated with oil's price. Over the period of 1965 to 1980, GDP grew an average of 10.6 percent per year. The collapse of oil prices resulted in an average decline in GDP of 1.2 percent per year during the 1980s, recovering to an average growth of 1.6 percent per year over 1991 to 1999. Still, the government accumulated significant wealth over this period and has used it to improve the living standards of the population. For instance, infant mortality fell from 119 per 1,000 births in 1970 to only 19 in 1999, and education has spread to a larger section of the population.

However, whether Saudi Arabia has developed in the sense that we mean it is debatable. The economy has diversified but not acquired a manufacturing base. In 1965, agriculture accounted for 8 percent of GDP, industry 60 percent, and services 31 percent, but of industry's 60 only 9 percent was in manufacturing, with the rest in oil. By 1990, agriculture accounted for 6 percent but still employed anywhere from 19 to 48 percent of the labor force (depending on the source of data). Only 50 percent of GDP was in industry—of which only 8 percent

was manufacturing—and services accounted for 43 percent. In 1999, only 10 percent of GDP was in manufacturing, 38 percent in other industry, and 45 percent in services. Government data from 1995 show 5.5 percent of the labor force in agriculture, 7.9 percent in non-oil industry, 15.5 percent in construction, and 69 percent in services. While this sounds a bit like development, the economic structure is not consistent with a balanced economy. Exports have been concentrated in oil: 98 percent in 1965, 99 percent in 1980, 89 percent in 1990, and around 80 percent in 1999. In part, the government has not found suitable domestic manufacturing worth pursuing. In 1980, at the height of oil prices, investment was 22 percent of GDP but saving was 62 percent, much of which went overseas. In 1996, the saving ratio was down to 32 percent, and investment was 20 percent.

In spite of the increasing reach of education and health, there remains a great disparity in the economic activity of men and women. While girls receive on the average almost as much education as boys, most employment is restricted. One source reports that women constituted 7 percent of the labor force in 1994; another reports 13 percent in 1995. While this outcome should be seen as a cultural more than an economic phenomenon, it raises questions about how we evaluate the results of economic policies.

A crucial difference between Taiwan and Saudi Arabia is the greater diversity of economic activity in Taiwan and the wide range of products it manufactures and trades. Another is the greater opportunity for a large majority of the population to freely enter into a variety of occupations. While the Saudi economy has grown, it remains highly vulnerable to the ups and downs in the oil market and delivers freedom of choice to a narrower range of the population. While Taiwan has not, until recent years, protected its environment from the consequences of growth, the Saudi dependence on nonrenewable oil raises grave questions about the sustainability of its path.

Sources: The usual sources of development data are not available for Taiwan. Because China claims the island, the World Bank and other organizations associated with the United Nations do not publish data for it. The data used here are taken from several of the chapters in Gustav Ranis, ed., *Taiwan: From Developing to Mature Economy* (Boulder, CO: Westview Press, 1992). For a dissenting opinion, see Walden Bello and Stephanie Rosenfeld, *Dragons in Distress: Asia's Miracle Economies in Crisis* (San Francisco: Food First Books, 1990). Information can sometimes be accessed on the Web at ⟨www.gio.gov.tw⟩ or ⟨www.stat.gov.tw⟩. Some data here come from ⟨www.britannica.com⟩. The Saudi government does not provide complete or timely data. The sources used here are the World Bank's *World Development Reports 1982* and *1992*, and *Indicators* of 2001; the UN Development Program's *Human Development Report* of 1998; and the Instituto del Tercer Mundo's *World Guide 1997/98* (Oxford: New Internationalist Publications). Some sketchy information is also available at ⟨http://www.saudinf.com⟩.

PURPOSE AND THEME OF THE BOOK

The World Bank's 1992 *World Development Report* claims that "The achievement of sustained and equitable development remains the greatest challenge facing the human race."[10] Not everyone would agree: Some will argue that the existence of certain shared values must first be achieved, after which development will be easier. Still, many would accept the crucial importance of economic development.

Why Study Economic Development?

Economic development affects the living standards and options of a vast majority of the planet's population. Students in the United States or other industrial countries may feel remote from these issues. The U.S.'s significant trade and investment relations with developing countries should argue otherwise. For example, in 1999 the United States sold 43 percent of its exports to, and bought 47 percent of its imports from, developing countries. Within the last few years, considerable publicity has attended U.S. participation in international conferences on trade, population, and the environment, with a great deal of focus on the developing countries. Increasing integration of financial markets brings the economic problems of Indonesia, Russia, and Brazil to our doorsteps.

Theme of the Book

A crucial underlying theme in all of economics is the role of government policy. While we will look at specific policies in specific areas, we usually come down to the same basic question: What are the proper roles of government and the market?

Once a society breaks out of the institutions that have guided it in the past, some form of a market mechanism—the use of prices to allocate scarce resources—generally takes over. One of the reasons that governments everywhere intervene in the operation of the market is to "promote the general welfare," although they may end up having a contrary purpose and effect. Perhaps the key challenge of economic policy in developing countries and elsewhere is to determine the most efficient combination of government and the market in pursuing (and changing) the goals of individuals within the society. Much of the controversy that has marked the last 50 years of debate in economic development has been over just this question. We will consider different responses to this debate throughout the book.

KEY CHARACTERISTICS OF ECONOMIC DEVELOPMENT

It will help us to take a brief look at how economists characterize development and envision the development process.

The Development Path

We can think of a country as following a path of economic development. One common approach is to look at patterns of output and relate them to historical development in the West. The first, least developed phase would consist of economies that use simple technologies to produce largely **primary products** (agricultural products or raw materials such as minerals and crude oil) and have very little manufacturing output. Most economies have already left this phase, but others have not. At the extreme is the African nation of Guinea-Bissau: In 1998 the agricultural sector accounted for 62 percent of its production. Four other African countries, three countries in Southeast Asia, and Albania each relied on agriculture for half or more of their annual product.

Development will take a nation's economy into manufacturing, as well as increasing the extent and sophistication of its service sector, including banking, insurance, and business and government services. Finally, those in an advanced phase (*a*) have de-emphasized agriculture in *relative* terms (but still produce and export food), (*b*) have sophisticated and varied manufacturing sectors, and (*c*) have significant service sectors (over half of U.S. output and two-thirds of U.S. employment). These are considered to be the "developed" countries. (The terms "advanced" and "industrialized" are often substituted for the term "developed.") Not all countries fit perfectly into the expected patterns. Some developed countries such as the Netherlands and New Zealand have maintained a strong primary sector with agricultural and mineral production. However, they also have mature manufacturing and service sectors, and primary activities are carried out with a high degree of technological sophistication.

A developing country in an early phase has the following characteristics: The overwhelming portion of the population is engaged in **subsistence agriculture**, in which families consume mostly goods they produce themselves and produce little more than enough to feed the family. Manufacturing is generally concentrated in a few cities and frequently is **labor intensive**, that is, its labor force has relatively little capital to work with. This production consists of assembly of imported components and concentrates largely on consumer goods, rather than capital goods. The services sector is either small or, in the case of modern services such as banking, is dominated by government operations or foreign firms.

Under these conditions, economic progress may be difficult because of the **vicious cycle** of poverty, illustrated in Figure 1–1. Low **productivity**—output per worker—brings low incomes, and people do not produce enough to save. Lack of saving means there is little to invest, especially in newer, more productive technology. Without investment and technological progress, productivity remains low and incomes remain low.

Some way must be found to escape this cycle. But even when this is possible, the result may simply be growth: an expansion of the size of the economy, producing a greater amount of the existing kinds of goods and services, either in the aggregate or measured per capita. Almost everybody wants growth. The question is: what kind of

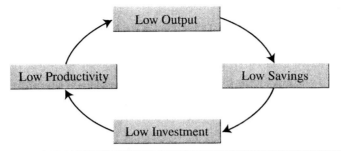

FIGURE 1-1 The Vicious Cycle of Poverty

The vicious cycle story typically begins with low productivity, which produces little output per person. Because incomes are not high, saving is difficult at best. If there is little surplus to be saved, net investment, or the building up of the capital stock, is also difficult. Therefore, companies are unable to increase productivity or output per person.

growth? *Development* implies a change in the structure of the economy—the division of production among agriculture, industry and services, and the extent and sophistication of capital goods used in production.

Economic Development and Structural Change

Studies of this kind of **structural change** began with investigation into historical patterns in those countries now considered developed. Simon Kuznets, who laid the groundwork for subsequent discussions of this issue, established the shift from agriculture to manufacturing to services as a nearly uniform pattern of development.[11] Figure 1–2 illustrates this change. As growth occurs, the demand for food grows more slowly than income, shifting demand to manufactured goods and inducing greater **investment**—the purchase of machinery by firms—in that area. A larger fraction of a country's resources become devoted to **infrastructure** (transportation, communication,

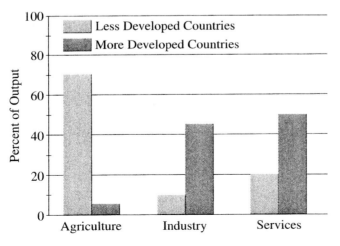

FIGURE 1-2 Structural Change

The typical developing country derives most of its production from the agricultural sector. As development proceeds, agriculture diminishes in importance, and both industry and services become prominent.

education), and production in all areas becomes more complex.[12] Although services are important in all economies, they change with development from largely personal services to more extensive business and financial services.

Economists suggest that a country's production is based on its resource endowment. In the early phases of development, those resources are primarily raw materials and low-productivity agricultural labor. Only after significant investment takes place are these resources supplemented by capital goods and more industrially skilled labor. Growth, accompanied by investment that changes the structural pattern of output, characterizes countries as they proceed along their development path. Expanding the range of output means acquiring the capacity to produce more and more sophisticated manufactured goods and services, and this has to be built up bit by bit. Development must improve the productivity of the land, people, and machinery, through improved technology. Countries often make use of foreign expertise and capital, but these must be channeled in directions that help a country move in the directions desired by its people. People must have access to education, health care, and economic opportunity. People must also be prepared to use new technology: India's first prime minister, Jawaharlal Nehru, claimed that an "ancient mind" could not use modern technology. These will also help alleviate the cycle of poverty.

The Values and Goals of Development

Even if we could settle on a definition of economic development, there is still a debate over its goals. This book does not claim that economic growth is the ultimate goal, nor does it suggest that poorer countries must copy the paths that others have taken before them. Some countries considered to be developed may experience high levels of environmental degradation, crime, and citizen apathy.

Nor is the goal of development simply the achievement of structural change, economic growth, and reasonable equality of income. The important goals of the development process are to expand the freedom and opportunities of individuals and to assure that both are widespread.[13] We assume that people generally do not wish to be poor, even though they may not need to be rich either. Economic development should create opportunities for individuals to choose productive activities that, in themselves and through the income they create, allow security and participation in the social life of the community.

Such goals are not easily attained, nor will they satisfy everyone. Change can be unsettling for many:

- Rukmani, of our Indian novel, is ambivalent about a tannery that was built near her village. At first it meant sudden growth and a change in the village's peaceful environment. Later, two of her sons were fired for organizing a strike, a third was killed while allegedly stealing from the tannery grounds, and finally it was the tannery that bought the land that she and her husband had worked for 30 years. So she muses that "some—a few—had been raised up; many others cast down, lost in its clutches."[14]
- A real woman in a Zambian village talks about the difficulties brought about by new farming techniques. Not only is money now needed for supplies, but her cosmos seems changed: "Even the rain falls differently now and the signs in nature which indicate when to do things are no longer the

ones we were used to. It seems that our old ways of cultivating are perishing as the government teaches us new ways of doing things."[15]

- A study of village life in Mexico describes a young man caught up in the "whirlpool" of social change. His village is no longer isolated but is now part of a larger world: "He no longer wore the clothing of the *indio*; he rarely spoke his primary language, Nahuatl; his dreams were of tomorrow rather than yesterday.... Yet there was something deep within that would not quite release him, and so his life hesitated, stuttering on the brink of a new world...."[16]

Most societal change finds some people left out, unable or unwilling to adapt to new forms of economic activity and relationships. Instead of working their father's land, they may now rent from a faraway landlord. Instead of sharing their crops with family and friends, they may sell to people they never see. Many fear that economic progress may be obtained at the cost of a sense of community, as individuals pursue their own self-interest, often at the expense of others. Perhaps the best justification for pursuing such progress, however, is that every form of society—whether changing or not—has problems; the best that can be hoped is that a people can retain the best of their cultural traditions while embracing new opportunities.[17]

A SIMPLIFIED VIEW OF THE DEVELOPMENT PROCESS

At the most fundamental level, then, what is required for economic development to occur?

Visualizing Development

Economists typically define their discipline as the study of allocating scarce resources. The Production Possibilities Frontier (PPF) (Figure 1–3) shows that production is limited by available resources at any time. The market mechanism, through interplay of

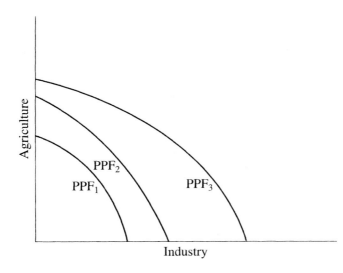

FIGURE 1–3 Growth and Development

The Production Possibilities Frontier (PPF) represents the physical limits of an economy's productive capacity. Growth extends the frontier (from PPF₁ to PPF₂) but does not guarantee a transformation to an industrial economy. Development changes the composition of output toward a greater focus on industry, while agriculture continues to grow, but more slowly (PPF₃).

producers and consumers, determines which point on the frontier best satisfies the desires of the society.

Increasing the ability to satisfy those wants requires that the economy grow over time. Through acquisition of raw materials, population growth, and the accumulation of capital and new technology, the economy's productive capacity increases and the frontier shifts outward; economic growth is achieved by a shift from PPF$_1$ to PPF$_2$. For an economy to achieve development or structural transformation, it must change the pattern of production so that the curve shifts faster on the industry axis than on the agriculture axis—a shift to PPF$_3$.

The Production Function

A **production function** is a mathematical expression of physical relationships between **factors of production**—the inputs into the production process—and the final result, the output. A simplified production function might take the form

$$Y = f(L, K, T)$$

in which output (Y) is a function of labor (L), capital (K), and technology (T).

A production function is a relatively reliable relationship: We can be reasonably sure that a specific amount of steel, rubber, plastic, machinery, electricity, and labor power will—time after time—result in the same automobile, and specific increases in inputs will lead to predictable increases in output. However, in a poor country newly producing automobiles, even were the company to import the same resources and capital goods and train a labor force in proper techniques, the same output could not be assured. It would be necessary to have a continuous power supply, certain standards of employee training, reliable transportation systems for regular delivery of supplies to and products from the plant, other individuals and firms throughout the economy operating on the same basis, and a stable set of government policies. We can then see development as a process of changing the way a society functions in order to make economic activity more reliable, more predictable.

Building Capital

Economic development requires an increase in the size, and change in the composition, of production and a new set of public and private institutions to accomplish the task. This means that resources must be redirected from traditional forms of consumption and saving, such as ceremonial displays and unused land, to the kinds of investment that will permit increased levels and new types of output. Additional resources must be made available to those who will invest in the means of production—capital. **Capital** involves an "indirect" or "roundabout" production method. Machinery is produced first in order to produce consumer goods, but the delay is accompanied by greater productivity than with simpler methods, and permits greater specialization and division of labor.

This shift to more **capital-intensive** production is not easily accomplished. As most development proceeds from an agricultural base, surplus resources can be transferred to other uses such as manufacturing only if producers are paid in a form that can be (1) channeled through savings institutions to would-be manufacturers or (2) taxed and invested by government. This is difficult without **monetization** of the economy. That is, economic transactions must be converted from largely subsistence and barter to the use of money.

In addition, manufacturing requires infrastructure: electricity, roads, ports, education, and credit. In all countries government provides much of the infrastructure, which means that effective and trustworthy public institutions are needed to keep production running smoothly.

It is quite likely that most capital goods will, at first, have to be imported: The agricultural surplus will have to be exportable and the proceeds used to import the requisite goods. Thus, the developing country is immediately plunged into the international economy.

But there may be an even more basic deficiency. Developing countries initially lack well-functioning market mechanisms and a trustworthy legal system that specifies the conditions of property ownership and enforces contracts. While any economic system uses agreed rules of behavior, development by way of the market relies increasingly on impersonal relationships among socially separated individuals, for example, formal laws that must substitute written contracts for customary trading relationships between individuals. Creation and acceptance of these new laws and attitudes may be a most difficult task.

Capital, such as machinery and factories, requires time to plan and build. Therefore, resources that are used to create capital must be saved to be available for investment. As we will see, saving requires a sound, trusted set of financial and regulatory institutions. It also requires that people can see the benefits of restricting their current consumption and that they have sufficient security to permit it.

People in developing countries tend to respect the future and go to great lengths to protect it when they can. Farmers do not sell the seed for next year's crop if they do not have to. Fields and forests are managed conservatively if at all possible. Families put aside money for their children's education when they can. But subsistence living is also an insecure living. In rural areas, flood or drought can wipe out a year's crop. If food is not kept on hand, there may be none in a crisis. Putting time, effort, and money into new farming techniques could be disastrous if they do not work. A job can be eliminated with an economic downturn, a change in the structure of a town or industry. Monetary savings can be wiped out by a family emergency. So the appropriate financial and regulatory institutions must provide the assurance to people that taking an economic risk does not mean that they might starve.

How Is the World "Divided?"

The title of this book addresses a world divided into "developed" and "developing" countries. The division stems from differences in per capita income and the degree to which the market is the primary mechanism for allocating resources. While some industrialized countries make extensive use of government to supplement the market mechanism, the market sets the pace. In developing countries, markets have often not had a chance to fully develop, and economic development is in part development of markets.

In some ways the world has become much less "divided" over the last few decades. Ideologically, the market-directed approach to development is now dominant, even in China where the state role in controlling the economy is extensive. We are more likely today to talk of the state taming the excesses of the market, rather than supplanting it. Many countries in Asia and Latin America are industrially developed, as in South Korea or Argentina, and some of their problems resemble more those of the business cycles familiar to the developed world.

But whereas Americans may refer to "pockets of poverty" and worry about whether the Social Security system or utility companies need more or less government involvement, over a billion people in Asia, Africa, and Latin America live on the equivalent of a dollar a day or less. While we debate whether the government should spend a few billion more or a few billion less, many in poor countries are the first of their generation to receive a primary education. They are not certain about what democracy should mean for them. They may be witnessing entire economies reeling under the impact of AIDS. Development is for them a hazy goal, not an accomplished fact.

MAJOR CONTROVERSIES IN ECONOMIC DEVELOPMENT

The field of economic development is full of controversy. Many points of dispute have been settled, although they frequently reappear in different disguises. For example, economists used to debate the usefulness of government planning of the economy. But while planning as such has not worked, the precise role of government is at issue over a wide range of topics. The following are some of the major disputes that still exist. Each will be taken up in later chapters.

What Is Development and How Do We Measure It?

As we have seen, development is much more difficult to define than economic growth. Some have reacted to the ambiguities of standard economic growth measures by adding to or even replacing them with indicators of well-being involving health and education. This is not an abstract argument. Promoting economic growth does not always ensure that the poorest segments of the population benefit. So if broader measures of development are chosen, this will help government pinpoint where money should be spent.

How Does Economic Growth Occur?

Even promoting economic growth as an objective is only a start for economic development. The mechanisms of growth—investment in capital, promoting technological change, improving the health and education of workers, opening to foreign trade—do not act in straightforward ways. So economists differ about which mechanisms are most important and how they might be combined. An important question about growth is whether there is, or could be, a tendency for growth rates to converge or diverge across countries. What should we expect to happen? Why is it happening or not happening? These questions continue to bring forth controversy.

Is There a Conflict Between Equality and Growth?

One of the key issues of economic development is the relationship between equality and growth of income. One popular economic viewpoint is that growth is spurred by inequality of income: Only wealthy people can save enough to provide the basis for investment needed for growth. That growth will "trickle down" to the rest of the population. Because unrestricted use of markets often brings unequal results, proponents of the market mechanism may be accused of being inegalitarian.

Recently, a number of economists have claimed that a certain type of equality—more equal access to resources such as land, credit, and education—has been associated with high rates of economic growth. Their conclusion is that, where necessary, markets must be complemented by government policies that make it easier for poor people to have access to these resources. So some types of equality are compatible with market mechanisms and can promote growth.

Is Population Growth a Threat to Economic Growth?

While population and economic growth have coincided in some eras, there has been concern for many years that rapid population growth in some of today's developing countries is retarding growth. Still, some argue that only economic development will reduce population growth rates. The implication for policy is clear: If we count on development to slow population growth, we need not take special steps to curb population. But if high population growth rates actually hold back growth and development through heavy demand for resources and a deteriorating environment, then the population problem must be tackled directly and quickly.

Is There a Trade-Off Between Growth and the Environment?

A debate similar to that about population growth is raging over the interaction between growth and the environment. Growth places heavy demands on the environment, but at the same time efforts to halt environmental deterioration often require resources that seem beyond the means of developing countries. Can countries "grow first and clean up second" as did many industrial countries? Will it be too late then? Are there ways that growth and development can be made compatible with easing environmental impacts?

On What Terms Should Developing Countries Accept Foreign Goods and Capital?

A debate on the appropriate degree of "openness" of developing countries has raged for over 40 years. Its first battleground was ordinary trade. Should poor countries try to enter the international arena with their limited range of export goods, hoping to earn enough to buy industrial goods? Should they try to produce as much as possible at home and minimize their reliance on trade? While those questions were being addressed, many in developing countries became suspicious of foreign companies on their soil, so they added the question of whether those companies should be allowed to enter and remain and, if so, on what terms. More recently, the debate has shifted to the impact of disembodied foreign capital, that is, foreign money that may come in to be invested locally and may just as quickly go out.

The addition of financial capital to flows of trade and physical capital has created a larger debate over globalization, the increasing integration of economic activity with little regard for national borders. This is not just an issue for developing countries but has engaged people throughout the world in a debate over whether national governments and cultures should become, or are becoming, subordinate to the economic decisions of large corporations.

What Should the Role of Government Be?

Through all these controversies runs the question of government's role. What should governments do to spur development and of what kind? Should they promote some kinds of equality? Should they encourage birth control? Should they intervene in private investment decisions that might be environmentally harmful? Should they try to keep some kinds of foreign goods, firms, or money out of the country?

In areas where government involvement is deemed essential, how should it go about participating in the economy? Should it plan in a way that many socialist countries attempted? Should it own its own companies? Stick to providing social services such as health, education, and infrastructure? Should it take the Hong Kong approach: focus on creating and promoting markets by improving the flow of information, standardizing measurements, and efficiently carrying out the responsibility of passing good laws and upholding private contracts? There is now a recognition that **market imperfection**—the failure of markets to function as they should—does not necessarily require government to replace markets, but often presents an opportunity for governments to promote market development and thereby contribute to the development process.

And how "good government" occurs is one of the latest questions to arise in the economics discipline. Economists realize that even if they can give good advice, governments must be willing to accept it and able to implement it. Are democratic governments best able to do that? How can bribery and corruption be minimized so that policy can be made effective? These questions have now become the subject of scrutiny by economists as well as political scientists.

Throughout the book, as we describe economic development, we keep an eye on strategy: evaluating attempts to promote development by the twin gauges of economic theory and countries' experiences. It will come as no surprise that many efforts have failed. But it will be less clear just what *should* be done. We do not trust simply to economic theory; we will find out that theory can only explain the likely results of specific efforts under specific circumstances. The first step is often simply to correctly interpret the circumstances, which is not always an easy task.

SUMMARY AND CONCLUSION

Economic development is a process of achieving sustained and sustainable growth in per capita income, accompanied by diversification of production, reduction of poverty, and expansion of economic opportunities for all citizens. Development encompasses economic growth and changes in the economy's structure—what it produces and how. Economies become both more self-reliant, in that they produce a greater range of goods, and more interdependent, in that their interaction with the rest of the world will increase. Finally, we look for a reasonably equitable distribution of income as a sign that most of the population is enjoying increased economic welfare in the process. We can act purposefully to improve the prospects for economic development, while realizing that other goals remain important.

A simplified economic view of development focuses on shifting resources from consumption to saving so they may be invested in capital goods. Increasing use of capital makes an economy more productive and enhances the prospect for continuous growth, if not development. Government can play at least a minimal role, building infrastructure and providing education and establishing the legal basis for secure market relations. Beyond that, the proper role of government is a matter of much debate.

In Chapter 2 we discuss how to measure development. Measurement helps to clarify the objectives of development and to assess progress in attaining those objectives.

Key Terms

- capital (p. 12)
- capital intensive (p. 12)
- development (p. 3)
- economic growth (p. 3)
- factors of production (p. 12)
- infrastructure (p. 9)

- investment (p. 9)
- labor intensive (p. 8)
- market economy (p. 4)
- market imperfection (p. 16)
- monetization (p. 12)
- per capita income (p. 2)

- primary products (p. 8)
- production function (p. 12)
- productivity (p. 8)
- structural change (p. 9)
- subsistence agriculture (p. 8)
- vicious cycle (p. 8)

Questions for Review

1. Distinguish between economic growth and economic development.
2. How do Taiwan and Saudi Arabia illustrate the differences between economic growth and development?
3. What is meant by "structural change," and what kinds of structural changes in economies have been typical in historical development?
4. What are some key characteristics of a "typical" developing country? Why might such a "typical" picture be unsatisfactory?
5. How would you describe, in the simplest terms, the process of and impediments to development?

Related Internet Resources

Economic development is a huge area of study, and we will note specific topic-related Web sites in each chapter. A good place to begin on the Web is the Virtual Library on International Development at ⟨http://w3.acdi-cida.gc.ca/virtual.nsf⟩. The site is sponsored by the Canadian International Development Agency and has links organized by topic, country, region, and organizations. One particularly interesting organization devoted to development research, focusing on "bottom-up" approaches, is the Institute of Development Studies at the University of Sussex in England. It can be accessed at ⟨http://www.ids.ac.uk/ids.⟩ One of the ongoing quests of development economists is for good data. In other chapters we will note international organizations that compile data for many countries, but it is often helpful to go to sites run by individual governments. Three academic sites provide collections of links to government sites. These are: ⟨http://www.library.northwestern.edu/govpub/resource/internat/foreign⟩, run by Northwestern University; ⟨http://www.lib.umich.edu/libhome/Documents.center/foreign.html⟩, run by the University of Michigan; and ⟨http://dpls.dacc.wisc.edu/crossroads/intlgov.html⟩, run by the University of Wisconsin. The government sites referenced in these libraries vary in their extensiveness and reliability, but they frequently have information not readily available from the international organizations.

Endnotes and Further Readings

1. See the introduction to Robert Heilbroner, *The Great Ascent* (New York: Harper and Row, 1963).
2. Kamala Markandaya, *Nectar in a Sieve* (New York: New American Library, Harper & Row, 1954).
3. These conditions are described in *ibid.*, pp. 141–142.
4. John Isbister, *Promises Not Kept: The Betrayal of Social Change in the Third World* (West Hartford, CT: Kumarian Press, 1998), p. 21.

5. Jennifer A. Elliott, *An Introduction to Sustainable Development* (London: Routledge, 1994), pp. 21–22. Also see David T. Sicular, "Pockets of Peasants in Indonesian Cities: The Case of Scavengers," *World Development* 19, no. 2/3 (February–March 1991), pp. 137–161. For varied pictures of urban life, see Susan Lobo, *A House of My Own: Social Organization in the Squatter Settlements of Lima, Peru* (Tucson: University of Arizona Press, 1982), and Hans Buechler and Judith-Maria Buechler, *The World of Sofia Velasquez: The Autobiography of a Bolivian Market Vendor* (New York: Columbia University Press, 1996).

6. The 1998 data come from the World Bank. The earlier estimates are provided in Lant Pritchett, "Divergence, Big Time," *Journal of Economic Perspectives* 11, no. 3 (summer 1997), p. 11.

7. Vinod Thomas, et al., *The Quality of Growth* (Washington: World Bank, 2000), pp. 11–12.

8. United Nations Development Program, *Human Development Report 1998* and *2000*, and the World Bank, *World Development Indicators 2000*.

9. Henry Bruton, "Import Substitution," in T. N. Srinivisan and H. B. Chenery, eds., *Handbook of Development Economics* 2 (Amsterdam: Elsevier Science Publishers, 1989), p. 1602.

10. The World Bank, *World Development Report 1992*, p. 1.

11. See Simon Kuznets, *Modern Economic Growth: Rate, Structure and Spread* (New Haven: Yale University Press, 1966), summarized in his Nobel lecture, "Modern Economic Growth: Findings and Reflections," *American Economic Review* 63, no. 2 (May 1973), pp. 247–258. Earlier writings were A. G. B. Fisher, "Production: Primary, Secondary and Tertiary," *Economic Record* 15 (1939), pp. 24–38, and Colin Clark, *The Conditions of Economic Progress* (London: Macmillan, 1940).

12. See Moshe Syrquin, "Patterns of Structural Change," in T. N. Srinivisan and H. B. Chenery, eds., *Handbook of Development Economics* 1 (Amsterdam: Elsevier Science Publishers, 1988), pp. 205–273.

13. See Amartya Sen, "The Concept of Development," in T. N. Srinivisan and H. B. Chenery, eds., *Handbook of Development Economics* 1 (Amsterdam: Elsevier Science Publishers, 1988), pp. 9–26, and *Development as Freedom* (New York: Alfred Knopf, 1999).

14. Kamala Markandaya, *Nectar in a Sieve*, p. 135.

15. Else Skjonsberg, *Change in an African Village: Kefa Speaks* (West Hartford, CT: Kumarian Press, 1989), p. 45.

16. Gregory G. Reck, *In the Shadow of Tlaloc: Life in a Mexican Village* (Prospect Heights, IL: Waveland Press, 1978), p. 66.

17. See Denis Goulet, *The Cruel Choice: A New Concept in the Theory of Development* (Lanham, MD: University Press of America, 1985), and *Development Ethics: A Guide to Theory and Practice* (New York: Apex Press, 1995).

CHAPTER

2

MEASURING ECONOMIC DEVELOPMENT

*Economic advance is not
the same as human progress.*
—SIR JOHN CLAPHAM (1873–1946)

INTRODUCTION

Now that we have some understanding of economic development, we should address the tools we can use to measure it. The kind of measurement an economist uses will depend on a particular view of development. In this chapter, we first discuss the problems of measuring output and comparing countries, then examine different approaches to measuring development. Finally, we look at some indicators of development, to see ways in which countries differ economically.

Why is measurement such an important issue? If we take development as a goal of public policy, measurement is essential to evaluate how well it is being achieved. Is the economy growing fast enough? Is it producing more efficiently? Are people healthier and better educated? We must be concerned with the accuracy and consistency of our measurements and the relevance of what we are measuring. None of this is easily achieved.

If measurement is not accurate, we do not really know how well our goals are being met. And, of course, it is essential to be able to repeat this process so our numbers mean the same thing at every attempt. When data gathering is reasonably sophisticated, statistical techniques can be used to make revisions of previous data to allow the numbers to be consistent over years or even decades. In developing countries, economic data are often unreliable, so what is being measured and how requires constant attention.

It is also crucial to know whether what we are trying to measure really tells us something important about economic development. In the first chapter we noted that development means not only higher income but also changes in economic structure. But are these our goals or just means to other goals, such as human well-being? If this broader objective is to be met, economic advance should translate into different kinds of end results, such as healthier, better-educated people, fewer of whom live in poverty and more of whom have an opportunity to choose better lives. Such goals make the measurement task more difficult and important.

In this chapter we review problems involved with measuring economic activity and how measuring development is more complex than simply measuring growth. We

19

then focus on poverty as a particular development problem and provide some ways of comparing the development progress of countries.

HOW CAN WE MEASURE DEVELOPMENT?

The more fully we express the term "economic development," the more difficult it becomes to measure.

Measuring Output

A number of difficulties appear in the attempt to measure an economy's output of goods and services. In the United States, the Department of Commerce simply measures the **Gross Domestic Product (GDP)**—the market value of final production in a year—and the population, and we have *per capita* output, a measure of economic well-being.* But GDP measurement is not completely trustworthy because it neglects nonmarket transactions such as services exchanged between friends and those provided in the home. It also includes the production of goods and services that may be harmful, such as cigarettes. Different measurement customs and fluctuating values of a country's currency cloud meaningful comparisons between countries. In developing countries the problems are of greater magnitude.

Data-Gathering Capabilities

Governments in developing countries are simply less able to measure what is going on, whether that activity is legal or meant to evade the eye of the official agencies. Even in the industrialized countries, GDP is the product of surveys and estimates. In developing countries, the necessary personnel, and experience on which to base sampling procedures, are less likely to be available. International organizations, including the United Nations and the **World Bank**, are the principal publishers of such data, but their sources are largely national agencies.

Unrecorded Transactions

Failure to record some economic transactions is a worldwide problem, exacerbated by conditions in developing countries. For example, home and child care services, often provided by a mother without pay, are not counted. A larger share of such domestic services is performed within the home in developing countries as compared to more developed countries. Barter of goods and services is also not recorded and therefore does not get counted in the GDP. When people attempt to avoid government regulation, for example, by selling from inside their homes, their transactions are not recorded. These transactions are more likely to occur in developing than in developed countries because data collection is less well developed, small businesses may find it more difficult to adhere to government regulations, and tax collection is difficult.

While this latter form of exchange is on the rise in the United States and Russia, it is virtually ubiquitous in developing countries. A recent survey reported on several at-

---

*A similar measure, **Gross National Income (GNI)** (changed from Gross National Product in 2001), includes income earned abroad by domestic resource owners. GDP, on the other hand, includes income created domestically by foreign resource owners, such as foreign investors.

tempts to measure this **shadow** or **second economy**. According to one set of estimates for 1989 to 1990, shadow production, encompassing virtually all categories of goods and services, was equal to 76 percent of recorded GDP in Nigeria and 71 percent in Thailand, compared to 9 percent for Norway. Deteriorating economic conditions in Russia are indicated by data that estimate shadow production equal to 15 percent of GDP for 1989 to 1990, 27 percent for 1990 to 1993, and 41 percent for 1994 to 1995.[1] When government does not know how much of what is being produced, development policy may be seriously misdirected.

Development economists have taken a special interest in the **informal sector**. This consists of economic activity carried out by mostly small businesses—personal services and small-scale production—that do not register with governments and may escape the network of regulation and taxation. In the informal sectors of the rural areas and cities, a vast amount of such activity takes place. The failure to count the relevant activities is higher in developing countries, so in any comparison among countries' GDP levels, the gap between the more and less developed will be exaggerated. Comparing output in a country over time could also be difficult. A study of Tanzania suggests the second economy accounted for 10 percent of total output in the 1960s but 20 percent by the mid-1980s, so changes in output would be understated.[2]

Capital-Intensive Production and Intermediate Goods

In more industrialized countries, production processes are more **capital intensive**; that is, they use more capital per worker than those in developing countries. For example, the same pair of shoes or dress is made with more machinery and so acquires more value in an industrialized country, increasing GDP compared to a poorer country. The gap is compounded because capital goods are ultimately counted twice in GDP. They are counted for the current year as final purchases by businesses of plant and machinery, and they are counted to some extent in succeeding years as part of the value of the goods they produce.

The Ambiguous Meaning of GDP

While we think of GDP as a good thing, not all activity that is counted is beneficial. Some brings unmeasured costs. For example, the processes that create pollution are counted in the GDP, as are the processes that clean up the pollution, so that the impact of environmental damage is twice counted as good. Dangerous substances that make people ill are likewise counted once when they are produced and again when the value of medical care enters the GDP. Advertising expenditure is counted, even if it creates new desires or just convinces people to buy Brand X instead of Brand Z. Cigarette production is a contribution to GDP, and a country that opens up a tobacco processing plant to replace imported cigarettes may celebrate a step forward in its development!

No deduction is taken for the permanent loss of raw materials or the damage done to the environment from the loss of species. The idea that some adjustment should be made to GDP to account for the depletion of natural resources, as we do to account for depreciation of machinery, has found increasing support among development economists and others.[3] A country that produces a large proportion of its GDP in the mining sector, or that uses environmentally more damaging agricultural practices, is sacrificing disproportionately for its output. We will encounter the issue of environmental accounting in Chapter 5.

Living Requirements

We in developed countries compare our level of well-being with other countries that have similar customs and living conditions. But how should we compare our expenditure on transportation with people who do not use private cars to the extent that we do? Or utilities usage by those who live in less variable climates that do not demand houses outfitted with both heating and air-conditioning? Or entertainment expenditures by people who place greater importance on communal living and leisure as opposed to our highly individualistic and equipment-oriented activities? Different types of development may make such comparisons less obvious than would be indicated by calculations of GDP.

Comparing Performance Over Time

Economic progress requires comparing a country's performance over time, but here too there are problems. For example, to know how today's developing countries compare to the past performance of more economically advanced countries, we might want to measure GDP for the rich countries 200 years ago. Such estimates are problematic. One such estimate reports real output per person in 1820 as $312 for Britain, $276 for the United States, and $254 for France. These numbers are roughly the same as 1980 figures of $235 for India, $257 for Pakistan, and $404 for China. A more recent attempt measures U.S. real GDP per person in 1820 as $1,287 in 1990 dollars, a figure matched by Japan in 1907, Spain by about 1860, Brazil in 1937, Indonesia in 1971, Ghana in 1963, and not yet matched in many countries.[4]

However, measuring any country's progress over decades or centuries runs into increasing difficulties. Not only are there fundamental changes in economic structure, but the availability and quality of data improves considerably over time. The use of index numbers, required for measuring price changes including the price components of GDP, brings its own set of problems, including decreased reliability over long time periods (see any statistics text for more on this topic).

Comparing Data Across Countries: The Purchasing Power Parity Approach

Comparing data across countries is difficult due to the dissimilarity of production processes, the impact of price-distorting trade barriers, and the impact of government-determined **exchange rates** (the price of one nation's currency in terms of another, such as 9.6 Mexican pesos per dollar). Even if exchange rates were determined by supply and demand, however, they do not accurately reflect price-level differences among countries because many goods and services are not traded internationally. The frequent use of indices to make comparisons involves difficulties of index number construction compounded by attempts at cross-country comparisons.

The **International Comparison Project (ICP)**, being undertaken under United Nations auspices, aims to reduce nations' GDP data from money values to quantities and prices in order to apply statistical methods that would permit better comparability among nations. This **Purchasing Power Parity (PPP)** approach gives a more accurate depiction of what can be bought in different countries for a given amount of dollars, pesos, or kwacha than the traditional method using exchange rates. The idea of PPP is that exchange rates ought to reflect the actual purchasing power of two currencies. If the dollar is worth 10 pesos, then a dollar and 10 pesos ought to buy the same bundle of goods in the United States and Mexico. An explanation of the methods of the ICP appears in the Appendix to this chapter.[5]

For example, the *Economist* magazine periodically gauges the correct valuation of national currencies by comparing the price of a Big Mac in different countries. If currencies are correctly valued, the local currency price of a Big Mac should translate into the U.S. price at the existing exchange rates (the number of dollars per unit of the local currency). In late 1998, the average price of a Big Mac in Chicago, New York, and San Francisco was $2.63. In Venezuela, the sandwich price, when transformed from pesos into dollars, was $3.33, indicating that the peso was overvalued. In Malaysia, however, the Big Mac cost only $1.10, indicating that the Malaysian ringgit was undervalued.[6]

One of the more significant findings to date is that the traditional method of comparing GDP figures by converting domestic currencies to dollars with exchange rates significantly overstates the gap between rich and poor countries, compared to the PPP method used by the U.N. Project. Table 2–1 shows some countries at different levels of income, ranked by the two methods. For example, in 1999 the World Bank's GNI per capita data, calculated in the traditional fashion, show $39,380 for Switzerland, ranked third, and $120 for Burundi, at number 205, a ratio of 328 to 1. The PPP data produce GNI per capita of $28,760 for Switzerland (seventh highest) and $570 for Burundi (number 203), a ratio of 50 to 1. The gap is tremendous but more realistic with the PPP data.

Another example of the impact of these comparisons is changes in countries' relative positions. The table shows, for example, that with the traditional method, Algeria's income is 5 percent higher than Romania's, with the two countries ranking 117 and 120. With the PPP measure, Romania's income is 23 percent higher than Algeria's, giving it a rank of 90 compared to Algeria's 105.

In the face of all these difficulties, it is easy to be skeptical about any set of GDP comparisons. Our only real alternatives, however, are to improve our methods or to

TABLE 2–1 Per Capita GNI, 1999

Country	Exchange-Rate Method GNI per Capita	Rank	PPP Method GNI per Capita	Rank
Switzerland	$38,380	3	$28,760	7
Denmark	32,050	6	25,600	13
United States	31,910	8	31,910	4
Greece	12,110	46	15,800	48
Chile	4,630	70	8,410	72
Algeria	1,550	117	4,840	105
Romania	1,470	120	5,970	90
Georgia	620	149	2,540	144
Nicaragua	410	164	2,060	156
Tanzania	260	187	500	206
Mozambique	220	195	810	192
Burundi	120	205	570	203

Source: World Bank, *World Development Indicators 2001.*

stop making comparisons. But policy makers and private individuals, as well as economists, are interested in how well economic goals are being achieved in different countries in order to appreciate what is being achieved and to correct problems that arise in meeting those goals. So we must improve what we can and use the figures carefully.[7] The problems become more complex, however, when we go beyond GDP to try and measure development.

Measuring Development: The Human Development Index

In contemplating development, more than access to goods and services is at stake. A number of organizations have therefore attempted to construct measures of social well-being. The Overseas Development Council in the United States proposed doing away altogether with measuring income and measuring instead a **Physical Quality of Life Index (PQLI)**: an equal weighting of infant mortality rate, life expectancy, and basic literacy.[8] However, because income does reflect access to goods and services, most economists prefer an index that incorporates an income measure, the most prominent of which is the **Human Development Index (HDI)**, constructed since 1990 by the United Nations Development Program (UNDP).

The Human Development Index

The Human Development Index ranks countries based on their scores in (1) health, for which life expectancy is taken as a reasonable gauge; (2) knowledge, expressed as a combination of literacy rates and average years of schooling; and (3) per capita income.

Originally, the rankings were based on the highest and lowest values measured throughout the world. This procedure gave only relative rankings that could not be compared over time because even an absolute improvement could leave a country at a lower ranking if others improved by more. Starting in 1994, the scales were changed to reflect absolute minimum and maximum levels. Economists considered historical data and projected forward 30 years, so that country performance could be measured by a set of fixed criteria. The range of average life expectancy worldwide, for example, is now from 25 to 85. Adult literacy rates could range from 0 to 100 percent, and average years of schooling could range from 0 to 15.

Finally, the ranking of per capita income levels has been revised to take advantage of the PPP approach by substituting **real income**, deflated by prices at purchasing power parity, for **nominal income** at current prices. The HDI method here has an interesting feature. Economists have long based their theory of demand on the proposition that consumption of an additional unit of a good in a fixed time period brings lower **marginal utility**, or additional satisfaction, for the consumer. Some have argued, by extension, that at higher income levels the marginal utility of the additional dollar earned is lower than earlier dollars. The HDI income-ranking system is based on that proposition: Actual per capita income levels are scaled so that higher income levels are given less than proportional weight. The current income ranges are from $100 to $40,000. Development Spotlight 2–1 shows how the index discounts higher levels of income.

One conclusion based on the HDI is that higher per capita income does not always correlate with a better life as measured by health and educational outcomes. Countries with lower income levels may provide better health and education possibilities than some countries with higher incomes. Table 2–2 gives a comparison of a

DIMINISHING MARGINAL UTILITY OF INCOME

The Human Development Index adjusts countries' per capita income by discounting higher incomes in order to emphasize decreasing marginal utility of higher income levels. For the 1999 Human Development Index, the range of incomes was $100 to $40,000. The gap between the rich and poor is narrowed by the adjustment shown in the table at right.

A country with per capita income of $5,000 has an income index almost two-thirds the value of a country whose income is eight times as high.

Actual Income	Index
$ 100	0.00
5,000	0.65
10,000	0.78
20,000	0.88
30,000	0.96
40,000	1.00

TABLE 2–2 Per Capita GDP and HDI, 1998

Country	Per Capita GDP*	HDI[†]	GDP – HDI[‡]
United States	$29,605	0.929	– 1
Kuwait	25,314	0.836	– 31
Hungary	10,232	0.817	– 1
Costa Rica	5,987	0.797	18
Cuba	3,967	0.783	40
Lebanon	4,326	0.735	3
Oman	9,960	0.730	– 42
South Africa	8,488	0.697	– 54
Tajikistan	1,041	0.663	43
Syria	2,892	0.660	– 1
Gabon	6,353	0.592	– 60
Ghana	1,735	0.556	0
Bangladesh	1,361	0.461	0
Angola	1,821	0.405	– 34

*By the Purchasing Power Parity method.

[†]Highest index was Canada (0.935) and lowest was Sierra Leone (0.252).

[‡]Numerical GDP rank minus numerical HDI rank: A positive value means the country ranks higher in human development, as measured by the HDI, than in GDP.

Source: Human Development Report 2000.

number of countries' GDP per capita and HDI. Countries are listed in order of their HDI, and while some are comparable in terms of GDP and HDI, some clearly are not, as indicated in the third column: A negative number indicates a country where income performance is better than human development, while a positive number shows a country where human development is relatively better than income performance. Gabon, for example, has a negative 60 indicating that its level of income is not matched by life expectancy and educational achievement. Cuba, on the other hand, has higher health and educational levels than might be expected on the basis of its per capita income. Ghana and Bangladesh rank equally in both measures.

Since 1992 the *Human Development Report* has been experimenting with measurements of personal and regional income distribution, gender disparities, poverty indices, and political freedom. None of these measurements is definitive, but they add to our understanding of peoples' situations and options. For instance, many economists accept the idea that widespread discrimination against females reduces a nation's quality of life.

Problems with the HDI

Such alternative indices have generated a great deal of debate. The PQLI ignored income, which is an important indicator of individuals' access to goods and services. The HDI has been criticized for the items it includes, how it measures them, and the equal weighting of those items. The individual items are highly correlated, that is, they are not statistically independent and together may not add more information than income levels alone. The results provide little usable information on the cause and effect between human development and economic growth.[9] Some of the data are out of date and incomplete, and one prominent critic contends that there is insufficient agreement on what constitutes human development for any one index to be acceptable.[10]

Ultimately, the usefulness of such composite indices depends on whether they suggest policies, other than a traditional focus on economic growth, to improve well-being. Supporters claim the HDI has in fact brought human dimensions of development to the front of the debate.[11] If the HDI serves as a conscience to policy makers it will have positive value, although there is no way to measure whether that value offsets the cost of the resources used to keep it going.

POVERTY AND INCOME DISTRIBUTION

In discussing economic development, we must give special consideration to poverty and **income distribution**, which shows the percentage of total income received by different portions of the population. The fact that a country's level of per capita income is low hides the fact that some of its citizens are wealthy, while many in the industrialized countries have income levels that allow only very low levels of consumption. Income is unequally distributed in every society, and each society has a portion of the population living below what it considers a poverty level. The question of poverty and income distribution has become more prominent in the last 20 years as economists wrestle with the possibility that income distribution may be an important factor in how an economy grows.

Poverty and Basic Human Needs

Many development economists have recognized that rapid rates of economic growth in some developing countries were not improving the quality of life for some of the poorest people. This led to the creation, in the late 1970s, to what is called the **Basic Human Needs (BHN)** approach to development. These basic needs include food, clothing, and shelter; health, including access to safe drinking water and adequate sanitation facilities; and the education necessary to allow a person to earn adequate income.

Advocates of this approach claim that meeting those needs would reduce poverty without sacrificing economic growth. The rationale is that very poor people who lack basic necessities such as health and education are not productive workers, so making an investment in those necessities will increase productivity and contribute to growth. The strategy is to aim development programs directly at basic levels of education, food, clean water, sanitation, and housing, rather than just promote growth and hope that the benefits would "trickle down" to eventually fill those basic needs. Proponents claim that the BHN is not only compatible with economic growth in the short run but produces superior rates of growth over the long run.[12] Little empirical evidence is available on which to evaluate this claim, but there is growing study of programs that "target" the poor.[13] A recent study suggests that rapidly growing countries in East Asia differed in the extent to which they had reduced poverty: Malaysia and South Korea took specific steps to combat poverty and succeeded, while Thailand and China grew without making a dent in poverty.[14] Because measures of income inequality are not highly correlated with measures of absolute poverty,[15] BHN proponents warn that unless the poorest *people* (rather than just poor countries or poor regions) are the beneficiaries of programs, income distribution can improve but still leave hundreds of millions of people without the basic necessities of life.[16]

The concern with **poverty** is important. Table 2–3 provides the most recent set of data from the World Bank. According to these estimates, almost half of the world's 6 billion people in 1998 lived on less than $2 a day. One-fifth of the world, about 1.2 billion people, lived in **absolute poverty** based on minimum requirements of food, clothing, and other basic needs yielding a consumption level of less than $400 per person in 1993 purchasing power parity dollars: just over a dollar a day.[17] The total was somewhat down from 1990 but actually up a bit since 1987. The percentage has fallen, however, as the total population has grown. The World Bank uses $1.08 per day as its poverty line, but when it sets guidelines for individual countries, it uses a figure equal to one-third of that country's average consumption level, if doing so yields a consumption level above $1.08.

Poverty is a significant statistical obstacle for social scientists. They consider the poverty line to be a barely subsistence level of income. But millions live just above that line, so many economists argue that attention should be given to those who have higher consumption levels but no surplus to save.[18] The poorest are more likely to be part of the group whose activities are most difficult to measure. For income alone, there is the problem of intermittent employment, informal-sector income, and, for

TABLE 2–3 Poverty in Developing Countries, 1990 and 1998

	People Living Below $1/Day		Percentage Living Below $1/Day		Poverty Line*	Percentage Below One-Third National Average Consumption	
	1990	1998	1990	1998		1990	1998
East Asia/Pacific	452.4	278.3	27.6	15.3	1.3	33.7	19.6
Excluding China	92.0	65.1	18.5	11.3	1.9	38.7	24.6
Europe/Central Asia	7.1	24.0	1.6	5.1	2.7	16.2	25.6
Latin America/Caribbean	73.8	78.2	16.8	15.6	3.3	51.5	51.4
Mideast/North Africa	5.7	5.5	2.4	1.9	1.8	14.5	10.8
South Asia	495.1	522.0	44.0	40.0	1.1	44.2	40.2
Sub-Saharan Africa	242.3	290.9	47.7	46.3	1.3	52.1	50.5
Total	1276.4	1198.9	29.0	24.0	1.6	37.4	32.1

*1993 PPP $ per day.

Source: World Development Report 2000/2001. Data for 1998 are preliminary.

farmers, the problem of estimating income from crop prices. Governments must supplement business firm data with household surveys that are subject to a great deal of error. Data on health and education must rely on institutional records, from hospitals and schools, which are not well kept and may reflect only a small portion of the relevant data.

Data on poverty are often not made public because they may indicate patterns of discrimination as well as general economic distress. A high incidence of poverty among families headed by women and among particular ethnic groups points to social policy that goes beyond economic measures.[19]

The World Bank despairs that some of the reported national data are "estimates made in national or international offices using assumptions and models" rather than actual counts.[20] While this is true for many other economic and social statistics, the measurement of poverty in developing countries is a particularly daunting problem. Nonetheless, many believe that until widespread absolute poverty is abolished, economic and human development cannot be considered a success.

Income Distribution

Simon Kuznets suggested that the early stages of growth might be accompanied by increasing inequality of income, followed in later stages by greater equality; a hint that others picked up and referred to as an **inverted U** pattern, or Kuznets curve (Figure 2–1). Presumably, inequality was necessary to permit the wealthy to save resources for investment. As development proceeded, a relative few in the more advanced sectors would gain, heightening inequality, until a larger middle class was formed. Some studies have found this pattern, but others have not supported it because of the wide variations in measurements of inequality at any level of per capita income. The consensus is that the particular policies and institutions guiding a country's development are more important than the stage in the development process or its income level.[21] Even

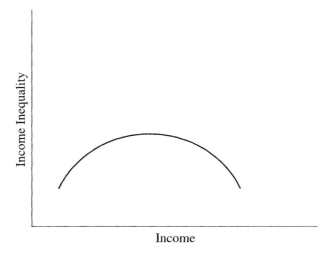

FIGURE 2–1 The Inverted "U," or Kuznets Curve

The inverted U represents a tendency for income inequality to increase as income grows but to fall back at higher levels. There is no recognized income level at which inequality is ordinarily reduced.

if early capitalist development does generate increasing inequality, this can be mitigated by careful government policies.

Why does an economist care about the distribution of income? Because distribution is not just a question of fairness but may have an impact on a country's ability to develop. Income is derived from assets, including **human capital**, or the income-earning potential derived from a person's education and training. Some recent studies show that relative equality in the distribution of key assets, such as land, can produce more rapid growth. Not only are the assets productive themselves, but they also ensure greater access to credit to improve productivity, including human productivity through education.[22]

We are less clear on the connection between income inequality and growth. A new study, using improved data and an expanded set of variables, concludes that at least over a five-year period and possibly longer, greater income inequality produces more rapid growth. The author is not certain why this should be true. He suggests that spending on health and education, which contributes to faster growth, is more important than previously thought and may be associated with greater inequality. Corruption, which increases inequality but stifles growth, has also been ignored in earlier studies.[23]

Two of the most commonly used measurements of income distribution are the Gini coefficient and the Lorenz curve from which it is derived. The **Lorenz curve**, shown in Figure 2–2, measures population percentiles on the horizontal axis and the cumulative percentage of income earned on the vertical axis. If each household earned exactly the same income, the curve would be a straight line at a 45-degree angle to the origin. As the curve sinks farther below this line, distribution becomes more unequal. The **Gini coefficient** is the ratio of the area between the line and the curve (Area A) to the entire area under the line (Area A+B). In a country characterized by perfect equality, the coefficient would be equal to zero; all the income going to one family would give a coefficient of one. Less equality gives a more bloated area between the line and the curve and a higher Gini coefficient.

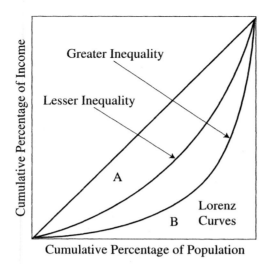

Cumulative Percentage of Income

Greater Inequality

Lesser Inequality

A

Lorenz
B   Curves

Cumulative Percentage of Population

TABLE 2-4 Income Levels and Measures of Inequality

Country	Per Capita Income 1999	Inequality	
		Gini	*Top/Bottom*
Burundi	$ 570	.33	5.3
Bangladesh	1,530	.34	4.9
Nicaragua	2,060	.60	27.6
India	2,226	.38	5.7
Honduras	2,270	.59	38.6
Sri Lanka	3,230	.34	5.4
Morocco	3,320	.40	7.2
Peru	4,480	.46	11.6
Venezuela	5,420	.49	14.4
Brazil	6,840	.59	24.2
Malaysia	7,640	.49	12.0
Poland	8,390	.32	5.1
Chile	8,410	.57	17.4
Hungary	11,050	.24	3.4
Czech Republic	12,840	.25	3.5
Greece	15,800	.33	5.4
New Zealand	17,630	.44	17.4
Sweden	22,150	.25	3.6
United Kingdom	22,220	.36	6.5
Ireland	22,460	.36	6.4
Germany	23,510	.30	4.7
Switzerland	28,760	.33	5.8
United States	$31,910	.41	8.9

Source: World Development Indicators 2000. Gini and top/bottom ratios are for varying years between 1987 and 1998.

Table 2–4 provides Gini coefficients for selected countries. The original data apply to different years (ranging from 1987 to 1998), and the estimation method is not precise. Nevertheless, they provide some idea of the differences that exist, and the lack of simple correspondence between level of per capita income and income distribution, as illustrated in Figure 2–3.[24] The data do show a greater consistency of low coefficients (relatively equal distributions) among higher-income countries than among those at lower incomes. But some high-income countries, such as Sweden, use taxes and government spending to enhance equality while others do not. Among the low- to middle-income countries, those with low coefficients tend to be either very poor (Bangladesh, Burundi) or have made significant efforts at greater equality under socialist governments (Poland, Hungary, and the Czech Republic). Some of the higher coefficients are in countries that have been growing rapidly, such as Malaysia, Colombia, and Brazil. Others, however, such as Venezuela and Costa Rica, have much more modest growth records. Case 2–1 gives a brief account of inequality in Brazil.

Table 2–4 adds another measure of inequality, the **top/bottom ratio**, a ratio of the share of income received by the top 20 percent of the population to the share received by the bottom 20 percent. A higher ratio would mean greater inequality. If we

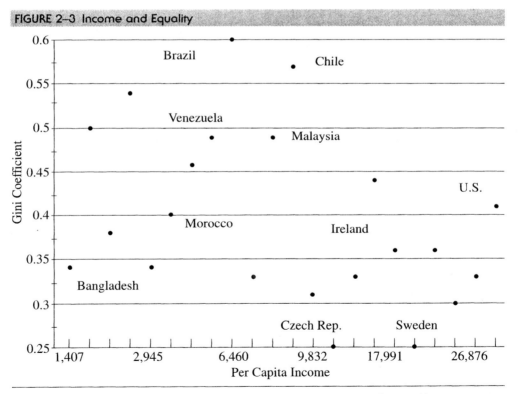

FIGURE 2–3 Income and Equality

There seems to be no close correlation between per capita income and the degree of income inequality. High-income countries tend to have relatively greater equality, but low- and middle-income countries may have more inequality or less.

CASE 2–1

INEQUALITY IN BRAZIL

FAST FACTS

On the Map: South America

Population: 168 Million

Per Capita GNI and Rank: $4,350 (73)

Life Expectancy: Male—63 Female—71

Adult Literacy Rate: Male—85%
Female—85%

Of all the countries for which the World Bank has calculated a Gini ratio, Brazil's .591 in 1997 was the sixth highest. Inequality in Brazil has been historically high but has worsened from a Gini of .50 in 1960 to 0.63 in 1990. The top 10 percent of the population earned 34 times as much as the bottom 10 percent in 1960, rising to 82 times in 1989 before falling back to 60 times in 1990.

Most of this worsening distribution occurred in two decades of rapid growth from 1960 to 1980. By 1980, landholdings of less than 10 hectares accounted for half of all holdings, but only 2.5 percent of the land area, while holdings over 100 hectares constituted less than 11 percent of the holdings but 80 percent of the land. (A hectare is a land area equal to about 2.5 acres.) The southeast province had 44 percent of the population in 1980 but earned 64 percent of the income in 1975 and contributed 73 percent of industrial output. The northeast province, with 29 percent of the 1980 population, earned 12 percent of the income in 1975 and contributed 8 percent of the industrial output.

What accounts for this degree of inequality? In its early years, Brazil imported considerable slave labor from Africa and followed policies to keep labor both cheap and illiterate (therefore unable to vote). Whether the government deliberately attempted to keep wages down during Brazil's "miracle" growth years (1964 to 1980) is a matter of debate, but the rapid structural changes increased the demand for skilled labor and held down the demand for unskilled labor while the population was growing rapidly: Wage differentials would naturally have spread. In the 1980s, inflation and stagnation contributed to further inequality.

In the midst of the debate about the impact of Brazil's economic policies, one fact stands out. Throughout its history, through the present day, good education has been available only to a few in Brazil. In the words of a recent study, unequal access to good education is "perhaps the main single cause of income inequality in Brazil."

Sources: Angus Maddison and Associates, *The Political Economy of Poverty, Equity and Growth: Brazil and Mexico* (New York: Oxford University Press for the World Bank, 1992); André Urani, "The Effects of Macroeconomic Adjustment on the Labor Market and on Income Distribution in Brazil," in Albert Berry, ed., *Poverty, Economic Reform, and Income Distribution in Latin America* (Boulder, CO: Lynne Rienner, 1998), pp. 205–231; Marcello Abreu and Dorte Verner, *Long-Term Brazilian Economic Growth 1930–94* (Paris: OECD, 1997); and Ricardo Barros, Rosane Mendonica, and Sonia Rocha, "Brazil: Welfare, Inequality, Poverty, Social Indicators, and Social Programs in the 1980s," in Nora Lustig, ed., *Coping with Austerity: Poverty and Inequality in Latin America* (Washington: Brookings, 1995), pp. 237–274.

compare the top/bottom ratios with the Gini coefficient for the same countries, we find that the two measures are highly compatible.

ALL DEVELOPING COUNTRIES ARE NOT ALIKE

The World Bank's ranking by per capita GNI (measured by the traditional exchange rate method) provides some dividing lines to distinguish low income (less than $755 per person in 1999), lower-middle income ($756 to $2,995 per person), upper-middle income ($2,996 to $9,266), and upper-income countries. The low-income group, containing most African countries along with some in Asia and Latin America, is a special category: Those countries are eligible for low-interest-rate loans from the International Development Agency, a special affiliate of the World Bank. Another special category, known as the **Newly Industrializing Countries (NICs)**, including Brazil, South Korea, Taiwan, and Argentina, identifies a group of countries that are considered on the brink of becoming developed in spite of some continuing problems. Then there are countries such as Saudi Arabia which are clearly rich but in many ways not developed.

There are also differences *within* countries. Whether the poor region is Appalachia in the United States, southern Italy, or the northeast in Brazil, differences in per capita income are prevalent within most countries. Many minority ethnic groups fare relatively poorly throughout the world. And the southern Indian state of Kerala, while sharing in the poor economic numbers of that country, has adopted policies that have dramatically improved the health, educational, and social status of the local population.[25] Case 2–2 summarizes the rather unusual case of Kerala.

Table 2–5 and 2–6 provide comparisons of key economic and social characteristics of countries in four income groups. China and India are often considered separately due to their size and importance. Until 1999, for example, the World Bank's *World Development Report* and *World Development Indicators* reported the low-income group with and without those two countries, but in that year China moved into the low-middle income group, dropped to the low-income group for the 2000 report, and up again for 2001. The average growth rate of these two has outpaced the high-income countries, but so have the growth rates of some other groups.

Agriculture accounts for almost one-fourth of output and two-thirds of employment in low-income countries. Agriculture declines in relative importance with higher incomes, while services tend to become more important. Savings and investment rates are relatively high in low-income countries in the years when China is in that group. In 1998, for example, the low-income countries had a 30 percent savings rate, but when China moved up in 1999 the rate fell to 20 percent. The 29 percent investment rate in 1998 likewise falls to 22 without China. Both savings and investment show declining shares at higher income levels. Life expectancy is significantly different only in the lowest-income countries, such as Rwanda, Haiti, and Laos, while population growth, infant mortality, and adult illiteracy evidently vary inversely with income.

A detailed examination of individual countries would bring even greater caution to designation by income groups. China and India, for example, have huge populations—more than 2 billion people between them—while many of the poorest countries have populations of around 1 million. Their low level of per capita incomes clash

POVERTY AND DEVELOPMENT: THE CASE OF KERALA

FAST FACTS

On the Map: South Asia

Population: 30 Million (1991)

Per Capita GNP and Rank: $324 (1996: Not Ranked)

Life Expectancy: Male—67 Female—72 (1996)

Adult Literacy Rate: Male—96 Female—90 (1997)

One of the more interesting stories in development is the state of Kerala in India. Although data are sometimes conflicting, they all indicate that Kerala is poorer than the average Indian state and may be growing more slowly as well. But in 1995, India's Human Development Index was 0.451; Kerala's was 0.628. By one estimate, adult literacy in 1994 was 90 percent, far above India's 51 percent and on a par with many of the rapidly industrializing economies of East Asia. Life expectancy in the early 1990s was about 10 years higher than the Indian average, and its population growth rate was lower. A 1973 to 1974 survey showed a poverty rate of 60 percent in Kerala and 55 percent in India: 20 years later India's rate had fallen to 36 percent and Kerala's to 25 percent.

This kind of comparison goes on and on. More education, more equality for females, better health: In generally every index that represents human well-being—other than income—Kerala outperforms the average for India. The important questions are why this has occurred and, because an economist must put the question this way, at what cost.

The first question has, to those who see Kerala as a better development "model," relatively easy answers. The state government in Kerala has seen to it that resources are distributed in ways that achieve their ob-jectives. In the average Indian state, representative data from the years 1960 to 1993 show that spending on education was almost 20 percent of all spending: In Kerala, the percentage never dipped below 25 percent and was often greater than 30 percent. In health care, Kerala was not unusual in the amount that it spent, but facilities were better and the higher levels of education permitted the public to make better use of information about health and disease. The state government also made poverty reduction a priority and has numerous programs to provide financial assistance to the poor.

Why all this occurred is also fairly clear, at least in general outline. The political culture of Kerala has from early on favored popular participation. An emphasis on literacy and activism, a greater willingness than in other parts of the country to put aside religious prejudices, and for many years strong left-wing governments have favored equity goals over those of economic growth.

The second question, at what cost has this been achieved, may never be answered to everyone's satisfaction. We would want to know, for example, how much lower economic growth has been in Kerala than in other similar states that pursued different policies. We would want some way to suggest whether different policies might have, in Kerala's circumstances, produced different results.

In fact, all is not well with Kerala. While growth rates have usually been satisfactory, they have often fallen below the average for all India. Many traditional economic activities have stagnated, and new ones have not always risen to take their place. Unemployment, however much alleviated by government programs, has been about three times the national average. The state government has faced fiscal difficulties; environmental destruction has been significant, particularly in the loss of forests; and some portions of the population have been left out.

These problems cannot all be put on the Kerala model: They afflict other countries and other states as well, and we cannot be certain that a different model might have worked better in Kerala. But even if the model is implicated in some of these difficulties, we would still have to weigh Kerala's achievements in the balance. If Kerala sacrificed growth over a 40-year period to achieve longer, healthier life, more education and greater equity, and political participation, one could argue both that this sacrifice was worthwhile and that it paved the

way for greater growth in the future. Searching for these answers, and others like them throughout the world, will occupy us for a long time.

Source: An excellent recent source on the Kerala experience is Govindan Parayil, ed., *Kerala: The Development Experience* (London: Zed Books, 2000). The data in this case come from several articles in the book. Data in the case text are from K. P. Kannan, "Poverty Alleviation as Advancing Human Capabilities: Kerala's Achievements Compared," pp. 40–65. For the Fast Facts, more current data were taken from other articles: population from Parayil's "Introduction: Is Kerala's Development Experience a 'Model'?", pp. 1–15; adult literacy from V. K. Ramachandran, "Kerala's Development Achievements and Their Replicability," pp. 88–115; GNP and life expectancy from Richard W. Franke and Barbara H. Chasin, "Is the Kerala Model Sustainable? Lessons from the Past, Prospects for the Future," pp. 16–39.

TABLE 2–5 Economic Indicators for Income Groups

Indicator	Low Income	Low-Middle Income	High-Middle Income	High Income
GNI Per Capita: 1999 By PPP Method	$1,870	$4,250	$8,770	$25,690
GDP Annual Growth (%)				
1980–1990	4.7	4.2	2.6	3.4
1990–1999	3.2	3.4	3.6	2.3
Saving as Percentage of GDP				
1980	28	na	25	24
1999	20	30	23	23
Investment as Percentage of GDP				
1980	28	na	25	25
1999	22	26	22	22
Shares of Output: 1999*				
Agriculture	26	14	6	2
Industry	30	39	33	30
Services	44	46	60	65
Percentage of Labor Force in Agriculture, 1990–1998[†]				
Male/Female	61/75	56/61	23/15	4/3
Commercial Energy Consumption per person (Kg. Oil Equivalent) 1998	550	1,116	2,025	5,366

*Share of output for high-income countries is for 1998.

[†]Most recent year for which data are available.

Source: World Development Indicators 2000, 2001.

TABLE 2-6 Social Indicators for Income Groups

Indicator	Low Income	Low-Middle Income	High-Middle Income	High Income
Life Expectancy, 1999	59	69	69	78
Population Growth Rate (1980–1999 (% per year)	2.1	1.4	1.6	0.7
Adult Illiteracy Rate, 1999				
Male	29	9	9	<5
Female	48	22	14	<5
Infant Mortality Rate (per 1,000 live births) 1999	77	32	27	6
Doctors/1000, 1990–1998*	1.0	2.0	1.5	2.8
Urban Population (%)				
1980	24	31	64	75
1999	31	43	75	77
Primary School Enrollments: Percentage of Relevant Age Group,[†] 1997	97	120	109	103

*Most recent year for which data are available.

[†]Percentages exceed 100 because those who are above the normal age are enrolled along with those from the primary school-age group.

Source: World Development Indicators 1999, 2000, 2001.

with high levels of social complexity and industrial production. Measured in total output, China had the seventh largest economy in the world in 1999 and may have the world's largest economy within a few years. Some East Asian countries, including South Korea and Taiwan, are strong competitors in world export markets and have proportionately large industrial sectors.

Sub-Saharan Africa was, perhaps most of all regions, shaped politically by European colonialism, with national boundaries separating and combining ethnic communities at the discretion of the colonizing countries. It is the poorest region in the world. Many Latin American countries have been nominally independent for well over a century, have large Catholic populations, and in some cases had levels of development equal to some European countries just a few decades ago. They vary considerably in the size of their land area, population, and level of income. Some still export largely agricultural commodities, while Brazil exports a large range of industrial goods including sophisticated military aircraft and computers. Additional differences will emerge, but we should understand that these countries range from the poorest peasant societies, some almost stagnant in recent decades, to modern, rapidly growing, and industrializing states.

Throughout the book we will be contrasting the experiences of developing countries. Their differences in economics, geography, and politics at the start of the postwar era are matched by tremendous differences in the policies they have followed and how successful they have been.

SUMMARY AND CONCLUSION

We have already seen the complexity of the economic development process. Measuring economic development is a difficult task. Even measuring the level of output of an economy is extremely difficult due to problems of definition, measurement, and comparing countries with different economic characteristics. Poverty tends to perpetuate itself and to hold back the development process by preventing people from acquiring productive assets. Supplementing data on per capita output with measurements of income distribution is useful. Severe inequality, especially for asset ownership, is now being recognized as a hindrance to growth and development.

The problems of measuring development should be a source of humility. We have only an approximate idea of what the world looks like. But even these approximations can tell us a significant amount about where the problems lie and give us some guidance as we look for ways to improve people's lives. As we accumulate a number of different measures of well-being, we become aware of significant differences among developing countries, but the comparison of countries along some development continuum becomes increasingly difficult.

Before turning to the key elements of development, however, it will be helpful to understand the different ways that economists have viewed the process as a whole. In Chapter 3 we review different models of economic growth and development. This will show how economists' understanding of these processes has evolved and allow us to highlight in advance some issues that will concern us in later chapters.

Key Terms

- absolute poverty (p. 27)
- Basic Human Needs (BHN) (p. 27)
- capital intensive (p. 21)
- exchange rate (p. 22)
- Gini coefficient (p. 29)
- Gross Domestic Product (GDP) (p. 20)
- Gross National Income (GNI) (p. 20)
- human capital (p. 29)

- Human Development Index (HDI) (p. 24)
- income distribution (p. 26)
- informal sector (p. 21)
- International Comparison Project (ICP) (p. 22)
- inverted U (p. 28)
- Lorenz curve (p. 29)
- marginal utility (p. 24)
- Newly Industrializing Countries (NICs) (p. 33)

- nominal income (p. 24)
- Physical Quality of Life Index (PQLI) (p. 24)
- poverty (p. 27)
- Purchasing Power Parity (PPP) (p. 22)
- real income (p. 24)
- shadow (second) economy (p. 21)
- top/bottom ratio (p. 31)
- World Bank (p. 20)

Questions for Review

1. What is Gross Domestic Product? What are some of the problems of measuring the GDP and comparing GDP levels among countries?
2. How does the International Comparison Project modify the usual method of calculating GDP?
3. What are some of the problems inherent in measuring economic development, as opposed to economic growth? How does the Human Development Index attempt to measure development, and what are some of its drawbacks?
4. How are the Lorenz curve and the Gini coefficient used to convey information about income distribution?
5. How does income distribution affect economic development?

6. Examine the following data for two hypothetical countries:

Measure	Country A	Country B
Per capita GDP	$350	$700
Gini coefficient	.29	.44
GDP growth rate	2.90	3.40
Population growth rate	2.20	3.30

Which country do you consider more developed? In which country would you rather live? Why? What other economic information would you like to have before making your decision?

7. Morocco fares much more poorly in the HDI ranking (125) than in its GDP (98) and has a moderately poor income distribution (Gini = 0.39). Costa Rica fares much better in HDI (34) than GDP (62) and has a more unequal income distribution (Gini = 0.47). Are these measurements consistent or conflicting? How would you explain this?

8. What is the rationale for the Basic Human Needs approach to development?

9. Why does Brazil have such a high degree of income inequality? Why is Kerala's performance in this area so different?

Related Internet Resources

Two of the major sources for statistics in development are the World Bank and the United Nations Development Program (UNDP). The Bank publishes its annual World Development Report and World Development Indicators, along with research papers, reports on Bank programs, and other data. Its Web site is ⟨http://www.worldbank.org⟩. The UNDP publishes its annual Human Development Report and other information as well. Its Web site is ⟨http://www.undp.org⟩. The data that are used to translate GDP into purchasing power parity values, along with other data, are in the Penn World Tables, sponsored by the United Nations. The data are made available through the National Bureau of Economic Research, at ⟨http://www.nber.org/pub/pwt56.html⟩. An interesting take on the question of quality of life is the Genuine Progress Indicator (GPI), published by a group called "Redefining Progress." Their data, contrasting the GPI to GDP, is calculated only for the United States, but the question is a more general one. Their Web site is ⟨http://www.rprogress.org⟩.

Appendix

THE INTERNATIONAL COMPARISON PROJECT (ICP)

The traditional way to compare income levels of different countries is to simply take the values of Gross Domestic Product in their own currencies and transform them into a common currency, usually the U.S. dollar, using the rate of exchange that prevails between the currencies, on average, for the year. However, this kind of comparison is distorted for a number of reasons, including the fact that exchange rates are not likely to reflect the actual relative purchasing power of the two currencies.

The **International Comparison Project** is attempting to eliminate that distortion by breaking down expenditure on GDP into categories based on detailed investigation of individual items, to gauge the relative purchasing power of currencies and compare GDP figures on that basis. At the end, the comparison is made not by using market exchange rates but by Purchasing Power Parity (PPP), which is the relative purchasing power of the currencies for similar items. If expenditure categories (E) are divided by their prices (P), the result is a ratio of the physical quantities of goods (Q) that can be purchased in the two countries. In the terminology used by Kravis (Endnote 5),

$$\frac{Qj}{Qb} = \frac{Ej}{Eb} \bigg/ \frac{Pj}{Pb}$$

where j and b stand for the two countries.

The project has divided GDP into about 150 expenditure categories, which it tries to make as comparable as possible in terms of component items and their qualities. Those items are assigned world average prices in order to obtain the E values. The E values are then divided by the individual countries' P values, in order to derive Q. The ratio of one country's Q to another then represents the ratio of their GDPs at Purchasing Power Parity.

As a final step, the project compares GDP ratios using PPP with the same ratios derived from the usual exchange rate (ER) comparison. A ratio of ER/PPP, called the Exchange Rate Deviation Index (ERDI), is determined, which allows us to see if there is any pattern to the differences between the two methods of calculating GDP; and it turns out that there is.

Since the usual exchange-rate comparisons of GDP have involved translating all other countries' GDP into dollars, it is not surprising that those countries with economic structures and trading patterns most like the United States have less deviation between the two methods of calculation. Those countries are the richer ones. In most cases, the lower the dollar GDP as traditionally measured, the more the distortion introduced by the exchange-rate method. As a rule, the *lower* a country's income, the more that income has been *underestimated* by the traditional exchange-rate measure.

Using the 1980 data, for example, the ERDIs for Japan and India were 0.95 and 2.91, respectively. This means that when making the adjustment from the traditional methods of comparing those countries' GDPs to that of the United States by the PPP method, Japan's GDP figure must be reduced by 5 percent, whereas India's must be nearly tripled.

The ICP is continuing to refine its methods and extend its estimates to larger numbers of countries. It will not remove all the problems of GDP comparisons but may be able to give us a somewhat more realistic measure of the differences among countries in this area.

Endnotes and Further Readings

1. Friedrich Schneider and Dominik H. Enste, "Shadow Economies: Sizes, Causes, and Consequences," *Journal of Economic Literature* 37, no. 1 (March 2000), pp. 77–114. Also see Shamim Hamid, "Non-Market Work and National Income: The Case of Bangladesh," *Bangladesh Development Studies* 22, no. 2/3 (June–September 1994), pp. 1–48.

2. M. S. D. Bagachwa and A. Naho, "Estimating the Second Economy in Tanzania," *World Development* 23, no. 8 (August 1995), pp. 1387–1399.

3. See John Miller, "A Green GNP: Taking the Environment into Account," *Dollars & Sense* 161 (November 1990), pp. 6–8, 22, and Ernst Lutz and Mohan Munasinghe, "Accounting for the Environment," *Finance & Development* 28, no. 1 (March 1991), pp. 19–21.

4. The first set of comparisons is from Angus Maddison, "A Comparison of the Levels of GDP Per Capita in Developed and Developing Countries, 1700–1980," *Journal of Economic History* 43, no. 1 (March 1983), p. 30. The second set is from Angus Maddison, *Monitoring The World Economy: 1820–1992* (Paris: OECD, 1995).

5. See Irving B. Kravis, "Comparative Studies of National Incomes and Prices" followed by Robin Marris, "Comparing the Incomes of Nations," a critique of the process, in the *Journal of Economic Literature* 22, no. 1 (March 1984), pp. 1–39 and 40–57; Irving B. Kravis, "The Three Faces of the International Comparison Project," *World Bank Research Observer* 1, no. 1 (January 1986), pp. 3–26; and Robert Summers and Alan Heston, "The Penn World Table (Mark 5): An Expanded Set of International Comparisons, 1950–1988," *Quarterly Journal of Economics* 81 (May 1991), pp. 327–368.

6. "Burgernomics," *The Economist* 349, no. 8099 (December 19, 1998), p. 150.

7. The June 1994 issue of the *Journal of Development Economics* was devoted to this issue. For a summary, see T. N. Srinivasan, "Data Base for Development Analysis: An Overview," *Journal of Development Economics* 44, no. 1 (June 1994), pp. 3–27.

8. See Morris David Morris, *Measuring the Condition of the World's Poor: The Physical Quality of Life Index* (New York: Pergamon Press, 1979).

9. See V. V. Bhanoji Rao, "Human Development Report 1990: Review and Assessment," *World Development* 19, no. 10 (October 1991), pp. 1451–1460, and Mark McGillivray, "The Human Development Index: Yet Another Redundant Composite Indicator?" *World Development* 19, no. 10 (October 1991), pp. 1461–1468.

10. T. N. Srinivasan, "Human Development: A New Paradigm or Reinvention of the Wheel?" *American Economic Review* 84, no. 2 (May 1994), pp. 238–243. Also see Michael Hopkins, "Human Development Revisited: A New UNDP Report," *World Development* 19, no. 10 (October 1991), pp. 1469–1473, and Sudhir Anand and Martin Ravallion, "Human Development in Poor Countries: On the Role of Private Incomes and Public Services," *Journal of Economic Perspectives* 7, no. 1 (winter 1993), pp. 133–150.

11. Paul Streeten, "Human Development: Means and Ends," *American Economic Review* 84, no. 2 (May 1994), pp. 232–237. Also see the *Human Development Report 1998* (New York: United Nations, 1998), pp. 16–19.

12. See Paul Streeten, et al., *First Things First: Meeting Basic Human Needs in Developing Countries* (New York: Oxford University Press, 1981). Early works are Irma Adelman and Cynthia Taft Morris, *Economic Growth and Social Equity in Developing Countries* (Stanford: Stanford University Press, 1973); Hollis Chenery, et al., *Redistribution with Growth* (London: Oxford University Press, 1974); the International Labour Organization, *Employment, Growth and Basic Needs: A One-World Problem* (Geneva: International Labour Organization, 1976); and David Morawetz, *Twenty-five Years of Economic Development: 1950–1975* (Washington: World Bank, 1977).

13. Pranab Bardhan, "Research on Poverty and Development Twenty Years After *Redistribution With Growth*," in *Annual World Bank Conference on Development Economics 1995* (Washington: World Bank, 1996), pp. 59–72.

14. Kwan S. Kim, "Income Distribution and Poverty: An Interregional Comparison," *World Development* 25, no. 11 (November 1997), pp. 1909–1924.

15. Suresh D. Tendulkar and L. R. Jain, "Economic Growth, Relative Inequality, and Equity: The Case of India," *Asian Development Review* 13, no. 2 (1995), pp. 138–168.

16. See N. Kakwani, "Measuring Poverty: Definitions and Significance Tests with Application to Côte d'Ivoire," in Michael Lipton and Jacques van der Gaag, *Including the Poor* (Washington: World Bank, 1993), pp. 43–66.

17. World Bank, *World Development Report 2000/01*, p. 3. Also see Shaohua Chen, Gaurav Datt, and Martin Ravallion, "Is Poverty Increasing in the Developing World?" *Review of Income and Wealth* 40, no. 4 (December 1994), pp. 359–376.

18. Michael Lipton, "Comment," *Annual World Bank Conference on Development Economics 1995* (Washington: World Bank, 1996), pp. 73–79.

19. See Robert Klitgaard, *Adjusting to Reality: Beyond "State vs. Market" in Economic Development* (San Francisco: ICS Press, 1991).

20. World Bank, *Poverty Reduction Handbook* (Washington, 1993), p. 242.

21. Articles by Simon Kuznets include "Economic Growth and Income Inequality," *American Economic Review* 45, no. 1 (March 1955), pp. 1–28, and "Quantitative Aspects of the Economic Growth of Nations: VIII, Distri-

bution of Income by Size," *Economic Development and Cultural Change* 11, no. 2, part 2 (January 1963); and chapter 4 of his *Modern Economic Growth*. Gary Fields's summary of this issue is "Income Distribution and Economic Growth," in G. Ranis and T. Paul Schultz, *The State of Development Economics: Progress and Perspectives* (Oxford: Basil Blackwell, 1988), pp. 459–485. Also see Gustav Papanek and Oldrich Kyn, "The Effect on Income Distribution of Development, the Growth Rate and Economic Strategy," *Journal of Development Studies* 23, no. 1 (September 1986), pp. 55–65. World Bank studies (*World Development Report 1990*, pp. 46–47) show no evidence of the inverted 'U'. But see Rati Ram, "Economic Development and Income Inequality: An Overlooked Regression Constraint," *Economic Development and Cultural Change* 43, no. 2 (January 1995), pp. 425–434, and Rati Ram, "Level of Economic Development and Income Inequality: Evidence from the Developed World," *Southern Economic Journal* 64, no. 2 (October 1997), pp. 576–583. More recently, see Albert Fishlow, "Inequality, Poverty, and Growth: Where Do We Stand?" *Annual World Bank Conference on Development Economics 1995*, pp. 25–39, and Sailesh K. Jha, "The Kuznets Curve: A Reassessment," *World Development* 24, no. 4 (April 1996), pp. 773–780.

22. See Albert Fishlow, "Inequality, Poverty, and Growth: Where Do We Stand?" *Annual World Bank Conference on Economics 1995*, p. 35, and Hans P. Binswanger and Klaus Deininger, "Explaining Agricultural and Agrarian Policies in Developing Countries," *Journal of Economic Literature* 35, no. 4 (December 1997), p. 1971.

23. Kristin J. Forbes, "A Reassessment of the Relationship Between Inequality and Growth," *American Economic Review* 90, no. 4 (September 2000), pp. 869–887. Also see Klaus Deininger and Lyn Squire, "New Ways of Looking at Old Issues: Inequality and Growth," *Journal of Development Economics* 57, no. 2 (December 1998), pp. 259–287.

24. The Gini coefficients are extremely sensitive to the data and methodology used and the year being reported. They can also be misleading because differently shaped Lorenz curves can yield the same Gini. See Klaus Deininger and Lyn Squire, "A New Data Set Measuring Income Inequality," *World Bank Economic Review* 10, no. 3 (September 1996), pp. 565–591.

25. See Richard W. Franke and Barbara H. Chasin, *Kerala: Radical Reform as Development in an Indian State* (San Francisco: Institute for Food and Development Policy, 1989), and Govindan Parayil, ed., *Kerala: The Development Experience* (London: Zed Books, 2000).

3

THE EVOLUTION OF DEVELOPMENT THOUGHT

In economics, the basic questions do not change—
it is the answers that change from time to time.
—ANONYMOUS

INTRODUCTION

Economists and public policy makers have been interested for centuries in how economies develop. Beginning in the middle of the twentieth century, many economists turned their attention to mathematical modeling, largely of the growth process, ignoring many of the development issues we discussed in Chapter 1. However, development-oriented modeling of a nonmathematical nature remains an important tool for explaining the problems facing developing countries. In this book we look at economic development largely from the viewpoint of economic theory. Concepts such as opportunity cost and the tools of supply and demand are applied to the problems that developing countries face. In this chapter we look first at some older visions of the development process, then discuss some of the formal models of economic growth, and return to development models. We will end the chapter by discussing a crucial debate about the role of governments and markets in developing countries.

APPROACHES TO DEVELOPMENT

Many economists have examined economic development from a broad perspective, reaching for explanations that go beyond the application of economic theory. A brief review of some of these approaches will help provide the context for our discussions and flesh out some aspects of the development process.[1]

Classical Visions

Classical economics refers to the period beginning in 1776 with the publication of the Scotsman Adam Smith's *Wealth of Nations* and ending in the 1870s with the emergence of **neoclassical economics**. Classical writers took a broad view of economics. To Smith, economics was part of what he called Moral Philosophy, a more general study of appropriate behavior. It then became a separate topic known as Political Economy.

Adam Smith and Classical Thought

Economic thinkers before Smith viewed the world in static terms. Wealth meant accumulating gold and silver, and the role of the state was to help the nation obtain as much of the world's presumably fixed supply of these metals as possible. Economic policy focused on promoting exports and domestic production of goods that would re-place imports.

Smith disagreed. To him, a nation's wealth consisted of its ability to use its natural and human resources for ever greater levels of production. Through individual spe-cialization and the social division of labor, production could become more efficient, increasing employment and income. This would increase the market for goods, lead-ing to further specialization and division of labor. The economy would grow through the accumulation of capital, more efficient economic organization, and expanding purchasing power: The production-possibilities frontier would shift out. Govern-ment's role was not to promote particular industries but to permit individuals maxi-mum opportunity to pursue their self-interest. Not only economic performance was maximized but individual freedom as well. Smith's discussion set the framework for the state vs. market debate that still occupies development economists over two cen-turies later.

Some classical writers focused on the distribution of resources among classes. David Ricardo, in particular, formalized the concept of **diminishing returns**. Figure 3–1 shows that with some resource—presumably land—in fixed supply, the addition of other re-sources—labor and capital—will result in declining **marginal product**, or additions to

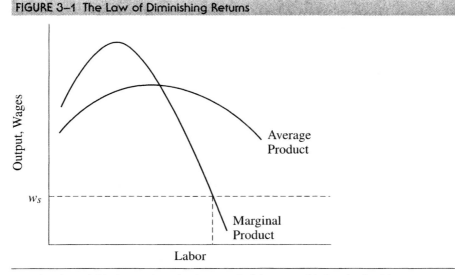

FIGURE 3–1 The Law of Diminishing Returns

As units of a variable factor of production, usually labor, are added to the fixed factors, output per person (Average Product) and the additional output from the additional person (Marginal Product) rise at first but eventually begin to fall. For Ricardo, land was ultimately fixed. In the long run, additions of labor and capital would drive production to the point where wages were as low as they could be (w_s), and profits were zero. All remaining revenue would go to landlords, and there would be no incentive for further investment.

production; presumably reaching a point where no more production was possible. Eventually, the economy would reach its stationary state, where growth stopped. Smith, Ricardo, and others did not discount technological progress completely, but they thought of it as an improvement in the organization of production, rather than advances in productive technology. Ricardo suggested that as countries became wealthy, profits would fall to zero, wages would fall to subsistence levels, and the economy would stall, with landlords the big winners due to the relative scarcity of good land. As better land became used up and agriculture spread to less productive land, the increasing demand for land allowed landlords to raise rents and the prices of their crops.

Thomas Malthus and Karl Marx

Thomas Malthus was even more pessimistic about the prospects for long-term growth. He is most famous for his view that population growth would ultimately outstrip the earth's productive capacity, leading to famine and war. He agreed that stagnation was inevitable but suggested that industrial production could be continued if there were sufficient investment. Ultimately, however, the increasing capital intensity of industry would shift income from wages (which were falling anyway due to population growth) to profits. Investment depended on demand for consumer goods. The poverty of workers put constraints on consumption. As consumption slowed, investment in industry would as well.

Karl Marx adopted some of the classical approach, especially in regard to the impoverishment of the labor force. He suggested that profit was possible only through exploitation of the workers. He concluded that periodic depressions would eventually bring capitalism to ruin, rather than just some stationary state. These depressions would result in the failure of smaller firms and the concentration of capital in ever fewer hands. After some number of these events, the concentration of wealth and the impoverishment of the workers would result in a political crisis. The resulting socialist revolution would provide a way for economies to harness the productive power of machinery, spread wealth equally, and presumably grow indefinitely.

Transition to Modern Development Thought

Classical economists provided some important insights into the problems of long-term economic progress. From the last quarter of the nineteenth century until the mid-twentieth, however, the attention of Western economists turned to the mathematics of general microeconomic equilibrium and to the business cycle.[2] Many who did worry about economic change concerned themselves with the possibility, seemingly real in the 1930s, that the stationary state had set in for the rich countries.

The situation was somewhat different in countries where pressing issues of development were taking center stage. In the Soviet Union, for example, the revolution of 1917 led at first to a vigorous debate on the role of the state and the importance of agriculture, heavy industry, and consumer goods in a development plan. Before the Communist revolution in China in 1949, nationalist leaders such as Sun Yat-sen looked to Western capitalism for answers. Before India's independence from Britain in 1948, its economists and politicians were debating questions of economic development and modernization. And European economists in countries with extensive colonies in Asia and Africa debated what sort of development was best for the colonies (usually as a way to enrich the colonial powers) and how to bring that about.[3]

But it was not until the end of World War II, recovery in the West, and the anti-colonial struggles in the developing countries that the mainstream of the economics profession began to focus on the discipline of economic development. However, they lacked an overview of the subject, so their first step was to describe characteristics of economies that were not developing.

Traditional Society

In discussing the problems of development, American economic historian Walt W. Rostow used the term **traditional society** to refer to non-Western societies that appeared to be "undeveloped" or "backward."[4] The traditional society was one in which there was a relative lack of geographic and social mobility and, consequently, a high degree of social cohesion; hereditary economic and social roles for the individual; production methods that use little capital and simple technology; a limited ability to produce an economic surplus above basic needs; and little trade, with the bulk of exchange taking place locally on terms dictated by custom. Under such conditions, economic development was prevented by the cycle of poverty. Economically, there was no way out. Although few societies were completely static, some showed little economic advance for centuries at a time.

Traditional societies were said to include the slave systems of early Greece and Rome; peasant societies in early Egypt, India, and China; and the feudal societies of medieval Europe. Even in the mid-twentieth century, many people in Asia, Africa, and Latin America had elements of this traditional orientation. These societies tended to be relatively static. To a large extent, economic activity was repeated generation after generation. People were accustomed to a relatively stable, low-output economy and frequently believed that no more was possible. Attempts at change would be resisted by ruling elites, whose power was based on religious authority and custom. High birth and death rates, widespread illiteracy, and lack of incentives for improvement were key characteristics of these societies.[5]

In the mid-twentieth century, economists drew different conclusions from this picture. One was that development was hopeless. Such conclusions were often based on hidden assumptions of racial inferiority, although phrased in terms of geography and climate. Other such approaches, relying on psychological or religious elements, extrapolated from German sociologist Max Weber's idea of the "Protestant Ethic," which claims that non-Christian or non-Western peoples were incapable of true economic development. These claims are clearly untenable, based both on historical and current evidence.[6]

Other writers believed that the introduction of some advanced techniques and institutions could bring about rapid growth and development.[7] This more optimistic approach led to the enthusiasm for development assistance from the rich countries, after which the poorer countries were expected to blossom quickly. This approach led to the establishment in the 1960s of foreign aid programs such as the United Nations Development Decade and the U.S. Alliance for Progress in Latin America.

Many economists suggested that development would take a long time to succeed, but this would be done as the poor countries traveled the path taken earlier by the rich. The process, some thought, might be speeded up. Robert Heilbroner, in *The Great Ascent*, saw development taking place through "... a pervasive social transformation ... a wholesale metamorphosis of habits, a wrenching reorientation of values ... an unweaving and reweaving of the fabric of daily existence itself ... [introduced and fostered by] ... regimes audacious enough to unleash social change."[8]

Most economists agreed that, slowly or rapidly, three key transformations in the social character of more traditionally oriented societies must take place to make economic development possible. One necessary change was in **factor mobility**: Labor must be able to move, both geographically and socially, land must be available for different crops or for industry, and people must be able to accumulate capital and direct it to profitable opportunities. Secondly, individuals must be able to reap the rewards of their own work or resources. Finally, there must be at least some people who could recognize the potential benefits of innovation—doing things in new ways. People must accept the validity and the desirability of change.

These three transformations could lead to a clash between new individualistic values and traditional values that put the community first. Denis Goulet emphasizes that development will be the more successful as new values do not present too stark a contrast with the old and can motivate new directions within a traditional social framework. Otherwise, the result may be success for just a few individuals, with the majority left behind.[9]

Dualism

One approach to understanding the coexistence of development and traditional economies was the idea of the **dual economy**, suggested in the early 1950s.[10] This is an economy with both modern and traditional sectors. The modern sector is one in which **capital-intensive** techniques (those using relatively large amounts of capital per worker) provide the means for high levels of production and exports and in which development is rapid. In the traditional sector, by contrast, production uses labor-intensive techniques and might be relatively isolated from the modern sector. Often, rural society was depicted as traditional and urban life was equated with modernization, although even 50 years ago urban life in many countries was a blend of modern and traditional.

Part of the debate over the dual economy scenario in the 1950s and 1960s concerned how quickly progress in the modern sector would trickle down to the traditional sector, but many questioned the extent of the separation. The modern sector in countries such as India relied on a pool of "surplus" labor from the traditional sector. This suggests that the two sectors are in fact integrated, not independent entities, and in the view of some Marxist-oriented economists, a social structure imposed from either a colonizing power or a modernized national elite would be content to keep the economy integrated in such a fashion.[11]

Stages of Development

The idea that human societies move in stages is an old one. The earliest economists saw society progressing from what Adam Smith in 1776 called "that early, rude state" of hunting and gathering, to increasing specialization and exchange, and then to modern industrial economies. Marx's "scientific socialism" described in the 1860s how the world would move to a new stage in which the industrialized countries would lead the way along a path from feudalism through capitalism and ultimately to socialism. In the years just before World War I, Russian revolutionary V. I. Lenin turned this idea around by suggesting that capitalists' overseas investment would spark development in the previously poor countries once capitalist expansion in Europe and the United States had reached the limit of their own markets. In 1962, Russian economist Alexander Gerschenkron gave that story a different twist by pointing out that economies that were latecomers to the development process could make tremendous strides and perhaps even overtake developed countries by taking advantage of the advanced technology that they did not have to produce.[12]

Rostow's Stages

Perhaps the most famous modern stage theory is Rostow's.[13] In the late 1950s he envisioned every society starting out in traditional fashion, in the vicious cycle of poverty. In order to break out of this cycle, a society must create "Preconditions for Takeoff" into self-sustaining growth. The preconditions included the rise of a class of entrepreneurs who would take risks, accumulating resources and investing them in more productive techniques. This required that a person would work diligently, often for someone else, and be able to save. There would have to be some degree of national unity, in order to widen the market and permit the specialization to make economically viable firms possible. The market would require increasing amounts of **social overhead capital**, such as transportation, communication, and education. Industrial expansion would require an increase in agricultural productivity, to provide enough food to feed those who must move to the cities to work, especially in **leading sectors**—those that were first industrialized. Finally, there would have to be increasing levels of monetization (use of money) and financial organization, to grease the wheels of commerce.

The combination of aggregate and sectoral change fuels Rostow's "Takeoff" stage, in which the key economic characteristic is an increase in investment from less than 5, to more than 10 percent of total output and a consequent increase in the rate of growth of output. The leading sectors, which need not be the same in each case, would grow rapidly; increased demand must be generated to support the new output; improvements in technology would result in greater productivity and output; profits would be reinvested and would permit the growth of new sectors; and new financial institutions, capable of mobilizing saving, would come into existence. The Western economies, in Rostow's estimation, had all achieved their takeoff stages by the beginning of the twentieth century: Britain between 1783 and 1802, the United States between 1843 and 1860, Japan from 1878 to 1900, and Russia over the period 1890 to 1914.

The economy then enters its "Drive to Maturity," characterized by relatively steady growth, with savings and investment ratios in the 10 percent to 20 percent range, increasing per capita output, and continuous shifting among the leading sectors. Britain, according to Rostow, had attained maturity around 1850, the United States by 1900, Japan by 1940, and the Soviet Union by 1950. Sustained activity of this sort would eventually lead to the "Age of High Mass Consumption." Figure 3–2 illustrates these stages. Rostow suggested that all countries would go through similar stages.

Rostow received a lot of criticism for this approach. Many economists considered it a highly simplistic representation of the development process. The theory he proposes ignores important issues such as how the transition from one stage to another is

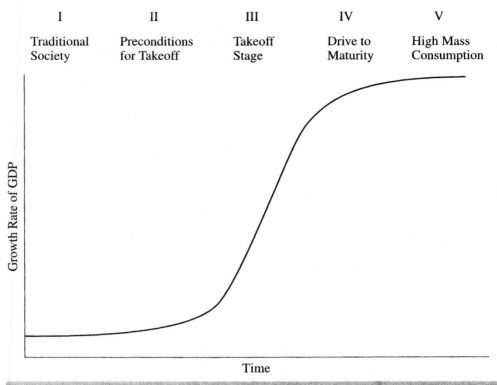

FIGURE 3–2 Rostow's Stages of Growth

Stage I is that of the traditional society in which little economic advance takes place. Stage II witnesses the creation of the preconditions for the "Takeoff": Infrastructure is built and entrepreneurial talent is no longer stifled. Stage III is the "Takeoff." The ratio of investment to income rises from 5 percent or less to more than 10 percent. Stage IV is the "Drive to Maturity." Investment to income ratios rise to 20 percent or more. Stage V witnesses "High Mass Consumption," and growth rates level off.

accomplished. Nevertheless, the stages approach remains a useful way of highlighting the importance of certain characteristics of the development process.

Dependency Theory

While Rostow focused on the internal dynamics of the development process, another set of authors blamed external factors for the failure of development to occur in many countries. This wholly different vision of development is embodied in the **dependency theory** of some Marxist-oriented social scientists, introduced in the 1960s and 1970s. A number of economists in developing countries endorsed this view of development. It constitutes one variety of the "world system" outlook that takes a global view of the development process, encompassing countries at different stages of development and the interaction among them.

Dependency theory, first outlined in some detail by Andre Gunder Frank in 1967,[14] considers the development of world capitalism as a whole from about the fifteenth century, with different results in the **center** (the metropolitan or developed countries) and the **periphery** (the satellite or developing countries). Dependency theory is rooted in Marx's idea that capitalism requires continual accumulation of capital, first at home and then globally. This idea was extended by Lenin's view that capitalists, having forced profit rates down at home, would seek outlets abroad, resulting in capitalist-oriented, but "uneven" development in poorer countries.

For dependency theorists, the development process is driven by a developed capitalist country that, resting on military superiority, shapes the developing country to suit its needs for raw materials and labor power. A company from a developed country exports raw materials from the developing country or transforms them into labor-intensive manufactures. Profits are either sent home or used to create a dependent business class in the satellite country. This group of local capitalists maintains a position of privilege, between its own people and the capitalists in the center. In this scheme, the development of the center and the "underdevelopment" of the periphery are opposite sides of the same coin. Frank referred to this process as the "development of underdevelopment." The center countries drain resources from the periphery, although within each peripheral region there are local centers, together with their own peripheries.

Frank's study of Brazil and Chile led him to the conclusion that the satellite countries are capable of development, but inversely to the strength of their ties to the center. Brazil and Chile, for example, developed largely under conditions dictated by European and U.S. capital until the period 1929 to 1945, when the West was distracted by the Great Depression and World War II. These countries then began a pattern of autonomous development, which came to an end when the West regained its economic footing.

Frank suggested that the most underdeveloped regions were those that historically had the closest economic ties to the developed countries, particularly Western Europe and the United States. So-called dual economies are composed not of more and less advanced sectors, but of local center-periphery relationships that are the result of a historical process related to *integration* into the world economy, not isolation from it.

The conclusion of Frank and others of this school is generally that poor countries can truly develop only by breaking the economic link with the West. In Chapter 12 we will discuss a less radical approach that arrived at similar conclusions and was a significant basis for the import substitution strategies pursued by numerous countries, especially in Latin America, during the mid-twentieth century.

Dependency theory was criticized by some Marxists, for its failure to emphasize class struggle as the basis of historical progress, and by more traditional economists, who claim it has not isolated a phenomenon peculiar to developing countries and responsible for their pattern of development or useful as a basis for policy. Nonetheless, the concept of dependency led to significant studies on the nature of interactions between the rich and poor countries of the world and to a greater understanding of the global nature of the development process.

GROWTH MODELS

In recent decades, many economists have become dissatisfied with the existing approaches that did not shed light on the sources of economic growth. Some now employ mathematical **models**, equations, or graphical approaches that represent key economic relationships to simplify the problem. Economists and other analysts try to break down complex realities into models that clarify key relationships.

Economic development is perhaps one of the most complex of these realities because we must consider not only what a society looks like and how it operates but also how it may change. A typical model contains one **dependent variable**, such as the rate of growth of per capita GDP, whose value or range of values is to be determined by the model. It then suggests several **independent variables** that are believed to cause, or at least be associated with, changes in the value of the dependent variable. The model can be expressed as an equation, such as $y = f(x_1, x_2)$, where y is the rate of growth and the x variables are such categories as the labor force and capital stock.

Two key questions for this book are which independent variables are most important in determining the rate of growth of output and what we can do to increase that growth rate. In this section, we look at some of the prominent ideas about economic growth and consider the rather abstract nature of these models. Note that early growth models were intended to explain the long-run behavior of relatively well-developed economies, not the year-by-year requirements of a developing economy.

The Harrod–Domar Growth Model and the Emphasis on Capital

The earliest growth model resulted from the separate but similar efforts of Sir Roy Harrod and Evsey Domar.[15] The **Harrod–Domar growth model** identifies capital investment and savings as the key conditions required for an economy to achieve steady growth. It relies on two important economic relationships that are derived from Keynesian economics. The **Marginal Propensity to Save (MPS)** is the proportion of any change in income that is saved, $\Delta S/\Delta Y$, where S is saving and Y is income. (Δ indicates "change in.") The **Incremental Capital-Output Ratio (ICOR)** is the addition to the capital stock necessary to produce an extra dollar of output, $\Delta K/\Delta Y$, where K is capital, or $I/\Delta Y$, where I is net investment (change in capital stock). For the economy to grow at a pace consistent with maintaining a full-employment equilibrium, aggregate demand and aggregate supply must grow at the same pace. The basic equations are set out in Development Spotlight 3–1.

Net investment leads to the growth of national income from one equilibrium position to the next, and income permits the saving that maintains the new equilibrium. The model produces an equilibrium growth rate equal to the ratio of the MPS to the ICOR. For example, if the ICOR is 4, and the MPS is 0.10, then the equilibrium growth rate would be 0.1/4 = 0.025, or 2.5 percent. From this result we can work backwards by, for example, picking a target growth rate of 5 percent and look at the conditions that would be required to achieve it. With an ICOR of 4, the MPS would have to rise to 0.2 (an increase in the economy's ability to mobilize resources), or with the old MPS, the ICOR would have to fall to 2 (improving the productivity of capital).

The model concludes that a certain savings rate and capital-output ratio permit only one viable growth rate for an economy. A lower growth rate would lead to depression and a higher rate to uncontrollable inflation. An economy has to walk on a

THE HARROD–DOMAR GROWTH MODEL

The model requires equal expansion of aggregate demand (Yd) and aggregate supply (Ys) to maintain an equilibrium growth rate for the economy.

$$Yd = I/\sigma = I/\text{MPS} \qquad (1)$$
$$Ys = K/\alpha, \text{ or } (K)(\Delta Y/\Delta K) \qquad (2)$$

Equation (2) can be reorganized to show that the rate of growth of output ($\Delta Y/Y$) must equal the rate of growth of capital stock ($\Delta K/K$) to maintain the equilibrium.

$$K/Y = \Delta K/\Delta Y, \text{ or } \Delta K/K = \Delta Y/Y \qquad (2a)$$
$$[\text{Note: } \Delta K/K \text{ is } I/K]$$

The static equilibrium condition is

$$Yd = Ys, \text{ or } I/\sigma = K/\alpha, \text{ so} \qquad (3)$$

$I/K = \sigma/\alpha$, which reads as MPS/ICOR. Equilibrium requires that the capital stock grow at a rate determined by the savings ratio and the ICOR. The absolute growth in aggregate demand and supply are determined by the following equations:

$$\Delta Yd = \Delta I/\sigma \qquad (4)$$
$$\Delta Ys = \Delta K/\alpha = I/\alpha \qquad (5)$$

The equilibrium growth path is then defined as:

$$\Delta Yd = \Delta Ys, \text{ or } \Delta I/\sigma = I/\alpha \qquad (6)$$

To attain this path, the rate of investment growth is

$$\Delta I/I = \sigma/\alpha = \text{MPS/ICOR} \qquad (7a)$$

while the rate of capacity growth is the same:

$$\Delta Ys/Ys = (I/\alpha)/Ys = (I/\alpha)/(K/\alpha) = I/K, \text{ and per equation 3, } I/K = \Delta K/K = \sigma/\alpha \qquad (7b)$$

and the rate of growth of demand is

$$\Delta Yd/Yd = (\Delta I/\sigma)/Yd$$
$$= (\Delta I/\sigma)/(I/\sigma) = \Delta I/I = \sigma/\alpha \qquad (7c)$$

"knife's edge" or fall in one direction or another. If we extend the model by incorporating the growth of the labor force, full employment is possible only if the growth rate of output and investment are equal to the rate of growth of the labor force. To grow faster, an economy must either save more of its income or increase the productivity of its investments.

Criticisms of the Harrod–Domar Growth Model

The Harrod–Domar growth model is a very narrow approach to growth, not to mention development. A major limitation, for example, is the assumption that savings is easily transformed into investment, implying a well-developed financial system. With respect to investment, the model makes no distinction among different kinds: They are assumed to be alike and, at least on average, have the same, unchanging impact on growth. In this model, the only things that matter are the proportion of income that is saved and the impact of investment on output. Not only are cultural matters ignored, and a functioning market assumed, but no allowance is made for monetary variables and prices. A closed economy is also assumed. Full employment is the initial condition. Finally, the rigid assumptions lead to an equally rigid conclusion: Any variation will result in either inflation or deflation. This is a highly restricted conclusion even for an industrialized country.

The Influence of the Harrod–Domar Growth Model

The Harrod–Domar model was extremely influential, despite its simplicity, because it focused attention on the availability and use of an unconsumed surplus of resources that could be invested. Further, it made clear that faster economic growth would require some combination of a higher propensity to save and a lower capital/output ratio. But this influence reinforced a tendency to equate development with growth and growth with industrialization. Its simplicity led to an emphasis on planning as a mechanism to coordinate and promote economic development.

In 1953, P. C. Mahalanobis of the Indian Planning Commission used an expanded version of the model to answer the question of how to divide available investment resources between the production of capital goods and consumer goods. His model demonstrated that promoting investment in the capital goods sector would accelerate growth. The problem was to find a necessary rate of investment growth in the capital goods sector while keeping investment in consumer goods industries high enough to satisfy the populace. While the model was simple, it was a serious attempt to apply some crucial lessons of economic growth and development to a real-world setting.[16]

Two Indian economists have estimated ICORs for India. C. Rangarajan and R. Kannan found an increase in their value between the early 1950s and the late 1970s, followed by a decline. The economywide ICOR rose from 3.37 in the early period to 6.56 thirty years later, showing a decrease in the productivity of capital. The ICOR then fell over the 1980s to a value of 3.82. They also estimated ICORs for different sectors of the economy and found values for the 1980s ranging from 0.48 in the banking and insurance industry to 10.33 in electricity, gas and water supply. This range supports our commonsense notion that service industries require relatively little capital while public utilities require more capital.[17]

The Neoclassical Model: Solow, the Steady State, and Convergence

Robert Solow in 1956 developed what is called the **neoclassical growth model**, sometimes referred to as the Solow model. This model uses many of the same basic ingredients as Harrod–Domar but reaches radically different conclusions.[18] In this model an economywide production function shows that both capital and labor produce the output, rather than just capital. Aggregate demand in this model includes consumption and investment, but investment is broken down into depreciation and net investment. Unlike the Harrod–Domar model, Solow's allows the capital-output ratio to vary with changes in the capital stock. It produces a steady state—a level of investment that is just equal to annual depreciation and which produces a stable ratio of capital to labor and level of output per worker. Development Spotlight 3–2 presents the technical aspects of the model.

The model tells us that an economy will grow by increasing its capital stock and that the limiting factor is the savings rate. Once the economy reaches its steady state, it will be investing, through its saving, just enough to replace the capital stock that has depreciated each year. Because the capital-output ratio can change, the economy does not face the daunting prospect of finding just the right "knife-edge" growth rate as in Harrod–Domar. Instead, it naturally tends toward a steady state of constant output

THE NEOCLASSICAL GROWTH MODEL

The neoclassical model rests on an aggregate **production function** and an aggregate demand function.

The initial form of the production function is

$$Y = F(K, L) \tag{1a}$$

where Y is total output, K is the capital stock, and L is the labor force. As a simplification, the terms are divided by L, so

$$y = f(k) \tag{1b}$$

where $y = Y/L$ and $k = K/L$. Because $L/L = 1$, it drops out of consideration.

Aggregate demand is

$$y = c + i \tag{2a}$$

where $y = Y/L$, $c = C/L$ (consumption per worker), and $i = I/L$ (investment per worker). We transform the equation by expressing consumption as income not saved (s = saving), so $c = (1 - s)y$.

Now we can restate equation (2a) as

$$y = (1 - s)y + i \tag{2b}$$

and solving the equation for i yields

$$i = y - (1 - s)y = y - y + sy, \text{ or} \tag{3a}$$

$$i = sy. \tag{3b}$$

Equation (3b) is an expression of macroeconomic equilibrium in which annual investment is equal to the portion of income that is saved. A further substitution of the production function for y gives us

$$i = sf(k). \tag{3c}$$

Finally, we add in depreciation by assuming that a fixed percentage (d) of k wears out each year. So the annual change in the stock of capital is net investment, or gross investment minus depreciation. Using the Δ to represent "change in," we get

$$\Delta k = i - dk, \text{ or} \tag{4a}$$

$$\Delta k = sf(k) - dk. \tag{4b}$$

The model then describes the "steady state" of the economy (stable capital stock and output per worker) as

$$\Delta k = sf(k) - dk = 0, \text{ or} \tag{5a}$$

$$sf(k) = dk, \tag{5b}$$

the point where investment is just equal to depreciation. In the model, investment grows until it produces a capital stock for which depreciation is just equal to investment. At that point, net investment and growth cease.

per person, which depends on the savings rate and rate of population growth. Therefore, the steady state can be higher if the savings rate increases. On the other hand, a growing population requires more investment to maintain the steady state: Investment each year must not only offset depreciation but also grow by the same rate as population to maintain the same output per person.

The idea of the steady state here is similar to that of the stationary state of the classical economists. Will people be satisfied with this? Is there any way to keep growing? It turns out that there is—through improved technology. Solow introduced technology through an increase in the efficiency of labor. If that improvement permits faster investment growth, output per worker can continue to grow.[19] Solow's work on growth theory earned him the Nobel Prize for economics in 1987.

Perhaps the most intriguing idea to come out of the neoclassical model is the possibility of **convergence**. Because poor countries have less capital, the productivity of capital should be higher there, and capital should flow to poor countries from rich countries. This more rapid investment should lead to faster growth: Thus, there should be a convergence, at least of growth rates if not actual income levels, between poor and rich.[20] A lot of study and debate has surrounded this possibility.

Unfortunately, even if convergence were established in the neoclassical sense, it would be of limited importance for development. What is really meant is that poor countries more rapidly approach their own steady state. But this steady state, as Robert Barro emphasizes, is specific to each country and depends on economic characteristics (savings rates, openness to trade), socioeconomic circumstances (population growth, health, and education of the labor force), and government policy. Looking at any country's actual growth rate and separating convergence from steady state components is a task economists have not yet accomplished.

Challenge to the Neoclassical Model: Endogenous Technological Change and the New Growth Theory

The Solow-type model was challenged in 1986 by Paul Romer and then by others[21] who incorporate technological change into the model—an **endogenous** factor—rather than the neoclassical model in which technological change is external, or **exogenous**.[22] This **new growth theory** is significant. It proposes that new knowledge, gained through learning, is produced by economic advance and, moreover, is not subject to diminishing returns. Innovations are a product of economic incentives—the possibility of at least temporary economic profits due to a patent or just the advantage of something new. They permit constant, instead of diminishing, returns to capital in the firm. This produces increasing, rather than constant, **returns to scale** in the economy; that is, a doubling of all inputs can permit more than a doubling of output. Some modern industries, such as production of semiconductors, are characterized by increasing returns to scale.

This change reverses an important conclusion of the neoclassical model: that economic growth must come to a halt in the absence of some fortuitous change. Instead, the endogenous growth models suggest that rates of growth may constantly increase, a proposition that Romer backs up with some preliminary evidence. Solow counters that his model was not restricted by constant returns to scale, nor did it require that technology was wholly exogenous. He also claims that the new approach reintroduces a rather extreme requirement that returns to capital be precisely constant: neither increasing nor decreasing.[23]

Nevertheless, this challenge to neoclassical growth theory suggests some important implications for developing countries. Solow-type models assumed that technology, once produced, was a free good that was available for any firm that wished to use it. However, if technology is the result of a firm's profit-seeking activities, it will not be so easily available to others. Firms that are in an economic and institutional environment that fosters invention and innovation, both forms of learning, are more likely to come up with and adapt new technologies. These environments are likely to be those of the industrialized countries, where widespread higher education and reward for innovation exist.[24] Still, some developing countries have invested heavily in human capital and have made considerable progress.

THE NEW GROWTH THEORY IN TAIWAN

FAST FACTS

On the Map: East Asia

Population: 22 Million

Per Capita GNI and Rank: $14,216 (Not Ranked)

Life Expectancy: Male—72 Female—78

Adult Literacy Rate: Male—94% Female—90%

One study of Taiwan uses the new growth theory to represent what that country has accomplished. Real per capita GDP grew at 6.54 percent per year over the period 1964 to 1986. At the same time, the top/bottom ratio fell from 5.33 to 4.55, indicating greater equality of income. The authors believe these results cannot be accounted for simply by growth in the capital stock (8.87 percent per year) and the labor force (1.38 percent per year). They credit public invest-

ment and exports but focus on improvements in labor skill and incentives to use labor.

To demonstrate this, the authors construct a labor-skill index by looking at the percentage of the population that completes a college or university education. Their index grows at 6.64 percent per year, leading them to conclude that, in keeping with the endogenous growth models, education has been a crucial factor in Taiwan's growth. In addition, since high interest rates encouraged firms to substitute labor for capital (lowering the ICOR), labor incomes grew very rapidly, reducing the degree of income inequality.

Source: Maw-Lin Lee, Ben-Chih Liu, and Ping Wang, "Growth and Equity with Endogenous Human Capital: Taiwan's Economic Miracle Revisited," *Southern Economic Journal* 61, no. 2 (October 1994), pp. 435–444.

One implication of the new growth theory is that the gap between rich and poor is likely to widen due to the superior knowledge and application of new technologies in the former: the opposite of convergence. However, these theories suggest an important requirement for development: Poorer countries need to provide appropriate institutions and incentives to facilitate learning and technological change. Countries such as South Korea, Brazil, India, and China that are acquiring these institutions can achieve some high-technology capabilities: Their economies may qualify for convergence. Those countries that cannot either acquire the requisite technological capability or induce foreign companies to bring technology with them may suffer from low income for a long time.[25] Case 3-1 summarizes a study that applied the new growth theory to Taiwan.

DEVELOPMENT MODELS: LEIBENSTEIN AND LEWIS

Development models are different from growth models. Whereas growth models tend to look for mathematical relationships, development models are often more concerned with process. They tend to address specific issues of importance to developing countries and look for explanations that are not obvious in typical micro- or macroeconomic thinking. One of the key issues frequently addressed is that of structural change. One recent defense of the study of economic development as a special subject notes that the neoclassical growth models, and by implication most models of just growth, ignore the significance of reallocation of resources among sectors.[26] Thus, some of the early models of development addressed breaking the cycle, the movement of labor from agriculture to industry, and the process of industrialization itself.

The Critical Minimum Effort Thesis

As we have seen, an underdeveloped economy may be envisioned as suffering from a vicious cycle of low productivity, low savings, low investment, and back to low productivity. Such economies were considered stagnant, or caught in a low-income stability. In 1957, Harvey Leibenstein objected that this picture was too simplistic and, if taken literally, would provide no escape.[27] In reality, the apparent vicious cycles hide fluctuations—random shocks and stimulants—combined with stabilizing forces. Whether development occurs depends on whether stabilizing influences are strong enough to offset changes introduced from the shocks and stimulants. For example, will an improvement in agricultural technology and output lead to growth, or just to an increase in population and consumption that cut off the surplus needed to sustain growth?

The critical minimum effort thesis states that a major improvement in technology, or increase investment, is needed to overcome the forces of stability. Growth is also more likely if the stabilizing forces, such as low education and traditional social patterns, could be changed in such a way as to make them contribute to growth, rather than to hinder it. If people were more accepting of change and, for example, willing to move from small villages to larger towns, growth and development could occur.

The Lewis Labor Surplus Model

One of the pathbreaking attempts to model economic development was W. Arthur Lewis's 1954 model of a labor surplus economy.[28] In the **labor surplus model**, Lewis divided the economy into subsistence and capitalist sectors, with quite different characteristics.

Agriculture, as a **subsistence sector** where food production is consumed largely by farmers themselves, may be so overcrowded that the marginal product of additional labor is below the average wage or even zero. Workers in this sector are likely to be **extended family** members who stay in the rural areas for reasons of custom rather than true economic advantage and, as family members, are sustained along with the more productive workers.[29] Some agricultural employment is therefore **disguised unemployment**, that is, workers' marginal output is less than the value of their wage. Technology is simple, and little capital is used. The profit motive does not prevail and little is saved. The industrial, or modern, sector in Lewis's model is small, uses more capital, and generally operates on a profit-making basis. Wages can be kept low because jobs are easily filled by the surplus labor from the agricultural sector. The surplus goes to capitalists in the form of profits.

Figure 3–3a illustrates the average and marginal productivity of labor in the subsistence sector, with a perfectly elastic labor supply at the level of the subsistence wage (w_s). Were people in this sector hired on the basis of normal profit-maximizing criteria, employment would be at Le, but under the conditions outlined above additional people are hired, conceivably to the point that marginal product is equal to or less than zero.

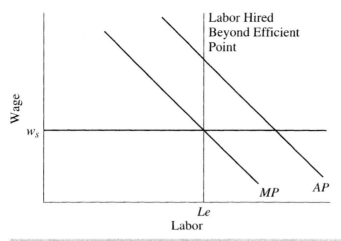

FIGURE 3–3A Lewis's Subsistence Sector

In the subsistence (agricultural) sector, the supply of labor is perfectly elastic at the subsistence wage, w_s, indicating an abundance of labor. The most efficient amount of labor would be Le, but because farmers may be part of an extended family or have other noneconomic goals, labor is likely to be hired beyond this point. In the extreme, MP could fall below zero. If so, the eventual departure of some of these workers would actually increase output.

Figure 3–3b shows the modern sector, with a series of marginal product curves (beginning with MP_1), and a labor supply curve that is initially perfectly elastic at a wage (w_m) that is likely to be a bit above the subsistence wage due to higher productivity.

The main action in the Lewis model takes place in the modern sector. The development process begins with migration of people (labor) from the rural sector to the modern

FIGURE 3–3B Lewis's Modern Sector

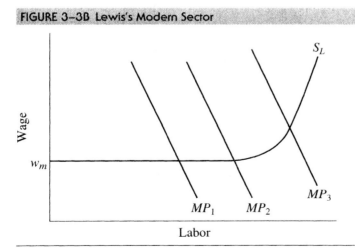

In the modern, or industrial, sector, labor supply is elastic for a long while at a minimum wage, w_m, as increasing demand brings additional workers from the subsistence sector. Growth occurs as new investment shifts the marginal product curve to the right. As surplus workers are drained from the subsistence sector, the labor supply curve in the modern sector begins to slope upward, cutting into profits and "easy" development.

sector. These people hope to receive higher wages and other advantages. Initially, a smaller rural labor force does not cause higher wages there because workers were not earning their full wage in the first place. Profits in the industrial sector generate new investment, but wages are kept low by increasing migration from the subsistence sector. As labor arrives, capitalists expand investment to absorb the numbers, thus steadily increasing employment and output. The marginal product of labor shifts to the right, reflecting the greater amount of capital. As we saw in Chapter 1, the economy's production-possibilities frontier shifts to the right. Profits grow absolutely and also as a share of national income. It is also important to note that for some period of time the decline in the agricultural labor force is not detrimental to the economy, because departing workers were consuming more than they produced. After all surplus labor is absorbed into the modern sector, the labor supply curve begins to slope upward, wages start to rise, and at some point capitalists have an incentive to substitute capital for labor. But this reduces the productivity of capital and profits begin to decline: "Free" development is at an end.

The Lewis Model in Perspective

The Lewis model injected some realism into the more traditional approaches to development. However, even for those developing countries that have large labor supplies, the picture of surplus labor may not fit the facts. For instance, some agricultural labor may be unneeded after the harvest is in but absolutely necessary at planting and harvesting times. In the latter case, withdrawal of labor from agriculture will hurt production unless new capital or technology is introduced. Also, some rural work is only part-time in farming, so marginal product may be positive and equal to the wage, whether in terms of money or subsistence. With a positive marginal product in the subsistence sector, moving labor into the cities without other improvements in agricultural production could lead to a decline in output.[30]

Another assumption is that the modern sector will introduce labor-using innovations to take advantage of the new workers pouring in from the countryside. In fact, this may be only a short phase, after which innovation is typically labor saving, leaving many urban dwellers either unemployed or underemployed. Industrial projects designed to take advantage of an abundance of labor may be expensive if they have a high capital/output ratio.

Further, the process of moving labor from agricultural to industrial employment is not easy. It may result in an increase in workers' consumption, thus requiring a higher industrial wage than the agricultural wage would indicate. Food must be shipped to urban areas, and urban living conditions will pose a costly problem. There must be also the promise of an effective demand for the output of the new workers, without which there will be little incentive to hire large numbers of even low-wage workers.

Perhaps the closest a country has come to actively employing the Lewis model is China during the 1960s and 1970s. The government directly mobilized agriculture workers, although without pay, for infrastructure projects. This succeeded for a time, but eventually the agricultural sector became drained of needed labor, and many returned to the farms.[31]

Lewis's model simplified an important observation that had been made about many developing countries at the time. Others have extended the model by introducing increases in agricultural productivity, showing how agriculture and industry might grow together, and dividing the rural sector into agriculture and nonagriculture.[32] It may be that Lewis's model was pressed into service to a far greater degree than he anticipated. But it has set the tone for a significant discussion of the development process in labor-surplus economies and was a useful step toward a more realistic investigation of that process.

One of the important implications of the model was that governments in labor-surplus economies could make use of migrants from the rural areas to create infrastructure at little social cost because agricultural output would not suffer. But whether the migrants would work on public works projects or find jobs in private industry, the goal was clearly to foster industrialization. Other economists focused their attention on how industrialization could be directly spurred by government action.

MODELS OF INDUSTRIALIZATION

Post-World War II debates on development strategy assumed that industrialization was the appropriate path to economic development. Two approaches to achieving industrialization were the Big Push and Unbalanced Growth.

The Big Push

Paul N. Rosenstein-Rodan suggested in 1943 that a massive effort would be required for industrialization to succeed. He concluded that neoclassical economic theory, focusing on the individual firm in an existing market environment, did not take into account the realities of the development process; what was required was a **big push**.[33] He gave five justifications for this approach: complementarity, indivisibility, market imperfections, infrastructure and savings.

Complementarity of Industries: Individual firms, or even industries, need suppliers and customers. A small number of firms or even industries might not find a large enough market, whereas the creation of numerous industries with a large urban labor force would furnish sufficient demand. A shoe factory, for example, would find few customers if there were no feet outside the factory that could afford shoes. **External economies** would be possible because labor trained in industrial habits and techniques would move among firms, increasing productivity and lowering costs for all.[34] Private investors who may be unwilling to take risks on their own would be more willing to do so in the presence of a large investment effort, especially with government support.

Indivisibilities: Many industrial undertakings, such as steel mills, require large production units. In these cases, one cannot simply proceed in small increments of capital, as assumed by neoclassical theory. This argument provided a rationale for heavy government investment in infrastructure and basic industries to stimulate smaller investments. The high fixed costs of such undertakings would lead to losses or failure under market conditions. Their long **gestation period**—the period in which construction would take place and before they would produce any measurable gains—would discourage private activity. As in Leibenstein's critical minimum effort, a minimum investment would be required. In the initial stages of industrialization, the only source of large investments might be government, or at the least government finance might be necessary.

Market imperfections: One characteristic of preindustrial economies is often the absence of well-functioning markets. While one response to this situation is for government to simply promote the spread and functioning of markets, this is a time-consuming undertaking that must be preceded by government investment until such time as large-scale private activity becomes feasible.

Infrastructure: Physical infrastructure might be insufficient to support private investment, especially for smaller firms. It must be created in advance of or along with directly productive activities. Infrastructure is a typical government undertaking, even when only to fund projects carried out by private contractors. **Positive externalities**—benefits beyond those accruing to the producer—have long been recognized as a rationale for such public sector activity.

Savings: In order to finance large investments, equally large amounts of financial resources were necessary, and these would be difficult to obtain from voluntary private savings.

Rosenstein-Rodan concluded that "Proceeding 'bit by bit' will not add up in its effects to the sum total of the single bits. A minimum quantum of investment is a necessary—though not sufficient—condition of success."[35]

Criticism of the Big Push

The big push idea was criticized on a number of points.[36] The key objections were that it ignored the role of foreign trade, was unduly pessimistic about the need for large investments, and that a big push would lead to a number of biases in development policy, including a state-oriented strategy that would be inefficient.

Trade, for example, would provide precisely the required outlet for individual firms through access to the world market for the new manufactured goods. Exports would make possible the import of capital goods for capital-intensive industries such as utilities, but it would be at best premature for developing countries to attempt to produce such equipment.

The argument that investments needed to be extremely large was also challenged. Investment in consumption goods production and services does not have to be as large as that required for capital goods and infrastructure. Since developing countries would start producing consumer goods, small investments were often practical. Nor are large investments required in agriculture. Further, unless demand is highly responsive to prices, large investments would reduce costs but would not guarantee much increased output: External economies would then not be realized. Finally, it is more important to sustain investment over time than to concentrate it. This does not require a big push.

In addition to the lack of urgency for a big push, critics stressed that the biases inherent in such a strategy were likely to be detrimental to development. The presumption of superiority of industry over agriculture, for example, could easily lead to neglect of agriculture. Further, development would be skewed toward capital intensity, when greater emphasis on the use of labor is required. And the clear implication of the big push is that the state must be heavily involved. While some might restrict the state's role to financing private-sector investment or making information available to the private sector, many of the early proponents of heavy investment did expect the state to play an active role.

Balanced Growth

A similar idea was Ragnar Nurkse's 1958 model of **balanced growth**.[37] His approach repeats the big push arguments that small markets discourage investment, that developing countries cannot rely on international markets for stimulus, and that the market mechanism may be too slow for the desired speed of development.

The pursuit of progress on many fronts simultaneously would require large amounts of investment and reliance on capital-intensive techniques. Labor intensity might correspond to factor endowments, but as Nurkse put it, "economic development must concern itself with changing these circumstances, not accepting them as they are." Balanced growth calls for a "pattern of mutually supporting investments over a range of industries wide enough to overcome the frustration of isolated advance."[38] The big push with a balanced pattern of investments provides mutually supporting markets. It has a positive impact on business psychology and allows income earned in one industry to be spent in others. This can be the result of either state planning or incentives to the private sector.

While proponents of balanced growth were more favorable than big push advocates to private investment, both shared an emphasis on capital intensity and a heavy volume of complementary investments. But while Rosenstein-Rodan's big push largely ignored agriculture in its focus on industrialization, Nurkse recognized that agriculture should be part of a balanced approach.

These approaches—big push and balanced growth—are recognizable in the development strategy pursued in South Korea. Although progress was already being made toward growth, the government became more active in the 1970s. Through a combination of public investment and incentives to the private sector, government promoted projects in iron and steel, machinery, chemicals, shipbuilding, and electronics, as well as urban infrastructure. Chemicals and heavy industry had increased their share of output from 24 percent in 1960 to 37 percent in 1970. This jumped to 52 percent in 1980 and 58 percent in 1986.[39] One study suggests that government investment and promotion had a big push effect by reducing costs and the degree of protection from imports than would have been necessary for individual firms to succeed on their own.[40]

Unbalanced Growth and Linkages

Is there a better approach than the big push to rapid industrialization? In 1958, Albert O. Hirschman proposed that it is more feasible to pursue **unbalanced growth**, which means to provide a boost to strategic, or leading sectors, which will create the **linkages** to bring others into existence. He suggested that initial investments be chosen in such a way that investors would have an incentive to establish new firms and industries in order to take advantage of what had been put into place earlier.[41]

Economists today commonly consider linkages to be a vital element of a development strategy. **Backward linkage** is the proportion of an industry's inputs that is purchased from other industries. For example, shoes require leather and machinery requires steel. **Forward linkage** is the proportion of an industry's output that is purchased by other industries, rather than the final consumer. For example, textile machinery requires textile producers. Linkages thus have a multiplier effect, increasing income by more than just the activities of the firm.

With linkages in mind, the concept of unbalanced growth suggests two alternative directions. Initial investments could create excess capacity, for example, by creating infrastructure, opening up the opportunities for private companies to take advantage of the available capacity. This is a clear forward linkage. The advantage of this approach is that governments do not have to predict the precise linkages that would occur and entrepreneurs would provide more specific direction through their own decisions. Hirschman disagrees with this approach and cites as an historical example the U.S. railroad system. The railroad system was created in piecemeal fashion, as demand for transport expanded, not in advance of that demand.[42]

Alternatively, initial investment could create shortages, thereby providing the incentive for firms to meet needs for backward linkages. For example, the shoe factory would create a demand for leather, and a clothing factory would create a demand for more cotton and cloth. The appropriate direction would vary with the linkages that were most significant for a particular country. It is necessary for economists and government officials to analyze the set of possible industries for those whose activities are most likely to create the desired linkages.

Those linkages could be anywhere, although initially, economists gave little thought to agriculture.[43] An attempt to measure such linkages was made in 1973, simulating the production structure of a typical developing country. It supported the view that agriculture has limited *backward* linkages. Manufacturing industries ranged from a high of 0.718 (food and beverages) to 0.481 (rubber). Agriculture measured only 0.368, although improvements in agricultural technique will eventually give rise to demand for new tools and inputs such as fertilizer. For *forward* linkages however, agriculture measured a below-average but respectable 0.502, well within the range for manufacturing from 0.980 (basic metals) to 0.025 (clothing).[44]

A study done in 1994, however, approached the matter differently. It supported the use of agriculture as a leading sector by showing that a dollar's worth of income produced in that sector in low-income countries led to new nonagricultural income of $2.75 and more when incomes rose. Industry did not return the favor, however. One dollar of nonagricultural income led to only $1.00 of agricultural income at low income levels, falling as income rose.[45] The concept of linkage, however, remained crucial to evaluating development strategies.

Proponents of unbalanced growth wanted, among other things, to reduce the role of government in developing-country investment programs. But others argued that governments could detect linkage possibilities more easily, that private-sector time horizons were not sufficiently long for firms to invest in needed industries, and that infrastructure and investments in critical industries were particularly large and not well suited for developing-country private sectors. Even if government were to leave the investment to private capital, it might be necessary to provide the incentives to guide firms along the way.

Governments have been heavily involved in many developing-country strategies, whether balanced or unbalanced. Government direction is needed more for a balanced strategy, such as that pursued by Mexico. However, many governments, including those of India and Brazil,[46] have pushed fairly unbalanced strategies, often directed at export markets.

IMPLICIT MODELS IN THE CURRENT DEBATE

Development economists pay less attention today to generalized models of development. These models rose to prominence in the middle of the century when formal critical thinking was brought to bear on development for the first time. But while the emphasis is now placed on policies, the debates involve implicit models of development. As we saw in Chapter 1, the key to policy debates is the extent of the government's role. In Chapter 2 we showed that the Basic Human Needs approach requires an active government to direct resources into health, education, housing for low-income families, and agriculture. Proposals for government protection of domestic firms, or more active support to specific industries, combine our industrialization models with questions about how developing economies should interact with the developed world.

The overarching issue of government's role is most starkly raised by what is now referred to as the **neoliberal** approach. Early modeling either assumed or concluded that government would play a significant role in the development process, usually because markets were either poorly organized or nonexistent. The neoliberal approach concentrates on the creation and proper functioning of markets.

This approach leads to what has been called the Washington Consensus, a set of policies broadly consistent with those advocated by the World Bank and International Monetary Fund, both based in Washington, D.C. These organizations want government policy to focus on the creation of efficient markets and minimize restrictions on markets for goods and services, labor, and capital. This applies to internal markets and those that link developing to developed countries.

The extremes of "market vs. state" tend to be blunted these days by an understanding that both types of institutions are vital, along with the private, nonprofit sector and community organizations. Still, when policies are debated, the neoliberal model tends to look to the development of markets as the fundamental answer, while what might be called the "neostatist" model emphasizes the downside of markets and looks for ways that other institutions should be called into play to mitigate the extremes of poverty, discrimination, and environmental damage. We will consider these debates in future chapters.

SUMMARY AND CONCLUSION

Economists have taken different approaches to development. Table 3–1 summarizes the key approaches to growth and development from this chapter. Classical economists tended to have a relatively gloomy view of long-run growth, assuming that eventually most economies would stagnate. Western economists virtually neglected long-run growth in the early part of the twentieth century, although interest continued in the Soviet Union and Asia.

After World War II, the end of colonialism put the problems of developing nations on the agenda of many economists, and numerous approaches to development appeared, including stage approaches such as Rostow's and varieties of dualism. Hope for economic progress in the developing countries was mixed, for a variety of culturally and politically oriented reasons, but economists outlined requirements for movement from traditional societies to more modern ones. Marxist-oriented theories, such as dependency theory, blamed the rich countries for the situation of the poor and recommended that developing countries break out of the prevailing world system.

In their attempt to explain economic growth and development, economists have used a number of models that isolate key variables. Growth models are relatively

TABLE 3–1 Approaches to Development

Approach	Authors/Dates	Description
Classical	Adam Smith, David Ricardo, Thomas Malthus, Karl Marx (1776–1865)	General term for the view that economic growth is self-limiting due to scarcity of natural resources or the inevitable poverty of workers.
Dualism	J. H. Boeke (1953)	Developing economies consist of a traditional, rural sector and a modern, urban sector.
Stages	Walt W. Rostow (1959)	Development occurs in relatively well-defined stages, from a more traditional economy in which activity takes place in the same way, and eventually takes off when social change permits greater saving and investment.
Dependency	Andre Gunder Frank (1967)	Large firms from rich countries dictate the kind of development that takes place in the poor countries, leading to underdevelopment of all but those sectors favored by foreign investors.
Harrod–Domar Growth Model	Roy Harrod, Evsey Domar (1939, 1947)	A mathematical growth model that produced a "knife-edge" growth rate from the relationship between the Marginal Propensity to Save (MPS) and the Incremental Capital-Output Ratio (ICOR).
Neoclassical Growth Theory	Robert Solow (1956)	Growth is a function of both labor and capital. An economy grows until it reaches a steady state in which high income is maintained. Higher growth rates may be achieved through technological improvement, arising outside the model.
New Growth Theory	Paul Romer (1986)	Followed the neoclassical model but made technological change a product of economic forces within the model. The ability to foster technological change thereby becomes a crucial element in promoting growth.
Critical Minimum Effort	Harvey Leibenstein (1957)	Development requires a major push, from new technology or foreign investment, for example, to overcome social inertia.
Labor Surplus Model	W. Arthur Lewis (1954)	Early development proceeds by moving labor out of the traditional, rural sector, where marginal workers produce less than their wage, to the modern, industrial sector where they help firms make a profit that can be accumulated for investment.
Big Push	Paul N. Rosenstein-Rodan (1943)	Industrialization requires a major effort in order to create a set of complementary industries in the initial absence of an integrated national market.
Balanced Growth vs. Unbalanced Growth	Ragnar Nurkse, Albert O. Hirschman (1958)	Balanced growth advocates a big push spread among numerous sectors. Unbalanced growth suggests that the push be concentrated in a small number of sectors, which would then create linkages, encouraging other sectors to emerge.
Neoliberal	World Bank, International Monetary Fund (late 1980s)	Restriction of government's role to the creation of markets. Otherwise, development proceeds best by promoting markets internally and internationally.

simplistic, but they allow us to focus on and debate some of these variables, including investment and technology. The neoclassical model proposes that economies might converge if capital moves from rich to poor, but they will converge on different steady states that are amenable to social change and government policy. The endogenous growth models point to technological change as a key to growth and the need for societies to be open to innovation.

Development models focus on specific characteristics of the development process and put the more general questions of investment and technology into the context of economies that have not fully entered the modern, or developed, stage. Lewis proposed a model for transferring labor from rural areas to industry, while other theories promoted a government-financed big push or, alternatively, unbalanced growth in order to accomplish more rapid industrialization. Modern models are more in the background of economic development analysis, but the debate between the neoliberal and more activist approaches finds its way into most issues of development policy.

All the models have something to teach us. From the early visions of societal change to the most abstract mathematical treatments, all point to crucial variables that are part of the development process. They are only the beginning, however. We must investigate these variables more closely, see how they apply to different situations, and draw policy conclusions in concrete circumstances.

One key weakness, however, is that economic models deal only with economic variables. They are not so good at understanding the impact of political and social institutions on economic outcomes. Although they can point the way to policies, they say nothing about why governments undertake some policies and not others. Many observers, economists and others, believe that economic success depends largely on how the economic, political, and social institutions of a country interact to use resources and technology.[47]

We now turn to some of the key ingredients in the development process. In Chapter 4 we address the financial requirements for development, a country's ability to save, and how saving can best be transformed into the investment necessary for economic growth.

Key Terms

- backward linkage (p. 61)
- balanced growth (p. 60)
- big push (p. 59)
- center (p. 49)
- capital intensive (p. 46)
- classical economics (p. 42)
- complementarity (p. 59)
- convergence (p. 54)
- dependency theory (p. 48)
- dependent variable (p. 50)
- diminishing returns (p. 43)
- disguised unemployment (p. 56)
- dual economy (p. 46)
- endogenous (p. 54)
- exogenous (p. 54)
- extended family (p. 56)

- external economies (p. 59)
- factor mobility (p. 46)
- forward linkage (p. 61)
- gestation period (p. 59)
- Harrod–Domar growth model (p. 50)
- Incremental Capital-Output Ratio (ICOR) (p. 50)
- independent variable (p. 50)
- indivisibilities (p. 59)
- leading sectors (p. 47)
- Lewis labor surplus model (p. 56)
- linkages (p. 61)
- marginal product (p. 43)
- Marginal Propensity to Save (MPS) (p. 50)

- market imperfections (p. 59)
- model (p. 49)
- neoclassical economics (p. 42)
- neoclassical growth model (p. 52)
- neoliberal (p. 63)
- new growth theory (p. 54)
- periphery (p. 49)
- positive externalities (p. 60)
- production function (p. 53)
- returns to scale (p. 54)
- social overhead capital (p. 47)
- subsistence sector (p. 56)
- traditional society (p. 45)
- unbalanced growth (p. 61)

Questions for Review

1. Briefly describe, and explain advantages and disadvantages to, the following views of economic development:
   a. Classical views
   b. Rostow's stage theory
   c. Dependency theory
2. Outline briefly the conclusions reached by the Harrod–Domar and Solow growth models. In what sense are they opposite?
3. According to the Harrod–Domar model, if an economy increases the proportion of new income that it saves from 10 to 20 percent, and improves the efficiency of new investment so that each dollar of new output requires only two dollars of equipment rather than three, what happens to the equilibrium growth rate?
4. What is the impact of technological change on the growth process in the neoclassical growth model? What are the implications for developing countries of a growth model that incorporates technological change as an endogenous factor?

5. How does an examination of growth in Taiwan show the contribution of the new growth theory?
6. What does convergence mean in the context of the neoclassical growth model? Why should convergence occur? Does convergence imply that poorer countries will catch up to richer countries?
7. What are the crucial assumptions of Lewis's labor surplus model of development, and what are the major problems with the model?
8. What was the rationale for proposals such as the big push and balanced growth? What were the problems associated with them?
9. Define the concept of forward and backward linkage and explain their relationship to the idea of unbalanced growth.

Related Internet Resources

Most development-related Web sites focus on data and issues. Theory is not a hot topic, unless related to specific issues. However, the New School for Social Research maintains a site called the History of Economic Thought Frontpage that, among other things, contains an alphabetical listing of the major figures in economic thought with brief summaries of their contributions. Numerous development-oriented economists are included. The Web site is ⟨http://cepa.newschool.edu/het/home.htm.⟩

Endnotes and Further Readings

1. See Walt W. Rostow, *Theorists of Economic Growth from David Hume to the Present* (New York: Oxford University Press, 1990); H. W. Arndt, *The Rise and Fall of Economic Growth: A Study in Contemporary Thought* (Melbourne: Longman Cheshire, 1978); and H. W. Arndt, *Economic Development: The History of an Idea* (Chicago: University of Chicago Press, 1987).
2. A major exception was Joseph Schumpeter, who focused on the entrepreneur who served as an innovator. See Joseph Schumpeter, *Theory of Economic Development* (Cambridge: Harvard University Press, 1934).
3. Chapter 1 of H. W. Arndt, *Economic Development: History of an Idea.*
4. See Walt W. Rostow, *The Stages of Economic Growth* (Cambridge: Cambridge University Press, 1960, 1971, and 1990).
5. See, for example, Daniel Lerner, *The Passing of Traditional Society: Modernizing the Middle East* (New York: Free Press, 1958); Guy Hunter, *Modernizing Peasant Societies: A Comparative Study of Asia and Africa* (New York: Oxford University Press, 1969); and George M. Foster, *Traditional Societies and Technological Change*, 2nd ed. (New York: Harper and Row, 1973).
6. Max Weber, *The Protestant Ethic and the Spirit of Capitalism* (New York: Charles Scribner's Sons, 1958). For opposing views, see Robert W. Green, ed., *Protes-*

tantism and Capitalism: The Weber Thesis and Its Critics (Boston: D. C. Heath, 1959); H. M. Robertson, *Aspects of the Rise of Economic Individualism* (Clifton, NJ: Augustus M. Kelley, 1973); R. H. Tawney, *Religion and the Rise of Capitalism* (New York: New American Library, 1954); and Kurt Samuelsson, *Religion and Economic Action* (New York: Basic Books, 1961).

7. See Harvey Leibenstein, *Economic Backwardness and Economic Growth* (New York: John Wiley, 1957).

8. Robert Heilbroner, *The Great Ascent: The Struggle for Economic Development in Our Time* (New York: Harper and Row, 1963), pp. 53–54.

9. Denis Goulet, *The Cruel Choice: A New Concept in the Theory of Development* (Lanham, MD: University Press of America, 1971, 1985).

10. See J. H. Boeke, *Economics and Economic Policy in Dual Societies* (New York: AMS Press, 1953, 1978); W. Arthur Lewis, "Economic Development with Unlimited Supplies of Labor," reprinted in A. N. Agarwala and S. P. Singh, *The Economics of Underdevelopment* (New York: Oxford University Press, 1963), pp. 400–449; R. S. Eckaus, "The Factor Proportions Problem in Underdeveloped Areas," *American Economic Review* 45, no. 4 (September 1955), pp. 539–565; Benjamin Higgins, "The 'Dualistic Theory' of Underdeveloped Areas," *Economic Development and Cultural Change* 4, no. 2 (January 1956), pp. 99–115; John Fei and Gustav Ranis, "A Theory of Economic Development," *American Economic Review* 51, no. 4 (September 1961), pp. 533–565; and Hla Myint, "Organizational Dualism and Economic Development," *Asian Development Review* 3, no. 1 (1985), pp. 22–42. A fairly technical review of the subject is Gustav Ranis, "Analytics of Development: Dualism," in Hollis B. Chenery and T. N. Srinivasan, *Handbook of Development Economics* 1 (Amsterdam: Elsevier Science Publishers, 1988), pp. 73–92.

11. For Marxist-oriented ideas on dualism, see Michael Barratt Brown, *The Economics of Imperialism* (Baltimore: Penguin Books, 1974), especially pp. 253–254 and 276–277.

12. Alexander Gerschenkron, *Economic Backwardness in Historical Perspective* (Cambridge: Harvard University Press, 1962). Also see V. I. Lenin, *Imperialism: The Highest Stage of Capitalism* (New York: International Publishers, 1939, 1969 [originally published in 1917]).

13. Walt W. Rostow, *The Stages of Economic Growth.*

14. See Andre Gunder Frank, *Capitalism and Underdevelopment in Latin America* (New York: Monthly Review Press, 1967), and *Latin America: Underdevelopment or Revolution* (New York: Monthly Review Press, 1969); the inaugural issue of *Latin American Perspectives* (Spring 1974) devoted to "Dependency Theory: A Reassessment"; Theotonio dos Santos, "The Structure of Dependence," in K. T. Fann and Donald C. Hodges, *Readings in US Imperialism* (Boston: Porter Sargent, 1971); Pierre Jalee, *The Third World in World Econ-*

omy (New York: Monthly Review Press, 1969); and Samir Amin, *Accumulation on a World Scale* (New York: Monthly Review Press, 1974).

15. See Roy Harrod, "An Essay in Dynamic Theory," *Economic Journal* 49 (March 1939), pp. 14–33; Evsey Domar, "Expansion and Employment," *American Economic Review* 37, no. 1 (March 1947), pp. 34–35; and Evsey Domar, "The Problem of Capital Formation," *American Economic Review* 38, no. 4 (December 1948), pp. 777–794. Also see Henry J. Bruton, "Growth Models and Underdeveloped Economies," *Journal of Political Economy* 63, no. 4 (August 1955), pp. 322–336.

16. Lance Taylor, *Macro Models for Developing Countries* (New York: McGraw-Hill, 1979), pp. 119–123.

17. C. Rangarajan and R. Kannan, "Capital-Output Ratios in the Indian Economy (1950–51 to 1989–90)," *Indian Economic Journal* 42, no. 1 (July–September 1994), pp. 1–16.

18. Robert M. Solow, "A Contribution to the Theory of Economic Growth," *Quarterly Journal of Economics* 70, no. 1 (February 1956), pp. 65–94. Also see N. Gregory Mankiw, David Romer, and David N. Weil, "A Contribution to the Empirics of Economic Growth," *Quarterly Journal of Economics* 107, no. 2 (May 1992), pp. 407–438, and N. Gregory Mankiw, *Macroeconomics*, 4th ed. (New York: Worth Publishers, 2000).

19. See Edmund Phelps, "The Golden Rule of Accumulation: A Fable for Growthmen," *American Economic Review* 51, no. 4 (September 1961), pp. 638–643; David Cass, "Optimum Growth in an Aggregative Model of Capital Accumulation," *Review of Economic Studies* 32 (July 1965), pp. 233–240; and Tjalling C. Koopmans, "On the Concept of Optimal Economic Growth," in *The Econometric Approach to Development Planning* (Amsterdam: North-Holland, 1965).

20. See chapter 1 of Robert J. Barro, *Determinants of Economic Growth: A Cross-Country Empirical Study* (Cambridge: MIT Press, 1997) and Jonathan Temple, "The New Growth Evidence," *Journal of Economic Literature* 37, no. 1 (March 1999), pp. 112–156.

21. See Paul Romer, "Increasing Returns and Long-Run Growth," *Journal of Political Economy* 94, no. 5 (October 1986), pp. 1002–1037; Paul Romer, "Capital Accumulation in the Theory of Long-Run Growth," in *Modern Macroeconomics*, R. Barro, ed. (Cambridge: Harvard University Press, 1989), pp. 51–127; and Paul Romer, "Endogenous Technical Change," *Journal of Political Economy* 98, no. 5 (October 1990), pp. 71–102. A "symposium" appears in the *Journal of Economic Perspectives* 8, no. 1 (winter 1994) with the following articles: Paul Romer, "The Origins of Endogenous Growth," pp. 3–22; Gene M. Grossman and Elhanan Helpman, "Endogenous Innovation in the Theory of Growth," pp. 23–44; Robert M. Solow, "Perspectives on Growth Theory," pp. 45–54; and Howard Pack, "Endogenous Growth Theory: Intellectual Appeal and Empirical Shortcomings," pp. 55–72.

22. Early approaches were Nicholas Kaldor, "A Model of Economic Growth," *Economic Journal* 67 (1957), pp. 591–624, and Kenneth J. Arrow, "The Economic Implications of Learning by Doing," *Review of Economic Studies* 29 (1962), pp. 155–173. For a review of growth models, see Nicholas Stern, "The Determinants of Growth," *Economic Journal* 101 (January 1991), pp. 122–133.

23. Robert M. Solow, "Perspectives on Growth Theory," pp. 48–50.

24. For a summary, see Jan Fagerberg, "Technology and International Differences in Growth Rates," *Journal of Economic Literature* 32, no. 3 (September 1994), pp. 1147–1175. For the institutional impact on technological development, see Richard R. Nelson and Sidney G. Winter, *An Evolutionary Theory of Economic Change* (Cambridge: Harvard University Press, 1982).

25. For an application of the new growth theories to developing countries, see Alessandro Pio, "New Growth Theory and Old Development Problems: How Recent Developments in Endogenous Growth Theory Apply to Developing Countries," *Development Policy Review* 12, no. 3 (September 1994), pp. 277–300.

26. Syed Nawab Haider Nagri, "The Significance of Development Economics," *World Development* 24, no. 6 (June 1996), pp. 975–989.

27. Harvey Leibenstein, *Economic Backwardness and Economic Growth*.

28. W. Arthur Lewis, "Economic Development with Unlimited Supplies of Labor." See also John C. Fei and Gustav Ranis in *Development of the Labor Surplus Economy: Theory and Policy* (Homewood, IL: Irwin, 1964); R. Albert Berry and Ronald Soligo, "Rural-Urban Migration, Agricultural Output, and the Supply Price of Labour in a Labour-Surplus Economy," *Oxford Economic Papers* 20, no. 2 (July 1968), pp. 230–249; and Lewis himself in a number of writings since then.

29. For the economic behavior of families under conditions of peasant agriculture, see Joseph Stiglitz, "Economic Organization, Information, and Development" in the *Handbook of Development Economics*, 1, H. Chenery and T. N. Srinivasan, eds. (Amsterdam: Elsevier Science Press, 1988), pp. 93–160, especially pp. 105–115.

30. See Folke Dovring, "Underemployment in Traditional Agriculture," *Economic Development and Cultural Change* 15, no. 2, part 1 (January, 1967), pp. 163–173. Jagdish N. Bhagwati and Sukhamoy Chakravarty, in "Contributions to Indian Economic Analysis: A Survey," *American Economic Review* 59, no. 4 (September 1969, supplement), pp. 54–60, define disguised unemployment as a situation where the Social Marginal Product of labor is zero. Also see Gustav Ranis, "Labour Surplus Economies," *Economic Development* (New York: W. W. Norton, 1989), p. 193; M. R. Rosenzweig, "Labor Markets in Low-Income Countries," *Handbook of Development Economics* 1, H. Chenery

and T. N. Srinivasan, eds. (Amsterdam: Elsevier Science Publishers, 1988), pp. 713–762; and Alan Richards, "The Egyptian Farm Labor Market Revisited," *Journal of Development Economics* 43, no. 2 (April 1994), pp. 239–261.

31. See K. N. Raj, "Mobilization of the Rural Economy and the Asian Experience," in Gustav Ranis and T. Paul Schultz, eds., *The State of Development Economics* (Cambridge: Basil Blackwell, 1988), pp. 252–280, especially pp. 261–264.

32. See Ranis and Fei, *Development of the Labor Surplus Economy: Theory and Policy*, and Richard Grabowski, "Commercialization, Nonagriculture Production, Agricultural Innovation, and Economic Development," *Journal of Developing Areas* 29, no. 5 (October 1995), pp. 41–62.

33. The initial paper was Paul N. Rosenstein-Rodan, "Problems of Industrialization of Eastern and South-Eastern Europe," *Economic Journal* 53, no. 2 (June–September 1943), pp. 202–211. See also Paul N. Rosenstein-Rodan, "Notes on the Theory of the 'Big Push,' " in Howard S. Ellis, ed., *Economic Development for Latin America* (New York: St. Martin's Press, 1961).

34. The basic concept is explored in Tibor Scitovsky, "Two Concepts of External Economies," reprinted in A. N. Agarwala and S. P. Singh, *The Economics of Underdevelopment* (New York: Oxford University Press, 1963), pp. 295–308. In that volume, also see J. Marcus Fleming, "External Economies and the Doctrine of Balanced Growth," pp. 272–294.

35. Paul N. Rosenstein-Rodan, "*Natura Facit Saltum*: Analysis of the Disequilibrium Growth Process," in Gerald M. Meier and Dudley Seers, eds., *Pioneers in Development* (New York: Oxford University Press, 1984), pp. 210–211.

36. See Howard S. Ellis, "Accelerated Investment as a Force in Economic Development," *Quarterly Journal of Economics* 72, no. 4 (November 1958), pp. 486–495.

37. Key sources include Ragnar Nurkse, "The Conflict Between 'Balanced Growth' and International Specialization," from *Lectures on Economic Development* (Istanbul: Faculties of Economics at Istanbul University and Political Sciences at Ankara University, 1958), pp. 170–176, excerpted as "Balanced Growth" in Gerald M. Meier, ed., *Leading Issues in Development Economics* (New York: Oxford University Press, 1964), pp. 250–254; Albert O. Hirschman, *The Strategy of Economic Development* (New Haven: Yale University Press, 1958); and Paul Streeten, "Balance versus Unbalanced Growth," *The Economic Weekly* (April 20, 1963).

38. Ragnar Nurkse, "The Conflict Between 'Balanced Growth' and International Specialization," in Gerald M. Meier, ed., *Leading Issues in Development Economics*, pp. 250–254. The citations are from pages 252 and 254.

39. Suk-Chae Lee, "The Heavy and Chemical Industries Promotion Plan (1973–79)," in Lee-Jay Cho and

Yoon Hyung Kim, eds., *Economic Development in the Republic of Korea: A Policy Perspective* (Honolulu: East–West Center, 1991), pp. 431–472. The data are from Byung-Nak Song, *The Rise of the Korean Economy* (New York: Oxford University Press, 1990), p. 107. Economic data for Korea are available at ⟨www.samsung.org⟩.

40. See Kevin M. Murphy, Andrei Shleifer, and Robert W. Vishny, "Industrialization and the Big Push," *Journal of Political Economy* 95, no. 5 (October 1989), pp. 1003–1026.

41. Albert O. Hirschman, *The Strategy of Economic Development.*

42. In his *Development Projects Observed* (Washington: Brookings, 1967), Albert O. Hirschman cites Albert Fishlow's *American Railroads and the Transformation of the Ante-Bellum Economy* (Cambridge: Harvard University Press, 1965).

43. See Albert O. Hirschman, *The Strategy of Economic Development*, pp. 109–110.

44. P. A. Yotopoulos and J. B. Nugent, "A Balanced Growth Version of the Linkage Hypothesis," *Quarterly Journal of Economics* 87, no. 2 (1973), pp. 157–171, reported in John Weiss, *Industry in Developing Countries: Theory, Policy and Evidence* (London: Routledge, 1990), p. 100.

45. Stephen J. Vogel, "Structural Changes in Agriculture: Production Linkages and Agricultural Demand-Led Industrialization," *Oxford Economic Papers* 46, no. 1 (January 1994), pp. 136–156.

46. Benjamin and Jean Downing Higgins cite Mexico and India in *Economic Development of a Small Planet* (New York: W. W. Norton, 1979), pp. 180–183, although Albert O. Hirschman cites India's early development plans as an attempt to pursue a more balanced growth, *The Strategy of Economic Development*, p. 80.

47. See Mancur Olson, "Big Bills Left on the Sidewalk: Why Some Nations Are Rich, and Others Poor," *Journal of Economic Perspectives* 10, no. 2 (spring 1996), pp. 3–24.

CHAPTER

4

FINANCIAL RESOURCES FOR DEVELOPMENT

What is . . . saved is as regularly consumed
as what is . . . consumed. . . . But it is consumed
by a different set of people.
—ADAM SMITH (1723–1790)

INTRODUCTION

Although models of economic growth have severe limitations when applied to development, their focus on investment and saving remains valuable. Whatever we conceive economic development to be, it is unlikely to occur without growth of physical capital and an increase in its productivity. Most investment requires the mobilization of financial resources: But the financial institutions to accomplish this, banks, bond markets, and the like, are likely to be absent or small in developing countries. In this chapter we consider the following questions: How important is capital for growth and development? How do we determine the best uses of capital resources? Since capital is required, how can we obtain financial resources from a poor population? To answer the latter question we look at the difficulties of mobilizing private-sector saving and carefully examine the role of financial institutions and interest rates.

CAPITAL AND GROWTH

Capital has long served as the economist's catchall term for anything that increases the productivity of labor. We describe it either narrowly as machinery, factories, and the like, or more broadly to include human skills and the economic infrastructure. Even consumption goods that make the difference between a person too weak to work and one fit for the rigors of productive life could be considered capital under some circumstances. The word "capital" is also used in a financial sense, as when a company raises capital by issuing stocks or bonds or borrowing from a bank. In this section we focus on physical capital, especially plant and equipment.

The Role of Capital

The Incremental Capital-Output Ratio (ICOR) was central to early growth models because capital plays a crucial role in the process of economic growth. Although high investment levels do not guarantee high income levels, one survey in 1989 found a

71

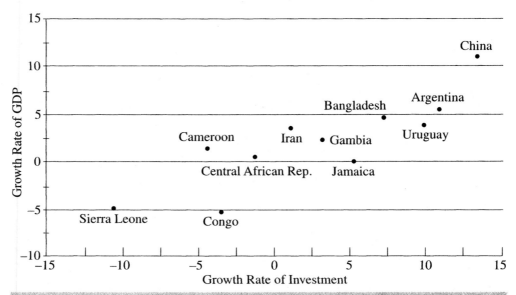

FIGURE 4–1 Investment and GDP Growth Rates (Selected Countries: 1990 to 1998)

A comparison of the growth rate of investment and GDP in a variety of countries reveals a positive correlation between the two. Economic reasoning suggests that higher investment produces higher growth.

positive correlation for countries within all income groups between ratios of investment to output and growth rates.[1] And some aggregate data show that for all the groups for which data are available, GDP growth rates are correlated with growth rates of investment. Figure 4–1 charts data for several countries for the period 1990 to 1998. While the correlation is not perfect, there is a clear direct relationship between the growth rate of investment and the growth rate of GDP.

Nonetheless, the link between investment and growth is a bit murky. As early as 1955, Alexander Cairncross[2] suggested that the industrialized countries' growth was the result of new technologies embodied in capital, rather than simply more capital. Studies showed that capital growth accounted for no more than one-fourth of output growth in those countries. Some recent research has even suggested that the contribution to growth from inputs of *all* factors of production may be as little as one-half in developed countries and one-fourth in developing countries. The remainder is due to residual, or unmeasured, factors that may represent technological change and economic organization.[3] For a brief explanation of **Total Factor Productivity**, see Development Spotlight 4–1. Another study suggests that growth leads to increases in capital stock, not the other way around.[4]

Finally, capital utilization is constrained by the economy's **absorptive capacity**; its ability to make use of all the capital that is available to it, based on the existence of complementary factors such as trained people and infrastructure.[5] There is ample evidence that, in the case of foreign aid for example, too much capital at once may not be usable and may be counterproductive if it wastes other resources such as time, materials, and labor.

TOTAL FACTOR PRODUCTIVITY

Total Factor Productivity (TFP) is a way of measuring the contribution of the quality, rather than the quantity, of factors of production to an economy's growth. While an economy grows by increasing the amount of capital and labor in use, it will grow faster if new machinery can produce more output per dollar than older machines and if better skills allow workers to produce more per hour than previously. To calculate TFP, subtract the growth rate of capital stock and growth rate of the labor force from the growth rate of GDP.

Using such calculations, one controversial study has concluded that East Asian economic performance, perceived by some as a "miracle," was due mainly to increases in the amount of capital and labor used, along with more educated labor. Growth of Total Factor Productivity, while respectable (2.6 percent in Taiwan, 1.7 percent in South Korea), was not significantly better than economies such as Japan (2.0), West Germany (1.6), and Brazil (1.6).

If capital is viewed as a means of introducing new technology, its importance is enhanced. A recent review of this topic supports the idea that increases in productivity are brought about as investment *reallocates* resources from less to more productive sectors. This reallocation contributes "a significant component of aggregate growth of output and Total Factor Productivity particularly in the industrializing stage."[6] Capital accumulation, especially investment in equipment, not only carries with it new technology but also requires training for workers, linking investment in physical and human capital.[7] Also, some technical progress permits lessening of capital intensity.

While there is no escaping the necessity of new investment for growth, investment may be wasted, so we should pay attention to making the best use of capital. Where government plays a role in allocating funds as an investing agency or just a source of encouragement to the private sector, officials must give careful consideration to the criteria for allocating those resources.

Investment Choice

A private firm considering a new investment will project a rate of profit on the basis of expected sales revenues and costs of production. A government policy maker, on the other hand, whether actually allocating resources to projects or simply concerned with incentives for private activity, may consider broader objectives in deciding which investments will be most desirable from the standpoint of society.

Social Objectives

Government investment decisions must start with certain choices: (*a*) what broad *sectors* or industries are important, (*b*) within those sectors, what specific *projects* are crucial, and (*c*) what *techniques* make sense, for example, how can ICORs be kept low and what capital/labor ratio is desirable, how sophisticated can the technology be. In making these choices, fundamental questions must be addressed. What are the primary objectives of the investment program; do we want to maximize output or employment (or other resource use)? How do we want to affect the distribution of income? What **bottlenecks**, or shortages, place a limit on absorptive capacity? What is the appropriate time horizon for the investment? A number of these objectives may be contradictory, and any particular choice will involve trade-offs.

In an authoritarian regime, the preferences of only a few people are relevant. Those preferences may be justified in the name of the "masses" but may have much more to do with the narrow personal gain to influential individuals and groups. In varying degrees, however, the political process may permit the needs of citizens to percolate up into economic decision making.

Alternative Criteria

Once the broad objectives are set, economists are involved in specifying the criteria to be applied to decision making. A key concept here is **social productivity**.[8] The important distinction between public and private criteria is attention to the broader social implications of investment projects. The concept is a simple one. Measurement of private profit or capital productivity is supplemented by an assessment of broader gains to society from, for example, improving the skill level of the labor force. Capital is then allocated among alternative projects in order to maximize increases in *social* welfare.

A project's ability to produce future investment can serve as a criterion for allocating capital. This means the project can produce an annual surplus (profit) over wages and depreciation. This criterion generally favors more capital-intensive projects such as highly mechanized factories for milling rice, stitching clothing, or producing steel. Alternative criteria may be considered superior: An investment could be evaluated primarily for its ability to produce employment or exports or for its use of particular technologies. Or, the goal may be stated in simple output terms, either in the aggregate or per capita.[9]

Project Appraisal

The literature on techniques for appraising and evaluating potential projects is quite technical.[10] The evaluation either uses a **cost-benefit analysis** or compares an expected rate of return to the interest rate. In the first, which is generally considered easier and more useful, costs and benefits are projected over the life of the project, and their values are discounted—by either the market interest rate or other suitable measure of the opportunity cost of capital—to obtain the **net present value (NPV)** according to the general formula:

$$\text{NPV} = \sum_{t=0}^{T} \frac{AB_t - AC_t}{(1 + r)^t}$$

where AB represents annual benefits, AC is annual costs, r is the **discount rate**, and t is the number of years of the project's expected useful life. Each year's costs are subtracted from benefits, and the net values, assumed to be received at year's end, are discounted; the discounted values are then summed over the life of the project. An NPV equal to zero means that all costs, including some normal return to capital, are covered. Any value greater than zero indicates a net benefit is received. For example, a two-year project that yields a net benefit of $10,000 with a discount rate of 6 percent has a net present value of $8,900 ($10,000 divided by 1.06^2). Ordinarily, calculations will be made for more than one project, and one with a greater positive NPV is favored. Development Spotlight 4–2 provides a more detailed example of how this type of cost-benefit analysis works.

Despite the conceptual simplicity, such a calculation is extremely difficult in practice. Even in a market economy, benefits and costs are based on difficult projections of future prices of the product and resources used in production. In countries whose markets do not work well, or where there may not currently be a market for the product, projecting relevant prices is even more difficult. Market imperfections—monopoly power in product and resource markets—will cause prices even in well-developed markets to deviate from the true opportunity cost of resources. A project will be affected by complementary projects and the overall economic environment. Should the public or private sector undertake the project?[11] Finally, the project itself and political judgments as to the distribution of the project's benefits are likely to cause a change in prices during the course of the project.

Discounting is a particularly difficult aspect of the capital allocation decision. The basic idea is that people normally prefer income today rather than at some time in the future. If income of 1,000 pesos is worth more than 1,000 pesos a year from now, then some smaller number of pesos today would be just as desirable as 1,000 pesos in one year. If the rate of interest is 10 percent, 1,000 pesos would be worth 1,100 in a year. A discount rate of 10 percent, applied to 1,000 pesos in a year, yields a present value of 909 pesos (1,000 divided by 1.1).

When discounting an investment project, the debate is over the rate at which future income should be discounted to determine its current value. In an economy where financial markets are not efficient, as we discuss shortly, the going interest rate will not be a very reliable guide. The case is often made that discount rates should be

---

DEVELOPMENT SPOTLIGHT 4–2

NET PRESENT VALUE ANALYSIS OF A PLOW FACTORY

Suppose a government decides to build a small plow factory. The factory will produce 10,000 plows per year after a year of construction. Plows are expected to sell for $10 each. The machinery will be simple, and the factory can be built for $100,000. Annual costs will start at $50,000 and increase slowly. The factory will last for five years after construction, and the interest rate is 8 percent. Using the formula

$$NPV = \sum_{t=0}^{T} \frac{AB_t - AC_t}{(1 + r)^t}$$

we would calculate the net present value as

Year	Revenues	Costs	Profit	NPV
1	$ 0	$100,000	–$100,000	–$92,593
2	100,000	50,000	+ 50,000	+ 42,867
3	100,000	50,000	50,000	39,692
4	100,000	55,000	45,000	33,076
5	100,000	65,000	35,000	23,820
6	100,000	70,000	30,000	18,905
Total	$500,000	$390,000	+$110,000	+$65,767

The project is profitable.

higher in developing countries. If the discount rate, like the interest rate, represents a reward for a willingness to wait for future returns, poorer people require a larger reward: Low and insecure incomes put a premium on income in the present and a greater sacrifice if present income is sacrificed for a future benefit.

Choosing any particular discount rate to assess an investment project will bias the project choice. Too high a rate will make the project less attractive by reducing the present value of future returns. Too low a rate will make it more attractive. In Development Spotlight 4–2, for example, a discount rate of 8 percent makes profit of $110,000 equal to a present value of only $65,767. At 7 percent, the present value is $70,304 and at 9 percent, only $61,465.

There are no easy answers. Interest rates set by government agencies may not be adequate as a guide to the true opportunity cost of capital in a country, but rates determined in international financial markets may not be any better. The field is open to bias on the part of those who either favor or oppose a project. We will apply this problem to the issue of environmental impact in the next chapter.

One author of a highly technical book on macroeconomic models suggests the following challenges to capital allocation:

> inadequate or downright dishonest technical consultants' reports, short-term considerations about which capital-goods supplier is giving better credits between this year and next, biases resulting from visions of national grandeur or regional growth through big, visibly expensive factory edifices, your political superior's concern about getting as much construction going as possible in an election year (it is always an election year). . . .[12]

Shadow Prices

Because poorly functioning markets and monopoly power often distort actual prices, economists have attempted to calculate hypothetical or **shadow prices** that differ from market prices. The shadow price is supposed to show the real opportunity cost involved in resource use, permitting more efficient allocation of resources than would otherwise occur. We might conclude, for example, that the **shadow wage**, or opportunity cost of low-productivity labor, is less than the actual wage. Development Spotlight 4–3 gives an illustration of how the use of shadow wages may affect the profitability of alternative technologies. This would justify using a greater amount of labor on a project than might be expected, even when the market wage seems high, because the loss of labor's alternative use is lower than indicated by the wage.

Another conclusion might be that the benefits of improved health and education may be greater than measurable returns indicate. Investment in these areas may be more productive than conventional accounting would indicate because it does not calculate the additional future productivity of healthier and better-educated individuals. Case 4–1 shows how trying to estimate a shadow wage may change the result of a project analysis.

Actually calculating shadow prices would be a daunting, perhaps even impossible task on a large scale. It would take a tremendous amount of information and a good deal of guesswork, and we could not be sure we were actually correct. The attempt, after all, is to evaluate the true opportunity cost of resources under hypothetical circumstances. The most efficient approach may be to look for an existing price that

DEVELOPMENT SPOTLIGHT 4–3

THE SHADOW WAGE

Wages have a dual role. They often represent a significant production cost, so a company wants to keep them low. But they are also income to most of the population, so workers want to see them rise. Governments often enact price floors—or minimum wages—so that working people can maintain a decent living standard on the wage. Wages may also be distorted by imperfections in labor and capital markets.

When evaluating a development project, however, using the legally mandated minimum wage will increase costs and lead to a bias against labor-intensive projects, although these are good for employment. To obtain a more accurate estimate of the true economic, or opportunity, cost of the project, we would use the shadow wage, or the true opportunity cost of a worker. When labor is abundant, and unemployment is high, the shadow wage—what the worker's best economic alternative would bring—may be close to zero, or at least to some subsistence level, and the true cost of the project would be much lower than the measured cost.

One means of estimating the shadow wage is suggested in the Lewis model, in which the rural wage is used as an approximation of the wage for unskilled urban labor, but living costs may be higher in urban areas.

Suppose we are choosing between two possible factories to manufacture shirts in a rural region of China. Each can produce shirts worth a million yuan a month. Factory A is automated, using sophisticated machinery and a few highly trained workers, at a cost of 900,000 yuan per month. Factory B would rely on simple sewing machines, hiring 100 workers. Using the legal minimum wage to calculate labor costs, this factory would cost 950,000 yuan per month, and the decision would be in favor of Factory A.

However, if the region has high unemployment, the opportunity cost—or production lost—from hiring the workers would be close to zero. Using zero as the shadow wage to calculate labor costs, total costs would be only 800,000 yuan per month, and Factory B would be chosen.

comes closest to reflecting competitively determined opportunity cost: usually **border prices**, which are prices determined in international markets.[13] Even these prices may be unreliable due to monopoly power and government restrictions on international trade, but where they are available they seem to offer a good compromise between guesses and a staggering job of economic analysis.

Some shadow prices are difficult to determine from border prices. This would be particularly true for the shadow wage and also for the discount rate. Interest rates determined in world financial markets might be used for assessing the appropriate rate, but domestic conditions might reduce their reliability. The discount rate probably should reflect market distortions, but future development will likely reduce those distortions.

In practice, some governments are quite arbitrary in the use of prices and discount rates in evaluating investment projects. The World Bank considers its evaluation methods to be fairly advanced, but a study of over a thousand World Bank projects found not only large discrepancies in the rates of return estimated at the

CASE 4–1

THE SHADOW WAGE AND TEXTILE PRODUCTION IN INDIA

FAST FACTS

On the Map: South Asia

Population: 998 Million

Per Capita GNI and Rank: $440   (163)

Life Expectancy: Male—62   Female—64

Adult Literacy Rate: Male—68%
Female—44%

Textiles in India are produced using three kinds of technologies: labor-intensive handlooms operated mostly by individuals or families, more capital-intensive powerlooms operated by hired labor in small enterprises, and very capital-intensive mills operated by factory workers. A comparison of costs in these sectors, using market wages, has shown that as interest rates rise, the more capital-intensive methods become relatively more costly. With low interest rates the mills are the most profitable, but powerlooms become more profitable than mills when interest rates rise above 13 percent and handlooms become more profitable when interest rates rise above 46 percent. These percentages are shown below under the column "market wage."

In the mill sector, wages are driven up by institutional influences such as unions and wage laws. The opportunity cost of labor, or shadow wage, is much lower. The powerloom sector does not suffer from this problem, and the study assumes that in this sector market and shadow wages are very close. In the handloom sector, however, as for mills, the shadow wage is below the market wage. Workers are helped by family members and have the flexibility of working at home, both of which reduce the sacrifice attributable to work and so the opportunity cost of working.

Because use of the lower shadow wages increases the (social) profitability of both mill and handloom production, the result should be to reduce the range of interest rates within which the powerloom sector is more profitable. The study suggests that mill production is preferred up to an interest rate of 30 percent, rather than 13.

We would expect that powerlooms, squeezed on one side by the mills, would be squeezed on the other side by the lower shadow wage in the handloom sector. However, the study *adds* half of the value of a handloom worker's land and buildings to more accurately reflect the shadow cost of *capital*. Increasing the cost of capital in this way maintains the cutoff interest rate of 46 percent between powerloom and handloom production with a shadow wage rate that is two-thirds the market wage. The interest rates at which different technologies are profitable are summarized below:

	Interest Rates at Which Different Production Methods Are Preferred	
Sector	*Market Wage*	*Shadow Wage (2/3 Market)*
Handloom	>46%	>46%*
Powerloom	13–46%	30–46%
Mill (Factory)	<13%	<30%

*Shadow capital cost above market is also used.

Source: Dipak Mazumdar, "The Issue of Small versus Large in the Indian Textile Industry: An Analytical and Historical Survey," World Bank Staff Working Papers, no. 645, 1984.

initiation and completion of the projects, but also that the Bank is largely unable to explain the discrepancies.[14]

Final Comment on Capital

In sum, capital plays a crucial—if sometimes misunderstood—role in the process of growth and development. Its association with improved technology and more efficient resource allocation may outweigh its purely production impact. It is essential to understand the limitations and objectives of investment so that we can allocate resources on the basis of criteria that further those objectives. Ultimately, well-informed judgment is called for in making investment decisions.

SAVINGS IN DEVELOPING COUNTRIES

Given the necessity of investment, it is crucial to assess the economy's ability to generate financial resources that may be put into investment. Typically, most resources for development come from within the domestic economy: personal, or household, saving, business saving via profits, and government saving accumulated by taxing or borrowing from the private sector.

Table 4–1 provides some data on savings as a percentage of GDP. In recent years, many developing countries such as Mauritius, Thailand, and Costa Rica have significantly increased their savings, while many higher-income countries such as Belgium, the Netherlands, and New Zealand have stabilized at a little over 20 percent. From 1965 to 1987, the countries with high GDP growth rates had the highest average savings ratios, but there was no significant difference between ratios of the groups with medium and low growth. On the other hand, a more recent study covering 1965 to 1995 did show a tendency for savings to be a larger share of per capita disposable income as

TABLE 4–1 Gross Domestic Savings (GDS) as a Percentage of GDP

Country	GDS as Percentage GDP		
	1965	*1980*	*1999*
Low Income (Average)	18	28	20
India	15	17	20
Tanzania	16	na	2
Nigeria	10	31	18
Lower-Middle Income (Average)	20	30	30
China	25	35	40
Kenya	15	13	7
Panama	16	31	24
Upper-Middle Income (Average)	25	25	23
Venezuela	34	33	22
South Korea	8	24	34
High Income (Average)	24	24	23
Singapore	10	38	52
United States	21	19	18

Source: World Development Report 1992 and World Development Indicators 2001.

income levels rose to about \$8,000. After that, savings rates leveled off and then fell.[15] The nature of developing countries makes the mobilization of those savings—collecting them and putting them in a form suitable for investment—a special problem.

Household Saving

The household is the original source of savings. In industrialized countries, large business firms also accumulate profits that are used to finance their own investments, but even then, ownership of stocks and bonds by the public and borrowing from accumulated household bank deposits play an important role. In developing countries where most firms are small, and often family owned, we look for savings in the household sector.

In general, savings are determined by income levels and income growth. Family composition is also important: Countries and families with a high **dependency ratio**—proportion of children and older people in the population—will save less than those with similar incomes but with a lower ratio.[16] In a poor country, especially where this ratio is high, a large portion of the population may earn little or no more than is required for basic consumption. Many of the poor, especially the rural landless poor, the urban unemployed, and many of the urban employed, achieve only a low level of consumption. Such groups are generally small in industrialized economies but are a significant portion of the population in many developing economies.

Further, much of the income earned in poor, agricultural economies is in the subsistence, or nonmonetary, sector. Especially in rural areas, much income is generated, and much trade takes place, with little or no money involved. Even though a surplus may be available, it may not take a form that is easily put into financial institutions and does not find its way to others who may have profitable investment opportunities but lack resources.

Savings may remain stashed away in forms that are necessary for the future (storage of surplus crops), used for ceremonial occasions, or in traditionally valued forms such as jewelry. These are not irrational uses from the point of view of an individual with traditional needs and assessment of the future, but from the point of view of economic development, resources would be better utilized if transformed into cash and put in a bank. Where wealth is traditionally measured in terms of possessions, be it land, livestock, art, or houses, wealthy individuals also may hold considerable resources that are not available for productive investment. These may be a decreasing portion of savings in developing countries, but some may retain a significant amount of wealth in jewelry, art, and land as a safeguard against the fragility of the emerging modern economy. Financial institutions with the capability and reputation to hold individuals' savings and make them available to investors may either not exist or may not function adequately.

Recent investigation into household saving in developing countries suggests a reason for both the pattern of saving behavior and for the difficulty of transferring that saving into investable form.[17] Whereas in wealthier countries household saving increases with income but also follows a life-cycle approach (low saving at the time of household formation, positive saving during the working years, and negative saving after retirement), many poor households suffer from extreme instability of income, and are likely to save as much as possible when income is earned and completely run down their asset stocks when income is discontinued. Accumulated assets are less likely to be put in investable form if they may be needed at any time, especially if financial institutions are not reliable.

In spite of all of these qualifications, in many developing countries the household sector not only finances its own investment, but is a net lender to the business and government sectors.[18] As we will see, this may require special institutions, such as Rotating Savings and Credit Associations (ROSCAs) that permit villages to collect savings from everyone to finance the investment of small businesses at different times.

Business Saving

In early stages of development, businesses tend to be relatively small and more oriented toward trade and quick profit than manufacturing and accumulation of reserves for investment. Profits may be quickly dissipated in consumption, family obligations, or new high-risk ventures that do not work out. The gradual, more efficient organization of developing economies generally involves the establishment of larger, production-oriented firms. This area is beginning to become a focus of policy: Developing-country governments and foreign assistance organizations are starting to train people in management and the long-term outlook that is essential for a modern business firm.

The Emergence of Pension Funds

In some of the wealthier developing countries, especially in Latin America, governments have established **pension funds** for workers in government and large private companies. These may be private funds to which workers in a particular firm and their employers contribute to provide for retirement pensions, or they may be large government-sponsored funds such as Social Security in the United States. Private pension funds in Latin America alone were reported to manage over $120 billion in mid-1997.[19] The accumulated funds are an increasingly important source of savings, and their revitalization since the 1980s has generated considerable debate.

Still, pension funds are uncommon in developing countries. Even in Latin America only about one-third of the population of those countries is covered, but in some countries coverage is nearly universal in large firms.[20] These systems initially were entirely government financed, but as in other areas, increasing fiscal pressures are leading to experiments in privatizing old-age pension systems. These systems are most extensive in Latin America, and some like Chile's have been getting mixed reviews.[21]

Pension programs may become significant sources of investment funds, and payments from them may reduce income inequalities. Where labor markets are fairly competitive from the supply side, social security payments required by government may result in lower money wages, so workers are actually trading off current income for future income.[22]

If these funds are to contribute to an increase in an economy's ability to mobilize savings, it is important to know the most efficient way of doing this, including the relative abilities of public and private management, and the extent to which they actually provide income security for retirees. These questions have not been fully answered yet but will bear watching over the next decade as retirees under systems in countries such as Chile and Argentina start to call on their contributed funds.[23]

MOBILIZING PRIVATE RESOURCES: THE ROLE OF FINANCIAL INSTITUTIONS[24]

Banking systems developed along with commerce and industry in Europe during the nineteenth century and became part of the landscape of industrialized countries. Early thinking on development assumed that the proper institutions would evolve during the development process, that finance followed real economic activity, and that no special measures were needed to encourage the formation of these institutions: Money was considered as having a passive rather than an active role in development. What was important was using real resources such as labor and capital.

What changed peoples' minds? For one thing, **inflation** became a major problem for some developing countries in the 1970s. Inflation acts as a tax on financial assets, reduces productive activity, distorts incentives, and brings unpredictable changes in peoples' use of their assets.

A second reason why banking systems began to receive more attention in developing countries was the increased internationalization of financial markets. The rapid increases in international trade and financial flows brought large sums of money into developing countries from North American and European money markets. Spurred on by dramatic advances in telecommunications, and the accompanying transmission of economic conditions in the "north" to countries in the "south," these flows brought increased instability to developing country markets and **capital flight**—the movement of large amounts of money from developing countries to safe financial institutions abroad.

At the same time, economists began increasingly to view money as a driving force in economic activity and one of a number of alternative assets whose attractiveness depended on rate of return and risk.[25] These changes encouraged some economists to apply new monetary approaches to the problem of growth and development.

Money and Financial Institutions

A country must have well-functioning financial intermediaries, beginning with banks, in order to achieve and sustain economic growth. For successful financial intermediation, resources must be in a transferable form such as money. Until the money economy is sufficiently extensive, intermediation is unlikely to be useful. Those with surplus resources must be able to easily transfer them to an intermediary, and those who need resources must be able to obtain them easily and on reasonable terms.

Financial intermediaries serve two key functions. First, they form a link between financial surplus units (savers) and deficit units (borrowers). This crucial function is illustrated in Figure 4–2.

The figure shows the benefits of financial intermediation by comparing two firms with different amounts of resources and resulting productivity. *MPRu* and *MPRr* are marginal productivity curves for capital in the urban and rural sectors. There is a larger resource base in the city. The two rates of return (u and r) differ because each is in an isolated market. Relative scarcity of resources in the countryside accounts for the higher returns there. A well-functioning financial system permits the transfer of resources from urban to rural markets, narrowing the differential sufficient to cover the cost of intermediation.

A second service of financial institutions is managing reserves and risk. Assets are always held for precautionary and speculative requirements. If not for the banking

Rate of Return

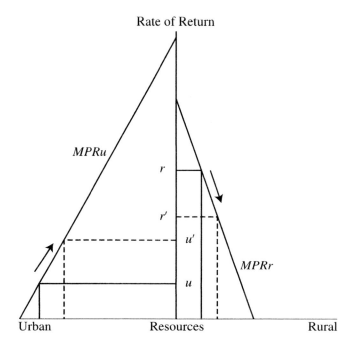

FIGURE 4–2 Financial Intermediation

Poor financial intermediation often results in poor farmers being unable to obtain credit. Suppose the urban (U) and rural (R) markets have different resources and marginal productivities, $MPRu$ and $MPRr$. The rates of return (u and r) differ because each is in an isolated market. A well-functioning financial system transfers resources from the city to the countryside, narrowing the differential. The remaining differential represents transaction costs.

system, such assets are held in nonproductive form such as idle land, jewelry, grain, and animals at great cost. Banks and other intermediaries provide an outlet to hold assets in financial form. They provide a channel for transferring foreign currencies so that transactions among countries can occur.

In order for these financial intermediaries to succeed, they must assure depositors that their resources will be returned to them as needed, and they must generate a sufficient spread between what they charge the borrower and what they pay the lender, to make a profit.

Industrialized countries maintain large, complex financial infrastructures that provide numerous ways for resources to be shifted from lenders to borrowers. These infrastructures include banks, insurance companies, and investment companies that permit trading in numerous financial instruments. In early stages of development, however, countries generally have few such institutions, and those that exist are generally located in a few urban areas. They are likely also to be foreign banks, providing mostly trade financing to foreign firms. For rural populations, informal moneylenders may exist who, due to the risk involved and the monopoly position enjoyed, charge high interest rates on loans. The problem is to build a financial intermediation infrastructure that can *both* collect surplus resources *and* make them available to others at relatively low cost.

As banking systems develop, however, they are vulnerable to failure. In the United States and Europe, regulations such as deposit insurance and capital reserve requirements have been created to maintain bank safety, helping bankers resist temptations to misuse depositors' money. This prudential regulation has taken time to develop and is still evolving in developing countries. Licenses to operate banks may be granted by multiple government authorities and those banks used to direct development funds or provide political patronage. There may not be enforceable guidelines to require the banks to keep sufficient capital as protection against failure of major borrowers. Nor are there always rules to prevent banks from concentrating their lending to particular individuals, firms, or sectors that may be prone to failure. Banks may be allowed to engage in risky activities, such as real estate speculation and ownership of firms. Developing-country banks often fail to recognize and provide reserves for problem assets, and bank examiners may not have authority to force banks to make provisions or write off bad loans. Some governments do not require external audits, and in others there may be no clear guidelines or standards. Banking rules and laws may be vague and difficult to enforce.[26]

Finance, Credit, and the Poor

A crucial issue in financial development is how to extend credit to the large portion of the population that is poor. Large urban banks prefer clients with large savings and borrowing needs. Government banks also have a preference for large projects. But the progress of the poor, like that of everyone else, depends on access to credit. Two issues stand out here: the traditional, or informal, credit mechanisms and small-scale credit from recognized financial institutions.

The Informal Financial Sector

Poor people have for centuries borrowed from local moneylenders, landlords, traders, and relatives. Folklore and observation provide horror stories of poor farmers everywhere paying interest rates of 100 percent or more to such informal lenders, losing all their assets when bad weather destroys a season's crops, and becoming permanently indebted over one loan gone bad. It is easy to believe that high interest rates are always evidence of exploitation and that there is an immediate need to extend full-scale banking operations to the poor.

Recent reappraisal of such informal credit mechanisms, however, finds that much of this activity is beneficial to the poor and the economy. A survey of informal financial markets in Bangladesh found that they complemented the more formal mechanisms because most of the informal credit was actually a leakage from the formal institutions: loans from banks being reloaned in smaller chunks to the poorer, less literate sections of the population that did not have access to banks. Higher interest rates in the informal sector actually reflected higher rates of return, so the entire process increased the efficiency of the system.[27] Another study shows how informal credit contributed to Taiwan's development by servicing small entrepreneurs that the banks found too costly to bother with.[28] The authors of these studies recognized the potential for abuse in informal credit systems but recommended that governments should try to remove the abuses while encouraging informal credit mechanisms. Ultimately, more formal financial institutions will spread their activities to the poor, but until then these other mechanisms should be encouraged to fulfill their role.

Financial Institutions for the Poor

The poor need not face a choice of moneylenders or traditional banks. The last two decades have seen the rise of **microfinance**—financial institutions designed to provide deposit and lending services to people with little collateral or earning potential. One of the more spectacular successes is the Grameen Bank in Bangladesh, featured in Case 4–2.

THE GRAMEEN BANK IN BANGLADESH

FAST FACTS

On the Map: South Asia

Population: 128 Million

Per Capita GNI and Rank: $370   (170)

Life Expectancy: Male—60   Female—61

Adult Literacy Rate: Male—52%
Female—29%

The Grameen Bank of Bangladesh is a model institutional mechanism for providing rural credit. The word "grameen" means "rural" in the Bengali language. Established in 1983 after some years of research, the bank lends money for very small noncrop agricultural projects: "everything from husking rice to making ice cream sticks, trading in brass, repairing radios, processing mustard oil, and cultivating jackfruit." Borrowers may own either no more than half an acre of cultivable land or assets equal to no more than one acre of land. The bank has over 1,000 branches serving 34,000 villages. Over the period 1985 to 1996, the bank's portfolio grew from $10 million to $271 million and its membership from less than 200,000 to over 2 million. It is owned largely (75 percent) by borrowers and the rest by the national government. About 95 percent of its members are women.

Bank loans require no collateral, carry a 16 percent interest charge, and have an excellent repayment record, with only about 2 percent of loans more than a year overdue. Because projects are not for planting crops, income is less affected by seasonal factors. Loans are made to members of small groups, which provides an incentive for good supervision of the use of funds and timely repayment. Group members must make minimum weekly savings deposits. Repayments are scheduled in small amounts to avoid large drains on borrowers. There is a strong, decentralized management, and bank workers are dedicated and well trained. The bank is also seen as a local institution, giving people a stake in its success.

Loans go primarily to those who cannot borrow elsewhere, with the gains thereby accruing to the poorest groups, although only a small portion of the poorest nationwide have so far been able to take advantage of this opportunity. While the interest rate is 16 percent, certain deposit requirements raise the effective rate to about 33 percent, which is still affordable for poor borrowers because projects generally use unemployed labor or workers with a low opportunity cost. Bank figures show that unemployment among borrowers has been reduced dramatically, and among borrowers there has been a substantial shift from labor for hire to self-employment.

Some have credited the bank's success to the stated policy of making all group members responsible for repayment of individuals within the group. A thorough survey, however, indicates that this policy is not enforced. It credits the bank's success to a culture of discipline and responsibility that is fostered within the groups and the training and oversight of bank employees.

The bank's proponents are cautious about whether the Grameen experience can be easily replicated elsewhere. The 16 percent interest rate does not cover costs; the bank receives a subsidy from the International Fund for Agricultural Development (IFAD) and earns income by putting its money in higher-interest deposits elsewhere. Personnel costs are high, but administrative costs are held down by the density of the population and are likely to be higher in more sparsely settled rural areas, such as in some parts of Africa. Nevertheless, advocates believe that the concept embodied in the bank carries important lessons that can be applied elsewhere.

Sources: Mahabub Hossain, "Credit for Alleviation of Rural Poverty: The Grameen Bank in Bangladesh" (Washington: Institute for Food Policy Research, Report 65, February 1988); *Grameen Dialogue*, the official newsletter of the Grameen Bank, no. 14 (April 1993); Pankaj S. Jain, "Managing Credit for the Rural Poor: Lessons from the Grameen Bank," *World Development* 24, no. 1 (January 1996), pp. 79–89; Jonathan Morduch, "The Microfinance Promise," *Journal of Economic Literature* 37, no. 4 (December 1999), pp. 1569–1614; and Muhammad Yunus, *Banker to the Poor: Micro Lending and the Battle Against World Poverty* (New York: Public Affairs, 1999). Current information is available at ⟨www.grameen-info.org⟩.

There have been numerous attempts to adapt the Grameen model to other countries.[29] Its success has been built on a highly personalized style of outreach to the poor, providing small loans to the rural, nonagricultural population, overwhelmingly women, in a context that emphasizes group solidarity among recipients and staff. Other bank-based successes include BancoSol in Bolivia and Bank Kredit Desa in Indonesia.[30]

Nonbank institutions are also widely used, however. These include Rotating Savings and Credit Associations (ROSCAs) in Bangladesh and accumulating savings clubs in Mexico. These institutions tend to organize relatively small groups of people to pool savings and lend them out to individual members in turn. Some actually require regular minimum deposits.[31]

There are of course problems with essentially local institutions. Larger organizations can spread risk, look further afield for lending opportunities, and lower costs. Small schemes that require minimum savings, while showing the willingness and ability of many poor people to save, still exclude the poorest segments of the population. One author objects that in many African countries, weaknesses in markets, governments, and property rights, and the lack of separation of business and family, severely limit the impact of microfinance. Borrowed money may be repaid, but there is little evidence that such small-scale credit pushes people up the income scale or increases the size of businesses.[32]

Still, growing evidence shows that the poor can be incorporated into a developing economy by financial institutions that are suited to their needs. Where the social and economic infrastructure are in place, small-scale credit can bridge some of the gaps between the poor and the more formal banking sector.

Why Governments Intervene

Governments often intervene in the financial sector for a number of reasons. Private banks are rare. Officials believe finance is ripe for extortion and private institutions will lend to the wealthy rather than the poor. At times governments may want to dispossess foreign banks. They may often direct credit to themselves or priority sectors of the economy. This intervention may take a number of different forms, including sectorally oriented lending requirements for banks (specific percentage of lending to go to agriculture or manufacturing, for example), easy refinancing of troubled projects, guarantees to cover default, preferential interest rates, and direct financing through special **Development Banks**. Through a variety of these methods, governments may ultimately direct as much as three-fourths of the credit in the economy: a figure approached by Turkey, Pakistan and Brazil at different times in the 1980s.[33]

Many of these interventions ultimately backfire. Banks often evade sectoral lending requirements by misclassifying their loans or by lending to a client who then re-lends to the ultimate borrower. Easy refinancing and credit guarantees provide an incentive to fund nonproductive or inefficient projects and to default. Development Banks—often funded through foreign aid in earlier years—have a generally poor record for picking profitable projects and have higher than average records for arrearages and default.[34] The results have often been bad projects, large debts, and delays in the development of well-functioning financial intermediaries. Although some Development Banks have had good records, the World Bank believes that "Rather than lay the foundations of a sound financial system, most governments concentrated on intervention designed to channel resources to activities that they felt were poorly covered by existing financial institutions" with poor results.[35] Ultimately, the market-oriented "sound financial system" must be established.

FINANCIAL DEEPENING AND ECONOMIC DEVELOPMENT[36]

Economic development normally is accompanied by an increase in the proportion of the economy's transactions that use financial instruments. This **financial deepening** means, at first, an increase in the proportion of transactions that are accomplished through money, rather than subsistence consumption and barter. For example, between 1955 and 1985, the ratio of money supply to GNP increased from 0.07 to 0.40 in South Korea and from 0.12 to 1.26 in Taiwan. With time and the development of financial intermediaries, a variety of financial assets emerges, from small savings accounts to bond and stock markets and sophisticated money markets. Although it is fair to wonder whether, at the extreme, much of this activity becomes a waste of resources, we may still be justified in looking to financial deepening as an indicator of development.[37]

Financial deepening ideally would be measured by the ratio of financial assets to total wealth. But as it is difficult to measure wealth, in practice it is common to use a ratio of financial assets or some other measure (the money supply, credit) to national income. Ronald McKinnon's early investigations showed that typical ratios of money supply to GNP are 0.1 to 0.3 for developing countries and 0.5 to 0.7 for wealthier countries.[38] More recent work, finding that simple money/GDP ratios may be higher in less financially developed economies, has looked at financial markets, the variability of interest rates, and other measures to further our understanding of this phenomenon.[39]

It appears that financial deepening is not only an *indicator* of development but also a contributing factor. A larger share of a society's surplus channeled into financial institutions means that the surplus is more likely to be used more productively. Higher productivity contributes to higher growth rates. Data show a significant positive correlation between rising indicators of financial deepening and (*a*) ratios of changes in GDP to Investment and (*b*) GDP growth rates over the period 1965 to 1985.[40] A recent survey of the literature concludes that the development of financial systems "is a good predictor of future rates of economic growth, capital accumulation, and technological change."[41]

FINANCIAL REPRESSION AND FINANCIAL SECTOR REFORM

Just as financial deepening is a sign of development, **financial repression**, or a declining ratio of financial assets to total output, is a sign that development is being stunted by government policies that hinder the workings of the financial system.[42] One of the latest indications is that during the economic woes in Asia in 1997 and 1998, many firms increased their use of barter to make exchanges when credit and financial systems failed.[43]

A key ingredient in both financial deepening and repression is the **real interest rate**. If r is the real rate, i is the nominal rate, and ρ is the rate of inflation, or more accurately the expected rate of inflation, then

$$\frac{1+i}{1+\rho} = 1 + r \qquad \text{and} \qquad r = \frac{i-\rho}{1+\rho}$$

For example, a nominal interest rate of 10 percent translates into a real interest rate of 10 percent only with zero inflation. An inflation rate of 10 percent makes the real interest rate zero, and an inflation rate of 20 percent yields a real interest rate of negative 8.3 percent. A fast approximation of the real interest rate is to simply subtract the inflation rate from the nominal interest rate.

The data show what common sense tells us: Market-determined real interest rates, while they do not necessarily increase the volume of saving above what is encouraged by artificially low rates, do increase the proportion of saving that makes its way into financial institutions.[44] Such an increase is one measure of financial deepening. Given this connection, we should now look at interest rates in some detail.

Interest Rate Policies[45]

Many developing-country governments deliberately hold interest rates below market levels. In macroeconomic terms, low interest rates stimulate investment, employment, and output. High interest rates are seen as increasing production costs and contributing to inflation. Government borrowing is obviously less expensive if interest rates are kept low, and where there is a significant government role in the economy, this justification is an important one. From a microeconomic perspective, low interest rates are said to crowd out informal moneylenders, thus expanding and easing small-scale borrowing.[46] They may compensate for other policies, such as import restrictions, that increase costs of production. If lowered selectively, they will promote particular sectors. Finally, low interest rates may be claimed to reduce the incomes of those who have money to lend.

But a fundamental question must be asked: Are interest rates in developing countries too high and should government keep them down? As with any price, interest rates are "too high" only if market distortions keep them above the competitive equilibrium, and the solution would be to reduce the distortions through greater competition among banks. If rates are so high as to stifle investment and growth, additions to the money supply are needed to reduce market rates. In many developing countries, however, even with appropriate monetary policies, the market rates themselves are considered excessive, and governments may impose interest rate ceilings.

The claim that interest rates are too high, and thus discouraging needed investment, comes from a macroanalysis typically applied to an industrialized country. In

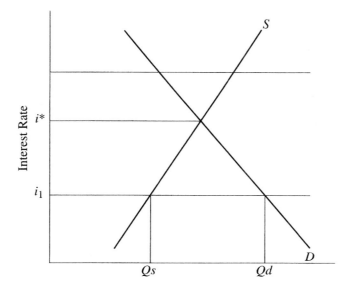

FIGURE 4–3 Disequilibrium Interest Rates

If a government imposes an interest rate such as i_1, which is below the equilibrium level ($i*$), the quantity of funds demanded (Qd) will exceed the quantity supplied (Qs). The excess demand cannot be satisfied, so the available funds must be rationed in some non-market fashion. Governments that hope to increase the amount of investment for development purposes will find they produce less and create the incentive for bankers to lend money to their friends.

Figure 4–3, a slow economy and (relative) deflation causes $i > i*$ where $i*$ is the equilibrium rate; excess savings show that i should be reduced to stimulate investment. Instead it is likely that, especially when inflation is factored in, real interest rates permitted in developing countries are too low, not too high. On the graph, $i_1 < i*$ due to government-imposed rate ceilings and inflation. There is an excess demand for funds, and i should rise. If it remains low, rationing will restrict investment to projects favored by either bankers or government officials, the excess demand for resources will contribute to inflation, and companies have less incentive to use these funds efficiently. According to one estimate, rationing may result in only about 5 percent of agricultural borrowers obtaining access to 80 percent of the available credit and 85 to 95 percent of farmers obtaining no credit at all.[47]

Developing-country governments have a variety of policies that result in (*a*) interest rates that are too low to either induce saving and allocate investment efficiently and (*b*) financial markets whose efficiency is lost to a maze of distortions. As with interest rates ceilings, high reserve requirements for banks distort financial markets because banks need to charge higher interest rates to compensate for inability to use those reserves. Thus, government's drive to keep rates low is even more difficult and distorting. There are also credit restrictions, necessitated by low interest rates, leading to administrative allocation that is frequently political in nature. High rates of inflation may make nominal interest rates meaningless as guides to saving and investment decisions.

Financial Repression

Financial repression is a situation in which economic policies or their outcomes discourage the use of money and financial instruments to facilitate economic transactions, resulting in a lower ratio of financial assets to GDP. Financial deepening and repression depend on the degree of regulation of the financial system, including whether real interest rates in the economy are realistic. Figure 4–4 shows nominal and real interest rates in Korea between 1963 and 1991. Deposit rates are official bank rates, and "curb"

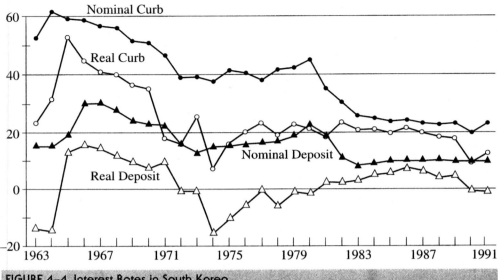

FIGURE 4-4 Interest Rates in South Korea

The difference between nominal and real interest rates in South Korea has declined over time, indicating lower inflation. Also, the difference between informal "curb" rates and bank-determined deposit rates has declined, indicating that the formal financial institutions are doing a better job of approximating rates determined by market forces.

Source: Amsden and Euh.

rates are those in informal lending markets. The gap between nominal and real rates is the inflation rate. Note that the nominal and real rates have similar patterns in both markets, and in both it is evident that inflation rates fell in the 1980s.

What are "appropriate" interest rate levels? Clearly we would expect markets to set those rates, if markets were reasonably competitive and unregulated. Where those conditions are not met, we would expect government to provide some guidance even as it does in industrialized economies. A recent survey by M. J. Fry found another inverted U, this time relating real interest rates to the growth of real GDP. Studying 85 countries over the 1971 to 1995 period, he found real interest rates just above zero to be associated with the highest growth rates; a range of from –5 percent to +15 percent was compatible with reasonable GDP growth. Lower real rates indicate financial repression, hindering growth, and higher rates indicate considerable uncertainty and risk, also hindering growth. In a smaller survey, he also found real interest rates of about zero compatible with highest ratios of saving to GNP.[48]

Policy Implications and Policy Reform

Financial repression occurs when high inflation makes financial instruments unreliable. One cause of inflation is excessive demand for credit caused by low official nominal interest rates. As inflation worsens, maintaining low nominal rates causes real interest rates to turn negative (early 1960s and mid-1970s in Figure 4–4), even while nominal interest rates in uncontrolled, or informal, markets may soar as lenders try to protect themselves from inflation. But financial repression also occurs when excessive regulation of formal financial markets drives people into alternative means of carrying on economic activity. Figure 4–5 illustrates the relationship between high inflation and financial repression with data from Argentina. Although the emergence of new financial instruments with development is expected to somewhat reduce the ratio of money supply to GDP, we see fairly dramatic reductions of M2/GDP in the middle and late 1980s that clearly coincide with inflation.

Interest rates are not the only culprits. In fact, studies of India suggest that banks can often get around fixed interest rates. Rate ceilings and floors, high reserve requirements and liquidity requirements for banks, and government direction of credit to favored industries and firms may be more serious problems.[49]

Under the circumstances, most economists recommend that governments do the following:

- Permit the market to determine interest rates
- Minimize the use of directed credit allocation
- Reduce reserve requirements to permit lower market interest rates
- Reduce taxes on financial transactions

In other words, financial institutions and financial markets should be liberalized, that is, subject to minimal interference. With suitable prudential oversight of financial

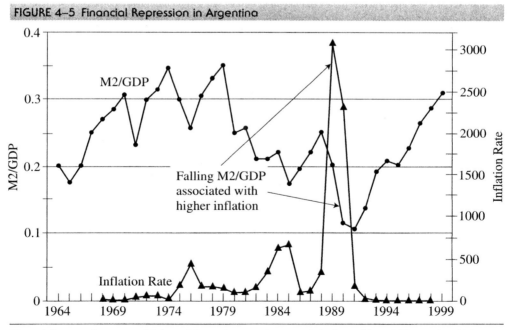

FIGURE 4–5 Financial Repression in Argentina

Financial repression, or a withdrawal from the use of money, is indicated by a falling ratio of Money Supply (M2) to GDP. This happens when inflation increases dramatically as in Argentina in 1976, 1984, and 1990.

Source: IMF/IFS.

institutions, a market-oriented financial system should funnel surplus resources into productive investment and enhance growth, if not development. Some countries, particularly those in East Asia, have had some success with mild financial repression, but a fair amount of discipline is required to keep it mild.

Such reform is not always easy, however. If an economy does not have a well-developed financial structure, if governments have large deficits and financial requirements, or if there is not a strong, well-functioning framework for normal prudential regulation of bank behavior, liberalizing the financial sector can produce chaos.

Debate over how fast to reform, and in what order, has been inconclusive. Gradual reform would lead to less instability, but if financial systems are interfering with growth, speed may be important. In general, a legal and regulatory system should be in place first. The financial system will work better also if governments have moderate borrowing needs and rely on markets, rather than pressure on banks, to obtain their funds. Again, however, the need for bank reform may be urgent and not able to wait for the "right" conditions.[50]

During the last three decades, numerous governments have attempted, some slowly, some rapidly, to deregulate their financial sectors. While part of the story must wait until we discuss foreign financial flows in Chapter 15, the lessons have been similar throughout the world. Interest rates have been increased too much, inducing excessively risky investments while not attracting sufficient savings. This prompted the government of Chile, for example, to renationalize the banks for awhile in 1982. Inadequate monitoring of bank behavior allowed Indonesian banks to lend to inefficient and corrupt firms in the 1990s. Continuation of government allocation of credit in Korea kept inefficient firms operating far too long. Lack of a strong legal framework, government intervention, and high government deficits have led to virtual financial collapse in some African countries. Interestingly, general economic liberalization in some African countries has worked to the benefit of informal and small-scale lending institutions while the formal banking sector has been unable to respond.[51]

SUMMARY AND CONCLUSION

Capital is crucial for growth, but the nature of its importance must be understood: Much investment can *accompany* growth, but when it comes to *causing* growth the most important role of capital is to introduce improved technology. Further, it is important to recognize that an economy's ability to use capital effectively depends on a number of other variables such as the skill of the labor force, the available infrastructure, and the mechanisms in the economy for allocating resources to their most efficient use. Those mechanisms must add development-oriented considerations to private profit criteria and call for careful judgment.

Capital goods must be purchased, so there must also be mechanisms for the economy to save resources and channel those savings toward those who can use them for investment. The most effective way of accomplishing this task is through financial intermediaries, starting with banks. A modern financial system operates by using interest rates to attract savings and allocate them among competing demands. It is therefore crucial that financial intermediaries develop and apply interest rates that reflect the true opportunity cost of capital.

Financial deepening is the increasing proportion of money and financial instruments in a country's overall economic activity. It helps promote, and is in turn promoted by, growth and development. Positive, though not high, real interest rates are necessary to funnel savings into financial institutions and to permit rational allocation of those savings. Governments can help financial institutions flourish and need to leave them relatively free to perform their functions. When inflation, negative real interest rates, and restraint of financial activity move an economy back toward barter and avoidance of financial instruments, financial repression takes place and is usually accompanied by a decline in real economic activity. Governments need to foster an efficient financial sector but must support corrective policies with a stable economy and a strong legal framework for preventing excesses of banking activity.

Key Terms

- absorptive capacity (p. 72)
- border price (p. 77)
- bottleneck (p. 74)
- capital (p. 71)
- capital flight (p. 82)
- cost-benefit analysis (p. 74)
- dependency ratio (p. 80)

- Development Bank (p. 86)
- discount rate (p. 74)
- financial deepening (p. 87)
- financial repression (p. 88)
- inflation (p. 82)
- microfinance (p. 84)
- net present value (NPV) (p. 74)

- pension fund (p. 81)
- real interest rate (p. 88)
- shadow price (p. 76)
- shadow wage (p. 76)
- social productivity (p. 74)
- Total Factor Productivity (p. 72)

Questions for Review

1. Explain the role, and limitations, of capital accumulation (investment) in the process of economic growth. Be sure to consider absorptive capacity and noneconomic factors.
2. Give some examples of factors to be considered if criteria for investment are to go beyond private profit.
3. Suppose a government is considering two projects: a steel mill and a flour mill. Given a discount rate of 10 percent and the cost and benefit schedules below, calculate the net present values to determine which project should be chosen.

| | Steel Mill | | Flour Mill | |
Project	Benefits	Costs	Benefits	Costs
Year 1	$ 0	$1,000	$500	$500
Year 2	1,000	500	500	100
Year 3	2,000	750	500	200

4. What are shadow prices? What difficulty are they designed to overcome, and how might one determine them?
5. If you hire an unemployed person in your factory, what would an economist say is the shadow wage, and why?
 6. How does the example of textile production in India show how project evaluation can be altered by using shadow wages instead of the market wage?
7. Explain the advantages of a well-functioning financial system.

8. For the following sets of data, calculate the real interest rate:

Nominal Interest Rate (%)	Inflation Rate (%)
10	3
10	10
10	18
100	50
100	200
100	2,000

9. Explain financial deepening and repression and the role of interest rates in these phenomena. What data would we consider to detect financial deepening and repression?
10. Why do governments often try to put ceilings on interest rates, and what impact is such a policy likely to have on the mobilization of savings and on investment?
11. Do "informal" financial institutions harm the economy? Explain.
 12. Search the Grameen Bank Web site (see below) for a typical small loan and discuss how such projects may play an important role in the development efforts of an economy like Bangladesh.

Related Internet Resources

 One of the fundamental discoveries of recent years is the possibility of success of small-scale savings and credit groups. The Grameen Bank has a Web site that looks at its founding and operations: ⟨http://www.grameen-info.org⟩.

Endnotes and Further Readings

1. Nicholas Stern, "The Economics of Development: A Survey," *The Economic Journal* 99, no. 397 (September 1989), p. 612.
2. The 1955 article, "The Place of Capital in Economic Progress," appeared in *Economic Progress*, L. H. Dupriez, ed. (Louvain, Belgium: International Economic Association, 1955), pp. 235–248. See also Alexander Cairncross, *Factors in Economic Development* (London: George Allen & Unwin, 1962).
3. Hollis B. Chenery, "Interaction Between Theory and Observation in Development," *World Development* 11, no. 10 (October 1983), pp. 853–861. A dissenting view is that of Maurice F. G. Scott, who claims that changes in relative prices have caused mismeasurements of capital, which have seriously underestimated its impact on growth. His ideas are presented in *A New View of Economic Growth* (Oxford: Clarendon Press, 1989) and summarized in "A New View of Economic Growth: Four Lectures," World Bank Discussion Paper #131 (Washington: World Bank, 1991). For the unreliability of most attempts to discern the causes of growth, see Ross Levine and David Renelt, "A Sensitivity Analysis of Cross-Country Growth Regressions," *American Economic Review* 82, no. 4 (September 1992), pp. 942–963.

They determine, however, that the most reliable correlate of growth is the share of investment in GDP.
4. Magnus Blomstrom, Robert E. Lipsey, and Mario Zejan, "Is Fixed Investment the Key to Economic Growth?" *Quarterly Journal of Economics* 111, no. 1 (February 1996), pp. 269–296.
5. For a summary of this concept, see Richard S. Eckaus, "Absorptive Capacity," in The New Palgrave, *Economic Development*, edited by John Eatwell, Murray Milgate, and Peter Newman (New York: W. W. Norton, 1989), pp. 18–20.
6. See Moshe Syrquin, "Patterns of Structural Change," in T. N. Srinivasan and H. B. Chenery, eds., *Handbook of Development Economics* 1 (Amsterdam: Elsevier Science Publishers, 1988), pp. 205–273. The quote is on p. 257.
7. Klaus Schmidt-Hebbel, Luis Serven, and Andres Solimano, "Savings and Investment: Paradigms, Puzzles, Policies," *World Bank Research Observer* 11, no. 1 (February 1996), pp. 94–96.
8. A discussion of this criterion can be found in "Criteria for Allocating Investment Resources Among Various Fields of Development in Underdeveloped Countries," United Nations *Economic Bulletin for Asia and the Far East* (June 1961). The article relies on the initial presen-

tations of the concept in A. E. Kahn, "Investment Criteria in Development Programmes," *Quarterly Journal of Economics* 65, no. 1 (February 1951), pp. 38–61, and H. B. Chenery, "The Application of Investment Criteria," *Quarterly Journal of Economics* 69, no. 1 (February 1955), pp. 76–96.

9. A number of different approaches are discussed in T. N. Srinivasan, "Investment Criteria and Choice of Techniques of Production" *Yale Economic Essays* 2, no. 1 (1962), pp. 59–63.

10. Two recent summaries of the field are Ivy Papps, "Techniques of Project Appraisal," in Norman Gemmel, ed., *Surveys in Development Economics* (Oxford: Basil Blackwell, 1987), pp. 307–340, and Lyn Squire, "Project Evaluation in Theory and Practice," in H. B. Chenery and T. N. Srinivasan, *Handbook of Development Economics* 2 (Amsterdam: Elsevier Science Publishers, 1989), pp. 1093–1137. Squire's summary is fairly technical, while Papps's is more accessible.

11. On the latter two points, see Shatayanan Devarajan, Lyn Squire, and Sethaput Suthiwart-Narueput, "Beyond Rate of Return: Reorienting Project Appraisal," *World Bank Research Observer* 12, no. 1 (February 1997), pp. 35–46.

12. Lance Taylor, *Macro Models for Developing Countries* (New York: McGraw-Hill, 1979), p. 196.

13. This is the approach used by I. M. D. Little and J. A. Mirrlees, *Manual of Industrial Project Analysis* (Paris: OECD, 1968), and I. M. D. Little, *Project Appraisal and Planning for Developing Countries* (London: Heinemann, 1974). An alternative, favored by the United Nations, is to make maximum use of consumer prices; see United Nations, *Economic Bulletin for Asia and the Far East* (June 1961). For a mathematical analysis of shadow prices, see Lynn Squire, "Project Evaluation in Theory and Practice," pp. 1102–1116. A recent suggestion to ease the burden is John MacArthur, "Shadow Pricing Simplified: Estimating Acceptably Accurate Economic Rates of Return Using Limited Data," *Journal of International Development* 9, no. 3 (May–June 1997), pp. 367–382.

14. Gerald Pohl and Dubravko Mihaljek, "Project Evaluation and Uncertainty in Practice: A Statistical Analysis of Rate-of-Return Divergences of 1,015 World Bank Projects," *World Bank Economic Review* 6, no. 2 (May 1992), pp. 255–277.

15. The first study is reported in *Financial Systems and Development*, Policy and Research Series No. 15 (Washington: World Bank, 1990), p. 9; a reprint of chapters 2 to 9 of World Bank, *World Development Report 1989*. The second study is in the World Bank's Policy and Research Bulletin, vol. 10, no. 1 (January–March 1999).

16. Paul R. Masson, Tamim Bayoumi, and Hossein Samier, "International Evidence on the Determinants of Private Saving," *World Bank Economic Review* 12, no. 3 (September 1998), pp. 483–501.

17. See Angus Deaton, "Saving in Developing Countries: Theory and Review," *The Proceedings of the Annual World Bank Conference on Development Economics 1989* (Washington: World Bank, 1990), pp. 61–96.

18. World Bank, *Financial Systems and Development*, p. 11. Some important references for the saving issue are Dale Adams, "Mobilizing Household Savings Through Rural Financial Markets," *Economic Development and Cultural Change* 26, no. 3 (1978), pp. 547–560; John D. Von Pischke, *Finance at the Frontier: Debt Capacity and the Role of Credit in the Private Economy* (Washington: World Bank, 1991); and Marguerite S. Robinson, "The Role of Saving in Local Financial Markets: The Indonesian Experience," an unpublished paper by Growth and Equity through Microenterprise Investments and Institutions, Washington, November, 1992.

19. Pamela Druckerman, "Latin American Firms Tap Region's Growing Sources of Funding," *Wall Street Journal*, September 29, 1997.

20. Carmelo Mesa-Lago, "Social Security in Latin America," *Economic and Social Progress in Latin America: 1991 Report* (Washington: InterAmerican Development Bank, 1991), pp. 179–216.

21. The literature on LDC social security systems has recently begun to proliferate. For a view of the relevance of industrialized country systems to the developing countries, see Ehtisham Ahmad, "Social Security and the Poor: Choices for Developing Countries," *World Bank Research Observer* 6, no. 1 (January 1991), pp. 105–127. African systems are reviewed in Jean-Victor Gruat, "Social Security Schemes in Africa: Current Trends and Problems," *International Labour Review* 129, no. 4 (1990), pp. 405–422. Reform in Latin American schemes is summarized in G. A. Mackenzie, "Reforming Latin America's Old-Age Pension Systems," *Finance and Development* 32, no. 5 (March 1995), pp. 10–13. For a major investigation of the issue, see World Bank, *Averting the Old Age Crisis: Policies to Protect the Old and Promote Growth* (New York: Oxford University Press, 1994). The World Bank sees Chile's system as a model, but more cautious reviews of that system are given in Colin Gillion and Alejandro Bonilla, "Analysis of National Private Pension Schemes: The Case of Chile," *International Labour Review* 131, no. 2 (1992), pp. 171–196, and Joseph Collins and John Lear, *Chile's Free-Market Miracle: A Second Look* (Oakland: Institute for Food and Development, 1995), pp. 167–180.

22. Lynn Squire, "Project Evaluation in Theory and Practice," pp. 117–118.

23. Two recent discussions of pension funds are G. A. Mackenzie, Philip Gerson, and Alfredo Cuevas, *Pension Regimes and Saving*, IMF Occasional Paper 153 (Washington: International Monetary Fund, August 1997), and Alberto Arenas de Mesa and Fabio Bertranou, "Learning from Social Security Reforms: The Different Cases; Chile and Argentina," *World Development* 25, no. 3 (March 1997), pp. 329–348.

24. The approach to financial intermediation provided here was outlined in a series of lectures given by Professor

Claudio Gonzalez-Vega attended by the author in 1986. See also World Bank, *Financial Systems and Development*, and Dimitri Germidis, Denis Kessler, and Rachel Meghir, *Financial Systems and Development: What Role for the Formal and Informal Financial Sections?* (Paris: OECD, 1991).

25. The significant early applications of monetary and financial considerations to developing countries are John G. Gurley and Edward S. Shaw, "Financial Development and Economic Development," *Economic Development and Cultural Change* 15, no. 3 (April 1967), pp. 257–268; U Tun Wai, "Interest Rates in the Organized Money Markets of Underdeveloped Countries," *IMF Staff Papers* 5, no. 2 (August 1956), pp. 249–278; U Tun Wai, "Interest Rates Outside the Organized Money Markets of Underdeveloped Countries," *International Monetary Fund Staff Papers* 6, no. 1 (November 1957), pp. 174–189; Hugh T. Patrick, "Financial Development and Economic Growth in Underdeveloped Countries," *Economic Development and Cultural Change* 14, no. 2 (January 1966), pp. 174–189; and Ronald I. McKinnon, *Money and Capital in Economic Development* (Washington: The Brookings Institution, 1973).

26. Vincent P. Polizatto, "Prudential Regulation and Banking Supervision: Building an Institutional Framework for Banks," World Bank Policy Research Paper 340 (Washington: World Bank, 1990), or search at ⟨www1.worldbank.org/finance/⟩.

27. Atiq Rahman, "The Informal Financial Sector in Bangladesh: An Appraisal of Its Role in Development," *Development and Change* 23, no. 1 (January 1992), pp. 147–168.

28. Shui-Yan Tang, "Informal Credit Markets and Economic Development in Taiwan," *World Development* 23, no. 5 (May 1995), pp. 845–855.

29. These have not always been as successful as the original. An overview of the problem is Atiur Rahman, "The General Replicability of the Grameen Bank Model," in Abu N. M. Wahid, ed., *The Grameen Bank: Poverty Relief in Bangladesh* (Boulder, CO: Westview Press, 1993), pp. 209–222. For case studies, see David Hulme, "The Malawi Fund: Daughter of Grameen," *Journal of International Development* 3, no. 4 (July 1991), pp. 29–37; Rebecca Fleischer, "Replicating Grameen in Papua New Guinea," *Pacific Economic Bulletin* 11, no. 2 (November 1996), pp. 23–38; and Helen Todd, ed., *Cloning Grameen Bank* (London: Intermediate Technology Publications, 1996).

30. Jonathan Morduch, "The Microfinance Promise," *Journal of Economic Literature* 37, no. 4 (December 1999), pp. 1569–1614.

31. Susan Johnson and Ben Rogaly, *Microfinance and Poverty Reduction* (Oxford: Oxfam, 1997). An economic analysis of ROSCAs is Timothy Besley, Stephen Coate, and Glenn Loury, "The Economics of Rotating Savings and Credit Associations," *American Economic Review* 83, no. 4 (September 1993), pp. 792–810.

32. Graeme Buckley, "Microfinance in Africa: Is It Either the Problem or the Solution?" *World Development* 27, no. 7 (July 1997), pp. 1081–1093.

33. For a discussion of these methods and their problems, see World Bank, *Financial Systems and Development*, pp. 37–43.

34. *Ibid.*, p. 43.

35. *Ibid.*, p. 37.

36. The associated concepts of financial deepening and financial repression are explored in Edward S. Shaw, *Financial Deepening in Economic Development* (New York: Oxford University Press, 1973) and Ronald I. McKinnon, *Money and Capital in Economic Development*.

37. For an example of how the process takes place, see Uwe Corsepius and Bernhard Fischer, "Domestic Resource Mobilization in Thailand: A Successful Case for Financial Deepening?" *Singapore Economic Review* 33, no. 2 (October 1988), pp. 1–20.

38. Ronald I. McKinnon, *Money and Capital in Economic Development*, pp. 92–95. These results are confirmed by the World Bank, *Financial Systems and Development*, p. 13.

39. David Lynch, "Measuring Financial Sector Development: A Study of Selected Asia-Pacific Countries," *The Developing Economies* 34, no. 1 (March 1996), pp. 3–33.

40. Ronald I. McKinnon, *The Order of Economic Liberalization* (Baltimore: Johns Hopkins University Press, 1993), pp. 15–17, and Panicos A. Demetriades and Khaled A. Hussein, "Does Financial Development Cause Economic Growth? Time-Series Evidence from 16 Countries," *Journal of Development Economics* 51, no. 2 (December 1996), pp. 387–411.

41. Ross Levine, "Financial Development and Economic Growth: Views and Agenda," *Journal of Economic Literature* 35, no. 2 (June 1997), p. 689. Also see P. Arestis and P. Demetriades, "Financial Development and Economic Growth: Assessing the Evidence," *Economic Journal* 107, no. 442 (May 1997), pp. 783–799.

42. Nouriel Roubini and Xavier Sala-i-Martin, "Financial Repression and Economic Growth," *Journal of Development Economics* 39, no. 1 (July 1992), pp. 5–30.

43. Darren McDermott and S. Karene Witcher, "Bartering Gains Currency in Hard-Hit Southeast Asia," *Wall Street Journal*, April 6, 1998.

44. For evidence that overall savings do not respond to interest rates, see Alberto Giovanni, "Saving and the Real Interest Rate in LDCs," *Journal of Economic Development* 18, nos. 2/3 (August 1985), pp. 367–382, and Klauss Schmidt-Hebbel, Steven B. Webb, and Giancarlo Corsetti, "Household Saving in Developing Countries: First Cross-Country Evidence," *World Bank Economic Review* 6, no. 3 (September 1992), pp. 529–547. For evidence that positive interest rates can bring resources from other assets into money saving, see Sylvanus I. Ikhide, "Positive Interest Rates: Financial

Deepening and the Mobilization of Savings in Africa," *Development Policy Review* 11, no. 4 (December 1993), pp. 367–382. One study concludes that interest rates become more effective in producing savings as income levels grow. See Masao Ogaki, Jonathan D. Ostry, and Carmen M. Reinhart, "Saving Behavior in Low- and Middle-Income Countries: A Comparison," *IMF Staff Papers* 43, no. 1 (March 1996), pp. 38–71.

45. The discussion of interest rates draws heavily on Claudio Gonzales-Vega, "Arguments for Interest Rate Reform," *Savings and Development* 6, no. 3 (1982), pp. 221–230. See also Anthony Lanyi and Rusdu Saracoglu, "The Importance of Interest Rates in Developing Countries," *Finance and Development* 20, no. 2 (June 1983), pp. 20–23.

46. For a full discussion of the relationship between the formal and informal financial sectors, see Germidis, Kessler, and Meghir, *Financial Systems and Development: What Role for the Formal and Informal Financial Sectors.*

47. Claudio Gonzales-Vega, "Arguments for Interest Rate Reform," p. 229.

48. "In Favour of Financial Liberalisation," *Economic Journal* 107, no. 442 (May 1997), pp. 754–770.

49. See two articles by Panicos O. Demetriades and Kal B. Luintel, "Financial Development, Economic Growth, and Banking Sector Controls: Evidence from India," *Economic Journal* 106, no. 435 (March 1996), pp. 359–374, and "The Direct Costs of Financial Repression: Evidence from India," *Review of Economic and Statistics* 79, no. 2 (May 1997), pp. 311–319.

50. See Alison Harwood and Bruce L. R. Smith, eds., *Sequencing? Financial Strategies for Developing Countries* (Washington: Brookings, 1997), especially R. Barry Johnston, "The Speed of Financial Sector Reform: Risks and Strategies," pp. 32–46, and David C. Cole, "Sequencing versus Practical Problem Solving in Financial Sector Reforms," pp. 47–59.

51. Study of financial sector reform has become quite popular. For Latin America in general, see Paul Holden and Sarath Rajapatirana, *Unshackling the Private Sector: A Latin American Story* (Washington: World Bank, 1995), chapter 6. For Chile in particular, see Carlos Diaz-Alejandro, "Good-Bye Financial Repression, Hello Financial Crash," *Journal of Development Economics* 19, no. 1–2 (September–October 1985), pp. 1–24. For Korea, Indonesia, and other East Asian countries, see United Nations, *Financial Sector Reforms in Selected Asian Countries* (New York: United Nations Economic and Social Commission for Asia and the Pacific, 1997); Joseph Stiglitz and Marilou Uy, "Financial Markets, Public Policy, and the East Asian Miracle," *World Bank Research Observer* 11, no. 2 (August 1996), pp. 249–276; Dimitri Vittas and Yoon Je Cho, "Credit Policies: Lessons from Japan and Korea," *World Bank Research Observer* 11, no. 2 (August 1996), pp. 277–298; and David C. Cole, "Sequencing Versus Practical Problem Solving in Financial Sector Reform." For Africa, see Diery Seck and Yasim H. El Nil, "Financial Liberalization in Africa," *World Development* 21, no. 11 (November 1993), pp. 1867–1881; Peter Lewis and Howard Stein, "Shifting Fortunes: The Policital Economy of Financial Liberalization in Nigeria," *World Development* 25, no. 1 (January 1997), pp. 5–22; and William F. Steel, Ernest Aryeetey, Hemamala Hettige, and Machiko Nissanke, "Informal Financial Markets Under Liberalization in Four African Countries," *World Development* 25, no. 5 (May 1997), pp. 817–830.

5

NATURAL BUILDING BLOCKS OF DEVELOPMENT: RESOURCES AND THE ENVIRONMENT

*That which is every bodies business
is no bodies business.*
—IZAAK WALTON (1593–1683)

INTRODUCTION

Are we in danger of running out of crucial natural resources? Are the rich countries taking up too much of the planet's resources and depriving the developing countries of the means to grow? Does protecting the environment cost too much and, therefore, is it a luxury that only rich countries can afford? Is there a conflict between economic development and the environment? Can we achieve a development path that is sustainable over the long term?

These are the kinds of questions that we hear frequently, although we often hear more answers than carefully formulated questions. Some environmentalists question the ability of economics to take the environment into account because it has often fallen outside traditional economic analysis or because costs and benefits are difficult to quantify. Some economists question the ability of environmentalists to form rational questions when they fail to realize that protecting the environment carries its own costs, as well as benefits.

Economic activity produces goods and services for consumption. But if land is used too intensively for too long its ability to produce food may decline. When chemicals and biological waste build up, water may be unfit to drink without costly treatment. When factories and homes burn fuel, pollution of the air may make breathing difficult for the young, the old, and the sick. In this chapter we incorporate environmental concerns into the analysis of economic development. We conclude that while development-oriented activities must take better account of their environmental impact, we have the tools to do so and can point development in a direction that improves life on earth and is sustainable.

THE ENVIRONMENT AND ECONOMIC ANALYSIS

Economists in the late eighteenth century viewed natural resources—land, water, and air—as free goods. However, in the first third of the nineteenth century, when food prices rose noticeably in Europe, political economists began to study the returns to land as a fixed factor of production. David Ricardo's theory of distribution focused on diminishing returns to land, but little attention was paid to substitutability of resources. In the twenty-first century, economists are divided. Some focus on the ability of technological change and market signals to guide us toward alternative resources. If this were true, the Earth would be an inexhaustible source of raw materials and the environmental consequences of resource use and depletion could be overcome. Many others, however, argue that these consequences are uncertain. Therefore, we need to supplement the market with public policy initiatives rather than wait until problems worsen. The economics of resources and the environment has now blossomed into a huge area of study.

But study of the environment poses some problems for economic thinking. Traditional microeconomic analysis tends to treat small changes and think of price increases as signaling the need for substitution of more plentiful for more scarce resources. But by the time this occurs in the case of an environmentally necessary resource, it is conceivable that it has passed the point where it can be recovered. Applied to any major ecosystem, this could threaten human survival: Many effects are irreversible and not capable of being detected until too late.[1] Species of plants and animals can become extinct, and water and land can become unusable for long periods. Economic analysis must be on the lookout for such problems.

Environmental Accounting

The environmental impact of economic growth may be considered through **environmental accounting**. This technique broadens conventional GDP accounting by treating natural resources and the environment itself (air, water, soil) as valuable **natural capital** that, like machinery, depreciates with use. Like human-produced capital, natural capital performs environmental "services": one recent estimate prices the water purification services of an acre of tidal marsh at $2,800 per year; $462 billion for the Earth's coastal wetlands. A more ambitious project estimated the value of the entire ecosystem's "services" at $33 trillion per year, almost twice the global GDP. Half of this was due to the recycling of nutrients in the soil.[2] The cost of replenishing or repairing this capital must be considered part of the cost of producing goods and services, just as we subtract capital depreciation from measures of gross investment to measure the net increase in our capital stock. When air quality is reduced, when nonrenewable resources such as oil are consumed, when soil is degraded, and when forests or fisheries are depleted, environmental accounting would inform us that our net national output has been diminished by such losses. Development Spotlight 5–1 outlines some of the modifications to traditional national income accounting considered in environmental accounting.

The result is a greater appreciation not only for a country's natural assets but also for the costs of alternative development projects or strategies. Attempts to account for some of these costs have been made in Norway, which is heavily dependent on petroleum, timber, and fish, and in developing countries such as Indonesia, Costa Rica, and China.[3]

DEVELOPMENT SPOTLIGHT 5–1

ENVIRONMENTAL ACCOUNTING AND THE NATIONAL ACCOUNTS

The traditional national income accounting framework can be modified using the Environmentally Adjusted Net Domestic Product (EDP) and Environmentally Adjusted Net Income (ENI). These terms are derived as follows:

Gross Domestic Product (GDP)

Less:	charges for depletion of mineral resources
Less:	costs of environmental degradation of land, water, and air due to productive activities
Equals:	Environmentally Adjusted Net Domestic Product (EDP)
Less:	environmental protection expenditures
Less:	environmental effects on health
Less:	environmental cost of government and household activities
Less:	environmental damage from discarded capital goods
Less:	negative environmental effects from overseas
Plus:	negative environmental effects sent abroad
Equals:	Environmentally Adjusted Net Income (ENI)

This type of calculation would be extremely difficult. To simplify the calculation, let us consider a country-specific example using Indonesia. Deducting losses in petroleum, forests, and soil brought 1984 GDP down from almost 16 trillion rupiah to only 13.3 trillion and reduced annual GDP growth over the 1971 to 1984 period from 7 to 4 percent.

Sources: The accounting framework is from Ernst Lutz and Mohan Munasinghe, "Accounting for the Environment," *Finance and Development* 28, no. 1 (March 1997), pp. 19–21. The Indonesia estimates are from Robert Repetto et al., *Wasting Assets: Natural Resources in the National Accounts* (Washington: World Resource Institute, 1989), reproduced in Mariano Torras, "Inequality, Resource Depletion, and Welfare Accounting: Applications to Indonesia and Costa Rica," *World Development* 27, no. 7 (July 1999), pp. 1191–1202.

SUSTAINABLE DEVELOPMENT

The concept of **sustainable development** focuses attention on the environment by evaluating the consistency of development with environmental preservation and enhancement.[4] In the most general sense, sustainable development means achieving improvements in living standards without sacrificing the ability of future generations to enjoy at least those same standards. This means that current development efforts should not reduce the Earth's natural capital. In practice, this means that our natural resource base should not be depleted, and our capacity to absorb waste should not be reduced. The use of some resources must be compensated for by improvement or creation of others.

Figure 5–1 illustrates the growth resulting from two development paths. Path A achieves rapid growth when logging companies clear tropical forests or mining companies rapidly exploit nonrenewable resources. These provide export revenue and, in the case of deforestation, permit rapid expansion of land areas for cultivation. But when the resources are gone, or when the land proves unsuitable for long-term agriculture, growth slows and may halt completely.

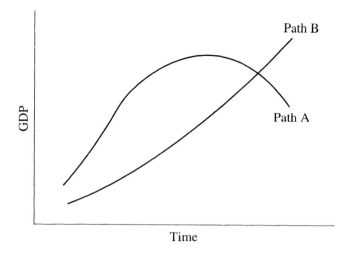

FIGURE 5–1 Sustainable and Nonsustainable Growth Paths

Path A permits faster initial growth but depletes resources too rapidly to be sustainable. Path B starts more slowly but can be sustained by conserving resources and investing in renewable resources and replacement of resources used.

Path B involves more careful use of forests to allow replacement while integrating agricultural use or slower exploitation of mineral resources and rehabilitating mined regions for later use. Growth could be slower initially, because resources are preserved, export opportunities are forgone, and costly investments are made to assure future alternatives. But the preservation, sacrifice, and investments may permit output to rise consistently over a longer period.

While there is no unique way to achieve this goal, the development process must be conceived holistically: We do not expect each investment or project to be environmentally neutral, but projects can be linked as programs that, taken together, would be. Environmental damage done by one project may be compensated for by another, as when a logging operation is combined with a reforestation project.

Is There a Trade-Off Between the Environment and the Economy?

Resistance to environmental protection arises from the view that production must be sacrificed for a somewhat vague notion of environmental improvement. In fact, some economic activities must be reduced or even eliminated to sustain the environment, while new ones may be required to reduce environmental damage or to return damaged resources to an earlier condition. For example, some polluting industries may be shut down or reduce output, and others will have to buy new equipment to reduce pollution. New jobs will be created in the production of pollution-control equipment and services, renewable energy, recycling services, and reclamation and conservation of resources.

Over the last few years, some economists have suggested that there is a common pattern to the environmental impact of economic growth. Early growth typically causes environmental deterioration, but environmental quality is what economists call a normal good: At higher levels of per capita income, people want, and an economy can afford to invest in, additional environmental improvement. This creates a Kuznets-like inverted U, also know as an **environmental Kuznets curve**, shown in

Figure 5–2: Environmental damage increases up to some income level, then decreases. It suggests that even if the market does not put a price on environmental services, it is not economically rational to use environmental capital past the point where its marginal productivity is zero. Empirical support was found in one study showing the inverted U-shaped pattern for parks and forests and another that found reverses in levels of fine smoke, suspended particles in the air, and sulphur dioxide (SO_2) in countries that had exceeded a per capita income of about $8,000.[5]

These studies have been challenged. One review suggests that the existence of some environmental improvement does not prove there is any natural or economic mechanism involved. Another suggests that the inverted U-shaped results obtained by comparing countries at different income levels cannot be interpreted as the natural path of any particular country. While the industrialized countries have improved their environmental performance, the reason is more complex than just economic change: It is more likely to involve political pressure from an environmentally aware population, which may not arise naturally as GDP increases.[6] However, the study of smoke, particles, and SO_2 had concluded the same thing: Politics combines with economics to reduce environmental damage. A recent study that focused on water, rather than air pollution, found somewhat different results. At higher income levels, the manufacturing share of GDP falls. The pollution intensity of manufacturing also falls as cleaner industries become more prominent, but this improvement does not continue much beyond middle-income levels. Finally, the pollution intensity of particular manufacturing processes does not keep falling at high income levels. The combined result is that while water pollution rises from lower- to middle-income levels (until about $9,000 per capita), it then levels off and does not fall with higher incomes.[7]

For any particular country, the challenge is to develop policies to achieve sustainable development. Not only will they have to make changes for the sake of their own environments but also to satisfy the requirements of the developed countries to whom they export their goods. On the other hand, short-term problems, such as heavy debt, may lead officials to ignore the environment in an effort to grow more rapidly. If they settle for lower environmental standards, developing countries could be the "benefi-

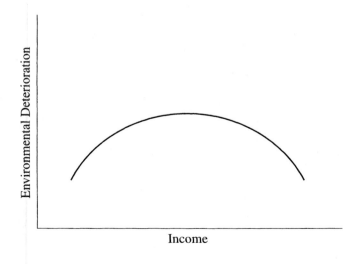

FIGURE 5–2 The Environmental Inverted "U"

The inverted "U" in this case represents a tendency for pollution, or environmental deterioration, to increase as per capita income grows but to fall back at higher levels.

ciaries" of polluting industries that leave developed countries, although this hardly seems like a long-run solution.[8] In the final analysis, however, the concept of sustainable development suggests that failure to account properly for the environmental impact of today's activities will significantly increase the cost of future development or even reverse beneficial trends. The crucial question is just how to go about minimizing the environmental damage from the development process.

Poverty and the Environment

The question of whether there is a trade-off between economic growth and the environment becomes particularly acute when considering the problem of poverty. Another vicious circle may be involved here. If poor people are unable to sacrifice their daily needs to environmental protection, their environment will continue to deteriorate and intensify their poverty.

The poorest people are most in need of environmental resources, and at the same time they are becoming more concentrated on the world's poorest land. If the poorest are defined as the low-income fifth of the developing world, about half of them live in South Asia, another 20 percent in Sub-Saharan Africa, and 11 percent in China. Approximately two-thirds of the nearly 800 million poorest people "do not live in areas of high agricultural potential."[9] In rural areas, population growth, consolidation of land ownership, and higher agricultural productivity have reduced the access of millions of people to productive assets, while in urban areas those assets are often restricted to skilled labor.

The World Bank calculates that rural areas of the world have an average population density of 519 per square kilometer. But Egypt has 1,177; Sri Lanka has 1,652; Oman has 2,967; and Papua New Guinea, 6,260. In Java, with a population density of only about 650, almost one-fourth of the population is landless, and landholdings average one acre or less.[10] Certain groups such as nomadic herders in Africa and the Middle East, forest dwellers in Brazil and the Philippines, mountain-dwelling peoples in Peru and Nepal, and those susceptible to periodic storms and flooding in India and Bangladesh may live at the brink of subsistence at almost all times. Any short-term deterioration in climate or soil quality can imperil their existence.

The extent to which poverty *causes* environmental deterioration will depend on just *how* poor people are and how well their particular environment provides for basic needs. One study of rural areas in the Philippines suggests that people who have a sense of permanence due to a long history in an area will not only preserve their environment but actively defend it against outside interests as long as that environment provides a stable and bearable existence. Only the poorest, or recent arrivals, will sacrifice the environment for temporary advantage.[11]

Strategies to reduce poverty should not come at the expense of the environment. Short-term economic improvements such as chemical fertilizers can worsen the environment, and conservation measures such as restricting access to land can increase poverty. Specific solutions must be found to local problems in order to address both poverty and environmental deterioration simultaneously.[12]

Such solutions are often referred to as **ecodevelopment**. They often involve specific projects designed to integrate development and environmental needs. For example, in Sierra Leone the Konta Agro-Forestry Project helped farmers replace older planting methods with ways of planting staple crops among trees. In Thailand, wastes from cassava, a plant with a starchy, edible root, are used to produce ethanol. And in Guatemala, farmers whose lands were on hillsides were taught contour planting and terracing techniques.[13] A controversial approach to ecodevelopment is ecotourism, where natural resources (the Serengeti Plain in Tanzania, coral reefs in the Caribbean and the South Pacific, mountains in Nepal) are used as the basis for tourist attractions, with particular attention to minimizing the potential environmental damage. Whether such activities can be both commercially successful and environmentally benign remains to be seen.[14]

THE ECONOMICS OF EXTERNALITIES

Externalities are the common thread that runs through economic consideration of the environment.[15] Externalities are costs and benefits that escape the normal price calculations of the individual producer or consumer: production costs that fall on the wider society rather than the producer or benefits received but not paid for by the consumer. They lead to inaccurate calculation of those costs and benefits, and are not included in pricing decisions of individuals and firms. We refer to such situations as **market failure**, where resources are misallocated.

Positive Externalities and Public Goods

Positive externalities are benefits obtained by individuals or firms without payment due to the activities of others. A firm whose costs are reduced by others' innovations, by government-provided infrastructure, or simply from the more diversified economic environment brought on by development obtains these economies. So does an individual who gains from a neighbor's property improvement. Such a firm or individual is referred to as a **free rider**. The investment has a **marginal social benefit** that exceeds the marginal private benefit. The fact that others reap part of the benefits means that

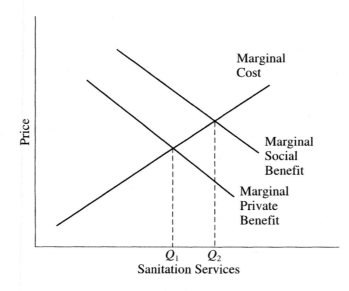

**FIGURE 5–3
Underproduction of a Public Good**

Marginal Private Benefit falls below Marginal Social Benefit, so production stops at Q_1 instead of Q_2, which would be optimal. If private firms are unable to obtain enough revenue from a poor population, the government must build the sanitation facilities required to make a city livable.

it is not possible for the producer to offset costs with the full social value of these benefits: In a competitive market, the good or service will be underproduced. For example, a private company might be willing to clean up a toxic spill by charging the polluter for cleaning services but may find it impossible to reap the future rewards of higher property values. The polluter may not be able or willing to make up that cost, so a private cleanup may not occur.

Activities that produce such externalities, such as education, police protection, or environmental improvement, are often produced by governments as **public goods**. Governments frequently provide primary education on the theory that the benefits are not only the individual's ability to read but also a more responsible citizen and one whose higher earnings will yield higher taxes. Figure 5–3 shows underproduction of sanitation services, where social benefits outstrip the private benefits to the purchaser. Public goods will be examined in more depth below.

Negative Externalities

Negative externalities are costs of economic activities that are imposed on others, and it is here that environmental damage is prominent. The simplest case is pollution of water or air. The pollution results in costs to those affected, for instance, through increased health care costs or taxes paid for government cleanup efforts. These are **marginal social costs** that exceed the private costs. Since the social cost is not paid by the producer, the good is produced in greater amounts than would be the case if all costs had to be incorporated into the price. In the case of negative externalities, the producer is the free rider because it receives a benefit (use of a river to dispose of waste) whose cost is borne by someone else. Figure 5–4 shows overproduction of timber when costs are not fully incurred by the producer.

Another common example is deforestation, where excessive removal of trees results in the inability of the soil to hold the normal amount of rainfall. Water runoff and soil erosion may then affect agricultural land, resulting in lower productivity and, in some hilly areas, severe mud slides such as those that in recent years have buried villages in Thailand and the Philippines. The inability or unwillingness of firms and

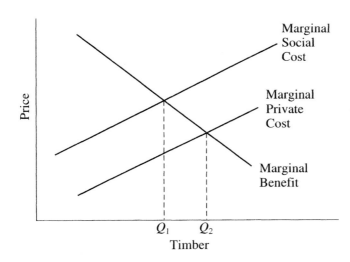

FIGURE 5–4 Overproduction of a Good with Negative Externalities

Marginal Private Cost falls below Marginal Social Cost, so production proceeds to Q_2 instead of stopping at Q_1, which would be socially optimal. If the soil degradation resulting from deforestation is not a cost to timber companies, they will cut too much forest.

governments to account for such externalities in their decisions has increased the concern about our ability to achieve sustainable development. It is necessary both to measure the environmental impact of economic activity and to devise the mechanisms to properly factor such costs into investment decisions.

Economic Values and the Environment

A firm or a government would normally determine the suitability of an investment project by measuring future net returns and using some rate of discount to calculate the present value of those returns. The challenge of fully accounting for all values is to appreciate and measure those costs and benefits that are not readily put into market terms.[16] Development Spotlight 5–2 explains some alternative methods of assigning a value to a natural resource.

What is the full economic value of a forest? We start by trying to identify alternative uses, because economists measure the cost of any particular use by what is given up. Benefit obtained from one use has the opportunity cost of the forgone uses. For example, the value of the trees as timber must be contrasted with the forest's value as a living environment and the trees' value as sources of food and other raw materials,

---

DEVELOPMENT SPOTLIGHT 5–2

HOW SCARCE IS A NATURAL RESOURCE?

How can we measure the opportunity cost of a nonrenewable resource? What permits us to say the resource is becoming more scarce? One text looks at three measurements of resource scarcity: the real unit cost of extraction, the real price, and resource rent.

The real *cost* method measures extraction costs directly. The resource, oil for example, is becoming more scarce if the marginal cost of extraction is increasing over time. But by this method, physical scarcity may be increasing even while costs fall due to technological improvement in extraction methods. Also, rising costs may indicate scarcity while substitutes are increasingly easy to find.

The real *price*—the price of the resource adjusted by some price index—is easier to calculate. But this requires care in choosing the right index, and it assumes competitive markets, undistorted by private or government agents. Also, prices may change over brief periods for reasons having little to do with scarcity.

The authors prefer the resource rent approach. The rent is derived by subtracting production costs from the price of the resource, thus indicating the scarcity of the resource itself, "in the ground." This method is said to account for technological change and substitution. It is still subject to distortion by imperfect markets and government policies and is difficult to measure consistently.

If sustainable development is the goal of resource-pricing policy, a conservative measure of scarcity makes sense. Too high a value placed on a resource will be an inducement to extract the resource for sale. A lower value, even if resources remain in the ground when they might be sold, at least has the virtue of preserving resources for future generations.

Source: John M. Hartwick and Nancy D. Olewiler, *The Economics of Natural Resource Use* (New York: Harper and Row, 1986), pp. 147–155.

including some not yet known such as the foundation for new medicines.[17] There is also an indirect value of maintaining the viability of surrounding soils and permitting recreational use. Loss of these values should be added to the cost of exploitation of the forest.

A more indirect way to assign a value to a forest is to calculate its option value—the value of future uses of the forest that are eliminated by current use. Trees that require 20 years to attain commercial value will not be available for use as timber later if they are cut today. Even more difficult to measure is the existence value—the value that some people will put on the forest's existence even if they never use it. For example, the Grand Canyon in the United States is considered a national treasure. Finally, the contribution of deforestation to global climate change must be factored in.

With the questions of externalities and values in mind, we can explore the solutions to environmental problems.

APPROACHES TO INCORPORATING EXTERNALITIES

Modern economies have two primary tools for making economic decisions: markets and governments. Our objective in this section is to look at the advantages and disadvantages of these tools for incorporating externalities into these decisions.

Using Markets

The existence of externalities has often led to the immediate search for nonmarket solutions, when what may be most needed is to make markets work better and to incorporate—or "internalize"—the externalities.

Making Ownership Rights Explicit

In many countries ownership rights are vague and many people do not own the land they work. Often, as a result, resources are overused or depleted because there is no clear, enforceable assignment of ownership or use rights to them. A first step would be to clarify those rights so that the right to earn income and the responsibility to incur costs are stable and enforceable. Theodore Panayotou, who has done considerable research into sustainable development issues, concludes that insecurity of the rights to ownership and use of land is "the single most severe policy failure in developing countries."[18] Lack of title, risk of eviction, and subsequent inability to use land as collateral for loans will often bias land use against investments in long-term sustainability in favor of quick-using endeavors that deplete the soil, sometimes referred to as mining the land.

Creating Markets

Markets can be created where none have existed, such as for forests, grazing and fishing areas, and for pollution rights. Creating a market results in imposing a price on economic activity, effectively *internalizing* the externality: Firms must become more efficient and reduce costs, or have higher prices that reduce their sales. For example, open land on which livestock have traditionally grazed unhindered will eventually become overgrazed if there are no controls imposed by the community. Pricing the land according to the number of animals would give farmers a truer picture of the cost of those resources and of the activity of livestock raising. To contain pollution, governments can create markets for polluting activities by setting emission levels and apportioning the right to pollute by seeing what firms are willing to pay. The firm then includes that cost when setting a price for the product. Alternatively, a tax would also force firms to add the cost of emissions into their prices.

Open Access and Common Property Resources

Small societies or groups often hold property in common: The forest, pond, or agricultural land is available for use by members of the community but is owned by the community. Such open access involves little overt regulation, but if a more formal set of rules exist we use the term **common property resources**. While these situations are being undermined by the spread of market relationships, both open access and common property resources still exist among farmers and fishermen in parts of Asia, Africa, and Latin America.[19] There is a danger of misuse of such resources unless there are recognizable and enforceable rules.

Government Regulation of Private Activity

In the face of significant externalities, governments may still have to regulate private market activity to promote sustainable resource use. When they do, they face a choice between direct controls and market-oriented incentives such as taxes and subsidies.

The use of **controls**, or the setting of specific **standards**, is generally a second choice among economists because it takes the place of market-oriented incentives that are considered more efficient. Controls may include requiring specific technologies in production processes, setting standards for emission of particular pollutants, or even eliminating certain pollutants entirely.

Standards may be necessary, for example, where monopoly or oligopoly power reduces sensitivity to market incentives, and where technological solutions "are relatively uniform and can easily be specified by regulators."[20] They may also be desired where a specific target is to be achieved, such as in the case of zoning to preserve particular areas or to direct land to specific uses, or when specific physical thresholds must not be exceeded (e.g., with toxic wastes or radioactivity). We may desire a certain level of safety, such as in protecting workers from injury or zero exposure to toxic waste.

In most cases, economists prefer incentives. These have the advantage of using the price mechanism that is more flexible, allowing individuals and firms to find their own most efficient solutions. Taxes on pollution, for example, produce revenue while imposing costs that inhibit certain behaviors. Such taxes are administratively easier if they are levied directly on resource use rather than on results such as emissions. The best taxes will not just discourage pollution and raise revenue but will actively encourage innovation in order to reduce the taxed activity and increase the efficiency of resource use.[21]

Neither standards nor taxes guarantee that objectives will be met. Governments, especially those in poor countries, often lack the personnel or desire to enforce their own laws. In the 1993 debate over the North American Free Trade Agreement (NAFTA), Mexican government claims that their environmental standards were fairly strict were met with concern in the United States over the Mexican government's ability and willingness to actually enforce them. Direct standards or controls may fail if a country does not punish company owners, if fines are set too low to deter violations, if monitoring is too difficult for thousands of small firms, or if underpaid government officials are willing to accept bribes below the level of fines to look the other way. On the other hand, they give the government a sense of control and hide the cost of enforcement from easy scrutiny. Taxes may also be difficult to enforce, and collecting taxes does not guarantee that specific standards are being met.[22]

Creation of a market for the right to pollute, mentioned earlier, is a complex undertaking. Not many developing-country governments yet have the ability to put such a system into place, although the government of Singapore does this for chlorofluorocarbons that are known to deplete ozone.[23] A positive approach is to provide incentives for activities that reduce pollution. Subsidies for unleaded gasoline and waste treatment equipment in Thailand and water treatment equipment in Indonesia are examples.

Direct Government Role: Public Goods

Although the potential efficiency of markets frequently argues for governments to create and enforce effective market mechanisms, there are cases where a more direct government intervention would be superior to imperfect markets.

The most widely accepted case for government involvement is for public goods. These are goods or services with positive externalities, as illustrated in Figure 5–3. They are characterized by **indivisibilities**, the inability of a producer to dole out small units of a product to individual consumers, and **nonexclusion**, the inability to prevent individual consumers from using the product. A service such as national defense cannot be allocated to specific individuals in specific amounts, and no one can be excluded from its benefits, so individuals cannot be charged for it—hence, there is no market. The same is true for the atmosphere. Public investment programs in infrastructure, such as road systems, have this character as well and are crucial components of a development effort.

Other goods, such as water, take on a public character in that many people believe this resource is so essential to life that it should not be owned by private firms. Clean water also has positive externalities, such as prevention of disease. But whereas water is an essential good, it remains a scarce resource with numerous competing uses. If the government takes on the chore of allocating water resources—as is true in most countries—it may choose from three methods: (*a*) ration water by amounts, perhaps giving individuals equal access or using some other formula; (*b*) use a first-come, first-serve approach; or (*c*) monitor use and charge accordingly. The last method is the closest to the market solution and is best able to account for opportunity cost if the government incorporates all relevant costs into its price. Conservation of water use would be encouraged. As with any resource, truly unusual exceptions could be permitted subsidies.

Another type of public good that is relevant to the environment is education. The traditional explanation of education as a public good is that the benefits include higher rates of literacy and acceptance of society's values, which make educated people more productive and less destructive. Thus, we all gain from others' education. The same is true to the extent that education improves one's awareness of and ability to deal with environmental problems.

This is particularly true of educating girls and women. In addition to equality and population issues, the role of women as producers—and thus creators and victims of pollution—requires that they not be left out of the provision of information and resources necessary to attack the problem. The World Bank notes that "In many parts of the world women play a central part in resource management and yet enjoy much less access to education, credit, extension services and technology than do men." Since their role in the health and education of children is crucial, and since they can control the size of the future population, "Improving education for girls may be the most important long-term environmental policy . . ." in developing countries.[24] (See Chapter 7 for more on this topic.)

Investment, Environment, and the Discount Rate

Governments play an important role in allocating investment resources; financing investment domestically from taxes and debt, and borrowing from foreign banks, governments, and multilateral institutions. They must evaluate projects or programs, and even if all relevant costs and benefits are accounted for in net returns, governments still must address the relative importance to be attached to future years' income.

In Chapter 4 we showed how the discount rate is used to reduce future returns to their present values. A higher rate reduces the present value of future years' incomes and reduces the attractiveness of long-term investments. The poor may prefer a higher discount rate because they have immediate income needs and are less able to wait years for trees to grow. Yet, some suggest that environmental deterioration is encouraged by the "discrimination against future generations" in high discount rates. Because environmentally benign projects have a greater emphasis on future benefits and so are more sustainable, they appear less attractive than those with higher up-front benefits. Some environmentalists and economists recommend that governments use a lower discount rate to evaluate projects that are environment friendly. An example of the problem is provided in Development Spotlight 5–3.

But high discount rates may not be as troublesome as they may appear, and environmental concerns can be taken into account in other ways. If high discount rates reflect appropriate market interest rates, they will discourage investment generally, thus reducing pressure on resources. Further, if the remedy is to have government use lower discount rates for environmentally benign projects, it may be difficult to exclude government projects that cannot be justified economically or to include relevant private-sector projects.

Economists usually favor specific remedies for specific problems, and the discount rate may be too broad an instrument for the targeting of environmental protection or enhancement. A better, though more complex, approach would include a careful assessment of the environmental impact of investment projects, so that it would be possible to offset projects yielding economic benefits and environmental degradation (say, adding to the pollution of water supplies) with compensating investments (such as waste treatment), which might restore the resource to its original state.[25]

The existence of negative externalities associated with some economic activity argues for careful consideration of total costs and benefits. Where markets are absent,

IMPACT OF THE DISCOUNT RATE ON PROJECT COMPARISON

In the Net Present Value (NPV) formula, future returns are discounted by a specific percentage. A higher percentage means that future years' returns are given less weight, reducing the attractiveness of the project. In example A, each of two projects is expected to yield a net return of one dollar a year for eight years. We compare the NPV with one project discounted at 10 percent and the other at 20 percent.

EXAMPLE A

Year	10%	20%	10%	20%
1	$0.91	$0.83		
2	0.83	0.69		
3	0.75	0.58	After 4 Years	
4	0.68	0.48	$3.17	$2.58
5	0.62	0.40		
6	0.58	0.33		
7	0.53	0.28	After 8 Years	
8	0.48	0.23	$5.38	$3.82

After four years the project discounted at 10 percent yields an NPV 23 percent higher. After eight years its NPV is 41 percent higher. The longer-lived a project, the more a high discount rate hurts its prospects.

Example B assumes that the eight-year returns of $10 are configured differently for two projects, both discounted at 10 percent. A steel mill is expected to have diminishing returns over time, while a project to develop environmentally friendly fertilizers will yield little at first but much more over time.

EXAMPLE B

Year	Steel Mill Returns Nominal	Steel Mill Returns Discounted	Fertilizer Returns Nominal	Fertilizer Returns Discounted
1	$ 2.0	$1.82	$ 0.2	$0.18
2	1.8	1.49	0.8	0.66
3	1.6	1.20	1.0	0.75
4	1.4	0.96	1.2	0.82
5	1.2	0.75	1.4	0.87
6	1.0	0.58	1.6	0.93
7	0.8	0.42	1.8	0.95
8	0.2	0.10	2.0	0.96
Total	$10.0	$7.32	$10.0	$6.12

The projects yield the same nominal return, but their time pattern makes the layer-yielding project less valuable. The higher the discount rate, the greater the disadvantage.

An additional problem is that the poorest people, for whom daily survival is problematic, are likely to have a higher discount rate than those who are better off: A dollar today is crucial, so a dollar a year from now may be considered equally to 85 cents a year from now, rather than 95 cents. Poor people may therefore be more likely to undervalue a project that protects future income at the expense of today's.

they should be created. When markets will not achieve the objective, regulation and public goods come into play. Few developing—or any—countries have been able so far to integrate environmental and economic policies. A beginning has been made in Taiwan, with some encouraging results, as shown in Case 5–1.

With these principles in mind, we can now address some specific environmental issues. We divide these into land, nonrenewable resources, water, and air.

CASE 5–1

INTEGRATING ENVIRONMENT AND DEVELOPMENT IN TAIWAN

FAST FACTS

On the Map: East Asia

Population: 22 Million

Per Capita GNI and Rank: $14,216   (Not Ranked)

Life Expectancy: Male—72   Female—78

Adult Literacy Rate: Male—94% Female—90%

Taiwan's extraordinary economic achievements have come at a considerable environmental cost. These include large-scale deforestation, decline in soil fertility due to heavy use of chemical fertilizers and pesticides, industrial pollution that went unchecked for decades, and lack of attention to the environmental hazards of nuclear energy.

Awareness of these problems began in the 1970s, but laws passed at the time were not well enforced by Taiwan's Environmental Protection Agency (TEPA). Beginning in the 1980s, the government has strengthened its laws and enforcement, and has begun integrating environmental concerns into its industrial strategy. While Taiwan has generally moved from a strategy of focusing on import replacement to export promotion, it has begun to use government to promote its own production of environmental goods and services. The government subsidizes firms' purchases of pollution control and abatement equipment, and finances research and technical assistance for firms that are trying to reduce pollution.

While the data necessary to track the impact of these programs are not easily accumulated, some evidence indicates that they are working. Firms' expenditures on pollution control and abatement equipment are rising, and are higher in those firms owned by the government. Some data on waste reduction at the firm level show significant improvement, and the pollution intensity of some industries has been falling.

The Taiwanese government has apparently been encouraged in these directions by more than the government's desire to clean up the environment. Public pressure against the spread of pollution has been growing, and greater democracy increases the chances that this pressure will be addressed. The demands of foreign customers for Taiwan's exports are pushing Taiwan toward cleaner products. The promise of a growing Asian market for environmental products provides an incentive for new export industries.

Taiwan's ability to make a significant shift over the period of a decade or so is due partly to the earlier successes at directing the country's development efforts. Also, a country that is rapidly growing is constantly improving its capital stock, affording numerous opportunities to upgrade technology and improve efficiency in the use of materials and energy.

Taiwan's experience shows some evidence for an environmental Kuznets curve bringing growth and environmental improvement. But this requires political will, the ability of the government to influence the direction of development in market-friendly ways, and a dynamic economy.

Sources: Walden Bello and Stephanie Rosenfeld, *Dragons in Distress: Asia's Miracle Economies in Crisis* (San Francisco: Institute for Food and Development Policy, 1990), pp. 195–214; Michael T. Rock, "Toward More Sustainable Development: The Environment and Industrial Policy in Taiwan," *Development Policy Review* 14, no. 3 (September 1996), pp. 255–272; and Pei-ing Wu, "Economic Development and Environmental Quality: Evidence from Taiwan," *Asian Economic Journal* 12, no. 4 (December 1998), pp. 395–412.

PRODUCTIVITY OF THE LAND

Land and natural resources are the material building blocks of production and development. Some classical economists concluded that, once profits had been driven to zero and wages to their subsistence level, the owners of land as the key limiting factor of production would reap the remaining rewards. But land is not necessarily fixed in amount or quality, nor is any single piece of land restricted to a single use. Land can be "used" but need not be "used up." Land is a **renewable resource**, but sustainable land use requires steps to maintain soil fertility so that it can be reused, at least over a cycle of years if not each year. Farmers see soil quality deteriorate with continued use and tend to appreciate conservation measures that preserve high-quality growing conditions. How is land used, and what principles ought to guide allocation of land to different uses?

Agricultural Land Use[26]

Table 5–1 shows one noticeable difference in land use among income groups. All low-income groups show significantly lower percentages of forestland than the middle-income countries. This is true not only for the Middle East and North Africa but also for Bangladesh and Pakistan. Sub-Saharan Africa, especially countries like Mali and Chad that include part of the Sahel Desert, has a smaller percentage of cropland and forest than other regions. Table 5–2, however, shows that at the regional level, population density is not strongly related to income. While low-income Bangladesh has a relatively high rural density at 1,204 people per square kilometer of arable land, India's density is only 438. Middle-income countries may also have high rural density: Costa Rica's is 824 and Sri Lanka's is 1,664.

Arable Land

The most relevant land in the agricultural context is **arable land**; land suited for cultivation. The United Nations reports that arable land was 36 percent of the total land area in developing countries over the 1984 to 1986 period and grew at only 0.33 percent per year, compared to recent population growth rates of 2.3 percent over the 1960 to 1990 period. The expansion of arable land is not an option everywhere but is still possible through irrigation and, to some extent, forest clearing. Both of these options, however, have significant environmental consequences.

Arable land, of course, is not all alike. Different types of soil are suited for different types of crops: Agricultural land-use patterns will differ for grasslands, hills,

TABLE 5–1 Utilization of Land, 1995 (%)

Countries	Cropland	Pasture	Forest	Other
Low Income	13	32	16	38
Low except China/India	9	32	16	43
Sub-Saharan Africa	7	34	17	40
Low-Middle Income	11	18	33	38
Upper-Middle Income	9	32	34	25
High Income	NA	24	21	NA

NA = Not Available.

Source: World Development Indicators 1998.

TABLE 5–2	Rural Population Density (People per Square Kilometer of Arable Land, 1998)
World	520
Low Income	507
Low-Middle Income	631
Upper-Middle Income	193
Low and Middle Income	
East Asia and Pacific	691
Europe and Central Asia	125
Latin America, Caribbean	252
Middle East, North Africa	534
South Asia	537
Sub-Saharan Africa	369
High Income	175

Source: World Development Indicators 2001.

wetlands, and semiarid areas. At present, despite the attention given to rain forests, it is dry and hilly land that is most endangered. According to United Nations reports, over three-fourths of "rangeland and dry forest" has been seriously degraded, leading to fuelwood shortages and less productive agriculture. At the same time, over half of prime agricultural land is considered degraded. "In India, Pakistan, Egypt, the Philippines, Sri Lanka and other countries, waterlogging and soil salinization have removed nearly as much irrigated agricultural land from production as has been opened by new irrigation projects in recent years."[27]

Older patterns of agriculture that allowed for portions of land to lie fallow (unused) periodically in order to be regenerated have often been abandoned. This is due to not only population pressure but also to varying types of "incorporation," including settler plantations, land-use restrictions, and incentive structures (pricing, taxes, etc.) that lead to alternative uses, particularly in Africa.[28] Along with changing land-use patterns come different capital requirements. All else equal, small plots of land will be more appropriately tilled with small handheld or ox-driven implements (hoes, small plows), whereas larger holdings can make good use of tractors. As land is used more intensively, its contribution to the development effort requires decisions regarding labor and capital as well.

Land Degradation

More intensive and extensive use of land is leading to greater environmental challenges. The most dramatic of these is **desertification**, or the making of land unsuitable for agriculture through removal of topsoil. The spread of people into fringe areas of Africa's Sahara Desert, often in wetter years, led to overuse that became unsustainable in normal years. Removal of plant nutrients leaves the land a desert. Satellite data show the Sahara moved south between 1980 and 1984 and receded in the late 1980s, but it was larger at the end of the decade than at the beginning. While it is clear that overgrazing has contributed to the extreme **degradation** of some soils in the Sahel region of the Sahara, we lack accurate measurements of climate and soil change over millennia that might indicate a cycle of desertification and improvement. Also, it is not clear whether drier climates help produce deserts or are in fact the result of desertification. Whether current rainfall patterns represent a long-term trend or a longer cycle that we are unaware of, desertification has become a threat to the near-term survival of some populations.[29]

Perhaps more important than desertification is the gradual degradation of soils due to erosion and loss of plant nutrients. Land loses its ability to produce when overused, either from planting or livestock grazing. Irrigation without proper drainage can raise the water table and bring more saline groundwater to the surface. The World Resource Institute reports that almost 2 billion hectares, or about 17 percent of all vegetated land, has been degraded due to human action over the period 1945 to 1990. Less than 1 percent of this area is classified as extremely degraded, over one-third is only lightly degraded, and almost one-half is moderately degraded.

The global distribution of soil degradation is uneven. Of the area considered degraded, 25 percent is in Central America and Mexico, 23 percent in Europe, 22 percent in Africa, 20 percent in Asia, and only 5 percent in North America. Additional degradation has taken place, but some land has been restored by soil conservation programs in industrialized countries. Degraded land requires additional cost to maintain its productivity.[30]

Degradation has occurred extensively in South and Southwest Asia and numerous areas in Latin America. Increased salinity of U.S. water flowing south was damaging Mexico's water until the United States built a desalinization plant in 1973.[31] The technology of the Green Revolution, including new high-yielding seed varieties, has improved yields dramatically but has brought increased use of fertilizers and pesticides, which may degrade the soil with prolonged intensive use. The Green Revolution is examined in more detail in Chapter 8.

Development projects involved with agriculture, forestry, and livestock must be evaluated for their impact on the land. For instance, governments and multilateral agencies have encouraged nomadic populations to turn to settled agriculture or animal husbandry, although these populations have likely adapted to land and climate patterns that were unable to support settled activity. The result has often been even greater soil degradation and pressure on water supplies.

Deforestation

A major global issue in land use is **deforestation**: reduction of forests can lead to agricultural productivity loss and the loss of numerous species of plants and animals, resulting in a reduction in **biodiversity**. Table 5–3 provides the World Bank's most recent estimates of the extent of forests lost each year, about 0.2 percent worldwide. Some estimates are higher than this, and the Bank believes that *tropical* forests were being lost at the rate of 0.9 percent per year in the 1980s. Even the Bank's estimates show Burundi losing 9 percent of its forests each year during the 1990s and Haiti over $5\frac{1}{2}$ percent.[32]

Forests have numerous economic and ecological uses:

1. Sources of timber (for construction, furniture, paper, fuel)
2. Providing food, materials, and habitat for people
3. Protection and enrichment of soils
4. Natural regulation of the water cycle
5. Impact on climate through evaporation control and carbon consumption
6. Impact on watershed flows
7. Current and potential sources of medical and other products

TABLE 5–3 Rates of Deforestation (% per Year)		
Countries	*1965–1989**	*1990–2000*
Low Income	0.4	0.8
Low-Middle Income	0.5	−0.1
Upper-Middle Income	0.4	0.5
Low and Middle Income		
East Asia/Pacific	0.7	0.2
Europe/Central Asia	NA	−0.1
Latin America/Caribbean	0.5	0.5
Mideast/North Africa	−0.2	−0.1
South Asia	−0.3	0.1
Sub-Saharan Africa	0.4	0.8
High Income	0.1	−0.1
World	0.2	0.2

*Data refer to forests and woodlands. Negative number means forest area increased during the period.

NA = Not Available.

Sources: *World Development Report 1992* and *World Development Indicators 2001*.

A major problem is determining the proper value to place on these uses and the discount rate appropriate to measuring the present value of future use.

Tropical forests are not the only ones to suffer decline, but they tend to be more fragile than temperate forests, so even the destruction of a few important trees imperils the entire forest. For the same reason, and due to the length of time to maturity, destruction of the rain forests tends to have a greater danger of being irreversible.

The pressure on tropical forests has been intense. In some countries, including Brazil, Indonesia, the Philippines, and Thailand, firms and governments have earned significant foreign exchange from the export of timber for furniture and paper. But although international attention is focused on the activities of the large forestry companies that are cutting large swaths of forest for timber, this represents probably less than 10 percent of global deforestation. While logging and destruction to make way for dams are concentrated geographically, land encroachment by farms and cattle ranches are the major causes of tropical forest destruction. Several Latin American countries, most notably Brazil, have cleared land for cattle grazing to help meet the demand for beef in North America and Europe. And some development has removed areas of forest that were simply in the way of new roads and towns.

Governments often contribute to the problem rather than the solution. The government of Brazil has opened new areas of settlement to relieve crowded regions and has developed new export products such as timber, minerals, and livestock to help reduce its foreign debt. In the process it has actively promoted deforestation in large portions of the Amazon, providing subsidies and tax breaks for cattle ranching.[33]

But in contrast to such frontier expansion, local overpopulation is an important cause of deforestation as people without easy access to farmland and commercial fuels slowly cut trees to grow crops and find wood to cook and heat their homes.[34] Population pressure has resulted in forest clearance for agricultural purposes, regardless of the inability of the soil to sustain agriculture for more than a few years. In Africa, rural population density worsens the situation. In Asia, on the other hand, significant replanting efforts are at least partially offsetting the impact of income and population density.[35]

The appropriate policies will depend on why forests are being removed and by whom. For small-scale deforestation, individual farmers often find their own alternatives when wood becomes scarce: Its higher value has encouraged private investment in trees on plantations and in small stands in countries such as Costa Rica, Kenya, Malawi, and Vietnam.[36]

Policy Failure and Success in Land Use

As with any resource, the allocation of land depends on the establishment of incentives to guide usage into efficient and/or socially desirable directions. Reductions in agricultural output, discussed more fully in Chapter 8, are frequently the result of deterioration of the soil caused by misguided policies. These include subsidies that encourage overuse of fertilizer, pesticides, water, and machinery. In addition, low returns to agriculture will depress land values and may discourage investment in soil maintenance.[37]

Mismanagement of land may often be due to a lack of clear designation of the ownership of or use rights to the land. Most analysis tends to focus on ownership as the key: Someone who uses but does not own the land (a free rider) is likely to abuse (overuse) it, leading to degradation. It was the problem of overgrazed common pastures in seventeenth-century Britain that prompted the quote from Izaak Walton at the beginning of the chapter.

Nonetheless, ownership is only the most obvious way in which land may be responsibly controlled. Experiments in villages around the world have shown that small communities holding land in common can, with vigilance, use it in a sustainable fashion. Conversion of land from communal to private property may generate confusion about ownership and lead to more significant degradation. People grow accustomed to land-use practices. For example, when Chinese reforms, intended to clarify land ownership, required land security by prohibiting periodic changes in boundaries of farming plots, the change was resented. While not denying the potential benefits of private ownership for responsible stewardship of the land, it is more important to recognize the need for a clear responsibility for sustainable land use: Security of land use or tenure is crucial. A recent study of Sub-Saharan Africa concluded that "In most cases, the tenurial security enjoyed by members of the community is sufficient to induce investment in land," and investment takes place when investors are confident in continued use of their resources. Cooperative behavior in managing common property resources has been successful throughout the world.[38]

Government directives to ensure sustainability, however, may fail. This is illustrated by the attempts of the government of Thailand to ban logging. By late 1988, over 30 years of logging had reduced forested area from 60 percent to 20 percent, and the ban was prompted by spectacular flooding and landslides. But underlying price incentives still made logging profitable, so lax enforcement and the failure to establish ownership rights in the forests failed to stop the logging.[39]

Singapore has successfully allocated urban land rights by increasing parking fees and taxing cars using downtown roadways during peak hours. Public transportation was enhanced to provide a viable alternative, and carpooling was exempted. The result was a significant reduction in rush-hour traffic, a reduction in pollution, and a more attractive city. In effect, the "overgrazing" of downtown streets was reduced by charging for the right to graze and by providing acceptable alternatives.[40]

Government correctives are sometimes necessary not for market failures but to undo previous government policies. Serious deforestation in the Brazilian Amazon has been the result of government-provided infrastructure, subsidies, and other policies. During 1987 to 1989, the rate of deforestation was reduced considerably by enforcing penalties on illegal burning, suspending tax incentives for activities such as ranching, and halting the requirement that forestland be improved before title could be given. Below-market pricing for land has created timber booms in Indonesia, Côte d'Ivoire, and the United States.[41]

Of course, things are not always this simple. Robert Repetto has used a series of concentric circles to illustrate how policies impact on deforestation. On the inside are direct policies such as those for land titling and timber pricing. Less direct are trade policies that encourage wood exports, agriculture policies that put pressure on farmland, and on the outside are general macroeconomic policies that affect resource prices and incomes.[42]

NONRENEWABLE RESOURCES

Biological resources in the land, water, and atmospheric environments are renewable as long as people are careful using them and appropriate incentives are in place. But many natural resources are **nonrenewable resources**: Once extracted and used they are gone forever.

Mineral Resources

Table 5–4 shows the global distribution of key mineral resources. Developing areas are short on some but have a significant share of the world's copper, manganese, chromium, and bauxite. In 1995, while Australia produced 39 percent of the world's bauxite (the raw material for aluminum), developing countries produced 55 percent,

TABLE 5–4 Distribution of World Metals Reserves (%): 1989

Region	Copper	Zinc	Iron Ore	Manganese	Chromium	Bauxite
U.S./Canada	21	28	19	0	0	Negligible
U.S.S.R.	12	7	36	29	10	1
Europe	7	18	5	0	3	6
Oceania	4	13	13	4	0	11
Developing Countries	56	33	26	66	87	83
Asia	9	16	11	3	6	5
Africa	13	6	4	61	80	38
Latin America	34	11	12	2	1	39

Source: World Resources 1994–95.

TO MINE OR NOT TO MINE?

The decision to either mine and sell a nonrenewable resource or keep it for the future requires a study of the alternative outcomes of the two actions. We compare the expected *future* value of income from the *current* sale with the possibility of a higher future price if we do not sell.

The expected future value of the income from sale can be estimated by assuming that the proceeds are invested at a market interest rate. We choose not to sell if we believe that the future price will rise sufficiently to offset the interest received on the proceeds of selling today: We compare the rate of interest (i) with the rate of expected price increase ($\rho = Pf - Pt$ where Pf is the expected future price and Pt is the current price).

If $i \geq \rho$, the decision will be to mine or sell the resource at the fastest pace possible, taking only private profit into account. If $i < \rho$, the resource is more valuable in the ground and mining slows or ceases. There are complications, of course, involving the uncertain future of the resource price, interest rates, and costs of mining the resource. In addition, new decisions will themselves have an impact on the current price and expectations of the future price.

Source: Richard Eden et al., *Energy Economics: Growth, Resources, and Policies* (Cambridge: Cambridge University Press, 1982), pp. 372–373. For variations on the theme, see Stephen W. Salant, "The Economics of Natural Resource Extraction: A Primer for Development Economists," *World Bank Research Observer* 10, no. 1 (February 1995), pp. 93–111.

with 23 percent alone from the small economies of Guinea and Jamaica. Chile produced 25 percent of the world's copper ore, and other developing countries added over 30 percent. These minerals are nonrenewable. A country must therefore decide how fast to extract them, how to address the environmental impact, and how to create incentives for firms to discover or create substitutes.

Minerals mined and sold this year will not be available in the future. A slower pace makes more sense when a resource is expected to be increasingly scarce and, thus, expensive. The drawback is that while reduced supply leads to higher prices, a high price encourages consumers to develop substitutes and other potential producers to search for deposits. A competitive producer, of course, has little choice of pricing policy. If a few producers control a world market, decisions of pricing policy are more discretionary. Such attempts to control prices through producer cartels and commodity agreements have generally not succeeded, but the Organization of Petroleum Exporting Countries (OPEC) can still affect world prices. Production cutbacks in late 1999 caused large price increases the following year. Development Spotlight 5–4 presents an economic analysis of the decision on mining a resource as opposed to keeping it in the ground.

Fossil Fuels

Nonrenewable fossil fuels, including coal, crude oil, and natural gas, serve a dual role as both consumer goods (for heating, cooking) and as inputs to manufacturing processes. Their significance became magnified with the large price jump during the

TABLE 5–5 Commercial Energy Production (%): 1997					
Region	*Coal*	*Oil*	*Gas*	*Nuclear*	*Electricity*
U.S. and Canada	27	15	30.0	31	31
Europe	18	18	37.5	48	29
Asia (except Middle East) and Oceania	47	12	14.5	19	28
Middle East and North Africa	1	35	11.5	—	4
South and Central America	1	14	5.5	1	6
Sub-Saharan Africa*	6	6	1.0	1	2
Developed Countries	59	35	73	93	72
Developing Countries	41	65	27	7	28
World Production (in million metric tons of oil equivalent)	2,274	3,530	1,917	624	1,200

*Data not given separately. Derived as a residual.
Source: World Resources 2000–01.

energy crisis of the early 1970s. High prices were sustained for awhile by increases in demand and removal of the artificially low prices that the multinational oil companies had set. Previously considered simply a cheap input to production, fossil fuels became looked on as a full-fledged factor of production to be carefully monitored and economized upon.

In this crucial category of fossil fuel resources, world reserves are noticeably uneven. Table 5–5 shows that Africa and Latin America have relatively low production of these resources. A few countries in the Middle East produce over one-third of the world's oil. While Asia outside the Middle East produces almost half of the world's coal, over 60 percent of that comes from China. Table 5–6 shows that consumption is also extremely uneven. The high-income countries and much of Asia consume more than they produce, whereas other regions export much of their production. Saudi Arabia has the world's largest excess reserves, and produces enough oil annually to exceed its energy consumption by a factor of five. On the opposite end, The Gambia, in West Africa, produces no oil or energy of any kind. Per capita consumption of commercial energy is almost 18 times higher in the United States than in South Asia. Commercial energy, mainly coal, oil, and gas, constitutes virtually all energy consumption in industrialized areas but only 36 and 76 percent of all consumption in Sub-Saharan Africa and South Asia, respectively. The remainder include charcoal, firewood, bagasse (waste from sugar cane and beet), and animal and vegetable wastes.

The development of the industrialized countries has involved increasing energy intensity until recently. In fact, until the energy crisis of the 1970s, economists often

TABLE 5-6 Commercial Energy Production and Use: 1998

	Production: Million Tons Oil Equivalent	*Use: Million Tons Oil Equivalent*	*Per Capita Use: Kg. Oil Equivalent*	*Annual Growth Rate Per Capita Use 1980–1998*
Low Income	1,291	1,179	550	2.5
Low-Middle	2,868	2,282	1,116	3.2
High-Middle	1,738	1,127	2,025	1.0
Low and Middle				
East Asia/Pacific	1,447	1,516	857	3.0
Europe/Central Asia	1,380	1,216	2,637	NA
Latin America/Caribbean	831	585	1,183	0.5
Mideast/North Africa	1,237	378	1,344	2.3
South Asia	483	569	445	1.9
Sub-Sahara Africa	517	324	700	−0.5
High Income	3,715	4,757	5,366	1.0
World	9,611	9,345	1,659	0.9

NA = Not Available.

Source: World Development Indicators 2001.

cited increasing energy use per person as an indicator of development. This outlook ended with the quadrupling of oil prices in the early 1970s. In spite of reduction in energy costs over the last 15 years, the more efficient use of energy and lower energy use per dollar of GDP remain goals of government policy in many countries. The 1970s price increases led to conservation and increased the search for additional supplies and the development of alternatives.

Development paths have important implications for energy consumption. It is common to think of ways to conserve energy in production (more efficient machinery) and in consumption (more efficient automobiles and appliances). Before such choices are made, however, it is wise to take energy use into account in deciding what goods to produce. Bauxite reserves may be a powerful incentive to produce aluminum, but the smelting process is extremely energy intensive; therefore, exporting bauxite should be considered as an option. For owners of small plots of land, energy requirements might argue for the use of handheld implements rather than tractors. Natural fertilizers are less energy intensive than chemical-based fertilizers. Bicycles and mass transit make more sense than automobiles for urban traffic.

The Market and Incentives

The case of oil holds a number of lessons for the economic approach to nonrenewable resources. Higher prices in the 1970s performed their economic function: They encouraged consumers to conserve and find substitutes, and they encouraged producers to search—successfully—for additional resources while increasing their rate of output. We know of more oil reserves now than we did at the beginning of the period. And while the price increases of the 1970s caused hardship for economies that depended on imported oil, they also encouraged energy conservation measures and

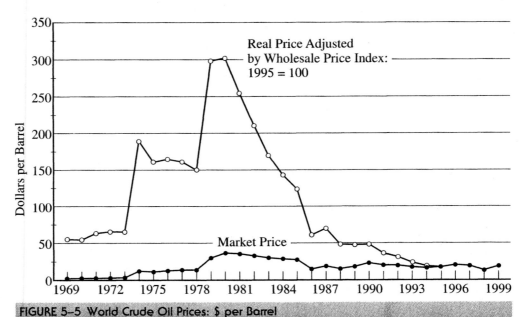

FIGURE 5-5 World Crude Oil Prices: $ per Barrel

World oil prices rose rapidly in the early and the late 1970s, then fell a bit and stabilized through the late 1990s. But when market prices are adjusted for inflation to obtain real prices, it becomes clear that the decline after 1980 was quite dramatic.

Source: IMF/IFS.

brought new income to countries that could find oil in their own territories. Figure 5–5 shows the trend in oil prices over the last 35 years. The decline from the early 1980s is all the more remarkable in real terms: The general level of prices has risen while oil prices have fallen.

This is not to say that we will continually find more of everything. But markets can help in our attempts to use resources wisely as long as they are allowed to signal resource scarcity.

Conflicting Needs: Renewable vs. Nonrenewable Fuels

Wood remains a significant source of household heating and cooking in many developing countries, but its continued use threatens forests and has made it increasingly inaccessible. Four countries—Burkina Faso, Nepal, Malawi, and Tanzania—rely on wood for over 90 percent of their energy consumption. Local depletion increases costs to households, mainly for women who must spend more of their time collecting wood. Unfortunately, the high price of imported oil in the 1970s and growing trade deficits in many developing countries have increasingly thrown poor households back to wood and manure as fuels. But while market pricing of domestic and imported oil and gas should be encouraged to reflect growing scarcity, there is some danger that all fuels will become prohibitively expensive for poor families and governments will be caught in a conflict with no palatable solution.[43]

"INALIENABLE RIGHTS": WATER AND AIR

It is in the use of traditionally "free" goods—water and air—that economics seems at times to collide with fundamental human values. How can we charge poor people for water? How can we allow factories to pollute our air? In fact, human societies routinely do these things. Water rights and prices have been fighting territory all over the world.[44] The value of economic production has been weighed against atmospheric pollution since at least the Industrial Revolution in Britain, and some evidence indicates that pollution from Greek and Roman lead mines drifted up to Sweden as early as 600 B.C.[45] Our objective is to see what light economic theory can throw on these questions and what we can learn from past mistakes.

Water

Water has numerous uses: Households need it for drinking, bathing, cooking, and sewage disposal. It is also essential to agriculture and forms part of many industrial and waste disposal processes. In 1990, more than 1.7 billion people did not have access to safe water and adequate sanitation. About 900 million people per year are afflicted by diarrheal diseases, with more than 3 million deaths, while at any time over 1 billion people are afflicted by worms and parasites from water. Resources are not equally available: Asia has less than 3.7 thousand cubic meters per person of "annual internal renewable (fresh) water resources," Europe about 4.0, and Africa less than 5.2, compared to a global average of 7.0, while the American continents have much more.[46]

Sustainable water use requires cleaning polluted water and not depleting the naturally occurring levels of water availability. Water naturally recirculates through the Earth's environment. Rain and snow penetrate the ground and may be absorbed, used, or run off to where water can evaporate. Very little of the total planetary supply of water is currently available for human use, the rest being in the oceans, ice sheets, and deep ground formations.

Development usually permits nations to invest in clean-water delivery systems, with consequent reduction in disease and reduced time required to bring water from its original source. Unfortunately, growing urbanization with insufficient water treatment has introduced considerable health problems, exacerbated by high population density. Where large cities have major rivers either in or near them, these waterways are used for all sorts of sewage disposal—household and industrial—as well as drinking and bathing for people and animals alike, creating immense health problems.[47] Water treatment may be considered too expensive in many countries.

In China, for example, only 5 percent of household waste and 17 percent of industrial waste were treated in 1996. About half the country's people are estimated to be drinking water that does not meet minimum health standards, leading to infectious diseases, cancers, and birth defects that are several times more prevalent in the more polluted regions than in cleaner ones.[48]

Water *scarcity* is an increasing problem. In many areas people are turning to groundwater as a cheaper source, but even this is expensive and contaminated from industrial seepage. The United Nations estimates that 1.5 billion people use groundwater for drinking.[49] Increasing reliance on groundwater further reduces its availability for agriculture and may even compromise the physical stability of the land. In

Sub-Saharan Africa, rainfall has been significantly below the long-term average for the last two decades, heightening the difficulties there.

Data for groundwater use and recharge, or replacement, are unavailable in many developing countries. But problems are huge in many countries for which data are available. In Libya, Pakistan, Saudi Arabia, and Iran, for example, groundwater use for 1998 was estimated higher than in the United States, due to lack of rainfall. Libya uses five times the amount of groundwater that is replaced, over four-fifths of it for agriculture. Major investments for replenishing water through desalinization have been made only in the wealthier Arab countries of Saudi Arabia, Kuwait, and the United Arab Emirates.[50]

Despite the universality of the need for water, governments must adopt policies that address the allocation of this increasingly scarce resource. The World Bank was late in emphasizing economic management of water resources. A review by the Bank of its own water projects showed that "the effective price charged for water is only about 35 percent of the average cost of supplying it."[51] Agricultural users are generally subsidized, although the value of a cubic meter of water for agricultural purposes is generally among the lowest of all uses. Another source estimates that irrigation projects financed by the World Bank show cost recovery at about 7 percent of the cost. Some critics remain concerned that the Bank's water-pricing principles, adopted in 1993, show little concern for environmental impacts of water usage.[52]

Market principles suggest how any resource may be allocated so as to maximize the total benefits of its use. All resources are presumed to be subject to diminishing marginal utility in a given period of time. Consumers or firms with limited spending power maximize utility from their spending by equating the marginal utility (MU) of the last dollar spent on each resource:

$$\frac{MUx}{Px} = \frac{MUy}{Py}$$

Any resource, such as water, that is priced below its market-clearing equilibrium will be used to a greater extent than would be efficient from the economy's standpoint. Utility-maximizing consumers will use additional amounts with less marginal utility because the price is too low. Raising the price will reduce consumption.

Subsidized water rates for farmers, businesses, or particular groups of consumers encourage use in less valuable ways. Under current conditions in many countries, market pricing of water is an essential step to reduce its use in agriculture and redirect it to urban and industrial users. One source cites a Chinese estimate that switching a given volume of water from agriculture to industry will increase its value by a factor of 60.[53] Market-oriented pricing of water will encourage conservation, compared to subsidized prices. This applies especially to government-owned or -run water systems that are a drain on budgets and do not perform efficiently due to lack of incentives. World Bank studies tend to show that even poor consumers are often willing to pay higher prices for water as long as the delivery system is safe and reliable. A survey of households in Morocco showed that, even with free water available from nearby standposts, families said they would be willing to pay more than 5 percent of their income for in-home water.[54]

Figure 5–6 illustrates the issue. In addition to the demand and supply curves for water, the horizontal line *Pc* shows a government-controlled price for water far below the equilibrium level. While *Qd* is the amount demanded, *Qr* is the available, rationed quantity. The shaded area represents the benefit to consumers of the water they obtain with a utility far above its price. In this case, raising the price to some extent

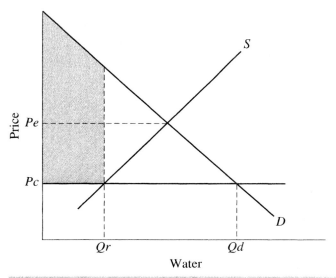

FIGURE 5–6 Impact of Water Subsidies

An initial price (*Pc*) below equilibrium encourages demand, but the small amount available requires rationing (*Qr*). Those farmers who manage to get the limited quantity available receive a large consumer surplus, or utility, indicated by the area between the demand curve and the subsidized price. Raising the price encourages greater efficiency in water use because farmers then have less purchasing power for other inputs. Until the equilibrium price (*Pe*) is reached, the higher price increases the available quantity. Only a price above *Pe* will begin to restrict water use, but it will be used more carefully with each price increase.

would not even reduce the use of water, although once the price reaches the demand curve, any further increases would cut back on use. Higher prices will provide greater incentive to use water efficiently, and an eventual end to bureaucratic rationing would reduce the incentive to bribe public officials for water allocations.

The World Bank's research concludes that the difficulty of establishing ownership rights, significant externalities arising from water use, and the monopoly element inherent in water supply provide a rationale for considering water a public good. Market mechanisms should be supplemented by water- and land-use planning, on the basis of "natural hydrological units such as river basins to ensure that the opportunity costs associated with different water uses are properly considered."[55] One attempt to completely privatize water-use rights shows the problems of going too far. Chile's 1981 Water Code has tried to make all rights to water use privately owned. The problems recognized by the World Bank have meant that, in practice, there is extremely little trading of rights in irrigation, indicating that the market is allocating very little.[56]

The human need for drinking, cooking, and bathing in safe water indicates the importance of going beyond simply allocating available water supplies. Large public investments are needed to obtain, treat, and distribute more water. The price mechanism can direct existing water to its greatest economic value if all social and private benefits and costs are considered, and public expenditures are essential when poor people cannot pay for water that would benefit their own health and the health of the economy.

Even public provision can be prejudicial to the interests of the poor unless specific measures are taken to ensure that the poor have access to the water, whether via irrigation schemes or placement of urban water facilities. Water projects in Burkina Faso tended to favor the wealthy until poor women organized to pressure the government in water allocation. In an attempt to ensure that the poor have access to water, South Africa is experimenting with a law that separates legal rights to land with the legal rights to the water on the land.[57]

The World Bank reports that "only 2 percent of sewage in Latin America is treated,"[58] but spending on improved sanitation has economic benefits and is a classic example of positive externalities and a public good. Clean water supplies for some can improve the health of others by limiting the spread of disease. Healthier people are more productive, increasing their economic contribution. Access to clean water supplies will reduce costs incurred by households trying to compensate for unhealthy water through drilling wells and buying bottled water.

Cleaning up water supplies is expensive. The millions of dollars spent on treating the highly polluted Ganges River in India would not handle the full load, even if all equipment were working full-time. The system must be closed for five months annually due to silt deposits from the monsoons. Hindu custom has contributed to the problem by resistance to charging for holy, and presumably free, water.[59] Still, the health impact of this pollution threatens the sustainability of India's development.

Air

The World Bank estimates that in the mid-1980s, 1.5 billion people, mostly in developing countries, lived in towns or cities that fell short of or only marginally met World Health Organization (WHO) standards for suspended particulate matter (SPM), and in the late 1980s 1.6 billion people lived in urban areas that fell short of or marginally met WHO standards for sulfur dioxide.[60] Air pollution is one of the classic examples of negative externalities. Although the polluting firm is the immediate source of the problem, governments that permit pollution that crosses national boundaries are also free riding to the extent that recipients of the pollution are stuck with the bill. To the extent that much pollution crosses national boundaries, solutions in this area must be global in nature.

The objective of sustaining the supply of clean air must be to keep its components in the proportions necessary for continued human survival: roughly 78 percent nitrogen; 21 percent oxygen; and only 1 percent carbon dioxide, water vapor, and everything else. This conservation has two components: (1) minimizing the encroachment of components such as carbon dioxide, sulphur dioxide, and various particulates on the total and (2) constantly renewing the oxygen supply. Maintaining a proper quantity and pattern of plant life helps maintain the oxygen while soaking up carbon dioxide.

The atmosphere can recycle a certain amount of pollutants, but its carrying capacity is limited; after a certain point these pollutants accumulate with adverse affects on human health and on economic development. Polluting activities range from burning vegetation (small-scale, to clear a field, or large-scale, to clear a forest) through mining and manufacturing activities to the consumption of the needs of daily life such as home fuel and gasoline. The three principal artificial sources are burning of fuel in the home, vehicles, and industrial production.[61]

Human health hazards are evident. Respiratory diseases result from breathing polluted air. Sick people work less and require additional resources to make them well. Children may be less able to learn and work productively. Should they die, they will never contribute to the production of goods after some years of consumption. Vegetation may be killed off by pollution, such as in the case of acid rain, when sulphur oxides combine with the air. Often considered a problem of the industrialized world, air pollution has caused significant damage in Mexico City, as we will see in Chapter 6; Bangkok; Sao Paulo; and numerous Chinese cities.[62]

Governments have used numerous approaches to control air pollution. Standards for factory emissions were early favorites, but the potentially greater efficiency of market allocation is pushing developed countries toward trying pollution-rights markets. In the United States, regional plans have been proposed for the Northeast and Southwest regions, incorporating not only factory emissions but automobiles and other emission sources as well. Developing countries are just beginning to struggle with this difficult problem, but solutions do not have to be exotic. Some progress has been made in reducing urban air pollution in Kathmandu, Nepal, by the introduction of electric minibuses, which run on the same types of batteries that have been used for years to power golf carts in the West.[63]

THE GLOBAL ENVIRONMENT AND MULTILATERAL ACTION

Environmental problems are not confined to their source. Water and air pollution travel. Even relatively confined problems have an impact on more than one country, and when agencies of foreign governments and multilateral lenders finance projects that affect the environment, they must share responsibility for the outcomes. Here we touch on some of the issues of greatest international significance, and give a flavor of how the industrialized countries have responded to environmental issues in the developing world.

Dams

Dams provide a way of regulating the flow of water for agriculture and production of electricity. In the process, they may incidentally create new opportunities, such as fishing and recreation. A dam may have an impact on only one country, if it is the only one downstream from the dam, but frequently regulating the water for one country may actually dry up water supplies for countries farther along the original waterway. Dams have significant environmental and human consequences, and the large size of many of them usually brings other governments or lending agencies into the picture.

The impact of a dam occurs both upstream and down. Above the dam, a reservoir is created, and it may deliberately inundate forests, farmland, and entire villages, as well as change the nature of the soil. Downriver, the remaining water flow may bring with it changes in the amount and composition of soil, changing the nature of the affected agricultural systems.

A classic case of the unintended consequences of dams is the Aswan High Dam in Egypt along the Nile River. In the late 1950s, the U.S. government backed away from the project to protest growing Egyptian friendliness to the Soviet Union. The Soviets then funded the project to solidify their influence with the Egyptian government. It has in many ways been a disaster. Sedimentation (accumulation of earth deposits) in Lake Nasser, created behind the dam, reduced the lake's capacity. This earth would normally have gone downstream to enrich the agricultural areas as it had done for millennia, but it now remains in the lake and has reduced the productivity of the land. Further, this loss of silt causes erosion in the Nile Delta, where the river approaches the Mediterranean Sea, causing significant damage to fishing, only partly compensated for by new fishing in the lake upstream.[64]

On a smaller scale, the Park Mun Dam in Thailand was completed in 1994 after extensive study and consideration of social and environmental impacts. In spite of assurances to the contrary, migrating fish species that provided the basis for the livelihood of villages upstream have been unable to use the "fish ladder" that was to enable them to bypass the dam. Village life is now in a shambles.[65]

The huge Itaipu Dam on the Paraná River in Brazil has been unsuccessfully opposed on the grounds that important indigenous populations would be relocated against their will, in areas dissimilar to the forests that had supported them for centuries. The Indian government plans to go ahead with a large project involving about 160 dams over the next half century on the Narmada River, giving up a $450 million World Bank loan for one component because the proposal failed to meet the Bank's environmental standards. Pressure from local groups has caused numerous changes in plans for this immense project. And China also is moving ahead with its Three Gorges Dam on the Yangtze River, despite opposition from environmental interests. That dam is expected to create a lake 375 miles long "that would inundate several scenic gorges and displace more than 1.1 million people . . . along the river."[66]

This list of problems suggests the need for a comprehensive evaluation of the environmental impact of any project of such magnitude. The result may or may not be to reject the project, but if it goes forward it may require modification to offset the negative externalities. As the case of the Park Mun Dam shows, even this may not be enough. One consequence of these problems is that aid agencies are increasingly reluctant to fund dam projects. Still, in 1996 there were over 800 large dam projects under construction around the world, 183 dams of all sizes in China alone.[67]

As in the case of the Narmada River project in India, China's Three Gorges, and other large dam projects around the world, the international community becomes involved through funding, even if other countries are not affected by the project itself. Lending agencies such as the World Bank and the export credit agencies of national governments must decide whether to provide or withhold funding. The competitive nature of national agencies such as the U.S. Export-Import Bank leads to funding pressure because U.S. firms may lose out to those in other countries if funding is denied. Only coordinated policy can successfully force the borrowing country to consider the environmental impact of large projects if they are not otherwise inclined to do so.

The Ozone Layer

The destruction of atmospheric ozone by chlorofluorocarbons, (CFCs, used for aerosols, refrigerants, and insulation) is a global environmental issue that is primarily of industrialized country origin so far. Depletion of upper-atmosphere ozone concentrations can reduce the Earth's protection against ultraviolet light, with uncertain impacts on plant and animal life, as well as direct harm to humans.

The use of CFCs may spread if goods produced but not saleable in the industrialized countries are exported to developing countries or if alternatives to CFCs are considered so expensive that the developing countries ignore them. The **Montreal Protocol** on Substances That Deplete the Ozone Layer (signed in 1987), although not accepted by all developing countries, is a framework to reduce CFC production and imports. Production was frozen at 1986 levels and was to be decreased by half by 1998. Countries were permitted to ban imports of CFCs, products that contain them, and products that require CFCs in their own production. An amendment in 1990 required the elimination of new CFC production and most other ozone-depleting substances by the year 2000. It is likely that only this kind of intergovernmental cooperation can address problems of international externalities. Some evidence indicates that atmospheric concentrations of ozone-depleting chemicals have been dropping since the protocol was put in place.[68]

Global Warming

Growing carbon dioxide (CO_2) and other greenhouse gas emissions make it more difficult for heat to escape the earth. CO_2 is produced when fossil fuels such as wood, coal, petroleum, and natural gas are burned and the carbon combines with oxygen. Animals also exhale carbon dioxide, although normally plants take it in and release the oxygen. The more fuel we burn, and the more plants we destroy (e.g., tropical forests), the more CO_2 accumulates in the atmosphere. The result could be the warming of the entire planet: **global warming**.

Global warming is a controversial issue. The Earth has gone through warming and cooling cycles before, and as recently as the early 1970s, some scientists were warning of global cooling.[69] Although measurements confirm that warming is occurring on the Earth's surface, it is not clear exactly what contribution humanity's emissions of greenhouse gases makes to the trend. Measurements of worldwide CO_2 emissions from the burning of fossil fuels and manufacture of cement show that the pace increased by a factor of two and a half from 1960 (9.4 billion tons) to 1996 (23.9 billion tons), while atmospheric concentration of CO_2 increased 16 percent to 367 parts per million in 1995. The World Bank is cautious: "Enough is known to discern a threat of climate change from increasing concentrations of greenhouse gases but not enough to predict how much will occur or how fast, the regional distribution of change, or the implications for human societies."[70]

If we would rather be safe than sorry, we should consider that it will be too late if we wait to see what the future holds before taking action to reduce CO_2 emissions. Yet, we are still left with the tricky questions of the costs and benefits of our actions in the face of uncertainty.

Developing countries are concerned with the implications of reducing greenhouse gas emissions. Reducing overall production seems unacceptable even in the industrialized countries. Changing the composition of production may or may not fit their development objectives. Finding ways to produce while using less fuel may be expensive at least initially. But finding solutions is crucial to developing countries. As Table 5–7 shows, while the high-income countries are the largest source of CO_2 emissions both in total and per person, low- and lower-middle-income countries are less efficient, requiring more emissions per dollar of GDP. Note the inverted U pattern of emissions per dollar, peaking in the lower-middle-income countries.

Continued global warming would result in a negative externality on a massive scale. Impeding or reversing it would require at a minimum that all economic activity producing greenhouse gases bear its full cost. This would be difficult to achieve, but a good start would be to ensure that fossil fuels are priced at full market value rather than subsidized. If that is deemed insufficient, then the use of those resources could be

TABLE 5–7 Carbon Dioxide Emissions: 1997

	Emissions in Million Tons	Per Capita Emissions in Tons	Efficiency in Kilograms per PPP $ GDP
Low Income	2,528	1.1	0.6
Low-Middle	6,958	3.4	0.9
High-Middle	3,048	5.5	0.6
Low and Middle			
East Asia/Pacific	5,076	2.8	0.8
Europe/Central Asia	3,286	6.9	1.2
Latin America/Caribbean	1,356	2.8	0.4
Mideast/North Africa	1,114	4.0	0.9
South Asia	1,201	0.9	0.5
Sub-Saharan Africa	502	0.8	0.6
High Income	11,335	12.8	0.5
World	23,868	4.1	0.6

Source: World Development Indicators 2001.

taxed in order to internalize the perceived external costs. The United States and some other oil-producing countries have objected to energy taxes: An attempt to install a tax on all fuels based on their energy ratings failed dramatically in the United States in 1993. Still, many economists suggest that something similar to a BTU tax, such as a carbon-based tax, be imposed nationally or internationally in an effort to force conservation in energy use.[71]

Some developing countries object to measures that would hurt them disproportionately, or even proportionately, given their more fragile economies and their relatively small current contribution to the problem. For example, in 1997, the global per capita emission of CO_2 was 4.1 metric tons, but Africa's contribution was only 0.8 tons per person compared to figures as high as 28.2 in oil- and gas-producing Kuwait, 20.1 in the United States, 15.6 in Norway, and 9.8 for the Russian Federation. Africa is responsible for less than 1 percent of humanity's methane emissions, and Asia, with 59 percent of the world's population, was responsible for only 48 percent.[72] Developing countries would rather see stricter measures taken in the countries that are most contributing to these problems.

In June 1992, at the meeting of the UN Conference on Environment and Development (UNCED) in Rio de Janeiro, a Framework Convention on Climate Change was adopted as a first step in addressing this issue on a global level. The convention focuses on the threat of global warming due to increased emissions of CO_2 and other greenhouse gases, and has as its objective the stabilization of such gases at a level that would preclude climate change induced by human activity. In pursuit of that goal, all governments are committed to do their best to limit emissions. Developed countries have additional commitments, including to apply the deadlines for CFCs in the Montreal Protocol to greenhouse gases, but this commitment is qualified in enough ways to effectively nullify it should any government wish to do so. Developing countries are urged to make what progress they can, and developed countries are to "provide such financial resources . . . needed . . . to meet the agreed full incremental costs of implementing measures" to which a developed and a developing country may agree. In essence, no government has to do anything, and developing-country governments cannot be asked to pay for any steps they agree to take.

Biodiversity

Biodiversity, shorthand for biological diversity, refers to the variety of plant and animal life on Earth. Scientists consider biological (and genetic) variety valuable because life has evolved as a complex system that is protected from local disasters by the adaptability of the system as a whole.[73] The study of ecology shows the interconnectedness of life: The loss of one species may lead to the loss of others. UN data suggest there are 1.7 million known species of plant and animal life and anywhere from 5 to 100 million overall. According to these estimates, one-fourth of all mammal species, one-ninth of bird species, and 6 percent of the estimated tree species on the planet are considered endangered to some extent.[74] And while we may be somewhat insulated from that loss, the continuous loss of species (we do not know how many there are or how many we are losing, but some estimates of loss are in the hundreds per year) reduces this diversity and makes us more vulnerable. Aside from the loss of resources that have potential value of which we are unaware, the reliance on fewer varieties of wheat or trees or fish or livestock increases the vulnerability to pests, disease, and climate change.

Efforts to preserve and enhance biodiversity will clearly require international cooperation. Still, many nations insist that the fate of local animal and plant life is a matter of national sovereignty, so that destroying species or habitats for economic gain is something they should not be denied or, at the least, should be compensated for. The Convention on International Trade in Endangered Species of Wild Fauna and Flora (CITES) is intended to protect certain endangered species, such as the elephant, but those countries with large elephant populations complain that the ban on international trade in ivory does not satisfactorily address the needs of national development and species protection. Some limited exceptions have been approved where elephant populations are proliferating.

The Rio meetings adopted a Convention on Biological Diversity. This convention establishes sovereign rights of a country over its biological resources and encourages national legislation to permit the sharing of the technological fruits and profits of those resources between companies that develop commercial uses and the countries in which the resources exist. Thus, for example, pharmaceutical companies that develop medicines from plant varieties taken from a country would be required—if appropriate legislation existed—to share the benefits with the country. The pharmaceutical company could be required to share its technology, although the convention calls for "adequate and effective protection of intellectual property rights." As in the climate convention, developed-country governments are called upon to provide additional financing for agreed steps taken by developing countries to fulfill the convention's obligations. An international mechanism is called for to provide money to developing countries for the purposes of complying with the convention, but developed-country governments have numerous protections against being forced to pay any particular amount.

As with the climate convention, no specific actions are required of any country in order to preserve biological diversity. No specific requirements are put on governments and private companies, although there is potential for governments to adopt legislation that would compel companies to share in the use of the resources, technology, and money involved in their operations.

Role of the International Community: The World Bank

Environmental protection is clearly an international concern. Conflicts exist between some national development goals and international environmental concerns, between some efforts to develop and efforts to protect the global environment. The existence of significant positive externalities would suggest that developed countries should help finance LDC policies that enhance the environment (conserving forests, maintaining biodiversity).

The World Bank lagged considerably in attending to the environmental impact of development activities. The Bank accepts the claim that it ignored the problem for years and contributed to the problem by ignoring environmental consequences of its projects but claims all this has changed. Now, ". . . the Bank's overall policy on environment is evolving into a two-pronged approach in which rigorous assessment of specific projects is increasingly being complemented by efforts to help governments build environmental concerns into policymaking at all levels."[75]

The World Bank has become more insistent on environmental awareness as a part of its lending requirements. Its parallel commitment to market principles, including market-oriented discount rates for environmental investments, puts it at odds with some environmentalists. And while its engagement in issues of environmental protection is more substantial than just 10 years ago, the Bank recently bowed to the demands from borrowers that a panel, set up to investigate claims of environmental damage from Bank-funded projects, be restricted in its preliminary investigation of those claims.[76]

A prototype Carbon Fund has been established by the World Bank in an effort to encourage investment in projects to reduce greenhouse gas emissions in developing countries. Developed-country firms agree to invest in these projects and receive in exchange credits that can be applied to future CO_2 emission limits as the Bank sets up a framework for trading emission rights. By early 2000, six governments—including Finland, Netherlands, Norway, and Sweden—and 15 companies—including BP Amoco, Shell Canada, and Hydro Quebec—have put $135 million into the fund.[77]

The International Community: From Rio to Kyoto

Concern about the environment has led to a number of international conferences, the most encompassing of which were the meetings in June 1992.[78] The main achievements were adoption of a statement of principles titled the "Rio Declaration on Environment and Development" and a longer document entitled "Agenda 21."

The Rio Declaration on Environment and Development and Agenda 21

The Rio Declaration is a statement of principles about the importance of international cooperation in addressing environmental concerns in the quest for sustainable development. It calls for governments to work toward this goal but imposes no specific requirements on them. The U.S. government, for example, was concerned that the acceptance of development as a right rather than as a goal could be taken to impose obligations on other countries to ensure those rights, and the idea that developed countries had a greater level of obligation in these matters would force the United

States to adhere to much greater obligations than most other countries. So the 27 principles for action in the areas of development and environment are nonbinding.

Agenda 21 outlines the key issues to be confronted in order to achieve sustainable development in the twenty-first century. These include resource management, population growth, health, consumption patterns, and poverty. In spite of its much broader scope and length (over 500 pages), and in spite of some seemingly specific language, Agenda 21 is basically a framework for considering the issue of sustainable development and imposes no requirements on any country. Perhaps the most visible outcome of that document has been local versions of the agenda that have been adopted by towns and villages in a number of countries.[79]

The Rio Summit and Sustainable Development

The documents signed at the Rio Summit amount to little more than statements of principles and objectives, but in the eyes of many they constitute a first step toward more binding agreements for protecting the planet from the potential consequences of unsustainable development. From our standpoint, they are an international affirmation of the concept of sustainable development and a new way of thinking about human progress.

The Kyoto Protocol on Climate Change

In November 1997, a follow-up conference to the Framework Convention on Climate Change was held in Kyoto, Japan, to commit governments to targets for greenhouse gas emissions. A number of governments committed themselves to specific targets, and agreement was reached to establish a mechanism for international trading of emissions rights. Countries are encouraged to help each other by providing assistance. A Clean Development Mechanism is envisioned to support projects to reduce greenhouse gas emissions. Any reduction in emissions in a poorer country can be partially counted as a reduction for the country that provides the assistance. Follow-up meetings were held in Buenos Aires (November 1998) and Bonn (November 1999).[80]

There is considerable controversy in some countries over this agreement, particularly because the developing countries made no commitments to reduce their greenhouse emissions. The U.S. government has signed the treaty but at present does not intend to submit it for ratification. The United States is also suggesting that it should receive credit against CO_2 emissions because its agricultural land and forests have considerable ability to absorb it. There is opposition to the accords from many industries in the United States, and without U.S. participation it is highly unlikely the treaty could be effective.[81]

SUMMARY AND CONCLUSION

The overuse of natural resources, including the land, water, and air, is of only recent concern to economists. Applied to economic development, these problems can be summed up in the goal of sustainable development, devising development strategies that preserve natural capital to the greatest extent possible. How that is achieved requires consideration of the roles of the market and government in the allocation of resources.

History shows us that both poverty and the development process produce pollution. A mass environmental movement arose only in the wake of a significant amount of development, but we cannot wait until developing countries have all developed to spread environmental awareness around the globe. Even if the environmental Kuznets curve exists, it still relies on conscious decisions of individuals, businesses, and governments. For some resources, we probably cannot wait to see if environmental degradation reverses itself automatically.

There need not be an inevitable opposition between the interests of development and the interests of the environment. We do need appropriate standards to guide sustainable development. While it seems clear that the existence of significant externalities makes the unaided market an inadequate guide for the production of public goods and environmentally degrading activities, it is not clear how far government intervention should go beyond internalizing the external costs and benefits of economic activity.

One of our primary concerns is finding mechanisms to guide our use of renewable resources—land, water, and air—and nonrenewables such as minerals and fossil fuels. All resources have alternative uses (including being saved for future use), and in each case the full opportunity cost of any use must be determined as accurately as possible. Even an "inalienable right" to the use of water and air must be qualified by recognition of their scarcity and the need to price them appropriately to permit both their use and maintenance.

People and business firms often have a tendency to be shortsighted in pursuit of their own welfare or profit. Governments can lengthen the time horizons of consumers and producers by appropriate combinations of building and strengthening markets, providing incentives and disincentives to promote more efficient and environmentally sensitive decision making, enforcing standards where necessary, and helping to account as accurately as possible for costs and benefits of public and private activity.

Most environmental problems have an international dimension, either because use of land, water, and air affects other countries or because multilateral agencies provide funding for development projects. The existence of externalities suggests that there should be international cooperation in the process of sustainable economic development.

Key Terms

- arable land (p. 113)
- biodiversity (p. 115)
- common property resources (p. 108)
- controls (p. 108)
- deforestation (p. 115)
- degradation (p. 114)
- desertification (p. 114)
- ecodevelopment (p. 103)
- environmental accounting (p. 99)
- environmental Kuznets curve (p. 101)
- externalities (p. 104)
- free rider (p. 104)
- global warming (p. 129)
- indivisibilities (p. 109)
- marginal social benefit/cost (pp. 104, 105)
- market failure (p. 104)
- Montreal Protocol (p. 128)
- natural capital (p. 99)
- negative externalities (p. 105)
- nonexclusion (p. 109)
- nonrenewable resources (p. 118)
- positive externalities (p. 104)
- public good (p. 105)
- renewable resources (p. 113)
- standards (p. 108)
- sustainable development (p. 100)

Questions for Review

1. Explain the concept of sustainable development. What kind of trade-off might face a country with marketable natural resources in an attempt to grow sustainably?
2. What is a public good, and how are free riders involved? How would you justify education for young women as a public good?

3. What is market failure? In your answer, distinguish between the failure of well-developed markets to work adequately and the lack of adequate markets. What are some environmental consequences of lack of rules governing the use of common land?

4. Explain the concept of externalities with reference to a project to clear large areas of forested hills to provide an outlet for population growth. What impact might this produce on agricultural populations in the valleys? On indigenous people already living in the forest? The soil in the forest?

5. Would you expect a poor society to have a higher or lower discount rate than a wealthier society? Explain.

6. How might a high discount rate "discriminate against" a development project whose environmental benefits are not evident for many years?

 7. How has the government of Taiwan reversed its previous indifference to the environmental consequences of growth?

8. What is an "economic" use of the air? What is the economic justification for putting a price on the use of supposedly "free" goods such as water and air?

9. Why is international action essential to deal effectively with environmental issues such as the ozone layer and global warming? Is environmental protection too expensive for poor countries?

Related Internet Resources

 Environmental issues are big on the Web. A first stop on any search for environmental information is the "Amazing Environmental Organization Webdirectory," at ⟨http://www.webdirectory.com⟩. Additional organizations devoted to environmental issues are the International Institute for Environment and Development, at ⟨http://www.iied.org⟩, and the Worldwatch Institute at ⟨http://www.worldwatch.org⟩.

Sustainable development is now seen by many as the essential reference point for economic activity in all countries. There are numerous Internet sites devoted to the issue, many of which are mainly links to other sites. Some of the private group sites are:

⟨www.greenyearbook.org⟩
⟨esa.sdsc.edu⟩ (Ecological Society of America)
⟨www.ulb.ac.be/ceese/meta/sustvl.html⟩ (the "Virtual Library" for Sustainable Development)
⟨www.oneworld.org/panos⟩

The World Resources Institute is on-line at:

⟨www.wri.org⟩

The United Nations Environment Program and Commission on Sustainable Development are at:

⟨www.unep.org⟩
⟨www.un.org/esa/sustdev⟩

Endnotes and Further Readings

1. See Bryan G. Norton and Michael A. Toman, "Sustainability: Ecological and Economic Perspectives," in *Land Economics* 73, no. 4 (November 1997), pp. 553–568, and Partha Dasgupta and Karl-Goran Maler, "The Resource Basis of Production and Consumption: An Economic Analysis," in Partha Dasgupta and Karl-Goran Maler, *The Environment and Emerging Development Issues,* vol. 1 (Oxford: Clarendon Press, 1997), pp. 1–32.

2. See Carl Zimmer, "The Value of the Free Lunch," *Discover* (January 1998), p. 104, and R. Costanza et al., "The Value of the World's Ecosystem Services and Natural Capital," *Nature* 387 (May 15, 1997), pp. 253–260.

3. See Ernst Lutz and Mohan Munasinghe, "Accounting for the Environment," *Finance and Development* 28, no. 1 (March 1991), pp. 19–21; Salah El Sarafy and Ernst Lutz, "Environmental and Natural Resource Accounting," in Gunter Schramm and Jeremy Warford, eds., *Environmental Management and Economic Development* (Washington: World Bank, 1989), pp. 23–38; and Martin Weale, "Environmental Statistics and the National Accounts," in Dasgupta and Maler, *The Environment and Emerging Development Issues*, pp. 96–128.

4. See Theodore Panayotou, *Green Markets: The Economics of Sustainable Development* (San Francisco: ICS Press, 1993); David Pearce, Edward Barbier, and Anil Markandya, *Sustainable Development: Economics and Environment in the Third World* (London: Earthscan, 1990); the UN-sponsored World Commission on Environment and Development (Brundtland Commission), *Our Common Future* (Oxford: Oxford University Press, 1987); Michael Redclift, *Sustainable Development: Exploring the Contradictions* (London: Methuen, 1987); and John Pezzey, *Sustainable Development Concepts: An Economic Analysis*, World Bank Environmental Paper No. 2 (Washington: World Bank, 1992).

5. For parkland, see John M. Antle and Gregg Heidebrink, "Environment and Development: Theory and Evidence," *Economic Development and Cultural Change* 43, no. 4 (April 1995), pp. 603–626. For air pollution, see Gene M. Grossman and Alan B. Krueger, "Economic Growth and the Environment," *Quarterly Journal of Economics* 110, no. 2 (May 1995), pp. 353–378.

6. J. Timmons Roberts and Peter E. Grimes, "Carbon Intensity and Economic Development 1962–91: A Brief Exploration of the Environmental Kuznets Curve," *World Development* 25, no. 2 (February 1997), pp. 191–198; Xiaoli Han and Lata Chatterjee, "Impacts of Growth and Structural Change on CO_2 Emissions of Developing Countries," *World Development* 25, no. 3 (March 1997), pp. 395–407; and Hemamala Hettige, Mainul Huq, Sheoli Pargal, and David Wheeler, "Determinants of Pollution Abatement in Developing Countries: Evidence from South and Southeast Asia," *World Development* 24, no. 12 (December 1996), pp. 1891–1904.

7. Hemamala Hettige, Muthukumara Mani, and David Wheeler, "Industrial Pollution in Economic Development: Kuznets Revisited," in Per G. Fredriksson, ed., *Trade, Global Policy, and the Environment*, World Bank Discussion Paper No. 402 (Washington: World Bank, 1999).

8. See A. S. Bhalla, ed., *Environment, Employment and Development* (Geneva: International Labour Office, 1992), especially Bhalla, "Conclusion and Future Perspectives," pp. 161–171.

9. H. Jeffrey Leonard, "Environment and the Poor: Development Strategies for a Common Agenda," in Leonard et al., *Environment and the Poor: Development Strategies for a Common Agenda* (New Brunswick, NJ: Transaction Books/Overseas Development Council, 1989), p. 18.

10. Pearce, Barbier, and Markandya, *Sustainable Development: Economics and Environment in the Third World*, p. 69.

11. Robin Broad, "The Poor and the Environment: Friends or Foes?" *World Development* 22, no. 6 (June 1994), pp. 811–822.

12. See Thomas Reardon and Stephen A. Vosti, "Links Between Rural Poverty and the Environment in Developing Countries: Asset Categories and Investment Poverty," *World Development* 23, no. 9 (September 1995), pp. 1495–1506.

13. See, for example, Robert Riddell, *Ecodevelopment: Economics, Ecology, and Development: An Alternative to Growth Imperative* (New York: St. Martin's Press, 1981); Margery Oldfield and Janis B. Alcorn, eds., *Biodiversity: Cultural Conservation and Ecodevelopment* (Boulder, CO: Westview, 1991); and D. Scott Slocombe et al., *What Works: An Annotated Bibliography of Case Studies of Sustainable Development* (Sacramento: World Conservation Union, 1993).

14. See Erlet Cater and Gwen Lowman, eds., *Ecotourism: A Sustainable Option?* (New York: Wiley, 1994); Michael V. Conlin and Tom Baum, eds., *Island Tourism: Management Principles and Practice* (New York: Wiley, 1995); Tensi Whelan, *Nature Tourism: Managing for the Environment* (Washington: Island Press, 1991); Olman Segura-Bonilla, "Ecotourism: A Hope But Not a Panacea," in *Ecological Economics Bulletin* 2, no. 1 (January 1997), pp. 12–13; and Krishna Ghimire, "Emerging Mass Tourism in the South," UN Research Institute for Social Development, Discussion Paper 85 (April 1997). The International Ecotourism Society can be accessed at ⟨www.ecotourism.org⟩.

15. See Tom Tietenberg, *Environmental and Natural Resource Economics*, 5th ed. (Reading: Addison Wesley, 2000) and *Environmental Economics and Policy* (Boston: Addison Wesley Longman, 2001).

16. The following discussion draws on David Pearce, *Economic Values and the Natural World* (London: Earthscan, 1993), pp. 13–17.

17. See Catherine Dold, "Tropical Forests Found More Valuable for Medicine Than Other Uses," *New York Times*, April 28, 1992.

18. Theodore Panayotou, *Green Markets: The Economics of Sustainable Development*, p. 77.

19. See Martin Fenton, *Common Pool Resources and Collective Action: A Bibliography*, vols. 1 and 2 (Bloomington: Indiana University Workshop in Political Theory and Policy Analysis, 1989, 1992).

20. *World Development Report 1992*, p. 73.

21. Kirit Parikh, "Sustainable Development and the Role of Tax Policy," *Asian Development Review* 13, no. 1 (1995), pp. 127–166.

22. See *Economic Instruments for Environmental Management in Developing Countries* (Paris: OECD, 1992), pp. 24–25 and 36, and Gunnar S. Eskeland and Emmanuel Jiminez, "Policy Instruments for Pollution Control in Developing Countries," *World Bank Research Observer* 7, no. 2 (July 1992), pp. 145–169.

23. *Economic Instruments for Environmental Management in Developing Countries*, pp. 36–39.

24. *World Development Report 1992*, pp. 31, 38.

25. See Pearce, Barbier, and Markandya, *Sustainable Development: Economics and Environment in the Third World*, pp. 24–47. A debate on the discount rate is in the March 1993 issue of *Finance & Development* 15, no. 1, in William R. Cline, "Give Greenhouse Abatement a Fair Chance," pp. 3–5, and Nancy Birdsall and Andrew Steer of the World Bank, "Act Now on Global Warming—But Don't Cook the Books," pp. 6–8.

26. See Mohamed Faris and Mahmood Hasan Khan, eds., *Sustainable Agriculture in Egypt* (Boulder, CO: Lynne Rienner, 1993); Vernon W. Ruttan, ed., *Sustainable Agriculture and the Environment* (Boulder, CO: Westview Press, 1992); and Organization for Economic Cooperation and Development, *Agriculture and Environmental Policies: Opportunities for Integration* (Paris: OECD, 1989).

27. H. Jeffrey Leonard, "Environment and the Poor: Development Strategies for a Common Agenda," p. 27. The data are taken by Leonard from the United Nations Environmental Program.

28. See the discussion by Chris Dixon in *Rural Development in the Third World* (London: Routledge, 1990), pp. 38–43.

29. Kevin Cleaver and Gotz Schreiber cite data from Compton Tucker et al., "Expansion and Contraction of the Sahara Desert from 1980 to 1990," in *Science*, no. 253 (1991), pp. 299–301. Their discussion of land degradation in Sub-Saharan Africa is on pp. 21–30 of their *Reversing the Spiral: The Population, Agriculture, and Environment Nexus in Sub-Saharan Africa* (Washington: World Bank, 1994). For the distinction between desertification and degradation in Africa, see Tony Binns, *Tropical Africa* (London: Routledge, 1994), pp. 56–58. For development strategies to reverse desertification, see Jean Eugene Gorse and David R. Steeds, "Desertification in the Sahelian and Sudanian Zones of West Africa," World Bank Technical Paper No. 61 (Washington: World Bank, 1987).

30. World Resources Institute, *World Resources 1992–93* (New York: Oxford University Press, 1992), pp. 112–113.

31. See Avijit Gupta, *Ecology and Development in the Third World* (London: Routledge, 1988), p. 23.

32. See Roger Repetto, "Macroeconomic Policies and Deforestation," in Dasgupta and Maler, *The Environment and Emerging Development Issues*, vol. 2, pp. 463–481.

The paper by Adelman, Fetini, and Golan is "Development Strategies and the Environment," in vol. 1, pp. 161–200. The World Bank's estimate of tropical forest loss is on page 6 of its *World Development Report 1992*. For a good summary of deforestation, see Avijit Gupta, *Ecology and Development in the Third World*, chapter 2.

33. See Dennis J. Mahar, *Government Policies and Deforestation in Brazil's Amazon Region* (Washington: World Bank, 1989). An overview of the issue throughout Latin America is Joseph S. Tulchin, ed., *Economic Development & Environmental Protection in Latin America* (Boulder, CO: Lynne Rienner, 1991).

34. See Tom Rudel and Jill Roper in "The Paths to Rain Forest Destruction: Crossnational Patterns of Tropical Deforestation, 1975–90," *World Development* 25, no. 1 (January 1997), pp. 53–65.

35. Maureen Cropper and Charles Griffiths, "The Interaction of Population Growth and Environmental Quality," *American Economic Review* 84, no. 2 (May 1994), pp. 250–254.

36. William F. Hyde, Gregory S. Amacher, and William Magrath, "Deforestation and Forest Land Use: Theory, Evidence, and Policy Implications," *World Bank Research Observer* 11, no. 2 (August 1996), pp. 223–248.

37. Robert Repetto, "Economic Incentives for Sustainable Development," in Schramm and Warford, *Environmental Management and Economic Development*, pp. 69–86.

38. The Chinese example is from James Kaising Kung, "Equal Entitlement versus Tenure Security Under a Regime of Collective Property Rights: Peasants' Preference for Institutions in Postreform Chinese Agriculture," *Journal of Comparative Economics* 21, no. 1 (August 1995), pp. 82–111. Other cases are reported in Theodore Panayoutou, *Green Markets: The Economics of Sustainable Development*, pp. 20–21 and 118–119. The African study is Cleaver and Schreiber, *Reversing the Spiral: The Population, Agriculture, and Environment Nexus in Sub-Saharan Africa*, p. 8. For cooperative resource management, see Martin Fenton, *Common Pool Resources and Collective Action: A Bibliography*; Elinor Ostrom, *Governing the Commons: The Evolution of Institutions for Collective Action* (Cambridge: Cambridge University Press, 1990); Edella Schlager, William Bloomquist, and Shui Yan Tang, "Mobile Flows, Storage, and Self-Organized Institutions for Governing Common-Pool Resources," *Land Economics* 70, no. 3 (August 1994), pp. 294–317; T. Anderson White and C. Ford Runge, "Common Property and Collective Action: Lessons from Cooperative Watershed Management in Haiti," *Economic Development and Cultural Change* 43, no. 1 (October 1994), pp. 1–43; and Klaus Deininger and Hans Binswanger, "The Evolution of the World Bank's Land Policy," *World Bank Research Observer* 14, no. 2 (August 1999), pp. 247–276.

39. Cleaver and Schreiber, *Reversing the Spiral: The Population, Agriculture, and Environment Nexus in Sub-Saharan Africa*, pp. 68–69.

40. *Ibid.*, pp. 92–93.

41. Repetto, in Dasgupta and Maler, *The Environment and Emerging Development Issues*, pp. 469, 473.

42. *Ibid.*, pp. 463–466.

43. The data on wood dependence are in P. K. Rao, *Sustainable Development: Economics and Policy* (Malden, MA: Blackwell Publishers, 2000), p. 44. Also see Elizabeth Cecelski, "Energy and Rural Women's Work: Crisis, Response and Policy Alternatives," *International Labor Review* 126, no. 1 (January–February 1987), pp. 41–64, and Jane Armitage and Gunter Schramm, "Managing the Supply of and Demand for Fuelwood in Africa," in Schramm and Warford, *Environmental Management and Economic Development*, pp. 139–171.

44. See G. Pascal Zachary, "Water Pressure: Nations Scramble to Defuse Fights Over Supplies," *Wall Street Journal*, December 4, 1997.

45. "Dumping on the Swedes," *Discover* 15, no. 7 (July 1994), p. 16.

46. The health-related data appear in the 1992 *World Development Report*, pp. 47, 49. For water availability, see *World Resources 2000–01*, Table FW–1.

47. See Gupta's brief case study on India's Ganges River, *Ecology and Development in the Third World*, pp. 38–41.

48. World Resources Institute, "The Environment and China: Water and Air Pollution," ⟨http://www.igc.org/wri/china/water.htm⟩.

49. United Nations Environmental Program, *Global Environment Outlook 1997* (New York: Oxford University Press, 1997), p. 4. Also see "The Drying Game," in *Der Spiegel*, May 25, 1992.

50. World Resources Institute, *World Resources 1998–99* (Washington: WRI, 1999), pp. 306–307.

51. *World Development Report 1992*, p. 104.

52. For the cost of recovery estimates, see David W. Pearce and Jeremy J. Warford, *World Without End: Economics, Environment, and Sustainable Development* (New York: Oxford University Press, 1993), p. 176. Criticism appears in P. K. Rao, *Sustainable Development: Economics and Policy*, p. 326.

53. World Resources Institute, *World Resources 1998–99* (New York: Oxford University Press, 1998), p. 189.

54. Alexander A. McPhail, "The 'Five Percent Rule' for Improved Water Service: Can Households Afford More?" *World Development* 21, no. 6 (June 1993), pp. 963–973. For China, see Theodore Panayoatou, *Green Markets: The Economics of Sustainable Development*, pp. 112–113.

55. Cleaver and Schreiber, *Reversing the Spiral: The Population, Agriculture, and Environment Nexus in Sub-Saharan Africa*, p. 191.

56. Carl J. Bauer, "Bringing Water Markets Down to Earth: The Political Economy of Water Rights in Chile, 1976–95," *World Development* 25, no. 5 (May 1997), pp. 639–656.

57. Barbara van Koopen, "Sharing the Last Drop: Water Scarcity, Irrigation and Gendered Poverty Eradication," Gatekeeper Series No. 85, International Institute for Environment and Development (London: 1999).

58. World Bank, *World Development Report 1992*, p. 16.

59. Melissa Everett, "A Sacred, Polluted River Gets Bostonians' Help," *Boston Sunday Globe*, February 23, 1992.

60. *World Development Report 1992*, p. 51.

61. *Ibid.*, p. 50.

62. Theodore Panayotou, *Green Markets: The Economics of Sustainable Development*, cites studies of the economic cost of air pollution in Sao Paulo, pp. 84–85. For Mexico City, see Matt Moffett, "In Mexico City, One Rarely Sees Anything as Lovely as a Tree," *Wall Street Journal*, March 4, 1993, and Gunnar S. Eskeland, "Attacking Air Pollution in Mexico City," *Finance & Development* 29, no. 4 (December 1992), pp. 28–30. An overview is Alan J. Krupnick, "Urban Air Pollution in Developing Countries: Problems and Policies," in Dasgupta and Maler, *The Environment and Emerging Development Issues*, vol. 2, pp. 425–459.

63. For the United States, see Richard W. Stevenson, "Facing Up to a Clean Air Plan," *New York Times*, April 3, 1989, and John J. Fialka, "Clear Skies are Goal as Pollution Is Turned into a Commodity," *Wall Street Journal*, October 3, 1997. For a critique, see Brian Tokar, "Trading Away the Earth," *Dollars and Sense* (March–April 1996), pp. 24–29. Nepal's experiment is reported in Miriam Jordan, "Electric Buses Put to Test in Nepal," *Wall Street Journal*, May 31, 2000.

64. Gupta's case study on the Aswan Dam, pp. 34–35, draws on D. Hammerton, "The Nile River—a Case History," in *River Ecology and Man*, R. T. Oglesby, C. A. Carlson, and J. A. McCann, eds. (New York, Academic Press, 1972).

65. Paul M. Sherer, "Thai Villagers Wish This Dam Was Never Built," *Wall Street Journal*, March 12, 1996.

66. James McGregor, "China Bulldozing Ahead on Dam Despite Opposition," *Wall Street Journal*, January 19, 1993. Also see Lena H. Sun, "In China, the Biggest Thing Since the Great Wall," *Washington Post Weekly Edition*, January 13–19, 1992, and Charles Radin, "Huge Dam May Alter River Forever," *Boston Globe*, August 2, 1993. For the Itaipu Dam, see Roberto P. Guimaraes, *The Ecopolitics of Development in the Third World: Politics and Environment in Brazil* (Boulder, CO: Lynne Rienner, 1991), especially pp. 121–124. For the dam project in India, see Steven A. Holmes, "India Cancels Dam Loan from World Bank," *New York Times*, March 31, 1993, and Joan Davidson and Dorothy Myers, *No Time to Waste: Poverty and the Global Environment* (Oxford: Oxfam, 1992).

67. Eduardo Lachica, "U.S. Aid to Dams Abroad Slows to Trickle," *Wall Street Journal*, March 12, 1996.

68. Amal Kumar Naj, "Chemicals That Destroy Ozone Layer Are Starting to Decline in Atmosphere," *Wall Street Journal*, May 30, 1996.

69. See Robert Root-Bernstein, "Future Imperfect," in *Discover* 14, no. 11 (November 1993), pp. 42–47. A sum-

mary of the evidence on global warming is J. F. Houghton, *Global Warming: The Complete Briefing*, 2nd ed. (Cambridge: Cambridge University Press, 1997).

70. The data are from Worldwatch Institute, *Vital Signs 2000* (New York: W. W. Norton, 2000), p. 67, and World Resources Institute, *World Resources 2000–01*. The Bank's approach is quoted from its *World Development Report 1992*, p. 21.

71. See Bjorn Larsen and Anwar Shah, "Combatting the 'Greenhouse Effect'," *Finance & Development* 29, no. 4 (December 1992), pp. 20–23.

72. *World Resources 1992–93*, pp. 346–49.

73. Two classic expositions of the place of humanity in a complex system are Theodosius Dobzhansky, *Mankind Evolving* (New Haven: Yale University Press, 1962) and Rene Dubos, *Man Adapting* (New Haven: Yale University Press, 1965).

74. United Nations Environment Program, *Global Economic Outlook 2000* (London: Earthscan Publications, 1999), pp. 39–40.

75. *The World Bank and the Environment: A Progress Report—Fiscal 1991* (Washington, 1991), p. 2.

76. Michael M. Phillips, "World Bank Board Agrees to Weaken a Watchdog Panel," *Wall Street Journal*, April 21, 1999.

77. John J. Fialka, "World Bank Emissions-Trading Venture May Expand to Accommodate Interest," *Wall Street Journal*, April 24, 2000.

78. See Michael Grubb et al., *The Earth Summit Agreements: A Guide and Assessment* (London: Earthscan, 1993). A gloomier assessment is a series of articles entitled "International Development and the Environment: Rio Plus Five," in the *Journal of International Development* 9, no. 3 (May–June 1997). Also see Patti L. Petesch, *North–South Environmental Strategies, Costs, and Bargains*, ODC Policy Essay No. 5 (Washington DC: Overseas Development Council, 1992).

79. For the text of Agenda 21, see ⟨www.igc.apc.org/habitat/agenda21⟩.

80. The text of this agreement and other official documents are available at ⟨http://www.unfccc.de⟩, and background information is available from the UN at ⟨http://www.unep.ch/conventions⟩.

81. See John J. Fialka, "U.S. to Argue Its Carbon-Absorbing Forests Should Reduce Need for Emissions Cuts," *Wall Street Journal*, August 2, 2000, and "Kyoto Treaty's Foes in U.S. Could Kill Pact Around the World," *Wall Street Journal*, October 19, 1999; and Andrew C. Revkin, "Bush's Shift Could Doom Air Pact, Some Say," *New York Times*, March 17, 2001.

CHAPTER

6

POPULATION GROWTH AND MIGRATION

As prosperity increases, so do the pleasures
that compete with marriage, while the feeling
towards children takes on a new character
of refinement, and both of these facts tend
to diminish the desire to beget,
and to bear children.

—L. BRENTANO (1844–1931)

INTRODUCTION

Together with natural resources, a country's population determines what a society is capable of producing and how. It is therefore useful to consider the population, together with its productive skills—its **human capital**. In this chapter we discuss population growth and its relationship to development. Is there a population problem? If so, can we expect it to be resolved naturally? Can government policy contribute to its resolution? Can the Earth feed everyone? We then discuss the migration of people from rural to urban areas and its importance for the growth of cities and the labor force.

We will find that population growth is not a major problem in all parts of the developing world: Growth rates are falling in many countries. The availability of food, while not assured worldwide, is often a matter of economic organization rather than global overpopulation. And urbanization, in spite of its contribution to development, has its grim side.

Just as important as the number of people is the quality of the population, determined by its access to health care and education. Economists point to these as some of the more important factors that contribute to a person's ability to work and earn. So in the next chapter we explore access to health care and education. Good health and education enable individuals to succeed, and their absence contributes greatly to poverty.

POPULATION: OLD IDEAS, NEW PROBLEMS

Much contemporary discussion of population views it as a problem: too many people clamoring for too few resources. Although better technology and better organization could more effectively extract and use resources, we often hear that population is growing faster than resources, technology, and organization can handle.

140

Nonetheless, the relationship between population and economic growth varies with time and place. The eminent economic historian Douglass North, for example, stresses the role of population growth in prehistoric times and in the ancient world (roughly up to the fall of Rome, around 400 A.D.) as a stimulus to economic growth and development. Population pressure led to the development of communal property rights that, in turn, permitted settled agriculture and the development of early agricultural technology. North calls population growth "the most fundamental underlying factor in ancient economic history."[1] There were limits, however, and no organizational or technological change saved Europe from the consequences of relative overpopulation in the late fourteenth century. The beginnings of the modern European economy may have begun only after plague wiped out a large portion of the population, leaving land in surplus once again.

The Malthusian Dilemma

The earliest systematic treatment of population—which in the nineteenth century earned economics the unenviable title of "the dismal science"—was the Reverend Thomas Malthus's[2] pessimistic view that in the natural course of events population would grow geometrically, overwhelming the Earth's ability to produce food which increased only arithmetically (Figure 6–1). In the absence of sufficient moral impediments

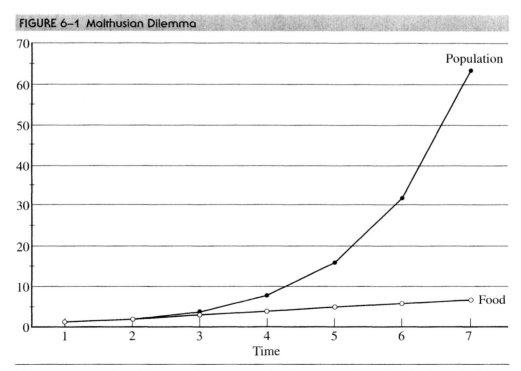

FIGURE 6–1 Malthusian Dilemma

Malthus suggested that while our ability to increase food supplies was limited, following a simple arithmetic progression, population, unless checked, would rise geometrically, resulting in increasing human hardship.

to population growth—later marriage and greater abstinence from sexual activity—the ultimate checks on population would be war and starvation.

However, Malthus was writing at a time when Europe was undergoing significant increases in its population growth rate—from nearly zero in the early eighteenth century to over 1 percent by century's end—and an apparent long-term increase in food prices. The classical economists, such as Ricardo with whom Malthus corresponded, were emphasizing diminishing returns to a fixed supply of land. The Industrial Revolution was just taking off and its full scope was not yet visible. Malthus was extremely skeptical of the fashionable intellectual currents of the time that looked toward the perfectibility of the human race.[3]

Our discussion can confront Malthus from both sides: first the relationship between development and population growth and then the issue of food supply. On the first count, it did not occur to him that economic improvement could actually reduce the demand for children. That possibility forms the basis of the current approach to population, referred to as the demographic transition.

Current Trends

How many people are there, where are they, and how fast is the number increasing? Table 6–1 shows a world population of just under 6 billion people in 1999 (that number was achieved in 2000), and a growth rate of 1.6 percent per year over the 1980 to 1999 period. Table 6–2 shows that by 1999 the growth rate had fallen to 1.3 percent, and the United Nations now estimates the world population could stabilize at 11 billion by the beginning of the twenty-third century.[4]

The major exceptions to declining population growth rates are Africa, the world's poorest region, and the Middle East. A population growth rate of 3 percent per year

TABLE 6–1 Population Growth and Population Size

Countries	Annual Growth Rates Percentage Per Year			Population (Billions)	
	1970–1980	*1980–1999*	*1999–2015**	*1999*	*2015**
Low Income	2.2	2.1	1.5	2.42	3.09
Low-Middle Income	3.5	1.4	0.8	2.09	2.38
High-Middle Income	2.5	1.6	1.0	0.57	0.67
Low and Middle Income					
Sub-Saharan Africa	2.8	2.8	1.9	0.64	0.88
East Asia/Pacific	1.9	1.4	0.8	1.84	2.10
South Asia	2.4	2.0	1.4	1.33	1.68
Europe/Central Asia	4.3	0.6	0.0	0.47	0.48
Mideast/North Africa	2.8	2.7	1.8	0.29	0.39
Latin America/Caribbean	2.4	1.8	1.3	0.51	0.62
High Income	0.8	0.7	0.3	0.90	0.94
World	2.2	1.6	1.1	5.98	7.08

*Projections.

Sources: World Development Report 1994 and *World Development Indicators 2001.*

TABLE 6–2 World Population Estimates

Year	Population (Billions)	Growth Rate (% Per Year)
1	0.30	
1000	0.31	
1250	0.40	
1500	0.50	
1750	0.79	
1900	1.65	0.5 (1750–1900)
1950	2.52	1.0 (1900–1950)
1980	4.44	1.7 (1950–1980)
1990	5.27	1.8 (1980–1990)
1999	5.98	1.3 (1995–1999)
2020	7.50	
2050	8.91	

Sources: J. D. Durand, "Historical Estimates of World Population," *Population and Development Review* 3 (1977), pp. 253–296, and United Nations Population Division, Department of Economic and Social Affairs, "The World at Six Billion," ⟨www.un.org/popin/wdtrends/6billion/toc.htm⟩.

will lead to doubling of population in less than 25 years. Jordan's population grew at 4.1 percent per year over the 1980 to 1999 period, and that of The Gambia grew at 3.5 percent. While China's growth rate of 2.2 percent over 1965 to 1980 diminished to 1.3 percent in the eighties and nineties, the growth rate within Sub-Saharan Africa has remained at 2.8 percent. Total fertility rates in the developing world have been falling from about 6.5 to about 4, but rates in Sub-Saharan Africa have hardly budged.

Some countries' populations are growing so rapidly that a large percentage of the population—40 percent in some developing countries—is under the age of 15.[5] This means that a very large group of people is about to enter its reproductive years as well as the job market.

The Demographic Transition

The rate of population growth is measured as the difference between the **crude birth rate**—the number of births per 1,000 people—and the **crude death rate**—or number of deaths per 1,000. The eventual decline of population growth rates in western Europe and the United States is usually taken as evidence of a **demographic transition**, illustrated in Figure 6–2, in which industrialization leads first to lower death rates and eventually to lower birth rates.

The decline in **mortality**, or death rates, occurs when higher income leads to improvement in the volume and nutritional value of food, along with increased public spending on sanitation, public health, and education. However, in nineteenth-century Europe, higher income and associated food intake played a greater role than in today's developing countries. Today, although incomes are not rising as rapidly, poorer people can still experience declining mortality because improvements in public

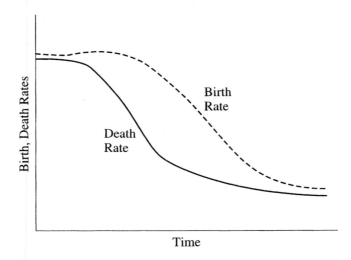

FIGURE 6–2 The Demographic Transition

In all parts of the world, birth and death rates were initially high. Death rates fall first, usually due to improvements in health-related infrastructure and medical advance. Birth rates may actually rise at first as traditional practices and values are abandoned, but soon economic factors lead to declining birth rates.

health disproportionately benefit children under five years of age, who represent a significant portion of the high death-rate group.[6]

Fertility (birth rate) decline is not as easily explained. At the beginning of the transition, birth rates may actually *increase* as traditional methods of limiting births—breast-feeding and temporary abstinence from intercourse after birth—are abandoned before modern contraception methods are adopted. Soon, however, fertility declines, due at least in part to the spread of modern contraception measures and an increase in the age of marriage.[7]

Fertility decline in developing countries now lags behind mortality decline by a longer period than in nineteenth-century Europe.[8] Developing-country populations are therefore growing much faster—at a rate of almost 2 percent per year with some countries in the 3 percent to 4 percent range—than Europe's average of only about 1.5 percent. (At 2.0 percent, population doubles in about 36 years, rather than 47 years at 1.5 percent.) Mortality is dropping faster now, fertility is higher, and the younger age structure of developing-country populations means continued population momentum: Even as birth rates fall, the large cohort of women of childbearing age ensures that population growth rates will not decline immediately. In addition, early Europe could count on more emigration than is permissible today.

Table 6–3 shows that the reality is a bit messier than the smooth curves in Figure 6–2. There are no countries today that really fit the picture of high birth and high death rates. In that sense, the transition has already begun as death rates are falling around the world. But where birth rates remain high and death rates start to fall, such as in many African countries, population begins to grow rapidly. Where birth rates start to fall from nearly 50 per 1,000 to 40 and less, and death rates fall from around 20 per 1,000 to the middle teens, growth rates will slow. But the situation can still become worse if countries make extreme progress in reducing death rates, say to below 10 per 1,000, while birth rates fall much more slowly. Therefore, countries such as Saudi Arabia will have population growth rates on the same level as countries where birth and death rates are much higher.

The demographic transition is accomplished as birth rates fall and death rates stabilize below 10 per 1,000, and the growth rate falls to below 1 percent. Positive aspects

TABLE 6-3 The Demographic Transition: 1999

Stage	Country	Crude Birth Rate	Crude Death Rate	Increase
CBR High	Niger	51	18	33
CDR Falls	Angola	48	19	29
	Malawi	46	24	22
	Rwanda	45	22	23
	Democratic Republic of the Congo	45	15	30
CBR Falls	Tanzania	40	17	23
CDR Falls Slowly	Lao Peoples' Democratic Republic	37	13	24
	Gabon	36	16	20
	Central African Republic	36	19	17
CBR Falls	Saudi Arabia	34	4	30
CDR Falls Rapidly	Honduras	32	5	27
	Paraguay	30	5	25
CBR Falls	Brazil	20	7	13
CDR Stabilizes	Thailand	17	7	10
	China	16	7	9
	United States	15	9	6
	Cuba	13	7	6
	France	13	9	4
	Canada	11	7	4
	Japan	10	8	2
Retrogress	Russian Federation	9	14	−5

Source: World Development Indicators 2001.

of today's situation, such as more effective and available contraception and greater education and other opportunities for women, reduce the desirability of early marriage and children. Still, the extent of our understanding of the transition is limited, and one leading authority concludes that we are unable to predict when a particular country would be ready for it.[9]

There are signs that many countries in Africa are now beginning this transition, but the evidence is mixed and the reasons behind some declining fertility rates are not yet clear.[10] We can, however, see the results of a modern demographic transition in East Asian countries such as Thailand and China. On the other hand, economic and social dislocation, such as has occurred in Russia over the last decade, can lead to negative population growth.

The Asian transition has been associated with not only a slowdown in birth rates but also another key characteristic, a reduction of the **dependency ratio**, or the ratio of nonworkers to the working-age population. The new population grew up to become workers, who added not only to production but also to saving and investment. A recent study estimates that from one-third to one-half of the growth of the East Asian

TABLE 6-4 Dependency Ratios

Country	Population Growth Rate 1980–1999	Dependency Ratio 1999	Percentage Over 65 1998
Saudi Arabia	4.0	0.8	2.8
Niger	3.3	1.1	2.4
Democratic Republic of the Congo	3.2	1.0	2.7
Angola	3.0	1.0	2.9
Tanzania	3.0	0.9	2.4
Honduras	3.0	0.8	3.2
Malawi	2.9	0.9	2.5
Gabon	2.9	0.8	5.7
Paraguay	2.9	0.8	3.4
Rwanda	2.5	0.9	2.0
Lao Peoples' Democratic Republic	2.4	0.9	3.6
Central African Republic	2.2	0.8	3.6
Brazil	1.7	0.5	4.9
Thailand	1.3	0.5	5.3
China	1.3	0.5	6.7
United States	1.1	0.5	12.3
Canada	1.1	0.5	12.3
Cuba	0.7	0.4	9.2
France	0.4	0.5	15.5
Japan	0.4	0.5	16.0
Russian Federation	0.3	0.4	12.2

Source: World Development Indicators 2000 and 2001.

economies over the last three or four decades is due to the lower dependency ratio. By implication, these economies may begin to slow down as the transition proceeds and these workers retire.[11] Table 6–4 shows that slowdowns in population growth rates are accompanied by reduced ratios. At the same time, the composition of the dependent category changes as children become a smaller proportion and people over 65 become a larger percentage of the population. There is some concern that this will lead dependency ratios back up, although there is no clear evidence yet.

A distinction should be made between a large population and rapid population growth. A large *number* of people may or may not be a problem, depending on the availability of resources and the efficiency of their use. Rapid *growth* of population, however, requires that efficiency and income growth must keep improving, just to keep the same level of income per person. Some African economies, for example, do not have large or even very dense populations. But their efforts to develop are made more difficult by the rapid growth of their populations.

The Benefits and Costs of Population Growth

Although concern is often expressed about a negative impact of rapid population growth on development, the case is not that strong for the majority of countries. While the pressure of people on resources *is* critical in some areas where political events and economic policies have caused living standards to deteriorate, a number of studies have reached contradictory conclusions: A major review of the problem concludes that "No consensus has emerged on the effects of the rapid population growth of developing countries on their economic growth."[12]

In the 1960s and 1970s, higher birth and population growth rates had no statistically significant relationship to economic growth. In the 1980s, however, problems emerged. High population growth in some countries incurred heavy costs in a decade marked by extreme economic hardship in many parts of the world. A strongly negative correlation existed between population growth and output growth (although not in the industrialized economies), but this may be due to the circumstances of the world economy and not to population growth. If positive economic growth in the 1990s spreads to some of the rapid population growth countries, we will be less concerned about the impact of population growth on economic growth.[13]

Does Population Growth Stimulate Development?

Since studies seem not to show any consistent relationship between per capita income growth and population growth, we are left with case studies and logical analysis. At one end of the spectrum is the claim that people as the "ultimate resource" are a positive factor in development.[14] A larger population, by earning income, will stimulate demand; in so doing it encourages economies of scale in manufacturing and reduces investment risk. It can encourage technological innovation, promote institutional change, and increase the demand for worker training.

Economist Nancy Birdsall finds little evidence that these things actually occur, except that larger rural populations may at times stimulate the construction of rural infrastructure. These results are more likely to be achieved by appropriate economic policies.[15] Further, the argument for this position ignores the conditions of heavily populated regions where many children die before their fifth birthday, providing none of the incentives suggested by the optimists. Nevertheless, while some negative impact of higher birth and growth rates exist, there are positive impacts as well. Population size and density do seem to stimulate economic activity, and there are lagged effects of higher births: For example, in east Asia, eventually most of those children entered the labor force and contributed to growth.[16]

Does Population Growth Depress Development?

The data give little support to the views of more pessimistic writers. Ansley Coale and others warned in the 1950s that population growth would lead to lower capital intensity of production and reduced labor productivity, large dependency ratios, and lower savings and investment in order to use resources for presumably less productive expenditures on health, education, and other consumption needs.[17]

Evidence from Asia does show that children, especially girls, suffer from large family size, with less food, health care, and education. Inequality within and among countries has worsened due to high population growth, the latter perhaps temporary due to high dependency ratios.[18] But despite some empirical evidence, there are reasons to doubt the more pessimistic conclusions. Like Malthus, some of these writers have downplayed the potential of technology to improve productivity and adapt for a more labor-abundant resource base, and the potential of substitution and market development to reduce pressure on crucial natural resources.[19] They neglected the possible links that run from development to lower fertility. They also may have misunderstood the availability of savings and the investment-like aspects of spending on health and education.

It may seem reasonable to suppose that more people means higher consumption (especially if many die before they contribute much to production) and, therefore, less saving available for investment, hence, less growth. However, there seems to have been little adverse correlation between population growth and savings until the 1980s. Some studies show that poor families with little savings reduce per capita consumption to provide for the extra child. At some income levels, saving may actually increase to provide for the child's future; even more so if parents work more hours. And once the dependency ratio falls, savings rates should actually rise. As for investment, resources diverted to health and education are productive and may even outperform more traditional physical capital investment.[20]

A key unresolved issue is the extent to which rapid population growth brings negative externalities. Additional people put a strain on the environment and on public goods (educational facilities, for example), while their additions to the labor force depress wages and may worsen unemployment and income distribution. On the other hand, when jobs are available at decent wage rates, more adults means more taxpayers to potentially support public goods and government programs to mitigate the negative impact on the environment and income distribution.[21] Study of this question is in its infancy, but the existence of externalities in this area is undeniable.

Why Population Grows Rapidly

Despite the lack of general conclusions, any given country may be concerned about the impact of population growth on its economic development. So it makes sense to investigate the underlying causes of rapid population growth and policies that might slow that growth.

High Birth Rates

In poor countries without significant social security systems, children *are* social security. Families tend to stay in intergenerational units, with the elderly being provided for by their adult children, and even small children are available for work on the farm or in the family firm. Families have more children because the chance of early death is great and because children are often a symbol of prestige and responsible adulthood. These habits and attitudes do not change rapidly when improvements in health bring rapid declines in death rates. Artificial means of controlling birth are not always available and are considered immoral by some people. In a period of rapid population growth, birth rates accelerate because the average age of the female population falls, leading to a larger percentage of the population in the childbearing age group.

Falling Death Rates

We have already noted that improvement in health care infrastructure is a significant factor in lower death rates, but no single factor accounts for declining mortality. It has "occurred as an integral part of overall economic development and improvement of living standards—including better water supply, sanitation, housing, medical services, education, and other social programs."[22]

Why Population Growth Should Slow with Development

Contemporary economic development brings with it access to modern means of contraception. Such devices—mainly condoms, the intrauterine device (IUD), and birth control pills—are made available and in some cases urged on the public. If effectively promoted and used they will help reduce fertility very quickly. But this will occur only if prospective parents are willing to use them, and it is important to understand why this willingness may arise.

The Role of Income

A key economic variable is income. Higher income usually increases the demand for goods and services, and there is some evidence that by itself this income effect increases the desire for children. But the overall impact is usually negative. Parents may substitute fewer children of higher "quality" (health, education, income opportunities) for a larger quantity.[23] In this sense, additional children—say, beyond the second or third—take on the characteristics of what economists call **inferior goods**. (The terminology is unfortunate, especially when applied to children.) These are goods such as lard for cooking and poorer cuts of meat that are purchased by poor people but replaced when higher incomes permit the substitution of better-quality goods. Extra children, who are necessary for contributing to the income of poorer families, are substituted for by greater expenditures on a smaller number of children.

We should also consider the increasing opportunity cost of children. Bearing and raising children is an alternative activity to education, work, and leisure. At higher income levels, the cost of work forgone is higher, and the leisure possibilities are greater, so additional children become less desired. Finally, the cost of raising children increases in modern urban life, providing an additional disincentive. One study of 79 countries demonstrated this link clearly. Lower fertility rates were associated with a higher percentage of women in paid employment, a lower percentage of women working as "unpaid family workers," and lower rates of illiteracy.[24]

In recent years, with increased urbanization and economic hardship in some African countries such as Kenya, Zimbabwe, and Senegal, birth rates are falling for those families that have lost traditional support systems and cannot make ends meet during hard times. High inflation and high unemployment seem to have reduced fertility rates in some African countries.[25]

Higher income brings improved maternal health. This produces healthier babies and lower infant mortality (deaths of children before their first birthday) and child mortality (deaths of children before their fifth birthday), so fewer births are required to obtain the same number of children living to adulthood. Alternative forms of social security become available for the elderly, reducing the need for children as a form of old-age support.

Education of Girls and Women

A crucial additional element in the decision to have children is the education of girls and women. When the benefits of development accrue mainly to males—which has been the case in most countries—fertility patterns do not change much or fertility rates actually rise.[26] In fact, some studies show that educating girls for three or four years actually seems to increase birth rates. The reasons are not clear, but it may be the income effect: Initial improvements in income and health increase the demand for children before a woman can earn enough to increase the opportunity cost of children significantly. Thereafter, however, girls' education is one of the strongest factors that has been found to reduce fertility rates. Some country studies show fertility rates falling 5 to 10 percent for each year of school. Better-educated women die less often, stay healthier, and have healthier children.[27]

In addition to the higher opportunity cost of time for a woman in the modern labor force,[28] women with more than four years of education tend to marry later, use contraceptives more (and more effectively), and acquire a taste for activities other than child rearing. And since child rearing remains overwhelmingly a female undertaking, the impact on fertility of higher educational levels for women is profound.

Government Role in Slowing Population Growth

Most governments embark on family planning efforts with at least initial caution. Even where morally sanctioned, efforts such as sterilization, contraception, and abortion may not be attractive to women and men for a variety of economic, social, and personal reasons. Educational efforts must be carefully designed to convey not only the methods for limiting births but also the reasons. The likelihood of at least some negative externalities to rapid population growth in some countries provides an economic rationale for government action, and family planning seems to be the most direct approach to the perceived threat.

Success and Lessons of Family Planning Programs

In spite of shifting international opinions on population policies, efforts to introduce modern methods of family planning have proceeded rapidly, funded by bilateral and multilateral donors, especially the United States, the World Bank, and the United Nations Population Fund. Although problems are often encountered at the initiation of programs, they have met with considerable success. The UN reports that contraceptive prevalence has increased in developing countries from the early 1960s to the early 1990s from 9 percent to 50 percent, compared to 71 percent in industrialized countries.[29] The world population growth rate declined from about 2.1 percent in the late 1960s to about 1.3 percent in the late 1990s.

Only part of the gains can be attributed to family planning programs; economic development must contribute to the *desire* for family planning before easier access to contraception can be effective. The World Bank, in a series of studies of eight countries, estimated that anywhere from two-thirds to three-fourths of the decline in total fertility (the number of children the average woman will bear in a normal lifetime) was due to increased use of contraceptives and most of the rest to an increase in the age of marriage. But the study estimates that contraceptive *availability* itself can reduce the total fertility rate only from six to four; to reduce the rate to a population-sustaining average of about two, either "strong social and economic change" or a new family planning strategy is required.[30]

The particular facets of social and economic change that most studies point to include the introduction of social security systems to reduce the need for more children to support their parents; a reduction in infant mortality and child labor; and, perhaps most important, an improvement in the educational, occupational, and legal status of women. Women's demand for fewer children becomes effective, and communicated to their husbands, when those children are healthier and women have access to alternative activities.

A number of lessons have been learned from family planning programs. A good personal relationship between program personnel and the target population is essential. Not only is it desirable to be physically close to the people being served, but an understanding of the individuals and their particular family planning needs is crucial in maintaining continued effective contraceptive use once begun.[31] One successful program, in the Muslim-dominated Matlab region of Bangladesh, employed a large number of educated young women to provide personal attention to families in their homes but also profited from the growth of output and employment in the area.[32] All studies have highlighted the necessity of substantial political and financial support for programs, and this is usually evident in high-profile advertising campaigns that promote the typical "modern" family with two children.

The more successful programs are integrated with health programs, especially those aimed at children and mothers. In this way the connection is made between family planning, prevention of sexually transmitted disease, prenatal care, and early intervention to sustain the health of the children that are born. Integration of family planning with overall development strategy is needed so that public resources are allocated, and private incentives shaped, in ways that support decisions to keep families small, such as easing the entry of women into education and the labor force and promoting public and private social security measures.[33] This also helps women win greater cooperation from their husbands.

Finally, attention to societal norms and close cooperation with the general population and civic and religious leaders may overcome significant social barriers to acceptance of contraception and family planning. For example, the disrepute of family planning in India following attempts by Prime Minister Indira Gandhi's government at forced sterilization contrasts with the Matlab program and highly successful efforts in Indonesia to promote family planning in areas with large Muslim populations.[34]

Policy Reversals: Nigeria, Mexico, and China

Governmental resistance to family planning has given way to a sense of urgency for limiting population growth in a number of countries. In Nigeria, for example, high birth rates are encouraged by what a United Nations report called a culture in which "the essence of marriage . . . is to have as many children as possible."[35] Not until the mid-1980s did government policy become more active in the face of significant deterioration of agricultural output and social infrastructure due to **rural–urban migration** and rapid population growth. Even then, plans did not go much beyond expanding formal education, promoting awareness of population as a problem, and supporting family planning efforts.

Mexico, in the 1930s "sought to advance its national objectives through population growth, by encouraging fertility and lowering mortality." By the 1970s, however, the Mexican government adopted an aggressive policy of promoting lower population growth. The ban on sales of contraceptives was lifted, help was provided to families that wanted to practice family planning, and population considerations became integrated into planning for health, education, employment, and public services.[36]

The Chinese government has gone both ways on population policy since the 1949 revolution, beginning somewhat pronatalist, switching to population growth reduction

CASE 6–1

CHINA'S ONE-CHILD POLICY

FAST FACTS

On the Map: Asia

Population: 1.25 Billion

Per Capita GNI and Rank: $780   (142)

Life Expectancy: Male—68   Female—72

Adult Literacy Rate: Male—91%
Female—75%

Perhaps one of the more controversial government campaigns for family planning—aside from India's flirtation with forced sterilization—has been the "one-child" policy of China. In the early 1970s, family planning policy consisted of exhorting people to marry late (the minimum age for marriage is 18), wait at least four years between children, and limit births to two per woman. Since 1974, contraceptives have been free. The one-child policy began after family planning was made part of the Chinese Constitution in 1978. Reducing the number of children per family from two to one was seen as necessary to overcome the population increases of the 1950s and 1960s. Local governments that administered the policy relied at first on persuasion but moved to coercive measures, including occasional forced abortion and sterilization, as well as social pressure. From the beginning, however, the policy has not been enforced among minority populations and has allowed more exceptions in rural areas. The program provided both incentives and penalties. Families with only one child received additional allowances in food and money, preferential treatment for allocation of land (in rural areas) and housing (in urban areas), priority access to medical and educational facilities, and the promise of preference in job assignment when the child became an adult. Also, if the parents promised to have only one

child, the mother received additional paid maternity leave. Once a family went beyond one child, penalties would kick in. There could be salary reductions, additional children might not be covered by public health programs, fines would be levied, the extra allowances granted for the first child were withdrawn, and after the second child the mother would not receive paid maternal leave.

China has had considerable success in reducing both fertility and population growth rates, but the one-child policy does not seem to have been the main cause. The birth rate fell from over 43 per 1,000 in 1963 to 17 in 1996, and population growth rate has fallen from 1.8 percent in the 1970s to 1.3 percent over the period 1980 to 1996. The percentage of births that were the third or later child fell from 50 percent in 1975 to 27 percent in 1981, as the average marriage age for women rose from 19 to 22 and couples spaced their children farther apart. But much of the improvement occurred before the one-child policy was put in place. The birth rate, particularly, fell to 19 per 1,000 by 1976 and has remained fairly stable since then. The policy has been evaded—often with the acquiescence of officials—when the first child was a girl. It would seem, therefore, that economic and social advance, not attempts to restrict births, has been largely responsible for China's progress in reducing its population growth. There have also been more abortions of girls and giving them up for adoption.

In addition, by operating in a cultural context that has favored male babies over female babies, China is now experiencing a worsening deficit in the female population that could have significant negative repercussions. And now it seems that the policy is being relaxed. Rural-urban differences, an aging population, and a concern for the psychology of the "only" children is causing a reduction of vigilance, even as the one-child family is becoming more acceptable for some urban Chinese.

―――――

Sources: United Nations, "Case Studies in Population Policy: China" (New York: United Nations, 1989); Peng Xizhe, *Demographic Transition in China* (Oxford:

Clarendon Press, 1991); *World Development Report 1994* (Washington: World Bank, 1995); Luise Cardarelli, "The Lost Girls: China May Come to Regret Its Preference for Boys," *Utne Reader*, no. 75 (May–June 1996), pp. 13–14; Jiali Li, "China's One-Child Policy: How and How Well Has It Worked? A Case Study of Hebei Province, 1979–88," *Population and Development Review* 21, no. 3 (September 1995), pp. 563–585; Joseph Kahn, "China Eases Up on Its One-Child Policy," *Wall Street Journal*, October 20, 1997; and China Rights Forum, "The Population Policy and Discrimination Against Women and Girls," *China Rights Forum* (Spring 1999), ⟨www.hrichina.org/crf/english/99spring⟩.

shortly thereafter but reversing again during the Great Leap Forward in 1958. The early sixties saw a return to population control policies, only to be overturned during the Great Cultural Revolution of 1966 to 1968. Family planning was reestablished in the 1970s and the one-child policy was inaugurated in 1980.[37] See Case 6–1 for more on China's policies.

POPULATION ISSUES

There are a number of important development-related issues surrounding population. Brief consideration of these issues provides a more complete perspective on the population problem.

AIDS and Population

The spread of Human Immunodeficiency Virus (HIV)/Acquired Immune Deficiency Syndrome (AIDS) has complicated the population issue in those countries, such as Uganda, Zambia, and Thailand, where it is widespread. AIDS raises mortality rates unevenly, with the largest impacts being at birth and between the ages of 20 and 40. It is estimated that by the year 2020, it could be the biggest single infectious killer of that age group in developing countries. It has reduced life expectancy drastically in some countries: by 22 years in Zimbabwe and by 11 years in Burkina Faso and Côte d'Ivoire.

The implications for population are serious. While AIDS will slow population growth rates in some poor countries, this will not be a "solution" in any meaningful sense of the word. By killing working-age adults, including women who have already had several children, it increases dependency ratios, increases the number of orphans, and slows economic growth.[38] We look at AIDS as a health-related issue in Chapter 7.

The Mystery of the Missing Women

Population pressure, combined with the greater earning power of men, seems to have caused a particularly pernicious problem: deliberate death of female babies. Worldwide, estimates suggest that there should be about 102 females for each 100 males, but given longer lives, something seems to be amiss. In the industrialized countries there

DEVELOPMENT SPOTLIGHT 6–1

FEMALE–MALE RATIOS AND MISSING WOMEN

In the original study by Dreze and Sen, about 95 million women were "missing" according to normal female–male ratios. Subsequent studies have revised this number downward, but the problem is still serious.

Region	F–MR	Missing Women (Millions)
Europe	1.050	
North America	1.047	
Sub-Saharan Africa	1.022*	
Southeast Asia	1.010	2.4

Region	F–MR	Missing Women (Millions)
Latin America	1.000	4.4
North Africa	0.984	2.4
West Asia	0.948	4.5
China	0.941	44.0
India	0.933	36.9

*Taken to be the norm.

Source: Jean Dreze and Amartya Sen, *Hunger and Public Action* (Oxford: Clarendon Press, 1989), p. 52.

are about 106 females for every 100 males but only 96 per 100 in the developing countries. When all explanations are put together, estimates of the number of "missing" females are as high as 100 million, as Development Spotlight 6–1 describes: some perhaps simply not counted, but others likely "missing" through more frequent abortions of female fetuses, and infanticide and neglect of female babies. Asia seems to be the major source of the discrepancies: In China and India alone in the early nineties, one source estimates that possibly 52 million females are missing, another estimates 81 million missing in 1986.[39] There is also "considerable evidence that intrafamily divisions often involve very unequal treatments" of food distribution, to the detriment of girls and women, especially in Asia.[40] Slowing of population growth, and improvement in the economic prospects of women, could go a long way to ending this problem.

Population, Food Supply, and Famine

How well did Malthus do on the question of food supply? While his views on population revolved around questions of social theory, his concern about food production seems to have been based on simple extrapolation of historical trends, with little consideration of the possibilities of technological change. Food production has expanded enormously in the last 200 years and, as shown in Figure 6–3, per capita output continues to increase. The trend in per capita grain production was up until 1984 but erratic since then. However, between 1990 and 1998, soybean production has increased by 44 percent while population has increased only 11 percent, and meat and fish production per person have risen somewhat.[41] The distribution of gains is very unequal: In Sub-Saharan Africa, cereal production grew only 60 percent, while population grew by 105 percent.

Much of the debate has moved from one of simply running out of land to quality of the land and the negative impact of the very technologies that were supposed to overcome the limits. Two opposing impacts are the degradation of soils from misuse and population pressure, and the improvement of soil fertility due to improvements in

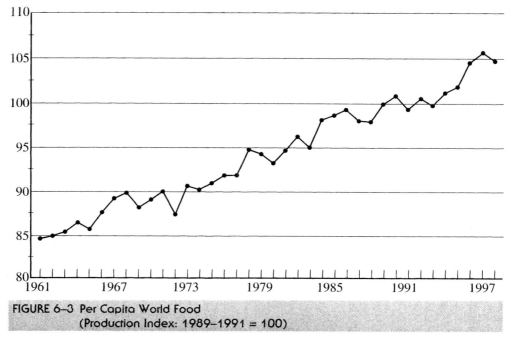

FIGURE 6–3 Per Capita World Food (Production Index: 1989–1991 = 100)

Despite periods of decline, the trend of world food production per person has been clearly up over the last several decades.

Source: UN FAO.

technique and technology. The gains up until now are impressive: During the period 1961 to 1987, world cereals production increased by 102.5 percent, land area increased by only 7 percent; and yields (measured in tons per hectare) improved by 89 percent.[42]

The impact on peoples' lives is difficult to measure accurately. Hunger may be defined as a level of food intake that is insufficient to maintain normal growth, activity, and health. Malnutrition is a chronic or seasonal absence of needed calories and protein from food. One estimate is that the proportion of the world's population that is considered to be hungry fell between 1950 and 1990, from about 23 percent to 9 percent. Another puts the percentage of malnourished, or "chronically underfed," people at 20 percent in 1990, down from 36 percent in 1970, and the absolute number at 786 million, down 190 million since 1975. A more recent estimate from the UN Food and Agricultural Organization (FAO) puts the number of people who are undernourished at an average of 825 million, of whom 791 million were in the developing world—18 percent of its population—over the period 1995 to 1997.[43]

While continuing the pace of food production is important, however, the problem is not simple scarcity of resources but intelligent resource use and providing everyone the ability to earn enough to afford basic necessities, including food. An income distribution that leaves a billion people poor will leave many people hungry despite the overall availability of food. Most recent studies conclude that our *ability* to feed the world well into the twenty-first century is not in doubt, although it is not clear that we will take advantage of that ability.[44]

Finally, we should not confuse the problem of hunger and malnutrition with that of famine. Famines are usually highly localized phenomena that may or may not involve soil degradation and long spells of dry weather but, more often, combine long periods of drought with political events such as civil war that deter either agricultural production or distribution of food from surplus areas, or both. Some of the more spectacular famines in this century—the Ukraine in the 1930s, India in the 1940s, Kampuchea and Bangladesh in the 1970s, and many parts of Africa in recent years—have combined either a history of inappropriate agricultural policies or inadequate channels of food distribution with bad weather and/or war.

For instance, Dreze and Sen, whose research first highlighted the problem of "missing" women, show data for food grain availability in Bangladesh over the 1967 to 1976 period and note that famine was *worst* in the *third best* year of the period. Despite floods, the famine had the most dire effects in many of the districts in which food availability was the highest. Instead, unemployment and disorganized markets caused most of the suffering. And the Independent Commission on International Humanitarian Issues, addressing famines in 1980s Africa, entitled its report *Famine: A Man-Made Disaster?* The answer was in the subtitle: "How Mistaken Policy and Inefficient Management Have Brought Starvation to Africa."[45]

The point is not to disregard the problems of feeding the population of the world. It is to put those problems into their proper sphere: agricultural policy; environmental degradation; and the economic, social, and political determinants of the distribution of incomes and productive assets in the world. The indications are that the simple comparison of people and resources is not the place to look if we are to banish hunger.

THE POPULATION POLICY DEBATE

Concern over the causes and consequences of population growth has engaged the international community for at least 40 years. In addition to the ongoing activities of the United Nations and the World Bank, there have been special World Population Conferences (now International Conferences on Population and Development) every 10 years since 1954: the first one that year in Rome, a second in Belgrade in 1965, followed by Bucharest in 1974, Mexico City in 1984, and Cairo in 1994. But divisions have plagued these conferences, with government positions changing substantially.[46]

While the Rome conference was of only academic interest to many, the Belgrade conference marked the first significant awareness of, and interest in, this problem for most of the developing countries. Still, as the 1960s and 1970s witnessed significant North–South differences in many areas of development policy, the Bucharest conference in 1974 involved conflict between a strong U.S. government interest in family planning programs and a suspicion among a number of developing countries that the West was simply interested in limiting the growth of nonwhite populations. That conference adopted an approach that emphasized development rather than population restraint.

Positions had reversed by the time of the Mexico City conference in 1984. By then, most developing countries had become convinced of the danger of rapidly growing populations and were engaged in numerous efforts to reduce fertility. In the United States, however, political winds had shifted away from government involvement, and there was particular sensitivity to any program that might show leniency toward abortion rights.[47] The United States eliminated support for the United Nations Population Fund due primarily to its association with the Chinese family planning programs, which are widely believed to involve coerced abortions. The United States reversed course again in 1993 to allow support for programs such as the UN Population Fund, but this was reversed again in 2001.[48]

The Cairo conference approved a broad "Program of Action" that focused on strengthening families, promoting sustainable development and gender equity, and improving health care, including the integration of family planning and health services for women and children. The program also called for paying special attention to adolescents in order to reduce early births and action in the areas of the environment and urbanization. As with the Rio conference on the environment, no specific commitments were required.[49]

State of the Academic Debate

Most economists now believe that Malthus went too far: Although rapid population growth can put pressure on economic development, does have environmental implications, and does lead to certain social stresses, economic development can also moderate population growth so there is no *necessary* conflict between the two. There is not likely to be a consensus on any maximum or optimum population for the planet, although many accept the proposition that ultimately a stable population level is necessary.

In some poor regions, population growth does put pressure on resources. This pressure is particularly intense in many African countries. It certainly makes life difficult at the individual and household level where fertility remains high. But technological change, improved education, economic and social opportunities, and attention to both markets and externalities open the way for continued economic progress without the inevitable threat of overpopulation.[50]

POPULATION SHIFTS: INTERNAL MIGRATION AND URBANIZATION

Rapid population growth is usually accompanied by population shifts: People migrate from rural areas, where economic prospects seem stagnant or less secure, to urban areas, where prospects seem brighter. In all countries economic advance tends to be accompanied by increasing concentration of populations in cities, or **urbanization**. Industrial cities such as Manchester, England, produced some of the more difficult living conditions in the nineteenth century, as well as some of the more evocative literature (Charles Dickens's *Hard Times*, for example) and worker protest of the period. In today's developing countries, urbanization is running much further ahead of the supporting infrastructure than was the case 150 years ago. It is a problem of massive proportions and getting worse. Many countries are urbanizing at rates of 3 percent to 6 percent per year, whereas in industrializing Europe the pace was 1 percent to 2 percent per year.[51] To understand this phenomenon, we now look at urbanization and informal labor markets.

The Urbanization Trend

Table 6–5 provides data on the trend of urbanization. Urbanization has increased among all country income groups, but the trend has slowed in the industrialized countries while upper-middle-income countries are approaching industrialized-country proportions. Much migration in low-income countries is initially intrarural: Rapidly rising populations are not immediately followed by intensification of land use but by the search for new land. Increasingly, men leave the land for work in the cities, sometimes followed by their families. Eventually, migration will become intraurban, although this does not replace rural-urban migration.

The problem is particularly acute in Latin America, where the population is now over 70 percent urban, matching the proportions of Europe and North America. In many African and Middle Eastern countries, rapid migration is taking place even without industrial development, which raises concerns for those economies' ability to provide jobs.[52] In the lowest-income countries, including Nigeria, India, and China, the trend is mitigated somewhat by the increase in the *number* of cities and the relatively low portion of the population living in cities of 1 million or more people. Still, estimates of rural-urban migration in China run as high as 100 million people between 1979 and 1994.[53]

In many developing countries however, while urbanization is proceeding at about the same pace as in nineteenth-century Europe, *city* growth is more rapid. (See Development Spotlight 6–2 for more on this subject.) The difference is that in these countries a more rapidly growing population has combined with other factors to draw—and keep—people into a relatively smaller number of rapidly growing cities, heightening the difficulties of dispersing development evenly throughout a country. Part of this is due to urban-urban migration, a much less well studied phenomenon.

TABLE 6–5 Percentage of Urban and Large City Population

Income Group	Percentage Urban		Percentage in Large Cities*	
	1980	1999	1980	1995
World	39	46	14	16
Low Income	24	31	7	10
Low-Middle Income	31	43	14	17
High-Middle Income	64	75	24	29
Low and Middle Income				
East Asia/Pacific	22	34	9	12
Europe/Central Asia	59	67	14	16
Latin America/Caribbean	65	75	24	28
Mideast/North Africa	48	58	17	21
South Asia	22	28	6	10
Sub-Saharan Africa	23	34	5	8
High Income	75	77	30	32

*Cities of at least 1 million.

Source: World Development Indicators 2001.

DEVELOPMENT SPOTLIGHT 6–2

MAJOR DEVELOPING-COUNTRY CITIES

Major cities in the developing world are rapidly becoming the largest cities in the world. The largest developing-country cities and their populations (in millions) are shown below according to their ranking in 1999, along with the largest developed-country cities in the latest ranking.

City	1950	1975	1999
Tokyo, Japan			26.4
Mexico City, Mexico	3.1	11.2	17.9
Bombay, India	2.9	6.9	17.5
Sao Paulo, Brazil	2.4	10.0	17.5
New York City, U.S.			16.6
Los Angeles, U.S.			13.0

City	1950	1975	1999
Shanghai, China	5.3	11.4	12.9
Lagos, Nigeria		3.3	12.8
Calcutta, India	4.4	7.9	12.7
Buenos Aires, Argentina	5.0	9.1	12.4
Dhaka, Bangladesh		2.2	11.7
Karachi, Pakistan		4.0	11.4
Delhi, India		4.4	11.3
Osaka, Japan			11.0
Beijing, China	3.9	8.5	10.8

Sources: United Nations, *World Urbanization Prospects: The 1994 Revision* (New York: 1995) and *The 1999 Revision*, ⟨www.un.org/popin/wdtrends/urbanization.pdf⟩.

Consequences of Urbanization

One of the most commonly suggested problems of large urban areas in developing countries is mass unemployment. While data are notoriously unreliable, it appears that there is little widespread, open unemployment in the cities.[54] What is more difficult to determine is the extent of **disguised unemployment**, or **underemployment**; that is, people working below their qualifications and producing less than the social value of their wage or income. The extended family operates here as well. Much of the apparently low-productivity employment of the urban informal sector—personal services—may not be disguised unemployment, because wages do reflect productivity; children as well as adults bustle around the cities, selling whatever goods they are able to obtain or whatever services are deemed desirable.

The increasing migration of women makes this picture more complicated. Probably more than half of women who migrate on their own do so in search of jobs, but they tend to be more isolated and more vulnerable to economic conditions than men. They are more likely to end up in informal jobs with low wages and no job security. Increasing numbers resort to prostitution, and some are virtually imprisoned and sold either domestically or internationally.[55]

Living conditions are very difficult in many urban areas. Land scarcity makes rents high, causing crowding among the poor. Pressure on urban and other local government budgets leaves inadequate resources to construct and maintain infrastructure, while lack of environmental controls makes much urban living dangerous to one's health. The advantages of industrial concentration quickly become the disadvantages of pollution and traffic congestion. Mexico City, described in Case 6–2, makes an excellent example, and while extreme, it serves as a warning to others.[56] In Lagos, Nigeria, city growth puts extreme strain on infrastructure, as demonstrated by bottleneck

CASE 6–2

MEXICO CITY

FAST FACTS

On the Map: North America

Population: 97 Million

Per Capita GNI and Rank: $4,440 (72)

Life Expectancy: Male—69 Female—75

Adult Literacy Rate: Male—93%
Female—89%

One of the largest, and probably most polluted, cities in the world is Mexico City, where more than 16 million people live and work, along with about 35,000 businesses and anywhere from 3 to 4 million automobiles and other vehicles. At an altitude of 7,300 feet, the city's atmosphere has about a 23 percent lower level of oxygen than is normal for breathing and burning fuel efficiently. The water supply is being rapidly exhausted (causing the ground to sink almost 1 foot per year in some places), with 20 percent of the city's supply being pumped in from outside the region.

The city is spreading physically, absorbing about 1,000 hectares of agricultural land and 700 hectares of forest every year. Immigration, mostly from rural areas, leads to occasional "invasions" of people who take up residence on state-owned lands: These can occur so swiftly that the squatters are known as *paracaidistas*, or parachutists. When the government has acknowledged these settlements by legitimizing them, the land has risen in value and middle-class residents force out the initial migrants, renewing the search for land.

The city creates 12,000 tons of garbage and 2,500 tons of hazardous waste per day, along with the waste from countless animals. "Snow" falls regularly as the residue from a nearby caustic soda plant. In 1990, atmospheric emissions measured 4.4 mil-

lion tons, more than three-fourths of which was from cars, buses, and trucks. About 30 percent of the residents have no sewerage service, and much of the existing service simply dumps sewage onto the ground and into the water: The Rio de los Remedios has been described as "a thick venomous stream of black sludge." In the winter, when atmospheric inversions are common, most days record ozone pollution well above internationally recognized danger marks: In mid-March of 1992, a pollution emergency caused the government to mandate a 70 percent reduction in production.

Piecemeal regulation before 1985 attempted to locate production of energy outside the metropolitan area, reduce the sulfur and lead content of refined petroleum products, and reduce the number of cars on the road. Since the 1985 earthquake, the government has attempted to make greater use of natural gas (rather than crude oil) in producing energy, add detergent to gasoline, and reduce emission standards for vehicles and industry. An integrated program in 1990 has involved fuel quality improvement; more efficient public transportation; better industrial pollution controls; reforestation and restoration of open land and dumping sites; and increased research, education, and communication in industrial areas.

This precarious situation reaches crisis proportions under abnormal conditions. A spate of wildfires in southern Mexico in early 1998 brought ozone readings to a level of 251, where 100 is harmful and 200 is considered dangerous. According to one estimate, almost one-third of the city's population suffered serious health problems, with doctor and hospital visits in the first five months up 20 percent over the same period a year earlier.

Sources: Rhona Mahoney, "Mexico City's Water Crisis," *E Magazine* 1, no. 5 (September/October 1990), pp. 17–18; Ellen M. Brennan, "Urban Land and Housing Issues Facing the Third World," in John D. Kasarda and Allan M. Parnell, eds., *Third World Cities: Problems, Policies, and Prospects* (Newbury Park, CA: Sage Publications, 1993), pp. 74–91; Stephen P. Mumme, "Clearing the Air: Environmental Reform in Mexico," *Environment* 33, no. 10 (December 1991), pp. 6–11, 26–30; Mark A. Uhlig, "Mexico City: The World's Foulest Air Grows Worse," *New York Times*, May 12, 1991; J. Garfias and R. Gonzalez, "Air Quality in Mexico City," in David A. Dunnette and Robert J. O'Brien, eds., *The Science of Global Change: The Impact of Human Activities on the Environment* (Washington: American Chemical Society, 1992), pp. 149–161; and "No Relief for Mexico's Air Pollution Crisis," ⟨www.cnn.com/WORLD/americas/9805/26/mexico.smog.pm/⟩.

traffic, frequent power outages, uncontrolled sewage disposal, clogged drainage systems, and the like. If economic activity cannot be more evenly dispersed, and if governments cannot provide adequate infrastructure, city environments will deteriorate.

The Push and Pull of Migration

Economists and demographers have long discussed rural-urban migration in terms of **push** and **pull** factors.[57]

Push refers to the deterioration of conditions in rural areas, including increasing population, lower incomes, and displacement due to construction of dams or incentives to develop forested areas. Even the good news, increases in agricultural productivity, exerts a push when fewer people are required to produce more food. This is often exacerbated by increasing concentration of land ownership. For example, a study of 16 Latin American countries showed that migration is higher when rural areas are dominated by large landholdings along with many small farms.[58] Pull refers to the attractions of the urban areas. Cities may provide more efficient environments for economic activity due to their concentrations of people. They generally offer higher-paying jobs, wider economic and social opportunities—a primary benefit of development—and a more sophisticated environment. Urban growth can be a positive factor in a country's development. In Delhi, India, during the 1970s, immigrants worked twice as many days and earned more than twice the income compared to the rural areas they had left. A survey of 22 countries in the late 1980s found infant and child death rates typically lower in urban areas, often by wide margins.[59]

On the other hand, perceptions of the pull factors may outrun the reality, so migration may continue long after the urban labor market has ceased to expand, and long after deteriorating living conditions make life more confining and restrictive than in the rural areas. There may not be education for the children or access to medical care or affordable food.

Jeffrey Williamson's review of the literature indicates that the wage gap between city and countryside (often 40 percent or more) is the main factor motivating rural–urban migration, and that, in fact, the gap tends to be *larger* than the migration stream would predict. Noting that "urbanization does not seem to have outpaced industrialization in the Third World since 1950," he concludes that, according to economic theory, cities are too small: The observed wage gap should draw larger numbers of people than in fact migrate to the cities. Nonetheless, urbanization can be a problem when city populations outgrow the ability to support themselves.[60]

TABLE 6–6 Distribution of Labor Force

Countries/ Year	More Developed			Latin America			Asia			Africa		
	Ag	*In*	*S*	*Ag*	*In*	*S*	*Ag*	*In*	*S*	*Ag*	*In*	*S*
1950	35	32	32	54	19	27	82	7	11	83	6	11
1960	27	36	38	49	20	31	76	10	15	80	7	13
1970	17	38	45	42	22	36	71	13	17	76	9	15
1980	12	37	51	34	25	41	66	15	19	69	10	21
1990	9	33	58	25	24	51	62	17	21	63	11	26

Ag = Agriculture.

In = Industry.

S = Services.

Source: International Labor Organization, *Economically Active Population (1950–2010)*, vol. V, World Summary (Geneva: ILO, 1996), pp. 109–118.

Rural–Urban Migration and Informal Labor Markets

One of the more significant issues of urbanization is the formation of labor markets. Table 6–6 shows that every region is experiencing a shift in employment from agriculture to industry and services; this generally implies a similar shift from rural to urban locations. And while population growth still accounts for most of city growth, the source and nature of the labor force are important questions for an understanding of how urban development proceeds.

Urban labor markets can be considered as consisting of two submarkets, called **formal** and **informal sectors**.[61] Development Spotlight 6–3 shows the contrast between the two markets. A key to this distinction is the degree of government regulation. The formal labor market consists of jobs in large, often more capital-intensive firms. It is subject to numerous government regulations, often minimum wage and pension laws,

DEVELOPMENT SPOTLIGHT 6–3

FORMAL VS. INFORMAL MARKETS

Although the boundaries often blur, the following may best illustrate the distinctions between the formal and informal markets.

Category	Formal	Informal
Entry	Difficult	Easy
Resources	Local/Foreign	Local
Ownership	Corporate	Family
Scale	Large	Small
Factor Intensity	Capital	Labor
Technology	Imported	Adapted
Training	Formal education	Informal education, experience
Markets	Often protected	Competitive, unregulated

Source: Adapted from Alan Gilbert and Josef Gugler, *Cities, Poverty and Development: Urbanization in the Third World*, 2nd ed. (New York: Oxford University Press, 1992), p. 96, adapted from the International Labor Organization.

conditions of employment, and perhaps rules with respect to hiring and firing. The informal market, including most self-employment and small, family run firms with labor-intensive methods, is assumed to operate largely outside these restrictions. We will consider the question of informal markets in greater detail later, but here we concentrate on their connection to labor migration.

Figure 6–4 illustrates some of the interaction between these labor markets. The market-clearing wage is expected to be higher in the formal market due to higher productivity. However, this gap is widened by the government-imposed minimum wage (Wmf) that reduces formal employment. The displaced workers spill over into the informal sector, increasing the supply and lowering the market wage (Wi_2).

The role of rural migrants in these markets was modeled first by Todaro and Harris.[62] They suggested migration from rural areas to cities was based not on an actual wage gap but the difference between rural wages and an *expected* urban wage: multiplying the actual urban formal-sector wage by the probability of obtaining a job indicated by the rate of employment in the urban labor force. This approach recognizes that a key benefit of moving to the city—higher income—is not guaranteed and that the possibility of not getting a job represents a cost of moving, in addition to what the migrant gives up by leaving. If urban unemployment rates rise, the probability of gaining a job falls, and presumably migration would slow. As long as this expected urban wage exceeded the rural wage, migration would continue, even if some migrants did not immediately find jobs in the formal sector. Those who did not were likely to enter the informal sector at a lower wage (perhaps little more than the rural wage), thus serving as a pool of labor available to fill formal-sector jobs.

FIGURE 6–4 Wages in the Formal and Informal Sectors

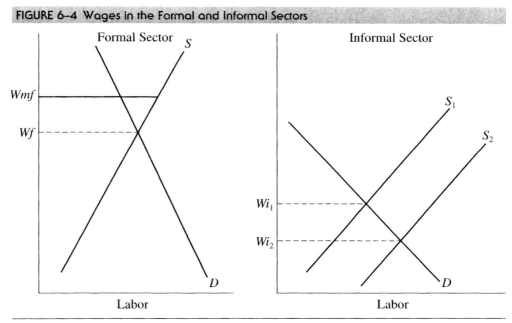

A minimum wage (Wmf) in the formal sector causes some unemployment, increasing the supply of labor in the informal sector and pushing wages down (Wi_2).

The reality is a bit more complicated. Some rural-urban migration is intentionally temporary: Migrants come to earn some money and return to the rural areas, as was typical of much migration in earlier decades. On the other hand, some informal workers are formal-sector workers who have saved enough to start their own businesses. Some workers hold jobs in both sectors simultaneously or move back and forth. At least one study has found that wages are higher in the informal sector.[63]

Characteristics of the informal labor force are in part determined by their origin. Thai migrants, often from the better-off sectors of the rural areas, have good educations and move easily from informal to formal jobs. Migrants in the Philippines, however, are largely from the poorer part of the rural population and remain confined to the informal sector on arrival in urban areas.[64]

In addition, many rural migrants have connections and move directly into positions in the formal sector. The costs of migration are significant: The migrant loses the benefits of home and income in the area of origin, must pay to get to the city and set up, and may find living difficult and expensive there. So permanent migrants may not gamble on a move without some assurance that a job awaits them. A study of Bombay, India, in the early 1970s showed that 90 percent of migrants obtained help from relatives and friends: Two-thirds received free room and board; two-thirds of blue-collar workers and one-third of white-collar workers got help in finding a job.[65] Such help significantly reduces the cost of migration and so helps to encourage it.

In fact, it is not any easier for an informal worker to penetrate the formal sector than it would be for a rural worker. Formal-sector hiring is conditioned by union rules, family relations, and employer preferences. Hiring is often determined by specific characteristics of workers such as their education, experience, and gender. A study of El Salvador, while noting more mobility for male than female workers, shows that conditions are better in the formal sector and stability is again rewarded. Men who move into the formal sector receive higher earnings, while moving back to the informal sector tends to lower earnings. Women have less mobility and less of an earnings differential between the two sectors, although formal jobs tend to be better. They make less money than men in both sectors.[66]

One critic of the Todaro–Harris model suggests that it was developed under the influence of the early stages of African urbanization in the late 1960s. At that time, economic expansion was rapid, expectations were high, and jobs were being created rapidly. Under current conditions, when major urban problems have emerged and urban unemployment is high, a model of rapid labor turnover may be inappropriate.[67] Todaro has recently suggested that migrant behavior is based on a longer-term perspective: Because migrants are young, they calculate the probability of succeeding in the city over a period of years. This accounts for continued rural-urban migration even while urban unemployment is high and short-term prospects seem bleak.[68]

Is There a Solution?

Urbanization is a complex phenomenon. While some large urban populations could be better supported with additional investment and better organization, without these the urban environment can threaten human well-being and sustainable development. The natural reaction to poor urban conditions is to want to improve them. Unfortunately, as widening highways has helped encourage more traffic, it is likely that increasing the benefits of migration by improving the urban environment will increase costs as well by attracting more capital, more labor, and more difficult conditions. So while improving urban conditions will continue to make a claim on resources, it will also be necessary to create new centers of economic activity and to refurbish old ones by improving the conditions of rural life.

INTERNATIONAL MIGRATION

The migration of people to foreign countries is a more complex situation, where push variables include not only the usual economic ones but political repression as well. A "best" guess of the number of migrants outside their own country in 1985 was 100 million, of whom over half were within the developing world. Such data are notoriously unreliable, as indicated by estimates for the number of refugees in 1993 ranging from 19 to 43 million.[69]

From an economic perspective, a key pull variable can again be seen as an expected wage that exceeds the current wage.[70] The perceived benefits may be more accurately assessed than previously as better communication between countries makes it easier to obtain information about job prospects, and more companies are now recruiting overseas. Improved communication and lower transportation costs also make the relocation process cheaper, as well as returning home if things do not work out.

For developing countries, emigration can mean the loss of relatively educated and skilled labor: the **brain drain**. The positive side is that the pressure on labor markets is eased: One estimate is that emigration from Pakistan drew off one-third of labor force growth between 1978 and 1983. Emigrants may be a significant source of income in the form of **remittances** to families at home, accounting in some cases for as much as 10 percent of GDP and 30 percent of the value of imports, with considerable variation from year to year. By one estimate, net transfers of this sort to developing countries amounted to $31 billion in 1989, two-thirds of the previous year's foreign aid. They played a major role in alleviating poverty in the Philippines, for example.[71] To the extent that migrants return, they will bring improved skills and new standards of health, education, and consumption.

The negative side, of course, is the loss of skilled labor, generally in short supply. Data are hardly precise, but a number of studies in this area are indicative:

- A 1970 study estimating that developing countries "were losing between 20 percent and 70 percent of their annual output of doctors" to the developed countries
- A study estimating the lost value of Indian technical personnel at $51 billion over the period 1967 to 1985
- A study showing that between 1974 and 1978 the proportion of foreign-born scientists and engineers in the United States rose from 5.8 percent to 10.5 percent, with the major sources being India, Britain, Taiwan, Poland, and China[72]
- A 2000 estimate that more than half of India's engineering graduates each year go to the United States, and of every 1,000 professionals to leave India, only 1 or 2 return[73]

The United States gives preference to certain types of workers, based on employer needs. In 1998, the United States admitted over 660,000 immigrants, although about half were already here and adjusted their status. As Europe and Canada accounted for only 100,000, most were from developing countries, including almost a quarter of a million from Mexico, China, India, and the Philippines. Although the available data do not identify which occupations come from which countries, the United States "imported" almost 4,000 doctors and over 4,000 other health care professionals in 1998, many of them from developing countries. Studies show that for most developing countries, migrants are disproportionately those with at least some college education.[74]

In some countries, political refugee flow has begun to be overwhelming. While Tibetan refugees are a small drop in the bucket of the Indian population, the tide of refugees that sometimes spills over from ethnic conflict in Burundi into Tanzania is a serious drain on a very poor country. International assistance has been of some help, but the adjustment problems of some permanent refugees remain serious.

The extent of our knowledge of the impact of migration on development is quite small. More study is required to take us beyond concerns about the brain drain to more detailed conclusions about that impact.

SUMMARY AND CONCLUSION

Economists have debated the relationship between population growth and economic advance for 200 years. Neither of the more extreme positions—that population growth must inevitably restrict economic growth or the more the merrier—has been borne out. For many countries and during many periods of history, the growth of population and per capita income have gone hand in hand, and this is true for many developing countries today. On the other hand, continued *high* rates of population growth, combined with failure to increase productivity and to put constraints on environmental damage, are a cause for concern in many countries. Governments play a role in making available the means to reduce population growth, although such means are not likely to be chosen voluntarily unless economic conditions make them desirable. Improved economic opportunity for women can reduce the desirability of large families, and family planning programs can make the means of prevention available for those who want them.

Globally, the production of food has more than kept up with population growth until recently. Still, the potential exists to feed a much larger population than now exists. Hunger may be best approached by looking at economic development generally rather than at food production per se. Famines tend to be the results of bad weather combined with political problems such as civil war, and inadequate infrastructure that prevent available food from being distributed.

A number of developing countries are experiencing rapid urbanization. While conditions in many cities are harsh, perceptions of improved economic opportunities bring millions into the cities and keep most of them there. People are attracted to cities by the belief that better jobs and better conditions are available. Once there, the distribution of labor between formal and informal markets is affected by the availability of jobs and different income-earning possibilities.

International migration is a complicated process resulting from a number of push and pull factors. It has the disadvantage of removing a number of often well-educated people from a country's population but often is the source of foreign exchange from remittances.

Key Terms

- brain drain (p. 165)
- crude birth rate (p. 143)
- crude death rate (p. 143)
- dependency ratio (p. 145)
- demographic transition (p. 143)
- disguised unemployment (p. 159)

- fertility (p. 144)
- formal sector (p. 162)
- human capital (p. 140)
- inferior goods (p. 149)
- informal sector (p. 162)
- mortality (p. 143)

- push/pull (p. 161)
- remittances (p. 165)
- rural–urban migration (p. 151)
- underemployment (p. 159)
- urbanization (p. 157)

Questions for Review

1. What was the basis for Malthus's predictions of overpopulation? What factors did he neglect?
2. Describe the "demographic transition," and explain what distinguishes the present transition in developing countries from the transition in Europe over 100 years ago.
3. If country A has 20 million people in the year 2000, with population growth of 1 percent, and country B has 10 million people, growing at $3\frac{1}{2}$ percent per year, which will have more people in the year 2025? 2050? Assuming other factors are equal, in which country would you rather live?
4. Is population growth a problem in developing countries today? What economic factors are relevant to this question?
5. What factors determine the "demand for children?" What kinds of economic change might alter that demand?
6. What economic factors limit the effectiveness of government-sponsored family planning programs?
7. Has China's one-child policy been effective in reducing population growth rates? Explain.
8. Distinguish between "push" and "pull" factors in rural-urban migration.
9. You are currently working on a farm in rural India, earning 22,000 rupees per year (about $500). Word comes that someone with little skill could earn 55,000 rupees per year in the city, but the chances of getting such a job are only 40 percent. Moreover, you do not know anyone in the city who can help, so your initial costs will be high. What would be a rational decision on whether to migrate?
10. What problems have been associated with the rapid urbanization that has been taking place in Mexico City?
11. What characteristics distinguish "formal" from "informal" activities in urban areas of developing countries?
12. Is there a global food shortage? What criteria might we use to determine the answer to this question?
13. What is the role of education in changing fertility patterns?

Related Internet Resources

The United Nations, through its United Nations Development Program, tracks population data and makes projections for different scenarios involving low, medium, and high rates of growth. Look for its work at ⟨www.undp.org/popin/popin.htm⟩. Data on population, urbanization, and related issues are at ⟨www.un.org/popin/wdtrends/⟩. The issue of food sufficiency and hunger is addressed by numerous groups. Try the work of the World Hunger Program at Brown University: ⟨www.brown.edu/Departments/World_Hunger_Program⟩. Data on food production are available from the UN's Food and Agricultural Organization at ⟨http://apps.fao.org/⟩. The general FAO Web site is useful for a variety of food-related issues, including hunger: See ⟨www.fao.org/⟩.

Endnotes and Further Readings

1. Douglass North, *Structure and Change in Economic Theory* (New York: W. W. Norton, 1981), p. 109.
2. Thomas R. Malthus, *An Essay on the Principle of Population*, edited by Anthony Flew (Baltimore: Penguin Books, 1970).
3. See W. W. Rostow, *Theorists of Economic Growth from David Hume to the Present* (New York: Oxford University Press, 1990), pp. 53–54, and Gary L. Peters and Robert P. Larkin, *Population Geography*, 6th ed. (Dubuque, IA: Kendall-Hunt, 1999), pp. 89–91.
4. Population data are available from the United Nations Web site, at ⟨http://www.un.org/popin/wdtrends⟩.
5. Allen C. Kelley, "Economic Consequences of Population Change in the Third World," *Journal of Economic Literature* 26, no. 4 (December 1988), p. 1691.
6. *Ibid.*, pp. 1689–1690, and Nancy Birdsall, "Economic Approaches to Population Growth," in Hollis Chenery and T. N. Srinivasan, eds., *Handbook of Development Economics*, vol. 1 (Amsterdam: Elsevier Science Publishers, 1988), pp. 481–482.
7. John Bongaarts, "The Transition in Reproductive Behavior in the Third World," in Jane Menken, ed., *World Population and U.S. Policy* (New York: W. W. Norton, 1986), pp. 106, 117.
8. Peters and Larkin, *Population Geography*, pp. 95–100.
9. John C. Caldwell, "The Soft Underbelly of Development: Demographic Transition in Conditions of Limited Economic Change," Proceedings of the World Bank Annual Conference on Development Economics, 1990 (Washington: World Bank, 1991), p. 210.
10. Matthew Lockwood, "Development Policy and the African Demographic Transition: Issues and Questions," *Journal of International Development* 7, no. 1 (January–February 1995), pp. 1–23, and Barney Cohen, "The Emerging Fertility Transition in Sub-Saharan Africa," *World Development* 26, no. 8 (August 1998), pp. 1431–1461.
11. David E. Bloom and Jeffrey G. Williamson, "Demographic Transitions and Economic Miracles in Emerging Asia," *World Bank Economic Review* 12, no. 3 (September 1998), pp. 419–455.
12. Nancy Birdsall, "Economic Approaches to Population Growth," p. 483. Also see Allen C. Kelley, "Economic Consequences of Population Change in the Third World," p. 1715.
13. Allen C. Kelley and Robert M. Schmidt, "Population and Income Change," World Bank Discussion Paper No. 249 (Washington: World Bank, 1994).
14. See Julian L. Simon, *The Ultimate Resource* (Princeton: Princeton University Press, 1981).
15. Nancy Birdsall, "Economic Approaches to Population Growth," pp. 491–493.
16. Robin Barlow, "Population Growth and Economic Growth: Some More Correlations," *Population and Development Review* 20, no. 1 (March 1994), pp. 153–165.
17. Ansley J. Coale and Edgar M. Hoover, *Population Growth and Economic Development in Low-Income Countries* (Princeton: Princeton University Press, 1958).
18. Satish C. Jha, Anil B. Deolalikar, and Ernesto M. Pernia, "Population Growth and Economic Development Revisited with Reference to Asia," *Asian Development Review* 11, no. 2 (1993), pp. 1–46, and Edmund J. Sheehey, "The Growing Gap Between Rich and Poor Countries: A Proposed Explanation," *World Development* 24, no. 8 (August 1996), pp. 1379–1384.
19. See Stephen D. Mink, "Poverty, Population, and the Environment," World Bank Discussion Paper No. 189 (Washington: World Bank, 1993).
20. Nancy Birdsall, "Economic Approaches to Population Growth," pp. 494–495, and Allen C. Kelley, "Economic Consequences of Population Change in the Third World," pp. 1705–1709.
21. See Ronald D. Lee and Timothy Miller, "Population Growth, Externalities to Childbearing, and Fertility Policies in Developing Countries," Proceedings of the World Bank Annual Conference on Development Economics 1990, pp. 275–304, and the critical comments of Marthe Ainsworth, pp. 305–308. Also see Nancy Birdsall, "Government, Population, and Poverty: A Win–Win Tale," in Robert Cassen et al., *Population and Development: Old Debates, New Conclusions* (New Brunswick, NJ: Transaction Publishers/Overseas Development Council, 1994), pp. 253–274.
22. *The World Bank and the Environment: A Progress Report—Fiscal 1991* (Washington: World Bank, 1991), p. 19.
23. Nancy Birdsall, "Economic Approaches to Population Growth," pp. 505, 516.
24. For an investigation of sociological variables, see Victor S. D'Souza, *Economic Development, Social Structure, and Population Growth* (New Delhi: Sage Publications, 1985). The study was carried out by the World Resources Institute and summarized in Partha Dasgupta, *An Inquiry into Well-Being and Destitution* (New York: Oxford University Press, 1995), p. 308.
25. Stephen Buckley, "Taking a New Line on Families," *Washington Post Weekly Edition* (May 4, 1998).

26. T. Paul Schultz, "Human Capital Investment in Women and Men: Micro and Macro Evidence of Economic Returns," International Center for Economic Growth Occasional Paper No. 44 (San Francisco: ICS Press, 1994), p. 25.

27. "Why Invest in Girls' Education," ⟨www.girlseducation. org/PGE_active_pages/GirlsEdResources/ EconandSocialDev/WhyInvest/b-right/asp⟩.

28. The term "modern labor force" hides numerous difficulties. If we seek to increase the opportunity cost of having children, women's employment must be sufficiently desirable to overcome customary roles. Earnings must be sufficiently high and conditions sufficiently attractive so that women are not expected to work *and* bear the usual number of children. I owe this insight to a former student, Amanda Quintal.

29. United Nations, *Population Policies and Programmes*, "Experience of 20 Years: Achievements and Challenges," p. 96.

30. World Bank, "Population and the World Bank: Implications From Eight Case Studies" (Washington: World Bank, 1992), p. 6.

31. See George B. Simmons, "Family Planning Programs," in Jane Menken, *World Population and US Policy* (New York: W. W. Norton, 1986), p. 195.

32. John Caldwell, "The Soft Underbelly of Development: Demographic Transition in Conditions of Limited Economic Change," p. 223. See also James F. Phillips, Ruth Simmons, Michael A. Koenig, and J. Chakraborty, "Determinants of Reproductive Change in a Traditional Society: Evidence from Matlab, Bangladesh," part 1, *Studies in Family Planning* 19, no. 6 (1988), pp. 313–334, and John Cleland, James F. Phillips, Sajeda Amin, and G. M. Kamal, *The Determinants of Reproductive Change in Bangladesh: Success in a Challenging Environment* (Washington: World Bank, 1994).

33. For an example of problems, see the report on *Integrating Development and Population Planning in India* (New York: United Nations, 1992).

34. In addition to the UN and World Bank articles mentioned earlier, see Rodolfo A. Bulatao, "Family Planning: The Unfinished Revolution," *Finance & Development* 29, no. 4 (December 1992), pp. 5–8. For Indonesia, see "Indonesia Slows Population Growth," *Boston Globe*, September 28, 1993, and Ines Smyth, "The Indonesian Family Planning Program: A Success Story for Women?" *Development and Change* 22, no. 4 (October 1991), pp. 781–805.

35. United Nations, "Case Studies in Population Policy: Nigeria," Population Policy Paper No. 16 (New York: United Nations, 1988), p. 22.

36. United Nations, "Case Studies in Population Policy: Mexico," Population Policy Paper No. 21 (New York: United Nations, 1989), p. 15.

37. United Nations, "Case Studies in Population Policy: China," Population Policy Paper No. 20 (New York: United Nations, 1989).

38. Lyn Squire, "Confronting AIDS," *Finance & Development* 35, no. 1 (March 1998), pp. 15–17, and "An Introduction to HIV/AIDS," ⟨www.worldbank.org/aidsecon/ toolkit/intro.htm⟩.

39. Ansley J. Coale, "Excess Female Mortality and the Balance of the Sexes in the Population," *Population and Development Review* (September 1991), cited in Irene Sege, "The Grim Mystery of World's Missing Women" *Boston Globe*, February 3, 1992. For revised estimates, see Stephen Klasen, " 'Missing Women' Reconsidered," *World Development* 22, no. 7 (July 1994), pp. 1061–1071.

40. For Asia, see Jean Dreze and Amartya Sen, *Hunger and Public Action* (Oxford: Clarendon Press, 1989), p. 51. The Africa case is more controversial. See also Kevin Cleaver and Gotz Schreiber, *Reversing the Spiral: The Population, Agriculture, and Environmental Nexus in Sub-Saharan Africa* (Washington: World Bank, 1994), p. 88; Peter Svedberg, "Undernutrition in Sub-Saharan Africa: Is There a Gender Bias?" *Journal of Development Studies* 26, no. 3 (April 1990), pp. 469–486; and the debate between Stephen Klasen, "Nutrition, Health and Mortality in Sub-Saharan Africa: Is There a Gender Bias?" and Svedberg, "Gender Biases in Sub-Saharan Africa: Reply and Further Evidence," in *Journal of Development Studies* 32, no. 6 (August 1996), pp. 913–943.

41. Crop production, yield, and trade data for most crops and most countries can be obtained at the UN Food and Agricultural Organization Web site, ⟨http://apps.fao.org/⟩.

42. Most of the data on production, area, and yields are from Stephen D. Mink, "Poverty, Population, and the Environment," pp. 20, 22.

43. The percentages of hungry people are estimates from the World Hunger Project at Brown University, reported by Charles A. Radin, "Proportion of World Hungry Is Down, Geographers Say," *Boston Globe*, August 16, 1992. The data on chronically underfed come from the UN Food and Agriculture Organization, reported by Liz Young, *World Hunger* (London: Routledge, 1997), pp. 27–28. The statistics on the undernourished are from FAO, *The State of Food and Agriculture 1999* (Rome: FAO, 1999). The World Hunger Program can be accessed through ⟨www.brown.edu/Departments/ World_Hunger_Program⟩.

44. See Vaclav Smil, "How Many People Can the Earth Feed?" *Population and Development Review* 20, no. 2 (June 1994), pp. 255–292; John Bongaarts, "Population Pressure and the Food Supply System in the Developing World," *Population and Development Review* 22, no. 3 (September 1996), pp. 483–503; and a review of several recent books by D. J. Shaw, "World Food Security: The Impending Crisis?" *Development Policy Review* 15, no. 4 (December 1997), pp. 413–420.

45. Jean Dreze and Amartya Sen, *Hunger and Public Action*, pp. 27–29. Independent Commission on International Humanitarian Issues, *Famine: A Man-Made Disaster?* (New York: Vintage Press, 1985).

46. See Kaval Gulhati and Lisa M. Bates, "Developing Countries and the International Population Debate: Politics and Pragmatism," in Robert Cassen et al., *Population and Development: Old Debates, New Conclusions* (New Brunswick, NJ: Transactions Publishers/ Overseas Development Council, 1994), pp. 47–78, and "Evolution of Population Policy Since 1984: A Global Perspective," in United Nations, *Population Policies and Programs*, pp. 27–41.

47. See Steven A. Holmes, "Clinton Seeks to Restore Aid for Family Planning Abroad," *New York Times*, April 1, 1993.

48. "Restoration of the Mexico City Policy," news release from the White House, January 22, 2001.

49. "Program of Action" of the 1994 International Conference on Population and Development (New York: United Nations, 1994).

50. See Robert Cassen, "Population and Development: Old Debates, New Conclusions," in the book of the same title, pp. 1–26, and Kevin Cleaver and Gotz Schreiber, *Reversing the Spiral: The Population, Agriculture, and Environmental Nexus in Sub-Saharan Africa*.

51. Reeitsu Kojima, "Introduction: Population Migration and Urbanization in Developing Countries," *The Developing Economies* 23, no. 4 (December 1996), pp. 349–369. The data cited here are on p. 356.

52. *Ibid.*, p. 353.

53. Lena H. Sun, "The Dragon Within: The Flood of Migrants to the Cities Is Threatening China's System," *Washington Post National Weekly Edition*, October 17–23, 1994. Also see "In China's Cities, Growth Takes Its Toll: Residents Are Forcibly Moved to Outlying Areas," *Wall Street Journal*, December 22, 1993; Keiko Wakabayashi, "Migration from Rural to Urban Areas in China," *The Developing Economies* 28, no. 4 (December 1990), pp. 503–523; and Guang Ha Wan, "Peasant Flood in China: Internal Migration and Its Policy Determinants," *Third World Quarterly* 16, no. 2 (June 1995), pp. 173–196.

54. Jeffrey G. Williamson, "Migration and Urbanization," in Hollis Chenery and T. N. Srinivasan, eds., *Handbook of Development Economics*, vol. 1 (Amsterdam: Elsevier Science Publishers, 1988), p. 447.

55. United Nations, *Women in a Changing Global Economy*, 1994 World Survey on the Role of Women in Development (New York: United Nations, 1995), p. 67.

56. See Adrian Guillermo Aguilar, Exequiel Ezcurra, Teresa Garcia, Marisa Mazari, and Irene Pisanty, "The Basin of Mexico," in Jeanne X. Kasperson, Roger E. Kasperson, and B. L. Turner II, eds., *Regions at Risk: Comparisons of Threatened Environments* (Tokyo: United Nations University Press, 1995), pp. 304–366; Peter Ward, *Mexico City: The Production and Reproduction of an Urban Environment* (Boston: G. K. Hall and Company, 1990); and Nigel Harris and Sergio Puente, "Environmental Issues in the Cities of the De-

veloping World: The Case of Mexico City," *Journal of International Development* 2, no. 4 (October 1990), pp. 500–532.

57. See Jeffrey G. Williamson, "Migration and Urbanization," pp. 425–465, and alternatively, Alan Gilbert and Josef Gugler, *Cities, Poverty and Development: Urbanization in the Third World*, 2nd ed. (New York: Oxford University Press, 1992).

58. Cited in Josef Gugler, "The Urban–Rural Interface and Migration," in Gilbert and Gugler, *ibid.*, p. 64.

59. These studies are cited in Gugler, "The Urban–Rural Interface and Migration," pp. 64, 67. Also see Eduardo Lachica, "Study Links Asia Megacities' Growth, Host Countries' Economic Performance," *Wall Street Journal*, November 6, 1995. The virtues of cities as centers of development and culture are outlined in great detail by Jane Jacobs, *Cities and the Wealth of Nations* (New York: Vintage Books, 1985), and *The Death and Life of Great American Cities* (New York: Vintage Books, 1992).

60. Jeffrey Williamson, "Migration and Urbanization." Also see Insan Tunali, "Migration and Remigration of Male Household Heads in Turkey: 1963–1973," *Economic Development and Cultural Change* 45, no. 1 (October 1996), pp. 31–68; Donald Larson and Yair Mundlak, "On the Intersectoral Migration of Agricultural Labor," *Economic Development and Cultural Change* 45, no. 2 (January 1997), pp. 295–320; and Nanda R. Shrestha, "A Structural Perspective on Labour Migration in Underdeveloped Countries," *Progress in Human Geography* 12, no. 2 (June 1988), pp. 179–207.

61. This distinction, and the term "informal" were introduced by K. Hart, "Informal Income Opportunities and Urban Employment in Ghana," *Journal of Modern African Studies* 11, (1973), pp. 61–89.

62. Michael Todaro, "A Model of Labor Migration and Urban Unemployment in Less Developed Countries," *American Economic Review* 59, no. 1 (March 1969), pp. 138–148, and J. R. Harris and Michael Todaro, "Mining, Unemployment, and Development: A Two-Sector Analysis," *American Economic Review* 60, no. 1 (March 1970), pp. 126–142. Also see Gary S. Fields, "Rural–Urban Migration, Urban Unemployment and Underemployment, and Job-Search Activity in LDCs," *Journal of Development Economics* 2, no. 2 (June 1975), pp. 165–187; Jeffrey G. Williamson, "Migration and Urbanization," pp. 445–448; and Dipak Mazumdar, "Microeconomic Issues of Labor Markets in Developing Countries: Analysis and Policy Implications," Economic Development Institute Seminar Paper No. 40 (Washington: World Bank, 1989), pp. 57–60.

63. See Douglas Marcouiller, Veronica Ruiz de Castilla, and Christopher Woodruff, "Formal Measures of the Informal-Sector Wage Gap in Mexico, El Salvador, and Peru," *Economic Development and Cultural Change* 45,

no. 2 (January 1997), pp. 367–392, and Gustavo Yamada, "Urban Informal Employment and Self-Employment in Developing Countries: Theory and Evidence," *Economic Development and Cultural Change* 44, no. 2 (January 1996), pp. 289–314.

64. Toru Nakanishi, "Comparative Study of Informal Labor Markets in the Urbanization Process: The Philippines and Thailand," *The Developing Economies* 34, no. 4 (December 1996), pp. 470–496.

65. Josef Gugler, "The Urban–Rural Interface and Migration," p. 70.

66. Edward Funkhouser, "Mobility and Labor Market Segmentation: The Urban Labor Market in El Salvador," *Economic Development and Cultural Change* 46, no. 1 (October 1997) , pp. 123–153.

67. Josef Gugler, "The Urban–Rural Interface and Migration," pp. 72–73.

68. Michael P. Todaro, *Economic Development*, 7th ed. (Reading: Addison Wesley Longman, 2000), pp. 307–308.

69. These estimates and the summary that follows are from Michael S. Teitelbaum and Sharon Stanton Russell, "International Migration, Fertility, and Development," in Cassen et al., eds., *Population and Development: Old Debates, New Conclusions*, pp. 229–252.

70. See Sharon Stanton Russell, "International Migration: Implications for the World Bank," HCO Working Paper 54, ⟨www.worldbank.org/html/extdr/hnp/hddflash/workp/wp_00054.html⟩, pp. 4–6.

71. *Ibid*, pp. 8, 10. See also M. G. Qibria, "Migrant Workers and Remittances: Issues for Asian Developing Countries," *Asian Development Review* 4, no. 1 (1986), pp. 78–99.

72. Ian Smillie, *Mastering the Machine: Poverty, Aid and Technology* (Boulder, CO: Westview Press, 1991), p. 81.

73. Henny Sender, "Soaring Indian Tech Salaries Reflect the Country's Brain Drain," *Wall Street Journal*, August 21, 2000.

74. The U.S. data are from the Immigration and Naturalization Service, Office of Policy and Planning, Statistics Branch, *Annual Report* (Washington: May 1999). The latest report can be accessed over the Internet through ⟨www.ins.usdoj.gov/⟩. For the educational level of migrants to the United States, see William J. Carrington and Enrica Detragiache, "How Extensive Is Brain Drain," *Finance & Development* 36, no. 2 (June 1999), pp. 46–49.

7

HUMAN CAPITAL: HEALTH AND EDUCATION

*Man is the most versatile of all
forms of capital.*
—IRVING FISCHER (1867–1947)

INTRODUCTION

Just as the number and distribution of people are crucial to the development effort, so too is the *quality* of the population. This quality is determined by the population's access to health care and education. Economists point to these as two key factors that contribute to a person's ability to work and earn. Access to health care and education provides the **human capital** that enables individuals to succeed, and their absence contributes greatly to poverty.

We can envision how health care and education impact production by looking again at our marginal product curve with one variable factor of production. Figure 7–1 shows the marginal product of increasing numbers of workers, where all are considered to be of equal ability. However the curve says nothing about the level of their ability. It is easy to imagine improving that ability, or productivity, through better education or more training. And while industrialized countries tend to accept that workers will normally be healthy enough to work productively, this may not be the case where hunger and malnutrition are prevalent. Achieving a certain basic level of health can help keep workers alert and on the job a standard number of hours per day, days per week, and weeks per year. The opposite change may occur if societal conditions lead to increases in alcoholism and decreasing productivity on the job.

A country with a healthy and educated population produces more goods and services. This helps us understand why governments have a legitimate role in provision of health care and education. The beneficiaries of these expenditures are not just the individuals who become healthier and better educated but the country as a whole. If the difference is between a less and a more productive worker, there are positive externalities that result in more, and more efficient, production of goods and services. We will see these externalities throughout the chapter.

We saw in Chapter 3 the role played by human capital in the endogenous growth theories. Technological progress is a crucial factor in continuous growth: An economy must be able to produce not only more but better. While this requires scientific and research institutions, incentives to innovate, and highly educated workers, it may well be said to start with the health and early education of each person.

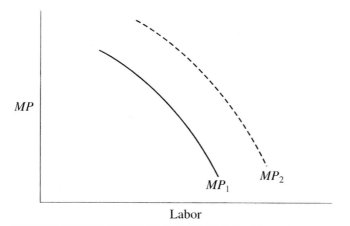

FIGURE 7–1 Human Capital and Productivity

Productivity of a variable factor of production (here labor) is measured by the marginal product achieved as units of the factor are increased. The curve MP_1 represents the initial situation, with capital fixed. An increase in the amount of capital increases labor productivity (MP_2). The same result can be achieved by improving the *quality* of the worker, through improved health, education, or training. Thus, the expression *human capital*.

In this chapter we look at the connections that have been so far observed between human capital and development and focus on the policies that might be pursued to ensure that every person has sufficient access to education and health care. We will find that much poverty can be avoided when human capital is enhanced.

HEALTH AND HEALTH CARE

Inadequate nutrition and frequent illness reduce the ability of people to learn, to produce goods and services, and to raise healthy children. So poor health contributes to poverty, and poverty in turn contributes to poor health. A basic requirement for the development of human capital, then, is good health.[1]

A few statistics give a good picture of the problem. In the 1990s (using the most recent data available on different countries), low-income countries on average had one doctor per thousand people, compared to 2.8 per thousand in the high-income countries. In 1999, low-income countries had an infant mortality rate of 77 per thousand, down from 114 in 1980, while among high-income countries the number was 6. Clearly, the discrepancies are large.

There has been considerable improvement. Life expectancy in developing countries increased from 40 to 64 between 1950 and 1999. The proportion of children dying before their fifth birthday fell from 22 percent in 1960 to 9 percent in 1999. Death rates between the ages of 15 and 60 fell from 450 per thousand in 1950 to 190 in 1999.[2] Unfortunately, there have been setbacks too. Deteriorating economic conditions in many African countries in the 1970s and 1980s have resulted in lack of resources to sustain health care. Some infant mortality rates have risen and life expectancy has fallen in some countries, particularly those suffering from AIDS,[3] as we see in Case 7–1).

CASE 7–1

THE AIDS THREAT TO DEVELOPMENT IN SUB-SAHARAN AFRICA

FAST FACTS

On the Map: Africa

Population: 643 Million

Per Capita GNI: $490

Life Expectancy: Male—46   Female—48

Adult Literacy Rate: Male—69%
Female—53%

A new public health threat has arisen in the last two decades in the form of the Human Immunodeficiency Virus (HIV), which is responsible for Acquired Immune Deficiency Syndrome (AIDS). It is transmitted largely through bodily fluids such as blood and semen. It is acquired primarily by adults through sexual intercourse and unsanitary needles. Babies acquire it in utero. In developing countries, heterosexual intercourse is the primary means of transmission. More than 90 percent of those infected are in developing countries.

The World Health Organization (WHO) estimates that 36 million adults were HIV positive at the end of 2000. Sub-Saharan Africa is particularly affected: WHO estimates about 25 million cases there and in some cities perhaps as many as one in three people. Countries vary widely, with fairly low rates of infection in Cameroon and particularly high rates in Botswana (36 percent of the 15 to 49 age group), Swaziland (25 percent), Zimbabwe (25 percent), and Lesotho (24 percent). In 2000, WHO estimates there were 5.3 million new cases worldwide, of which 3.8 million were in Sub-Saharan Africa and 0.8 million in South and Southeast Asia. The lack of any known cure for the foreseeable future adds emphasis to what is already a need for preventive health care services. Religious barriers to the use of

contraceptives and sex education in schools have retarded efforts in some African countries to effectively spread information about prevention.

The dire economic consequences are primarily twofold: the cost of prevention and care and the loss of the productive services of those infected, who are primarily working-age adults. For example, one attempt to estimate the impact for Tanzania suggests that without decisive action, by the year 2010 that country's working-age population would be 20 percent lower and its per capita GDP as much as 10 percent lower than the no-AIDS estimate. If these results are repeated in other high-risk countries, a tremendous amount of economic and social progress could be lost.

AIDS presents challenges to governments and international organizations. Governments need to become involved as early as possible in prevention campaigns. They need to provide information on the nature of the disease and urge changes in private behavior: abstinence from and protection during intercourse, avoidance of intravenous drugs, use of sterile needles in medical facilities, and protection from sexual assault. Once AIDS has become widespread in a country, the entire health care system needs to be strengthened and mobilized to provide treatment and care. And government must help in the battle of discrimination against AIDS victims.

Developing-country governments need outside help. Sources of help include aid donors (national governments, the World Bank), nongovernmental organizations (such as the International Red Cross), and health-care-related corporations. The World Bank is making emergency funds available to poor

African countries. Large pharmaceutical companies such as Merck, Abbot Laboratories, Pfizer, Bristol-Myers, and Boehringer Ingelhorn are engaged in activities such as providing free or low-cost drugs and donating money for national programs to fight AIDS. These early initiatives have had some difficulties but attest to the worldwide attention now being given to the problem.

Sources: Data on AIDS are available at the World Health Organization Web site at ⟨http://www.who.int/emc-hiv⟩. The current data are from WHO, "AIDS Epidemic Update: December 2000." Also see *World Development Report 1993*, pp. 99, 101; Susan Okie, "The Deepening Shadow of AIDS Over Africa: Widespread Fear Hasn't Translated into Change," *Washington Post National Weekly Edition*, October 17–23, 1994; John T. Cuddington, "Modeling the Macroeconomic Effect of AIDS, with an Application to Tanzania," *World Bank Economic Review* 7, no. 2 (May 1993), pp. 173–190; Martha Ainsworth and Mead Oliver, "AIDS and African Development," *World Bank Research Observer* 9, no. 2 (July 1994), pp. 203–240; Lyn Squire, "Confronting AIDS," *Finance & Development* 35, no. 1 (March 1998), pp. 15–17; World Bank, *Confronting AIDS: Public Priorities in a Global Epidemic* (Washington: 1997); Michael Waldholz, "Makers of AIDS Drugs Agree to Slash Prices for Developing World," *Wall Street Journal*, May 11, 2000, "Bristol-Myers Finding Pledging AIDS Aid Is Easier than Giving It," *Wall Street Journal*, July 7, 2000, and "AIDS Initiatives Planned for Poor Nations," *Wall Street Journal*, July 10, 2000; Michael Phillips, "World Bank Is Targeting AIDS in Africa," *Wall Street Journal*, September 12, 2000; and Michael Phillips and Rachel Zimmerman, "U.N. to Unveil Sweeping Attack on AIDS," *Wall Street Journal*, April 25, 2001.

Causes of Poor Health in Developing Countries

Table 7–1 compares causes of death in developing and more developed countries. In developed countries, the biggest killer is circulatory disease: those of the heart. Together with cancers, these causes account for 68 percent of all deaths. These are primarily diseases of later life, and they are noninfectious. In developing countries, by contrast, over 40 percent of deaths are due to infectious and parasitic diseases, led by respiratory infections, diarrhea, and dysentery in children under the age of five; tuberculosis; malaria; measles; and hepatitis. Death from these causes is unusual in the developed countries.

It is clear that poor health in developing countries is related more to environmental causes and dietary deficiency than to the stresses and infirmities that come with

TABLE 7–1 Causes of Death: 1993

Cause of Death	Developed Countries* (Percent)	(Thousands)	Developing Countries (Percent)	(Thousands)
Infectious and Parasitic	1.2	135	41.5	16,310
Lower Respiratory	7.8	905	5.0	1,938
Cancers	21.6	2,523	8.9	3,490
Circulatory	46.7	5,454	10.7	4,222
Maternal	Negligible	Negligible	1.3	508
Perinatal, Neonatal	0.7	83	7.9	3,097
External	7.5	879	7.9	3,118
Other, Unknown	14.5	1,692	16.8	6,602

*Includes transition economies of Eastern and Central Europe.

Source: World Health Report 1995 (Geneva: World Health Organization 1995).

age. It is due to problems that can be corrected with attention to environmental factors and better access to health care.

Environmental Factors

Peoples' health depends on their physical environment and access to preventive medical care. Water is crucial for drinking, cooking, and bathing; waterborne diseases such as bilharzia kill large numbers of people every year. Poor sanitation contributes to the spread of diseases such as cholera. Yet in low-income countries in 1995, only an estimated 76 percent of the population had access to safe water supplies and 28 percent to adequate sanitation. The same environment leaves people vulnerable to insects and pests and the diseases they carry.[4]

Pollution of water and air are particularly dangerous. In Africa, water and indoor air pollution account for 30 percent of disease. In 11 Chinese cities, the cost of illness and early death is estimated to be more than 20 percent of urban incomes. Waterborne disease and pollution cause 50,000 infant deaths every year in Vietnam.[5] Basic medical care, both preventive and curative, is not within easy reach of a large portion of the population. In the high-income economies, four-fifths of children are vaccinated against diphtheria and measles, and while the figure for China is about 95 percent, in Sub-Saharan Africa it is just over half.

Women and Health

Even when some medical care is available however, low levels of literacy make proper use of medical information difficult. This is particularly the case for the lower levels of education received by women. Women are usually the primary caregivers in a family, and their awareness of health issues is crucial for the health of infants and older children. And health care is offered disproportionately to boys. The United Nations reports that when fees are charged for clinic visits, more boys are brought than girls, even though visiting officials find greater health problems among girls in the villages.[6]

Another health-related issue that affects women disproportionately is violence. Domestic abuse of women is tolerated in some societies. Such abuse—from beating to rape and other sexual abuse—not only inflicts damage upon the victim and impairs economic activity, but when carried out against pregnant women, increases the risk of miscarriage and premature babies. It also increases the frequency of sexually transmitted diseases. Of particular recent concern is the practice of female genital mutilation, which the World Bank estimates has been inflicted on anywhere from 85 million to 114 million women worldwide.[7]

Poverty and Malnutrition

Poverty is generally associated with malnutrition: Although poor people spend much of their income on food, they may not be able to afford what they need, and cheaper foods often have lower nutritional value. But nutritional shortfalls are difficult to measure. Nutrient intake, perhaps the most direct evidence, is only one possible measure of a person's health status. Accurate measurements, taken over a large enough group of people for a long enough period of time, are difficult to obtain, and a standard, varying by gender, size, activity, calorie conversion rates, etc., is difficult to establish.[8] Nonetheless, estimates are routinely made based on estimated minimum standards of calorie and protein needs. According to standards suggested by the World Health Organization, between 600 and 800 million people—between 11 percent and 15 percent of the world's population—suffer from hunger and malnutrition.

The effects of malnutrition include high infant mortality rates, low weight and height for the person's age, and low weight for the person's height. This is due not only to the child's nutritional intake but to the mother's. Poor health of the mother leads to low-birth-weight babies and greater chance for poor physical performance of the child. The results generally include disease and early death, lower intelligence, and lower capacity to work. In 1999, the under-five mortality rate was 85 per 1,000 in developing countries (down from 135 in 1980) and only 6 in high-income countries.[9]

However, it is also not clear exactly how much impact poor nutrition and health have on economic growth or development. Malnourished women do not necessarily have fewer children, although babies are more likely to have low birth weights. There is evidence suggesting a positive impact of better childhood nutrition on productivity due to ability to learn and succeed in school.[10] Some studies do show that nutritional supplements improve the health of children and permit increased energy expenditure for adults.[11] Some show healthier people are more productive, but others show no difference. Studies in Brazil and elsewhere show that taller men, presumably taller due to higher income and better nutrition, are more likely to have jobs and make higher incomes.[12] Still, while the logical link is clear, the quantitative impact is only a matter of conjecture at this time.

Approaches to Improving Health

Poor countries do not have vast resources to devote to health care. In allocating those resources, two issues are important: prevention vs. treatment, and the role of governments and the private sector in providing services.[13]

Prevention vs. Treatment

Efficient allocation of health-related resources suggests concentration on prevention and those types of treatment that are cheaply and easily made available. Prevention measures would include effective prenatal care, routine vaccinations and other public health measures, adequate provision of basic food and shelter, and a concerted effort to attack the conditions that help spread disease, including lack of running water and the means of controlling insects that carry disease.[14]

One example is a World Bank campaign to control river blindness in Africa. Blindness results when a blackfly bites a person, depositing the larvae of a parasitic worm. The campaign involved the use of insecticide to kill the blackflies. It has not only cured a million and a half people, but it is estimated that another half million cases will have been prevented over a quarter of a century, at low cost.[15] Information on prevention and treatment, and the education that allows people to use information effectively, are crucial.

With respect to treatment, a choice is often possible between sophisticated, expensive means of treating relatively uncommon diseases, and cheaper, easily delivered treatments for common problems such as childhood diseases and diseases caused by lack of proper nutrition. The choice is often made for the former because decisions are made by relatively well paid government officials in cities who tend to take their lead from the most advanced facilities in the industrialized countries.

The outcome of such decision making is an **urban bias**. The World Bank reports that

> in virtually every developing country, facilities, equipment, human resources, and drugs are skewed toward [specialized treatment facilities]. Yet . . . cost-effective public health and clinical interventions . . . are best delivered at the level of the district hospital or below. . . . In many countries public investments are concentrated unduly on [specialized] services, and public spending subsidizes high-end facilities, equipment, and human resources for private markets.[16]

In India, for example, the two wealthiest states have 1,500 and 1,100 hospital beds per million people, while the two poorest have 300 and 400. Urban bias can be reduced. The government of Pakistan in the 1980s implemented an immunization program that expanded coverage from 5 percent to 75 percent over a five-year period. It funded the immunization campaign by simply postponing for that five years the construction of a large urban hospital.[17]

Urban bias in the distribution of medical facilities is replicated in the location of medical personnel. Doctors, like other individuals, tend to move to urban areas in response to higher incomes. Even though those incomes are quite high by local standards, medical education and training are usually subsidized. Not only are rural areas and public health generally deprived of health care workers, but there is a net migration of doctors from their home countries. Of all migrating doctors, 11 percent go to developing countries, while 56 percent leave them.[18]

The benefits of a low-end, comprehensive approach to health care are visible in East Asia where many countries have made an epidemiological transition. As populations have become healthier and live longer, the prevalence of disease has switched from common developing-country diseases, such as those caused by parasites, to common developed-country diseases, such as those of the circulatory system. These countries spent heavily to provide universal access to primary and preventive health care.[19]

The Role of Government in Health Care

Health care is an area in which the public and private sectors typically share responsibility in many countries. But spending money does not guarantee results. So it is useful to examine three rationales for government action.[20] First, governments have a role in the reduction of poverty generally. The case can be made that the existence of any significant percentage of poor people in a country is a drag on the overall economy by depriving the rest of the population of normal levels of productivity that contribute to the general well-being. Poor people are more likely to have health problems and are less able to afford health care services. Health care investment by governments has underfunded basic medical care for some, mainly poor, sections of the population while making lavish facilities available for more unusual illnesses. This suggests a government role in the provision of basic health services to the poor, either directly through its own agents or by subsidizing the means of prevention and cure. In rural areas, especially given past incentives for urban location of health care facilities and personnel, the government may be the primary source of these services.

Second, the existence of public goods and externalities is a common rationale for government action. Provision of clean water and sanitation, prevention of disease through immunization, control of insects carrying disease, and provision of information on diet and nutrition are very much public goods and are usually recognized as legitimate government responsibilities. Large positive externalities are associated with the treatment of infectious diseases and may also justify family planning programs and treatment of alcohol and drug abuse, as well as improvement of water and sanitation facilities and measures to curb pollution.

A final rationale is the existence of market failures in the provision of health insurance. Because medical bills are uncertain and can be suddenly very large, insurance can help smooth out such irregular spending requirements. Better-off populations often have access to health insurance through employment or can more easily afford it on their own. Not only will insurance be too expensive for most of the poor, but higher incidence of illness among the poor means their rates are most likely to be highest. This problem, a variety of **adverse selection**, justifies some government subsidy of health insurance for the poor.

Government expenditures, as we note in Chapter 9, are always constrained: Limited taxing ability and the many claimants on public spending often put public health at a disadvantage. Over the period 1990 to 1998, public spending on health care accounted for less than 2 percent of GDP in developing countries, compared to more than 6 percent in high-income countries.

Unfortunately, government spending may not translate easily into improvements in public health. Differences in health-related outcomes, statistically, seem to have no relationship to government health-related spending, either as a percentage of GDP, of total government spending, or of total health spending. Even locating public health clinics and services close to small communities seems to have little impact. This leads to the conclusion that much spending is inefficient or ineffective.[21]

Examples of such ineffectiveness include lack of equipment, medicines, and qualified health care workers and poor management of medical facilities. A local study in El Salvador showed that the clinic was open only twice a week and then only until noon. The doctor was often absent and the wait was three hours, all inferior to a local private facility. Public facilities often lack incentives for good performance, and personnel are not held accountable for poor performance.

In general, the impact of public services is low when people have no alternatives. This would indicate the need for competition, but in the absence of incentives and accountability, public-sector facilities may not respond to competition from private services. In a study of 32 low-income countries, private spending was 63 percent of all health care spending, compared to only 33 percent in a number of high-income countries. Public health services can improve conditions when there is no alternative. In the Philippines, public spending improved infant mortality in poor regions but not in rich regions, where presumably the availability of private services made the public services redundant.

Public spending is clearly required in poor countries. To maximize its impact, that spending should focus on areas where market failure is greatest, that is, public goods and high externalities, such as sanitation facilities, pest and infectious disease control, health information, and unavailability of insurance. In countries that have been successful in reducing mortality and improving health, governments have provided immunizations, training in the most common health problems, clean water and sanitation, and basic nutrition.[22]

When, as is common, public resources are squeezed, incentives should be given for private health care.[23] Given the number of urgent needs, and the varying capacities of developing countries, governments in the poorest countries should focus their limited resources on the provision of essential public health services and more education, especially for women and girls. For middle-income countries, it would make sense to redirect government expenditures from the more exotic branches of health care to those services on which a majority of the population depends, and foster the private market for both health care and health insurance.[24] In East Asian countries, heavy government funding of primary health care in early stages of development was followed by health insurance schemes that, while publicly regulated, have been financed privately once higher income levels made this possible.[25]

EDUCATION AND TRAINING

The productivity of healthy human beings, in economic terms, is usually a function of the amount and quality of the capital that they have to work with. But with given capital, the ability of an economy to use it productively depends on the skills of the people. No less than physical abilities, the intellectual skills of the population are important.

In high-income countries, virtually every child of elementary- and secondary-school age attends school, although the maintenance of educational quality remains a concern. In low-income countries, apart from China and India, only 82 percent are enrolled in primary education and perhaps one-third in secondary education. Significant improvements have been made, but there is clearly a long way to go. Overall, girls have lower enrollment rates—about 94 percent of male rates at the primary level and 83 percent at the secondary level, with some countries having much lower rates.[26]

The link between education and human capital is revealed in studies that show income levels for groups with different educational levels. Figure 7–2 shows typical pat-

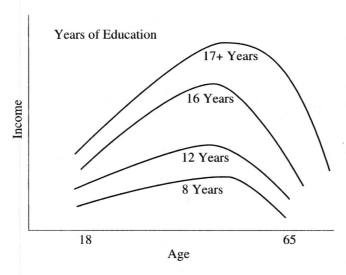

FIGURE 7–2 Education and Earnings

Typical lifetime earnings patterns show income rising throughout an individual's life until near the end of the working life, then declining. The amount of earnings, however, varies with education so that higher levels of education bring more income at each age (except that those without college will earn more during the time when others are in college).

terns of lifetime earnings. At all educational levels, earnings rise throughout most of life, declining in old age. But there are dramatic differences due to education: Those with more education generally earn more at every age.

The Importance of Literacy

Ability to read and write (literacy) and work with numbers (numeracy) are a crucial link to the knowledge required for increased productivity. Few are the jobs whose performance would not be improved by the ability to read. Farmers want to learn better ways to plant, factory workers want to understand their machines and their role in the production process, and service workers have jobs that often require reading and interpreting complex instructions. Numeracy is required for most people and anyone who might work with money. Using computers requires both literacy and numeracy. While clearly some jobs can be learned through observation and practice alone, their number and importance are declining. Finally, the increasingly complex social and political structures in which people live demand an understanding of the workings of government and the economy if people wish to take advantage of what society offers and, perhaps, avoid the pitfalls.

Investment in Education

People can easily find reasons to make their education a low priority or to put it off until the "right" time. Education takes time and money. It therefore has a significant short-run opportunity cost because the time required reduces current earnings or other contributions to the maintenance of the household. Parents may see even less gain from their children's education. Financially hard-pressed governments may see a higher priority in investments that have a quick, easily observable payoff. Why invest in education?

Estimates of the benefits of education have been questioned on the basis that more education may simply reflect greater abilities (more able people get more education) and that educational credentials are not always essential but are used largely to screen for employees who have social values related to education: the ability to work, conform, and interact on the job.[27] It is likely, however, that while ability and education are mutually reinforcing, education does have productive value of its own on the job. **Screening** seems to uncover virtues that are complementary to higher education. The evidence that more highly educated workers are more likely to keep their jobs (so labor turnover is lower), and that education increases the productivity of farmers (where screening is less likely to occur), testifies to the independent value of education.[28]

Returns to Investment in Education

Studies indicate very clearly that education brings economic returns that often exceed the opportunity cost of physical capital. More education leads to better jobs and higher income, in part because education improves the worker's ability to understand and work with new technologies. It turns out that education—especially if expanded to include informal education and on-the-job training—seems to improve the productivity of capital as well because more educated workers make better use of machinery.[29] This finding complements the suggestion in Chapter 4 that one of the indirect benefits of capital accumulation and improvement is the corresponding improvement in the capabilities of workers.

The difficulty of accurately measuring the gains to educational investment lies in the fact that there are social benefits, over and above the benefits to the educated person. These include greater productivity, a larger tax base, the inculcation of citizenship virtues, and family oriented benefits associated particularly with the education of girls and women. Returns to educating females include a greater desire to limit families and ability to care for children, as well as enabling women to earn more money. One estimate shows that doubling secondary school enrollments for girls in 72 countries in 1975 could have reduced fertility rates 10 years later from 5.3 to 3.9 children per woman and reduced the infant mortality rate from 81 per 1,000 to 38. The gains from education were estimated to be far more significant than doubling family planning services, the number of doctors per person, or per capita GDP.[30] Development Spotlight 7–1 illustrates successful attempts to increase school attendance for girls.

Research suggests that investment in education can have rates of return that easily justify the resources allocated to it by governments. The basic approach is to see how earnings vary with the amount of education. Earnings are "net," that is, they are offset by costs. For private rates of return, these costs involve the income forgone by students who (if old enough to earn income) substitute school for work. Social costs also include the value of resources used to provide education.

DEVELOPMENT SPOTLIGHT 7–1

EDUCATING GIRLS IN BANGLADESH

The benefits of improving access to education for girls span the range from healthier babies to a higher degree of participation in all areas of the economy and society. The Fourth World Conference on Women, in Beijing in 1995, advocated gender equality on the premise that it promotes economic efficiency. A number of public and private agencies are now focusing on projects to encourage the education of girls.

Two programs in Bangladesh are aimed at different levels of education. The Bangladesh Rural Advancement Committee (BRAC), along with outside donors, has developed a Non-Formal Primary Education Program that increased some local female enrollment rates from 53 percent in 1985 to 100 percent in 10 years, decreasing the gender gap from 19 percent to 0. It hires female teachers, keeps schools close to home, and has flexible schedules to allow children to attend to chores at home.

At the secondary level, the government of Bangladesh and the World Bank undertook the Female Secondary School Assistance Program. It provides stipends to girls, increases the number of female teachers, and builds public awareness of the need for girls' education. It assists more than a million girls a year and has succeeded in achieving near parity for girls' education. Girls outnumber boys in some schools.

Sources: Caroline O. N. Moser, Annika Tornqvist, and Bernice van Bronkhorst, "Mainstreaming Gender and Development in the World Bank: Progress and Recommendations" (Washington: World Bank, 1999), and ⟨www.girlseducation.org/⟩.

Although the calculations are approximations, they do give a general impression of high returns. Because of relatively low cost and low initial educational levels, returns are higher in developing than in developed countries. One set of estimates, provided in Table 7–2, shows that *private* returns are highest in primary education, followed by higher (university-level) education, and lowest in secondary education. Net *social* returns are again highest for primary education, followed by secondary and, last, university-level education.

The high returns to primary education are due to its relatively low cost (in resources and forgone income) and the large increases in productivity that come with basic literacy. The high private returns to university-level education come from the increase in earnings power of graduates. Social returns are lower because higher education is extremely costly and, in many developing countries, university graduates do not obtain the jobs they train for.[31] The higher private returns to education occur because private costs are frequently subsidized by governments.

Returns vary widely by country. Where relatively low percentages of students have received an education, initial returns can be high: 66 percent social return to primary education in Uganda (1966) and 50.5 percent in Morocco (1970). Diminishing returns sets in as a larger portion of the population is educated: social rates of return to primary education of 6.6 percent in Singapore (1966) and 8.1 percent in Chile (1989). For secondary education, social rates of return range from 47.6 percent in Zimbabwe (1987) to 5.1 percent in Brazil (1989). For higher education, the range was 24 percent in Yemen (1985) to –4.3 percent in Zimbabwe (1987)! Of course, rates of return vary within the population as well. A study of Sri Lanka showed returns on educational investment to be greater for women than for men at the primary and secondary levels, although not at the university level. Returns were also higher in urban than in rural areas.[32]

In addition, some tentative studies suggest a positive impact of education on agricultural productivity. Evidence from Mexico suggests rates of return above 20 percent from primary education, although other Latin American countries show lower returns. In Ghana, cognitive skills, rather than years of schooling, were shown to increase farm productivity, and this permits farm families to earn higher nonfarm income.[33]

TABLE 7–2 Rates of Return to Education

Income Group	Social Returns (%)			Private Returns (%)		
	Primary	Secondary	Higher	Primary	Secondary	Higher
Low	23	15	11	35	19	24
Lower Middle	18	13	11	30	19	19
Upper Middle	14	11	10	21	13	15
High	na	10	8	na	13	8
World	20	14	11	31	18	19

Primary = primary education.

Secondary = secondary education.

Higher = university-level education.

Source: George Psacharopoulos, "Returns to Investment in Education: A Global Update," *World Development* 22, no. 9 (September 1994), p. 1328.

Allocating Scarce Resources in the Educational System

All educational systems need not be alike: The needs of people at any point should dictate the structure and needs of education.

Educational Choices

As in the case of health care, resources may be either spread out, giving high priority to primary education for all, or may be relatively concentrated among the urban elite who are permitted and encouraged to take their training all the way through the university level. Rates of return provide a strong economic rationale for poor country governments to provide as much basic education as possible, limiting resources allocated to higher education.

We can apply economic analysis to the content of education as well. For example, at the primary level, the likelihood that most rural students will attain only a basic education and remain in agriculture suggests that those students should receive the preparation they need for farming. Even many of those who move out of farming will acquire jobs that require fundamental skills associated with literacy and numeracy, including jobs as mechanics, technicians, bookkeepers, etc. At the secondary level, however, many graduates of "technical" education find jobs that do not use their skills, leading some experts to support more general education. Technical training is expensive and may be more effective when provided by employers than by schools.[34] Subsidies for employer training would be more effective in this case than paying for technical secondary schools.

What about the content of higher education? The allocation of public resources should consider the country's needs: How many research physicists are likely to be needed? How many lawyers and philosophers? How many teachers, nurses, and accountants? How many economists, sociologists, and political scientists? While making these estimates with any precision will be time wasted, the use of public resources might well be focused on increasing the number of teachers, medical technicians, statisticians, and agronomists, rather than lawyers and philosophers. As mentioned earlier, subsidizing the education of doctors who are likely to be well paid and more likely than others to emigrate may not be a wise use of the government's educational resources.

Of course, development will alter a country's educational needs. As agriculture diminishes in importance, industrial work skills will become proportionally more important. The need for management skills in public, private, and nonprofit endeavors will increase, and the ability to work with computers will be essential in virtually every occupation. More generally, people will need broad-based knowledge that will enable them to change jobs occasionally, and the importance of liberal arts will increase. But many countries are still in desperate need of basic literacy and work skills.

The Delivery of Education

The choices made with respect to allocation of resources in the education sector are likely to dictate how education is delivered. A commitment to needs-oriented education implies:

- A delivery system made up of many small schools, located throughout the country, with teachers who in some cases may have little more formal edu-

cation than their students but who are able to teach them what they need to
know.

- Little spending on graduate programs in any but the most crucial fields and
  little incentive to students to take more schooling than may be appropriate
  at a given time.
- That the mechanisms of "education" are not strictly "schools": They include
  agricultural extension and trade schools, adult literacy programs, and special
  programs in areas such as nutrition for all family members.

The World Bank's experience in lending for education suggests that qualitative investments in curriculum development, better books, and teacher training often provide higher returns than putting up more buildings and providing the latest educational equipment.[35]

This type of prescription often sounds elitist: Let the developing countries continue to provide the farmers and factory workers while the industrialized countries
move into services and more creative ventures and innovation. But just as the
United States began its development with agricultural extension and schools for
mechanics, it does no good to educate people for jobs that do not exist while the
things that need to be done go unattended. Education, like other areas of investment, must be concentrated on where the social returns are highest for any particular country.

Again, East Asian experience is helpful. Some countries in the region had
achieved 100 percent primary enrollments by 1960, then concentrated on the secondary level. About 40 percent of the students were on vocational tracks during the
major growth phases, declining thereafter. Not all these countries had exceptionally
high investments in education, but some performed well by paying teachers well to
teach large numbers of students.[36]

Financing Educational Investment

The question of financing is difficult because the traditional comparison of costs
and benefits is more ambiguous in the case of education. Benefits of education are
spread out among the individual, the family, and society at large. The actual recipient
may not even recognize education as a benefit until a much later age. And especially
at the primary level, the recipient of educational services has no income at present, so
any fees or taxes are paid by parents and other citizens. The bias toward public funding of education in many countries has been justified economically by the presumed
social benefits associated with citizenship, productivity, fertility reduction, and by the
virtue of providing equal opportunity. But given the data in Table 7–2 that show private benefits exceeding social benefits in virtually all country groups for all levels of
education levels, how is public funding for education justified?

Largely, the rationale revolves around distributional questions. For one thing, the
poor have less discretionary income and may discount the future more heavily. Since
the benefits of education are in the future and may not accrue to the families directly,
poor children are more likely to be deprived of education. A recent study in Vietnam
has confirmed and strengthened earlier conclusions that the association between income level and education is strong: Poorer children receive less education than those
in higher-income families, and this is even more true for girls than for boys.[37]

Both rich and poor may take advantage of public rather than private education, although the poor are more likely to do so. A couple of small studies have suggested in fact that while the poor are the primary beneficiaries of primary education, the middle class and upper-income families now receive greater benefits at the secondary and university levels. To the extent that government subsidizes public education, the higher income levels are being subsidized more than are the poor. But the extent to which different income groups pay the cost depends on the kinds of taxes that finance public education and the degree to which those taxes fall on different income groups.[38]

Governments everywhere are facing difficult budgetary constraints, and the very real private benefits of education may suggest that students or their families should pay directly for some portion of the expenses. This would seem more reasonable for higher-income families and for university-level education where private gains may be much more significant when a college degree is the gateway to higher salaries. If students are unable to pay at the time of their education, loans or perhaps a tax levied on graduates would be preferable to outright grants.

Payment becomes more difficult when the family is poor and when time for school is already putting a strain on the family's income-earning power. Some privatization of education has been harmful to the poor when fees necessary to recover costs are more than a family can afford.[39] Still, government fiscal problems are already forcing families to pay fees for a portion of primary and secondary education, including for books, uniforms, and meals. Some rural schools have experimented with small farm plots cultivated by children as part of school time, to help feed the students. Shifting technical education from schools to employers is another device for privatizing education, as are ordinary private schools.[40]

Educational Inequality

While returns to education are high, there is surprisingly little association between a country's educational level—average years of schooling—and per capita income: Some studies have shown a negative correlation.[41] This is all the more startling if we consider that economic growth and higher levels of education should be mutually reinforcing: More education should contribute to growth, and growth should make available more resources for education.

The puzzle can be explained partly by the distribution of educational opportunity. A report for the World Bank has calculated Gini coefficients for distribution of educational opportunity, like those we saw in Chapter 2 for income generally. For 12 countries in 1970, these coefficients ranged from 0.279 (relatively equal) in Chile to 0.450 (relatively unequal) in China. By 1995, some countries had made significant progress: Most notably, South Korea's Gini fell from 0.439 to 0.189 through a policy of heavy investment in primary and then secondary education. But some countries' educational achievement became less equal: India's Gini coefficient rose from 0.370 to 0.452, the highest of the countries surveyed.

India had not ignored education: In 1997, it was spending 3.2 percent of its GNP on education, not too far below Korea's 3.7 percent. But India seems to have gotten less for its money due to the lack of educational access for the poor. In 1999, that country still had adult illiteracy rates of 32 percent for males and 56 percent for females: This must be considered a major hindrance to development.

THE FEMINIZATION OF POVERTY

We have already seen that the poor are becoming increasingly concentrated in ecologically vulnerable portions of Asia and Africa. It is useful to link health and education to the problem of poverty and address the **feminization of poverty** as a human capital issue. Table 7–3 summarizes some pertinent data.

The data show patterns of gender inequality. For industrialized countries, women outlive men on the average by over five years. In the developing world, this advantage is three years. Female literacy rates in the developing world were 81 percent of male rates in 1998, up from 54 percent in 1970, although their enrollment in primary and secondary education was 94 and 83 percent, respectively, of male enrollments. Literacy and education are virtually equal for women and men in the industrialized countries. Education for women is particularly neglected in South Asia and the Arab nations, while East Asia and Latin America do a much better job. By the United Nation's index of economic activity for people over the age of 15, the rate for women was 66 percent that of men in the developing world, below the 71 percent for the industrialized countries. But for the Arab nations, South Asia and Latin America, rates were much lower; only about one-third in Arab countries and one-half in South Asia and Latin America.[42] But because of the lower educational base, the role of women in the family, and their potential in the labor force, social returns to women's education are higher than those for men.[43] Educated women marry later; have fewer children; and bring knowledge to bear on problems of nutrition, and thus health, especially of children.

The disadvantage faced by women in the labor force, and their greater susceptibility to economic retrenchment, is beginning to be more thoroughly investigated. We will note later the lack of access of women to productive resources, and, for years, the frequent failure of foreign aid programs to make their benefits available to women. Worldwide, households with no adult males are poorer than others: They have fewer workers and resources, more dependents, lower education, and less help raising children.[44]

The UN reports that over the decades of the 1970s and 1980s, the increase in rural poverty was 50 percent for women and 30 percent for men, due to a combination of worsening economies and male migration to cities. To the extent that many gov-

TABLE 7–3 Gender and Human Capital

	Developing		High Income	
	Female	*Male*	*Female*	*Male*
Adult Literacy Percentage 1998	65	80	98	99
Youth Illiteracy Percentage 1998	19	11	NA	NA
Life Expectancy 1998	66	63	81	75

	Females per 100 Males	*Females per 100 Males*
Primary School Enrolled 1997	94	100
Secondary School Enrolled 1997	83	98
Economically Active 1998	66	71

NA = Not Available.

Source: Human Development Report 2000.

ernments have discriminated against the agricultural sector in their economic policies and in the ways in which agricultural policies have been carried out, women have received a smaller share of resources than their role would require. Different studies in Bangladesh have shown that when poor women do have access to credit and income, they not only do well but want fewer children and make greater use of contraceptives.[45]

The extent of the feminization of poverty is in dispute. Some United Nations reports in the mid-1990s used a rough proportion of 70/30, that is, 70 percent of the world's poor were women. In an attempt to verify this through a combination of data, estimates suggest that such a high percentage is not feasible.[46] A survey of 14 developing countries concluded that, at least for the rural poor, the female ratio was only half of what would be needed to produce the 70 percent figure. The rural poor populations in these countries was about 53.5 percent female in 1995, not terribly far above women's share of the population.

But poverty affects women disproportionately in a different way. Data routinely report whether a household is headed by a female (which means that no adult male is present) or by a male (which means usually that both adult male and female are present). Worldwide, poverty afflicts 16.6 percent of male-headed households and 25.3 percent of female-headed households. This disproportion is, if anything, likely more pronounced in developing countries where male migration is significant. Regardless of whether the children are male or female, women family heads bear a greater burden of poverty than male family heads.

This is only one of the areas where we note the special problems faced by women in developing economies. The case for an emphasis on the role of women in development and development programs has now become clear to virtually all researchers and practitioners in the field.[47] This case was emphasized at the 1995 World Conference on Women in Beijing. While the conference Platform did not commit governments to act, the final Declaration called for efforts to "Promote people-centered sustainable development . . . through the provision of basic education, life-long education, literacy and training, and primary health care for girls and women."

SUMMARY AND CONCLUSION

Economic development builds on the natural and human resources of a society. To do the work of the present, and to learn the work of the future, people must be healthy and increasingly well educated. The resources available to an economy must be allocated as efficiently as possible in these areas, and choices are inevitable and difficult. But if the fundamental nature of health and education are recognized, public resources can be focused on those—especially the poor and women—in greatest need. The externalities generated from both public and private spending in these areas will well repay the investment.

One cause of high birth rates in many countries is continued high death rates of infants and children. Health care, especially preventive care, can significantly reduce mortality rates and ultimately reduce fertility rates. Each country's circumstances will dictate the best combination of public and private efforts, but the poorest countries can make significant progress with basic public spending on water, sanitation, information, and modest public health facilities.

Education, particularly for girls and women, is one of the best investments to promote lower fertility and to enrich the quality of life of many of the poor in developing countries. Educational services should be geared to the current needs of each country and to realistic prospects for advance. Developing country governments, mindful of their budgetary burdens, need to find the appropriate combination of private and public provision and funding of education.

Low levels of health care and education are key factors in perpetuating poverty in developing countries (and indeed everywhere). These services are still distributed disproportionately to males, despite significant progress over the last quarter century. Thus, poverty has become increasingly burdensome to women, which is one reason why development researchers and policy makers must become increasingly aware of gender implications.

In the following chapters we switch to a discussion of the paths that development might take and the government policies that influence those paths. Agricultural development has been distorted by government policies that ignored or discriminated against it. Industrialization has often been promoted heedlessly through inappropriate policies. Both the agricultural and industrial sectors are affected by how a government leads a country into participation with the rest of the world, so trade policy is a crucial area for exploration, as are other means of obtaining resources from abroad. And the size and direction of government intervention is an area of concern by itself. It is to these topics that we now turn.

Key Terms

- adverse selection (p. 179)
- feminization of poverty (p. 187)
- human capital (p. 172)
- screening (p. 181)
- urban bias (p. 178)

Questions for Review

1. In what ways has spending on education and health been distorted from the perspective of developing-country needs? What types of spending make most sense?
2. In what ways is human capital development particularly important for girls and women? What differences exist in their current situation? What are the special advantages to redressing these inequalities?

 3. How does the AIDS epidemic illustrate the threat of poor health to development success in Africa?
4. In what ways is poverty an especially difficult situation for women?

Relevant Internet Resources

 The worldwide problems of health and health care are the focus of the United Nations' World Health Organization, whose Web site is ⟨www.who.int/⟩. WHO's reports on AIDS are at ⟨www.who.int/emc-hiv⟩. The World Bank also addresses AIDS, at ⟨www.worldbank.org/aidsecon⟩. A united effort to address the problems associated with providing greater educational opportunities for girls has a site at ⟨www.girlseducation.org⟩.

Endnotes and Further Readings

1. This section relies heavily on the World Bank, *World Development Report 1993: Investing in Health* (Washington: World Bank/Oxford University Press, 1993).
2. Good sources of such data are the World Bank's annual *World Development Reports/Indicators* and the United Nations's annual *Human Development Reports*. The data marking improvements come from Dean T. Jamison, "Investing in Health," *Finance & Development* 30, no. 3 (September 1993), p. 2, extended from the 2000 *Indicators*.

3. Simon Appleton, John Hoddinott, and John MacKinnon, "Education and Health in Sub-Saharan Africa," *Journal of International Development* 8, no. 3 (May–June 1996), pp. 309–310.

4. See Sarah Richardson, "The Return of the Plague," *Discover* 16, no. 5 (January 1995), pp. 69–70.

5. Vinod Thomas et al., *The Quality of Growth* (New York: World Bank/Oxford University Press, 2000), pp. 9, 85.

6. United Nations, *Women in a Changing Global Economy* (New York: United Nations, 1995), p. 40.

7. See *World Development Report 1993*, p. 50; Cynthia Dickstein, "Breaking the Silence," *Boston Globe*, March 20, 1994; and "A Traditional Practice that Threatens Health—Female Circumcision," *WHO Chronicle* 40, no. 1 (1986), pp. 31–36. See also Lori L. Heise et al., "Violence Against Women: The Hidden Health Burden," World Bank Discussion Paper No. 255 (Washington: World Bank, August 1994), and Anne Tinker et al., "Women's Health and Nutrition: Making a Difference," World Bank Discussion Paper No. 256 (Washington: World Bank, July 1994).

8. See Jere R. Behrman and Anil B. Deolalikar, "Health and Nutrition," in Hollis Chenery and T. N. Srinivasan, eds., *Handbook of Development Economics*, vol. 1 (Amsterdam: Elsevier Science Publishers, 1988), p. 650.

9. See Phillips Foster, *The World Food Problem: Tackling the Causes of Undernutrition in the Third World* (Boulder, CO: Lynne Rienner Publishers, 1992), and Jean Dreze and Amartya Sen, *Hunger and Public Action* (Oxford: Clarendon Press, 1989).

10. Jere R. Behrman, "The Economic Rationale for Investing in Nutrition in Developing Countries," *World Development* 21, no. 11 (November 1993), pp. 1749–1771.

11. Jere R. Behrman and Anil B. Deolalikar, "Health and Nutrition," p. 699.

12. John Strauss and Duncan Thomas, "Health, Nutrition, and Economic Development," *Journal of Economic Literature* 36, no. 2 (June 1998), pp. 766–817. These studies are reported on pp. 799 and 811–812.

13. See Anthony B. Zwi and Anne Mills, "Health Policy in Less Developed Countries: Past Trends and Future Directions," *Journal of International Development* 7, no. 3 (May–June 1995), pp. 299–328.

14. See Santosh Mehrotra and Richard Jolly, eds., *Development with a Human Face: Experiences in Social Achievement and Economic Growth* (Oxford: Oxford University Press, 1998), pp. 100–102.

15. *World Development Report 1993*, p. 19.

16. *Ibid.*, p. 134.

17. Mahbub ul Haq, *Reflections on Human Development* (New York: Oxford University Press, 1995), p. 9.

18. *Ibid.*, p. 141.

19. Sudipto Mundle, "Financing Human Development: Some Lessons from Advanced Asian Countries," *World Development* 26, no. 4 (April 1998), pp. 659–672.

20. *World Development Report 1993*, especially pp. 55–57.

21. See Deon Filmer, Jeffrey Hammer, and Lant Pritchett, "Health Policy in Poor Countries: Weak Links in the Chain," World Bank Policy Research Working Paper 1874 (Washington: World Bank, 1997).

22. *Ibid.*, p. 38, and Santosh Mehrotra and Richard Jolly, *Development with a Human Face: Experiences in Social Achievement and Economic Growth*, pp. 100–102.

23. See Peter A. Berman, "Rethinking Health Care Systems: Private Health Care Provision in India," *World Development* 26, no. 8 (August 1998), pp. 1463–1479.

24. *World Development Report 1993*, p. 147. See also the September 1993 issue (vol. 30, no. 3) of *Finance & Development*, particularly Dean T. Jamison, "Investing in Health," pp. 2–5; Robert Hecht and Philip Musgrove, "Rethinking the Government's Role in Health," pp. 6–9; and Jose-Luis Bobadilla and Helen Saxenian, "Designing an Essential National Health Package," pp. 10–13.

25. Sudipto Mundle, "Financing Human Development: Some Lessons from Advanced Asian Countries," p. 669.

26. Data are from the 1998 *World Development Indicators* and *Human Development Report*.

27. For screening, see Joseph E. Stiglitz, "The Theory of 'Screening,' Education and Distribution of Income," *American Economic Review* 65, no. 3 (June 1975), pp. 283–300. Also see David E. Sahn and Harold Alderman, "The Effects of Human Capital on Wages, and the Determinants of Labor Supply in a Developing Country," *Journal of Development Economics* 29, no. 2 (September 1988), p. 175.

28. George Psacharopoulos and Maureen Woodhall, *Education for Development: An Analysis of Investment Choices* (New York: Oxford University Press/World Bank, 1985), pp. 44–50. See also George Psacharopoulos, "Education and Development: A Review," *World Bank Research Observer* 3, no. 1 (January 1988), pp. 99–116, and Wim Groot and Hessel Oosterbeck, "Earnings Effects of Different Components of Schooling: Human Capital versus Screening," *Review of Economics and Statistics* 76, no. 2 (May 1994), pp. 317–321.

29. The pioneer works were T. W. Schultz, "Education and Economic Growth," in N. B. Henry, ed., *Social Forces Influencing American Education* (Chicago: University of Chicago Press, 1961), and E. F. Denison, *The Sources of Economic Growth in the United States and the Alternatives Before Us* (New York: Committee for Economic Development, 1962). For recent extensive reviews, see T. Paul Schultz, "Education Investments and Returns," in Hollis Chenery and T. N. Srinivasan, eds., *Handbook of Development Economics*, vol. 1 (Amsterdam: Elsevier Science Publishers, 1988), pp. 534–630; George Psacharopoulos and Maureen Woodhall; *Education for Development: An Analysis of Investment Choices*; George Psacharopoulos, "Returns to Investment in Education: A Global Update," *World Development* 22, no. 9 (September 1994), pp. 1325–1343; and Rati Ram, "Level of Development and Rates of Return to Schooling: Some Estimates from Multicountry Data," *Economic Develop-*

ment and Cultural Change 44, no. 4 (July 1996), pp. 839–858. A different approach is outlined in Paul Glewwe, "The Relevance of Standard Estimates of Rates of Return for Schooling for Educational Policy: A Critical Assessment," *Journal of Development Economics* 51, no. 2 (December 1996), pp. 267–290. The impact on capital productivity is reported in George Psacharopoulos and Maureen Woodhall, *Education for Development: An Analysis of Investment Choices*, pp. 16–20.

30. See K. Subbarao and Laura Raney, "Social Gains from Female Education," World Bank Discussion Paper No. 194 (Washington: World Bank, 1993). See also Rosemary Bellew, Laura Raney, and K. Subbarao, "Educating Girls," *Finance & Development* 29, no. 1 (March 1992) pp. 54–56.

31. George Psacharopoulos and Maureen Woodhall, *Education for Development: An Analysis of Investment Choices*, pp. 23, 55, and Dipak Mazumdar, "Microeconomic Issues of Labor Markets in Developing Countries: Analysis and Policy Implications," pp. 75–77.

32. David E. Sahn and Harold Alderman, "The Effects of Human Capital in Wages, and the Determinants of Labor Supply in a Developing Country."

33. For Mexico, see Ram D. Singh and Maria Santiago, "Farm Earnings, Educational Attainment, and Role of Public Policy: Some Evidence from Mexico," *World Development* 25, no. 12 (December 1997), pp. 2143–2154. For Ghana, see Dean Jolliffe, "Skills, Schooling, and Household Income in Ghana," *World Bank Economic Review* 12, no. 1 (January 1998), pp. 81–104.

34. George Psacharopoulos, "Education and Development: A Review," pp. 109–110. Disputing this conclusion is Paul Bennell, "General versus Vocational Secondary Education in Developing Countries: A Review of the Rates of Return Evidence," *Journal of Development Studies* 33, no. 2 (December 1996), pp. 230–247.

35. George Psacharopoulos and Maureen Woodhall, *Education for Development: An Analysis of Investment Choices*, pp. 314–415.

36. Positive aspects of East Asian policies are in Sudipto Mundle, "Financing Human Development," and Alain Mingat, "The Strategy Used by High-Performing Asian Economies in Education: Some Lessons for Developing Countries," *World Development* 26, no. 4 (April 1998), pp. 695–715. Cautions are expressed in Jere R. Behrman and Ryan Schneider, "An International Perspective on Schooling Investments in the Last Quarter Century in Some Fast-Growing East and Southeast Asian Countries," *Asian Development Review* 12, no. 2 (1994), pp. 1–50.

37. Jere Behrman and James C. Knowles, "Household Income and Child Schooling in Vietnam," *World Bank Economic Review* 13, no. 2 (May 1999), pp. 211–256.

38. See George Psacharopoulos and Maureen Woodhall, *Education for Development: An Analysis of Investment Choices*, pp. 138–143.

39. Christopher Colclough, "Education and the Market: Which Parts of the Neoliberal Solution are Correct?" *World Development* 24, no. 4 (April 1996), pp. 589–610.

40. George Psacharopoulos and Maureen Woodhall, *Education for Development: An Analysis of Investment Choices*, p. 146.

41. See Ramón López, Vinod Thomas, and Yan Wang, "Addressing the Education Puzzle: The Distribution of Education and Economic Reforms," World Bank Policy Research Working Paper No. 2031 (1998).

42. United Nations, *Human Development Report 1999*.

43. K. Subbarao and Laura Raney, "Social Gains from Female Education: A Cross-National Study," *Economic Development and Cultural Change* 44, no. 1 (October 1995), pp. 105–128.

44. United Nations, *Women in a Changing Global Economy*, 1994 World Survey on the Role of Women in Economic Development (New York: United Nations, 1995), pp. 33–34.

45. These studies are reported in Ruhul Amin, A. U. Ahmed, J. Chowdhury, and M. Ahmed, "Poor Women's Participation in Income-Generating Projects and Their Fertility Regulation in Rural Bangladesh: Evidence from a Recent Survey," *World Development* 22, no. 4 (April 1994), pp. 555–565, and Sidney Ruth Schuler, Syed Mesbahuddin Hashemi, and Ann P. Riley, "The Influence of Women's Changing Roles and Status in Bangladesh's Fertility Transition: Evidence from a Study of Credit Programs and Contraceptive Use," *World Development* 25, no. 4 (April 1997), pp. 563–575.

46. "Feminization of Poverty: Facts, Hypotheses, and the Art of Advocacy," ⟨www.un.org/popin/fao/womnpoor.htm⟩.

47. Start with Ester Boserup, *Woman's Role in Economic Development*, initially published in 1970, reprinted by Earthscan Publications Ltd., London, 1989. Then see Lourdes Beneria and Shelley Feldman, eds., *Unequal Burden: Economic Crises, Persistent Poverty, and Women's Work* (Boulder, CO: Westview Press, 1992); Jeanne Bisilliat and Michele Fieloux, *Women of the Third World* (Rutherford, NJ: Fairleigh Dickinson University Press, 1987); Mayra Buvinic and Margaret Lycette, "Women, Poverty and Development in the Third World," in John Lewis et al., *Strengthening the Poor: What Have We Learned?* (New Brunswick, NJ: Transaction Books/Overseas Development Council, 1988); Susan Joekes, *Women in the World Economy* (New York: Oxford University Press, 1987); Janet Momsen, *Women and Development in the Third World* (London: Routledge, 1991); Janet Momsen and Janet Townsend, eds., *Geography of Gender in the Third World* (New York: State University of New York Press, 1987); Irene Tinker, *Persistent Inequalities* (New York: Oxford University Press, 1990); and World Bank, *Women in Development* (Washington: World Bank, 1990).

CHAPTER

8

THE KEY ROLE OF AGRICULTURE IN DEVELOPMENT

While agriculture prospers all other arts alike are vigorous and strong, but where the land is forced to remain desert, the spring that feeds the other arts is dried up.

—XENOPHON (440–355 B.C.)

INTRODUCTION

One of the nearly universal characteristics of economic development is the long-term shift of populations and production from agriculture to industry and services. Only a small fraction of the population in the industrialized countries makes its living in agriculture.

Many of us take for granted that modern farmers use heavy machinery, chemical fertilizers, and extensive irrigation systems to grow food, with only an occasional blip when there is a flood or drought, or when a farm depression causes numerous smaller farmers to sell out to large agro-industrial firms. Traditional agriculture takes place on a much smaller scale than modern farming and uses technology that is often less productive. In this chapter, we will explore the development literature on agriculture, the requirements for successful agricultural development, and key public policy issues. We emphasize that successful agriculture is essential for successful development and that governments must work carefully with farmers to achieve that success.

AGRICULTURE AND THE DEVELOPMENT PROCESS

Table 8–1 shows World Bank data on the structure of production. Higher-income countries have smaller percentages of output from their agricultural sectors, and in developing countries the share of agriculture has declined since the mid-1960s. Agriculture's share of the labor force fell between 1950 and 1990: from 83 to 63 percent in Africa, from 82 to 62 percent in Asia, and from 54 to 25 percent in Latin America.

This trend is consistent with **Engel's Law**: As income rises, people spend smaller portions of that income on food. Agriculture expands but more slowly than the rest of

TABLE 8–1	Structure of Production in Developing Countries (Percentage of Output Derived by Sector)					
	Agriculture		*Industry*		*Services*	
	1965	*1999*	*1965*	*1999*	*1965*	*1999*
Low Income	41	26	29	30	30	44
Lower-Middle Income	22	14	32	39	44	46
Upper-Middle Income	16	6	36	33	47	60
High Income*	5	2	42	30	54	65

*Data for high-income countries are for 1998, not 1999.

Sources: World Development Report 1992 and *World Development Indicators 2001.*

the economy. For the most part developing countries with higher rates of agricultural growth also have higher rates of overall growth.[1] This shows the challenge that faces today's developing countries: They strive for rapid *industrial* development, but this is rarely achieved without rapid *agricultural* development.

Much early development thinking, however, focused on industrialization and displayed an urban bias.[2] Governments favored cities over rural areas in policies ranging from taxation to investment of all kinds: infrastructure, manufacturing, and public services. Development was viewed in the light of extensive industrialization in the West and the Soviet Union, and it was assumed that the agricultural sector would easily provide food and raw materials for development. However, this ignored the reality of historical development. The industrialization of England in the eighteenth and nineteenth centuries was accompanied by rural–urban migration made possible only *after* significant improvements in **agricultural productivity** (increasing yields per person and per hectare, or acre). America's growth was spurred in part by its huge agricultural capabilities. In the Soviet Union, industrial growth was conditioned on the most brutal type of exploitation of peasant producers,* and during most of its history the USSR had to import large amounts of food.

We can now specify the nature of agriculture's contribution to the development process and discuss approaches to ensuring that contribution.

Agriculture's Contribution to Development

Agriculture's central role in the process of economic development implies that improving the lives of farmers improves the conditions for a substantial portion of the population *and* enables them to contribute to the country in industry and services.[3]

Increasing Food Supplies

We expect the demand for food to rise rapidly with increases in both population and per capita income. Because food is essential to survival, demand for food grows rapidly at low levels of income. The **income elasticity of demand**, measured

---

*Throughout this chapter and elsewhere, we use the term "peasant" to refer to a rural producer who tends to be more isolated, to produce primarily for subsistence, and whose contact with formal markets tends to be intermittent. We use the term "farmer" to mean one who has more connections with the urban sector and produces for urban or international markets. While reality tends to be less clear-cut, the distinction is conceptually useful.

by the percentage change in quantity divided by the percentage change in income, is likely to be very high. For example, a family earning the equivalent of $500 a year, spending half on food, may use an increase of $100 (20 percent) just on food, increasing its consumption by 40 percent, for an income elasticity of 2.0. At higher incomes, people may change the kind of food they eat, but the quantity consumed is generally limited: Increasing income from $50,000 to $60,000 may not lead to the consumption of any more food (even if expenditures actually rise to buy more expensive food). Therefore, a developing economy must have access to rapidly increasing amounts of food, supplied primarily from its own agricultural sector.

In the absence of infrastructure and resources, price elasticity of supply may be low: Price increases will not bring forth much increase in production immediately. We would expect a rapid increase in demand to result in rapidly rising food prices. Such increases are likely to be politically damaging and produce pressures to offset shortages through imports at a time when the economy's ability to import may be limited. Nonetheless, it is crucial that food prices provide farmers with sufficient incentive to increase output steadily.

Export Revenue

Economic development has always depended on the ability to import what a country cannot produce efficiently. The best way to pay for these imports is to earn foreign exchange through exports, and until manufactured products such as clothing, tools, and small appliances are competitive in world markets, agriculture is likely to provide the best source of revenue. Even Brazil, which exports large amounts of manufactured goods, relies on earnings from coffee to finance much of its imports. Southeast Asian countries export large amounts of food and raw materials to fuel their industrialization.

Transfer of Labor to Industry

While the Lewis model shows that there are constraints to the effective transfer of labor from agriculture to industry, this transfer is an inevitable and important result of development. Such a transfer requires the agricultural sector to be sufficiently productive to increase output as it loses some of its labor.

Capital Formation

Since agriculture usually has a lower capital/output ratio than does industry, and is initially the largest sector of the economy, increased agricultural productivity can permit the accumulation of surplus for capital formation in both the agricultural and industrial sectors. Higher incomes in agriculture spur greater saving, and the portion that is not reinvested in agriculture can be transferred, through financial institutions, to industry. Lower agricultural prices, achieved by expanded supplies, can ease pressure on industrial wages, thereby funneling resources into private investment via profits and public investment via tax revenues.

Demand for Manufactured Goods

Higher cash income stimulates demand for consumer goods as farmers buy clothing, utensils, furniture, radios, and the like. Also, increased agricultural output requires additional inputs in the form of fertilizer, tools, and machinery.

TABLE 8–2 Importance of Agriculture-Sector Growth

Sector	Share of GDP	Slower Growth	Faster Growth
Agriculture	0.60	0.03	0.06
Industry	0.15	0.06	0.06
Services	0.25	0.10	0.10
Total GDP	1.00	0.42	0.70

Agriculture and Overall Growth

Table 8–2 illustrates the importance of agriculture in the growth of an economy dominated by that sector. In 1999, the West African country of Guinea-Bissau derived about 60 percent of its GDP from agriculture, 15 percent from industry, and the rest from services. If industry grows at 6 percent a year, and services at 10 percent, doubling agricultural growth from 3 percent to 6 percent would increase the overall GDP growth rate from 4.2 percent to 7 percent. Since population growth was 2.4 percent in 1998, doubling agricultural growth increases per capita GDP growth from 1.8 percent to 4.6 percent.

Agriculture and Poverty

According to the United Nations, about 1 billion of the 1.2 billion people living in absolute poverty in developing countries are in the rural sector. The World Bank has recognized the conjunction of population, agriculture, and environment as a key to understanding the problems facing Sub-Saharan Africa, one of the world's poorest regions.[4] Rapid population growth, while partly offset by urbanization, has put increasing pressure on agricultural land, and agricultural technique has not progressed sufficiently to ease the situation. The results include increasing soil degradation, and reduced per capita food production and intake. Thus, the performance of agriculture is crucial for poverty reduction.

Reversing the trend will not be achieved easily. The agricultural sector will require not only significant financial resources, but also improved technology and infrastructure. Government discrimination against agriculture impedes the entire development effort.

The Agricultural Transformation

A healthy agricultural sector is not only a *means* to development, but an *end* as well. While we expect agriculture's share of total output and employment to diminish as income rises, low-income countries may have initially 80 percent to 90 percent of their people in rural areas. Agriculture will for the foreseeable future provide a livelihood for billions of people. These people should be the beneficiaries of development, as well as its contributors. Achieving a transformation of the agricultural sector involves (1) increasing agricultural productivity, (2) using resources generated there for development outside the sector, and (3) integrating agriculture with the national economy through infrastructure and markets. Getting from here to there is one of the most important tasks of development in many countries today.

By one estimate, agricultural productivity in Asia and Africa during the 1970s was 45 percent below the level of the Western countries at the beginning of the Industrial

TABLE 8-3 Growth Rates (%): Agriculture, GDP, and Population

Years	Agriculture			GDP			Population		
	1965–1980	1980–1990	1990–1999	1965–1980	1980–1990	1990–1999	1965–1980	1980–1990	1990–1999
Low Income	2.6	3.0	2.5	4.9	4.7	3.2	2.3	2.0	2.1
Low-Middle Income	3.6	4.0	2.0	5.5	4.2	3.4	2.4	2.2	1.4
Upper-Middle Income	3.2	2.9	2.0	7.0	2.6	3.6	2.2	1.7	1.6
High Income	NA	2.2	NA	3.7	3.4	2.3	0.8	0.6	0.7

NA = Not Available.

Sources: World Development Report 1992 and *World Development Indicators 2001*.

Revolution.[5] Unfortunately, over the last several decades, agricultural output has grown less than overall output. What is particularly disturbing is that, as shown in Table 8–3, agricultural production in low- and lower-middle-income countries has grown just a bit faster than the rate of population growth, largely due to slow agricultural output growth in Sub-Saharan Africa.[6] Figure 8–1 shows that regional experience has been decidedly mixed, with Asia making steady progress, South America progressing more slowly, and Sub-Saharan Africa slowly reversing a long decline.

FIGURE 8–1 Per Capita Food Output
(Index: 1989–1991 = 100)

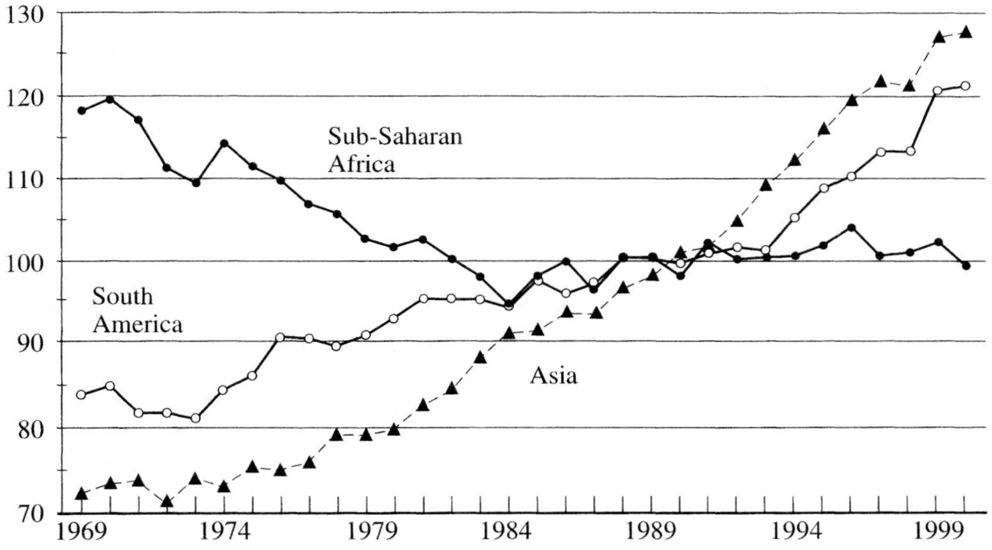

Both Asia and, to a lesser degree, South America have experienced steadily rising levels of food output per person. Sub-Saharan Africa, however, underwent a serious decline during the 1970s and has leveled off only slightly above the record lows of 1984.

Source: ⟨http://apps.fao.org⟩.

Exploitation of Agriculture

Mistreatment of farmers has been common in the twentieth century. In the Soviet Union in the 1920s, Stalin used compulsory sale of grain to the government at prices dictated by the state.[7] Low purchase prices combined with higher sales prices would provide revenue for the government. Peasants were ordered into large common or **collective farms** in a futile effort to increase efficiency and output. China also followed a policy of collectivization, as did some others on a smaller scale.

But force is not the only means to exploit farmers. Many developing countries have kept farm prices low; many have levied high taxes on agricultural activity, deprived the rural sector of capital, and in general put industrialization above all other objectives. Lewis's model of the labor surplus economy led some economists and policy makers to think of agriculture only in terms of how to use its excess labor to provide workers for industrialization. Improving the performance of the agricultural sector receded behind the assumption that agricultural development would occur naturally.

Sectoral Terms of Trade and Agricultural Development

Resources will flow into agriculture in response to economic incentives. Government can provide some of those, in the form of technical advice and improved infrastructure. However, the prices of crops must be high enough to encourage farmers to increase their output. In addition, the prices of goods that farmers *buy* should not be so high as to discourage consumption.

If Pa is an index of prices of agricultural goods, and Pi is an index of prices of industrial goods, the **sectoral terms of trade** for agriculture is the ratio Pa/Pi. An increase in this ratio means that food prices are rising faster than the prices of goods such as clothing and fertilizer: Farmers can buy more of what they need with the same output and are encouraged to increase output. A study of Indonesia, for example, calculated a Pa/Pi ratio over a series of years and the growth rate of agricultural GDP with a year time lag. When the price ratio was 0.78 over a three-year period, growth

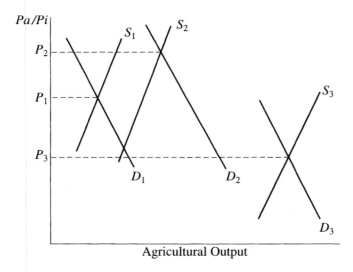

Agricultural Output

FIGURE 8–2 The Progress of Agricultural Prices

As development spurs the demand for food, relative prices should rise (P_2), providing the incentive for increasing production. At higher income levels, the increase in food demand will slow down while increasing productivity expands supply, causing a shift in relative prices toward the industrial sector (P_3). The initial improvement encourages agricultural development. Eventually, agriculture will become a smaller portion of national income.

was 0.9 percent per year. As the ratio increased to 0.83 and 1.06, agricultural growth climbed to 4.3 percent and then to 8.3 percent.[8]

Increasing terms of trade for the agricultural sector should be a transitory phase. Figure 8–2 illustrates how relative agricultural prices (expressed as the ratio *Pa/Pi*) should be expected to change over time. In response to initially high agricultural prices (P_1), resources will be drawn into agriculture, thus increasing output (S_2). This may well continue as the initial increase in the demand for food (D_2) outpaces production. As demand for food and raw materials grows more slowly (D_3), and agricultural productivity and supply increase (S_3), these terms of trade will reverse and industry will be encouraged. But in the initial stages of economic development, agriculture should be a priority. To keep and attract resources in agriculture would require that its terms of trade rise to reflect scarcity or at least not fall.[9]

FARM PRICES: MARKET AND GOVERNMENT

"Farmers the world over," notes economist Peter Timmer, "talk primarily about two topics: the weather and prices." One of the key issues of agricultural policy is the pricing of agricultural products.[10] Developing-country governments have frequently taken control of pricing decisions. Assertions of Western economists that poor countries should let the market work sound insincere, given significant subsidies to agriculture in rich countries. Government officials have sometimes assumed that peasants' agricultural practices are the result of custom and that they would not respond significantly to changing prices.

Evidence from all over the world disputes that claim.[11] Whether the decision is what to plant, where to sell, where to work, or any of a number of other questions, small farmers respond, sometimes quickly, to changing relative prices. Resistance to change is largely a function of economic insecurity. Anyone whose life hangs on the balance of sun and rain is likely to be extremely cautious about trying some new crop or technique. Improved income prospects may not be attractive if that income also fluctuates greatly, leaving the family open to starvation in the bad years. Theodore Schultz's valuable work[12] shows the rationality and efficiency of peasant agriculture within the constraints of available resources and institutions.

The Consequences of Price Ceilings

Mistaken views of peasant behavior have led governments to set below-market prices for agricultural commodities. Officials have believed that traditional ways of life (or coercion, if necessary) would maintain agricultural production; that lack of available surpluses for market would make prices irrelevant for some farmers; or even that fixed money needs would encourage peasant farmers to sell less food at higher prices. A low-price policy taxes agriculture and subsidizes politically vocal urban populations. Governments may also tax agricultural production directly, especially exports.

Figure 8–3 shows how imposing a **price ceiling** reduces the incentive to produce food while encouraging consumption. In the figure, when a price ceiling (P_c) is imposed rather than the equilibrium (P_e), production (or at least marketed production) falls from Q_e to Q_s, and farmers' income falls from rectangle $PeXQ_e0$ to $PcYQ_s0$. Consumers are willing and able to buy Q_d, and the excess demand will either be frustrated or satisfied by imports, both legal and illegal.

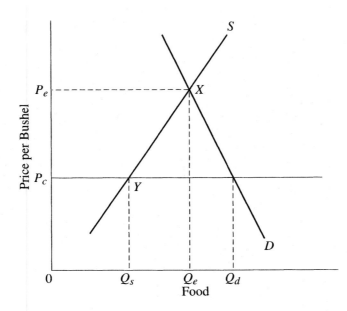

FIGURE 8–3 Price Ceiling on Farm Output

A price ceiling (P_c) will increase the quantity of food demanded but reduce incentives for production. If this applies to only one crop, such as maize, production may be simply shifted to wheat or cotton next year. If all crops are similarly affected, excess demand ($Q_d - Q_s$) will be frustrated or supplied either illegally or through imports, or both.

The graph is simplified in two ways. First, it shows a market for "food" in which supply and demand are relatively price inelastic. Most studies of the *overall* price elasticity of agricultural supply do indicate a fairly weak response to price changes, especially in the short run. However, there are much stronger supply responses to *relative* price changes. Thus, lower prices for maize may encourage farmers to plant wheat or cotton instead. Supply and demand curves for individual products and, over a longer time period, should be more elastic. Second, since the graph shows a price ceiling set by the government, the supply and demand responses refer only to the markets in which those prices are relevant. Lower official prices may cause not lower production but lower *reported* production, while farmers sell privately.[13]

Lower farm income reduces the agricultural sector's demand for manufactured goods, including agricultural inputs and household items. Incentives to support research in the agricultural sector are reduced, even when that activity is sponsored by the government. When price ceilings are placed on exportable commodities, exports will either fall or be sold illegally, depriving the country—or perhaps just the government—of some of its export receipts.

A good example of the difficulties caused by price controls is the policy of pan-territorial pricing formerly used by some countries in Eastern and Southern Africa. Government officials tried to encourage maize (corn) production in regions where it was not normally grown by purchasing it from farmers at the same price in all regions: This price was higher than equilibrium in remote regions and lower than equilibrium closer to urban areas. Since the cost of setting up purchasing stations and transporting the crop was much higher in the more remote regions, the government lost large amounts of money. At the same time, farmers closer to the city did not receive a high enough price and, so, resorted to either illegal markets or crops that were more appropriately priced.[14]

Why have many developing-country government officials wanted to keep farm prices low? In addition to misconceptions about peasant responsiveness to prices, some government officials believed that only the wealthier, capitalist farmers would benefit from higher prices. They knew that lower food prices (and lower prices for cotton, hides, etc.) would have a favorable impact on consumers and business profits. Through their **marketing boards**, organizations that paid low prices to farmers and collected higher prices from consumers (especially foreign consumers of export crops), governments thought they could accumulate funds for development. Finally, they believed they could quickly induce industrialization, to everyone's benefit.

Most of these assumptions were incorrect. While low prices for food and raw materials benefit consumers and industrial users, sustained pricing below market levels has hurt agriculture in numerous countries, especially in Africa, by limiting production and putting a brake on the accumulation of capital in the economy as a whole. Poor farmers are hurt most because they have fewer alternative uses of their land.

Despite these failures, some governments remain reluctant to let the market alone determine agricultural prices. Government officials often suspect that markets allow middlemen to exploit poor farmers. Uncontrollable events such as droughts and floods result in wide fluctuations in prices. Such fluctuations limit the effectiveness of prices as signals to producers and cause great uncertainty for consumers. Producer response to prices is less reliable (and supply less elastic) when new price levels are expected to be temporary.

Market-determined farm prices imply openness to foreign trade, and world agricultural prices are volatile. Recessions and subsidies in the industrialized countries can depress price levels. Developing-country exporters are concerned that unreliable prices will depress export revenues, while domestic production that competes with subsidized grain from rich countries may be lost to imported wheat, corn, and rice. Finally, the ability to provide inexpensive food to the cities is a political problem for regimes whose backing lies more in the urban than rural areas. High or erratic food prices lead to demands for higher wages, which in turn stimulate, or exacerbate, inflation.

Additional Consequences of Price Interventions

Many developing-country governments have tried to bridge the gap between agricultural prices that are too high for consumers and too low for producers by intervening in pricing decisions at different levels. Governments may set farm-gate prices (those received by the farmer) in an attempt to maintain or increase production. This process is complicated because there is a large number of crops, with opportunities for farmers to substitute one for another. Price controls are placed also on processed crops (flour, meal) at the retail level, in order to satisfy the perceived needs of the urban population.

Mistakes in price setting cause numerous problems. Low farm-gate prices result in either insufficient production or in production that is sold outside official distribution channels, at home or to neighboring countries. Low retail prices require large government subsidies through state-owned enterprises. They also encourage illegal sales from those, generally in the larger cities, who have easy access to controlled-price goods, to consumers, often in the rural areas, who do not.

Governments often attempt to offset low farm-gate prices through subsidies on the prices of inputs, but this creates its own problems. Subsidies to inefficient state-owned fertilizer companies permit high-cost production and inefficient delivery. Subsidies for the purchase of machinery promote overmechanization. Promoting credit, either through subsidized interest rates or attempts to force banks to lend given percentages of their funds to farmers, has generally failed to efficiently allocate funds to farmers.

Prices Aren't Everything

Prices can do only so much. Peter Timmer suggests that their major function is not just to stimulate production in the short run, but "in conditioning the investment climate and expectations of all decision-makers in the rural economy about the future profitability of activities in the sector."[15] Prices must be put in context.

A study of agricultural price policy in Asia concludes that "profitability, not just prices, is what drives production."[16] A long-range study of agricultural policy by the World Bank concludes that "While favorable price incentives based on appropriate macroeconomic and sectoral policies played a key role in explaining performance, the quality of natural resources and of technological, institutional, political, and human and physical investments critically determined the ability of small farmers to mobilize land and labor, the two most important factors explaining growth."[17]

Problems of Liberalizing Agricultural Markets

Government control of agricultural pricing and marketing has been particularly prominent in some African countries. Newly independent governments often intensified the colonial pattern of directing these markets but at increasing cost and with decreasing effectiveness. Many have begun liberalization attempts since the 1980s, under pressure from the World Bank and other aid donors. More pricing decisions have been left to the market, and governments have permitted greater private marketing efforts.

Gains have been limited, in part because many governments have not loosened controls enough. Private marketing efforts have been fairly successful in delivering food to urban and rural areas. However, there has not been nearly the increase in supply anticipated by reform proponents. The most likely explanation is that "getting prices right" is only part of the answer. Lack of infrastructure, research, market information, and legal and organizational support have weakened the ability of farmers to react to higher prices.[18]

LAND, LABOR, AND CAPITAL IN AGRICULTURAL DEVELOPMENT

The factors of production—land, labor, and capital—combine to permit turning raw materials into final goods and services. Their interrelations are sketched out in Figure 8–4. In the figure, the farmer combines a variety of inputs with the soil to produce crops. These crops pass through additional stages on their way to final use by people and companies. As food or industrial inputs, crops provide and enhance employment in the production of goods and services used by farmers.

Land

Agricultural policy requires attention to questions beyond the environmental issues discussed in Chapter 5. Two aspects of the land are important here. First is physical understanding of the soil and second is the legal relationship between soil and cultivator. The latter will take us into a discussion of land reform.

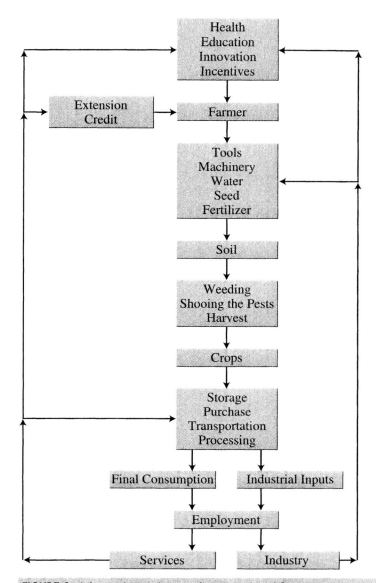

FIGURE 8–4 Interrelationships in the Agricultural Sector

The farmer combines agricultural inputs with the soil to produce crops. The output goes through a number of stages before becoming either final goods or raw materials for industry. All contribute to employment, producing goods and services, many of which reward and improve the life of the farmer.

The Soil

Farmers must understand the soil before choosing which crops to grow and which techniques to use. There are often extreme ecological variations in a small area, requiring different approaches, or similar conditions over vast areas. There are dangers in **monocropping** (planting large areas with a single crop), as has been done extensively in North America, and in Southeast Asia where large areas are devoted to wet rice production. Bad weather, insects, disease, or declining consumer demand may wipe out regions dependent on a single crop. Appropriate crop diversification maintains the nutrient content of the soil and protects farmers against lower prices for individual crops.[19] The need for highly specific knowledge about geography and ecology means that research is needed to assure the compatibility of land, crop, and technique. Technique here includes the proper choice and use of fertilizers, the appropriateness of machinery, and farming practice itself such as the timing of planting and need for crop rotation.

Population pressure and changes in crops or farming methods have often led to soil degradation. A recent study of Kenyan agriculture evaluated a number of crops, from staples such as maize and beans to exports, including tea, coffee, vegetables (such as tomatoes), and cut flowers. Maize and beans replaced natural ground cover, providing less protection against soil erosion. Vegetables, often encouraged for export to Europe, come up short on many counts: They provide poor protection for the soil; make massive use of fertilizers and insecticides, which are carried to other locations by irrigation ditches; and use imported seeds, which may bring in foreign pests. Tea, which has been exported for decades, is relatively benign except that a good deal of fuel is required in the drying process.[20] Such considerations argue for a careful assessment of what is planted and where.

Land Tenure

We have discussed the importance of ownership and careful management of land in Chapter 5. Now we must address **land tenure**. Landholdings can be very large, such as plantations in Africa and Latin America. Some are very small (as are some individual plots everywhere) and some in-between. The people who work the land may be the owners, most likely on small- to medium-sized plots, but this is not necessarily true. According to the UN Food and Agricultural Organization, over 1 billion people in rural areas have either no land or, more often, too little land for their own subsistence.[21] Landowners hire workers for a wage or under a **tenancy** agreement that requires payment to the landlord of either a rent or a share of the output—**sharecropping**—for the use of the land. The diversity of conditions is enlarged because those who hire labor are not necessarily large landowners. Small holders may hire some labor, and some cultivators may both own some land and work for others.[22]

Farmers are more productive when they have a direct stake in the land. But as land ownership is often expensive, wage-labor and tenancy are quite common. Sharecropping, giving a portion of the crop yield to a landlord, would seem to reduce the farmer's motivation. However, sharecropping has two advantages. First, it reduces risk, which is particularly important when the small farmer has few assets and is exceptionally vulnerable to bad weather and weak markets. Second, sharecropping may give tenants access to the landowner's credit, which they can use to eventually acquire land of their own.[23] Table 8–4 compares the position of landlord and farmer under rental contract (the farmer pays rent to the landlord), wage contract (the farmer is hired by the landlord), and sharecropping.

Industrialized countries use pure rent or pure wage arrangements rather than sharecropping. Under a rental contract, the farmer receives the entire value of the product except for the fixed rent, but there is a risk that lower production or sales will

TABLE 8–4 Risk and Incentive Under Alternative Contracts

Contract Party	Type of Contract		
	Rent Contract	*Labor Contract*	*Sharecropping*
Landlord	No Risk	All Risk	Shared Risk
Farmer	All Risk	No Risk	Shared Risk
	Production Incentive	No Production Incentive	Shared Production Incentive

Under a rental contract, a farmer bears the entire risk and has a strong incentive to produce in order to gain all the income in excess of the rent owed. Under a labor contract, the farmer gets a wage and neither takes a risk nor has an incentive to produce any more than will guarantee continued employment. Sharecropping, in which the farmer owes a fixed percentage of the crop, spreads the risk between farmer and landlord.

reduce revenues below costs. If the farmer is simply hired labor, all risk is taken by the landlord, but the farmer has no incentive to produce more under a set wage. Share-cropping involves a farmer who splits the output with the landowner. This arrangement splits the risk of shortfalls between the farmer and landlord, while still providing the farmer with some incentive to increase production. Because some incentive exists, sharecropping provides a relatively costless way for the landlord to monitor the farmer's efforts, as opposed to a wage contract in which the farmer may have an incentive to work less efficiently.[24]

Land Reform: The Issues

The importance of the relationship between cultivator and soil leads to one of the more politically explosive issues in economic development: **land reform**, or changes in the legal structure of land ownership.

Throughout the developing world, colonialism had left its mark on the land. The Japanese in Korea and the Europeans and Americans in Africa, Asia, and Latin America obtained large areas that were often devoted to a single crop: coffee, tea, sugarcane, bananas, and others grown largely for export. Settlers usually claimed the most productive land. Even after independence, these plantations often remained in foreign hands. Therefore, the most frequent demand for land reform has been for the breakup of those plantations.[25]

The beneficiaries of these reforms were people who owned no land of their own (or had lost what they had) and had to work for landlords under conditions often little different from slavery. The economic justification for the breakup of the plantations and *latifúndios* (literally, wide lands) combined a number of claims. Absentee owners, often foreigners, frequently kept large portions of their land out of production, thereby making no contribution to development. Plantation crops tended to be for export, with the proceeds concentrated in a few hands, so that the population's need for food and the economy's development requirements were not being addressed. Ownership of land by individual peasants would provide them the incentive to find more productive methods of farming and would give them greater access to credit. Finally, spreading income more evenly would promote demand for consumer goods.

Experience in Japan, Taiwan, and South Korea has shown that a more equitable distribution of land, what Bruce Johnston has called a "unimodal" pattern of medium-sized holdings as opposed to a "bimodal" combination of very large and very small holdings, often promotes efficiency, production, and equity. Such reforms are never easy because they require taking land from large holdings and redistributing it. Radical political change may provide a context. After World War II, for example, the removal of Japanese control from Korea allowed redistribution of land taken from Japanese owners and Koreans who had cooperated with the Japanese.[26]

Another economic argument supports consolidation of very small farms. In some countries, including the populous regions of southern Asia and many African countries, farmers subdivided land among their sons for generations, creating numerous small plots that were inefficient, especially if one wanted to apply newer technology.[27] The ownership of several small noncontiguous plots by some individuals increased their time requirements as well. However, diversity of land and crops has some advantages for a small landowner in case of local weather problems, low prices for specific crops, and when credit and food markets are fragmented.[28]

If plots are too small, land reform could mean consolidating the smaller plots under individual or group ownership. If some farmers lose their land in the process, arguments for efficiency and equity may be in conflict, unless land reform is accompanied by stringent efforts to permit individual peasants to make up what they might lose in land. In cultures where landownership increases an individual's social status, in addition to its economic value (including most cultures in the world), land reform can be difficult. Intermediate solutions—such as common ownership—may be difficult to manage successfully.

However, there is also evidence that small farms are efficient. Some studies have calculated small-farm productivity as high as five and a half times that of large farms.[29] One of the earliest of such studies, whose results appear in Table 8–5, looked at yields in Colombia. Value added per hectare clearly declined as the size of landholdings

TABLE 8–5 Farm Productivity in Colombia: Value Added in 1,000 Pesos, 1960

Hectares*	Value Added per Hectare	Value Added per Effective Hectare[†]	Value Added per Worker
0–3	1.37	0.75	1.67
3–5	0.86	0.79	2.08
5–10	0.73	0.50	2.71
10–50	0.44	0.57	3.47
50–200	0.25	0.38	5.35
200–500	0.21	0.35	8.61
>500	0.13	0.35	15.07
Total	0.28	0.46	3.71

*A hectare is a unit of land equal to 2.47 acres.

†This adjustment takes account of land quality.

Source: Albert Berry, "Farm Size Distribution, Income Distribution, and the Efficiency of Agricultural Production: Colombia," *American Economic Review* 62, no. 2 (May 1972), p. 406.

rose. When land was adjusted for fertility to obtain value added per "effective hectare," the results, while less striking, showed the same trend. On the other hand, value added per worker clearly rose with the size of landholdings, likely due to greater mechanization.

If farmers profit from working the land more intensively after reform, output per acre can rise even if output per worker is falling, and this will be profitable up to the point where the marginal product of labor equals the wage. Family labor on small farms can be more efficient than hired labor on large farms, which is why large landowners have often rented land to families. If effective markets provide small farmers with access to credit, technical information, and machinery to rent for periodic use, they can make very effective use of small plots of land. If land is abundant and labor scarce, as in the United States, large holdings make sense. Where labor is abundant, as in India and China, smaller holdings should prevail.

From an ecological standpoint, land reform should aim to provide the security necessary to encourage sustainable use of the land. Use rights, whether individual or group, that can be taken away encourage users to seek maximum immediate gain, often at the expense of sustainability in the long run.[30]

Land Reform: Experience

Many studies conclude that land reform has largely failed. The more successful cases—Japan after World War II, Taiwan upon the flight of the Nationalist government from the mainland after the Communist revolution, and South Korea immediately after the Korean War—occurred under exceptional circumstances. In each case, there was better political organization among beneficiaries than among victims and a government bureaucracy capable of carrying out the reform. Failure has often been due to a combination of insufficient political power to carry out a reform (which usually requires a fairly thorough displacement of former owners) and lack of appropriate economic policies to support the new owners. Numerous reform attempts in Latin America, the Philippines, Egypt, and India failed through one or more of these problems.[31] Initial successes may be reversed when new small landholders are still economically vulnerable and can be bought out by former landlords. And even when successful in terms of providing "land to the tiller," the resulting land tenure system may disadvantage women who exercised traditional rights of land use but are not considered eligible to legally own property or are not served by government programs meant to help new landowners.[32]

Over the last few decades, a different debate on land tenure has taken place. Tanzania, in the late 1960s and early 1970s, embarked on a program—at first voluntary but later compulsory—to move peasants from their scattered homes to villages—called *ujamaa* villages, for the Swahili word adopted for "socialism." The avowed purpose was to promote agricultural development, rather than drain resources for industrialization. The government hoped to bring services such as education and medical care to villagers more efficiently, and to promote a more communal and efficient agriculture that was thought to correspond to traditional African practices.

That experiment failed. The government could not deliver on its promises to provide inputs and social services. In the absence of strong social or financial incentives, people spent more time on their private plots.[33] Peasant farmers have greater incentive to produce for their own gain, however cooperatively they may participate in other activities: Secure tenure is necessary, even if not sufficient, for successful agricultural development. This often means they will own their own land, but other arrangements such as use rights to land (see Chapter 5) and sharecropping can be efficient if the rules are clear and incentives are strong.

Labor

There are two key characteristics of labor in agriculture. First, people who cultivate land must possess numerous skills. Second, women and children make up a significant percentage of the labor pool.

Labor Activities

Agricultural tasks are numerous: soil preparation, planting, weeding, applying pesticide, scaring off the birds and animals, and harvesting.[34] Farmers must make preparations before the season. They must obtain the necessary inputs, and after harvesting they must store the crops (against weather and pests), prepare them for sale, and maintain their equipment. Since not all crops are planted and harvested at the same time, these tasks often take place more than once a year, and activities may overlap for different crops. Much agriculture involves caring for livestock, whether on a large scale for commercial purposes or on a smaller scale for farm work and food.

Aside from these activities, people have other responsibilities. They must maintain homes, care for children and the elderly, seek out loans, deal with government officials, and participate in village political and social organizations. Planning the use of labor must also account for the seasonal variations in labor requirements and the possibilities for division of labor within the family. For example, educating children either takes valuable labor away from important activities or must be scheduled to fit around the requirements of economic life. Children may need to work on the farm, and the opportunity cost of their education will be higher at times of peak labor need, such as at harvest.

Women in Agriculture

One of the more difficult problems facing projects to improve agricultural productivity has been the gender-based division of labor. Women grow roughly one-half of the food in developing countries; about three-fourths in Africa. They also do virtually all the processing and preparation of food.[35] Reported statistics usually understate the percentage of women in the rural labor force. A UN survey of 13 Latin American countries reported that in Panama, for example, the official estimate was 5 percent while the survey estimated 26 percent. In Peru, the official estimate was 45 percent and the unofficial estimate 70 percent.[36]

In many countries, particularly in Africa, small rural businesses are predominantly owned by women. Women and children bear some of the physically heaviest burdens, including walking long distances for fuelwood and water, preparing the soil, and weeding and harvesting, often while carrying the younger children. Women may sell some or all of the crops and do the housework. In many Asian and African villages, men tend to politics and less strenuous activity but may well claim the proceeds from sale of the crops. A summary of 12 detailed studies of daily work hours in rural areas shows that in only 2 cases did men work longer hours, and only marginally (8.54 hours per day to 8.50 for women), while in the other 10, women worked longer hours by a substantial margin (9.93 hours per day to 7.13 for the men).[37]

Although production systems vary widely, women in many African countries grow crops necessary for food while also working on the farms of their husbands growing crops for sale. They are less able to hire labor, often because labor shortages occur when men migrate and other women are taking care of their own families. When land use shifts from a primarily food crop to a primarily cash crop, or when a traditionally consumed crop begins to become marketable, men may take over the plots. Whenever new machinery or new technologies are introduced, men frequently take over. In one Nigerian village studied, women took on new farm tasks as men went to work off the farm, but men maintained control of productive resources.[38]

In bringing technical assistance and extension services to villages, official agencies often insist on dealing with the men, even though women do the work. Laws may not permit women to own land or be eligible for loans, and lack of formal legal standing may preclude their signing any contract. Projects oriented to women's needs including health care, education, and agricultural skills often struggle for recognition. If incorporated into overall assistance programs, they may be subordinated to similar male-oriented programs. If separated out for special consideration, they are often marginalized, rather than integrated into the full benefits of assistance projects. Development agencies frequently walk a fine line, having to either breach well-entrenched social customs or risk ineffectiveness by dealing with people who are not going to implement innovations.[39]

Physical Capital: The Trouble with Machines

Differences exist between past agricultural development in the industrialized countries and that of today's developing countries. In the West, the capital intensity (ratio of capital to labor) of agriculture increased slowly, usually as a response to abundant land resources. The use of capital corresponded to the relative scarcity of labor, as opposed to the sometimes overcrowded rural sectors today. Early capital-intensive agriculture usually proceeded along with a country's industrial capacities and did not depend on imports of agricultural machinery, spare parts, and fuel (until later on). It proceeded apace with technological capacity and did not depend on much imported expertise. Finally, capital-intensive agriculture in some industrialized countries did not have much competition from cheap food imports.

Agricultural machinery must be appropriate to the patterns of land and labor use. Some older patterns of cultivation permitted much of the land to lie fallow. For example, in the "slash and burn," or swidden system, a plot was burned after the harvest and not used for some years to allow soil nutrients to build up. As population pressure increases, these patterns often give way to new methods and new crops that have an annual cycle or even use the same land for two or three crops per year. That transition increases the need for plowing, fertilizing, and watering the soil, and the appropriate machinery (including construction of irrigation facilities) may actually make use of more labor than previously.[40]

As the size of plots decreases under population pressure, handheld tools, small machines (such as rototillers), and animal-drawn implements are more efficient than large tractors and combines. Innovative social arrangements might permit large groups of people to rent and share machinery.

Attempts in some developing countries to apply capital-intensive methods to agriculture have led to a number of adverse consequences, including abrupt shortages of fuel and spare parts in times of foreign exchange scarcity, additional rural-urban migration (and concentrated ownership of land), production of crops not suited to local land and diets, and counterproductive use of local and foreign capital. Like any other decision, the use of machinery requires farmers to consider a whole range of costs and benefits. These can be best evaluated when market criteria are extended to the cost of capital, including the provision of credit for its purchase.[41]

Financing Agricultural Development

The lack of reliable, low-cost credit has often prevented farmers from adopting new agricultural technologies. As we saw in Chapter 4, formal financial institutions were not established in rural areas because bankers thought savings were low and profitable investments rare. Government institutions frequently embodied the same attitudes.

But while the potential savings do exist in the rural economy, individuals' savings tend to be small in amounts and scattered among the population. In some regions, particularly Central America and the Caribbean, attempts to find savings in rural areas have been successful.[42] As we saw in Chapter 4, the Grameen Bank in Bangladesh, lending mainly for nonagricultural projects in rural areas, is an example of what can be accomplished. Projects in Malaysia and Malawi have shown that similar results can be obtained in other countries. The Bank Rakyat Indonesia established a Village Bank system that has reached "millions of low-income rural clients without relying on subsidies."[43]

The primary objective of credit policy should be to create a self-sustaining set of financial institutions in the rural areas. The objectives of these institutions is not simply to provide credit but to mobilize savings as well. They provide market interest rates for savers, with the knowledge that sufficiently productive agricultural investment will be able to afford market rates. Such full-service institutions can provide rural areas with local sources of funds and provide a greater sense of community, which fosters saving and investment.

A visible portion of savings collected in an area should be reinvested there, showing people the fruits of their efforts and encouraging a sense of responsibility in which failure to repay a loan can be seen as hurting their neighbors. Banks with their base in the urban areas must overcome their reluctance to lend to small farmers. Small farmers and entrepreneurs, with just a little bit of backing, are capable of invigorating an economy.

Financial institutions must be familiar with the local economy and the local people. Bank personnel must take an "outreach" approach, going to where the people are.[44] They must be committed to their task and make efforts to ease the processes of depositing money and obtaining loans. Transportation time and long delays in processing will cause the opportunity cost of the loan to increase dramatically, especially when the amounts are small.

Attempts to force banks to devote a certain amount or percentage of their loans to agriculture have either been resisted or circumvented. Banks end up lending to large farmers and not even ensuring that the loans are used for agricultural or even rural investment.

One summary concludes that "Whether the private market is capable of meeting the demand for credit at reasonable rates of interest, or whether the government should supplement private credit with official credit, is one of the unsettled questions in agricultural development." The author cites research that supports market-determined interest rates as the best way to allocate scarce credit while also suggesting that viable, independent peasant cooperatives, by pooling resources and skills, can reduce the risk associated with individual loans and bring down interest rates.[45]

Informal finance has existed in rural areas for centuries. Although terms were sometimes difficult, due to high costs and monopoly power, this has not been universally true. Credit is a way of life in agriculture. Traditional arrangements may have involved a good deal of reciprocity: Community needs were recognized along with individual needs.[46] Newer institutions that replace informal financial arrangements must make conditions better, not worse.

Adaptation of Technology: Agricultural Extension

Machinery is only one aspect of technology. Agricultural technology involves more fundamental issues like methods of planting, soil-specific fertilizers, and the proper application of new varieties of seeds. Significant research into seeds is required to take advantage of local soil conditions and climate. Farmers must consider the relation of fertilizers to soil types and the ecology. The effectiveness of fertilizer must be balanced against its cost, especially in foreign exchange.

Agriculture specialists have paid increasing attention to what kind of agricultural research takes place and how information is conveyed to farmers. **Agricultural extension** is a way for trained government officials to help farmers learn about and use new technologies. Small demonstration plots, sown by local extension agents under conditions faced by farmers, can give the evidence of results. In turn, these agents must be open to the techniques that local people have used for generations. Experience confirms that farmers will adopt new seed varieties and new techniques that are proven to be technically and economically reliable. Years of experience in Turkey and India have shown that agents must make frequent visits to farms. The World Bank's "training and visit system" has shown the benefits that can be derived from regular, long-term contacts between agent and farmer.[47]

The environment of innovation has become so important that some economists explicitly follow what has been called the **induced innovation model** of agricultural development.[48] This model highlights the incentives to save on scarce resources. In labor-scarce economies such as the United States and Canada, early technological development emphasized heavy use of machinery so a few workers could farm large land areas. In the land- and capital-scarce economies of Asia, the inducements to innovation focus on biological and chemical means to increase the productivity of the land. This is the sort of innovation that has characterized the Green Revolution.

The Social Character of Technology: The Green Revolution

The **Green Revolution** refers to the combination of high-yielding seed varieties along with more intensive use of water and fertilizers to increase production. The application of this new technology has social consequences.[49]

Progress and Problems

The Green Revolution of the 1960s and 1970s was a response to global concern about the slow growth of food production in the developing world. It was the result of agricultural research carried out mainly by the International Rice Research Institute (IRRI) in the Philippines and the International Maize and Wheat Improvement Center (CIMMYT is the acronym in Spanish) in Mexico. It introduced new high-yielding varieties (HYVs—sometimes referred to as MVs, for "modern varieties") of seed for both these crops and was hailed as the savior of developing-country agriculture. An example is provided in Development Spotlight 8–1. Difficulties arose, however, when it became clear that the use of these seeds required amounts of land, water, fertilizers, and machinery that were often unavailable to many small farmers. Some saw in this combination yet another way of impoverishing the small producer, stacking the deck in favor of rich landowners and those in wealthy countries who would supply the new inputs.[50]

Research into these questions has not absolutely resolved the distributional questions. Resource requirements of new seed varieties may have widened income disparities among regions in India and between landowners and tenants. The new agricultural technology seems to have reduced food prices and increased income and employment. Ultimately, if a society is determined to distribute the gains of innovation more equally, it will do so despite the nature of the technology. One study in the Philippines concludes that while large farms gained disproportionately, this could have been avoided by programs aimed at helping small farmers. Another study suggests that as the new technologies spread rapidly, they encouraged interregional migration that tended to equalize wages.[51]

A major study by Inderjit Singh provides some results of the yields in Bangladesh, India, and Pakistan showing output per acre as much as double that of traditional varieties. Even *without* the use of fertilizers, some HYVs had yields that were as much as one and a half those of traditional varieties for rice and one and two-thirds those for wheat. He concludes that many of the social ills attributed to the HYV "packages" were the result of implementation policies and not of the technology itself. For instance, he found that "small farmers have adopted and continue to adopt HYVs when they are suitable and profitable." They were slower to do so than larger farmers, because the risks from failure would be greater and because they lacked access to credit, but eventually caught up. Small farmers did have more trouble affording the fertilizers but were able to substitute more intensive labor with good results. Even landless cultivators benefited through greater employment, higher wages, and lower food prices. The mechanization accompanying some experiments, like the fertilizers, could be separated from the HYVs and did not have to cause unemployment. Finally, increasing concentration of land, and consequent removal of poor peasants from their landholdings, once again were due to policies that accompanied the HYVs but were not inevitably caused by them.[52]

A series of articles evaluating the Green Revolution in Bangladesh concluded that it resulted in greater and more consistent output of grains but not enough to increase per capita consumption. Consumption of grain to some extent only replaced consumption of other foods such as fruit, vegetables, and fish. Agriculture remains heavily labor intensive, because the nonagricultural labor market has not expanded rapidly enough to absorb rural labor that might have been freed up by new technologies.[53] Case 8–1 provides detail on the Green Revolution in Bangladesh.

The "revolution" has raised longer-term issues as well. The rest of the rural economy has generally lagged behind production. Governments did not anticipate such large increases in output and were not prepared with milling or transportation facilities needed to take advantage of supply. Some crops went to waste. Some previous importers and marginally self-sufficient countries started to accumulate surpluses that they wanted to export. This brought them into conflict with the developed grain-exporting

DEVELOPMENT SPOTLIGHT 8–1

IMPROVED VARIETIES OF WHEAT AND MAIZE

A good deal of the research into wheat has taken place in Mexico. The following data give the average potential yield (kilograms per hectare) of several varieties of bread wheat released in Mexico over the period 1950 to 1985.

Decade	Number of Varieties	Average Yield
1950s	1	3,500
1960s	7	5,900
1970s	16	7,250
1980s*	7	7,790

*Through 1985.

The spread of high-yielding varieties may be limited due to expense, natural conditions, peasant resistance, etc. There is a direct, although not perfect, relationship between average yields (tons per hectare) and the percentage of area planted in high-yielding varieties of maize. (Other factors are also important, of course.)

Region	Percentage Area in HYVs	Average Yield
South America, Southern Cone	76	2.1
East Asia	72	3.7
North Africa, Middle East	47	2.7
Mexico, Central America, Caribbean	42	1.6
Southeast Asia, Pacific	37	1.2
East/Southern Africa	36	1.2
South Asia	34	1.3
South America, Andean	29	1.7
West/Central Africa	22	0.9

Sources: Dana Dalrymple, *Development and Spread of High-Yielding Wheat Varieties in Developing Countries* (Washington: United States Agency for International Development, 1986), and David H. Timothy, Paul H. Harvey, and Christopher R. Dowswell, *Development and Spread of Improved Maize Varieties and Hybrids in Developing Countries* (Washington: United States Agency for International Development, 1988).

CASE 8-1

THE GREEN REVOLUTION IN BANGLADESH

FAST FACTS

On the Map: South Asia

Population: 128 Million

Per Capita GNI and Rank: $370   (170)

Life Expectancy: Male—63   Female—74

Adult Literacy Rate: Male—52%
Female—29%

A study of the impact of the Green Revolution in Bangladesh provides an optimistic view of what is possible. The improvements began with an increase in the area planted with Modern Varieties (MV) of rice and wheat, along with increased inputs of water, through irrigation, and chemical fertilizer.

Share of Wheat and Rice Area Planted with MV Seed

1967/1968	0.6%
1970/1971	4.6%
1985/1986	31.0%

Share of Land Under Modern Irrigation

1960/1961	0.3%
1973/1974	7.2%
1984/1985	21.5%

Sales of Chemical Fertilizer: Kilograms of Nutrients Per Acre

	All Seasons	Dry Season
1960/1961	0.9	2.6
1970/1971	4.6	15.2
1984/1985	18.1	44.8

One result was higher rates of growth of both overall production and the yield per unit of land.

Growth Rates (Percentage per Year) for All Crops

	Yield/Unit of Land	Production
1950–1971	1.40	2.52
1971–1985	2.02	2.92

Independent Estimates of Crop Yields for Rice (Tons/Acre)

	1980–1982	1981–1982	1982–1985
Traditional	0.67	0.65	0.65
Modern	1.31	1.33	1.41

While seed costs remained the same, the modern seeds produced more and so cost less as a portion of output.

Cost of Seed for Rice, 1982

	Taka* Per Acre	Percentage of Output
Traditional	156	6.3%
Modern	156	3.0

*Taka is the unit of currency in Bangladesh.

Total costs per acre rose, but cost per ton of output was down and profits were up.

Total Cost and Estimated Profits, 1984/1985

	Total Costs (Taka)		Estimated Profits	
	Per Acre	Per Metric Ton	Per Acre	Percentage of Costs
Traditional	2,425	3,720	1,038	43
Modern	4,200	2,990	2,296	55

The higher costs per acre reflect better seed, more fertilizer, and irrigation. The higher yield gives not only lower cost per ton but higher profits, even though inflation between 1975 and 1985 hit the modern varieties harder due to their more intensive use of inputs.

The net return to family labor is 75 taka per day with the traditional varieties and 87 taka per day with the modern varieties. Small farmers and tenants have been somewhat *more* likely to adopt the modern varieties than medium and large farmers. They have found the package less profitable than larger farms but still fare better than under traditional varieties. "The comparative patterns of income distribution for all rural households (including the landless) show a neutral affect for the new technology" as the top 20 percent took away slightly from the middle 40 percent with no change in the share of income going to the poorest 40 percent. Land-less laborers have actually improved their status due to greater employment and higher wages. The downside noted in the study was that higher profits seem to have led to greater concentration of landholdings, and the entire process does not seem to have increased agricultural investment noticeably.

Source: Mahabub Hossain, "Nature and Impact of the Green Revolution in Bangladesh" (Washington: International Food Policy Research Institute, Research Report 67, July 1988).

countries, such as the United States and France, which support their agriculture by subsidizing overseas sales, often in aid programs. Farmers and environmentalists are also concerned about the impact of both the new seed and the new technology on the environment. If soil fertility is damaged and genetic diversity is dramatically reduced, there could be long-term ecological problems. In countries such as India, variety is being reduced as high-yielding wheat, maize, and rice replace cotton, legumes, and oilseeds.[54]

Much of this perceived difficulty might be considered an opportunity, however. When food supplies are relatively assured, the government can shift its attention to other development needs. Less need for government subsidies could free resources for research, education, and infrastructure.

Second-Stage Green Revolution

Some agricultural specialists have been concerned that the Green Revolution has run its course. Fertilizers are being used intensively, irrigation is showing diminishing returns, the flood of new scientific results is drying up, and production increases are slowing. Yields in cereals production are still rising but at a slower rate. Comparing Asian yields in the 1986 to 1995 period with the previous 10 years, growth rates were down in rice (from 3.5 percent per year to 1.5 percent), in wheat (from 5.4 percent to 2.1 percent), and in maize (from 3.9 percent to 3.4 percent). Sustainability is a concern because of the intensive input use associated with modern varieties.[55] And the early promise of biotechnology is being reconsidered in the face of legal battles between companies and farmers over the ownership of genetically engineered plants and concerns about safety.[56]

But there should be additional gains, even if the revolutionary impact of the 1960s and 1970s is somewhat diminished. Supporters of continued research point to possibilities in pest resistance, drought tolerance, and promoting genetic diversity in spite of some early tendencies to reduce it. There is a limit to extending improved varieties to marginal soil, but some are doing well with rain-fed agriculture, as well as with irrigation.

Biotechnology holds promise to address these problems. Genetic engineering research is being aimed at increasing the ability of plants to take up nitrogen from the soil, resist disease, and increase their nutritional value. Biofertilizers are being used to help plants absorb more nitrogen from the atmosphere, and plant-based "green" manures may also replace some chemical fertilizers. As long as the benefits of continued research outweigh its costs, and research investment yields returns comparable to other investments, we can expect further help from the Green Revolution.[57]

ADDITIONAL ASPECTS OF AGRICULTURAL DEVELOPMENT

Agricultural development is an integral part of economic development. Industry must provide goods for farmers to buy. Nonfarm employment is necessary to keep families in rural areas. And food production must be consistent with consumer tastes.

Incentive Goods

Farmers do not produce a surplus simply to make money. The money is valuable only if there are goods to buy, sometimes called **incentive goods**. These include bicycles, radios, clothing, construction materials, furniture, cookware, and education. The rural population represents a large volume of potential consumption. Insufficiency of incentive goods, or inability to deliver them to rural areas, could lead to reductions in agricultural output or smuggling of raw materials outside the country to be exchanged for consumer goods; it could also cause an exodus of more active members of the population from the rural areas.

Rural Industry

Agriculture is not the only activity that takes place in rural areas. What others are appropriate?

Service activities related to agriculture include marketing, finance, provision of social services, machine maintenance, retail services, government, and managerial and administrative services. In addition, villages will need manufacturing, based on raw materials produced in the agricultural sector, that meet the needs of consumers who are far from the cities. These activities include grain milling and other food processing, clothing, leather goods, construction material, and farm implements.

There are a number of reasons to pay attention to rural industry:

> The accumulating empirical evidence indicates that these activities not only generate a significant amount of rural employment and output but also provide an important source of income for rural households. Moreover, there is mounting evidence that several kinds of rural industries may be more economically efficient than their larger-scale urban counterparts.[58]

Local activities are likely to center on rural demands. It is also important to provide a variety of economic activity to retain people in the rural areas. Farming will not be for everyone, especially as people become aware of alternatives.

Migration to cities has positive and negative effects. Studies of the Uttar Pradesh region of India showed that migrants remit substantial earnings to their rural relatives. But although the Lewis model hypothesized that outflow of surplus labor would increase farm productivity, this depends on who leaves and who stays. Without options, the more energetic portions of the population are likely to stream into the towns and cities, as happened in a very short span of years in Nigeria, resulting in stagnation of agriculture.[59]

Rural towns will not hold everyone, of course, but for viable alternatives to cities, to maintain family life, and for the sake of the extra help that is required seasonally on the farm, there should be a normal mix of population—by age, gender, and skills—in the rural areas. Financial institutions will be crucial, not only as part of the new rural landscape themselves but as agents of rural development.

A large portion of nonfarming enterprise in rural areas is managed by women. Whether as an adjunct to growing food, such as food marketing, or as off-peak employment in handicrafts or factory work, women's income is crucial to whether the family lives below or above the poverty line. Supporting women's education, legal status, and access to credit will go a long way to supporting their position in rural industry.

Food Consumption: Agricultural Change and Diet

Consumption needs are frequently left out of the discussion of agriculture in developing countries. Dietary habits may be difficult to change: New crop varieties and food aid may be rejected by local people because they do not cook properly or quickly, or have adverse social connotations, or just plain do not taste good.[60] The desirability of new crops, like new technology, should be gauged according to market criteria rather than outside advice on what consumption patterns represent development.

The opposite problem may also occur. When developing countries turn to the industrialized countries for food assistance, they are pressed to buy (at concessional rates) whatever the seller has in surplus that year. The result has often been the introduction of relatively new grains, such as rice or wheat, for which people quickly acquire a taste. This may skew local production to those commodities despite higher capital costs and greater vulnerability to drought. Proponents of food aid maintain that the increasing openness of the world economy is naturally changing peoples' tastes as they acquire more information. Governments should be careful, however, not to use the price system to artificially encourage costly dietary substitutes.

THE ROLE OF GOVERNMENT

Government intervention in agriculture is a worldwide phenomenon.[61] Farm subsidies and supports in the rich countries not only encourage inefficiency by drawing excess resources *into* agriculture and require budgetary outlays, but hurt poorer countries by encouraging surplus output, much of which is sold in the international market at below-market prices with which the poor cannot compete. Many developing-country governments have gone much further into the business of agriculture; not content to regulate prices and provide technical advice, they have engaged in many production and commercial activities in this sector. The results have often been disastrous, as illustrated by the example of Tanzania in Case 8–2. On the other hand, reform

CASE 8–2

STATE-DIRECTED AGRICULTURE IN TANZANIA

FAST FACTS

On the Map: East Africa

Population: 33 Million

Per Capita GNI and Rank: $260   (187)

Life Expectancy: Male—44   Female—46

Adult Literacy Rate: Male—84%
Female—66%

Tanzania has a reasonably diverse agricultural base. In addition to producing food crops, primarily maize, millet, some rice, and cassava, it has exported coffee, tea, pyrethrum (from which insecticides are made), tobacco, sisal (from which rope and the like are made), and, from the island of Zanzibar, cloves. However, it has remained largely agricultural with few minerals and a poorly developed manufacturing sector. For over 20 years, the government of Tanzania moved progressively along a state-directed path of agricultural development.

Tanzania is one of the poorest countries in the world. In the first decade after independence from Britain in 1962, significant progress was made in improving health and access to education. But agriculture produced about one-half of total national product, the same as in 1965. Exports declined by over 4 percent per year between 1965 and 1980 and about the same in the 1980s, before recovering to grow rapidly in the 1990s. In 1999, foreign aid was equal to 66 percent of gross domestic investment.

At independence, the country had no overarching economic plan, but from 1967 the government committed itself to an agrarian socialism (*ujamaa*), accompanied by exhortations to peasants to move from scattered plots into villages. Some villages were formed voluntarily and performed well. But by the early 1970s, millions of peasants were

more or less forcibly moved. Under the circumstances, peasants minimized their time on communal plots.

By the 1980s, government was in charge of:

- Producing fertilizers and providing inputs to farmers
- Setting prices for major crops
- Buying and transporting the crops
- Milling the major foodcrop (maize)
- Selling the milled flour and all export crops
- Running all wholesale trade and even numerous retail stores in the villages
- Running all social services in the villages, including education and medical care
- Maintaining infrastructure and owning the largest manufacturing operations in the country

With the help of foreign aid, agricultural research institutes were set up, and almost every region of the country had its own integrated rural development project. But food production per person was sluggish, and agricultural exports declined.

Agricultural inputs were very costly (subsidized fertilizer cost twice the world price) and frequently late in arriving. Mechanization was expensive, especially when oil prices shot up and foreign exchange shortages made spare parts difficult to get. Inadequate attention to crop storage resulted in losses of as much as one-fourth of the crop in some years. Collection of crops was frequently late—resulting in more losses—and often the government could not pay farmers on time. The main company responsible for processing the food—the National Milling

Corporation (NMC)—was inefficient and a major drain on the government's budget for its annual subsidy.

The government took on the task of setting prices for all major food and export crops. For several years the government deliberately set prices low with an eye on the consumer, but eventually it attempted to approximate market prices, although with little success. The data that might show the impact of these problems are extremely unreliable because we know only how much food was collected and not how much peasants kept for themselves or smuggled across the borders to Kenya, Zaire, Zambia, and Mozambique.

The list of all the government tried to do—in a country with only a handful of college graduates at independence—suggests that major problems were bound to occur. At the end of the 1980s the country had been transformed from a net exporter of food to a net importer, with no appreciable improvement in the standard of living of the

peasantry. A study comparing Tanzania with five other low-income countries concluded that "the sheer magnitude of the burden imposed on both agricultural sub-sectors . . . short-circuited the development process and, more specifically, jeopardised the desired industrialisation."

Sources: Reginald Green, D. Rwegasira, and Brian Van Arkadie, *Economic Shocks and National Policy Making: Tanzania in the 1970s* (The Hague: Institute of Social Studies, 1980); "Political–Economic Adjustment and IMF Conditionality: Tanzania 1974–81," in John Williamson, *IMF Conditionality* (Washington: Institute for International Economics, 1983), pp. 347–380; Alex Duncan and Stephen Jones, "Agricultural Marketing and Pricing Reform: A Review of Experience," *World Development* 21, no. 9 (September 1993), pp. 1495–1514; and T. S. Jayne and Stephen Jones, "Food Marketing and Pricing Policy in Eastern and Southern Africa: A Survey, *World Development* 25, no. 9 (September 1997), pp. 1505–1527. The final quote is from J. Lecaillon et al., *Economic Policies and Agricultural Performance of Low-Income Countries* (Paris: OECD, 1987), p. 193. Much of the situation in the early 1980s comes from observations made by the author during two years in Tanzania, 1980 to 1982.

measures have achieved significant progress, as illustrated by the Chinese example in Case 8–3.

We have focused on government policies throughout this chapter. However, agricultural policies warrant a separate discussion. Governments have both a microeconomic and macroeconomic role in the agricultural sector.

Government's Microeconomic Role

One good rule of thumb is that "independent private firms have a comparative advantage over public agencies in carrying out *commercial* functions such as production or marketing farm products or distributing farm inputs."[62] The closer we come to the individual decisions that farmers must make about their specific circumstances, the more sense it makes to put decision making in the hands of the private firm. The debate over public ownership in these areas has arisen in part because so many governments have intervened where private activities did not exist but have remained to discourage, not encourage, private activity. In Tanzania, Zambia, and some other African countries, governments started taking control of finance, major industry, and export-import operations. Within 10 to 15 years, in the name of eliminating exploitation by private enterprise, these governments were operating local bus services, small retail establishments, and a variety of small-scale firms. Much of this activity quickly deteriorates due to incompetence and corruption.

CASE 8–3

COLLECTIVIZATION AND REFORM IN CHINESE AGRICULTURE

FAST FACTS

On the Map: Asia

Population: 1,254 Million

Per Capita GNI and Rank: $780　(142)

Life Expectancy: Male—68　Female—72

Adult Literacy Rate: Male—91%
Female—75%

China's agricultural policies have undergone considerable changes over the last 50 years. The postrevolutionary period saw the implementation of classic state-centered policies including collectivization of production, government-controlled prices, and government monopolization of the distribution system. By 1958, 120 million households were organized into 24,000 communes to better organize crop production, irrigation, and infrastructure. From 1952 through 1958, grain output grew by one-fourth, outpacing population growth. The government was the sole buyer of grain, and food was rationed to ensure low prices and deliveries to urban centers.

However, a major drop in production over the next three years brought output below the 1952 level, and 1958 output was not surpassed until 1966. This disaster, which resulted in about 30 million deaths from starvation from 1959 to 1961, brought some experimentation. Aside from modernizing inputs of fertilizer, seed, and irrigation, however, no major policy changes took place until new government leadership arrived in 1978.

Between 1978 and 1995, the Chinese government made three major changes: (1) Production was removed from communal production teams to households, under the "household responsibility system." This

was virtually complete by 1983. (2) The right to buy and sell grain was opened to the private sector, although the state still handles most of the activity. (3) The government became more sensitive to pricing, starting with huge increases in procurement prices.

The pricing system is constantly being modified. Peasant households are still given production quotas. The government, however, is unwilling to rely on markets for pricing and must continually decide what prices it should offer. It has been caught between keeping prices high enough to sustain farmers' incentives and its policy of subsidizing food prices for consumers. The more it pays for grain, the more is produced and the more expensive it is to subsidize and store food. In 1984, for example, a peak production year to that point, food subsidies accounted for over 20 percent of the government budget. When it reduces grain prices to farmers, however, production often suffers because households now have greater freedom to switch to other crops or even nonagricultural activities.

On the whole, production continues to outpace population growth, and China has even exported grain in good years. But its commitment to achieving self-sufficiency has been costly to the government budget. Grain prices at both the procurement and resale points were finally freed in 1993, but households still have grain quotas to meet. When production is below expectations, the government becomes more intrusive in decisions at the local level. The future of this approach is increasingly in doubt. As China's land/labor ratio falls, and as the economy becomes increasingly oriented toward industry and services, grain self-sufficiency becomes a less realistic goal for the Chinese economy.

Another crucial aspect of China's rural areas is the increasing importance of small enterprises. While good data are elusive, it is clear that the number of such enterprises has increased dramatically, especially since 1984 when private enterprise took off. Most enterprises remain collective, however, owned by townships and villages. Such collective enterprises accounted for about two-thirds of rural nonagricultural output in 1990. In most industries, productivity advance in collective rural enter-prises has exceeded that of the large state enterprises.

Sources: Justin Yifu Lin, "Agricultural Development and Reform in China," in Carl Eicher and John Staatz, eds., *International Agricultural Development*, 3rd ed. (Baltimore: Johns Hopkins University Press, 1998), pp. 523–538; Gary H. Jefferson, "Are China's Rural Enterprises Outperforming State Enterprises? Estimating the Pure Ownership Effect," in Jefferson and Inderjit Sing, *Enterprise Reform in China: Ownership, Transition, and Performance* (New York: Oxford University Press/World Bank, 1999), pp. 153–170; and Michelle S. Mood, "The Impact and Prospects of Rural Enterprise," in Christopher Hudson, ed., *The China Handbook* (Chicago: Fitzroy Dearborn Publishers, 1997), pp. 122–136.

But when *should* a government intervene? Here we anticipate the arguments in Chapter 10. Structural rigidities in agriculture—factors that prevent change in response to market pressures—are prevalent in the early stages of development. Government intervention is extremely difficult, due to the large number of small, private actors, but is essential for the same reason: Some activities are likely beyond the scope of individual small farmers.

Infrastructure

Government, both national and local, has a key role in provision of infrastructure, especially where it may be able to obtain external funding for capital projects. Such projects, including roads, power, communications, and irrigation, have been in the public domain since Adam Smith, due to their high capital requirements, long gestation periods, and creation of external economies. Much of this infrastructure makes agriculture more productive and breaks down barriers to markets, thereby improving the efficiency of resource allocation throughout the economy.

Information

Provision of information is a multifaceted undertaking. Farmers need information about market conditions, new technologies, and even what to expect from the weather. So research and development becomes a prime target for focused government spending, as does extension services to bring the results of research to the farm. Education and training help farmers improve productivity and manage their operations.

Market Building

Governments can help create and improve markets by providing accurate measurements for crops, providing insurance against crop failures, and encouraging small-scale credit activities that make saving and borrowing easier for farmers. In some cases, when areas are truly isolated, governments may have to take the initiative in making transportation, storage, and marketing facilities available, although such activities should eventually be undertaken by private firms and individuals as the barriers between markets are broken down.

Public Policies

Government officials should remain aware of the incentive effects—positive and negative—of taxes, subsidies, and services that are offered. For example, taxes are necessary but should not reduce production incentives; they should not cause a decline in the rural/urban terms of trade.

Government's Macroeconomic Role

Studies of government's impact on agriculture frequently point to macroeconomic problems that seem far removed from the farm.[63] This impact is felt through the five macro prices—wages, interest rates, land rents, the agricultural terms of trade, and foreign exchange rates. When governments make budgets, engage in deficit spending, and determine monetary policy (see Chapter 11), they affect these macro prices. The budget process is an obvious starting point, because it determines the extent to which resources will go to agriculture and other sectors of the economy. But seemingly neutral macro policy decisions affect agriculture, especially when their result is inflation.[64]

Interest rates are an obvious link that we have discussed in Chapter 4. Even if manipulated for their macro impact, they affect the cost and availability of credit for farmers. If interest rates are too low, nonmarket allocation of credit often bypasses politically marginal farmers. If rates need to be raised dramatically to fight inflation, credit will be too expensive for those farmers who lack high-yielding investments.

Inflation has a negative impact on real purchasing power. Urban residents may then put pressure on governments to keep food prices below market levels. Rents too may rise with inflation, because people may convert financial assets into land to protect the value of their wealth. When that happens, land values will rise, especially if land acquired for these purposes is kept out of production. The resulting increases in rents will leave poorer farmers without access to land.

The agricultural terms of trade are subject to unpredictable pressures in the presence of inflation. Not all prices rise equally, and urban bias often ensures that governments exert more effort to control food prices than those of manufactured goods that farmers must buy. Inflation also discourages investment and slows down increases in agricultural productivity. Distortions of product prices, wages, and interest rates can also confuse the choice of appropriate technology in unpredictable ways.

Finally, governments can also distort economic decisions by manipulating the rate of exchange between the country's own currency and foreign currencies. If the domestic currency is priced above its market value in foreign markets, this causes greatest damage in agriculture. First, it discourages agricultural exports because foreigners have to pay more to get the currency to buy these goods that are sold in highly competitive international markets. Second, it encourages imports by making foreign currencies cheaper: Food imports are encouraged, providing downward pressure on domestic production, prices, and incomes. Imports of capital goods and intermediate goods are encouraged, which tends to bias domestic production toward industry and away from agriculture.

All these problems have damaged agriculture in developing countries. However, there is a growing awareness of these linkages between macro- and agricultural policies. Significant progress has been made in reducing inflation, especially in Latin America, and in promoting more realistic interest rates and exchange rates. Improved macro policies will not themselves produce agricultural development, but they clear away very real impediments and allow governments to address the agricultural sector directly without having their efforts negated by the inadvertent fallout from macro-policies.

FOOD VS. AGRICULTURE: A QUESTION OF BALANCE

There is a fundamental question about the goals of agricultural development. Agriculture is, after all, more than just the production of food. It includes industrial crops such as cotton, jute (for rope and bags), pyrethrum (for insect repellent), and tobacco. Not all the food grown is meant for domestic consumption: Much will be exported. So a debate arises as to whether a poor country should concentrate on the production of basic foodstuffs (**food crops** or **staples**, such as corn and beans) or—if a choice must be made—on crops for export (**cash crops**, such as coffee and cocoa) to earn foreign exchange. Some crops—such as wheat, corn, rice, and cotton—may be put in both categories. The choice of crops is more than a matter of producer profit and consumer demand. The dependence of many countries on agriculture means that the kind of crops planted has a great impact on the country's development.

Colonial Policy

Under colonial governments, indigenous farmers could not always choose which crops to grow. The colonial powers frequently developed agriculture in these countries according to the needs of the home country, either for direct consumption or for trade. Sugar plantations in the Caribbean and Africa; sisal plantations in Africa and Asia; and vast areas of land devoted to such "first world" tastes as coffee, tea, and cocoa were often a direct result of decisions made by colonial governments and backed up by a combination of threats and price incentives. The requirement to pay taxes in money forced farmers to grow crops for which money, rather than barter, was received and often prodded men to leave their families for months to work on faraway plantations. But independence, and the accompanying distrust of the colonial powers and the world market, raised the question anew: Should a country reorient its production to satisfy its own food requirements, or should it continue to rely on export crops to earn the foreign exchange with which to import food?

Self-Sufficiency vs. Food Security

Much of the damage done to agricultural production and the new dependence on food imports has been the result of government policies intended to achieve self-sufficiency in basic foodstuffs. However, even if policies toward that end could be successful, the question still arises as to whether it is a worthy goal.

Self-sufficiency is important to countries that are reluctant to depend on outsiders for food in critical situations or to depend on fluctuations of international food prices. In 1973 world rice prices rose 85 percent, followed by 90 percent the following year, only to fall by a third in 1975 and another 30 percent in 1976. Many economists prefer **food security** to self-sufficiency.[65] This involves a mix of domestic production and reliance on international markets as an important supplement, on the basis of the old economics standby, comparative advantage. By producing mainly those goods for which the country has a relative cost advantage and importing the rest, it will use resources more efficiently and thus produce more output and income: Imported food will be cheaper than inefficient use of domestic resources.

In other words, self-sufficiency is costly. Are there political benefits that make it desirable? Under what circumstances? It is worthwhile repeating that the industrialized countries engage in significant protection of their agricultural sectors and developing countries could, with the right policies, do so in ways that would encourage food production rather than discourage it, although when *everyone* does that, global misallocation of resources is obvious. We should also recall that a number of developing countries were developed not simply toward export agriculture per se, but also toward relatively specialized export production, to the extent that some countries relied on one, two, or three crops for the bulk of their foreign exchange earnings.[66] The evidence indicates that an appropriate agricultural policy that balances diverse export and food crops can be successful.[67] These are the issues that governments must address.

The Food Situation

Hunger is a local phenomenon. The World Bank, in its 1986 report on *Poverty and Hunger* began by noting "The world has ample food. The growth of global food production has been faster than the unprecedented population growth of the past forty years."[68] Nonetheless, food production has stagnated in many of the low- and middle-income countries, and production per capita has fallen in many of the poorest. The data in Table 8–6 indicate the dimensions of the problem. Per capita food production fell during the 1980s in Sub-Saharan Africa.[69] Cereals imports increased dramatically between 1974 and 1999. Food aid to Africa increased by a factor of two and a half between 1974 and 1989. Some of the shortfall was "filled" by people eating less.

Proponents of food security might consider the increase in food imports a positive sign, except that in Sub-Saharan Africa it is due to lower production decline in the face of serious attempts to increase food output. Proponents of self-sufficiency consider these imports evidence that self-sufficiency is even more necessary, except that production has dropped in spite of—or because of—those very attempts at self-sufficiency.

An economy should develop on the basis of its current resources and a realistic assessment of its near- to middle-term capacity for change. But it is sobering to suggest that a country whose ability to import food, medicine, machinery, and other goods depends on the export of a few crops should deepen that dependence in the name of food security. A more diverse and stable export base is necessary to allow secure funding for food imports.

TABLE 8–6 Food Production and Imports

	Food Output per Capita (1989–1991 = 100)			Cereals Imports (1,000 Metric Tons)		
	1974	*1986*	*2000*	*1974*	*1986*	*1999*
Sub-Saharan Africa	114.3	99.7	99.2	4,629	8,885	13,675
Developing Asia	72.9	93.8	127.6	35,065	53,941	86,822
South America	84.3	95.7	121.2	7,488	12,359	20,307

Source: United Nations Food and Agricultural Organization, ⟨http://apps.fao.org⟩.

SUMMARY AND CONCLUSION

Governments often took agricultural development for granted because development was defined as industrialization. The failure of agricultural policies to permit the greatest contribution of that sector to development has caused a reorientation of theory and policy. Farmers must be encouraged and given appropriate incentives to increase productivity and output, permitting both the improvement of their condition and the release of surplus food, labor, and capital to the industrial and service sectors.

A key part of agricultural policy is permitting agricultural prices to be largely market driven. High food prices at an early stage of development will increase incomes for the rural majority and elicit greater production. When supply begins to expand faster than demand, the agricultural terms of trade can fall for the betterment of growing urban populations.

A healthy agricultural sector requires attention to the efficient use of land, labor, and capital, with due regard for existing factor proportions. Governments can encourage agriculture with research, extension services, and creation of a climate for rural finance to flourish. They should be more cautious when it comes to actually engaging in productive or distribution activities, leaving as much as possible to the private sector. They also need to design macroeconomic policies that do not discourage agricultural development.

Key Terms

- agricultural extension (p. 211)
- agricultural productivity (p. 194)
- cash crops (p. 223)
- collective farms (p. 198)
- Engel's Law (p. 193)
- food crops (staples) (p. 223)
- food security (p. 223)
- Green Revolution (p. 212)
- income elasticity of demand (p. 194)
- incentive goods (p. 216)
- induced innovation model (p. 211)
- land reform (p. 205)
- land tenure (p. 204)
- marketing boards (p. 201)
- monocropping (p. 203)
- price ceiling (p. 199)
- sectoral terms of trade (p. 198)
- sharecropping (p. 204)
- tenancy (p. 204)

Questions for Review

1. What is "urban bias" in development, and what does such a view imply for the role of agriculture in the development process?
2. What are "terms of trade" as applied to agricultural development? What trend in those terms seems most compatible with successful agricultural development?
3. What are the principal contributions that agriculture can make to the development process?
4. Suppose that a government that is the sole buyer of a crop offers farmers $2.00 per ton for maize, while the market price across the border is $2.50 per ton. What will be the impact on production of maize? Will this affect production of other crops? Will the government likely be able to buy all the output?
5. What was the Green Revolution? What were some of the benefits that it brought to a country like Bangladesh? What problems came with it?
6. How can encouragement of rural industry contribute to agricultural development?
7. What guidelines can be used in evaluating how government support for agricultural development should be provided directly or through reliance on markets?
8. How did the Tanzanian government's attempts to direct agricultural development backfire?

9. What lessons for agricultural price policy can be gained from the Chinese experience?

10. If inflation refers to an increase in an economy's general price level, why should it be particularly problematic for agriculture?

11. How can economic analysis be used to clarify the debate between "self-sufficiency" and "food security?"

Related Internet Resources

Information on agriculture is key to a number of the Web sites on the environment and sustainable development presented in Chapter 5. For information on food production trends and practices, the UN's Food and Agricultural Organization is a basic resource. The main site is ⟨www.fao.org⟩, and its data are at ⟨http://apps.fao.org⟩. Public policy related to food is the primary activity of the International Food Policy Research Institute, at ⟨www.ifpri.org⟩. Important research on how to increase food yields and production is conducted by numerous international organizations. Many of them cooperate under the Consultative Group on International Agricultural Research, at ⟨www.cgiar.org⟩.

Endnotes and Further Readings

1. *World Development Report 1982: Agriculture and Economic Development* (New York: Oxford University Press, 1982), pp. 44–45.

2. Michael Lipton, *Why Poor People Stay Poor: Urban Bias in World Development* (Cambridge: Harvard University Press, 1976), popularized the expression. Also see Shutosh Varshnay, ed., "Beyond Urban Bias," *Journal of Development Studies* 29, no. 4 (July 1993), and John Staatz and Carl Eicher, "Agricultural Development Ideas in Historical Perspective," in their *Agricultural Development in the Third World*, 2nd ed. (Baltimore: Johns Hopkins University Press, 1990), pp. 3–38.

3. See Bruce Johnston and John Mellor, "The Role of Agriculture in Economic Development," *American Economic Review* 51, no. 4 (September 1961), pp. 566–593, and J. Lecaillon, C. Morrison, H. Schneider, and E. Thorbecke, *Economic Policies and Agricultural Performance of Low-Income Countries*, OECD Development Centre Study (Paris: OECD, 1987).

4. Kevin Cleaver and Gotz Schreiber, *Reversing the Spiral: The Population, Agriculture and Environment Nexus in Sub-Saharan Africa* (Washington: World Bank, 1994).

5. Paul Bairoch, *The Economic Development of the Third World Since 1900* (Berkeley: University of California Press, 1975), cited in C. Peter Timmer's chapter, "The Agricultural Transformation," in the *Handbook of Development Economics*, vol. 1, Hollis Chenery and T. N. Srinivasan, eds. (Amsterdam: Elsevier Science Publishers, 1988), p. 284.

6. Data are contradictory. See Steve Wiggins, "Change in African Farming Systems Between the Mid-1970s and the Mid-1980s," *Journal of International Development* 7, no. 6 (November–December 1995), pp. 807–840.

7. For example, see Roger Munting's *The Economic Development of the USSR* (New York: St. Martin's Press, 1982).

8. C. Peter Timmer, "Indonesia: Transition from Food Importer to Exporter," in Terry Sicular, ed., *Food Price Policy in Asia: A Comparative Study* (Ithaca, NY: Cornell University Press, 1989), pp. 22–64.

9. See Kevin Cleaver, "The Impact of Price and Exchange Rate Policies on Agriculture in Sub-Saharan Africa," World Bank Staff Working Paper No. 728 (Washington: World Bank, 1985).

10. *Ibid*. Also see Inderjit Singh, Lyn Squire, and James Kirchner, "Agricultural Pricing and Marketing Policies in an African Context," World Bank Staff Working Paper No. 743 (Washington: World Bank, 1985); C. Peter Timmer, *Getting Prices Right—The Scope and Limits of Agricultural Price Policy* (Ithaca, NY: Cornell University Press, 1986); Ojetunji Aboyade, "Administering Food Producer Prices in Africa: Lessons from International Experiences" (Washington: International Food Policy Research Institute, 1985); World Bank, "Trade and Pricing Policies in World Agriculture," *World Development Report 1986: Trade and Pricing Policies in World Agriculture* (New York: Oxford University Press, 1986); and Maurice Schiff and Alberto Valdes, *The Political Economy of Agricultural Pricing Policy*, vol. 4, *A Synthesis of the Economics in Developing Countries* (Baltimore: Johns Hopkins University Press, 1992).

11. Robert Stevens and Cathy Jabara, *Agricultural Development Principles* (Baltimore: Johns Hopkins University Press, 1988), p. 66.

12. Theodore Schultz, *Transforming Traditional Agriculture* (New Haven: Yale University Press, 1964). Also see Joseph E. Stiglitz, "Sharecropping," in John

Eatwell, Murray Milgate, and Peter Newman, eds., *The New Palgrave Economic Development* (New York: W. W. Norton, 1989), pp. 308–315.

13. See Frank Ellis, *Agricultural Policies in Developing Countries* (Cambridge: Cambridge University Press, 1992), especially chapter 4, "Price Policy."

14. T. S. Jayne and Stephen Jones, "Food Marketing and Pricing Policy in Eastern and Southern Africa: A Survey," *World Development* 25, no. 9 (September 1997), p. 1510.

15. C. Peter Timmer, "The Agricultural Transformation," in *Handbook of Development Economics*, 1, H. Chenery and T. N. Srinivasan, eds. (Amsterdam: Elsevier Science Publishers, 1988), pp. 275–380. Also see Timmer, *Getting Prices Right—The Scope and Limits of Agricultural Price Policy*.

16. Terry Sicular, "Conclusion: Structure and Motifs in the Food Price Policy Story," in Terry Sicular, ed., *Food Price Policy in Asia: A Comparative Study*, pp. 289–296. Also see Dharam Ghai and Lawrence D. Smith, *Agricultural Prices, Policy, and Equity in Sub-Saharan Africa* (Boulder, CO: Lynne Rienner Publishers, 1987).

17. Uma Lele, "Agricultural Growth, Domestic Policies, the External Environment, and Assistance to Africa: Lessons of a Quarter Century," World Bank MADIA Discussion Paper 1 (Washington: World Bank, 1989).

18. See Alex Duncan and Stephen Jones, "Agricultural Marketing and Pricing Reform: A Review of Experience," *World Development* 21, no. 9 (September 1993), pp. 1495–1514, and T. S. Jayne and Stephen Jones, "Food Marketing and Pricing Policy in Eastern and Southern Africa: A Survey."

19. See "Agricultural Diversification: Policies and Issues from East Asian Experience," World Bank Policy and Research Series, No. 11 (Washington: World Bank, 1990).

20. Anil Markandaya, Lucy Emerton, and Sam Mwale, "Preferential Trading Arrangements Between Kenya and the EU: A Case Study of the Environmental Effects on the Horticulture Sector," in Per G. Fredriksson, ed., *Trade, Global Policy, and the Environment* (Washington: World Bank, 1999), pp. 83–100. Also see Cleaver and Schreiber, *Reversing the Spiral: The Population, Agriculture, and Environment Nexus in Sub-Saharan Africa*, pp. 16–31.

21. Cited in H. Jeffrey Leonard, "Environment and the Poor: Development Strategies for a Common Agenda," in Leonard et al., *Environment and the Poor: Development Strategies for a Common Agenda* (New Brunswick, NJ: Transaction Books/Overseas Development Council, 1989), p. 13. Also see Hans P. Binswanger and Klaus Deininger, "Explaining Agricultural and Agrarian Policies in Developing Countries," *Journal of Economic Literature* 35, no. 4 (December 1997), pp. 1958–2005.

22. See Polly Hill, *Development Economics on Trial: The Anthropological Case for a Prosecution* (Cambridge:

Cambridge University Press, 1986), especially chapters 2, 6, and 10 on inequality of wealth and on labor systems in rural areas.

23. Yujiro Hayami, "Community, Market, and State," in Carl K. Eicher and John M. Staatz, *International Agricultural Development*, 3rd ed. (Baltimore: Johns Hopkins University Press, 1998), pp. 90–102.

24. Joseph E. Stiglitz, "Sharecropping," in *The New Palgrave Economic Development*, John Eatwell, Murray Milgate, and Peter Newman, eds. (New York: W. W. Norton, 1989), pp. 308–315.

25. See Peter Dorner and Don Kanel, "The Economic Case for Land Reform: Employment, Income Distribution, and Productivity," in *Land Reform, Land Settlement and Cooperatives*, no. 1 (United Nations Food and Agricultural Organization, 1971); Alain de Janvry, "The Role of Land Reform in Economic Development," *American Journal of Agricultural Economics* 63, no. 2 (May 1981), pp. 384–392; case studies in Roy Prosterman, Mary Temple, and Timothy Hamstad, eds., *Agrarian Reform and Grassroots Development* (Boulder, CO: Lynne Reinner, 1990); and Hans P. Binswanger and Miranda Elgin, "Reflections on Land Reform and Farm Size," in Eicher and Staatz, *Agricultural Development in the Third World* (1990), pp. 342–354. See also Clive Bell, "Reforming Property Rights in Land and Tenancy," *World Bank Research Observer* 5, no. 2 (July 1990), pp. 143–166.

26. Bruce F. Johnston and P. Kilby, *Agriculture and Structural Transformation: Economic Strategies in Late Developing Countries* (New York: Oxford University Press, 1975). The Korean example is provided in Byung-Nak Song, *The Rise of the Korean Economy* (New York: Oxford University Press, 1990), p. 176.

27. See S. K. Jayasuriya, A. Te, and R. W. Herdt, "Mechanisation and Cropping Intensification: Economics of Machinery Use in Low-Wage Economies," *Journal of Development Studies* 22, no. 2 (January 1986), pp. 327–335. But see Polly Hill, *Development Economics on Trial: The Anthropological Case for a Prosecution*, chapter 9.

28. See Benoit Blarel, Peter Hazell, Frank Place, and John Quiggin, "The Economics of Farm Fragmentation: Evidence from Ghana and Rwanda," *World Bank Economic Review* 6, no. 2 (May 1992), pp. 233–254.

29. See Hans P. Binswanger and Miranda Elgin, "Reflections on Land Reform and Farm Size," pp. 316–328; Subrata Ghatak, "Agriculture and Economic Development," in Norman Gemmell, ed., *Surveys in Development Economics* (Cambridge: Basil Blackwell, 1987); Stevens and Jabara's data on India, Taiwan, and Brazil in the 1960s, *Agricultural Development Principles*, pp. 67–68; K. N. Raj, "Mobilization of the Rural Economy and the Asian Experience," in Gustav Ranis and T. Paul Schultz, eds., *The State of Development Economics: Progress and Perspectives* (Oxford: Basil Blackwell, 1988), pp. 260–278; Dwayne Benjamin,

"Can Unobserved Land Quality Explain the Inverse Productivity Relationship?" *Journal of Development Economics* 46, no. 1 (February 1995), pp. 51–84; Andrew Newell, Kiran Pandya, and James Symons, "Farm Size and the Intensity of Land Use in Gujarat," *Oxford Economic Papers* 49, no. 2 (April 1997), pp. 307–315; and R. Heltberg, "Rural Market Imperfections and the Farm Size–Productivity Relationship: Evidence from Pakistan," *World Development* 26, no. 10 (October 1998), pp. 1807–1826.

30. Cleaver and Schreiber, *Reversing the Spiral: The Population, Agriculture, and Environment Nexus in Sub-Saharan Africa*, p. 150.

31. A. K. Bagchi cites Mexico, Egypt, and India in *The Political Economy of Underdevelopment* (Cambridge: Cambridge University Press, 1982). Other examples are provided in Prosterman et al., *Agrarian Reform and Grassroots Development*. For Japan, see Ronald Dore, *Land Reform in Japan* (Oxford: Oxford University Press, 1958). For India and Bangladesh, see Ronald Herring, *Land to the Tiller: The Political Economy of Agrarian Reform in South Asia* (New Haven: Yale University Press, 1983). This overview is based in part on Yugiro Hayami, "Land Reform," in Gerald M. Meier, ed., *Politics and Policy Making in Developing Countries* (San Francisco: ICS Press, 1991).

32. Ellis, *Agricultural Policies in Developing Countries*, credits this point to C. D. Deere, "Rural Women and State Policy: The Latin American Agrarian Reform Experience," *World Development* 13, no. 9 (September 1985), pp. 1037–1054.

33. Friendly critics abound: See Goran Hyden, *Beyond Ujamaa in Tanzania: Underdevelopment and an Uncaptured Peasantry* (Berkeley: University of California Press, 1980); International Labor Office, *Towards Self-Reliance—Development, Employment and Equity Issues in Tanzania* (Addis Ababa: ILO, 1978); Deane McHenry, Jr., *Tanzania's Ujamaa Villages: The Implementation of a Rural Development Strategy* (Berkeley: Institute of International Studies, 1979); and Michaela von Freyhold, *Ujamaa Villages in Tanzania: Analyses of a Social Experiment* (London: Heinemann, 1979). Also see Gershon Feder and Raymond Noronha, "Land Rights Systems and Agricultural Development in Sub-Saharan Africa," *World Bank Research Observer* 2, no. 2 (July 1987), pp. 143–170.

34. See, for example, Y. Hayami et al., *Anatomy of a Peasant Economy: A Rice Village in the Philippines* (Manila: International Rice Research Institute, 1978), especially chapter 3.

35. Data cited in H. Jeffrey Leonard, "*Environment and the Poor: Development Strategies for a Common Agenda*," p. 12.

36. United Nations, *1999 World Survey on the Role of Women in Development* (New York: United Nations, 1999), p. 39.

37. See Mayra Buvinic and Rekha Mehra, "Women and Agricultural Development," in Eicher and Staatz, *Agricultural Development in the Third World* (1990), pp. 290–308, and Janet Henshall Momsen, *Women and Development in the Third World* (London: Routledge, 1991), chapter 4 on "Women and Work in Rural Areas."

38. For male "takeover," see Cleaver and Schreiber, *Reversing the Spiral: The Population, Agriculture, and Environment Nexus in Sub-Saharan Africa*, chapter 5. See also Nkoli N. Ezumah and Catherine M. DiDomenico, "Enhancing the Role of Women in Crops Production: A Case Study of Igbo Women in Nigeria," *World Development* 23, no. 10 (October 1995), pp. 1731–1744.

39. See Mayra Buvinic, "Projects for Women in the Third World: Explaining Their Misbehavior," *World Development* 14, no. 5 (May 1986), pp. 653–664; Katrine Saito and C. Jean Weidemann, "Agricultural Extension for Women Farmers in Sub-Saharan Africa," World Bank Discussion Paper No. 103 (Washington: World Bank, 1990); and Katrine A. Saito and Daphne Spurling, "Developing Agricultural Extension for Women Farmers," World Bank Discussion Paper No. 156 (Washington: World Bank, 1992).

40. See Mary Tiffen and Michael Mortimore, "Malthus Controverted: The Role of Capital and Technology in Growth and Environment Recovery in Kenya," *World Development* 22, no. 7 (July 1994), pp. 997–1010.

41. See Hans Binswanger, "Agricultural Mechanization: A Comparative Historical Perspective," *The World Bank Research Observer* 1, no. 1 (January 1986), pp. 27–56, and "Agricultural Mechanization: Issues and Options," World Bank Policy Study (Washington: World Bank, 1987), and chapter 8 of Ellis, *Agricultural Policies in Developing Countries*.

42. I am indebted to some lectures by Professor Claudio Gonzalez-Vega for stressing the potential—and the requirements—for mobilizing savings in the rural sector of Caribbean countries. See Dale Adams and Robert Vogel, "Rural Financial Markets in Low-Income Countries," in Eicher and Staatz, *Agricultural Development in the Third World* (1990), pp. 355–370. Also, see Avishay Braverman and Monika Huppi, "Improving Rural Finance in Developing Countries," in *Finance & Development* 28, no. 1 (March 1991), pp. 42–44, and chapter 7 in Ellis, *Agricultural Policies in Developing Countries*.

43. Jacob Yaron, McDonald Benjamin, and Stephanie Charitonenko, "Promoting Efficient Rural Financial Intermediation," *World Bank Research Observer* 13, no. 2 (August 1998), pp. 147–170. Also see David Hulme, "The Malawi Mundi Fund: Daughter of Grameen," *Journal of International Development* 3, no. 4 (July 1991), pp. 29–37. On Grameen, see Muhammad Yunus, "The Grameen Bank Story: Rural Credit in Bangladesh," in Anirudh Krishna et al., eds., *Reasons for Hope: Instructive Experiences in Rural Development* (West Hartford, CT: Kumarian Press, 1997), pp. 9–24.

44. See Virginia de Guia-Abiad, "Borrower Transaction Costs and Credit Rationing in Rural Financial Markets: The Philippine Case," *The Developing Economies* 31, no. 2 (June 1993), pp. 208–219.

45. Christopher Gerrard, *Promoting Third World Agriculture: Lessons of Recent Experience* (Ottawa: North–South Institute, 1983), pp. 14–15. Also see Monika Huppi and Gershon Feder, "The Role of Groups and Credit Cooperatives in Rural Lending," *World Bank Research Observer* 5, no. 2 (July 1990), pp. 187–204.

46. See Polly Hill, *Development Economics on Trial: The Anthropological Call for a Prosecution*, chapter 8.

47. See Dean Birkhaeuser, Robert E. Evenson, and Gershon Feder, "The Economic Impact of Agricultural Extension: A Review," *Economic Development and Cultural Change* 39, no. 3 (April 1991), pp. 607–650; Daniel Benor, James Q. Harrison, and Michael Baxter, *Agricultural Extension: The Training and Visit System* (Washington: World Bank, 1984); and Joseph Mullen, "Training and Visit System in Somalia: Contradictions and Anomalies," *Journal of International Development* 1, no. 1 (January 1989), pp. 145–167.

48. This model was developed by Yujiro Hayami and Vernon Ruttan in *Agricultural Development* (Baltimore: Johns Hopkins University Press, 1971, 1985). More recent sources include Larry L. Burmeister, "The South Korean Green Revolution: Induced or Directed Innovation?" *Economic Development and Cultural Change* 35, no. 4 (July 1987), pp. 767–790; Ian Coxhead, "Induced Innovation and Land Degradation in Developing Country Agriculture," *Australian Journal of Agricultural and Resource Economics* 41, no. 3 (September 1997), pp. 305–332; and Ruttan, *Technology, Growth, and Development: An Induced Innovation Perspective* (New York: Oxford University Press, 2000).

49. See, for example, Harry Cleaver, "The Contradictions of the Green Revolution," *American Economic Review* 62, no. 2 (May 1972), pp. 177–186; Walter Falcon, "The Green Revolution: Generations of Problems," *American Journal of Agricultural Economics* 52, no. 5 (December 1970), pp. 698–710; M. Prahladachar, "Income Distribution Effects of the Green Revolution in India: A Review of the Empirical Evidence," *World Development* 11, no. 11 (November 1983), pp. 927–944; Yujiro Hayami, "Assessment of the Green Revolution," in Eicher and Staatz, *Agricultural Development in the Third World* (1984), pp. 389–396; S. K. Jayasuriya and R. T. Shand, "Technical Change and Labor Absorption in Asian Agriculture: Some Emerging Trends," *World Development* 14, no. 3 (Marcy 1986), pp. 415–428; Edward C. Wolf, "Beyond the Green Revolution: New Approaches for Third World Agriculture," Worldwatch Paper 73 (Washington: Worldwatch Institute, 1986); Derek Byerlee, "Technological Challenges in Asian Agricul-

ture in the 1990s," in Eicher and Staatz, *Agricultural Development in the Third World* (1990), pp. 424–433; Gordon Conway and Edward Barbier, *After the Green Revolution: Sustainable Agriculture for Development* (London: Earthscan Publications, 1990); and chapter 6 of Chris Dixon's *Rural Development in the Third World* (London: Routledge, 1990). The revolution has been much slower in coming to Africa; see the *Journal of International Development* 1, no. 1 (October 1989).

50. See Alain de Janvry, *The Agrarian Question and Reformism in Latin America* (Baltimore: Johns Hopkins University Press, 1981).

51. Romeo M. Bautista, "Income and Equity Effects of the Green Revolution in the Philippines: A Macroeconomic Perspective," *Journal of International Development* 9, no. 2 (March–April 1997), pp. 151–168; R. Sathiendrakumar and W. K. Norris, "The Green Revolution, Biotechnology and Environmental Concerns: A Case Study of the Philippines," in Iftikhar Ahmed and Jacobus A. Doeleman, eds., *Beyond Rio: The Environmental Crisis and Sustainable Livelihoods in the Third World* (New York: St. Martin's Press, 1995), pp. 195–220; and Michael Lipton and Richard Longhurst, "MV Research and the Poor," excerpted in Ron Ayres, ed., *Development Studies: An Introduction Through Selected Readings* (Kent, England: Greenwich University Press, 1995).

52. Inderjt Singh, *The Great Ascent: The Rural Poor in South Asia* (Baltimore: Johns Hopkins University Press, 1990). Newer studies are reported in Abe Goldman and Joyotee Smith, "Agricultural Transformation in India and Northern Nigeria: Exploring the Nature of Green Revolutions," *World Development* 23, no. 2 (February 1995), pp. 243–263.

53. On consumption patterns, see Mohammad Alauddin and Clem Tisdale: "Impact of New Agricultural Technology on the Instability of Foodgrain Production and Yield," *Journal of Development Economics* 29, no. 2 (September 1988), pp. 199–227; "Poverty, Resource Distribution and Security: The Impact of New Agricultural Technology in Rural Bangladesh," *Journal of Development Studies* 25, no. 4 (July 1989), pp. 550–570; and "Welfare Consequences of Green Revolution Technology: Changes in Bangladeshi Food Production and Diet," *Development and Change* 22, no. 3 (July 1991), pp. 497–517. On labor utilization, see Keijiro Otsuka, Fe Gascon, and Seki Asano, "Green Revolution and Labour Demand in Rice Farming: The Case of Central Luzon 1966–90," *Journal of Development Studies* 31, no. 1 (October 1994), pp. 82–109; Mohammad Alauddin and Clem Tisdale, "Labor Absorption and Agricultural Development: Bangladesh's Experience and Predicament," *World Development* 23, no. 2 (February 1995), pp. 281–297; and T. Islam and M. A. Taslim, "Demographic Pressure, Technological Innovation and Welfare: The Case of Agriculture of

Bangladesh," *Journal of Development Studies* 32, no. 5 (June 1996), pp. 734–770.

54. See Vandana Shiva, *The Violence of the Green Revolution: Ecological Degradation and Political Conflict* (London: Zed Books, 1991); Abe Goldman and Joyotee Smith, "Agricultural Transformation in India and Northern Nigeria: Exploring the Nature of Green Revolutions," pp. 246, 254; and Kartik C. Roy and Clement A. Tisdell, "Technological Change, Environment and Sustainability of Rural Communities," chapter 4 in Roy, Tisdell, and Rajkumar Sen, eds., *Economic Development and Environment: A Case Study of India* (Oxford: Oxford University Press, 1992).

55. See Derek Byerlee and Akimal Siddiq, "Has the Green Revolution Been Sustained? The Quantitative Impact of the Seed–Fertilizer Revolution in Pakistan Revisited," *World Development* 22, no. 9 (September 1994), pp. 1345–1361; Mubarik Ali, "Institutional and Socioeconomic Constraints in the Second-Generation Green Revolution: A Case Study of Basmati Rice Production in Pakistan's Punjab," *Economic Development and Cultural Change* 43, no. 4 (July 1995), pp. 835–862; Michael Morris and Derek Byerlee, "Maintaining Productivity Gains in Post-Green Revolution Asian Agriculture," in Eicher and Staatz, *International Agricultural Development*, pp. 458–473; David Dawe, "Reenergizing the Green Revolution in Rice," *American Journal of Agricultural Economics* 80, no. 5 (December 1998), pp. 948–953; and Prabhu L. Pingali, "Confronting the Ecological Consequences of the Rice Green Revolution in Tropical Asia," in Eicher and Staatz, *International Agricultural Development* (1998), pp. 474–493.

56. Legal issues are illustrated in Rick Weiss, "Seeds of Controversy," *Washington Post National Weekly Edition*, March 1, 1999. Health (and profitability) issues are summarized in David L. Chandler, "Down on the Farm," *Boston Globe*, September 24, 2000.

57. Sathiendrakumar and Norris, "The Green Revolution, Biotechnology and Environmental Concerns: A Case Study of the Philippines," and Derek Byerlee, "Modern Varieties, Productivity, and Sustainability: Recent Experience and Emerging Challenges," *World Development* 24, no. 4 (April 1996), pp. 697–718. The Consultative Group on International Agricultural Research (CGIAR) supports 16 research centers, including IRRI and CIMMYT. Its Web site is ⟨www.cgiar.org⟩. Its policy-oriented center, the International Food Policy Research Institute, is at ⟨www.ifpri.org⟩. See, for instance, its Focus 2 briefs on "Biotechnology for Developing-Country Agriculture: Problems and Opportunities," Gabrielle J. Persley, ed. (October 1999).

58. Enyinna Chuta and Carl Liedholm, "Rural Small-Scale Industry: Empirical Evidence and Policy Issues," in Eicher and Staatz, *Agricultural Development in the Third World* (1990), page 338. See also Earl P. Scott,

"Home-Based Industries: An Alternative Strategy for Household Security in Rural Zimbabwe," *Journal of Developing Areas* 29, no. 2 (January 1995), pp. 183–212, and Deborah Fahy Bryceson, "Deagrarianization and Rural Employment in Sub-Saharan Africa: A Sectoral Perspective," *World Development* 24, no. 1 (January 1996), pp. 97–111. An overview is Malcolm Harper and Shailendra Vyakarnam, *Rural Enterprise: Case Studies from Developing Countries* (London: Intermediate Technology Publications, 1988). For a particularly successful case, see Rizwanul Islam and Jin Hehui, "Rural Industrialization: An Engine of Prosperity in Postreform Rural China,' *World Development* 22, no. 11 (November 1994), pp. 1643–1662.

59. The study of India is K. N. S. Yadava, Surendar S. Yadava, and R. K. Sinha, "Rural Out-Migration and Its Economic Implications on Migrant Households in India: A Review," *Indian Economic Journal* 44, no. 2 (October–December 1996), pp. 21–38. The Nigerian case is reported in S. M. Essang and A. F. Mabawonku, "Impact of Urban Migration on Rural Development: Theoretical Considerations and Empirical Evidence from South Nigeria," *The Developing Economies* 13, no. 2 (June 1975), pp. 137–149. Also see *International Labour Review* 128, no. 6 (1989), a special issue on "Rural Labour Markets and Poverty in Developing Countries."

60. See Jonathan Karp, "Adding U.S. Soybeans to India's Spicy Diet Faces Big Roadblocks," *Wall Street Journal*, December 8, 1998.

61. See Odin Knudsen, John Nash et al., "Redefining the Role of Government in Agriculture for the 1990s," World Bank Discussion Paper No. 105 (Washington: World Bank, 1990), and C. Peter Timmer, ed., *Agriculture and The State: Growth, Employment, and Poverty in Developing Countries* (Ithaca: Cornell University Press, 1991). For an overview see Robert Bates, *Markets and States in Tropical Africa: The Political Basis of Agricultural Policies* (Berkeley: University of California Press, 1981).

62. Bruce Johnston, "The Political Economy of Agricultural and Rural Development," in Sisay Asefa, ed., *World Food and Agriculture—Economic Problems and Issues* (Kalamazoo: W. E. Upjohn Institute, 1988), p. 41. Italics in the original.

63. See Schiff and Valdes, *The Political Economy of Agricultural Pricing Policy*, but also Roland Herrmann, "Agricultural Policies, Macroeconomic Policies, and Producer Price Incentives in Developing Countries: Cross-Country Results for Major Crops," *Journal of Developing Areas* 31, no. 2 (winter 1997), pp. 203–220.

64. C. Peter Timmer, "The Macroeconomics of Food and Agriculture," in Eicher and Staatz, *International Agricultural Development* (1998), pp. 187–211. The quote is on pp. 189–190.

65. See the World Bank Policy Study, "Poverty and Hunger: Issues and Options for Food Security in Devel-

oping Countries" (Washington: World Bank, 1986). See also Uma Lele and Wilfred Candler, "Food Security in Developing Countries: National Issues," in Carl Eicher and John Staatz, *Agricultural Development in the Third World* (1984), pp. 207–221.

66. Some countries depend on a single agricultural export for more than three-fourths of their revenues. This was true in 1985 for Burundi (coffee, 85 percent); Cuba (sugar, 86 percent); Ethiopia (coffee, 77 percent); Ghana (cocoa, 75 percent); Somalia (livestock, 87 per-

cent); and Uganda (coffee, 86 percent). (Numbers reported by Dixon from UNCTAD data.) This dependence exists also for countries that rely on a few mineral exports, such as oil or copper, for a large portion of their foreign earnings.

67. See Andrew Storey, "Food vs. Cash Crops in Africa," in Ayres, ed., *Development Studies: An Introduction Through Selected Readings*, pp. 652–664.

68. *World Bank, Poverty and Hunger*, p. 1.

69. But see Endnote 6.

9

INDUSTRY, TECHNOLOGY, AND EMPLOYMENT

*Improvements in machinery are always
more advantageous to the labourers,
regarded as a class, than to capitalists.*
—J. R. McCulloch (1789–1864)

*The instrument of labor, when it takes the
form of a machine immediately becomes a
competitor of the workman himself.*
—Karl Marx (1818–1883)

INTRODUCTION

Development requires that an economy move from reliance largely on an agricultural base to one based on industry and services. Industrialization has accompanied development everywhere and is an objective of policy, even in an industrialized country like the United States seeking to preserve its industrial base. However, without renouncing industrialization, we must be careful to state it in terms that make economic sense; to understand what it is and how best to go about it. This chapter outlines a balance between ends and means; putting industrialization in a perspective that accounts for the current situation in many poor countries and offers a reasonable guide to development.

We first look at the state of industrialization in the developing world. Next, we examine the role of technology and its relevance for the scale of industry. Are some technologies better suitable for developing countries, and if so, what determines what they are? How well can technologies be transferred among countries, and how should they be adapted? Finally, we look at labor market and employment issues in both the formal and informal sectors. Who is unemployed in developing countries and why? Are formal labor markets unduly distorted? How can countries get the most from their small firms? We stress throughout that industrialization must use a nation's current resources even as it attempts to transform and enhance them.

INDUSTRIALIZATION IN PERSPECTIVE

Industrial development has long been the objective of many government officials and economists.[1] Rosenstein-Rodan's Big Push was conceived in the 1940s as a way to restart industrialization in Eastern Europe after World War II. Lewis's surplus-labor model in the 1950s was the first formal attempt to understand how a largely rural economy could industrialize by drawing resources from where they were less productive. Rostow's stages showed how industrialization typically took place, highlighting the need to increase savings, investment, and entrepreneurial ability and offering the hope that communism would not be necessary to accomplish this goal in a relatively brief period. What these models have in common is the idea that development is synonymous with industrialization. Industrialization is said to have many advantages. It:

- Produces more output, savings, and employment per dollar of investment than does agriculture
- Brings modern technology
- Provides local substitutes for imports
- Increases competitiveness in export markets
- Helps create infrastructure
- Attracts foreign capital[2]

Early postwar development strategies counted on industrialization to produce a significant amount of employment as well as increased output. Many economists focused on manufacturing output as the key indicator of development. The road to development led not only through more capital but also through "better" capital, which meant "modern," or state-of-the-art, technology. Modernization meant increasing capital intensity of production processes.

For an economist, however, increases in capital intensity of production—more capital per unit of output (K/Y), or a greater ratio of capital to labor (K/L)—is not always desirable. We often think of technologies matching certain products: steel as capital intensive and circuit-board assembly as labor intensive. However, a single product, such as cotton shirts, milled rice, or steel, can use either large amounts of labor with simple machinery or a lot of heavy machinery with fewer workers.

Which technologies are appropriate for a given situation? One approach is that each firm decides for itself, on the basis of the profitability of different technologies. From the perspective of the whole economy, as we will see later in this chapter, appropriate technologies are those whose **factor intensities**—the degree to which they use one factor of production relative to another—match the economy's **factor endowments**—the existing quantity and quality of labor and capital. So an economy in which there is a large population but little capital should focus on technologies that are labor intensive, at least until more capital has been accumulated.

Attempts at industrialization have not always worked out very well. They have often been inconsistent with nations' resources, leading to an even greater dependence on imports, and have lured people into cities that could not meet infrastructural needs or provide adequate employment. India, for example, became dependent on imports for its industrialization, while neglect of agriculture increased the need for food imports. Algeria made an early attempt to import complete factories but did not have the trained personnel to operate them.[3] Industrialization has been more difficult than anticipated, and the benefits that were perceived to follow have not matched expectations, to the detriment of not only the new cities but rural areas as well.

Misreading History

To some extent, this focus on industrialization resulted from a misunderstanding of what actually happened in the Industrial Revolution. Increasing capital-*output* ratios were not always synonymous with rapidly increasing capital-*labor* ratios because both capital and industrial employment were expanding rapidly. In Western economies, displacement of labor in pre-industrial or handicraft production through capital accumulation and industrialization was quickly made up in new industries and expansion of old ones. Unemployment and relocation of labor was considered by many to be an acceptable price for growth, while workers could do little about it as labor unions were for a long time illegal. However, in many developing countries, industrialization appears to produce less employment and growth than was the case 150 years ago.

Developing Country Industry Today

Tables 9–1 and 9–2 show the industrialization that has taken place in the last 35 years. Note that "industry" in the broad sense includes manufacturing, mining, construction, and utilities. It is common, however, to use the terms "industry" and "manufacturing" interchangeably. Our discussion focuses on manufacturing.

Patterns of Industrialization

Tables 9–1 and 9–2 give a general impression that historically industry has been a more significant part of output in higher- than in lower-income countries and that high-income countries count on manufacturing for a much higher portion of their exports. Since 1980, however, manufacturing's importance has been diminishing in many countries, largely due to the rapid expansion of service industries. Developing countries generally are expanding industrial output, although in some cases a higher percentage of output coming from industry may indicate that the performance of agriculture is worsening. Analysis of the composition of manufacturing in developing countries shows a shift from **light** (labor-intensive) into **heavy** (capital-intensive) **industry**: from consumer nondurable goods (processed foods, clothing) to intermediate, capital, and consumer durable goods (appliances, autos). Between 1963 and 1980, the proportion of heavy industry in developing countries' manufacturing increased from

TABLE 9–1 Progress of Manufacturing

Countries	Growth of Manufacturing (Percentage per Year)			Industry* (As Percentage of GDP)		
	1965–1980	*1980–1990*	*1990–1999*	*1965*	*1990*	*1999*
Low Income	6.7	7.7	2.7	26	31	30
Lower-Middle Income	NA	6.7	9.0	32	39	39
Upper-Middle Income	8.9	3.4	4.1	36	40	33
High Income†	3.2	NA	2.6	43	37	30

*Industry includes manufacturing, mining, construction, and utilities.

†Manufacturing growth data refer to 1990–1998 instead of 1990–1999. Industry as percentage of GDP refers to 1980 and 1998 rather than 1990 and 1999.

NA = Not Available.

Sources: World Development Report 1992 and *World Development Indicators 2000* and *2001.*

TABLE 9–2 Importance of Manufacturing in Merchandise Trade

Countries	Percentage of Imports			Percentage of Exports		
	1965	*1980*	*1999*	*1965*	*1980*	*1999*
Low Income	70	55	63	31	33	52
Lower-Middle Income	65	58	70	16	NA	62
Upper-Middle Income	63	57	76	32	39	73
High Income	51	53	77	69	73	82

NA = Not Available.

Sources: World Development Report 1992 and *World Development Indicators 1999* and *2001.*

43 percent to 57 percent.[4] Developing countries have also been increasingly attracted to assembly operations, spurred by favorable trade arrangements with industrialized economies.[5]

On the other hand, the developing countries' share of world industrial production, although up in recent decades, at 14 percent in 1984 was no higher than in 1948. By 1997, low- and middle-income countries produced less than 12 percent of the value of world manufacturing.[6] The rapid increase in manufacturing in developing countries has been concentrated in a small number of countries, including South Korea, Taiwan, Thailand, India, Argentina, Mexico, and Brazil.

Employment Prospects

In spite of increasing industrialization and migration to urban areas, employment prospects are grim. In most developing countries, labor forces are growing from 1.5 percent to 3.5 percent per year, with urban labor forces probably growing more rapidly. However, according to one estimate, the demand for labor is increasing at $\frac{1}{2}$ percent per year or less.[7] So the nature of the technology that is being used becomes crucial if output and employment are both to increase.

Some of the excess labor is taken up in **Export Processing Zones (EPZs)**, which will be discussed at greater length in Chapter 12. These areas offer special incentives to labor-intensive firms that will produce for the export market. In 1997 there were 634 such zones in developing countries, employing over 20 million people. The largest numbers are in China (124) and the **maquiladora**, or border export processing industries of Mexico (107), but smaller economies participate as well. Costa Rica has created nearly 50,000 jobs since 1981, and the state of Penang, Malaysia, created nearly 200,000 jobs between 1970 and 1997. The entire economy of Mauritius is a single EPZ.[8]

In recent decades many developing countries such as Algeria and Tanzania have had to scale back grandiose ideas of rapid industrialization. The main issues now are how to choose the industries, technology, and scale of operation most appropriate to an individual country's circumstances.

TECHNOLOGY AND SCALE

Why have some countries had better success than others in their efforts to industrialize? Countries certainly differ with respect to how long they have been independent, their resource base and trade histories, the size of their markets, their openness to foreign investors, and their commitment to infrastructure and education.

However, here we look at the type of industrialization that has been attempted; that is, to what extent countries promote the production of goods and technologies that are suited to their own resources. We start by examining the economics of production and the role of technology in making use of the resources of the firm and the nation.

Factor Endowments and Technology

What determines the most efficient use of resources in production; that is, the most appropriate technologies to use? Figure 9–1 illustrates the typical economic analysis of the firm's choice of how to best produce a particular product. An isoquant represents a given level of output (say 10 shirts per week) that can be produced with different combinations of capital and labor, measured on the vertical and horizontal axes, respectively. It is assumed that there is an infinite number of available production processes capable of producing that output, and that the firm will choose the process that minimizes cost given factor prices determined by relative scarcity of those factors.

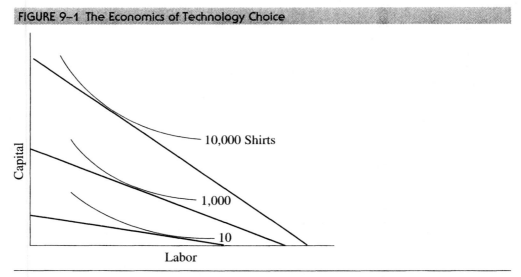

FIGURE 9–1 The Economics of Technology Choice

The isoquants show continuous sets of alternative capital/labor ratios that may be used to produce a specific number of shirts. There are as many isoquants as there are output levels. The slope at any point is the ratio of the marginal product of labor to the marginal product of capital (MP_l/MP_k). If production uses a lot of capital and little labor (high K/L), the marginal product of labor will be high and the marginal product of capital low (high MP_l/MP_k).

The straight lines represent the ratio of the price of labor (wage, w) to the price of capital (rental, r). If labor is plentiful relative to capital, we would expect the w/r ratio to be low.

The tangency point is the most efficient combination of capital and labor at the given price ratio. As output increases and technology changes, it is common for production processes to become more capital intensive.

On the graph, little initial capital and a large amount of unskilled labor result in a low wage/rental ratio: Wages are low and labor-intensive technology makes sense. As investment causes capital stocks to rise faster than the workforce, wages become relatively higher and capital-intensive techniques become more appropriate at higher output levels.

Each point on the curve has a slope equal to the ratio of the marginal product of labor (MP_l) to the marginal product of capital (MP_k), also known as the **Marginal Rate of Technical Substitution (MRTS)**.[9]

The straight lines show how much labor and capital can be hired with a given amount of expenditure. The slope of such a line represents the ratio of the price of labor, or wage (w), to the price of capital, or rental (r). Since only one relative price line is assumed to exist in an economy at any time, the economically most efficient production technique is the one for which the price ratio is equal to the MRTS, where the price line is tangent to the isoquant.

Under competitive conditions, countries with relatively high ratios of labor to capital will have relatively low wage to rental ratio (w/r), and firms will more likely choose more labor-intensive production methods. This is a typical situation for an economy in an early stage of development with relatively little accumulated capital.

As the firm expands, the optimum capital-output ratio does not necessarily change. New technology, however, may be either capital or labor using. The changing factor demand, along with growing factor supplies, will shift relative prices. Thus, the economy's growth path may veer toward either axis. As development proceeds, it is common to veer toward the capital (vertical) axis as production increases to, say, 10,000 pair of shoes per week. Greater capital intensity is associated with a higher wage-to-rental ratio.

An important qualification of this analysis is that at any given time there does not exist an infinite number of technologically feasible production processes. Figure 9–2 shows an isoquant with only four feasible techniques. Point A is the most capital intensive and Point D the most labor intensive. Recall also that dualistic development models suggest there may be at least two sets of relative price ratios: Rural sectors with relatively abundant labor supplies should have lower w/r ratios than modern manufacturing sectors that, despite abundant labor, have relatively more capital. Of course, urban areas may also have dual economies: formal and informal sectors with different capital/labor and w/r ratios.

A classic illustration of the question of technology use in a developing country is Peter Timmer's study of rice milling in Java.[10] He studied five techniques ranging from hand pounding of rice to large "bulk" facilities, with capital requirements per unit of output ranging from 0 to over $120,000. If we use the dollar value of investment per employee as an indicator of the capital-labor ratio, these ranged from 0 for hand pounding to $662,000 for large bulk operations.

Employing the kind of economic analysis we have presented, Timmer showed that the small rice mill, the second most labor-intensive technique at $673 per worker, was more efficient than either more capital-intensive techniques or the highly labor-intensive pounding by hand. There was considerably less employment compared to hand pounding, but Timmer maintains that a number of factors (including the drudgery and difficulty of hand pounding) offset that loss and that proper policies could mitigate it further. More capital-intensive techniques employed by large mills and bulk facilities were not efficient in the face of low wages, high interest rates, and the low price of rice. The only large mills operating (at $5,655 per worker) were either run by the government, which was not concerned about making a profit, or run privately near urban areas where minimum wages, cheaper credit, and a higher price of rice made capital-intensive techniques profitable.

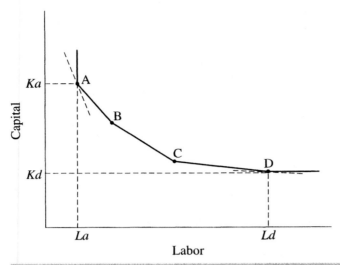

FIGURE 9-2 Limited Technology Choice, Multiple Price Ratios

As in Figure 9–1, the isoquant represents alternative factor proportions that may be used to produce a specific amount of the product. Here, however, given the indivisibility of capital, there are only a limited number of actual ratios possible. Those possibilities are at the points where the slope of the isoquant changes. Point A is more capital intensive than Point D.

Different sets of factor price ratios will determine the most efficient technology choice. Point A has a higher MP_l/MP_k ratio than point D and will use relatively more capital, corresponding to a higher w/r ratio.

A dual economy may use capital-intensive techniques in the industrial sector and labor-intensive techniques in agriculture. However, even two firms in an industry such as clothing or steel may use different techniques efficiently.

A number of economists have worried, however, that a developing country firm, or a foreign firm operating in a developing country, may use a relatively capital-intensive technique (*Ka, La*) that is inappropriate for its resource endowment, rather than the more appropriate labor-intensive technique (*Kd, Ld*). Such industries as food processing and textile manufacture often are found operating with factor combinations that are more capital intensive than the country's endowments would suggest. When this occurs on a regular basis, a "modern" sector, firms using capital-intensive techniques, uses a disproportionately large share of the nation's capital and financial resources and a disproportionately small share of the nation's labor, while a "traditional" sector, firms using labor-intensive techniques, receives relatively little investment. Why might this occur?

Appropriate and Inappropriate Technology

The term **appropriate technology** has been at the center of a debate over technology choice since the early 1970s.[11] Technology is appropriate when it involves a capital–labor ratio that is consistent with the ratio that exists in an economy; that is, consistent with the country's factor endowments. The issue is not just the existence of economically inappropriate technologies in developing countries. Some claim that they are used commonly because foreign investors bring in techniques with which they are familiar, and local firms actively pursue modernization by using production techniques developed in the industrialized countries for higher capital–labor ratios. Further, the pursuit of modernization has likely led to a developing-country preference for the *products* consumed in the industrialized countries, which skews the production *processes* before a decision about relevant technology is even encountered.

Proponents of adopting the most modern technologies point to their high productivity, linkages, and potential for creating strategic industries, especially in the context of import-substitution policies. Opponents contend, however, that in the face of developing-country factor endowments, such technology can be successfully adopted only in the face of market imperfections such as minimum wages and subsidized credit and that removing such imperfections will reveal the superior productivity of more appropriate techniques. Also, such technologies will not benefit small-scale firms. The determination of linkages and strategic industries must have a strong economic basis, not simply a desire for modernization.[12] A study of Indian manufacturing even suggests that high fixed-capital usage in some industries is inefficient when it does not account for the need for skilled labor and other requirements.[13]

Characteristics of Inappropriate Technologies

Aside from capital–labor ratios that seem out of line with a country's factor endowments, other telltale signs of inappropriate technologies include:

- Products that are tailored to the needs and desires of rich-country consumers
- The use of imported materials when local materials might be suitable
- A scale of operation so great that excess capacity is common
- The use of specific labor skills not locally available along with wage scales greatly at odds with prevailing wages
- Considerable use of imported machinery that is ill-adapted to local conditions and "high" cost of technology[14]

An example from the food-processing industry is machinery that removes the hull, or covering, from grain. A machine called the Engelberg has been adapted for this task in some African countries, but a more sophisticated machine, the Nogueira, made in Brazil, is also in use. However, the Nogueira breaks down more often in semiarid lands, is more difficult to repair, and requires imported parts, whereas the Engelberg has parts that can be fabricated locally. (Ironically, the inappropriate machine is produced in a developing country, albeit an advanced one.) Likewise, the use of motorized agricultural machinery would be uneconomic in very poor areas where plots are small and animal-powered implements are more efficient.[15]

One very important implication of inappropriate technologies is that they are suitable for a few large firms but not for many small ones. In some developing countries, of course, large and small firms produce similar goods side by side, so both types of technology could be in use simultaneously.[16]

Firms will not use techniques that force them to lose money, so at some level so-called inappropriate technologies must be appropriate to the firm. If so, we should be able to detect market distortions that make profits possible.

Market Distortions

Market distortions, or prices set by governments above or below equilibrium levels, cover a wide range of topics. For example, labor market distortions may include minimum wage laws, union-negotiated wages, hiring and firing restrictions, and legally mandated benefits such as social security contributions. If such regulations are effective, they increase the price of labor and induce a shift toward capital use.

Capital–market distortions such as interest rate ceilings and administered credit allocation benefit large firms and skew factor-use decisions toward capital. Large firms also often receive tax concessions for machinery purchases, but small firms are less subject to tax, so the overall impact may well be minimal. Foreign trade regimes generally favor large, capital-intensive firms. Their products are more likely to be protected by tariffs, and their machinery imports are more likely to be exempt from tariffs, while machinery imported by small firms, such as sewing machines and small motors, are often classified as consumer goods and subject to tariffs.

One of the first systematic studies of factor market distortions, which measured a large range of policies in seven countries, calculated impacts on the wage/rental ratio ranging from 0 in Hong Kong in 1973 to an increase of 316 percent in Pakistan in the early 1960s. The other five countries had increases between 11 percent and 87 percent. A review of numerous studies concludes that market distortions give large-scale firms, more likely to be capital intensive and use inappropriate technology, a 30 percent to 65 percent advantage over small-scale firms in their capital costs.[17] In addition, discrimination against agriculture described in the last chapter has given an overall boost to industrial development in many countries.

Output and Employment in Technological Choice

At times, the choice of technique has been posed as a choice between competing objectives: maximizing output as opposed to maximizing employment. Capital-intensive techniques may give more output per dollar invested (lower capital--output ratio) and thus increase the growth of GDP, even while ignoring factor scarcities. The use of older, more labor-intensive techniques will produce smaller increases in output per dollar of investment but may provide significantly higher employment.

This dilemma would be overcome if, for instance, employment fosters learning of new skills, making labor more efficient and productive over the long term. Higher employment and higher incomes, especially for relatively lower-paid workers, may increase demand sufficiently to stimulate much higher output levels. On the other hand, there are likely to be situations where choosing the more capital-intensive technology will increase output, savings, and investment and ultimately lead to greater output *and* employment.[18]

Rich-Country Goods, Poor-Country Consumers

A final aspect of the appropriate technology question concerns the choice of goods produced. One approach to consumer theory suggests that people do not so much buy particular goods as they buy things that have certain desirable characteristics; therefore, it may be useful to think of the characteristics people want and to ask what alternatives exist—in the form of products—to provide those characteristics. In the simplest case of domestically produced goods for which there is no imported competition, appropriate goods will be made of local resources and appeal to local tastes, using local factor proportions.

However, when imports are available, even if to a very few, additional characteristics may appear; perhaps just the desire to have the modern product, as with soap in Ghana reported in Case 9–1. The attempt to compete with those goods requires domestic production of goods that will be affordable to a relatively small portion of the population and therefore require a relatively unequal distribution of income. These goods are also more likely to have capital-intensive production processes. The pressure for imitation is even stronger if a country contemplates producing for the export market where firms will attempt to match the highest standards available in international markets.[19]

The attempt to imitate rich-country tastes means that the need to serve large numbers of people at a very basic level may be squeezed out by investments that provide more expensive goods to a smaller number. Should resources be used to provide clean water or a Coca-Cola bottling plant? Should local materials and standards be used to produce inexpensive clothing or should different standards be used to satisfy a licensing agreement with Calvin Klein? The worldwide uproar in the late 1970s (and not yet resolved) over the aggressive marketing by Nestlé of infant formula in developing countries, often replacing healthier breast-feeding, is a good example of some of these problems. Basic multipurpose, multipassenger vans would make more sense than manufacturing five-passenger Peugots; inexpensive solar cookers will make more sense for rural populations than electric stoves.

The advice of economic theory is clear. Efficient manufacturing sectors will produce goods and use technologies that fit a country's resource endowment and demand pattern, with some allowance for exports. In labor-abundant countries, labor-intensive techniques make sense where factor markets are reasonably competitive and demand is not influenced by the tastes of industrialized countries. Governments can provide some assistance by reducing factor market distortions and supporting adaptive R&D. The basic principles usually lead to technologies that are compatible with factor intensities.

Innovation, Adaptation, and Technology Transfer

Much of our discussion of appropriate technology has been predicated on the idea that modern technology is developed in the industrialized countries and purchased or licensed whole by firms in the poorer ones. While this is to a large extent true—the industrialized countries spend 96 percent of the world's R&D budget—it hides a more interesting and promising reality: the process of innovation in developing countries.

Innovation and Development

An increasing number of authors have placed great emphasis on the role of technological improvement—invention and innovation—in economic development.[20] Invention is the creation of a new product or production process. **Innovation** is the successful commercial use of such a product or process, or even the successful introduction of some other element of commerce that enables goods to be more efficiently advertised, transported, sold, and used.

Innovation in developing countries has patterns that differ from those in the industrialized countries. Research and Development (R&D) and innovation in the wealthier countries has been concerned with new goods and new ways of making goods. In many developing countries, R&D is largely concentrated on adapting imported technology to local needs.[21]

Adaptation includes modifying and redesigning products for local consumer tastes; adapting local materials to replace imported materials; reducing the scale of manufacturing plants to fit smaller markets; using more labor-intensive techniques in such ancillary activities as packing and shipping; and modifying, simplifying, and stretching the capacity of machinery for local conditions. Increased labor intensity should move some developing-country firms away from point A in Figure 9–2 in the appropriate direction of point D. At the same time, however, development of local skills and capital goods moves other firms from point D back in the direction of point A, and improved overall efficiency allows given amounts of labor and capital to increase output.

Appropriate adaptations will be the more difficult as the nature of the technology becomes more complex. However, developing countries such as South Korea, Taiwan, India, China, Brazil, Mexico, and Argentina have sophisticated scientific establishments: In the mid-1990s, South Korea ranked second in the world in percentage of GDP spent on R&D.[22] And business firms in many countries are good at adaptive work. In Colombia, for example, under pressure of import restrictions, local firms were capable of producing agricultural machinery, pumps, stoves, and integrated kitchen appliances.[23] South Korea is an important manufacturer of semiconductors, and numerous small Indian software firms are drawing customers from industrialized countries.[24] Singapore was the world's fifth largest exporter of high-tech products in 1998.

Firms and governments must cooperate in order to improve the technological capacity of those firms. A study of the capital goods industries of Pakistan emphasizes the importance of education, training, technical assistance, and an active policy of seeking out new information in acquiring those capacities. A similar conclusion was reached with respect to increased efficiency in Taiwan.[25] A major study of Chilean manufacturing concludes that despite significant liberalization of the economy and favorable macroeconomic policies, manufactured exports have remained in "easy" industries such as food processing, furniture, and clothing. Compared to South Korea, for example, there has not been an effort to improve labor skills and promote greater technological capacity among exporters.[26]

Problems of Technology Transfer

Many developing-country firms can incorporate imported, appropriate technologies into their products and incorporate their own innovations as well. Korean manufacturing firms have been able to substitute for imports as a result of their own R&D activities. One study of India showed that firms that imported technology were also more likely to undertake their own R&D. Another showed that technology imports will help those firms that invest in R&D to improve their production of goods incorporating new technology, while those firms that rely only on their own R&D efforts are less successful. However, important Indian industries that were protected from foreign competition failed to develop their own R&D activities, preferring to rely on imports.[27]

With advice and assistance, technologies from crop processing to basic engineering can be transferred to even small companies.[28] Could this process move more rapidly? The contention of some proponents of intermediate or appropriate technology is that more than market distortions keeps developing-country firms using inappropriate technologies: They point to the conditions attached to imported technology by the creators of those technologies in the developed countries.

Simon Teitel's survey of developing-country technology importers indicates that the reasons for insufficient adaptation of imported technologies start with the fact that foreign firms provide a specific technology as part of an overall investment package, which they may be unwilling to modify. Second, import protection provides high enough profits that there may be little incentive to adapt foreign technology. Next are the expense of modifying technology and the requirements of foreign lenders that tie loans to purchases of specific equipment. Other reasons include import subsidies, lack of incentive for adaptation, unrecognized needs, and lack of requisite skills.[29] A study of Mexico and Pakistan suggests that the balance of benefits, costs, and negotiating power determine the ability of developing-country firms to obtain technology on good terms.[30] A combination of economic conditions, domestic policies, and foreign restrictions thus conspires to reduce adaptive innovation.

Technical assistance organizations, often maintained by outside donations, play a major role in promoting small-scale technology in a number of countries. They provide technical assistance, training, and often finance for the research, introduction, and support of new production techniques.[31] Case 9–1 looks at the Technology Consultancy Centre in Ghana that worked with local entrepreneurs to develop an efficient, attractive alternative to both traditional and foreign production of soap.

The pace of technological change worldwide argues in favor of a much more flexible approach to technology transfer than some countries have taken in the past. In this area, governments are likely to move much too slowly, and private firms will have to have access to technologies developed in other countries. While students and workers will go overseas and return with new knowledge, the speed of knowledge upgrades will require constant interaction with the foreign firms and research institutes that produce that knowledge.

The Potential for Public Policy

Government can help in the promotion of adaptive innovation in developing countries.[32] The existence of market distortions indicates some immediate policy reforms that would bring market prices into line with factor endowments, reduce the incentive to remain with inappropriate technologies, and perhaps tip the balance toward smaller firms. Paradoxically, lifting ceilings on interest rates would help small firms. It would help foster small-scale financial institutions by allowing them to attract more savings, thereby increasing the availability of credit and allocating it to the most creditworthy enterprises. Restrictions on the import of used machinery are also harmful to small firms that cannot afford new machinery and do not have the skills to match it.[33]

Provision of technical information to small firms and help in training workers would increase firms' awareness of possibilities and capacity to innovate. In addition, government might consider supporting its firms in their negotiations with larger

CASE 9–1

SOAP PRODUCTION IN GHANA

FAST FACTS

On the Map: West Africa

Population: 19 Million

Per Capita GNI and Rank: $400   (166)

Life Expectancy: Male—57   Female—59

Adult Literacy Rate: Male—79%
Female—61%

At the beginning of the 1970s, Ghanians had only two choices for soap: locally made soap of very poor quality, produced by traditional methods, and soap manufactured by Lever Brothers with imported raw materials and imported machinery, providing one-half of the country's demand from a single factory. Beginning in 1972, the Technology Consulting Centre (TCC) started to work with local small-scale entrepreneurs to develop an intermediate process.

TCC helped small companies develop intermediate-capacity machinery, using mostly local materials for both raw materials and machinery, and provided training for workers. Problems included inconsistent government policies that periodically restricted imports and controlled output prices and exchange rates, and the erratic halting

and restarting of production by Lever. By 1975 there were seven local firms producing soap with the new technology, although differences in management resulted in large variations in quality; soap coming from the poorly run companies gave a bad name to all the locally produced soap.

By 1981, 17 companies were producing the local soap, and a partial rationalization of government policies in 1983 eased the operating environment. The local companies often found it difficult to compete with the reentry of Lever because large portions of the urban population preferred to pay twice as much for the "foreign" soap as for comparable local soap. By 1985, however, dozens of small producers were sharing the market with Lever, operating locally produced machinery at low fixed cost and with one-tenth the amount of capital per worker of the Lever operation.

Source: Ian Smillie, "The Transfer of Sustainable Appropriate Technology in Ghana's Industrial Sector—The Experience of the Technology Consulting Centre," in Marilyn Carr, ed., *Sustainable Industrial Development: Seven Case Studies* (London: Intermediate Technology Publications, Ltd., 1988), pp. 101–127.

foreign technology suppliers. Removal of subsidies and import protection, however, could require some cost-saving innovation so that firms could be competitive with imports. Case 9–2 shows how government regulations held back India's electronics industry and how that industry began to prosper as regulations were eased.

More direct support is possible as well. The uncertainty of returns, the potential for free riders to use privately produced knowledge, and the great expense sometimes required for the effort indicate market failure in the production and use of knowledge and an economic basis for greater government support for, or direct carrying out of, R&D.[34] In fact, R&D activity is supported by government in every industrialized country. Direct support of R&D activities would be more efficient than import protection aimed at the same goal.

DEVELOPING THE INDIAN COMPUTER INDUSTRY

FAST FACTS

On the Map: South Asia

Population: 998 Million

Per Capita GNI and Rank: $440   (163)

Life Expectancy: Male—62   Female—64

Adult Literacy Rate: Male—68%
Female—44%

India, along with Brazil and South Korea, produces micro- and minicomputers and software. Although the industry appeared in the 1960s, it grew slowly at first. In 1975, 15 computers were sold, worth $4.2 million. By 1986, however, over 12,000 computers were sold at a value of almost $140 million. The explosion had more to do with government policies than with advance in the industry itself.

The Indian government had started with the traditional approach of fostering its own production, while allowing foreign firms as well. But the two foreign firms (IBM and ICL of Great Britain) were content to stick with older technologies, and the Indian government company did poorly. Even after a new government company, Electronics Corporation of India, Ltd., (ECIL), began making progress, imports remained popular, twice ECIL's output in the late 1970s in spite of import restrictions. The government sponsored R&D, but little of this did more than permit production of technologies already in existence.

One of the key problems was lack of competition. Government licensing requirements were used to restrict new entrants, so that only three licenses had been issued by 1976/77, and in 1978 IBM left rather than give control to domestic interests. But a series of policy changes in the late 1970s and early 1980s led to the existence of 43 firms by 1980/81 and 300 by 1984/85.

Indian firms were further held back by restrictions on collaboration with foreign firms and restrictions on the import of any component that could be produced by an Indian firm. These two policies kept Indian firms isolated from the technological advances sweeping the world. But they too were modified: Tariffs were reduced and limits raised in 1981, and collaboration with foreign firms was being increasingly permitted in 1982. These changes gave Indian firms greater access to newer technologies but increased the extent to which computers themselves were protected from import competition. An unfortunate consequence was that Indian firms carried out very little R&D on their own, and the government provided no incentives for them to join forces to promote research into new technologies.

The less restrictive approach was extended to software in the mid-1980s. Restrictions on imports were reduced in order to promote exports, and foreign companies could open wholly owned subsidiaries.

All these changes contributed to the rapid growth of the industry. The Indian electronics industry grew faster than the South Korean industry during the 1980s, although from a lower base. (Comparable data show India's sales in 1986 roughly one-third of Korean sales.) One study showed that prices of Indian computers were the same as that of comparable American models by 1986. Hardware exports expanded in the late 1980s, in part due to demand from the Soviet Union.

Government in India remained heavily involved in the industry. Investment

245

decisions still had to be approved and imports were still regulated. Thirteen central government firms and 20 state government firms existed. The state was still the biggest source of demand for computers, provided capital to domestic firms, and was a major source of infrastructure (such as the telecommunications industry). But despite government competition, much of its role supports the private sector, fostering its development.

Sources: Hans-Peter Brunner, "Building Technological Capacity: A Case Study of the Computer Industry in India, 1975–87," *World Development* 19, no. 12 (December 1991), pp. 1737–1751, and Peter B. Evans, "Indian Informatics in the 1980s: The Changing Character of State Involvement," *World Development* 20, no. 1 (January 1992), pp. 1–18.

But some types of government involvement can be counterproductive. Government officials too are often attracted by modern technologies and may ignore more appropriate possibilities and small firms. A study of Indonesia in the mid-1970s showed government agencies routinely choosing the most capital-intensive technologies for their program proposals. In East Pakistan (now Bangladesh), one author concluded that

> it was the organizational requirements of the implementing agencies,
> including the aid donors, that determined . . . [the technology] . . . such
> factors as risk avoidance, appearance of modernity, established procedures,
> familiar techniques, and by no means least, control, outweighed development
> policy objectives.[35]

A historical study of technological development in early and late developing countries concluded that while government agencies can help in the process of searching for and evaluating foreign technologies, the most promising government contribution would be to help firms develop their own capacities to carry out these tasks and create a business environment in which entrepreneurs are confident that their rewards from technological innovation will be protected by government.[36] The World Bank's 1998/1999 issue of the *World Development Report* focuses on openness to foreign goods and knowledge, protecting intellectual property rights, support for public and private R&D, and promoting education specific to acquiring greater technological capacities.[37]

It is particularly crucial that modern information-processing technologies be made available to firms and individuals in developing countries. The World Bank estimates that high-income countries have one computer with Internet connection for every 10 people. In the low-income countries, there is one for every 20,000 people.[38] With a sound telecommunications infrastructure, Internet capability is becoming less expensive. Those who are not connected could fall behind rapidly.

EMPLOYMENT IN THE FORMAL AND INFORMAL SECTORS

Decisions on technology and scale have important implications for the size and quality of the labor force. Both large manufacturing firms and small enterprises producing traditional products in traditional ways can employ large numbers of semiskilled workers. As both the products and the technologies become more oriented to modern requirements, the needed skills may become greater and labor requirements per unit of output are often reduced.

TABLE 9–3 Growth of Output and Labor Force
(Percentage per Year)

	GDP		Manufacturing		Labor Force	
	1980–1990	*1990–1999*	*1980–1990*	*1990–1999*	*1980–1990*	*1980–1999*
Low and Middle Income	3.5	3.5	4.9	5.8	1.9	2.0
East Asia/Pacific	8.0	7.5	10.4	10.2	1.9	1.9
Europe/Central Asia	2.9	–2.3	NA	NA	0.5	0.5
Latin America/Caribbean	1.7	3.4	1.3	2.6	2.6	2.7
Mideast/North Africa	2.0	3.0	NA	2.8	2.9	3.0
South Asia	5.6	5.6	7.1	7.0	2.0	2.2
Sub-Saharan Africa	1.7	2.2	1.7	1.6	2.5	2.6

NA = Not Available.

Source: World Development Indicators 1998 and 2001.

Developing countries must provide employment for growing populations. The International Labor Organization estimates that over the period 1980 to 1991, while GDP grew at about 2 percent per year in Latin America and Sub-Saharan Africa, manufacturing jobs were stagnant in the first region and declined about ½ of 1 percent in the second. GDP grew almost 6 percent per year in South Asia, but manufacturing jobs grew at only 1 percent per year. The East and Southeast Asian region had GDP growth of almost 8 percent and job growth of about 6½ percent.[39] Table 9–3 shows that for most regions where data are available, manufacturing is growing more rapidly than GDP. Typically, the labor force is growing more slowly, but in both the Middle East and in Africa the labor force is growing more rapidly. Assuming some increase in labor productivity, these regions are particularly vulnerable to high unemployment. More recently, Table 9–4 shows employment growing faster than the labor force in Asia but more slowly in Latin America.

More and better jobs mean rising incomes. More widespread employment is also a means of promoting a more even income distribution. This is especially true in labor-abundant countries where capital-intensive production techniques ordinarily widen the gap between owners of capital and workers. A tendency toward more capital- and technology-intensive production will swell the ranks of the disguised unemployed and

TABLE 9–4 Growth of Labor Force and Employment
(Percentage per Year)

	Labor Force	*Employment*
Developed Countries, 1987–1997	1.1	1.1
Latin America, Caribbean, 1990–1997	3.2	2.9
China, 1990–1994	1.5	2.2
India, 1987–1993	2.2	2.4
Other Developing Asia, 1990–1996	1.9	2.0
Africa	NA	NA

NA = Not Available.

Source: International Labour Organization, *World Employment Report 1998–99* (Geneva: ILO, 1998).

reduce wages among the unskilled. Unemployment is demoralizing: Useful work is an important human need. Long-term unemployment leads to loss of skills and lower productivity when people are once again employed. And, of course, unemployment, especially urban unemployment, may be politically explosive. But there are difficulties in studying labor conditions in developing countries; not only of getting good data on employment and unemployment but even of obtaining useful definitions.

Who Is in the Labor Force?

Even in industrialized countries there is some ambiguity about who is or is not part of the labor force. The **labor force participation rate** is usually defined as the percentage of the working age population (frequently from 16 to 64) outside of institutions or correctional facilities who are either working or actively looking for a job. This is usually taken to eliminate full-time students and those, generally women, who work full-time in the home. The **unemployment rate** is the percentage of that population that has not worked over the relevant period, with those who have worked at least a few hours a week considered to have been employed.

The data that we have for developing countries show participation rates ranging from 40 percent to 80 percent with differences caused in large part by educational levels and cultural factors that sometimes inhibit the participation of women in the labor force. For example, a survey of female participation rates in the mid-1980s found a figure of 45.6 percent in non-Muslim countries and 27.5 percent in Muslim countries, a pattern that occurred in all income categories.[40] In Oman, an estimate for 1995 was 87 percent for men and 10 percent for women. In China, on the other hand, the figures were 96 percent and 80 percent, respectively.[41] Still, the UN believes the female participation rate in developing countries now exceeds 60 percent, compared to over 70 percent in Canada, the United States and the Scandinavian countries.[42]

The difficulty of agreeing what constitutes employment, especially in rural areas, makes all these data suspect. As we have seen, a significant portion of economic activity in developing countries may be either outside of formal markets or not picked up by government surveyors, so that employment in unrecorded production may be significant.[43] By the definitions of the industrialized countries, a majority of rural women might not be considered part of the labor force, when they actually work longer hours than men. David Turnham concludes that "part of the substantial differences in reported female participation rates between countries . . . reflects the application of varying criteria rather than differences in the objective reality."[44]

Evaluation of the developing-country labor force has also been confused by the incentive to work among populations in transition from subsistence agriculture to industrial employment. Figure 9–3 illustrates a backward bending supply curve for labor, which has sometimes been used to characterize portions of the labor force. The explanation was that new industrial workers had low aspirations and that once a target level of income was obtained, higher wages led to reduced hours. Most economists now believe that this is, at best, a very limited phenomenon. A study from Bangladesh concludes that when workers move out of agriculture to industrial jobs, a reduction of hours cannot be seen as a result of a limited desire for income. Workers may now have more assets and better living conditions, even with fewer work hours.[45] Workers may also undertake other productive activities after their factory workday is finished.

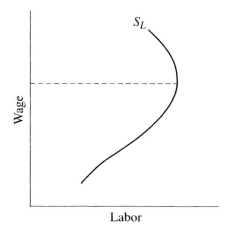

FIGURE 9–3 Backward Bending Supply Curve for Labor

Workers have a specific target income. Once wages rise enough to permit that income to be earned, any increase in the wage would result in a corresponding reduction in time worked, as long as the target income were maintained.

If we are not sure just who is in the labor force, estimates of unemployment will be based on arbitrary criteria. Given these constraints, however, the best estimates are that unemployment tends to be higher in developing than in the industrialized countries, although there is considerable variation among regions within countries. Table 9–5 reports unemployment rates. In developing countries, the largest single category of the unemployed is frequently young people, including those with above-average educations, excluding many who are in school but might well leave if jobs were available. In one group of studies, the average urban unemployment rate in 22 countries surveyed was 18 percent in the 15 to 24 age group and 5 percent for those over 24. Most of the data come from urban surveys, but it seems that unemployment is lower overall in rural areas: 5.4 percent as opposed to 8.1 percent urban unemployment in a survey of 18 countries.[46]

TABLE 9–5 Unemployment Rates

Countries	1987	1993	1997
United States	6.2	6.9	4.9
Western Europe	10.4	10.6	10.5
Japan	2.8	2.5	3.4
Developing Countries			
China*	2.0	2.6	3.0
India	3.4	2.3	NA
Other Asia*†	4.3	4.4	4.2
Latin America/Caribbean†	5.7	NA	7.4
Central/Eastern Europe*	NA	7.2	9.6

*Data are for 1996 rather than for 1997.

†Data are for 1990 rather than for 1987.

NA = Not Available.

Source: International Labour Organization, *World Employment Report 1998–99* (Geneva: ILO, 1998).

Reasons for Unemployment in Developing Countries

We are used to thinking about employment in the context of the overall growth of the economy, amenable to the volume of aggregate demand in the short run, and to the gradual accumulation of capital over a longer period. Even here, however, structural unemployment—caused by inability of workers to adapt quickly to new skill needed in new industries—can result in significant hardship.

We should not then be baffled when unemployment rates in developing countries stay high despite growing aggregate demand. Reasons may include unequal access to education that makes employment qualification for many jobs impossible, especially for poor people; social changes, such as the increasing proportion of women in the labor force; the use of capital-intensive technologies; and structural change, in which changing demand for labor creates jobs in new sectors while reducing opportunities in older sectors. Jobholders from traditional employment categories may not yet be trained for newer jobs, and many may be no longer employable because new skills take long periods of education and training. For women, of course, discrimination in employment is pervasive.

While there are significant cyclical fluctuations such as in many Latin American countries, the constraints on output in the poorer countries are often due less to insufficient demand than to problems from the supply side when saving is insufficient to provide the capital needed to create employment in the new formal sector. And investment in capital-intensive technologies creates relatively little employment. High unemployment rates among young people with high levels of education may be due to lack of jobs at the level they expected to see after many years of school. High unemployment rates in Arab countries, for example, are a consequence of rapid population growth, the slowing of oil-related growth, and already bloated public-sector payrolls.[47]

This contrasts to some earlier claims that unemployment was not likely to be an important issue for developing countries because poor people simply could not afford to be unemployed and that labor markets were flexible enough to absorb people at some market-clearing wage. Most unemployment was considered to reflect people's voluntary search for better jobs. This view has now been overturned by a growing amount of research on unemployment in developing countries. David Turnham's review suggests we still do not know with any degree of confidence how different macro- and microeconomic variables affect unemployment in developing countries.[48]

Under these circumstances, government policies to reduce unemployment may not hit the mark. Traditional macropolicies, addressed in Chapter 11, tend to focus on fostering growth with low inflation. Microlevel policy changes—considered in the next section—will be hit-or-miss because we cannot be certain which policies are in fact causing unemployment. To the extent that factor prices can be brought into line with evolving factor endowments, it is conceivable that unemployment will be reduced at the cost of lower wages and benefits in the short run, problems that may be resisted by workers.

Labor Market Issues in the Formal Sector

The formal sector has conditions of employment that resemble those in industrialized countries. These include minimum wages, high professional salary scales, unions, social insurance, and benefits. In theory, such conditions should raise the cost of labor above market levels and lead to a bias against labor-intensive production methods.

While we do not know exactly how important these conditions are in determining employer decisions among production techniques, we can sketch out some of the issues.

Minimum Wages

Minimum wages were a relatively late development in industrial countries, justified by the spirit that working people should be able to earn enough to live decently and supported by the notion that higher wages strengthen aggregate demand. However, there has always been a concern that, in the absence of growing aggregate demand, an above-equilibrium wage floor would lead to lower employment among those sectors of the labor force that qualified only for minimum-skill employment, as shown in Figure 9–4. In a developing country, where that category includes a majority of the population, there is a tendency for minimum wages also to place urban formal workers at an economic level above that of rural workers, even considering the extra expenses of urban living.

Above-equilibrium wages attract workers to the modern sector and may induce substitution of capital for labor, especially when government policy at the same time places ceilings on interest rates. The minimum wage becomes a political tool for pacifying the urban proletariat, which quickly becomes a liability when inflation brings demand for ever-increasing minimum wages. Further, minimum wages at the bottom of the skill ladder may govern all wage scales, so when the minimum is increased, all levels may obtain increases to keep their relative positions.

The evidence on the impact of minimum wages in developing countries is inconclusive. Minimum wages are sometimes expensive for governments and firms that hire excess workers, but they are often below wages that firms in the formal sector are already paying for their skilled labor and so have little impact.[49] This impact may be minimal

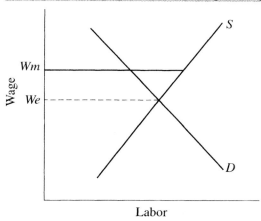

FIGURE 9–4 Impact of a Minimum Wage: Competitive Market

A government-enforced minimum wage (*Wm*) above the equilibrium level (*We*) will increase the quantity of unskilled labor supplied and reduce the quantity demanded, creating unemployment. This can be reduced by some combination of reducing the minimum wage; expanding demand for this labor, through higher industry or aggregate demand; and reducing supply by training people for jobs for which wages are not controlled.

due to shortages of skilled labor and the theory of the efficiency wage, which suggests that employers may pay more than absolutely necessary to acquire and keep happy, productive workers.[50] Minimum wages in some developing countries may apply to such a narrow group of workers, or be so loosely enforced, that their impact is very small. For example, a study of Mexico and Colombia concluded that there was virtually no impact in Mexico: The minimum wage was too low to be effective in the formal sector and was largely ignored by employers in the informal sector. In Colombia, however, the minimum wage did appear to reduce employment.[51]

Economic analysis suggests another qualification to the impact of minimum wages. Figure 9–5 provides the typical illustration of a **monopsony** situation in a factor market. In competitive labor markets the labor supply curve is very elastic: Firms are too small to exert any pressure on wages and they have to pay whatever market conditions dictate. When a relatively small number of employers exists, there may not be effective competition for workers and the labor supply curve is less elastic. The resulting levels of wage and employment are below the competitive equilibrium, so a minimum wage can, up to a point, increase both, improving economic efficiency. A number of developing countries are very small (59 whose 1999 populations are at or below 1 million), and the existence of large employers would almost guarantee some monopsony power.

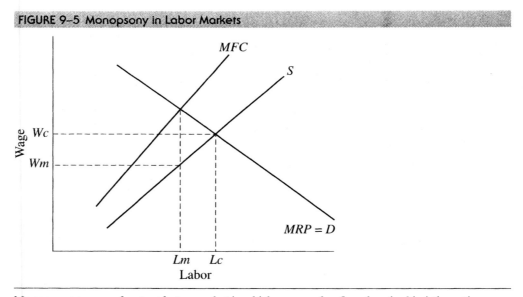

FIGURE 9–5 Monopsony in Labor Markets

Monopsony power refers to a factor market in which one or a few firms buy (or hire) the entire supply. If monopsony power exists, such as in this labor market, new workers receive higher wages. Also, previous employees get the benefit of a higher supply price, so the marginal cost to the firm is greater than the wage: The Marginal Factor Cost (*MFC*) curve lies above the factor Supply Curve.

A profit-maximizing firm determines employment by equating the Marginal Factor Cost and the Marginal Revenue Product (*MRP*), which is the additional revenue brought in by the production of the last employee hired. The result will be that, compared to a competitive situation, the monopsonist will hire fewer people (*Lm*) than in a competitive market (*Lc*). The wage, determined by supply curve (*Wm*), is less than the competitive wage (*Wc*).

Under these circumstances, a minimum wage above the monopsony wage but below the competitive wage will increase both wages and employment.

Even a large country may exhibit similar conditions. A study of Indonesia concluded that a doubling of the minimum wage in real terms caused considerable employment losses in small firms but may possibly have increased employment in large firms.[52]

Professional Salary Scales

Salaries at the upper levels of formal-sector companies and the government were set high for expatriate employees during the colonial period. In the private sector they may continue in order to attract highly trained expatriate workers. When compared to positions that have been held by the local populations, these wages create a distinct gap between upper-level positions and all others. Since it was impolitic, during the earlier days of independence, for new governments to accept dual wage rates at upper-level positions, many of the local replacements for expatriates received similar salaries and never let go of them. This begins to exert pressure on the lower levels, which resent the extreme separations. While inflation and the informal economy have eroded some of these discrepancies for government officials,[53] some government employment has become more lucrative through opportunities to receive bribes.

Unions

Workers in developing countries have often formed, joined, and put pressure on firms and governments through labor unions. Although in most developing countries these unions are rendered ineffective or are even subservient to the government or ruling political party, they may at times be a major source of pressure, especially in the context of urban-oriented development and political support. Table 9–6

TABLE 9–6 Labor Force and Union Membership (Millions)

	1999 Labor Force	1995 Union Membership
High Income (Including High-Income Asian Countries)	595	
North America		21
Northern Europe		8
Western Europe		24
Southern Europe		11
Central/Eastern Europe		14
Europe/Central Asia	318	
Latin America/Caribbean	319	
Central America		11
South America		22
Middle East/North Africa	172	7
East/Southeast Asia		24
South Asia	797	10
East Asia/Pacific (Excluding High-Income Asian Countries)	1,220	
Sub-Saharan Africa	340	10
Totals	3,761	162

Sources: Labor force data from *World Development Indicators 2001.* Union membership data from *World Labor Report 1997/98.*

provides some data on the portion of the labor force belonging to unions throughout the world.

The argument for unions in developing countries is no different from that in other countries: If workers do not look after their interests, no one else will. Private employers and governments have greater economic power than workers, and have no innate desire to provide wages and conditions (safety, fringe benefits) that are any more generous than necessary to maintain a productive labor force. Unions can improve workers' wages and working conditions. They also can promote higher productivity and greater satisfaction among workers.

Unions in some Latin American countries, such as Mexico, Chile, and Argentina, have been a strong base of support for left-of-center regimes that were supportive of laws favorable to workers. But some of these same unions have been suppressed, or their support withdrawn, when those regimes were replaced. As Latin American governments have become more attuned to the problems of international competitiveness, union concerns have been placed after those of companies.[54]

There is significant variation in the ability of unions in developing countries to affect labor market flexibility.[55] Developing-country governments are in a perpetual state of trying to squeeze as much surplus out of the population as is consistent with politically acceptable consumption standards. If unions are weak, as in many countries, they may have little impact on government policy. If they have political influence, however, they may win concessions that are out of proportion to labor's contributions to development. In fact, the power of unions may be felt less at the level of the individual firm than at the macro level, where they may mobilize large groups of people for such objectives as higher minimum wages or political change.

Unions, and the rigidities they can impose on labor markets (overstaffing, rigid job classifications, restrictions on firing workers) have hurt the ability of some firms to adapt to market pressures.[56] In Argentina, for example, employers are required to pay severance equal to one month's pay per year worked, with a two-month minimum.[57] Throughout Latin America, governments are attempting to reform labor markets by making collective bargaining less centralized, and changing legal requirements in areas such as severance payments and unemployment insurance.[58] As in the industrialized world, the balance between corporate adaptability and worker rights is constantly being tested.

Social Insurance

Workers, especially those in the formal private sector and government, tend to want conditions they observe in the West. They may press for retirement pay and medical care at levels commensurate with those of workers in the industrialized countries. As societies become more monetized and more urban, as family size falls and some family cohesion weakens, the need for social security increases. Such benefits may be beyond the government's capability to service the bulk of the population and thus further reinforce the inequities that exist in the employment arena.

The Impact of Regulations

It seems unlikely that these problems significantly, and by themselves, interfere with the development of a formal sector and labor force. On the other hand, regulations may well drive some activity into the informal sector, as we will see in the discussion of small firms. A survey of seven countries in different regions of the developing

BUILDING A MODERN LABOR FORCE IN INDONESIA

FAST FACTS

On the Map: Southeast Asia

Population: 207 Million

Per Capita GNI and Rank: $600   (150)

Life Expectancy: Male—64   Female—68

Adult Literacy Rate: Male—91%
Female—81%

Indonesia, with severe financial problems and under attack for poor labor conditions, would seem a bad example for developing a modern labor force. Yet significant strides have been made. Between 1965 and 1990, the labor force grew at 2.7 percent per year. Over that time, agriculture's share of GDP fell from 73 percent to 50 percent, industry's share rose from 8 percent to 17 percent, and services from 19 percent to 33 percent. Between 1975 and 1988, real earnings per worker in manufacturing grew at 4.9 percent per year. What factors were responsible for this progress?

A major factor was rapid growth of output, fostered by macroeconomic stability and a favorable climate for investment. Also, the government invested heavily in infrastructure and education and funneled oil revenues to agriculture, services, and public works. Family planning was part of the mix, reducing birth rates and permitting more women to work.

Another lesson of the Indonesian experience is that labor market restrictions will not greatly retard job and wage growth when output and labor demand are growing rapidly. The eight-hour day (six days a week) and hiring/firing regulations were in force, among others, although in view of violations of child labor laws, these other regulations may have been evaded as well. Minimum wages were not introduced until the 1990s.

The picture has flaws of course. Protection of domestic industry and an emphasis on capital-intensive projects reduced potential employment and widened wage gaps while encouraging informal-sector growth. Less educated and older workers were not well incorporated into the labor market. Many of the new workers labored under exploitative conditions: Unions were suppressed, work conditions were poor, much employment was irregular, and child labor was used. Despite this, however, Indonesian wage rates were representative of levels throughout Southeast Asia.

The Indonesian experience is not a perfect model, but it does point to the benefits of heavy infrastructure and human capital investments, and macroeconomic stability to foster labor market development.

Source: Chris Manning, *Indonesian Labour in Transition: An East Asian Success Story?* (Cambridge: Cambridge University Press, 1998).

world revealed "great diversity" in the extent to which regulations are complied with. Especially for small enterprises, governments often fail to enforce regulations considered unrealistic.[59] A study of Latin America concluded that overall wage rates, investment, and macroeconomic variables such as the exchange rate, not labor market regulations, are the main determinants of industrial competitiveness.[60] A thorough study of Indonesia, summarized in Case 9–3, supports these conclusions and provides a degree of optimism about what can be achieved.

Discrimination Against Women

Discrimination against women is common in developing-country labor markets. Women are disproportionately represented in informal markets and, within formal markets, in low-wage occupations. In those developing countries for which data are available, female unemployment rates are typically higher than rates for men, while they are often lower in industrialized countries. Job security is less, as are training and benefits. Women tend to work disproportionately part-time as well, likely both as a matter of personal choice and employer policy. Lower levels of education, as well as education and training less applicable to formal markets, hinders the qualifications of women. Technological change sometimes works against women by upgrading jobs to areas from which they are excluded. Finally, the relatively greater acceptance of women in public sector employment has made them disproportionately affected by cutbacks made in that sector as part of structural adjustment measures taken during the eighties and nineties.[61]

It is not clear whether rising female labor force participation rates bode a greater acceptance of women as workers or just a preference for a lower-waged, easily controlled group in such settings as export processing zones. A positive sign can be seen in the booming high-tech sector of the Indian economy. Women are moving into some managerial positions and generally enjoying work conditions previously reserved for male workers.[62]

Child Labor

One of the most troublesome aspects of labor markets in many developing countries is the use of children under the age of 15 as part of the labor force. Child labor was prevalent in the factories of the West's Industrial Revolution, providing the rallying cry for many social reformers. In rural areas, and the informal sector of developing countries, child labor is common as part of family-run enterprises. More disturbing, however, is the use of children as full-time workers in formal-sector firms, often under conditions that are exploitative, detrimental to their health, and heedless of their education.[63]

The extent of this phenomenon is not clear, but a recent estimate puts child labor in developing countries at 250 million.[64] The highest rate of labor force participation among children ages 5 to 14 is in Africa, over 40 percent, but the figure is over 20 percent in Asia and Latin America. Most of the activity, of course, is in the agricultural sector (about 70 percent), but over 8 percent of child labor is estimated to be in manufacturing and 10 percent in services. Most work at least six days a week, primarily at unpaid labor for the family, and often in hazardous jobs. Children making clothing, bricks, or cigarettes may work from six in the morning to six or eight in the evening, for only a few dollars a week. Girls tend to work longer and for lower pay than boys, many as household domestics.[65]

Children work in mines without protective equipment; in glass factories with temperatures over 100 degrees, broken glass on the floor, and exposed electrical wires; in fields exposed to biological and chemical agents; as domestics as young as five, for as long as 15 hours a day; and in construction carrying loads much too heavy for their size and age.[66] This is not in the long-run interest of a country's development: By producing uneducated children in poor health, reducing employment opportunities for adults, reducing the incentive for innovation, and threatening reaction among Western consumers of certain exports, child labor is a shortsighted approach to immediate profit. The International Labor Organization is spearheading an International Program on Elimination of Child Labor (IPEC), working with individual governments to provide educational and other options for children.[67]

The Urban Informal Sector

The dynamism of the informal sector in developing countries underscores its importance for employment.

Characteristics of Informality

Informal enterprises are often characterized by ease of entry; the use of local resources; family ownership; small scale; labor intensity; adapted technology; informally acquired skills; and relatively unregulated, competitive markets. A particularly significant differentiation has to do with the informal sector's location outside of (or antagonistic to) government regulation. This is not always clear-cut. Some firms may act in accordance with regulations, some may evade them, and in some cases the government may not actually try to enforce regulations on small firms. Firms may comply with some but not other regulations. Perhaps the most useful, and common, distinction between the two sectors has to do with the number of employees in a firm, although this fails in the case of professional services such as doctors and lawyers. Nevertheless, it seems to be a good general reference point.[68]

A good way to envision the informal sector is through some of its activities. A visitor's perspective is only partially valid. You are met at the airport by someone—often a child—who wants to carry your bags, shine your shoes, be your guide, or sell you food and inexpensive manufactured goods. Driving your own car and parking on the street, a child will offer to "watch your car" for a small sum, and perhaps it is worth your while to pay. Such small-scale "street" services are not only the most visible but are also the first line of entry for many into the informal labor force.

Development Spotlight 9–1 suggests some key activities of the informal sector. One review, summarizing a number of Latin American studies, breaks down the activities of the informal-sector labor force into the categories of services (38 percent), commerce (20 percent), manufacturing (19 percent), construction (6 percent),

---

DEVELOPMENT SPOTLIGHT 9–1

ACTIVITIES OF THE INFORMAL SECTOR

The informal sector consists mainly of small, family-owned firms that operate outside of, or on the fringes of, legal standards established for other firms. The informal sector is usually an important source of employment in developing nations. Typical activities include:

Services—tailoring, barbers, loans, machinery repair

Commerce—retail sales, restaurants, lodging

Manufacturing—food processing, textiles and clothing, materials processing, brewing

Construction

Transportation—taxis, buses

Miscellaneous—recycling, prostitution

transport (3 percent), and other (14 percent).[69] Small family firms produce much of the clothing, processed food, and beer. The taxi drivers, construction workers, auto maintenance, and other service workers are part of the informal sector, as are messengers and others who fill in the cracks for large firms. Studies in the late 1960s and early 1970s for Latin American cities indicated that typically the share of urban employment considered informal was 40 percent or more.[70] Another review estimates the informal sector's share of the labor force in Latin America to have been 46 percent in 1950 and 42 percent in 1980. In the small West African country of Benin, the informal sector accounted for an estimated 41 percent of all employment and 93 percent of nonagricultural employment in 1993. A recent study of small firms in five Southern African countries concluded that over a 10-year period they accounted for half of the new entrants into the labor force. A multicontinent survey found the same to be true for national employment in the 1990s. An estimated 83 percent of new jobs created in Latin America and the Caribbean between 1990 and 1993 were in the informal sector.[71]

The informal sector typically has higher unemployment levels. A survey of 13 Latin American countries in 1996 found informal unemployment rates higher than formal rates in 9 countries. Because informal firms operate outside some government regulation, often employing family members, wages are low. Because they may have a harder time getting loans, and rely on informal financing, capital costs are higher. The lower wage/rental ratio, combined with smaller scale, explains why these firms are relatively labor intensive and operate with simpler technology. With these characteristics in mind, an examination of the informal sector's role is revealing of much of the commercial and industrial activity in developing countries.

The Informal Sector and Small-Scale Industry

The informal sector is important because of the size distribution of firms in developing countries.[72] If we define a small firm as one with fewer than 10 employees and a large firm as one with more than 50, industrialized countries tend to have a positive correlation between the number of firms and their size. In developing countries, there tends to be a large number of small and large firms, with relatively few in between.

There are a number of reasons for this. Small, fragmented markets, high transportation costs, little access to capital, and the prominence of labor-intensive industries such as food processing and apparel tend to keep down the size of firms. Once these barriers are overcome, firms can become quite large. In addition, a high degree of government regulation is also a factor. The cost of regulations frequently discourages firms from crossing the invisible line that separates informal from formal, while the large firms are better able to withstand those costs; thus, there are few midrange firms.

There is little evidence, however, that small firms are inefficient. Given their technology, small firms in developing countries seem to be as efficient as those in higher-income countries. Industries where small scale predominates show easy entry and exit (especially where regulations are not onerous), and many new firms match the efficiency of established firms in a few years.[73]

Informal firms provide some services that are otherwise not available at all or are available to only a small part of the population through the formal sector. They fill in the cracks by providing ancillary services (transportation, repair) that permit the formal sector to run and a variety of services to individuals who work in the formal sector. Sometimes they may work directly for formal-sector enterprises, through various types of subcontracting arrangements.[74]

Informal firms are an extremely important source of inexpensively acquired skills, including managerial and organizational skills. As a sort of informal business school and vocational institute, they are often the only source of training available to poor workers in developing countries. Pay tends to be below similar jobs in the formal sector, but heads of informal enterprises (sometimes the only employee as well) often earn more than the average wage in the formal sector through a combination of return to both labor and capital. Informal firms may compete with some formal firms, especially in services, transportation, and commerce, but they may also provide strong backward linkages to the formal sector by purchasing their machinery and raw materials.[75]

Informal finance through moneylenders and organizations formed by poor people are crucial. In both rural and urban areas, there are informal rotating credit organizations in which funds are contributed by members and are available to them either on a regular basis or as needed. The importance of such organizations is attested to in the Cameroons where these "tontines" constitute the largest source of savings, with a combined membership of almost three-fourths of the adult population.[76]

Women in the Informal Sector

In a number of developing countries, informal enterprises are a significant source of economic opportunity for women. They are primarily involved in small-scale trade, selling food, clothing, and other nondurables (at which some in West Africa have become quite wealthy) or work at home in family-run businesses such as textile and clothing manufacture and restaurants. The downside of many of these activities is that discrimination in formal and high-value-added activities has restricted women to trade and services that are often limited as paths to greater productivity and advancement.[77]

Women in the informal sector face all the disadvantages of that sector in addition to the usual double burden of home and family care, legal discrimination in employment and ownership, and lower levels of education. A study of small-scale enterprises in southern Africa shows women's enterprises to be less dynamic and in more traditional areas than men's. Some success has come from special organizations by which women pool resources.[78] But women's activities in some environments are vulnerable to takeover. A United Nations report on small-scale rural women's activities notes that "most activities remain women's exclusively only as long as they are carried out traditionally . . . As soon as a new technology is introduced and material gains can be made, the activity is taken over by men."[79]

Child Labor in the Informal Sector

Because many informal firms are family based, children form an important part of the labor force. The dividing line is often impossible to draw between a child's household chores and tasks that would constitute labor in the family firm. In urban manufacturing (such as clothing) and services (such as food preparation or product delivery), children may be indispensable to survival of the firm. However, beyond the use of the family's own children, others under the age of 15 may be hired as apprentices, and that employment may be the only type of vocational training available to those who cannot afford to continue their education beyond the primary level.

Small Firms and the Government

The impact of government policies on the use of appropriate technology applies with full force to the informal sector. Advantages to formal firms reduce opportunities for informal firms, while the inducements to capital use in the formal sector may cause labor spillover into the informal sector, lowering wages there. Government could promote the informal sector by reducing its own bias toward large formal firms, reducing legal and regulatory barriers, and by paying more attention to the infrastructure needs of these activities and to overall macroeconomic stability.[80]

Development is often seen not only in terms of changing economic structure but also of changing the nature of business enterprises from primarily small to primarily large. Still, the persistence of small (often informal) enterprises in developing countries and evidence from all over the world indicate that the informal sector continues to grow. Informal sectors pose numerous challenges to government policy. Their vulnerability to economic downturns is likely to be greater than for other sectors: In Latin America during the 1980s, while medium- and large-scale output shrank by 7 percent, formal small-scale enterprise output fell by 30 percent, and informal activity declined by an estimated 42 percent. However, they sometimes prove quite resilient.[81]

There has been increasing interest among foreign aid donors in assisting small firms, or microenterprises. This has been a particular focus of the Inter-American Development Bank, World Bank, the United Nations, the U.S. Agency for International Development (USAID), and many nongovernmental organizations (NGOs). Experience with these programs indicates that the availability of credit is a key variable in success or failure. Credit must be combined with technical assistance to improve the chances for success. Contrary to some preconceptions, lending to small firms has not run unusual repayment risk, and can lead to significant output and employment opportunities.[82]

However, a USAID survey of its programs for microenterprises notes that there are limits to this assistance. Government restrictions on credit markets may make continued borrowing difficult once the foreign assistance program has been withdrawn, while needs beyond some money and technical assistance have not yet been addressed very well. Managerial performance requires considerable attention, especially if individual small firms are to grow while others take their place.[83]

Providing employment for growing developing-country labor forces will be difficult for a long time. The formal sector may be treated much like industrialized-country labor situations, dealing with issues such as sufficient aggregate demand, minimum wages, and social insurance. Employers must pay attention to education, training, and the match between skills and jobs. The informal sector, however, disadvantaged by government policies and lack of skills, requires a greater degree of attention to make its full contribution to development.

SUMMARY AND CONCLUSION: EVOLVING FACTOR ENDOWMENTS AND DEVELOPMENT

Industrialization, per se, has moved from a central focus in the field of economic development to the background. No one doubts that increasing industrialization is a likely and desirable outcome of the development process in most countries: Indeed, we define development in part as a shift from an agricultural to an industrial focus. But the questions of the kind of industrialization and the requirements for it have become much more complex and subtle. In this chapter, we have noted the necessity for each country to undertake the process of industrialization by looking at its particular resource endowment, including its labor force. Development economics has turned away from grand schemes of large-scale manufacturing in favor of looking for ways to grow industries appropriate to what each country can sustain with current and near-term resources.

This approach does not mean that we are satisfied with things as they are. It does not mean that people and their governments should not strive to develop new industries. It does not mean abandoning modern industry to North America, Western Europe, and Japan. It does mean that we no longer expect that tremendous strides in industrialization will take place in all countries at a rapid pace. Time is required to develop labor skills and appropriate technology to produce sustainable industrialization.

In deciding which investments are most appropriate, businesses look at the potential demand for a product, and we expect them to proceed along a path that uses factors of production in such a way as to match their relative productivities. In so doing, however, firms are initially limited to existing technologies or modifications or adaptations of those technologies. Some developing-country firms are misled into inappropriate technologies: those that use factors of production in combinations inconsistent with their country's factor endowments.

Inappropriate technologies may be used due to ties to foreign firms or finance, distortions in labor and capital markets, protectionist policies that provide no incentive to adapt foreign technologies to local conditions, or the desire to imitate firms in industrialized countries. Governments can adopt policies that provide maximum incentive to firms to use more appropriate technologies.

Providing employment for growing labor forces is one of the greatest challenges of development, and most developing countries have not yet succeeded. Unemployment is due to a combination of demand- and supply-side factors, exacerbated by capital-intensive technologies. More attention to midrange technologies, plus relevant education, is necessary to correct this problem.

A significant portion of the output and employment in developing countries exists in the informal sector. That sector is more labor intensive than the formal sector, and less technologically sophisticated, but may use more appropriate technologies. As it is also a dynamic portion of many developing-country economies, governments should take pains to encourage its activities and help those in the informal sector to prosper.

The spectacular performance of countries such as South Korea need not be repeated everywhere for us to conclude that industrialization is on the way. If local production of soap in Ghana, cement in India, and kitchen appliances in Colombia does not sound like a significant change in world history, it is nevertheless an indication that economic development is proceeding. If we then throw Korean autos, electronics, and ocean vessels; Brazilian electronics and military equipment; and Indian software and machine tools into the mix, it is clear that worldwide industrialization is, however unevenly, on the move.

We still have to pay close attention to the international context of development, which will take up most of the remaining chapters. Before that, however, we need to focus more closely on changing notions of the economic role of the government (or the state) in development and the problems of macroeconomic policy.

Key Terms

- appropriate technology (p. 238)
- Export Processing Zone (EPZ) (p. 235)
- factor endowments (p. 233)
- factor intensities (p. 233)
- heavy industry (p. 234)

- innovation (p. 241)
- labor force participation rate (p. 248)
- light industry (p. 234)
- maquiladora (p. 235)

- Marginal Rate of Technical Substitution (MRTS) (p. 237)
- market distortions (p. 240)
- monopsony (p. 252)
- unemployment rate (p. 248)

Questions for Review

1. What is the relationship between "industrialization" and "development?" Is it more useful to see industrialization as a cause or effect of development?
2. What economic considerations determine the production technique chosen by a business firm? Explain, on microeconomic grounds, why one might expect any particular good to be produced by different techniques in industrialized and developing economies.
3. Define the concept of "appropriate technology" and apply it to Question 2.

4. How does the Ghanaian soap industry illustrate the difficulties that small local firms must overcome in competing with imports from multinational firms?
5. Explain how market distortions can lead to the adoption of "inappropriate" technologies. What additional factors may be involved in such adoption?
6. How does innovation in developing countries differ from innovation in more industrialized countries?

7. How did the Indian government stifle growth of an indigenous computer industry in spite of an ostensible desire to promote it?
8. What are the main causes of unemployment in developing countries? To what extent do labor market imperfections affect unemployment?

9. What policies were or were not important in the improvement of the Indonesian labor force?
10. List some typical informal-sector activities and ways in which the informal sector interacts with the formal sector.
11. What are some typical differences between formal and informal firms, including such areas as technology, employment, and relationship to the government?

Related Internet Resources

The United Nations has created an agency to promote industrial development. The UN Industrial Development Organization (UNIDO) reports on projects and progress on its Web site at ⟨www.unido.org⟩. Labor conditions worldwide are monitored by the UN's International Labour Organization. Data on the labor force and employment by country are available at ⟨http://laborsta.ilo.org⟩. The activities of the ILO, including efforts to improve the working conditions of women and children, are reported on at the main Web site, ⟨www.ilo.org⟩.

Endnotes and Further Readings

1. For an overview, see John Weiss, *Industry in Developing Countries: Theory, Policy and Evidence* (London: Routledge, 1990).
2. See Alyn Young, "Increasing Returns and Economic Progress," *Economic Journal* 38, no. 152 (1928), pp. 527–542, and Rajesh Chandra, *Industrialization and Development in the Third World* (London: Routledge, 1992), pp. 1–4.
3. For India, see Tom Kemp, *Industrialization in the Non-Western World* (London: Longman, 1989), chapter 4.

Algeria is mentioned in Tom Hewitt, Hazel Johnson, and Dave Wield, eds., *Industrialization and Development* (Oxford: Oxford University Press, 1992), p. 214.

4. John Weiss, *Industry in Developing Countries: Theory, Policy and Evidence*, p. 10, provides this breakdown of data collected by the United Nations Industrial Development Organization (UNIDO).

5. For example, Leslie Sklair, *Assembling for Development* (San Diego: Center for U.S.–Mexican Studies, 1993).

6. The 1948 and 1984 data are reported in Rhys Jenkins, "Industrialization and the Global Economy," in Tom Hewitt, Hazel Johnson, and Dave Wield, eds., *Industrialization and Development*, pp. 13–40. The data for 1997 are from the *World Development Indicators 1999*.

7. Ian Smillie, *Mastering the Machine: Poverty, Aid and Technology* (Boulder, CO: Westview Press, 1991), p. 198.

8. International Labour Organization, *World of Work*, no. 27 (December 1998). This report can be accessed at ⟨www.ilo.org/public/english/bureau/inf/magazine/27/news.htm⟩.

9. See James Pickett, D. J. C. Forsyth, and N. S. McBain, "The Choice of Technology, Economic Efficiency and Employment in Developing Countries," in Edgar O. Edwards, ed., *Employment in Developing Nations*, Report on a Ford Foundation Study (New York: Columbia University Press, 1974), pp. 83–132, and Simon Teitel, "On the Concept of Appropriate Technology for Less-Industrialized Countries," in his *Industrial and Technological Development* (Washington: Inter-American Development Bank, 1993), pp. 161–187. An early paper is A. K. Sen, "Choice of Techniques of Production: With Special Reference to East Asia," in Kenneth Berrill, ed., *Economic Development with Special Reference to East Asia* (New York: St. Martin's Press, 1964), pp. 386–396.

10. C. Peter Timmer, "Choice of Technique in Rice Milling on Java," *Bulletin of Indonesian Economic Studies* 9, no. 2 (1974), reprinted in Carl K. Eicher and John M. Staatz, eds., *Agricultural Development in the Third World*, 2nd ed. (Baltimore: The Johns Hopkins University Press, 1990), pp. 309–319. Also see Howard Pack, "The Substitution of Labor for Capital in Kenyan Manufacturing," *Economic Journal* 86, no. 341 (March 1976), pp. 45–58, and "Employment and Productivity in Kenyan Manufacturing," *East African Economic Review* 4, no. 2 (December 1972), pp. 29–52.

11. See E. F. Schumacher, *Small Is Beautiful: Economics as If People Mattered* (New York: Harper and Row, 1973), printed on 100 percent recycled paper, long before this was popular; Denis Goulet, *The Uncertain Promise: Value Conflicts in Technology Transfer* (New York: IDOC/North America, Inc., 1977); and Ian Smillie, *Mastering the Machine: Poverty, Aid and Technology*.

12. See Gustav Papanek, "Industrialization Strategies in Labor-Abundant Countries," *Asian Development Review* 3, no. 1 (1985), pp. 43–53.

13. Buddhadeb Ghosh and Chiranjit Neogi, "Productivity, Efficiency, and New Technology: The Case of Indian Manufacturing Industries," *The Developing Economies* 31, no. 3 (September 1993), pp. 308–328.

14. See Teitel, *Industrial and Technological Development*, pp. 163, 180–182, and Frances Stewart, "Technology and Employment in LDCs," in Edwards, *Employment in Developing Nations*, pp. 86–90.

15. United Nations, "Local Production of Appropriate Technology for Rural Women" (New York: UN Industrial Development Organization (UNIDO) document, November 14, 1989), pp. 19–21. Also see Fong Chan Onn, "Appropriate Technology: An Empirical Study of Bicycle Manufacturing in Malaysia," *The Developing Economies* 18, no. 1 (March 1980), pp. 96–115.

16. See U. Hiemenz, "Growth and Efficiency of Small and Medium Industries in ASEAN Countries," *Asian Development Review* 1, no. 1 (1983), pp. 101–118, and A. H. M. Nuruddin Chowdhury, "Small and Medium Industries in Asian Developing Countries," *Asian Development Review* 8, no. 2 (1990), pp. 28–45.

17. See *Trade and Employment in Developing Countries*, vol. 3, *Synthesis and Conclusions*, Anne O. Krueger, ed. (Chicago: University of Chicago Press, 1983), p. 150; Steve Haggblade, Carl Liedholm, and Donald C. Mead, "The Effect of Policy and Policy Reforms on Non-Agricultural Enterprises and Employment in Developing Countries: A Review of Past Experiences," in Frances Stewart, Hank Thomas, and Tom deWilde, *The Other Policy: The Influence of Policies on Technology Choice and Small Enterprise Development* (Washington: Intermediate Technology Publications, 1990), pp. 58–98; and in the same volume, Frances Stewart and Gustav Ranis, "Macro-Policies for Appropriate Technology: A Synthesis of Findings," pp. 3–42. Some distortions may help growth. See Jene K. Kwon and Hoon Park, "Factor Price Distortions, Resource Allocation and Growth: A Computable General Equilibrium Analysis," *Review of Economics and Statistics* 57, no. 4 (November 1995), pp. 664–676.

18. An example is Gerald C. Nelson, "Labor Intensity, Employment Growth and Technical Change: An Example From Starch Processing in Indonesia," *Journal of Development Economics* 24, no. 1 (November 1986), pp. 111–117. A survey is Jeffrey James, "New Technologies, Employment and Labour Markets in Developing Countries," *Development and Change* 23, no. 3 (July 1993), pp. 405–437.

19. See Stewart and Ranis, "Macro-Policies for Appropriate Technology: A Synthesis of Findings," pp. 25–27.

20. See Joseph A. Schumpeter, *Theory of Economic Development* (Cambridge: Harvard University Press, 1955); Nathan Rosenberg, *Perspectives on Technology* (Cambridge: Cambridge University Press, 1976); Raymond

Vernon, "Technological Development: The Historical Experience," Economic Development Institute (EDI) Seminar Paper No. 39 (Washington: World Bank, 1989); W. W. Rostow, *Theorists of Economic Growth from David Hume to the Present* (New York: Oxford University Press, 1990), especially pp. 451–470; and Joel Mokyr, *The Lever of Riches: Technological Creativity and Economic Progress* (New York: Oxford University Press, 1990).

21. See articles by Simon Teitel in his *Industrial and Technological Development.*

22. *World Development Indicators 2000.*

23. See Mariluz Cortes, Albert Berry, and Ashtaq Ishaq, *Success in Small and Medium-Scale Enterprises: The Evidence from Colombia* (New York: Oxford University Press/World Bank, 1987), pp. 178–187.

24. For the growing R&D capacity in East Asia, see Dan Biers, "Asian Countries Aim to Boost Research," *Wall Street Journal*, October 24, 1995. On India's software industry, see "Bangalore Bytes," *The Economist* (March 23, 1996).

25. Henny Romijn, "Acquisition of Technological Capability in Development: A Quantitative Case Study of Pakistan's Capital Goods Sector," *World Development* 25, no. 3 (March 1997), pp. 359–377, and Bee Yan Aw and Geeta Batra, "Technological Capability and Firm Efficiency in Taiwan (China)," *World Bank Economic Review* 12, no. 1 (January 1998), pp. 59–79.

26. Carlo Pietrobelli, *Industry, Competitiveness and Technological Capabilities in Chile: A New Tiger from Latin America* (New York: St. Martin's Press, 1998).

27. Jaymin Lee, "Technology Imports and R&D Efforts of Korean Manufacturing Firms," *Journal of Development Economics* 50, no. 1 (June 1996), pp. 197–210; Homi Katrak, "Imported Technologies and R&D in a Newly Industrializing Country: The Experience of Indian Enterprises," *Journal of Development Economics* 31, no. 1 (July 1989), pp. 123–139; Nagesh Kumar, "Technology Imports and Local Research and Development in Indian Manufacturing," *The Developing Economies* 25, no. 3 (September 1987), pp. 220–233; Homi Katrak, "Imports of Technology, Enterprise Size and R&D-Based Production in a Newly Industrializing Country: The Evidence from Indian Enterprises," *World Development* 22, no. 10 (October 1994), pp. 1599–1608; and Homi Katrak, "Developing Countries' Imports of Technology, In-House Technological Capabilities and Efforts: An Analysis of the Indian Experience," *Journal of Development Economics* 53, no. 1 (June 1997), pp. 67–83.

28. See Thomas Fricke, "High Impact Appropriate Technology Case Studies" (Washington: Appropriate Technology International, 1984), and Sosthenes Buatsi, *Technology Transfer: Nine Case Studies* (London: Intermediate Technology Publications Ltd., 1988).

29. Teitel, *Industrial and Technological Development,* chapter 8, pp. 183–184.

30. Homi Katrak, "Imports of Technology of the Newly Industrialising Countries: An Inter-Industry Analysis for Mexico and Pakistan," *Journal of International Development* 2, no. 3 (July 1990), pp. 352–372. For Asian country experiences, see UN Conference on Trade and Development (UNCTAD), *Technology Transfer and Development in a Changing International Environment: Policy Challenges and Options for Cooperation* (New York: United Nations, 1992).

31. See Nicolas Jequier and Gerard Blanc, *The World of Appropriate Technology: A Quantitative Analysis* (Paris: OECD, 1983), and Farrokh Najmabadi and Sanjaya Lall, *Developing Industrial Technology: Lessons for Policy and Practice* (Washington: World Bank, 1995).

32. See Sanjaya Lall, "Understanding Technology Development," *Development and Change* 23, no. 4 (October 1993), pp. 719–753.

33. Giorgio Barba Navaretti, Isidro Soloaga, and Wendy Takacs, "When Vintage Technology Makes Sense: Matching Imports to Skills," World Bank Policy Research Working Paper No. 1923 (Washington: World Bank, 1998).

34. Teitel, *Industrial and Technological Development,* chapter 9, pp. 197–199.

35. John Woodward Thomas, "The Choice of Technology for Irrigation Tubewells in East Pakistan: An Analysis of a Development Policy Decision," in Timmer et al., *The Choice of Technology in Developing Countries: Some Cautionary Tales* (Cambridge: Harvard Center for International Affairs, 1975), pp. 31–67. For Indonesia, see Timmer in the same volume, pp. 1–29. Also Howard Pack, " Appropriate Industrial Technology: Benefits and Obstacles," *Annals of the American Association of Political and Social Sciences*, no. 458 (November 1981), pp. 27–40.

36. Vernon, "Technological Development: The Historical Experience."

37. *World Development Report 1998/1999: Knowledge for Development* (New York: Oxford University Press, 1999).

38. The data are from the *World Development Indicators 2001.*

39. *World Employment 1995* (Geneva: International Labour Organization, 1995), p. 61.

40. David Turnham, *Employment and Development: A New Review of Evidence* (Paris: OECD, 1993), p. 37.

41. *World Development Report 1995: Workers in an Integrating World* (Washington: World Bank, 1995), Table A-1.

42. United Nations, *1999 World Survey on the Role of Women in Development: Globalization, Gender and Work* (New York: United Nations, 1999), p. 8.

43. See Luisella Goldschmidt-Clermont, "Economic Measurement of Non-Market Activities: Is It Useful and Feasible?" *International Labour Review* 129, no. 3 (1990), pp. 279–299.

44. *Ibid.,* p. 45.

45. Mohammed Sharif, "Landholdings, Living Standards, and Labour Supply Functions: Evidence from a Poor Agrarian Society," *Journal of Development Studies* 27, no. 2 (January 1991), pp. 256–276.

46. Turnham's survey is on pp. 56–71 of *Employment and Development: A New Review of Evidence*. The data are on pages 80 and 86.

47. Radwan A. Shaban, Ragui Assaad, and Sulayman S. Al Qudsi, "The Challenge of Unemployment in the Arab Region," *International Labour Review* 134, no. 1 (1995), pp. 65–82.

48. David Turnham, *Employment and Development: A New Review of Evidence*, pp. 56–60.

49. Haggblade et al., "The Effect of Policy and Policy Reforms on Non-Agricultural Enterprises and Employment in Developing Countries: A Review of Past Experiences," p. 68.

50. See Dipak Mazumdar, "The Marginal Productivity Theory of Wages and Disguised Unemployment," *Review of Economic Studies* 26 (June 1959), pp. 190–197, and Joseph E. Stiglitz, "Alternative Theories of Wage Determination and Unemployment in LDCs: The Labor Turnover Model," *Quarterly Journal of Economics* 88, no. 2 (May 1974), pp. 194–227.

51. See Lyn Squire, *Employment Policy in Developing Countries: A Survey of Issues and Evidence* (New York: Oxford University Press, 1981), p. 112, and Linda Bell, "The Impact of Minimum Wages in Mexico and Colombia," World Bank Policy Research Working Paper No. 1514 (Washington: World Bank, 1995).

52. Martin Rams, "The Consequences of Doubling the Minimum Wage: The Case of Indonesia," World Bank Policy Research Paper No. 1643 (Washington: World Bank, 1996).

53. See Derek Robinson, "Civil Service Remuneration in Africa," *International Labour Review* 129, no. 3 (1990), pp. 371–386.

54. Patrice Franko, *The Puzzle of Latin American Economic Development* (Lanham, MD: Rowman and Littlefield, 1999), pp. 253–257.

55. Joan M. Nelson, "Organized Labor, Politics, and Labor Market Flexibility in Developing Countries," *World Bank Research Observer* 6, no. 1 (January 1991), pp. 37–56.

56. See, for example, Jonathan Friedland, "In This Mexican Union, Changing a Lightbulb Is a Three-Man Job," *Wall Street Journal*, December 3, 1999.

57. René Cortázar, Nora Lustig, and Richard H. Sabot, "Economic Policy and Labor Market Dynamics," in Nancy Birdsall, Carol Graham, and Richard H. Sabot, eds., *Beyond Trade-Offs: Market Reform and Equitable Growth in Latin America* (Washington: Inter-American Development Bank, 1998), p. 200.

58. See *ibid*. in its entirety, pp. 183–212.

59. Christian Morrisson, Henri-Bernard Solignac Lecomte, and Xavier Oudin, *Micro-Enterprises and the Institutional Framework in Developing Countries* (Paris: OECD, 1994). On this point see p. 139.

60. Adrianna Marshall, "Economic Consequences of Labour-Protection Regimes in Latin America," *International Labour Review* 133, no. 1 (1994), pp. 55–74.

61. See the UN's *Women in a Changing Global Economy*, 1994 World Survey on the Role of Women in Development (New York: United Nations, 1995), pp. 60–67 and 68–77.

62. Chen May Yee, "High-Tech Lift for India's Women," *Wall Street Journal*, November 1, 2000.

63. See "The Littlest Workers" (May–June 1994), p. 20; Michel Bonnet, "Child Labour in Africa," *International Labour Review* 132, no. 3 (1993), pp. 371–390; Christian Grootaert and Ravi Kabu, "Child Labour: An Economic Perspective," *International Labour Review* 134, no. 2 (1995), pp. 187–204; Skip Barry, "Taking Aim at Child Slavery," *Dollars & Sense* (July–August 1997), p. 10; and Kebebew Ashagrie, "Statistics on Working Children and Hazardous Child Labour in Brief," ⟨www.ilo.org/public/english/comp/child/stat/stats.htm⟩.

64. The main ILO report is "Child Labour: Targeting the Intolerable," International Labour Conference Report VI (1)—86th Session (Geneva: International Labour Organization, 1998). A summary appears in *World of Work*, no. 18 (December 1996), ⟨www.ilo.org/public/english/bureau/inf/magazine/18/child.htm⟩.

65. See ⟨www.ilo.org/public/english/bureau/stat/child/childhaz.htm⟩.

66. ILO, "Child Labor: Targeting the Intolerable."

67. ⟨www.ilo.org/public/english/standards/ipec/about/index.htm⟩.

68. However, see Josef Gugler, "The Urban Labour Market," in Alan Gilbert and Josef Gugler, *Cities, Poverty and Development: Urbanization in the Third World*, 2nd ed. (Oxford: Oxford University Press, 1992), pp. 87–113.

69. Harold Lubell, *The Informal Sector in the 1980s and 1990s* (Paris: OECD, 1991). The data are on p. 54 and are derived from Victor E. Tokman, "Politicas para el sector informal en America Latina," *Revista Internacional del Trabajo* 97, no. 3 (July–September 1978), p. 314. For a later evaluation, see Victor E. Tokman, "The Informal Sector in Latin America: 15 Years Later," in David Turnham et al., eds., *The Informal Sector Revisited* (Paris: OECD, 1990).

70. The first set of studies is cited by Lubell, *ibid*. The second review is from Manuel Castells and Alejandro Portes, "World Underneath: The Origins, Dynamics, and Effects of the Informal Economy," in Alejandro Portes, Manuel Castells, and Lauren A. Benton, eds., *The Informal Economy: Studies in Advanced and Less Developed Countries* (Baltimore: Johns Hopkins University Press, 1989), pp. 11–37.

71. Donald C. Mead, "The Contribution of Small Enterprises to Employment Growth in Southern and Eastern Africa," *World Development* 22, no. 12 (December 1994), pp. 1881–1894. The 1990s data are reported in

the ILO *World Employment Report, 1998–99*, p. 167. The data for Benin are from the UN *1999 World Survey*, p. 29, and for Latin America/Caribbean, from ILO, "Unemployment Threatens World Cities: Jobs are Needed to Check Growth in Urban Poverty, Says ILO," May 29, 1996, ⟨www.ilo.org/public/english/bureau/inf/pr/96-15.htm⟩.

72. See James R. Tybout, "Manufacturing Firms in Developing Countries: How Well Do They Do, and Why?" *Journal of Economic Literature* 38, no. 1 (March 2000), pp. 11–44. Also see *Asian Development Review* 6, no. 2 (1988), and A. T. M. Nurul Amin, "The Role of the Informal Sector in Economic Development: Some Evidence from Dhaka, Bangladesh," *International Labour Review* 126, no. 5 (September–October 1987), pp. 611–623.

73. See also Bee Yan Aw, Xiaomin Chen, and Mark J. Roberts, "Firm-Level Evidence on Productivity Differentials, Turnover, and Exports in Taiwanese Manufacturing," National Bureau of Economic Research (NBER) Working Paper No. W6235 (1997), which can be accessed at ⟨http://papers.nber.org/papers/W6235⟩.

74. See Lourdes Beneria, "Subcontracting and Employment Dynamics in Mexico City," in Portes, Castells, and Benton, *The Informal Economy: Studies in Advanced and Less Developed Countries*, pp. 173–188.

75. Lubell, *The Informal Sector in the 1980s and 1990s*, p. 64.

76. *Ibid.*, p. 101.

77. See Ann Leonard, ed., *SEEDS: Supporting Women's Work in the Third World* (New York: The Feminist Press of City University of New York, 1989), and Ian Smillie, *Mastering the Machine: Poverty, Aid and Technology*, p. 189.

78. Jeanne Downing and Lisa Daniels, "The Growth and Dynamics of Women Entrepreneurs in Southern Africa," report to U.S.A.I.D. by GEMINI (Washington, Technical Report No. 47, August 1992).

79. United Nations, *Women in a Changing Global Economy*, p. 12.

80. Carl Liedholm, "The Dynamics of Small-Scale Industry in Africa and the Role of Policy," Working Paper No. 2, GEMINI Project (Washington, January 1990); Walter Elkan, "Policy for Small-Scale Industry: A Critique," *Journal of International Development* 1, no. 2 (April 1989), pp. 231–260; and Barbara Grosh and Gloria Somolekae, "Mighty Oaks from Little Acorns: Can Microenterprise Serve as the Seedbed of Industrialization?" *World Development* 24, no. 12 (December 1996), pp. 1879–1890.

81. The Latin American data are from Turnham et al., *The Informal Sector Revisited*, p. 137. See also Harold Lubell and Charbel Zaron, "Resilience Amidst Crisis: The Informal Sector of Dakar," *International Labour Review* 129, no. 4 (1990), pp. 387–396.

82. See Brent Bowers, "Third-World Debt That Is Almost Always Paid in Full," *Wall Street Journal*, June 7, 1991; Michael Korengold, "Micro-Enterprise: Credit Where It's Due," *Utne Reader* (November–December 1991), pp. 44–46; and Andy Jeans, Eric Hyman, and Mike O'Donnell, "Technology—The Key to Increasing the Productivity of Microenterprises," Working Paper No. 8, GEMINI Project (Washington, March 1990).

83. See Lubbell, *The Informal Sector in the 1980s and 1990s*, pp. 83–95, and an OECD study *New Directions in Donor Assistance to Microenterprises* (Paris: OECD, 1993). Also see Steve Onyeiwu, " 'Graduation' Problems Amongst Micro and Small Enterprises in Eastern Nigeria, 1960–91," *Journal of International Development* 5, no. 5 (September–October 1993), pp. 497–510.

10

THE AMBIGUOUS ROLE OF THE STATE IN DEVELOPMENT

*A government could print a good
edition of Shakespeare's works,
but it could not get them written.*
—ALFRED MARSHALL (1842–1924)

INTRODUCTION

In this chapter and the next we consider the various economic roles of governments. The "magic of the market" alone cannot rid the world of terrible poverty and despair, but governments have often done more harm than good.

We look at the rationales for both general and specific government activities. We begin with planning, then investigate the role of government-owned companies and the debate over whether to reform or privatize them. Government action is then put in the context of social services and market development, where its role is crucial. Finally, we analyze government's regulatory role, with a focus on the negative consequences of rent seeking and corruption. We find that while the role of government should be limited, there remain important areas where government can be effective and should participate actively.

MARKET FAILURE AND THE GOVERNMENT'S ROLE

There are a number of economic reasons for government activity, ranging from provision of the legal infrastructure to facilitating the efficient allocation of resources. Once these reasons are laid out, we can better evaluate specific government interventions.[1]

Market-Facilitating Institutions

Markets operate reliably only when buyers and sellers can be confident that they are free to exchange and that the terms of those exchanges are legally enforceable. When communities grow so large that social pressure cannot be relied upon to enforce adherence to agreements, legal contracts and a system of justice become necessary. Parties to contracts must trust that they can obtain equal treatment under laws that are fair to all sides.

Only with such institutions in place will any significant investment take place. Buyers will be hesitant to buy if they do not expect redress from a faulty product. People who lend money or take other kinds of risk will do so only if they are reasonably sure that they can keep whatever profits they make. So one inescapable rationale for government is to set and enforce rules that encourage production and exchange.

Large-Scale Economic Activity

We have already reviewed Rosenstein-Rodan's Big Push approach to development.[2] Among the rationales for this government-oriented approach was that a poor society composed of small-scale businesses cannot generate either the savings or investment to undertake large projects, such as transportation infrastructure or even large-scale manufacturing. While there are arguments against this, such as the need to start small, and the possibility of imports and foreign investment, many newly independent governments generated large projects under the conviction that only they could raise and organize the necessary resources.

A related argument was that development required a series of projects, even if none was big in itself, to create the necessary linkages for coherent development. Individual entrepreneurs might not see the potential for profit from their individual pieces of the puzzle, perhaps not envisioning a large enough market to generate returns to scale and profitability. Under these conditions, the state would at least coordinate such investment and perhaps even carry it out.

Market Failure

Most of the contemporary focus on the role of government revolves around the concept of **market failure**. Its most general meaning is the inability of a competitive market to efficiently allocate resources, although it also encompasses situations in which the conditions for competition do not exist.

Monopoly

Markets are not competitive if one or a very few firms have control of the market. Output may be less and prices higher than if there is a large number of sellers. Monopolies are large only relative to their market. Thus, although firms in developing countries may be small, isolated markets may be common so that monopoly power is widespread. In rural areas, for example, there may be only one source of fertilizer, seed, or roofing materials. Or there may be a monopsony—one buyer of grain for storage and transportation to the cities. Here, the role of the government might be to enforce competition, either by breaking up monopolies, breaking down barriers to entry of new firms, or breaking down the barriers that separate markets. Some governments might want to compete with private firms with their own companies.

A more complicated situation is that known as **natural monopoly** (Figure 10–1). Electricity, for example, requires a large initial investment (fixed cost) in generation (a dam, for example) and transmission (transforming stations, network of lines). Once this is complete, however, the marginal cost of an additional kilowatt hour delivered to your home is extremely low. The same would be true for a water treatment plant. In such cases, the technical requirements for production would entail a firm so large that it encompasses the entire market, so having competition would be inefficient. If production scale is such that marginal and average costs are declining along the entire relevant range of production, competitors could not gain a foothold, and the market would be overcrowded if they did. Solutions here could be either government provision of such goods or services, or government regulation of private companies. In the

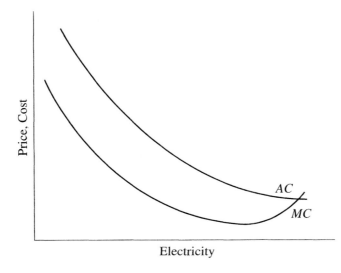

FIGURE 10–1 Natural Monopoly

High fixed costs, implied by the large downward-sloping range of marginal and average cost, allow the initial market entrant to capture economies of scale. Newer entrants cannot compete on cost, so the industry is effectively limited to one firm, the natural monopolist. When such conditions exist, most governments will at least regulate the pricing decisions of the firm, and some will find a justification for takeover. Examples include power generation and transportation infrastructure.

latter case, it is quite common for private firms to submit requests for price increases to a government agency.

Externalities and Public Goods

We have discussed externalities thoroughly in Chapter 5. The existence of costs not borne by the producer (negative externalities such as pollution) or benefits received by a free rider (positive externalities such as education or agricultural research) argue for government intervention. The typical case is in the regulation of pollution, where government has a host of potential measures to force the polluter to pay for, or reduce, the costs imposed on outsiders.

Public goods are those that are considered to have large positive externalities. In addition, they are impossible to produce for just one person. Sewage treatment and national defense, for example, require expenditures meant to benefit a large number of people. These goods and services are **nonrivalrous**—which means that consumption by one person does not restrict consumption by another—and **nonexcludable**—meaning that it is impossible, or extremely costly, to exclude individuals from their use. The latter term implies that all consumers are in a sense free riders, so that the only way to fund such expenditures is through taxes. (We could disconnect a home from the sewage system, but this would be expensive and would impose high costs on surrounding homes.)

Imperfect Information

A more recent addition to the list of market failures is imperfect, or absent, information. The usual analysis of competitive markets usually presumes that all buyers and sellers have perfect information about products in the market. If consumers lack information, they are prey to pressure from sellers who gain from the consumer's inability to compare price and quality. In extreme cases, lack of reliable information will cause a market to deteriorate, to the disadvantage of buyers and sellers alike. Case 10–1 provides an example.

Imperfect information is likely to be more common and more severe in developing countries and, as the case shows, is amenable to government interventions that are

CASE 10–1

IMPERFECT INFORMATION IN THE MARKET FOR MILK IN INDIA

FAST FACTS

On the Map: South Asia

Population: 998 Million

Per Capita GNI and Rank: $440 (163)

Life Expectancy: Male—62 Female—64

Adult Literacy Rate: Male—68%
Female—44%

The quality of milk in India was deteriorating during the 1960s. Milk production was increasing and production was moving out of rapidly growing urban areas. Greater supply led to lower prices, but higher costs of shipping milk into the cities led some producers to dilute their milk, causing a drop in demand and losses to dairy farmers. Milk consumption per capita fell by one-fourth between 1950 and 1970.

Part of the problem was a lack of understood, enforceable standards for the fat content of milk. The Indian National Dairy Development Board (NDDB) approached this problem as one of creating standards and helping farmers maintain them. It created quality standards and made the technology for measuring the fat content in milk available to dairy farmers and consumers. It then helped farmers to maintain those standards by helping them improve milk production, and helping improve transportation and marketing standards. The NDDB even set up its own brand name for dairy products, certified to meet the standards.

The NDDB did not take control of dairy production. By setting standards, helping producers to meet them, and warning consumers to be sure of what they were getting, it induced a rapid increase in consumption and production, and provided an incentive for private milk processors to match those standards in order to compete.

Source: Robert Klitgaard, *Adjusting to Reality: Beyond "State Versus Market" in Economic Development* (San Francisco: ICS Press, 1991), pp. 51–55.

widely recognized as beneficial and often essential. Providing acceptable standards to measure quantity and quality, and enforcing requirements for producers to tell consumers the proper use of a product and where to get help when a problem arises, are activities that are even more essential when consumers are unfamiliar with new products and more accustomed to face-to-face transactions than with less personal transactions with large corporations.

In some cases it is the producer who is ill-informed. This is particularly common in financial transactions where the bank or other financial institution often has incomplete or even deliberately inaccurate information about the borrower. We examine problems of this sort in Chapter 15.

REACTION AGAINST THE MARKET AND THE LURE OF PLANNING

The attempt to manage an entire national economy through planning has been the most ambitious type of government intervention. In principle, little more would seem to be required than managing a large conglomerate firm where managers make decisions on what to produce, how to produce most efficiently, how much to produce, and at what price to sell. In practice, even with modern information systems, successful planning at this level would seem to be unattainable. In fact, whereas the discipline of economic development looked to government action for much of the post-World War II era, there has been a significant shift back to interest in the market since the early 1980s. How far that shift ought to go is one of the underlying questions of this chapter.

Away from the Market

It should not be surprising to learn that the leaders of many developing-country governments took early steps away from the market. The markets they were most familiar with, outside of purely local activities, were the world markets for their exportable products, either agricultural or mineral goods. Those markets can be highly unstable. Demand shifts in consuming countries, vagaries of weather in producing countries, the development of substitutes for primary products, and other factors have led to great fluctuations in output, prices, and revenues.

Many developing-country governments could not easily follow the path of the West. From a position of superior force, Western countries used not only their own resources but those of the countries they colonized or traded with. Europe and the lands of European settlement took their time to develop. Today's developing countries are in a hurry.

With most developing economies structured by European and American firms to serve home-country markets, it was common for a poor country to earn virtually all of its revenue from one or a few such commodities. Drastic swings in foreign exchange earnings made industrialization difficult.

The developing economies in the 1950s and 1960s were often not only behind the Europe of the 1800s but were bound up in an existing international division of labor. If they wanted to process their own raw materials, they had to challenge the multinational processing and trading firms that had established channels for large-scale operation and who sometimes refused to deal with them. If they succeeded in light manufacturing, they would find barriers created to their goods. Their economies were often too small to set up large-scale production of items such as machinery and steel, especially when the developed-country industries were established and efficient or protected by trade barriers. The existing technology was not always available and for most companies was not suited to their resources. Those developing-country industries that succeeded were often able to take advantage of help from their governments.

If we then add the arguments about market failure, the temptation to find another path was often overwhelming. And if one must create institutions from the ground up, the direct approach—such as have a government decide to build a dam or a steel mill—may seem much more attractive than an attempt to create the incentives for capital to move in the appropriate direction. It seems safer as well if private capital is foreign owned and comes with conditions that are not conducive to the government's own idea of the direction of development. Therefore most developing countries in Africa and Asia that attained formal independence after World War II turned to some form of planning, while even the long-independent countries of Latin America looked to government to give direction to their economic development.

The Lure of Planning

The original impetus to a **planned economy**, in the Soviet Union and those who followed its path, was the desire to both develop rapidly and be rid of the "irrationalities" of the capitalist system where production is motivated by private profit rather than national development. The motivations of the developing-country governments today, although containing some elements of the anticapitalist urge, are geared largely to rapid development—that is, development at a pace that might allow them to catch up with the wealthier countries. It is important to remember also that in the two decades after World War II, governments were associated with some impressive economic achievements. The performance of the Soviet economy, the mobilizations for war in Western Europe and the United States, and the recovery of Western Europe with Marshall Plan assistance were widely admired. The new international concern for development, as expressed by World Bank programs and the U.S. Alliance for Progress in Latin America, gave governments a strong role in devising projects that they were encouraged to integrate into a wider plan of development.[3]

The early Soviet success with comprehensive national economic planning gave way to inefficiency and stagnation.[4] Developing-country governments did not have the resources for that level of planning anyway. Instead, they drew up five-year "plans" that were usually just lists of priority projects that required government money and some government-owned corporations for implementation. This kind of "planning," including controls over imports, exports, and external capital flows, often fails because those countries have few skilled people, little capital, and insufficient infrastructure. Whereas the best hope of such attempts would be for a government to take a few sectors and try to lay the groundwork for additional development, it was common for them to try everything at once and end up doing most of it badly.

PLANNING IN TWENTIETH-CENTURY DEVELOPING ECONOMIES

What is required for effective planning? Why has so much of what has been called planning failed?

Requirements of Planning

Plans require information about the country's financial, physical, and human resources. This means taking (and updating) surveys of land and natural resources, the labor force, capital equipment, and income for both its spending and taxing potential.

Initially, planning focused on the national economy. A comprehensive plan would help governments decide what consumer and capital goods should be produced, and at what rate. It would have to address the relative importance of output versus employment (choice of technology), and which goods to produce at home and which to import.

An aggregate target for the country's rate of growth would be of little use. More critical for *development* is where growth should take place: what targets should be set for the specific sectors of the economy. Then the requirements for those targets must be determined: how much investment is required, and how much is required to operate these projects, in both physical and financial terms.[5]

Sectoral targets must then be subjected to a project-by-project analysis of costs and benefits. An accurate assessment of costs requires realistic prices or reliable methods of estimating shadow prices. Estimating benefits is more difficult. Benefits in economics are usually the outcomes experienced by consumers, along with positive externalities that benefit society as a whole. But how are these measurements to be taken in advance? They end up being political judgments from which ordinary consumers are removed.

Governments also need a good understanding of how the economy works as an integrated whole; that is, the relationships among sectors. Projects will be vying for specific resources. **Input–output tables**—which show the relationships among sectors of the economy—might help to determine if governments are realistically planning the sectors that produce inputs (coal, iron, steel) so that they meet the needs of the sectors that produce the outputs (cars, railway track, buildings). But this information is unlikely to be available. Are all these plans consistent with respect to their physical characteristics? Timing? Financial requirements? Are mathematical tools such as linear programming and General Equilibrium models able to capture the messiness of the real world? Then there are political aspects of the planning process.[6] Planners have their own interests; different departments within governments have to mesh their interests and work together. Governments must assess their ability to properly implement these plans.

It is then essential to decide how the private sector should be involved, and the relationship between state and market. How will the private sector be encouraged to cooperate with the plan; what incentives will be offered and under what conditions? What is the appropriate combination of macro-level policies (fiscal and monetary policies) and micro-level policies (subsidies, tax incentives, and tariff rebates)? Will we be better off making maximum use of markets by influencing relative prices, or should we use the more direct but less reliable approach of setting physical goals and quotas? What should be the role of foreign firms?

The Failures of Planning

Even where growth and planning have coincided, it is not easy to show that planning was the cause of growth. Most plan targets were not achieved, and the policy instruments often caused problems. Of course, circumstances that originate outside the country can upset plans: changes in the demand for a country's exports, changes in the prices it pays for imports (including interest rates on borrowed money), sudden reductions in foreign aid, natural disasters, or political upheaval.

However, there are typically inherent weaknesses in the plan itself. It may have been based on incorrect data or a faulty economic model; it may be overambitious or inadequately prepared, have insufficient means for implementation, and ignore noneconomic factors. Many plans "were often made not merely without there being investment projects, but without examination of whether any potential investments in that sector would be likely to be adequately socially profitable."[7]

But there may be more fundamental problems as well. Planners may simply not understand the development process sufficiently to make any kind of a reasonable plan. How big a role is played by capital, education, technology? What is the appropriate mix between agriculture and industry? How should we measure future benefits and costs of social infrastructure or alternative capital/labor ratios? How will people react to changes in government policy or changes in living standards

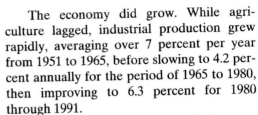

CASE 10-2

PROBLEMS OF PLANNING IN INDIA

FAST FACTS

On the Map: South Asia

Population: 998 Million

Per Capita GNI and Rank: $440   (163)

Life Expectancy: Male—62   Female—64

Adult Literacy Rate: Male—68%
Female—44%

Indian economist P. C. Mahalanobis was ready for planning before India's independence, having studied with some of the famous mathematical economists of the Soviet Union. Early Indian plans (the first five-year plan covered the period 1951 to 1956) were based on his elaborations of relatively simple growth models: The key objective was economic growth that required investment and, in turn, savings. Growth was seen largely in industrial terms. In the absence of a well-developed market system, industrialization would require detailed direction from the public sector in terms of what projects would be chosen, how resources should be allocated, and how foreign exchange should be allocated for all projects, public and private.

Such plans could hardly be flexible. Detailed allocation of materials and imports through licensing systems could not be changed frequently if they were to be effective. The first Indian plan in 1951 outlined its own sort of socialism through public investment and control of private investment, but the bureaucracy simply created an avenue for political power and patronage.

The economy did grow. While agriculture lagged, industrial production grew rapidly, averaging over 7 percent per year from 1951 to 1965, before slowing to 4.2 percent annually for the period of 1965 to 1980, then improving to 6.3 percent for 1980 through 1991.

But many problems reduced plan success. Intentions to improve agriculture, which was in practice neglected for the first two plans, were nullified by failure to implement land reform and lack of resources devoted to rural construction. Intentions to reduce dependence on foreign resources were overpowered by the increased need for imports to carry out plan projects and overvaluation of the exchange rate, which hurt exports. Protection simply led to greater inefficiency of protected industries. Intentions to improve the distribution of income were also nullified by the lack of growth and the incentives to inefficiency.

In the middle 1980s, the Indian government began a long trip down the path of "liberalizing" its economy so planning is less relevant now, but the obstacles erected by the system of private and public protection and privilege have made it slow work.

Source: Jagdish N. Bhagwati, "Planned Development in India" (1973), in Gerald M. Meier, ed., *Readings in Economic Development*, 4th ed. (New York: Oxford University Press, 1984), pp. 747–753. Data are from Lloyd G. Reynolds, *Economic Growth in the Third World, 1850-1980* (New Haven: Yale University Press, 1985), and *World Development Report*, 1991, 1993.

and social relationships? How can government officials decide the correct combination of purely domestic activity and goods that may be exported to or imported from other countries? As the case of India (Case 10–2) shows, even a relatively well developed bureaucracy with considerable intellectual skills and motivation is likely to falter in the face of such problems.

These problems illustrate how inherently complex planning is. It is unlikely that any activity that we would describe accurately as "planning" is capable of accomplishing more than a small bit of what it sets out to do.[8] For those that prefer a strong state role but have given up the urge to plan, there is another option, to which we now turn.

NOT-QUITE PLANNING: STATE-OWNED ENTERPRISES

Many countries at different levels of development still provide significant economic activity through their governments. One important instrument of government control is the government-owned company known as state-owned enterprise (SOE).

State-Owned Enterprises

State-owned enterprises[9] are set up when government officials believe private enterprise cannot, will not, or should not undertake a particular activity, or at times simply as a means to provide political patronage. Table 10–1 shows the prominence of SOEs in a number of countries. A recent World Bank survey showed that, despite a growing sentiment in the 1980s toward selling SOEs to private investors, little change occurred during that decade. In a group of 40 market-oriented developing countries, the share of SOE output in GDP remained at about 11 percent from 1978 to 1991, compared to 8 industrial countries where the share fell from 9 percent to 7 percent. In a group of 55 developing countries, SOE investment as a share of national investment fell only from 23 percent to 19 percent. As Table 10–1 shows, SOEs are more prominent in low- rather than in middle-income countries.[10]

The range of possible government activity is broad, although there are some guidelines from economic theory that could be used to limit its scope. The potential for positive government involvement is generally recognized where there are significant positive externalities (public goods) and economies of scale that might result in natural monopolies.[11]

TABLE 10–1 State-Owned Enterprise in Developing Countries

	1978–1991 Average	1978	1991
Share in Valued Added (%)			
Low Income (15)	14		
Middle Income (25)	9		
Developing (40)	11	11	11
Share of Gross Investment (%)			
Low Income (18)	29		
Middle Income (37)	17		
Developing (55)	21	23	19
Share of Employment (%)			
Low Income (10)		15	16
Middle Income (11)		5	6
Developing (21)		9	11

Source: Luke Haggarty and Mary M. Shirley, "A New Data Base on State-Owned Enterprise," *World Bank Economic Review* 11, no. 3 (September 1997), pp. 497–513.

Rationales for Public Ownership

We have already noted economic rationales such as the paucity of entrepreneurs or lack of a well-developed capital market that are often put forward for developing countries; reasons which should fade from view as development proceeds. Other rationales have combined economic and political goals. For example, concern that foreigners or a few wealthy citizens could essentially ignore larger public needs has led to SOEs in the mining of natural resources such as oil, copper, and tin. The same concerns have motivated public ownership in areas considered the "commanding heights" of the economy: public utilities (often natural monopolies), steel, and banking. The extension of development priorities has led governments to control import/export activities (to ensure appropriate use of foreign exchange) and the distribution of agricultural inputs and crop marketing.

The Case for Some State Ownership

Although governments are able to levy taxes, borrow money, and receive aid, so their enterprises may lack the incentive to operate efficiently, it is not at all impossible. They must obtain the resources and management skills, enforce the necessary internal incentives, and take advantage of (or create) profitable opportunities.

Some Successes

Some countries have, in fact, run successful SOEs for long periods of time. Examples include the Chilean Copper Corporation (CODELCO); Brazil's iron company CVRD and petroleum company Petrobras; Venezuela's oil company Petroleos de Venezuela (PDVSA) and its iron and steel conglomerate Corporacion de Guayana; India's Hindustan Machine Tools; South Korea's steel corporation POSCO; and Malaysia's National Electricity Board. Even the overburdened SOE network of Tanzania has produced some efficient companies, including the Tanzania Investment Bank and the electric power company, Tanesco. A major study of SOEs in Kenya, from independence in 1963 into the mid-1980s summarized in Case 10–3, concludes that a number of firms performed efficiently and profitably for over 25 years. Instances of bad performance were often due to government policies such as price controls rather than inherent inefficiency. Most of the failures occurred after the late 1970s, when high oil prices and interest rates hurt so many developing countries. A study of Brazil's state enterprises before the crisis of the 1980s concluded that its experience "demonstrated that state ownership of basic industries can be an effective substitute for private enterprise in stimulating rapid and sustained economic growth," at least under Brazilian conditions.[12] Public firms, even when losing money, may still create local technologies and other economic opportunities that promote development.[13]

Based on the long-term development record, Lloyd Reynolds summarized the experience of state-owned manufacturing firms to 1980 as largely negative. But he suggested that efficient government companies are possible where labor scarcity reduces the incentive to overstaff the company and where governments are "stable, pragmatic and outward-looking," circumstances that have existed in some East Asian countries.[14] Writing for a U.S. foreign policy audience, Raymond Vernon concluded that "Where governments have been reasonably competent and responsible, and where comparisons between private enterprises and state-owned enterprises have been possible, the technical performance of state-owned enterprises has not appeared much

SUCCESS AND FAILURE IN KENYAN SOEs

FAST FACTS

On the Map: East Africa

Population: 29 Million

Per Capita GNI and Rank: $360   (172)

Life Expectancy: Male—47   Female—48

Adult Literacy Rate: Male—82%
Female—75%

The government of Kenya has run numerous SOEs over the years, some successful and some not. Two successful companies were the Kenya Pipeline Company (KPC) and the Kenya Power and Lighting Company (KPL).

Over the period 1978 to 1988, KPC ran at nearly full capacity. In early years there were losses, but cost reductions and a price increase in 1980 reversed that situation. Profit plus interest was usually 25 percent of net assets after 1979, although prices fell after 1980. The high profits are difficult to evaluate, however. The price received for shipping bulk oil products was set by the government, in part as a means of imposing a consumption tax on oil. But unit costs dropped by half between 1978 and 1980, then fluctuated around a flat trend during the remainder of the period studied. Even the World Bank deemed it an efficient operation. The company consistently upgraded its financial position by increasing the ratio of its equity to assets.

KPL kept costs steady over the period 1964 to 1988. Inflation-adjusted prices fell from 1967 to 1975 but even after rising remained below 1970 levels through 1988. The rate of return on equity exceeded 8 percent every year but one. Performance was excellent even though KPL was in charge of operating rural electrification projects that were relatively more expensive than urban electricity provision.

Two failures were both in the transportation sector. The Kenya National Transport Company (Kenatco) engaged in freight transport by truck and taxi service. Management was terrible, records nearly nonexistent. The company appears to have been somewhat profitable in the early and mid-1970s, but the breakup of the East African Common Market (EACM) in 1977 interrupted commerce with Tanzania while Uganda was politically unstable. At the end of 1983 the company was put under receivership, and the trucking operation disbanded.

Kenya Railways was likewise hurt by the dissolution of the EACM. Much of its former freight business went to roads and pipelines. Labor productivity fell and unit costs soared. Government policies take a lot of the blame. Much of the bulk freight was basic commodities on which the government deliberately kept prices low. When the railway tried to compensate with higher prices on other goods, it could not compete with trucks that did not have to pay for the roads. Foreign exchange shortages resulted in unavailability of spare parts for engines and prevented the railway from keeping up with the transition to containerized shipments. Road shipment was more expensive, but the railway did not have capacity to meet the demand. The government's practice of bailing out the firm, by transforming debt into equity, provided no incentive to improve performance.

These cases raise more questions than they answer about SOEs. It is tempting to see the success of KPC and KPL as due to their monopoly status, especially as Kenatco failed miserably in a field crowded with competition. But monopolies are supposed to be breeding grounds for inefficiency and this was not true for either KPC or KPL. And a study of state-owned banks in Kenya shows many of them competing successfully against both Kenyan and foreign banks.

It seems possible therefore, "to appoint capable and public-spirited managers who will do a good job without punitive or restrictive controls." In other words, with the proper incentives and a government that does not interfere with operations, success is possible. The importance of government restraint is emphasized by the problems faced by Kenya Railways. Aside from problems with efficiency, the loss of the EACM, and foreign exchange shortages, the company was put in an untenable situation by government subsidization of bulk agricultural commodities. Even a private, regulated firm faced with the same constraints might have suffered the same fate. A private, unregulated firm might have fared better, but it is not clear that a private firm would have been willing to operate under such unpromising market conditions.

The situation is clearest for Kenatco. Trucking and taxi services are highly individualistic enterprises, even more so in a country with an underdeveloped transportation and communications infrastructure. In a situation of relatively fragmented markets, freight hauling is a lucrative, if sometimes risky, enterprise. Government should concentrate its resources on cutting transport costs by improving infrastructure and count on the private sector to carry the goods. The desire to run a taxi system is even less understandable, except that the Kenyan capital of Nairobi is a key destination for international tourism. The government kept up the taxi service after Kenatco's trucking operations were given up, but it is doubtful that government taxies will ever serve more than a small part of the market. Governments are clearly able to manage some kinds of firms better than others. But the study of other Kenyan SOEs confirms these results: Dedicated personnel and the ability to make business-oriented decisions can make for success.

Source: Barbara Grosh, *Public Enterprise in Kenya: What Works, What Doesn't, and Why* (Boulder, CO: Lynne Rienner, 1991), pp. 123–151.

different from that of private enterprise."[15] Such "reasonably competent and responsible" governments do exist, but many governments fall short.

Typical Problems of SOEs

A state-owned enterprise can be insulated from political pressure by the legal system. An SOE may have a board of directors composed of nongovernment officials and may have a legal mandate to be managed according to commercial criteria, as if it were private. For instance, Bolivia has experimented with performance contracts between the government and various SOEs. Such separation is difficult to accomplish unless a government is willing to employ a hard budget constraint (no subsidies or bailouts), allow SOE managers autonomy in decision making, and provide effective monitoring and accountability.[16]

Most SOEs remain under government control. Their managers, compared to those in highly bureaucratized private companies, may be less oriented toward efficiency and profit. They are subject to perverse incentives in that SOEs are expected to promote government objectives such as low prices and high employment, and respond to conflicting demands of several government agencies. SOEs often have no competition, either because they are natural monopolies or because competition is deliberately prohibited to protect government revenues, and no fear of bankruptcy due to the availability of government subsidies.[17] The lack of profit-oriented incentives in the firm and greater tendency to bureaucratic organization may make SOE managers less likely to take normal commercial risks.

As long as the government has a stake in the successful operation of the enterprise, or at least avoiding bankruptcy, subsidies and bailouts may become the norm. Under such conditions, the enterprise loses the incentive to perform efficiently and will not be run on a commercial basis. Subsidies may become a significant drain on the government's budget: One extreme is reported in a study of eight government companies in Togo where combined losses in 1980 were equal to 4 percent of GDP.[18]

Some of these problems become clear when SOEs are compared to private companies operating in the same market or even to other SOEs. A World Bank comparison of two public municipal bus lines in the Indian cities of Calcutta and Coimbatore is instructive. In Calcutta, the bus company had no performance-oriented incentives and was regularly bailed out by the government. In a market where private buses make profits, the public Calcutta company operated its fleet at less than 65 percent of capacity, had 20.7 employees per operating bus, lost more than 15 percent of its revenues from people not paying its fares, and regularly incurred losses. In Coimbatore, the public bus company had accountable management, operated on a commercial basis, and provided performance incentives to employees. It operated its fleet at more than 95 percent capacity and had 7.3 employees per operating bus: It consistently made a profit while charging competitive fares.[19]

In some cases, governments have taken over failed companies whose loans those governments have guaranteed. But much government ownership has been the result of the government's desire to extend its realm. Eventually, the government may end up trying to do so many things that it can do none of them satisfactorily. Especially where governments spread themselves thin, SOEs suffer from insufficient capital and, most significantly, skilled labor (including everything from mechanics to general managers).

Quantification of the impact of SOEs on an economy is fairly new. The World Bank contends that there is an inverse relationship between the size of the state enterprise sector and an economy's growth rate, but critics have reworked the data and deny that this is true.[20] A different approach looks at the state share of manufacturing as a clue. One study notes that while Bangladesh and Denmark both have 6 percent of GDP produced by public enterprises, in manufacturing Bangladesh has 70 percent and Denmark 0. The study concludes that very low GDP per worker is associated with a high share of SOEs in the manufacturing sector.[21] The largest comparative study of firm performance looked at 1,100 Indian firms and found that rates of return fell as the share of government increased.[22]

In sum, public ownership can be justified on a number of grounds but is difficult to carry out efficiently. Development Spotlight 10–1 provides a summary of the rationales and problems. The question then becomes where and how to move toward private ownership.

Privatization

The overreach of some governments has resulted in inefficiency and the collapse of production. Reforms include reducing the size of the public sector, increasing competition and financial discipline in SOEs, and increasing the operational autonomy of the firms.

PROS AND CONS OF STATE-OWNED ENTERPRISE

Arguments for and against the existence of state-owned enterprises (SOEs) often have an ideological basis but also consider very practical issues. The pros and cons include the following:

Pro	Con
Lack of private capital	Inhibit competition
Few local entrepreneurs	Lack profit incentive

Pro	Con
Natural monopoly	Subsidies breed inefficiency
Target development needs	Rent seeking, corruption
Promote public policy goals (low prices, high employment)	Constrained by public policy goals

Of all the proposed reforms, the one most endorsed by aid donors, led by the United States and Britain, has been **privatization**, the selling off of state-owned enterprises to private individuals and groups. The U.S. Agency for International Development calls privatization "a key intervention in support of A.I.D.'s overriding goal of stimulating economic efficiency" and puts "a high priority on . . . assistance to privatization efforts." So intent has the U.S. government been in this area that its "policy prohibits assistance to physical, organizational, or financial restructuring if the principal purpose is to increase the price of the SOE when privatized or to increase efficiency of the SOE devoid of any plan for eventual privatization."[23]

Privatization has taken place and sometimes in large doses, although not necessarily because of countries' concern over the companies' performance. The burden on government budgets from subsidies to SOEs was brought into sharp focus by the debt crisis of the 1980s. In response to this crisis, in the structural adjustment programs instituted by the World Bank and International Monetary Fund, governments have initiated privatization and improvements in the public sector.

For example, by early 1989, Mexico had sold 180 companies, liquidated 260, merged 70, and transferred 25 to local governments. By the end of 1991, more than 900 of the 1,155 Mexican state-controlled companies that existed in 1982 had been sold or closed. In Latin America alone, between 1990 and 1995, 716 companies were privatized—mostly in Mexico and Argentina—and yielded revenues of almost $63 billion. Privatizations of multi-billion-dollar companies include Argentina's oil and gas firm YPF, Mexican telecommunications giant Telmex along with telecommunications companies in Indonesia, Peru, and Venezuela; oil and gas companies in Russia; Korea Electric Power; and China Steel of Taiwan. Brazil's state oil company, Petrobras, has not been privatized but by 2000 has sold $4 billion worth of shares that trade on the stock exchanges in São Paulo and New York, while it conducts 44 joint ventures.[24]

While conceptually very simple, privatization in practice has proven difficult for legal, political, and economic reasons. These include lack of the proper legal and financial expertise and institutions, government reluctance, and technical issues (how should sales take place? at what price? to whom?). Private firms of any size will usually issue stock to raise capital, and many countries do not have well-organized capital markets that would allow shares of stock to be traded easily.[25] At the same time, unsettled macroeconomic and pricing policies have obscured the immediate impact of privatization. These problems have also significantly slowed the pace of reform in Eastern Europe and the former Soviet Union.[26]

Privatization has two major goals: reducing the financial burden on the state and increasing efficiency of the economy. The experience so far has been mixed. One problem with the first objective is that SOEs that are losing money are not easy to sell; some early privatizations have been companies that were profitable, thus increasing the overall financial burden on the government.[27] It may be necessary to simply close some companies and sell whatever bits and pieces can obtain a price. Chile's first round of privatizations in 1974 seemed successful, but the conditions of sale coupled with recession in 1982 led to bankruptcies and government reacquisition of many of the properties. (The same thing occurred in Mexico, where new owners were not always competent, and the 1994 financial crisis forced the government to buy corporate assets owned by banks.) A new round of privatization in 1985 included the sale of many profitable companies, often at prices far below their actual value. A careful series of privatizations in Bangladesh went more smoothly.[28] A broader study of Latin American experience cautions that sales proceeds are generally not a significant help to budget deficits,[29] although selling loss-making firms should reduce the annual drain of subsidies.

It is not always possible to determine the impact of privatization on efficiency. The structure of competition in the industry may be as important as ownership. Trading a government monopoly for a private monopoly may be of little help, so there must be ways of encouraging competition and permitting price flexibility before the economy will receive the full benefit of privatization. Here too, the hasty Mexican sell-off disregarded questions of market power and traded government monopolies for private ones.[30] Privatized public utilities in Chile showed improved performance, but without effective regulation there was no significant reduction in prices to consumers. On the other hand, privatization and regulation combined to bring down prices in electricity and gas distribution, and in telecommunications in Argentina.[31]

Governments must also consider the impact of privatization on the social goals that SOEs had been charged with achieving. One reason often given for poor profitability of some efficient SOEs is that they are constrained from normal profit-maximizing behavior by government direction to, for example, keep prices low as a way of helping the poor or keep employment high. A company can then be technically efficient but unprofitable. Privatizing a company should eliminate these practices. An OECD study of 10 privatizing countries points out that evaluation of these social goals must consider the extent to which those objectives were in fact being achieved, at what cost, and whether the government could find other ways of achieving these objectives.[32]

A recent World Bank conference presented studies of twelve privatization cases, almost all in developing countries. A summary of "winners and losers" concluded that 11 of the 12 cases showed unambiguous gains from privatization. Even where product prices rose subsequent to sale of the companies, the resulting profits financed investment that increased output. Workers were also judged to be better off in every case, although the reference was to those who remained employed: One of the sources of increased efficiency was the "shedding of excess labor," which normally exists in public enterprises.[33] The study of Argentina concluded that gains from privatization were greater at higher income levels, but gains from regulation were somewhat more beneficial to those with lower incomes.[34]

In Latin America especially, a significant amount of privatization has taken place in the context of debt-equity swaps (foreign debt is traded for equity in domestic companies) that are one of the features of debt-reduction plans. One of the leaders in this area has been Argentina, which by May 1993 had reduced its foreign debt by $6.7 billion and raised another $5.3 billion through privatizations. Although haste and lack of preparation have caused some major problems, including sale of the national airline to Spain's state-owned Iberia, the initial verdict is largely positive. In 1993, Argentina became the first developing country to privatize a national petroleum company.[35]

One of the negative aspects of recent economic liberalization in Latin America and Eastern Europe is the corruption associated with privatization. Beyond the inadequate valuation placed on some SOEs for sale to favored individuals, enterprise officials have taken advantage of the confusion to divert enterprise assets to their own and others' uses. The relationships between government and private officials with respect to enterprise sales and government contracts has taxed the weak judicial systems in many countries.[36]

There is a qualitative difference between privatizations in many developing countries and those in Eastern Europe and the former Soviet Union. Most developing countries have, in varying degrees of adequacy, market-determined prices. The market framework for operating private firms exists. However, for most of the formerly socialist countries, private ownership on a large scale has long been illegal, so individuals are not familiar with operating or investing in large enterprises. Price systems have been largely artificial.[37]

A recent summary of the post-Communist experience shows benefits to a strategy of (*a*) eliminating barriers to private enterprise; (*b*) enforcing a hard-budget constraint on state firms, forcing those losing money to close; and (*c*) selling other SOEs to investors who can afford to buy them. This strategy allowed successful privatization in Hungary and Poland. The alternative was to promote immediate distribution of SOE assets, through vouchers and other means, to large numbers of people, often including workers in the firms. The results of this approach, as in the Czech Republic and Russia, was that firms were not in the hands of capable investors; SOE managers were able to control the firms' assets, often for their own benefit; and the citizen owners ended up selling their shares to investment funds that were incapable of managing the companies. Those companies remained inefficient.[38]

These options illustrate, at least in the near term, one of the pitfalls of privatization. Wide distribution of ownership, no matter how socially beneficial, is impractical because poor owners of a few shares need short-term benefits that induce them to sell their shares. Whether firms are sold to wealthier individuals initially or not, wealth that used to belong to the state becomes concentrated in private hands. Wide share ownership most likely must wait until a large middle class emerges that can afford to participate in the process.

Alternatives to Privatization

Some studies have concluded that firm performance depends as much on the degree of competition and the government's willingness to allow a company to operate on a commercial basis and go bankrupt if unsuccessful. In Indonesia, for example, the contribution to improved performance in the 1980s involved only a minor reduction in the number of enterprises. Most came from permitting competition with the private

SOE TRANSFORMATION IN CHINA

FAST FACTS

On the Map: Asia

Population: 1.254 Billion

Per Capita GNI and Rank: 780   (142)

Life Expectancy: Male—68   Female—72

Adult Literacy Rate: Male—91%
Female—75%

A rising debate among China experts concerns SOE reform and privatization. Economic liberalization has been a measured process, with private companies permitted to start up and create competition while the state-owned firms remain in place. In manufacturing, SOEs accounted for one-third of output in the mid-1990s compared to three-fourths in 1981. A dual pricing system has allowed the SOEs to sell output greater than planned amounts at market prices above state-controlled prices.

Competition from private Chinese firms, new Chinese SOEs, and foreign private firms has significantly reduced profitability of small and medium Chinese SOEs, and those that lose money are no longer automatically financed by state banks. SOEs as a group lost money in 1995 and 1996, and laid off 10 million workers in 1996.

For larger SOEs, the picture is not clear. In many cases, losses occur in the face of rising sales because firms are required to pay wages to laid-off workers and very high taxes. In a ringing endorsement of competi-

tion, the government recently broke up its telecommunications firm into four separate SOEs and encouraged competition in mobile phone technologies produced by one of them.

But some studies, while cautious about the quality of their data, indicate that larger SOEs have been improving their productivity through at least the early decades of reform. The government has increased their autonomy in the areas of marketing and wage decisions, permitted them to contract with private firms, and to be more responsible for their own profit and loss. These changes have transformed many large SOEs to the point where the boundaries between state and private ownership are difficult to discern, with favorable results.

Sources: Barry Naughton, "What Is Distinctive About China's Economic Transition? State Enterprise Reform and Overall System Transformation," *Journal of Comparative Economics* 18, no. 3 (June 1994), pp. 470–490; Wei Li, "The Impact of Economic Reform on the Performance of Chinese State Enterprises, 1980–89," *Journal of Political Economy* 105, no. 5 (October 1997), pp. 1080–1106; "Beijing Rules," *The Economist* (May 3, 1997), pp. 54–55; Ian Johnson, "How China Redefined Reform with Breakup of Telecom Monopoly," *Wall Street Journal*, June 8, 1999; Yiping Huang and Ron Duncan, "How Successful Were China's State Sector Reforms?" *Journal of Comparative Economics* 24, no. 1 (February 1997), pp. 65–78; and Peter Nolan and Wang Xiaoqiang, "Beyond Privatization: Institutional Innovation and Growth in China's Large State-Owned Enterprises," *World Development* 27, no. 1 (January 1999), pp. 169–200.

sector, removing SOE employees from the civil service, reduction in government budget support for SOE investment, greater price flexibility, and other market-oriented changes.[39] Mexico's giant oil company, Pemex, has improved its performance in order to avoid privatization.[40] In China, many SOEs are going bankrupt while others are improving their performance, as shown in Case 10–4.

As an alternative to the SOE, government might impose regulation on private firms in order to achieve public policy objectives: Price controls may be needed, or firms could be required to provide subsidized services to poor areas. But the advantage of private decision making is nullified if political objectives interfere too much with the firm's operation. One study suggests that public enterprises may be preferred to regulated private enterprises when the economic activity in question, such as sanitation services, is one that has a significant public interest.[41] Another option, referred to earlier, is the performance contract.

A number of Latin American countries have experimented with ways of improving public utility performance. Public provision of water, for example, has suffered in many countries because subsidized prices have not provided sufficient resources for maintenance of the system. In Chile, prices to consumers are set to cover the full cost, but the government provides subsidies to the company that in turn credits them to consumers' accounts on the basis of income. Parts of Brazil have experimented with coproduction arrangements by which poor communities pay low prices but contribute labor to the upkeep of the local water system. In Buenos Aires, private firms compete with government to supply some water. In all these experiments, government still provides water but the system is made more efficient.[42]

PUBLIC GOODS AND SOCIAL SERVICES

Usually the government's role does not require owning actual companies. Governments everywhere make investments in physical infrastructure and provide social services such as health and education. Where market institutions are lacking or weak, government can help strengthen them.

Public Services

Public goods include education and public health services, whose benefits accrue to the citizenry as a whole over and above benefits received by any individual, and those like police protection and national defense, whose benefits are provided to the public at large because it would be impractical to ask individuals to buy their share on an open market.

While there are some arguments in favor of private provision of certain public goods,[43] and while developing-country governments frequently lack the necessary resources to provide desired levels of services, there is a close enough connection between provision of these services and development to warrant a strong government presence. Not only are there positive externalities in the provision of education and health facilities, but our analysis in earlier chapters has highlighted the positive impact of a healthier, better-educated population on the development process. Theories of endogenous growth, which focus on the acquisition and use of new knowledge and technology to spur growth, acknowledge the importance of human capital.

Some World Bank conclusions in this area sound very close to arguments made by proponents of the Basic Human Needs approach: Direct government action to target the needs of the poor for health and education will improve productivity and growth. The Bank concluded in its 1990 *World Development Report* that "social progress is not merely a by-product of economic development." With respect to education, "most of the schools in developing countries are public schools that are built, financed, and staffed by the government." Health programs are also important. For both, access is essential for the poor to take advantage of the programs: "The biggest obstacle for the poor in gaining access to health and education services is the lack of physical infrastructure, especially in rural areas."[44]

Table 10–2 shows some tendency for government consumption spending—current spending on goods and services excluding state enterprises—to be a higher share of GDP at higher income levels, but the connection between such spending and growth is not clear. A cross-country study has made a start toward attempting to determine whether more public services would be an expected *consequence* of economic growth, in which case governments would be well advised to simply push for higher growth, or whether those services should be targeted directly as *determinants* of growth. This preliminary study indicates that "the importance of growth lies in the way that its benefits are distributed between people and the extent to which growth supports public health services," meaning that while economic growth *is* important, it must be directed at least partially toward public services (in this case health) for it to have the desired impact. (Such consumption spending is actually investment when the result is an increase in human capital.) When the method was applied to the infant mortality rate in Sri Lanka, the conclusion was again that "*both* income growth and public spending matter."[45]

This is not to say that relevant government programs are as effective as they should be. For both health and education there remains a bias toward services like hospital care and higher education that tend to be of greater benefit to the middle and upper classes, as opposed to services such as preventive care and primary education that would be of greater benefit to the poor. Pakistan has illustrated the trade-offs that could benefit the poor with little sacrifice. Between 1983 and 1988, half of the country's villages were connected to the national power grid at the cost of occasionally cutting power an hour or two in the cities.[46] A recent study[47] confirms that in Africa both health care and education programs provide more benefits to the rich than the poor, although the poor do receive benefits out of proportion to their income. And there are some findings that health and education spending may be negatively associated with growth rates, although the reasons are not clear.[48] As we saw in Chapter 5, government programs tend to be overextended and often not well executed, so that governments ought to be looking for more efficient ways of providing services to the poor.

TABLE 10–2 General Government Consumption as Percentage of GDP			
Income Category	*1980*	*1990*	*1999*
Low Income	12	12	11
Lower-Middle Income	NA	13	14
Upper-Middle Income	11	15	15
High Income	16	16	16

General government consumption is defined as current spending on goods and services by governments, generally excluding state-owned enterprises. Current spending usually includes health- and education-related spending, which is investment in human capital.

NA = Not Available.

Sources: World Development Indicators 2000 and 2001.

Decentralization and privatization are often suggested, but each has problems. The key advantage of decentralization should be greater local familiarity with specific problems and greater interest in their resolution. Chile, for example, has decentralized much of the responsibility for health and education from federal to regional and to municipal governments and has encouraged private provision of some higher-level education. But decentralization works only if local governments have the competence and the means to improve services: In Chile some of these services have deteriorated badly, especially in poorer regions. Privatization also has its risks when applied to public goods: Chile's higher education is slighting the poor and skewing education toward more lucrative occupations.[49]

The debate around government provision of some social services now centers on finding appropriate means of delivery. A key issue that exists in all countries is whether to make certain programs such as basic medical care cheaply available to all, knowing that some of the nonpoor will take advantage of them, or to attempt a more narrow **targeting** of poor populations and run the risk that some deserving people will be missed in the process.

The broader approach assures more beneficiaries, increasing the productivity of larger populations. The nonpoor may be willing to pay more for (presumably) better private services, but widespread availability may make these programs more politically acceptable. That availability may also make them more expensive, and broader programs may miss more specific needs of the poor. Narrow targeting, while more focused on needy recipients, has high costs of monitoring (are the poor and only the poor receiving the benefit? Who are the poor?) and implementation, and may be less politically acceptable to nonpoor voters. Each case must be judged on its own merits.[50]

REGULATION AND ITS CONSEQUENCES: RENT SEEKING AND CORRUPTION

Every government imposes certain regulations on business, from the simple requirement to incorporate to complex regulations for operation. Thus, the nature and extent of regulation provide another area of debate over government policy in all countries. We look at different kinds of regulation throughout the book. Here we cover the problem of regulation and the implications of excessive regulation.

Types of Government Regulation

Government **regulation** of private economic activity may be a substitute for planning. We exclude here social regulation such as protection of health, safety, and the environment, and regulation of foreign trade and investment. Rather, our concern is with regulations that set the rules for certain types of economic transactions.

Factor Markets

Labor force regulations include minimum wages and other conditions of employment, and rules about hiring and firing. Although companies frequently list such rules as obstacles to business operation, our discussion in Chapter 9 was unable to conclude that such regulations significantly affected employment or the operation of firms, especially when regulations went unheeded or did not impose serious constraints on firms. The minimum wage puts additional stress on government budgets. The impact of interest rate ceilings and the allocation of credit, examined in Chapter 4, are more important for businesses, and such regulations are likely to result in improper allocation of capital resources.

Price Controls and Subsidies

Governments put price ceilings on products that are important expenditure items for the poor, such as flour, electricity, water, bus fares, and fuel. When these items are produced by SOEs, they cause losses to be subsidized by government budgets. When these items are produced by private companies, they reduce incentives to invest in those products. Either way, scarcity is not properly signaled and resources will likely go to less efficient uses.

Permits and Fees

Most governments require businesses to file papers to incorporate, obtain permits to construct facilities, and attest to the safe operation of machinery. Such requirements may have a fee attached to them.

Is the Whole Greater than the Sum of Its Parts?

Many regulations satisfy legitimate purposes. However, the multiplicity of regulations, and the control that they give government officials over private activity, run the risk of stifling enterprise, inducing illegal activities in order to avoid them, and providing a source of control and financial gain for government officials.

Consequences of Overregulation: Rent Seeking

Extensive regulation can be just as disruptive to the private sector as actual planning. Regulation tends to be ad hoc; responsive to special interest group pleading, and frequently contradictory. By distorting market signals, regulation may make accurate calculations of costs and benefits impossible, thus hiding the actual waste and inefficiency of the system. And when prices of products, labor, and capital are set administratively, the true costs of production are difficult to determine.

Rent-seeking* describes economic activity devoted to seeking out the sources of monopoly profit due to government-created scarcity in a highly regulated economy.[51] Government control over licences and permits makes the hunt for these items a profitable activity. Regulations by their nature tend to restrict activity, and restrictions by their nature reduce competition.

Figure 10–2 shows two approaches to the allocation of a resource called a business permit. In Figure 10–2a, anyone may purchase a permit at the fee set by the government: There is a perfectly elastic supply at the going price. Clearly, the number of permits may be reduced by raising the fee (here from $100 to $500), but at least in this case anyone who can afford the fee will receive a permit, and an increase in the demand for permits will be matched by an increasing number. In Figure 10–2b, however, the number of permits is fixed; possibly allocated at the whim of the public official if there is not effective oversight. An increase in the desire to do business itself drives up the price, with the greater possibility of corruption. Such a system puts someone in charge of deciding how many permits will be offered at any time, allowing the supply curve to be shifted according to any desired criterion.

---

*Economists use the term "rent" in a general sense to mean any income created by restricting competition and increasing in scarcity. This can be the result of private monopolizing activity or public policy, such as restricting the number of licenses to carry out an activity.

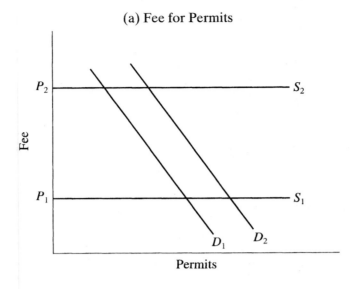

(a) Fee for Permits

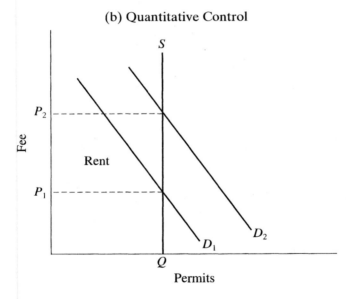

(b) Quantitative Control

FIGURE 10-2 Alternative Regulation of Business Permits

(a) Elastic supply curves allow the number of permits to be determined by the quantity demanded at the official price.

(b) An inelastic supply, regardless of the quantity, not only limits the permits but determines the fee solely by demand, opening the door to corruption. Economic rent is created, measured by the total revenue above a minimal price required for creating and administering the permits.

When an activity becomes restricted, the potential for rents increases. In Figure 10–2b, almost any price above a nominal fee may be considered rent. The number of permits is fixed in amount, like a natural resource. But unlike a resource that has real extraction costs, the economic cost of "producing" a permit is minuscule, so any higher price extracts significant rents. As areas of regulation proliferate, people will have to spend an increasing amount of money and energy simply complying with the regulations and obtaining permits. Some take advantage of these opportunities to make more than competitive profits, even if that means bribing government officials to dispense special

CASE 10–5

THE COST OF REGULATION: THE INFORMAL SECTOR IN PERU

FAST FACTS

On the Map: South America

Population: 25 Million

Per Capita GNI and Rank: $2130   (101)

Life Expectancy: Male—66   Female—71

Adult Literacy Rate: Male—96%
Female—85%

The case against overregulation has been vividly made in Hernando de Soto's *The Other Path: The Invisible Revolution in the Third World.* De Soto set up an Institute for Liberty and Democracy in Lima, Peru, to investigate the cost of regulation. Institute employees not only studied regulations in housing, retail trade, and transport but also set up companies so that they could go through the process of obtaining approvals to operate in these areas. The theme of the book is that the "formal" economy has been so constricted that the informal sector has become the most dynamic part of the urban economy, providing rapid gains in employment and production of goods and services. This sector was harassed by the government, and endured higher costs in order to stay ahead of the bureaucracy, and still manages to succeed.

In demonstrating the problem, de Soto traced the process of setting up a formal industry in Lima. There were 11 approvals required, which took an average of 289 days and cost an amount equal to 32 times the monthly minimum wage. To obtain approval for a new housing development, the time required was 83 *months*, almost 7 years; to set up a store, 43 days; a marketplace, 17 *years*; a minibus company, 27 months. One need not be an advocate of complete laissez-faire to agree with his conclusion: "What we have here is bad law."

Source: Hernando de Soto, *The Other Path: The Invisible Revolution in the Third World* (New York: Harper and Row, 1989).

favors. The more people turn to such rent-seeking activity, the less time, energy, and capital they devote to productive activity. Government officials can also be rent seekers, especially where planning or an extensive SOE network makes them key players in the system of production and distribution. Regulation can thus be destructive both by deterring productive activity and by encouraging rent seeking. Case 10–5, describing the informal sector in Lima, Peru, is a classic illustration of the cost of regulation.

Consequences of Overregulation: Corruption

Corruption occurs when officials in the government or private sector require extra payment to perform their services or use the organization's resources for their personal gain. Whether it is a local official who expects a bribe in exchange for a business permit or a president who awards contracts to his friends, corruption breaks down respect for law and introduces incentives for unproductive rent seeking. It is usually a product of scarcity, whether real or contrived through regulation, and benefits from poorly trained and underpaid officials.[52]

One of the most basic functions of government is to provide enforceable rules and regulations that limit individual and corporate activities. Within these limits, prices are determined by supply and demand. Governments in market economies are expected to foster competition so that prices accurately reflect production costs. The fewer the suppliers, the greater the scarcity and the more a price will exceed marginal cost. When products and services are monopolized, and sellers are not accountable to anyone, prices will less efficiently allocate scarce resources.

But government regulations frequently make government officials the authorized source of scarce goods or services. We have already considered the consequences of having a fixed supply of permits, but government officials may also control distribution of fertilizer to farmers, seating on airplanes, installation of telephones, beds in hospitals, and bank loans. If these officials are not accountable for their actions, they have an incentive to take bribes, such as for a building permit or access to a construction contract.

While corruption exists in virtually every country, it is often assumed to be more common in developing countries. Economic logic supports this perception. Regulation is often extensive, providing opportunities. Lax controls and low-paid, poor-quality civil servants are additional incentives that suggest that greater corruption is likely.[53] When market mechanisms are relatively new, and opportunities for profit relatively few, the opportunities for corruption are greater. In a recent survey of Eastern Europe and former Soviet republics, the percentage of firms reporting that they bribe "frequently" varied between 8 percent in Croatia and Slovenia, to 60 percent in Azerbaijan. Bribes varied between 2 percent of firms' annual revenue in Croatia and 8 percent in Georgia.[54] Some have argued that bribes are merely additional "prices," which supplement the market mechanism and thus promote efficiency. On the other hand, they reallocate resources from productive to rent-seeking activity, lead to additional corruption, make bureaucratic systems less flexible, and lead to a system based on arbitrariness rather than the rule of law.[55]

It is logical to expect that corruption would be negatively associated with growth. Some evidence has been presented,[56] but the difficulty of quantifying corruption makes these claims difficult to support statistically. One study suggests that impacts vary based on the type of corruption. When Zaire's president Mobutu systematically looted the treasury from the 1960s until fleeing the country in 1997, extorted bribes from companies and then sent the money to Switzerland, there is little doubt that he reduced the economy's well-being. When Philippine President Marcos used the government to set up moneymaking enterprises for himself and his friends between 1965 and when he was forced to flee in 1986, much (not all) remained in the country. But the companies did little to help the economy while diverting resources that could have been used more productively elsewhere. In South Korea, however, private companies received favors from government officials, but these improved those companies' ability to do business and were often productive. Whether alternative resource uses would have been more productive is not clear.[57]

A recent study has identified a statistically significant negative association between an index of "corruption perception" and both GDP and its growth.[58] Because corruption itself is impossible to measure, the perception index, based on surveys, is taken as a reasonable approximation. The authors provide some evidence that corruption causes lower growth through three paths: (*a*) increased production costs, especially for potentially more dynamic small- and medium-sized firms; (*b*) distortions of investment—domestic investment is reduced, foreign investment is more likely to seek domestic partners, and public investment is less productive; and (*c*) diversion of individual talents into rent-seeking activities. Evidence points in the direction we might expect: Corruption leads to worse economic performance.

Many steps are possible if governments are dedicated to reducing corruption. The World Bank, in addition to projects to improve the effectiveness of government agencies, also helps countries improve their own efforts to fight corruption.[59] Increasing government salaries, removing excess government positions, greater transparency of regulation and penalties for corruption, and reducing the number of regulations are all likely possibilities.[60] Development itself should help. By increasing incomes and widening the availability of goods and services through greater competition, the need to resort to extortion and the opportunities for restricting profitable undertakings will diminish. But government reform must go hand in hand with economic progress.

MARKET INSTITUTIONS

The question we have posed is how far a government ought to go in dealing with market failure. But a key role of government is creating the conditions under which markets can work effectively. Economists stress that when markets function properly they are the most efficient way to allocate resources and promote economic growth. To do so they must be reasonably competitive. Competition requires a clear set of enforceable rules governing contracts and property rights. Governments are in the best position to set and enforce those rules. The government role takes place in a number of areas:

Infrastructure: To improve mobility of resources, products, and information, adequate transportation and communication are necessary. While trucks and telephones will be privately provided, roads, rail lines, airports, and some communications infrastructure take on the character of public goods because positive externalities exist.

Security: Governments must pass laws and regulations related to contracts and property ownership. Douglass C. North, one of the preeminent economic historians of our time, has argued that the Industrial Revolution itself would not have been possible without secure property rights that allowed inventors and innovators to expect they would obtain the profits of the improvements they introduced.[61] Governments must enforce the rules and resolve disputes that arise: As economic activity expands and markets become more impersonal, peer pressure becomes less able to govern everyday transactions. Without formal enforcement, there will be some degree of insecurity about ordinary transactions, and people will be less willing to invest resources in production and innovative activity.

Information: Information about market conditions is essential for competitive markets. Robert Klitgaard[62] cites agricultural markets specifically, noting that ignorance of prices and conditions of product quality is widespread in developing countries. Governments have a crucial role in making information available to market participants by, for example, publishing commodity prices or by enforcing the use of standardized weights and measures in these markets (see Case 10–1). Creating infrastructure in the area of transportation and communication also promotes the spread of information.

GOVERNMENT FAILURE AND THE "WASHINGTON CONSENSUS"

In reaction to the overuse of market failure as a justification for state action, much has now been written on large-scale **government failure** in many countries. Governments are often inflexible and incapable of performing a true entrepreneurial role in an economic environment that requires significant adaptability.[63] The poor results of economic planning are perhaps the most extreme example of this, but the problems of SOEs and the close association of governments and private companies (see Chapter 15) are more common.

On the other hand, from issues of externalities to questions of social justice, market solutions are not trustworthy as the sole criterion for resource allocation. Governments are still the favored mode of providing infrastructure, social services, and programs to support the poorest sections of the population.[64] Some elements, such as infrastructure construction and technical education, can be contracted out to private companies, but governments will still decide to allocate resources for these activities.

Market-oriented economists and others believe that economic incentives are the chief motivator and means of ensuring rational resource allocation. The state provides the wrong kinds of incentives; those based on bureaucratic power and political interests are most powerful. But skeptics cite the limitations of economic incentives to obtain broader social goals and doubt that those incentives are effective in translating economic success into wider objectives.

The debate over government's role has taken shape over the last decade in the context of what John Williamson has called the "Washington Consensus".[65] This was a set of guidelines for the kinds of policy reforms required for Latin American governments to restore economic stability after the debt crisis of the 1980s. They include:

- Fiscal restraint (i.e. zero or small government budget deficits—Chapter 11)
- Shifting government spending to development-oriented areas as infrastructure, health care, and education (this chapter)
- Tax reform (Chapter 11)
- Market-determined interest rates (Chapters 4 and 15)
- Market-determined foreign exchange rates (Chapter 14)
- Trade liberalization (Chapter 12)
- Freer inflows of foreign direct investment (Chapter 13)
- Privatization of state enterprises (this chapter)
- Deregulation (this chapter)
- Secure property rights (this chapter)

How fast and how far such reforms should go is a matter of debate. Taken as a whole, however, they suggest a considerable redirection of government activity toward providing an environment within which private-sector activity could prosper. Unfortunately, the policy debate among economists often takes the form of a simple market vs. state argument, rather than guidelines for an effective government role.

While a large number of development economists lean toward a return to the market (the counterrevolution against proponents of a strong state role), the assumptions and conclusions of these neoliberals are again being challenged.[66] While this challenge does not propose government planning, economists are interested in examining particular market defects such as risk and imperfect information to determine how the state can best work with—or, if need be, instead of—markets to guide policy toward sustainable growth that helps the poor. Government failures do not automatically translate into market solutions if such markets do not exist. And even well-functioning markets must operate in some regulatory framework. Competent, if authoritarian, governments such as in Taiwan and South Korea (both becoming more democratic) have had exceptional successes, and one observer concludes that there are "few instances of major countries growing without government playing a seemingly vital role."[67] Because governments must be involved, outside agencies such as the World Bank should strengthen their competence, not undermine it.

SUMMARY AND CONCLUSION

The question of the proper roles of the state and the market permeates every nook and cranny of economics. Developing-country governments, suspicious of markets and impressed with Soviet planning, gravitated after World War II toward attempts to plan economic development. In most cases, developing countries lacked the knowledge, skills, and resources to carry out full-fledged planning. However, given the requirements for successful planning, and given Soviet experience, it is unlikely that any government is capable of doing it.

Even without planning, many developing-country governments have taken a major role in directing development by operating companies. These SOEs are largely plagued by inefficiency due to lack of fiscal accountability and competition. In response to such failures, governments are increasingly privatizing their SOEs, and in spite of difficulties most privatization results in economic gains. Still, when government resources are not overextended, and when some competition exists, SOEs can be efficient and contribute to economic development.

Government spending for infrastructure and social services can be beneficial and is essential in all countries. Governments also regulate private-sector activity. While some kinds of regulation are beneficial, there is again a tendency to go too far. Overregulation may encourage individuals to engage in rent-seeking activity and corruption by providing incentives to evade regulation. This results in misallocation of resources and higher costs for all economic activity.

The overextension of the state in developing countries, not to mention the former socialist countries, has seriously weakened advocates of national planning and extensive regulation of the private sector. But governments play a crucial role in establishing and strengthening the institutional framework in which markets can operate. Market and state always combine in some fashion, and the question is whether there should be a predisposition to market solutions until they are shown to fail. The World Bank states that position clearly: "It is not enough to know that the market is failing; it is also necessary to be convinced that the government can do better." Of course, the criteria are themselves open to debate. Experience of the last 40 years has shown that "government failure" is much more prevalent than previously admitted and that some mechanism for social decision making can be combined with market-oriented activities, even in the public sector.

The type and degree of government involvement can vary significantly. We return to this debate in the last two chapters, especially as it has played out in East Asia. Next, however, we turn to one of the universally acknowledged roles of government—fiscal and monetary policies that are needed to achieve the macroeconomic stability that is required for successful growth and development.

Key Terms

- corruption (p. 289)
- government failure (p. 292)
- input–output tables (p. 273)
- market failure (p. 268)
- natural monopoly (p. 268)
- nonexcludable (p. 269)
- nonrivalrous (p. 269)
- planned economy (p. 272)
- privatization (p. 280)
- regulation (p. 286)
- rent seeking (p. 287)
- state-owned enterprises (SOEs) (p. 275)
- targeting (p. 286)

Questions for Review

1. Why might governments in developing countries be interested in a strong state role in economic development?
 2. How did the Indian government solve the problem of deteriorating milk quality without imposing controls on the industry?
3. What problems confront any government that might contemplate a planned economy? Why might developing countries' problems be worse?
 4. How has planning in India exposed some inherent difficulties with the planning process?
5. Why might we expect an SOE to operate less efficiently than a comparable private firm? Are there ways around these problems?
 6. How does Kenya's experience with SOEs suggest the circumstances best suited for government enterprise?
 7. How has the Chinese government attempted to reform its SOE sector without privatization?
8. What are the potential benefits of privatization? What economic conditions are most likely to contribute to these benefits?
9. What, in general, is meant by government "regulation?"
10. Explain rent seeking and give an example.
 11. How did overregulation in Peru lead to significant disincentives for small firms? How does this case illustrate rent seeking?
12. What are some of the conditions that lead to corruption?

Related Internet Resources

Most current research and discussion on the role of the state is centered around either privatization or improving the performance of government activities. The main source of information in this area is the World Bank, whose site, ⟨www.worldbank.org/publicsector⟩ is organized around such topics as civil service reform, decentralization, anticorruption efforts, SOE reform, and the Legal Institutions of the Market Economy. The only major site on privatization, the Privatization Center, ⟨www.privatization.org⟩, is concerned almost exclusively with issues within the United States. An internationally oriented organization concerned with corruption issues is the Internet Center for Corruption Research, at ⟨www.gwdg.de/~uwvw/icr.htm⟩.

Endnotes and Further Readings

1. See Pedro Belli, "The Comparative Advantage of Government: A Review," World Bank Policy Research Working Paper 1834 (1997), and Daniel W. Bromley, *Economic Interests and Institutions: The Conceptual Foundations of Public Policy* (New York: Basil Blackwell, 1989).

2. An early approach is Paul N. Rosenstein-Rodan, "Programming in Theory and in Italian Practice," in MIT, Center for International Studies, *Investment Criteria and Economic Growth* (Cambridge: MIT Press, 1955).

3. See Ian M. D. Little, *Economic Development: Theory, Policy, and International Relations* (New York: Basic Books, 1982).

4. See Morris Bornstein, "The Soviet Centrally-Planned Economy," in Morris Bornstein, ed., *Comparative Economic Systems: Models and Cases*, 7th ed. (Burr Ridge, IL: Irwin, 1994), pp. 411–443, and Richard E. Ericson, "The Classical Soviet-Type Economy: Nature of the System and Implications for Reform,'" *Journal of Economic Perspectives* 5, no. 4 (fall 1991), pp. 11–27.

5. See various articles in Max Millikan, ed., *National Economic Planning* (New York: Columbia University Press, 1967).

6. Albert Waterston, "What Do We Know About Planning," from *International Development Review* 7, no. 4 (December 1965). Also Waterston's book, *Development Planning: Lessons of Experience* (Washington: World Bank, 1969).

7. See Little's review of planning failures, *Economic Development: Theory, Policy, and International Relations*, pp. 57–58 and pp. 126–136. The quote is on p. 127.

8. See Waterston, "What Do We Know About Planning," and Tony Killick, "The Possibilities of Development Planning," *Oxford Economic Papers* NS 28, no. 2 (July 1976), pp. 161–184, and Ramgopal Agarwala, "Planning in Developing Countries: Lessons of Experience," World Bank Staff Working Paper No. 576 (Washington: World Bank, 1983).

9. See Leroy P. Jones, ed., *Public Enterprise in Less Developed Countries* (Cambridge: Cambridge University Press, 1982); Mary M. Shirley, "Managing State-Owned Enterprises," World Bank Staff Working Paper No. 577 (Washington: World Bank, 1983); Robert H. Floyd et al., *Public Enterprise in Mixed Economies: Some Macroeconomic Aspects* (Washington: International Monetary Fund, 1984); and V. V. Ramanadhan, *The Economics of Public Enterprise* (London: Routledge, 1991).

10. Luke Haggarty and Mary M. Shirley, "A New Data Base on State-Owned Enterprises," *World Bank Economic Review* 11, no. 3 (September 1997), pp. 497–513. Also see O. Bouin and Ch.-A. Michalet, *Rebalancing the Public and Private Sectors: Developing Country Experience* (Paris: OECD, 1991), pp. 64–65.

11. See Deepak Lal, "Public Enterprises," in John Cody, Helen Hughes, and David Wall, eds., *Policies for Industrial Progress in Developing Countries* (New York: Oxford University Press, 1980), pp. 211–234.

12. Barbara Grosh, *Public Enterprise in Kenya: What Works, What Doesn't and Why* (Boulder, CO: Lynne Rienner Publishers, 1991), and Thomas J. Trebat, *Brazil's State-Owned Enterprises: A Case Study of the State as Entrepreneur* (Cambridge: Cambridge University Press, 1983).

13. See John Rapley's arguments, *Understanding Development: Theory and Practice in the Third World* (Boulder, CO: Lynne Rienner, 1996).

14. Lloyd G. Reynolds, *Economic Growth in the Third World, 1850–1980* (New Haven: Yale University Press, 1985), p. 432.

15. "Introduction: The Promise and the Challenge," in Raymond Vernon, ed., *The Promise of Privatization: A Challenge for American Foreign Policy* (New York: Council on Foreign Relations, 1988), p. 4.

16. Richard D. Mallon, "State-Owned Enterprise Reform Through Performance Contracts: The Bolivian Experiment," *World Development* 22, no. 6 (June 1994), pp. 925–934.

17. See Ahmed Galal, "Public Enterprise Reform: Lessons from the Past and Issues for the Future," World Bank Discussion Paper No. 119 (Washington: World Bank, 1991), pp. 4–5, and Leroy P. Jones, "Performance Evaluation for Public Enterprises," World Bank Discussion Paper No. 122 (Washington: World Bank, 1991).

18. John R. Nellis, "Public Enterprises in Sub-Saharan Africa," World Bank Discussion Paper No. 1 (Washington: World Bank, 1986), p. 19.

19. Mary M. Shirley, "Managing State-Owned Enterprises."

20. The Bank report is *Bureaucrats in Business: The Economics and Politics of Government Ownership* (Washington: World Bank/Oxford University Press, 1995). Critics include Ha-Joon Chang and Ajit Singh, "Can Large Firms Be Run Efficiently Without Being Bureaucratic?" *Journal of International Development* 9, no. 6 (September–October 1997), pp. 865–875, and in the same issue, Hossain Jalilian and John Weiss, "Bureaucrats, Business and Economic Growth," pp. 877–885.

21. James A. Schmitz, Jr., "The Role Played by Public Enterprises: How Much Does It Differ Across Countries?" Federal Reserve Bank of Minneapolis *Quarterly Review* (spring 1996), pp. 2–15.

22. Pradeep Chhibber and Sumit K. Majumdar, "State as Investor and State as Owner: Consequences for Firm Performance in India," *Economic Development and Cultural Change* 46, no. 3 (April 1998), pp. 561–581.

23. "Implementing A.I.D. Privatization Objectives," USAID Policy Determination PD-14 (Washington: USAID, January 1991), pp. 1–2, 4.

24. See Pedro Aspe and Jose Angel Gurria, "The State and Economic Development: A Mexican Perspective," *Proceedings of the World Bank Annual Conference on*

Development Economics (Washington: World Bank, 1992), p. 12; Patrice Franko, *The Puzzle of Latin American Economic Development* (Lanham, MD: Rowman and Littlefield, 1999), p. 160; "The Big Deals," *Wall Street Journal*, October 2, 1995; and Pamela Druckerman, "Brazil's Oil Giant Seeks to Evolve," *Wall Street Journal*, August 11, 2000.

25. See Ademola Ariyo and Afeikhaena Jerome, "Privatization in Africa: An Appraisal," *World Development* 27, no. 1 (January 1999), pp. 201–213.

26. Roman Frydman and Andrzej Rapaczynski, "Privatization in Eastern Europe: Is the State Withering Away?" *Finance and Development* 30, no. 2 (June 1993), pp. 10–13, and in the same issue, Gerd Schwartz and Paulo Silva Lopes, "Privatization: Expectations, Trade-Offs, and Results," pp. 14–17; and Claudia Rosett and Steve Liesman on Russia, "Starting from Scratch," *Wall Street Journal*, October 2, 1995.

27. *Bureaucrats in Business: The Economics and Politics of Government Ownership*, and Bouin and Michalet, *Rebalancing the Public and Private Sectors: Developing Country Experience*, p. 181.

28. For Chile, see Felipe Larrain, "Public Sector Behavior in a Highly Indebted Country: The Contrasting Chilean Experience," in Larrain and Marcelo Selowsky, *The Public Sector and the Latin American Crisis* (San Francisco: ICS Press, 1991), pp. 89–136; Dominique Hachette and Rolf Lüders, *Privatization in Chile: An Economic Appraisal* (San Francisco: ICS Press, 1993); Joseph Collins and John Lear, *Chile's Free-Market Miracle: A Second Look* (Oakland: Institute for Food and Development, 1995), pp. 50–60; and Jonathan Friedland, "The Master Plan," *Wall Street Journal*, October 2, 1995. For Bangladesh, see Tawfiq E. Chowdhury, "Privatization of State Enterprises in Bangladesh, 1975–1984," in Geoffrey Lamb and Rachel Weaving, *Managing Policy Reform in the Real World: Asian Experiences* (Washington: World Bank, 1992), pp. 57–70. Also see Steven H. Hanke, ed., *Privatization and Development* (San Francisco: ICS Press, 1987).

29. Armando Castelar Piñeiro and Ben Ross Schneider, "The Fiscal Impact of Privatisation in Latin America," *Journal of Development Studies* 31, no. 5 (June 1995), pp. 751–776.

30. Craig Torres, "Fallen Star," *Wall Street Journal*, October 2, 1995.

31. Eduardo Bitran and Pablo Serra, "Regulation of Privatized Utilities: The Chilean Experience," *World Development* 26, no. 6 (June 1998), pp. 945–962, and Omar Chisari, Antonio Estache, and Carlos Romero, "Winners and Losers from the Privatization and Regulation of Utilities: Lessons from a General Equilibrium Model of Argentina," *World Bank Economic Review* 13, no. 2 (May 1999), pp. 357–378.

32. Bouin and Michalet, *Rebalancing the Public and Private Sectors: Developing Country Experience*, p. 195. Also see Jonas Praeger, "Is Privatization a Panacea for LDCs? Market Failure versus Public Sector Failure," *Journal of Developing Areas* 26, no. 3 (April 1992), pp. 301–322.

33. Leroy Jones, "Winners and Losers in Privatization," in Ahmed Galal and Mary Shirley, eds., *Does Privatization Deliver?* (Washington: World Bank, 1994). Also Rolph Van der Hoeven and Gyorgy Sziraczki, eds., *Lessons from Privatization: Labour Issues in Developing and Transitional Countries* (Geneva: International Labour Office, 1997).

34. Chisari et al., "Winners and Losers in Privatization and Regulation of Utilities: Lessons from a General Equilibrium Model of Argentina."

35. See World Bank, "Argentina's Privatization Program: Experience, Issues, and Lessons" (Washington: World Bank, 1993). A review of the Latin American experience is Manuel Sanchez and Rossana Corona, eds., *Privatization in Latin America* (Washington: Inter-American Development Bank, 1993).

36. See Matt Moffett and Jonathan Friedland, "A New Latin America Faces a Devil of Old: Rampant Corruption," *Wall Street Journal*, July 1, 1996. Also see John Rapley, *Understanding Development: Theory and Practice in the Third World*, pp. 85–87.

37. See, for example, Cheryl W. Gray, "In Search of Owners: Privatization and Corporate Governance in Transition Economies," *World Bank Research Observer* 11, no. 2 (August 1996), pp. 179–197.

38. Janos Kornai, "Making the Transition to Private Ownership," *Finance & Development* 37, no. 3 (September 2000), pp. 12–13.

39. World Bank, *Sustaining Rapid Development in East Asia and the Pacific* (Washington: World Bank, 1993), pp. 34–35. Also see J. A. Kay and D. J. Thompson, "Privatisation: A Policy in Search of a Rationale," *Economic Journal* 96 (March 1986), pp. 18–32; Mahmood A. Ayub and Sven O. Hegstad, "Management of Public Industrial Enterprises," *World Bank Research Observer* 2, no. 1 (January 1987), pp. 79–101; and World Bank, *Bureaucrats in Business, The Economics and Politics of Government Ownership*.

40. Jonathan Friedland, "Mexico's Oil Company Becomes Businesslike to Avoid Privatization," *Wall Street Journal*, May 24, 1999.

41. Robert D. Willig, "Public versus Regulated Private Enterprise," *Proceedings of World Bank Annual Conference on Development Economics* (1993), pp. 155–170.

42. Raquel Alfaro, Ralph Bradburd, and John Briscoe, "Reforming Former Public Monopolies: Water Supply," in Nancy Birdsall, Carol Graham, and Richard Sabot, eds., *Beyond Trade-Offs: Market Reform and Equitable Growth in Latin America* (Washington: Inter-American Development Bank/Brookings Institution Press, 1998), pp. 267–304.

43. See Sherwin Rosen and Bruce A. Weinberg, "Incentives, Efficiency, and Government Provision of Public

Services," in *Annual World Bank Conference on Development Economics 1997*, Boris Pleskovic and Joseph Stiglitz, eds. (Washington: World Bank, 1998), pp. 139–166.

44. World Bank, *World Development Report* (Washington: World Bank, 1990), pp. 74–84.

45. Sudhir Anand and Martin Ravallion, "Human Development in Poor Countries: On the Role of Private Income and Public Services," *Journal of Economic Perspectives* 7, no. 1 (winter 1993), pp. 133–150. The quotes cited are on pages 142 and 144, italics in the original.

46. Mahbub ul Haq, *Reflections on Human Development* (New York: Oxford University Press, 1995), p. 9.

47. Florencia Castro-Leal, Julia Dayton, Lionel Demery, and Kalpana Mehra, "Public Social Spending in Africa: Do the Poor Benefit?" *World Bank Research Observer* 14, no. 1 (February 1999), pp. 49–72.

48. Trish Kelly, "Public Expenditures and Growth," *Journal of Development Studies* 34, no. 1 (October 1997), pp. 60–84, and Stephen M. Miller and Frank S. Russek, "Fiscal Structures and Economic Growth: International Evidence," *Economic Inquiry* 35, no. 3 (July 1997), pp. 603–613.

49. Joseph Collins and John Lear, *Chile's Free-Market Miracle: A Second Look*, pp. 94–124 for health care, and pp. 125–148 for education. Also see World Bank, "Development Brief," No. 60 (August 1995), and Robert Klitgaard, *Adjusting to Reality: Beyond "State versus Market" in Economic Development*, pp. 139–145.

50. See Giovanni Andrea Cornia and Frances Stewart, "Two Errors of Targeting," *Journal of International Development* 5, no. 5 (September–October 1993), pp. 459–496, and Dominique van de Walle, "Targeting Revisited," *World Bank Research Observer* 13, no. 2 (August 1998), pp. 231–248.

51. See Anne Krueger, "The Political Economy of the Rent-Seeking Society," *American Economic Review* 64, no. 3 (June 1974), pp. 291–303, and Jagdish Bhagwati, Richard A. Brecher, and T. N. Srinivasan, "DUP Activities and Economic Theory," *European Economic Review* 24, no. 3 (April 1984), pp. 291–307.

52. See Susan Rose-Ackerman, *Corruption: A Study in Political Economy* (New York: Academic Press, 1978).

53. Vito Tanzi, "Corruption Around the World: Causes, Consequences, Scope and Cures," *International Monetary Fund Staff Papers* 45, no. 4 (December 1998), pp. 566–576. Also see Pranab Bardhan, "Corruption and Development: A Review of Issues," *Journal of Economic Literature* 35, no. 3 (September 1997), pp. 1320–1346, and Andrei Shleifer and Robert W. Vishny, "Corruption,"*Quarterly Journal of Economics* 108, no. 3 (August 1993), pp. 599–617.

54. John Reed and Erik Portanger, "Bribery, Corruption Are Rampant in Eastern Europe, Survey Finds," *Wall Street Journal*, November 9, 1999.

55. *Ibid*, pp. 578–584. Also see M. S. Alam, "Some Economic Costs of Corruption in LDCs," *Journal of Development Studies* 27, no. 1 (October 1990), pp. 89–97.

56. Tanzi, "Corruption Around the World: Causes, Consequences, Scope and Cures," p. 585, and Paolo Mauro, "Corruption and Growth," *Quarterly Journal of Economics* 110, no. 3 (August 1995), pp. 681–712.

57. Andrew Wedeman, "Looters, Rent-Scrapers and Dividend Collectors: Corruption and Growth in Zaire, South Korea, and the Philippines," *Journal of Developing Areas* 31, no. 4 (summer 1997), pp. 457–478.

58. Vito Tanzi and Hamid R. Davoodi, "Corruption, Growth and Public Finances," IMF Working Paper WP/00/182 (2000).

59. See page 12 of the *World Bank Annual Report 1999* (Washington: World Bank, 1999).

60. Tanzi, "Corruption Around the World: Causes, Consequences, Scope and Cures," p. 586, and Susan Rose-Ackerman, *Corruption: A Study in Political Economy*, pp. 45–51.

61. Douglass C. North, *Structure and Change in Economic History* (New York: W. W. Norton, 1981), chapters 11 and 12.

62. Robert Klitgaard, *Adjusting to Reality: Beyond "State versus Market" in Economic Development*.

63. See Joseph E. Stiglitz, "Alternative Tactics and Strategies for Economic Development," in Amitava K. Dutt and Kenneth P. Jameson, *New Directions in Development Economics* (Hants, U.K.: Edward Elgar, 1992), pp. 57–80.

64. See, for example, Harsha Aturupane, Paul Glewwe, and Paul Isenman, "Poverty, Human Development, and Growth: An Emerging Consensus?" *American Economic Review* 84, no. 2 (May 1994), pp. 244–249.

65. First see John Williamson, "What Washington Means by Policy Reform," in John Williamson, ed., *Latin American Adjustment: How Much Has Happened?* (Washington: Institute for International Economics, 1990), then Williamson, "What Should the World Bank Think About the Washington Consensus," *World Bank Research Observer* 15, no. 2 (August 2000), pp. 251–264.

66. See Tony Killick, *A Reaction Too Far: Economic Theory and the Role of the State in Developing Countries* (Boulder, CO: Westview Press, 1989), and Christopher Colclough and James Manor, eds., *States or Markets? Neo-Liberals and the Development Policy Debate* (Oxford: Clarendon Press, 1991), especially Colclough's opening article, "Structuralism Versus Neo-Liberalism: An Introduction," pp. 1–25.

67. Stiglitz, "Alternative Tactics and Strategies for Economic Development," p. 62.

11

MACROECONOMIC POLICY, INFLATION, AND STABILIZATION

Inflation is like sin;
every government denounces it
and every government practices it.
—SIR FREDERICK KEITH-ROSS (1887–1968)

INTRODUCTION

In the 1980s, economic problems in many developing countries reached crisis proportions. In Latin America and many other countries, inflation attained record rates, sometimes thousands of percent per year. While everyone recognized the seriousness of the situation, there were differences of opinion about how inflation started, who was responsible, and how to combat it. Were developing countries especially prone to inflation? Were government policies primarily responsible, or were they just responding to economic and political pressures? What could macroeconomic policy do to control inflation? Could the International Monetary Fund help, or did its policies exacerbate the situation?

Governments use macroeconomic policy to stabilize the economy. Since the Great Depression of the 1930s, most economists have recognized a responsibility of government in overseeing the rates of economic growth, unemployment, and inflation. Key activities of macroeconomic policy are revenue collection, purchases, transfer payments, and regulation of the money supply. We start our investigation by looking at government spending and analyzing the efficiency of the tax system, then put most of our emphasis on the impact of the government's budget on the economy. Governments typically run budget deficits, spending more than they take in from taxes. The size of these deficits, and their financing through borrowing and/or printing money, are crucial for macroeconomic stability. Lack of stability—indicated by high inflation rates—can kill investor confidence and a country's hopes for development.

MACROECONOMIC POLICY

Macroeconomic policy consists of fiscal and monetary policies. The former are concerned with the relationship between government expenditures and tax revenues, the latter with changes in the money supply and interest rates.

Fiscal Policy

Fiscal policy refers to the government's expenditures, the amount of taxes levied to finance these expenditures, and the relationship between them. Spending usually exceeds tax revenues, leaving governments to finance **deficits** by either borrowing or printing money.[1]

Given that criticism of economic performance in developing countries often focuses on spending, one might conclude that developing-country governments spend much more of their country's income than do developed-country governments. In fact, the reverse is true. The data in Table 10–2 show that government consumption expenditures as a share of GDP rise somewhat at higher income levels. When all government spending is accounted for, the trend becomes even more striking. In 1998, national governments in low-income countries spent 17.0 percent of GDP. For middle-income countries, spending was 20.5 percent, and for high-income countries, 30.2 percent. On the other hand, developing-country governments do spend proportionately more than developed-country governments did at similar stages of development.[2] Many factors affect whether a government will spend a greater or smaller portion of GDP, but no one stands out. There seems to be no discernible relationship between the percentage of government spending in total output and economic growth or between the size of the deficit and growth.[3] More important is *what* the government buys with its money, how sensible and effective that spending is, and what impact other policies have on growth.

Data for 1998 (Table 11–1) show lower incomes associated with a greater portion of expenditures on goods and services, especially wages and salaries. A greater portion, however, also goes to investment, or capital expenditure. The data on subsidies and transfers are difficult to interpret because they include very different items: subsidies to SOEs, which are typically more important in poorer countries, and transfers to households, which are more relevant in richer ones. The World Bank reports data on defense expenditures for most countries but does not aggregate them by income group.

The effectiveness of this spending may be less in developing countries. Inefficient investments require large ongoing maintenance expenditures. With insufficient quality control, spending on health and education may produce inadequate results.[4]

Tax Policy in Developing Countries

Just as developing-country governments spend a smaller portion of GDP than do their more developed counterparts, ratios of tax revenues to GDP are also smaller but to an even greater extent. Whereas the richer countries collected almost 30 percent of

TABLE 11–1 Patterns of Central Government Expenditure (%): 1998

	Goods and Services	*Wages and Salaries**	*Interest*	*Subsidies/ Transfers*	*Capital Spending*
Low-Middle Income	39	24	10	38	12
Upper-Middle Income	28	16	10	49	11
High Income	29	12	8	58	5

Note: Aggregate data for low-income countries are not available.

*Part of goods and services.

Source: World Development Indicators 2001.

output in taxes in 1996, the averages are a bit over 14 percent for low- and 17 percent for middle-income countries.

Objectives of Tax Policy

While taxes are clearly a means of obtaining revenue, there are other objectives as well.[5] In many countries, taxes are used as a way of manipulating the price system toward some favored allocation of resources. Objectives include increasing certain kinds of industry and employment, redistributing income, and attempting to increase growth by providing resources for public investment. The problem with pursuing numerous objectives through a single policy instrument such as taxes is that interests conflict. Too much caving in to one or another interest results in a chaotic system where it is difficult to determine if anything positive is being accomplished.

Using a simple model in which growth requires capital, capital requires investment, and investment requires saving, we would then have to ask whether—and how—to use tax policy to increase saving. Even if we were confident of increasing the government's saving and investment through taxation, we would also have to know the impact of taxes on private saving. A World Bank review of studies on this matter concludes that about one-third of tax revenues is offset by reductions in private saving.[6] Also, it appears unlikely that deliberately using the tax system to distribute income toward upper-income levels—on the theory that the rich save a greater portion of income than the poor—has any *positive* impact on saving.[7]

Can tax policy be used to generate employment? The evidence, according to one reviewer, "does not lead to very optimistic conclusions." Reducing taxes overall may at times do so, but jiggling the tax structure seems to be ineffective. While tax breaks for some sectors may increase employment there, it may just be displaced from somewhere else.[8] Wage or employment subsidies (negative taxes) as a whole seem to do little good, in part because there is a complex interaction among particular types of outputs, inputs, technology, and income distribution that dilutes the impact of such a broad approach. The same can be said for attempts to decrease the use of labor (by subsidizing capital). Richard Bird, a prominent practitioner in this field, concludes that taxes should be neutral as between factors of production.[9]

Another frequent objective of taxation is redistribution of income. Here again, the current state of our knowledge gives no cause for optimism. Income taxes can be levied on only a small portion of the population and if too high will encourage evasion. Taxes on specific products may be counterproductive in the absence of reliable data on who buys what. A tax on a productive input will be passed on to some extent to consumers.

Types of Taxes

Tax structures show some consistent patterns that distinguish poorer and richer countries. Table 11–2 provides a breakdown for revenues collected by central governments. The table shows that the richer countries have relied to a greater extent on **direct taxes** on personal and corporate income and social security taxes, while developing countries have had a much greater dependence on **indirect taxes** (sales, excise, and foreign trade taxes). The reasons why this has been so, and what this implies for improving revenue collection in LDCs, have been the subject of a great deal of investigation.

TABLE 11-2 Central Government Revenue Sources (%): 1998

	Direct Taxes*	*Social Security*	*Goods and Services*	*Foreign Trade*	*Other Taxes*	*Nontax Revenues*
Low-Middle Income	15	9	40	9	1	12
Upper-Middle Income	17	22	33	4	2	9
High Income	28	20	28	0	3	8

Notes: Aggregate data for low-income countries are not available. Sums do not add to 100 percent due to what the source calls "adjustments to tax revenue."

*Direct taxes are those on personal income, corporate profits, and capital gains.

Source: World Development Indicators 2001.

Problems of Collecting Taxes

Our picture of a developing country generally includes a significant portion of economic activity that takes place outside the market or at least outside the formal sector. Collecting taxes from the subsistence economy is difficult given greater illiteracy, lack of record keeping, a greater proportion of income received from nonmonetary transactions, and people's distrust of governments. Even when transactions are monetized, a small company employing many family members and engaged in different types of activities will have ample opportunity to hide revenues. And if hiding just a few hundred dollars moves a taxpayer to a lower tax bracket, or to below the minimum taxable income, the incentive to do so is large. Some governments' reputation for corruption reduces taxpayers' enthusiasm for paying what is owed. Even if corruption is not involved, individuals may not see the benefits from government activity and they may have little sense of community with other sectors of the economy, especially in multiethnic societies. Foreign companies, who prefer their books not be examined, have incentives to maintain two sets of books, with lower income reported to the host government.

Assessing and collecting taxes is a complicated task. Even in countries where record keeping is reasonably consistent and honest, tax officials review only a small percentage of tax returns, and taxpayers will interpret the tax laws in ways that result in lower taxes than the authorities believe should be paid. In order to successfully apply the laws to assess taxes (such as on income, sales, and land value) and determine whether taxpayers are complying with the law, tax authorities must be well trained and well enough compensated to resist temptation.

Some General Lessons of Tax Policy

Where does all this leave us if we are searching for some principles to guide tax policy?[10] Some lessons that might be applicable anywhere are particularly relevant for developing countries. One of these is simplicity of the tax structure. Simple structures (e.g., few brackets for income taxes, few tax rates for sales taxes) give less incentive to evade. They are also easier to administer: The more complex the tax structure becomes, the greater the chance for confusion and conflicts of interest that ultimately reduce the system's effectiveness.

Another lesson is that taxes should be as broadly based as possible in order to reduce resentment against those not covered, and tax rates kept low enough to achieve revenue objectives without providing incentives for evasion. Broadening the base, however, is particularly difficult for developing economies, especially those with large informal sectors.

Direct Taxes

The *income tax* is difficult to assess in the rural and urban informal sectors. However, high marginal tax rates in the formal sector will drive activity into the informal sector (or hinder entrance into the formal sector) and thus be counterproductive to the goal of raising revenues. Foreign companies may also be difficult to tax, especially if rates are higher than in their home economies.[11]

Economists commonly recommend that there be relatively few income brackets (ranges) and that the top marginal rate fall between 30 and 50 percent. The brackets should be indexed; that is, they should rise with inflation in order to prevent the bulk of the population from quickly entering the top bracket when incomes rise due to inflation. If greater **progressivity** (higher marginal tax rates at higher incomes) is desired, or if the difficulties of taxing the informal sector are overwhelming, it makes sense to exempt incomes below some level, thereby relieving poverty and preventing the waste of time of chasing after millions of individuals whose tax bills would be minimal anyway. Direct taxes are more elastic, that is, revenues increase automatically with higher GDP. Another way to simplify the tax system is to treat income from all sources—wages, rent, interest, profits—equally. Although there is often public sentiment for higher rates on "unearned" (nonwage) income, the benefits of simplicity and decreased evasion may well argue for such **horizontal equity**.

A recent study of the Bulgarian income tax concluded that the 7 brackets in place in 1992 could have been replaced by 3. Such a system would likely have collected more revenue and been more equitable and efficient. Unfortunately, the system became more complex, moving to 10 brackets, before dropping to 5 in 1997. At that time the top tax rate was reduced from 52 percent to 40 percent, and the income level for a zero rate was increased significantly.[12]

Another approach to direct taxation is the "presumptive" approach, which can be applied to individuals and companies. The tax is based on the income presumed to be realizable from an individual's wealth or business sales. Some form of this tax has been applied successfully in Colombia and Bolivia and is recommended especially where record keeping is poor. If, as in Bolivia, accurate records show income to be lower than presumed, the tax is then lowered accordingly.[13]

Indirect Taxes

The major source of tax revenue for most developing-country governments is *indirect taxes*: some sort of sales tax, excise taxes, and taxes on foreign trade, particularly imports. In the next chapter we review recommendations for simplifying a country's tariff structure, so here we discuss indirect taxes on goods produced at home.

The principles of simplicity and equity are as useful for indirect taxes as they are for direct taxes. Have few tax rates, perhaps just one for most goods, and achieve progressivity by exempting goods such as basic foodstuffs and cooking oil that require large portions of the incomes of poor people. The form of indirect taxation is also important. Taxes on consumption are useful to increase national saving but may have a negative impact on productive inputs, and on the production and distribution chain.

The earliest tax of this sort to be used was a sales tax levied at the point of final sale. More recently, however, favor has turned to a **Value Added Tax (VAT)**, which taxes each step in the production/distribution chain according to what that step adds to the value of the product. Such a tax has been levied for some time by Western European countries and is often rebated when goods are exported. Tax experts often suggest a common rate of between 10 and 20 percent together with a broad base. A number of developing countries, including Indonesia, Turkey, Chile, and a number of other Latin American countries, have now turned to this tax.

Another form of sales tax is the excise tax, which is levied on a specific product or products rather than all sales. About 90 percent of excise revenue in most countries is derived from taxes on tobacco products, alcoholic beverages, and petroleum products, often with the additional objective of discouraging consumption.[14] Some economists would favor higher tax rates on "luxuries," but this is tricky when poorer people consume such so-called luxuries as cigarettes, alcohol, and cosmetics. There may be a conflict between discouraging such consumption and reducing real incomes of the poor. These are perhaps the least costly taxes to administer, but if imposed on too many products they can make the entire tax system much too complex.

One significant debate about indirect taxes is their **incidence**, that is, the extent to which the consumer actually pays the tax.[15] Since any indirect tax will raise the price to the consumer, there will be an incentive for consumers and producers to shift from the taxed product to another. If the government's objective is simply to raise revenue, rather than to shift resources among industries, officials must be aware of the overall impact of such a tax.

Figure 11–1 provides a simple example of the impact of different elasticities of demand and supply on the incidence of an excise tax. On the graphs, the more elastic demand and supply curves are labeled *De* and *Se*, and the more inelastic *Di* and *Si*. The prices and quantities are labeled to correspond to which curve is relevant (with the original position labeled *Po* and *Qo*). Those products generally subject to excise taxes have relatively inelastic demand because fewer substitutes are available.

In Figure 11–1a, a tax shifts the supply curve upward to *St*. The less elastic the demand, the more the tax will be borne by the consumer (*Pi > Pe*), and the less negative impact it will have on production and use of inputs (*Qi > Qe*). If a product has many substitutes, demand will be more elastic and a tax will simply shift spending to those substitutes unless all, including imported substitutes, are equally taxed. One rationale for taxing imported products is precisely to shift spending to the domestic product. But if revenue is an important objective, taxing the elastic product will shift spending to such an extent that little revenue is obtained because less of the product is bought.

In Figure 11–1b, the two supply curves shift by an equal amount (measured vertically—the amount of the tax). The less elastic the supply, the less impact on output: *Qi > Qe*, although the share of the tax borne by the consumer will be less (*Pi < Pe*).[16] Taxes on agricultural commodities, especially for those where consumption substitution is great and growing periods last over many years, will be burdensome on farmers.

Tax incidence, therefore, depends on how easily consumers and producers can shift away from the taxed activity. Not surprisingly, research indicates that some of

(a) Different Demand Elasticities

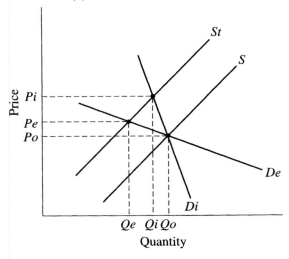

(b) Different Supply Elasticities

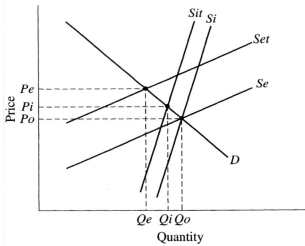

FIGURE 11–1 Elasticities and Tax Incidence

(a) The tax is the vertical distance between the two supply curves. For the more elastic demand curve, such as for imported beer, consumers shift to substitute goods, in this case, domestic beer. The increase in price is much less than the tax, and most of the tax burden is borne by the producer, which in this case is a foreign company. For a less elastic product, such as maize meal, a staple in some countries, there is less ability to switch and the consumer bears a greater burden of the tax.

(b) For any given demand curve, tax incidence depends on the elasticity of supply. For a more elastic supply, such as for polyester shirts, from which firms can shift production easily, the increase in price is greater and consumption shifts to a substitute, such as a cotton shirt. When supply is inelastic, such as for many agricultural commodities in the short term, the producer absorbs more of the tax.

the most regressive taxes—whose burden is disproportionately on poorer people—are those on basic commodities essential to the poor. Studies in Ghana and Madagascar showed taxes on kerosene consumption were among the most regressive. Taxes on the productive activities are also regressive. Export taxes—on cocoa in Ghana and on vanilla in Madagascar—were highly regressive because consumers in importing countries had other sources of supply.[17]

Tax on Wealth

Those who suspect that people with higher incomes and accumulated wealth are better able to evade income taxes will favor wealth taxes. A tax on accumulated wealth may have fewer disincentive effects than taxes on income, although tax rates that are too high may cause wealth holders to shift the form of wealth to something less easily taxed, such as foreign assets.[18]

One form of wealth tax that many economists tend to favor is a tax on land. This is particularly the case if much of the land in question is not being well utilized. Although land can be put to different uses, its overall supply tends to be fairly inelastic. A land tax will encourage more intensive use of the land if this is feasible, and in the rural sector particularly, this may result in greater employment.[19] A government seeking to encourage small-scale agriculture may well put a lower limit on the amount of land that is taxed, although as with all wealth this opens a door to evasion by having large landholders divide up their property's legal ownership. Of course, clear legal title and a simple, consistent method of valuing land must exist; problems that may account for the fact that land taxes typically account for only 1 to 2 percent of the total revenues of developing countries.

A land tax, which could be made progressive on the basis of size or productivity, may be a good candidate for taxing the agricultural sector. It would overcome some of the usual difficulties of taxing that sector: A substantial portion of its activity is not monetized, and its population may be very poor. The political difficulty of assessing and collecting taxes on large landholders is notorious,[20] but the potential rewards (unless taxes are so high that the land is abandoned) should make the effort worthwhile, given the inelasticity of supply. One study of Pakistan concludes that a tax based on land productivity is the best approach to taxing agriculture there. It could be easily administered and would be equitable, especially if the least productive land were untaxed.[21]

Export Taxes

One of the more harmful types of taxation is a tax on exports. These taxes have often been imposed as a way of taxing agricultural incomes and/or when it was imagined that the world market would absorb them. The result, however, has usually been to hurt exports, especially agricultural exports that have been most often subject to these taxes. Farmers may switch to non-export crops, or other exporting countries may capture more of the market. Nigeria, for example, lost a large portion of its share of the world market for both cocoa and palm oil through export taxes on these products in the early 1960s.[22] Many developing countries have now reduced or eliminated export taxes, but many exports are indirectly taxed through tariffs on the imported inputs used for exports.

Taxes as a Tool of Environmental Policy

The benefits of environmental taxes, or charges, can be great. Such taxes are a way of internalizing externalities and raising revenue and do not require setting up emissions markets, which may be administratively complex. Still, there are many difficulties. Monitoring is hard, especially as each source may emit many different kinds of pollutants, including factory smoke and chemical runoffs. The incidence of such taxation has yet to be studied throughly, and any such studies will require separating out the impact of the pollution tax and other taxes on a product that pollutes in the course of production and use.[23]

A tax on fuel or energy use—such as a carbon tax—could raise revenue and provide an incentive toward energy efficiency. This is especially true given the existence of strong negative externalities of energy consumption and the difficulties of monitoring pollution. Some countries tax leaded fuel more heavily than nonleaded. Costa

Rica taxes all oil products at 15 percent. Singapore "taxes" import and use of chloro-fluorocarbons (CFCs) by reducing the number of permits given out—thereby raising their price. Fuel taxes are likely to hurt the poor disproportionately, but this can be offset by subsidies or exemptions.[24]

Applying the Lessons: Tax Reform

Tax systems may be changed gradually, but there may be occasions when they cannot be rationally attacked in small bites and must be completely overhauled. In fact, economic crisis may be the best environment in which to accomplish this task. At that point, governments can heed the general types of advice that have been suggested earlier: simplify, broaden, and lower. Tax systems should be simplified to ease the administrative burden and reduce evasion. The base should be broadened to reduce shifting of resources from taxed to nontaxed activities and provide a sense of fairness. Rates should be lowered to reduce evasion, especially if broadening the base will permit revenues to increase. Case 11–1 summarizes tax reform efforts in Bolivia and Indonesia.

Monetary Policy

Governments can increase (or decrease) economic activity by adding to (or subtracting from) the total amount of spending. **Monetary policy** involves changes in the money supply and the extent to which the government borrows through sales of new bonds to the public, firms, and government agencies.[25] Increasing the money supply will lower interest rates and induce more private spending as well. The economy will expand through some combination of higher production and prices. Reducing the money supply, or slowing its growth, should reverse this process. When the government borrows, however, its impact depends on the availability of funds. With a slow economy, the government may simply add spending and increase production. But if funds are fully utilized by the private sector, government borrowing will cause interest rates to rise and its spending will replace (crowd out) some private activity.

Borrowing

To the extent that a government's desire to spend outpaces its ability to tax (a condition that is well known to people everywhere), governments resort to borrowing, issuing bonds where possible. But the less developed a country is, the less extensive are its financial resources. Developing economies have fewer financial instruments, and the ability of a government to borrow is restricted by the limited role of formal bond markets. In more developed economies, government bonds are not merely purchased and kept until maturity, but are also bought and sold on open markets. Where such a market does not exist, bonds are less attractive as a means of holding wealth. Poor and unstable governments do not inspire the confidence necessary for their bonds to be attractive. In addition, the tendency toward inflation in many countries robs these instruments of most of their value by the time of maturity unless they are indexed or adjusted for inflation.

In some developing countries, governments enforce this kind of borrowing by requiring the purchase of their bonds by businesses and workers. Those most susceptible to this pressure are government employees and any individual or firm that wishes to conduct significant business with the government. The government may also sell bonds to the banking system, as is done in Korea, Nepal, and Sri Lanka.[26]

TAX REFORM IN BOLIVIA AND INDONESIA

FAST FACTS

Bolivia on the Map: South America

Population: 8 Million

Per Capita GNI and Rank: $990   (134)

Life Expectancy: Male—60   Female—64

Adult Literacy Rate: Male—92%
Female—79%

Indonesia on the Map: Southeast Asia

Population: 207 Million

Per Capita GNI and Rank: $600   (150)

Life Expectancy: Male—64   Female—68

Adult Literacy Rate: Male—91%
Female—81%

Bolivia's economy lay in devastation in 1985, with inflation just under 12,000 percent. The tax system, which had yielded revenues of nearly 13 percent of GDP in 1974, brought in only 1 percent of GDP in 1985 following a year in which the government's budget deficit had reached 30 percent of GDP. One part of the overall answer was tax reform.

In 1986, the entire system, except for import and export taxes, was replaced. The entire set of direct taxes on personal and corporate income was eliminated, the indirect tax system was revised, and simplification was introduced where possible. The main burden fell on a Value Added Tax (VAT) of 10 percent, excluding housing and financial services and the informal sector. A complementary VAT, at 10 percent of the basic VAT, was also withheld, although it could be returned if receipts from the original transactions could be produced, an incentive to good record keeping. To this was added a 1 percent tax on transactions; a 30 percent tax on alcohol, perfume and cosmetics; a 50 percent tax on tobacco and jewelry; and a 2 percent tax on personal and corporate wealth, based on presumptions of profits from that wealth. Additional aspects of the reform included simplification of small-business taxes, the elimination of investment incentives, a uniform tariff rate (originally 20 percent then lowered to 10) on imports, a simpler formula for sharing revenues with cities and government enterprises, and the use of the banks as collection agents to cut government bureaucracy and reduce opportunities for corruption.

There were some immediate signs of success. Revenues returned to 13 percent of GDP in 1987, rising to 17.5 percent in 1998. There is some concern that the turn away from direct taxes will make the system more regressive, but exemption of the informal sector and the likelihood of significant evasion from the previous regime suggest that the new one may be no worse for the poor. It is also likely that the new system is more neutral with respect to different activities than the earlier one.

The Indonesian government did not wait for a crisis. The country's finances had become largely dependent on oil exports, and in 1981 the government began to plan a complete overhaul that served it well when oil prices fell in the mid-1980s. The government officials who reported on the reforms said the old system had

become so complicated and so open to evasion that it could not provide any guarantee that a target level of revenues could be achieved... [C]ollection procedures were so poor that they easily led to embezzlements. Some of the sanctions imposed for failure to pay taxes were so unrealistic that they were seldom applied, while others were so light that they failed to function as deterrents.

After almost three years of study, drafting, and sending officials for training, a new

307

system was put into place in 1984 with the following features:

1. Income from all sources—individual and corporate—was taxed at the same rate.

2. Previous income tax rates of 25 percent, 30 percent and 45 percent were lowered to 15 percent, 25 percent and 35 percent, with few exemptions.

3. Exemption for low income effectively excluded the poorest 90 percent of the population from the income tax.

4. The requirement that government officials would have to assess each taxpayer's income was replaced by taxpayer self-assessment to save administrative costs and remove opportunities for collusion between officials and taxpayers.

5. A VAT was initiated that exempts agriculture, distribution, and most services. This rationalized the previously confusing indirect tax system and has caused no significant increase in prices.

The new system was inaugurated with an interim amnesty to allow taxpayers to make up deficiencies owed under the old system. The entire tax system was computerized, officials were trained, and stricter discipline imposed on officials who would break the rules. Revenue targets were achieved, with the major increases realized through the VAT. Table 11–3 shows some relevant data.

TABLE 11–3 Indonesian Tax Reform

	1979	1989
Non-Oil Tax Revenues (Trillion Rupees)	2.2	15.4
Percentage of Total Revenues	35	65
Percentage of GDP	5.99	8.86
Breakdown of Non-Oil Tax Revenues (%)		
Income Tax	41	36
Sales/Excise Taxes	37	47
Import Duties	13	10
Other	9	7

Sources: Wayne Thirsk, "Bolivia's Tax Revolution," in Wayne Thirsk, ed., *Tax Reform in Developing Countries* (Washington: World Bank, 1997), pp. 33–55; Stephen C. Smith, *Case Studies in Economic Development*, 2nd ed. (Reading: Addison-Wesley, 1997), pp. 211–217; R. Mansury and Ismail Tamsir, "Tax Reform in Indonesia, 1984," in Geoffrey Lamb and Rachel Weaving, eds., *Managing Policy Reform in the Real World* (Washington: World Bank, 1992), pp. 71–85; and Mukul Asher, "Reforming the Tax System in Indonesia," in Thirsk, *Tax Reform in Developing Countries*, pp. 127–166.

The Money Supply

In industrialized countries, monetary policies target changes in the money supply and interest rates in an attempt to promote steady, noninflationary growth. In many developing countries, governments prefer rapid rather than steady growth, and inflation is frequently the result. Money is created as needed to fund private and public investment, and interest rates are deliberately kept low to encourage industrialization.

As the legal issuer of money, a government obtains real resources. Governments obtain purchasing power at nominal cost through their role as monopoly suppliers of money. To the extent that they borrow, inflation reduces the value of government debt. This gain to the government is referred to as **seigniorage**, originally the fee extracted by rulers for making coins from gold and silver.[27] Although the relationship is not precise, where economies experience higher inflation, governments gain more by seigniorage, which is estimated by measuring the increase in the amount of currency as a percentage of the country's GDP. A major study of 90 countries covering 1971 to 1990 estimated seigniorage from 0.4 percent of GDP (New Zealand, Denmark, the United States, and Canada) to 15 percent in Israel and from 1 percent of government spending (in several countries) to 149 percent in Yugoslavia and 62 percent in Argentina.[28]

There is not much agreement on the causes. One author suggests that the variation among countries is due to inefficient tax systems, fluctuations in government spending, and lack of central bank independence. Another relates seigniorage directly to the usual monetary policy variables; rapid money-supply growth and high reserve requirements.[29] But while the gains from this practice may be significant, a study of moderate inflation countries (15 percent to 30 percent per year) finds little evidence that seigniorage gains are a goal of government policy.[30]

There is a significant difference between monetary policy as it is practiced in developed and developing countries. In industrialized countries, the **central bank** (the Federal Reserve, or Fed, in the United States) can easily change the ratio of reserves that ordinary commercial banks are required to maintain behind their deposits, change the discount (interest) rate that banks have to pay to borrow reserves for new lending, and regularly buy and sell government securities (Open Market Operations) as a way of injecting new reserves into or draining reserves from the system. Reserve ratios and discount rates are changed infrequently, and Open Market Operations are relied upon for frequent small changes in the rate of growth of the money supply. While all of these instruments are in principle available to developing-country central banks, the most flexible, Open Market Operations, is often impractical due to the very small market for government securities. Governments are therefore left with only the more drastic measures, not suitable for marginal changes in money supply growth.

There is an even more important difference between monetary policy in developed and developing countries. In industrialized countries there is usually a clear distinction between fiscal and monetary policies because governments finance most of their domestic debt by the issuance of new government securities to individuals, firms, and financial institutions. New government debt can either draw on excess savings or compete for financial resources by driving up interest rates without having a significant impact on the money supply per se. In those developing countries that lack large markets for government securities, government domestic debt is financed by borrowing from the central bank and printing money, thus injecting new spending into the system. Fiscal and monetary policy may be virtually synonymous, and government debt has a more dramatic impact on inflation.

One recent line of inquiry into the pressures on monetary policy focuses on the independence of the central bank from the executive branch of the government. Where the president controls the central bank, money can be created at will to finance expenditures. If the bank is independent, government spending must rely on taxes or legitimate borrowing. Formal or legal independence, however, is not always a realistic criterion for evaluating this independence, nor does it seem to be associated with low inflation rates. Some authors believe a high turnover rate of central bank governors suggests lack of true independence and that lack of independence is associated with high inflation rates.[31]

THE INFLATION DEBATE

Inflation is normally considered undesirable. Yet some developing-country policy makers have welcomed inflation. Where savings are difficult to encourage, and taxes difficult to collect, they contend that inflation creates **forced saving**, based on the distinction between money and real resources. The usual way of looking at inflation is that the same goods are bought for a higher price. But this also means that, for the same expenditure in money terms, less is actually purchased. Real resources are thereby taken away from consumption and thus saved. The first beneficiaries of inflation are the sellers, and inflation amounts initially to an increase in the share of profits in income (and a reduction in the share of wages). If these profits are not eliminated by subsequent increases in costs, they can be used for private investment or taxed by the government and used for government spending. Often, governments are the primary beneficiary of inflation as higher incomes lead to higher tax payments. Development Spotlight 11–1 summarizes the "winners and losers" from inflation.

In this section we look at the causes and cures of inflation. Is some inflation "normal" or even beneficial? What are the problems associated with high inflation? How does inflation get to be too high? What can government do about it?

DEVELOPMENT SPOTLIGHT 11–1

WINNERS AND LOSERS FROM INFLATION

Inflation benefits owners of resources whose prices rise first or faster, or those who can easily shift toward those resources. Those who lose own resources whose prices rise later or more slowly (or not at all) and cannot shift.

Typical winners own resources—such as land and foreign assets—which are viewed as safe havens. Land, due to relative scarcity and productive value, is generally considered safe, so people will often sell other assets to buy land, thus increasing its value. Precious metals have the same property. Foreign assets, including bank accounts and securities, can be reconverted to domestic assets at a favorable rate after the inflationary surge has passed (unless inflation occurs in the foreign country as well).

Borrowers also come out ahead because the purchasing power of repayments during inflation is lower than when borrowed—although lenders may reduce their losses through variable interest rates. Those who sell goods at a quick turnover also gain—particularly traders whose capital is not tied up for too long. Governments may gain initially as the purchasing power of its debt repayments diminishes and revenues based on income or sale rises.

Typical losers are those on fixed incomes—such as retirees—or those whose income lags inflation, such as workers without full cost-of-living adjustments or with infrequent adjustments. Lenders who were not protected by variable interest rates will lose. Even producers of normal goods with long production processes will lose to the extent that their capital is "tied up" for long periods—hence, large investments in plant and machinery are discouraged if money can be used to make a quick profit. Domestic competitors to foreign goods will be disadvantaged if inflation is lower overseas. Government may lose in the long run if tax collection lags assessment and its own purchases become more expensive.

Taken together, these factors indicate that inflation disproportionately hurts the poor. They own fewer assets, spend all their income on items often hit hard by inflation, and may work for the minimum wage or have less power over their wages.

Inflation as a "Normal" Part of Development

Some amount of inflation can be justified as the inevitable result of development.[32] Economic *growth* at its most basic is simply an increase in the (per capita) production of goods and services. Often, growth is a response to higher demand; firms expand in size when the market indicates that investment will be profitable. Demand therefore puts pressure on existing resources, to which businesses respond by investment, producing growth. The increasing pressure of demand on existing supplies results in price increases. When this is a general phenomenon (aggregate demand grows faster than aggregate supply), we have inflation.

Development adds a change in economic structure. New areas of economic activity bring a greater likelihood that demand will put pressure on the limits of capacity. Unless prices in other sectors are sufficiently flexible to fall, and fall enough to offset increases in new areas, there will be a general price-level increase, or inflation. As supply expands demand may well accelerate, continuing the inflationary pressure.

Clearly some inflation exists everywhere. A key question is at what rate this inflation interferes with growth. The answer is not precise. One study suggests inflation at or below 8 percent can be harmless or even have a positive impact on growth. Another suggests inflation below 20 percent will not interfere, while a third limits beneficial inflation to less than 5 percent.[33]

The Record of Inflation in Developing Countries

Developing countries are clearly more inflation-prone than the more industrialized countries, with Latin America having the worst record and Asia the best. Table 11–4 shows recent data on these differences. Fluctuations around the inflation trend

TABLE 11–4 Inflation Rates (GDP Deflator)

	1965–1980	*1980–1990*	*1990–1999*
Africa			
Côte d'Ivoire	9.2	2.8	8.2
Kenya	7.3	9.1	14.9
Morocco	5.8	7.1	3.2
Zambia	6.4	42.2	57.4
Asia			
China	Negligible	5.9	8.2
India	7.4	8.0	8.5
Republic of Korea	18.4	6.1	5.8
Thailand	6.2	3.9	4.6
Latin America			
Argentina	78.4	391.9	6.2
Bolivia	15.7	327.2	9.1
Brazil	31.6	284.0	263.9
Costa Rica	11.2	23.6	16.7
Mexico	13.2	71.5	19.5
Other			
Japan	1.2	1.7	0.1
Russian Federation	NA	NA	190.4
United States	5.3	4.2	2.1

NA = Not Available.

Sources: World Development Report 1987 and *World Development Indicators 2001.*

are also greater in developing countries. There is a positive relationship between level and variability of inflation in developing countries with Latin America the most volatile. Some countries have learned to live—and grow—with moderate to high inflation, but once inflation rates exceed 50 percent or especially 100 percent per year, the instability associated with high rates is likely to make sustained growth impossible.[34]

Problems with Inflation

If in fact inflation provides a means of forcing savings, of releasing resources from consumption toward investment, governments would rationally see inflation not just as an accompaniment to development but as a tool, or means of pushing development: They could use government demand to inflate prices, tax away the profits, and use the revenues to finance development projects. Were inflation sufficiently gradual, there might be little difficulty in maintaining such an ongoing policy. If profits are used to increase capacity, employment, and output, inflation might thereby lead to growth to the benefit of everyone. However, inflation in developing countries may be rapid. In this case, a number of problems will occur.

Wage earners will push for at least matching increases. This will not only counteract the real resource transfer but may also overshoot the mark, causing further price increases and an upward spiral.

Price instability destroys confidence in the economy. Fear of continuing inflation leads to hoarding, as consumers buy preemptively ahead of the next round of price increases. Such demand behavior leads to further inflation. Inflation also encourages attempts to borrow, as individuals and firms expect to pay back in money that has lost considerable value. This increase in the demand for funds leads to higher interest rates, as lenders seek to protect themselves. For example, at the end of 1989 the Central Bank discount rate in Brazil was over 38,000 percent. If interest rates are controlled by governments, loanable funds become scarce and are allocated by political considerations including development strategy and favoritism.

Inflation encourages investment in items whose value is expected to rise quickly (gold, land, art, finished goods for trade, foreign currencies) and discourages investment in long-term productive activities, such as producing capital goods. Thus, resources are shifted from more- to less-productive activities. Another inflation-induced spending shift is the increasing attractiveness of foreign goods over domestic goods, leading to increased imports and lower exports, unless the currency is devalued, which many governments are hesitant to do.

A further cost of inflation is what one author has called the "shoe-leather" cost: People spend a lot of time going to (and waiting in line at) the banks and other financial institutions to undertake the transactions necessary to preserve the real value of their wages, while companies' resources tend to shift somewhat from production to cash flow management. Throughout the economy, resources are shifted toward the financial sector and away from production and distribution.[35]

Rapid inflation robs money of its value, so the advantages of using money are lost and trade reverts to barter. Financial deepening is reversed.[36] Those whose assets are disproportionately in the form of money—the poorest parts of the urban population—fare worst as the value of money declines. Wide variations in price changes for different goods and services reduce the ability of the price mechanism to accurately reflect scarcity.

As inflation proceeds more rapidly, one of the losers is the government itself. Although government is generally presumed to gain from higher taxes on inflated earnings, there is always a lag between the imposition of taxes and their collection. In that period, the (real) value of tax revenues diminishes, forcing governments to borrow even more to support their spending.

Generally, once inflationary expectations are generated, any benefits collapse and an upward spiral begins. But how exactly does inflation start? What are the most important steps governments can take to stop it? Differences of opinion exist about the fundamental cause of inflation in developing countries and therefore about the solution. As one might expect from the data in Table 11–3, this debate has taken place largely in the Latin American context. The contending parties are monetarists and structuralists.[37]

Causes of Inflation and Its Cure: The Monetarist View

Monetarists follow the reasoning developed by economists from the University of Chicago. They see inflation as resulting primarily from excessive increases in money supply, frequently caused by governments deliberately trying to promote development through inflation or simply bowing to political pressures to make more money available. Figure 11–2 illustrates how to avoid this problem. *AS* and *AD* are the aggregate supply and demand curves for an economy. Monetarists suggest that Latin American governments have held back aggregate supply by overregulating their economies and discouraging efficiency through protection from foreign competition. Instead, governments have rapidly increased money supplies, thereby shifting aggregate demand and producing inflation. A more flexible economy could minimize inflation.

Two examples are Brazil and Bolivia. In 1990 Brazil's money supply grew by over 2,000 percent and inflation approached 3,000 percent. In 1985 Bolivia's money

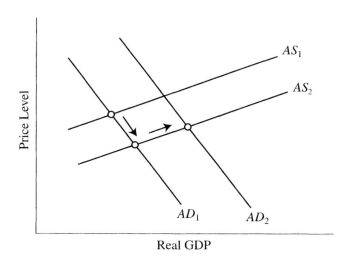

FIGURE 11–2 Monetarist Approach to Avoiding Inflation

Monetarists believe aggregate supply can be made more elastic and shifted to the right through market-oriented policies. If aggregate supply shifts first (AS_2), higher income will increase demand without much inflation from increases in aggregate demand (AD_2).

supply grew by almost 6,000 percent and inflation was almost 12,000 percent. By one estimate, the seigniorage created in Bolivia accounted for two-thirds of the government's revenue in that year.[38]

Monetarists point out the severe limits of inflation as a development strategy: Forced saving disappears when peoples' expectations adjust, resources transferred are not used efficiently by businesses or government, and inflation discourages long-term risk taking. Once begun, inflation may encourage even more government spending and lead to more inflation.[39] In addition, inflation discourages the inflow of foreign capital, discourages capital-intensive investments with long gestation periods, discourages the development and efficient use of capital markets, and stimulates investment in inventories or speculation.

Orthodox anti-inflationary policy is, in principle, fairly simple. Based on monetarist assumptions, it recommends that the government reduce its deficit, thereby removing demand and money from the economy. The advantages are not only the removal of excess demand and money but also the particular kinds of reforms that would be implied by a balanced budget. Most favored is a reduction in military spending and in government subsidies of its own SOEs. If those firms are to continue without subsidies, they would have to raise prices to market levels. Although this may be a one-time boost to inflation, the result would be a more efficient allocation of resources. Subsidies on goods that are important to the poor would have to be cut as well. The poor may be protected by more efficient policies, such as direct payments: The World Bank suggests protecting the poorest on equity grounds and as a means of obtaining political support for the program.

The other side of the budget lever is taxes, and most monetarists would join others in calling for a more rational tax system. But if inflation fell, many believe that *real* government revenues would rise, as they would no longer be whittled away by the effects of inflation. This could permit tax rates to fall over time and thus to improve incentives.

This traditional solution was implemented successfully by Bolivia. Government spending was reduced through privatizations and payroll reductions. Tax reform restored confidence and increased revenues significantly. The public sector deficit fell from 18 percent of GDP in 1984 to 2 percent in 1986. International transactions were liberalized to spur competition and attract foreign capital. Inflation, which had hit almost 12,000 percent in 1985 was down to 15 percent two years later and has remained below 20 percent. GDP growth, negative in 1983, 1985, and 1986, turned positive in 1987 and has remained so in most years since.[40]

Causes of Inflation and Its Cure: The Structuralist View

Traditional **structuralist** arguments were developed by economists at the UN Economic Commission for Latin America (ECLA).[41] They do not deny the link between government spending and inflation but suggest that government deficits, rapid expansion of the money supply, and inflation are *symptoms* of bottlenecks: Crucial shortages of land, capital, and skilled labor prevent output from responding rapidly to increases in demand. For example, agricultural supply may be price inelastic, so that higher demand and higher prices do not result quickly in greater output. Expansion of industrial supply to remove structural imbalances in the economy is difficult because investment and output require imports, for which the needed foreign exchange is scarce. And there is a simple lack of internal financial resources. Slow and unstable export growth requires costly import substitution and does not supply sufficient government revenues. Figure 11–3 illustrates this idea: The aggregate supply curve is extremely inelastic in the short run. An increase in demand causes inflation, but presumably this is the only way to encourage an increase in supply over time.

In addition to the structuralist argument there is a **neo-structuralist** view[42] that focuses on societal conflict resulting from changes in income distribution among wage earners, capitalists, and landholders. In this view, inflation is largely **inertial**: An economic shock such as an increase in oil import prices or interest rates may change the existing distribution of income and cause disadvantaged groups to try to catch up. As real wages fall, labor groups will push for higher money wages, which puts pressure on profits, leading to higher prices and a new round of wage increases. "Clearly, inflation is fundamentally a struggle among groups for the redistribution of real income, and the rise in the price level is merely the external expression of that struggle." Referring to the Brazilian experience in the 1940s and 1950s, one author claims that expanded money supply was not the cause. Instead, "the banks almost always act in a completely passive manner," supplying money to meet the demand of firms to finance this struggle.[43]

Monetarists do not accept the structuralist argument. They deny that agricultural supply is as inelastic as is claimed: Higher producer prices will in fact result in higher output that can ultimately channel resources back into investment, if governments will only permit prices to be set by the market. They oppose the structuralists' gloom over trade possibilities with arguments that exports are discouraged by overvalued exchange rates, and intermediate goods imports are sustained through protection of consumer goods production and increased indebtedness. Other inappropriate policies, including labor market restrictions, may also be the cause of structural problems.[44]

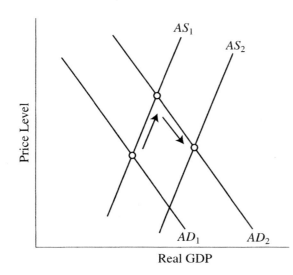

FIGURE 11–3 Structuralist View of Inflation

In the structuralist view, aggregate supply is highly inelastic in the short run. Stimulating demand (AD_2) inevitably causes inflation, but this will ultimately increase aggregate supply (AS_2).

Further, monetarists believe that regardless of the type of shock to the economy, further rounds of wage and price increases can be sustained *only if* the government expands the money supply to accommodate the higher demands. But increasing demand first still causes inflation. Monetarists suggest that instead of government maintaining expenditures on inefficient SOEs and other programs, it should allow markets to reduce inefficiencies in resource allocation and shift the supply curve ahead of increases in demand. Once supply has shifted, increasing incomes will shift demand with less inflationary impact.

Monetarists suggest that structuralist concerns are not always borne out. In 1986, Bolivia reduced money growth from 6,000 percent to 86 percent and its fiscal deficit from 9 percent to 2 percent of GDP. Inflation fell from nearly 12,000 percent to 276 percent. While output declined by $2\frac{1}{2}$ percent, this was no more than the average for the previous four inflationary years and began a steady upward trend in 1987. In Brazil, money supply growth fell from 2,195 percent in 1994 to 26 percent the following year. Inflation fell from 2,076 percent to 66 percent, and GDP growth slowed but was still 4.2 percent.

Structuralists do not oppose monetary restraint in principle. However, they worry that reducing credit and the money supply will reduce demand without bringing a corresponding increase in output, thereby reducing income, and employment. The cost of halting inflation may be greater than the benefit; monetary expansion and demand-led growth are necessary, even at the cost of inflation. Structuralists would look for government spending policies to break the bottlenecks in those sectors where supply is inelastic. They fear that overstrict control of the money supply will instead bring down demand and make overcoming the bottlenecks impossible. Economist Lance Taylor concludes that "the outcomes of orthodox [stabilization] packages ranged from moderately successful to disastrous."[45] The more successful cases studied, moreover, all included important elements of government intervention. Ultimately, he believes that each economy has features that make it unique, and that the appropriate combination of orthodox and more ad hoc approaches must be determined for each one.

Structuralist explanations of inflation are more complex than those of monetarists and cast doubt on the easy solution of demand restraint. Their preferred approach is to expand the economy's productive capacity and remove the bottlenecks that they believe cause inflation. If economic stability requires regaining international competitiveness by eliminating price differentials between domestic and foreign goods, lower demand may not work if many domestic and foreign goods do not compete. Industrial prices may not be demand driven but based on fairly rigid rules by which firms simply add a percentage markup to their costs, so reducing demand may be of limited use. Reducing demand by reducing public investment may be counterproductive to growth if private investment is complementary to, rather than competitive with, public spending. For example, government investment in infrastructure and education may stimulate private investment.

Finally, the monetarist emphasis on slower money growth and higher interest rates may be incorrect. Ronald McKinnon, one of the creators of the financial repression/deepening concept, suggests that *increasing* interest rates will *increase* the demand for money, because higher real rates will bring more resources into the monetary sector, part of which will be held as money.[46] This would worsen inflation.

In recent years, a number of countries that had inflation rates in the hundreds and thousands of percent have had limited success with what have been called **heterodox**, or unconventional, policies aimed at inertial inflation. The chief of these policies is **indexation** of wages, wherein wages are automatically adjusted to inflation in order to offset its impact. But this intensifies price pressures, and high real wages are an incentive for employers to replace labor with capital. Indexation is often part of a politically approved pact against redistribution of income, and its removal could bring political turmoil.

A further complication involves expectations. Groups of workers whose wages are not indexed, especially those in the private sector, and businesses whose prices are the items that actually inflate will respond to expectations of inflation by pushing those wages and prices upward to protect themselves from anticipated increases in other wages and prices. Once the process begins, more than simply restrictive fiscal and monetary policies may be required to squeeze inflation out of the system, at least without heavy costs.

One response has been drastic measures to freeze wages and prices, end indexation, and freeze some other key economic variables including the exchange rate. These are intended to shock the system back to a lower-inflation stability or growth path, and avoid the adverse impact of orthodox demand-restraint policies on the level of output and employment. While wage and price controls interfere with market operations and distort resource allocation, even the relatively conservative International Monetary Fund concedes that at a certain point they may have a temporary justification, *provided* that they are accompanied by strong fiscal restraint.[47] Cases 11–2 and 11–3 summarize the experiences of Argentina and Israel in using heterodox policies to stabilize their economies. An article from the World Bank[48] accepts the conclusion that these programs can remove inertial inflation, at least temporarily, and can limit the recessionary costs of inflation reduction under these circumstances, as compared to orthodox programs. It also recognizes that such reduced inflation can contribute to fiscal discipline by restoring the real value of tax collections.

But there are warnings here as well. Wage/price freezes and other controls cannot be permanent if the economy is to respond flexibly. Inflation cannot be held down permanently without controls in the absence of fiscal discipline. Eventually, controls must be relaxed. Moreover, reliance on controls could, in the view of the World Bank and IMF, merely highlight the inability of the government to commit to fiscal discipline, thereby raising inflationary expectations and making discipline harder to achieve. If the inertial explanation is not accurate in a particular country, heterodox policies will not be appropriate.[49] One study of 13 anti-inflation programs categorizes two orthodox and five heterodox plans as unsuccessful while two orthodox and four heterodox plans were successful. However, the successful heterodox plans were accompanied by fiscal and monetary control, while the heterodox failures were unable to maintain such control.[50]

Inflation and Financial Liberalization

Financial repression, discussed in Chapter 4, is both cause and consequence of inflation. Attempts to keep interest rates below market levels, maintain high reserve requirements for banks, and otherwise overregulate financial markets hurts the availability of

HETERODOX EXPERIMENTS IN ARGENTINA

FAST FACTS

On the Map: South America

Population: 37 Million

Per Capita GNI and Rank: $7,550   (58)

Life Expectancy: Male—70   Female—77

Adult Literacy Rate: Male—77%
Female—56%

Argentina suffered under inflation that, during the second quarter of 1985, reached an average rate (wholesale prices) of 35 percent per month. The austral plan, intro-duced in June, combined attempts at deficit reduction with a fixed exchange rate and a freeze on most wages and prices. A new currency, the austral, equal to 1,000 pesos Argentinos (which had been introduced two years previously to equal 10,000 old pesos), was introduced.

Figure 11–4 shows some key variables. The growth rate of the money supply was considerably reduced, as was the fiscal deficit as a percentage of GDP, and, together with the freeze, these actions had an immediate and beneficial but temporary impact on the

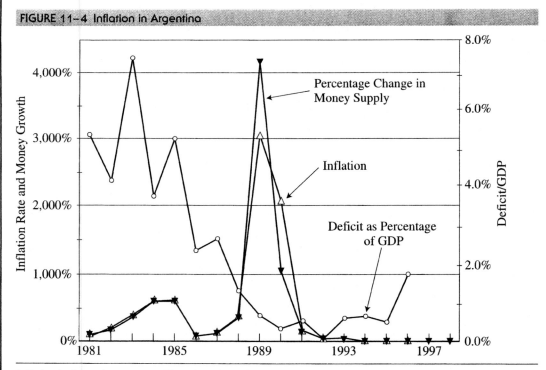

FIGURE 11–4 Inflation in Argentina

Inflation in Argentina, measured here by the GDP Deflator, was "only" around 600 percent in the mid-1980s, but soared to about 3,000 percent in 1989 and 2,000 percent in 1990. Inflation closely tracks annual increases in the money supply. In the early 1980s, those increases may have been attributable to high government budget deficits.

Source: IMF/IFS.

inflation rate. The figure shows that growth of the money supply and the fiscal deficit increased starting about the last quarter of 1986, following the relaxation of wage and price controls in April, and higher inflation levels soon followed. Recession had put pressure on the government to depart from its restraint, and some external shocks abetted the inflation, which was stopped briefly by short freezes in February and October of 1987.

In August 1988 the government again made some attempts to reduce its deficit and provide pricing guidelines, but the high government debt, high interest rates, and the difficulty of financing a large foreign debt fueled speculation against the austral.

Under the austral plan, the government was unable to maintain either the controls or fiscal discipline, and both internal and external factors led to inflationary expectations that could not be removed. The plan was itself incomplete in that it had no medium-term plan for moving from shock therapy to true stabilization and growth.

As inflation returned and expectations of future inflation heightened, Argentines increasingly opted to hold dollars, first pulling the government toward higher interest rates to keep money home, then lower rates to encourage investment. Argentina had moved from military rule to democracy only in 1983, and the entire economy, from taxes to spending to wage negotiations, was in a state of flux. Financial repression was evident in the people's lack of trust in domestic securities and money.

Considerable success was achieved later when a new government introduced a drastic program with largely monetarist tones accompanied by liberalization. When the new president took over in mid-1989, inflation was 200 percent per month. In addition to significant privatization, the currency was again changed—to a new peso—and made fully convertible to dollars at a fixed rate. A new law prevented the printing of any new

money not backed by dollars or gold. Trade was liberalized, major sectors of the economy were deregulated, many SOEs were privatized, and significant tax reform helped to eliminate the fiscal deficit. In the 17 months following peso convertibility, inflation was a total of 38 percent, and economic activity picked up. The inflation rate was 4,200 percent in 1989, 800 percent in 1990, 56 percent in 1991, and close to 20 percent for 1992.

Problems remained. Rising prices of public utilities and greater international competition hurt some companies and workers. Government health and education services suffered. Even the lower inflation rates were higher than those in the United States, so the real value of the peso continued to drop although it was nominally fixed. The result was Argentina's first trade deficit in some years.

The Argentine economy regained an important measure of stability that it had lacked for some time. The more dramatic actions of 1989, monetarist in nature, seem to have had better results, and inflation virtually disappeared in the late 1990s. Unfortunately, economic growth has also slowed.

Sources: From Michael Bruno et al., eds., *Lessons of Economic Stabilization and Its Aftermath* (Cambridge: MIT Press, 1991); Daniel Heymann, "From Sharp Disinflation to Hyperinflation, Twice: The Argentine Experience, 1985–1989," pp. 103–130; and Miguel A. Kiguel and Nissan Liviatan, "The Inflation-Stabilization Cycles in Argentina and Brazil," pp. 191–232. From Michael Bruno et al., eds., *Inflation Stabilization: The Experience of Israel, Argentina, Brazil, Bolivia, and Mexico* (Cambridge: MIT Press, 1988); Jose Luis Machinea and Jose Maria Fanelli, "Stopping Hyperinflation: The Case of the Austral Plan in Argentina, 1985–87," pp. 111–152; and Alfredo J. Canavese and Guido Di Tella, "Inflation Stabilization or Hyperinflation Avoidance? The Case of the Austral Plan in Argentina, 1985–87," pp. 153–190. Also, Ricardo Lopez Murphy, "Stabilization Programs: Recent Experience in Latin America," in *Policies for Growth: The Latin American Experience* (Washington: International Monetary Fund, 1995, pp. 9–49, and Evan Tanner and Pablo Sanguinetti, "Structural Reform and Disinflation: Lessons from Argentina's Convertibility Plan," *Journal of Developing Areas* 31, no. 4 (summer 1997), pp. 529–552.

CASE 11–3

HETERODOX STABILIZATION POLICY IN ISRAEL

FAST FACTS

On the Map: Western Asia (Middle East)

Population: 6 Million

Per Capita GNI and Rank: $16,310 (36)

Life Expectancy: Male—76 Female—80

Adult Literacy Rate: Male—98%
Female—94%

A reasonably successful heterodox program was put in place in July 1985 in Israel. Table 11–5 provides some key data. Israel had escaped the worst results of moderate-to-high inflation through an arrangement that included indexing of wages, pensions, long-term debt instruments, and, de facto, the exchange rate. But by 1984 the cost of inflation brought on the program that turned a fiscal deficit into a surplus, and temporarily froze wages, prices, credit, and the exchange rate.

The shekel was devalued by 26 percent and fixed to the dollar. Government subsidies were reduced, forcing rices up by 27 percent the first month, but prices were then subject to controls that permitted an increase of 4 percent per month for three months and then 1 percent per month over the next two years.

Nominal wages were also increased by 26 percent immediately, then frozen for three months. The supply of money and credit was frozen for six months, and government spending was reduced to keep the deficit below 5 percent of GNP.

Helped by a sense of crisis, a decline in oil prices, and the decline in the dollar's value against European currencies and the Japanese yen (reducing the price of Israeli exports), the program was a clear success initially. Inflation was sharply reduced and economic growth actually quickened, while an initial increase in unemployment was reversed. After two years the economy slowed considerably, and inflation remained stuck in the 15 percent to 20 percent range until falling to under 10 percent in 1992.

Israel suffered from some difficult political problems. The Intifada uprisings that began in 1987, and subsequent restrictions on the activities of Palestinians, reduced labor supply, tourism, and exports to the occupied territories. The recession of 1988 and 1989 is also linked to lost competitiveness resulting from an end of the wage freeze, high interest rates, and delays in devaluation of the shekel in the face of these problems. In-

TABLE 11–5 Key Macroeconomic Data for Israel

Period	GDP Growth	Unemployment Rate	Inflation Rate	Deficit (% GDP)
1980–84	2.8	5.1	189.2	10.9
1985	5.3	6.7	304.6	−1.1
1986	5.8	7.1	48.1	−3.5
1987	7.2	6.1	19.9	−0.1
1988	1.8	6.4	16.3	1.9
1989	1.5	8.9	21.0	6.1

Source: Michael Bruno and Leora (Rubin) Meridor, "The Costly Transition from Stabilization to Sustainable Growth: Israel's Case," p. 242.

flation has been reduced over the longer term. After averaging over 100 percent per year throughout the 1980s, it averaged only about 10 percent between 1990 and 1999.

Sources: Michael Bruno and Leora (Rubin) Meridor, "The Costly Transition from Stabilization to Sustainable Growth: Israel's Case," in Bruno et al., *Lessons of Economic Stabilization and Its Aftermath*, pp. 241–275, and Stanley Fischer's "Comment" on the Bruno/Meridor paper, in the same source, pp. 276–280; Michael Bruno and Sylvia Piterman, "Israel's Stabilization: A Two-Year Review," in Bruno et al., *Inflation Stabilization: The Experience of Israel, Argentina, Brazil, Bolivia, and Mexico*, pp. 3–47 and, from the same source, Alex Cukierman, "The End of High Israeli Inflation: An Experiment in Heterodox Stabilization," pp. 48–94; and Don Patinkin, "Israel's Stabilization Program of 1985, Or Some Simple Truths of Monetary Theory," *Journal of Economic Perspectives* 7, no. 2 (spring 1993), pp. 103–128.

funds that are needed to invest in development. As Figure 11–5 illustrates, below-market interest rates create excess demand and the need to ration scarce supplies of funds. The excess demand pushes up prices and lowers real interest rates. While governments gain by issuing bonds at low rates and accessing required reserves (on which interest is not paid), the economy suffers a cost in lost growth from inflation.

Table 11–6 shows 11 Asian countries' inflation performance in the 1980s. There is some tendency for countries with lower inflation rates to have higher real interest rates and lower government deficits. Also, most countries that improved their inflation performance did so with higher real rates and lower deficits.

So it is clearly in a nation's interest to consider moving toward **financial liberalization**, the freeing up of market forces in the financial sector. The removal of interest rate restrictions will raise those rates to market levels. But once an economy has become financially repressed and inflation prone, the way out is not at all easy. Some liberalization attempts have failed because of immature banking systems and capital markets. And while financial growth seems to lead to real growth, the case that higher real interest rates encourage saving is less well accepted.

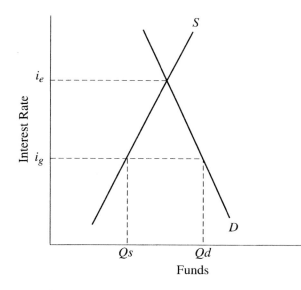

FIGURE 11–5 Below-Equilibrium Interest Rate

When the interest rate is set by government (i_g) below the equilibrium rate (i_e), the result is an excess demand for funds ($Qd > Qs$). The shortage is corrected by administered rationing, either by government or the banks.

TABLE 11–6   Inflation, Interest Rates, and Deficits

Country	Inflation		Real Interest Rate		Budget Deficit as Percentage of GDP	
	1979–1984	*1984–1989*	*1975–1981*	*1982–1988*	*1979–1984*	*1984–1989*
Philippines	17.9	9.9	−0.16	−0.32	2.3	2.7
Sri Lanka	15.7	8.1	0.27	4.08	15.6	11.4
South Korea	11.4	4.1	−2.58	5.13	2.2	0.3
Indonesia	10.9	5.9	−5.80	7.57	4.0	5.7
Bangladesh	10.8	11.0	−3.19	2.23	6.9	6.2
Nepal	10.4	10.3	4.04	3.36	7.8	9.5
India	10.0	7.8	0.07	1.13	4.2	5.3
Pakistan	8.8	5.8	−1.15	2.96	5.9	7.0
Thailand	8.0	3.4	1.52	7.67	3.5	1.1
Taiwan	7.4	1.3	2.88	5.48	0.2	−0.1
Malaysia	5.7	1.4	1.79	5.37	14.0	7.8

Source: Maxwell Fry, *Money, Interest, and Banking in Economic Development*, pp. 423, 431. Interest rates are deposit rates.

Attempts at premature financial decontrol have run into serious difficulties, with Chile as a prime example.[51] In the early 1970s, a socialist government attempted to restrain the role of the private sector, including foreign companies. This led to a reduction in investment and a withdrawal of foreign funding, leaving Chile with high inflation. When the military took power, the new regime attempted to liberalize financial markets before inflation was controlled. As inflation then began to slow, interest rates remained high, but due to a breakdown of bank supervision there was no monitoring of the creditworthiness of borrowers.

Under these conditions, **adverse selection** sets in. Adverse selection refers to perverse incentives that favor less productive active economic activity. Too-high interest rates encourage the less trustworthy investments. Ordinary borrowers with worthy investment projects may still face rates of return below the interest rates. Those most willing to borrow at rates that are too high are those with extremely risky investments, who are more likely to fail and default. So liberalization initially channels investment to risky and less productive activities unless price stability is first achieved. In Chile, international financial transactions were permitted, and large industrial conglomerates, or "Grupos," made money by borrowing dollars at low interest rates and changing them into pesos, which they lent at high rates to high-risk borrowers.

This led to the **moral hazard** problem. Moral hazard occurs when people feel they are protected from the consequences of inappropriate action and proceed to risk such action. Here, high, unstable interest rates and large losses increase the perception that the government will bail out financial institutions, and such a perception makes the institutions less cautious. This could easily become a self-fulfilling prophecy as the lack of caution leads to bank failure and increased pressure for a government bailout. Although the Chilean government had insisted that it would not bail out the banks, it lost its nerve and finally did so. When banks were renationalized, depositors were saved, but the ongoing assumption that the banks would be saved actually permitted them to behave recklessly.

From many of these episodes, economists have drawn the conclusion that sustained price stability is required before significant liberalization is safe.[52] A major reason is that an atmosphere of instability requires that nominal interest rates be high enough to assure adequate real interest rates. Such high rates reinforce financial repression rather than cure it.

For financial liberalization to succeed, inflation must be brought down first. This, most agree, requires at a minimum fiscal control—reduction of government deficits. Only with inflation under control can a liberalized banking system provide reasonable and stable interest rates, although government must carefully monitor financial institutions to assure that their practices are safe. When these steps have been taken and the domestic economy is stabilized (with growth, one hopes), it then makes sense to relax controls on foreign transactions.[53]

Inflation, then, is a double-edged sword. Its existence, in moderation, may be an indicator of structural change in progress, and it has at least a theoretical justification as a development tool. However, it is unpredictable and, outside of narrow boundaries, prone to be out of control. Like the genie out of the bottle, it may require extraordinary measures to tame.

A "Middle Road" on Inflation and Stabilization?

The inflationary episodes and anti-inflationary policies of the 1980s and 1990s have added new dimensions to the monetarist-structuralist debate over inflation. Structuralists have accepted the legitimacy of fiscal discipline as a crucial part of the approach, while continuing to point to key structural rigidities in developing economies that require more complex policies to bring inflation down to tolerable levels. Monetarists in turn have taken more seriously the importance of structural issues, while continuing to point to the essential role of government deficits and excessive money creation in maintaining inflation apart from structural or inertial conditions. The IMF and the World Bank, through their Structural Adjustment Programs (Chapter 14) have pushed fiscal and monetary restraint. They have accepted heterodox solutions in individual cases where orthodox restraint is present as well. Most agree that a country must have an independent central bank that can resist the government's desires for more money and credit if a plan based on reduced government spending and money supply is to have credibility with the public.

SUMMARY AND CONCLUSION

Governments use fiscal and monetary policies to promote growth and low rates of unemployment and inflation. For developing countries, the level of government spending is pushed upward by the desire to develop quickly. Although developing-country governments do not collect taxes at higher rates than those in wealthier countries, many of them have run large budget deficits through borrowing and printing money.

Tax systems may be weak and chaotic. Developing countries still rely heavily on indirect taxes but should anticipate switching over time. Tax systems must be structured in ways that do not discourage monetized activity and that promise the greatest revenues. The design of tax systems must account for the difficulty of collecting income taxes, the tendency for individuals and firms to switch to less productive activities in order to avoid taxes, and the structure of consumption in the economy. In most cases, low uniform rates applying to wide sectors of the economy will be more efficient than higher, differential rates.

The dangers of inflation have been sufficiently demonstrated and serve as a warning against comfortable attitudes about the desirability of moderate inflation. Immature bond markets in many developing countries have left many governments to finance their deficits by printing money. Rapid money growth, alone or combined with structural and inertial factors, has caused extremely high rates of inflation in many countries, especially in Latin America. Proposals to reduce inflation must include slower growth of the money supply and government spending, some deregulation to allow markets to respond reliably to price signals, and sometimes wage and price freezes to break inflationary spirals.

Key Terms

- adverse selection (p. 322)
- central bank (p. 309)
- deficit (p. 299)
- direct tax (p. 300)
- fiscal policy (p. 299)
- financial liberalization (p. 321)
- forced saving (p. 309)
- heterodox policies (p. 317)
- horizontal equity (p. 302)
- incidence of tax (p. 303)
- indexation (p. 317)
- indirect tax (p. 300)
- inertial inflation (p. 315)
- monetarist (p. 313)
- monetary policy (p. 306)
- moral hazard (p. 322)
- neo-structuralist (p. 315)
- orthodox (p. 314)
- progressivity (p. 302)
- seigniorage (p. 308)
- structuralist (p. 314)
- Value Added Tax (VAT) (p. 303)

Questions for Review

1. Why might the pattern of taxation in developing countries differ from that of the United States? Do developing countries tax more than the wealthier countries?

 2. How do the successful tax reforms in Bolivia and Indonesia illustrate general rules that promote more efficient tax systems?

3. Why might the distinction between fiscal and monetary policies be less clear in developing countries than in industrialized countries?

4. How do different segments of the economy gain or lose from inflation?

5. What are the fundamental arguments for and against the deliberate use of inflation as a method of financing economic development?

6. What are the monetarist and structural explanations of inflation in LDCs? What does the inertial explanation add?

7. What are the principal dangers of "orthodox" anti-inflation measures? What conditions in developing countries may call for "heterodox" measures? What are the drawbacks of such measures?

 8. How did heterodox anti-inflationary policies of Argentina and Israel illustrate the difficulties in eliminating inflation?

Related Internet Resources

 There is surprisingly little that is readily available on the Net on these topics. Probably the largest selection of items relating to fiscal and monetary policies and inflation can be found on the Web site of the International Monetary Fund, at ⟨www.imf.org⟩. You can also access the sites of most countries' central banks. For example, the search engine ⟨www.directhit.com⟩ offers a full list. Click on "Business," then Financial Services, Banking Services, Banks and Institutions, and finally "Central Banks," which has (at last check) 144 links to various central banks.

Endnotes and Further Readings

1. See William Easterly and Klaus Schmidt-Hebbel, "Fiscal Deficits and Macroeconomic Performance in Developing Countries," *World Bank Research Observer* 8, no. 2 (July 1993), pp. 211–237.

2. David L. Lindauer and Ann D. Velenchik, "Government Spending in Developing Countries: Trends, Causes, and Consequences," *World Bank Research Observer* 7, no. 1 (January 1992), pp. 59–78.

3. See Zaidi Satter, "Public Expenditure and Economic Performance: A Comparison of Developed and Low-Income Developing Economies," *Journal of International Development* 5, no. 1 (January–February 1993), pp. 27–49. Also, Michael A. Nelson and Ram D. Singh, "The Deficit–Growth Connection: Some Recent Evidence from Developing Countries," *Economic Development and Cultural Change* 43, no. 1 (October 1994), pp. 167–192.

4. George T. Abed et al., "Fiscal Reforms in Low-Income Countries: Experience Under IMF-Supported Programs," Occasional Paper No. 160 (Washington: IMF, 1998).

5. See Richard Bird, *Tax Policy and Economic Development* (Baltimore: Johns Hopkins University Press, 1992); Nicholas Kaldor, "Taxation for Economic Development," *Journal of Modern African Studies* 1, no. 1 (March 1963), pp. 7–24; Richard Goode, *Government Financing in Developing Countries* (Washington: Brookings, 1984); World Bank, "Reforming Tax Systems," in *World Development Report 1988* (New York: Oxford University Press, 1988); Bird and Oliver Oldman, eds., *Readings on Taxation in Developing Countries*, 4th ed. (Baltimore: Johns Hopkins University Press, 1990); and Robin Burgess and Nicholas Stern, "Taxation and Development," *Journal of Economic Literature* 31, no. 2 (July 1993), pp. 762–830.

6. *Lessons of Tax Reform* (Washington: World Bank, 1991), p. 19. Also, Vittorio Corbo and Klaus Schmidt-Hebbel, "Public Policies and Saving in Developing Countries," *Journal of Development Economics* 36, no. 1 (July 1991), pp. 89–115.

7. World Bank, *Lessons of Tax Reform*, p. 25; Bird, *Tax Policy and Economic Development*, p. 10; and Norman Gemmell, "Taxation and Development," in Norman Gemmell, ed., *Surveys in Development Economics* (Oxford: Basil Blackwell, 1987), p. 281.

8. Gemmell, "Taxation and Development," pp. 284–285.

9. Bird, *Tax Policy and Economic Development*, pp. 62–65.

10. See World Bank-sponsored studies, *Tax Policy in Developing Countries*, Javad Khalilzadeh-Shirazi and Anwar Shah, eds. (Washington: World Bank, 1991), and *Tax Reform in Developing Countries*, Wayne Thirsk, ed. (Washington: World Bank, 1997).

11. See Chad Leechor and Jack Mintz, "Taxation of International Income by a Capital-Importing Country: The Perspective of Thailand," pp. 100–124, and Anwar Shah and Joel Slemrod, "Taxation and Direct Foreign Investment," pp. 125–138, *Tax Policy in Developing Countries*, in Javad Khalilzadeh-Shirazi and Anwar Shah, eds. (Washington: World Bank, 1991).

12. Fareed M. A. Hassan, "Revenue-Productive Income Tax Structures and Tax Reforms in Emerging Market Economies: Evidence from Bulgaria," World Bank Policy Research Working Paper No. 1927 (Washington: World Bank, 1998).

13. Charles E. McLure, Jr. et al., "Net Wealth and Presumptive Taxation in Colombia," pp. 288–295, and Richard A. Musgrave, "Income Taxation of the Hard-to-Tax Groups," pp. 299–309, in Richard M. Bird and Oliver Oldman, *Taxation in Developing Countries*, 4th ed. (Baltimore: Johns Hopkins University Press, 1990).

14. Bird, *Tax Policy and Economic Development*, p. 122.

15. See Anwar Shah and John Whalley, "The Redistributive Impact of Taxation in Developing Countries," in Khalilzadeh-Shiraze and Shah, *Tax Policy in Developing Countries*, pp. 166–187.

16. But see Shah and Whalley (*ibid.*) on the reliability of such studies.

17. Stephen D. Younger, David E. Shan, Steven Haggblade, and Paul A. Dorosh, "Tax Incidence in Madagascar: An Analysis Using Household Data," *World Bank Economic Review* 13, no. 2 (May 1999), pp. 303–331.

18. For wealth taxes, see Bird, *Tax Policy and Economic Development*, pp. 130–144.

19. *Ibid.*, pp. 80, 136.

20. See Ehtishan Ahmad and Nicholas Stern, "Taxation for Developing Countries," in *Handbook of Development Economics*, vol. 2 (Amsterdam: Elsevier Science Publishers, 1989), p. 1074.

21. Ehtisham Ahmad and Nicholas Stern, *The Theory and Practice of Tax Reform in Developing Countries* (Cambridge: Cambridge University Press, 1991), chapter 8.

22. *World Development Report 1988*, p. 91.

23. See Nick Hanley, Jason F. Shogren, and Ben White, *Environmental Economics in Theory and Practice* (New York: Oxford University Press, 1999), chapter 4; and Robert W. Hahn, "Economic Prescriptions for Environmental Problems: How the Patient Followed the Doctor's Orders," *Journal of Economic Perspectives* 3, no. 2 (spring 1989), pp. 95–114.

24. David Malin Roodman, *Getting the Signals Right: Tax Reform to Protect the Environment and the Economy*, Worldwatch Paper No. 134 (Washington: Worldwatch Institute, May 1997).

25. See Maxwell J. Fry, *Money, Interest, and Banking in Economic Development* 2nd ed. (Baltimore: Johns Hopkins University Press, 1995).

26. *Ibid.*, p. 431.

27. See references to the term in *ibid.*

28. Reid W. Click, "Seigniorage in a Cross-Section of Countries," *Journal of Money, Credit and Banking* 30, no. 2 (May 1998), pp. 154–171.

29. *Ibid.*, and Joseph H. Haslag, "Seigniorage Revenue and Monetary Policy: Some Preliminary Evidence," Federal Reserve Bank of Dallas *Economic Review* (3rd quarter 1998), pp. 10–20.

30. Rudiger Dornbusch and Stanley Fischer, "Moderate Inflation," *World Bank Economic Review* 7, no. 1 (January 1993), pp. 1–44.

31. See Alex Cukierman, Steven B. Webb, and Bilin Neyapti, "Measuring the Independence of Central Banks and Its Effects on Policy Outcomes," *World Bank Economic Review* 6, no. 4 (September 1992), pp. 353–398, and Alberto Alesina and Lawrence H. Summers, "Central Bank Independence and Macroeconomic Performance: Some Comparative Evidence," *Journal of Money, Credit and Banking* 25, no. 2 (May 1993), pp. 151–162. These findings have been contradicted by Robert J. Barro in his *Determinants of Economic Growth: A Cross-Country Empirical Study* (Cambridge: MIT Press, 1997), pp. 104–111.

32. See Harry G. Johnson, "Is Inflation the Inevitable Price of Rapid Development or a Retarding Factor in Economic Growth," *Malayan Economic Review* 11, no. 1 (April 1966), and Graeme S. Dorrance, "The Effect of Inflation on Economic Development," *International Monetary Fund Staff Papers* 10, no. 1 (March 1963), pp. 1–47.

33. Michael Sarel, "Nonlinear Effects of Inflation on Economic Growth," *International Monetary Fund Staff Papers*, 43, no. 1 (March 1996), pp. 199–215; Barro, *Determinants of Economic Growth: A Cross-Country Empiral Study*, pp. 95–118; and Atish Ghosh and Steven Phillips, "Warning: Inflation May be Harmful to Your Growth," *International Monetary Fund Staff Papers* 45, no. 4 (December 1998), pp. 672–710.

34. See Dornbusch and Fischer, "Moderate Inflation," as well as *World Development Report 1991*, p. 110, and Barro, *Determinants of Economic Growth: A Cross-Country Empiral Study*, p. 93.

35. Don Patinkin, "Israel's Stabilization Program of 1985, Or Some Simple Truths of Monetary Theory," *Journal of Economic Perspectives* 7, no. 2 (spring 1993), pp. 103–128.

36. See B. J. Moore, "Inflation and Financial Deepening," *Journal of Development Economics* 20, no. 1 (January–February 1986), pp. 125–133.

37. See Roberto de Olivera Campos, "Economic Development and Inflation with Special Reference to Latin America," in *Development Plans and Programmes* (Paris: OECD Development Center, 1964); Colin Kirkpatrick and Frederick Nixson, "Inflation and Stabilization Policy in LDCs," in Norman Gemmell, ed., *Surveys in Development Economics*, pp. 172–202; and Andres Velasco, "Monetarism and Structuralism:

Some Macroeconomic Lessons," in Patricio Meller, ed., *The Latin American Development Debate: Neostructuralism, Neomonetarism, and Adjustment Processes* (Boulder, CO: Westview Press, 1991), pp. 43–58.

38. See Juan-Antonio Morales, "Inflation Stabilization in Bolivia," in Michael Bruno et al., eds., *Inflation Stabilization: The Experience of Israel, Argentina, Brazil, Bolivia, and Mexico* (Cambridge: MIT Press, 1988), pp. 307–346, and Colin D. Campbell, "Seigniorage and Bolivia's Runaway Inflation, 1982–1985," *Eastern Economic Journal* 21, no. 3 (summer 1995), pp. 399–409.

39. See Bijan B. Aghevli and Mohsin Khan, "Government Deficits and the Inflationary Process in Developing Countries," *International Monetary Fund Staff Papers* 25, no. 3 (September 1978), pp. 383–416.

40. See Patrice Franko, *The Puzzle of Latin American Development* (Lanham, MD: Rowman and Littlefield, 1999), pp. 126–128.

41. An early statement of the structuralist thesis was Raul Prebisch, "Economic Development or Monetary Stability: The False Dilemma," *Economic Bulletin for Latin America* 6, no. 1 (March 1961).

42. See Lance Taylor, *Varieties of Stabilization Experience: Towards Sensible Macroeconomics in the Third World* (Oxford: Clarendon Press, 1988).

43. Celso Furtado, *The Economic Growth of Brazil: A Survey from Colonial to Modern Times* (Berkeley: University of California Press, 1963), pp. 253, 255.

44. See Chihan Bilginsoy, "Inflation, Growth, and Import Bottlenecks in the Turkish Manufacturing Industry," *Journal of Development Economics* 42, no. 1 (October 1993), pp. 11–131.

45. Lance Taylor, *Varieties of Stabilization Experience: Towards Sensible Macroeconomics in the Third World*, p. 147.

46. See Ronald McKinnon, *Money and Capital in Economic Development* (Washington: The Brookings Institution, 1973), pp. 86–87.

47. See Peter T. Knight, F. Desmond McCarthy, and Sweder van Wijnbergen, "Escaping Hyperinflation" (in Argentina, Brazil, and Israel), *Finance & Development* 25, no. 4 (December 1986), pp. 14–17, and "Hyperinflation: Taming the Beast" (in those three countries and Bolivia), *The Economist* (November 15, 1986), pp. 55–64.

48. Miguel A. Kiguel and Nissan Liviatan, "When Do Heterodox Stabilization Programs Work? Lessons from Experience," *World Bank Research Observer* 7, no. 1 (January 1992), pp. 35–57. For an earlier evaluation, see Mario I. Blejer and Adrienne Cheasty, "High Inflation, Heterodox Stabilization, and Fiscal Policy," *World Development* 16, no. 8 (August 1988), pp. 867–881.

49. Ana Dolores Novaes, "Revisiting the Inertial Inflation Hypothesis for Brazil," *Journal of Development Economics* 42, no. 1 (October 1993), pp. 89–110.

50. Edward J. Amadeo, "Distributive and Welfare Effects of Inflation and Stabilization," in IMF, *Policies for Growth: The Latin American Experience* (Washington: International Monetary Fund, 1995), pp. 54–72.

51. See Carlos Diaz-Alejandro, "Good-Bye Financial Repression, Hello Financial Crash," *Journal of Development Economics* 19, no. 1–2 (September–October 1985), pp. 1–24.

52. See Ronald I. McKinnon, *The Order of Economic Liberalization: Finanicial Control in the Transition to a Market Economy* (Baltimore: Johns Hopkins University Press, 1991), pp. 67–77.

53. See Mario I. Blejer and Silvia B. Sagari, "Sequencing the Liberalization of Financial Markets," *Finance & Development* 25, no. 1 (March 1988), pp. 18–20. For Argentina and Uruguay, see Roberto Zahler, "Financial Strategies in Latin America: The Southern Cone Experience," in Patricio Meller, ed., *The Latin American Development Debate: Neostructuralism, Neomonetarism, and Adjustment Processes*, pp. 101–127.

CHAPTER

12

FOREIGN TRADE AND DEVELOPMENT STRATEGY

*Trade is in its nature free, finds its
own channel, and best directeth its
own course: and all laws to give it
rules and directions, and to limit and
circumscribe it, may serve the particular
ends of private men, but are seldom
advantageous to the public.*

—CHARLES D'AVENANT (1656–1714)

INTRODUCTION

One of the basic tenets of economics is that growth and development require specialization, division of labor, and growing markets. Even large countries such as the United States and the former Soviet Union needed, increasingly, access to the outside world. Today, trade is essential for economic development.

It would be logical to conclude, therefore, that the more trade the better. This conclusion has been challenged, however, and the objectives of this chapter are to outline the arguments and show how countries are moving toward a greater emphasis on foreign trade. Experience generally supports the contention of economic theory that an "outward" orientation is better than an "inward" orientation in promoting economic development.

Table 12–1 shows significant changes in world trading patterns over three decades. In 1965, developing-countries' exports were largely based on primary commodities such as unprocessed food and minerals, as opposed to manufactured goods in the high-income group. By 1999, patterns were more similar, although many developing-countries' manufactures were often more traditional goods such as textiles, clothing, and shoes. Table 12–2 shows that exports have grown continuously but with no consistent patterns among income groups over time.

Debate over the role of trade in economic development has centered around the contention that trade has been and will be the **engine of growth**—the key factor that can propel a country to higher levels of development. This view is supported by historical examples, including the economies of Taiwan and South Korea in our own time. Those who disagree point to a number of African countries to claim that although trade may have been an engine of growth for the currently industrialized countries, today it serves only to entrench an international division of labor in which

329

TABLE 12–1   Composition of Merchandise Trade (%)

	Primary Goods		Manufactures	
Exports	**1965**	**1999**	**1965**	**1999**
Low Income	69	48	31	52
Lower-Middle Income	82	38	16	62
Upper-Middle Income	70	27	32	73
High Income	31	18	69	82
	Primary Goods		**Manufactures**	
Imports	**1965**	**1999**	**1965**	**1999**
Low Income	30	37	70	63
Lower-Middle Income	34	30	65	70
Upper-Middle Income	37	24	63	76
High Income	48	23	52	77

Primary goods include food, agricultural raw materials, fuel, metals, and minerals.

Sources: World Development Report 1992 and *World Development Indicators 2001*.

TABLE 12–2   Growth of Exports (% per Year)

	1965–1980	**1980–1990**	**1965–1997**
Low Income	5.1	5.4	4.2
Lower-Middle Income	NA	7.2	4.0
Upper-Middle Income	3.9	1.9	6.9
High Income	7.3	4.3	5.5

Data for 1965–1980 and 1980–1990 are merchandise trade only. The 1965–1997 data include goods and services. Another possible reason for the incongruities in the data come from the changing country composition of the categories over time.

NA = Not Available.

Sources: World Development Report 1992 and *World Development Indicators 1999*.

poor countries supply the materials for the manufactures of the rich. If this were the case, countries should reduce the role of trade in their economies by promoting development that will substitute for imports, either alone or in regional associations. The debate over how trade relates to growth and development is an important one.

DEVELOPMENT AND THE THEORY OF INTERNATIONAL TRADE

We will now review some trade theory, examine the arguments and evidence for both views, and look at the role of the developed countries.

Comparative Advantage

David Ricardo described in detail, almost 200 years ago, how even countries with generally inferior capabilities could benefit by specializing in those activities in which they had the greatest relative cost advantage.[1] This principle of **comparative advantage** shows that productivity is enhanced if each country specializes in those goods for which it has lowest opportunity cost. The result of such a system is a more efficient global use of resources, greater output and consumption, and lower prices. This is true even in the short run when resources are fixed, apart from any growth that occurs over longer periods. Appendix 12A provides an advanced analysis of the benefits of trade.

What determines the goods for which a country has a comparative advantage? Eli Heckscher and Goran Ohlin pointed to the correspondence between a country's **factor endowments**—that is, how much land, labor, and capital it has—and the **factor intensity** of the goods it produces. Products that require much land and relatively little labor (such as wheat) should be produced by those countries with high ratios of land to labor, while those goods that have higher labor requirements (such as inexpensive clothing) should be produced by countries with high ratios of labor to land and labor to capital. Capital-intensive goods, such as jet aircraft, should be produced in those countries that have accumulated significant amounts of capital goods.

This approach helps us anticipate trade patterns between developed and developing countries. It reinforces the common assumption that developing countries would naturally produce food, raw materials, and cheap manufactures. Whether they could do so and still develop is a question that persists.

The theory of comparative advantage also suggests that free trade should increase the relative income of the factor of production that is abundant in each country. Countries that specialize in labor-intensive goods find that labor's income will increase over time as more of these goods are exported. Developing countries would export goods that require less skilled labor and less capital, while importing more capital-intensive goods from the industrialized countries. They could take advantage of world markets to achieve economies of scale in their best industries, thus earning the foreign exchange necessary for their imports.

As the problems of the developing countries came to prominence with the post-World War II economic recovery, some economists emphasized the *dynamic* benefits of trade.[2] Developing countries could import not only raw materials and intermediate goods to pursue production, but also capital, technology, ideas, and skills through both products and foreign investment. Imported goods would provide needed competition for domestic producers. These advantages would not only spur domestic production, but also enable countries to be efficient exporters and to then import still more goods and technology. As the currently developed countries had gained from trade, so trade would be the engine of growth for developing countries.

Objections to the Engine of Growth Thesis

Some economists have objected to the notion that comparative advantage provides either a clear criterion for evaluating modern trade outcomes or a sound basis for recommending how today's developing countries should proceed. We can consider these criticisms as variations on **export pessimism**, the idea that developing countries cannot count on exports to propel their development.

Hla Myint,[3] a Burmese economist, suggested that developing-country exports could best be explained by a theory that preceded Ricardo: Adam Smith's **vent-for-surplus** theory. At least in the early stages of development, local production is less than optimal because the lack of integrated markets limits the demand for goods. The introduction of Western firms and new infrastructure helps somewhat to link markets, and foreign demand brings additional production. However, Myint noted that little feedback is provided to the rest of the economy. He concluded that colonialism in developing countries created dual economies. Initially, colonial policy pursued development through expanding agricultural and mineral exports, which failed to achieve linkages with the colony as a whole. Roads and railroad lines, for example, ran directly from the plantations or mines to the main port where the product would be sent back to Europe or America. The export sector was capital and land intensive, with little skilled labor needed. Where this was not true, for example in mining, production units often were economically isolated, using as little labor as possible.

Gunnar Myrdal[4] also focused on dualism, suggesting that these exports, instead of generating more equal incomes due to increases in the price of labor, increased inequality within and among countries. The only spread of incomes outside the areas of production occurred in the cities where colonial governments were located, accounting partly for the growth of national capitals in port cities, far from much of the local population. Local industries were frequently destroyed or used in the service of primary exports, the abundance of labor kept wages down, and low domestic demand prevented the domestic market from widening. Capital flowed *out* of the colonies, despite its scarcity, because of insufficient markets and the risks of reinvestment.

Finally, Ragnar Nurkse[5] suggested that modern developing countries should not rely on trade in the same way that Europe had a century earlier. Nineteenth-century trade consisted of primary commodities that Europe imported from Asia, Africa, and Latin America, in exchange for simple manufactured exports. In the twentieth century, however, the industrialized economies dominated the world with trade among themselves, largely in manufactured goods, leaving developing countries still on the margin.

Terms of Trade: The Prebisch Controversy

The principal assault on the engine of growth thesis was the charge that the terms of trade between developed and developing countries were deteriorating for the latter.[6] In the simplest case, a country's terms of trade are measured by comparing an index of the prices of its export goods to an index of the prices of its import goods. This ratio, Px/Pm, known as the **net barter terms of trade**, can then be traced over time and gives one view of the purchasing power of a country's exports in terms of its imports. For example, a developing country may export coffee and tea while importing a broad range of manufactured goods. If the prices of coffee and tea decline, say from an index of 100 to 90, while manufactures prices are rising, say from an index of 100 to 110, the net barter terms of trade decline from 1.00 (or 100) to 0.82 (or 82). A dollar's worth of exports could have originally purchased a dollar's worth of imports but now buys only 82 cents' worth.

The Prebisch–Singer Thesis

Raul Prebisch was an Argentine economist who became interested in trade between developing and developed economies. He worked for the UN Economic Commission for Latin America (ECLA) and became the first Secretary General of the UN Conference on Trade and Development (UNCTAD). He suggested in the 1950s that the prices of primary exports of the poor countries were deteriorating *as the result* of trade, while prices of the manufactured products of the industrialized countries were either constant or increasing; developing countries were suffering from worsening living standards and also becoming stuck in a pattern of producing and exporting primary products, which would keep them poor. Similar findings were reported by Hans Singer. The Prebisch–Singer thesis became the basis of a broad approach to development policy in many countries.

Economic theory generally suggests that the opening of trade will lower the price of a country's imports (and the domestic goods that substitute for imports) by reducing barriers and increasing competition and the supply of those goods. On the other hand, by adding foreign demand to the domestic demand for a country's export goods, those prices should rise. The static conclusion (that is, assuming no economic impact apart from the changes in production and trade from the reduction of barriers) is that the ratio Px/Pm should rise for all countries. Prebisch concluded from his research that while this was in fact true for the developed countries, the developing countries' terms of trade were falling. He suggested a number of reasons for this conclusion:

First, **Engel's law** suggests that the income elasticity of demand is lower for primary commodities than for manufactured goods. As income rises, the demand for primary products tends to rise more slowly than the demand for manufactures. Unless the supply of primary products is sharply reduced, which is unlikely in most cases, prices for primary products remain low and prices for manufactured products rise more quickly.

Second, improvements in technology do not have parallel benefits. In the industrialized countries they result in higher labor productivity, which should reduce the cost and prices of manufactured goods. However, the relatively high demand for labor, union pressure, and the oligopolistic nature of product markets ensure that the prices of their exports do not fall. For developing countries however, with lower labor demand and more competitive world markets for their primary products, the result of better technology is reduced wages and prices.

Third, there has been a trend, especially since the end of World War II, for the substitution of synthetics for natural resources, thus slowing the industrialized countries' demand for the products of the developing countries. In addition, more efficient production has reduced the materials component of many manufactured products.[7]

Finally, Prebisch pointed to **protectionism** in the industrialized countries: barriers to the entry of developing-country products.

The Prebisch–Singer thesis is an example of **immiserizing growth**. It is conceivable that large volumes of exports, for example, Brazilian coffee, could lower the world price and shift the terms of trade to such an extent that the exporting country has lower utility due to greater exports. We can extend the principle to apply to many small countries exporting the same commodity and to developing countries as a group. For example, if several developing countries specialized in and produced more cocoa or bananas, increasing supplies could bring lower commodity prices and a decline in the terms of trade.

Challenges to the Prebisch Analysis

Prebisch claimed that the data for the period 1870 to 1936 supported his thesis. A number of weaknesses, summarized in Development Spotlight 12–1, showed up in his analysis, but following many years of skepticism, there is increasing appreciation for

THE PREBISCH THESIS: CHALLENGING THE DATA

While Prebisch's thesis remains a matter of controversy, his original study had many flaws. Lack of data caused him to infer Argentina's exports to Britain from Britain's import statistics. The data did not separate out transport costs, which were falling rapidly. Also, the trade data are misleading because changes in quality of goods, which was increasing over time, are not always reflected in higher prices. Exchange rates changed over the period, so lower prices paid by Britain may not have meant lower prices received by Argentines. And Prebisch's data ended in 1936—in the midst of the Great Depression—when world agricultural prices were exceptionally low. Finally, Prebisch used the net barter terms of trade (Px/Pm). In order to reflect the ability of countries to afford imports on the basis of export revenues, it may be more relevant to use the **income terms of trade** (($Px \times Qx)/Pm$).

the difficulties of countries that rely on primary exports. Aside from price instability (addressed later in this chapter) the evidence seems to support a long-term decline in prices of many primary commodities in the twentieth century.[8]

Significant downward slides during World War I and the Great Depression of the 1930s were followed by major improvements, but a quantum leap in commodity prices during World War II began a new downward trend until the early 1970s. Long-term downward price trends have occurred for specific commodities. A recent study of the 1900 to 1992 period shows secular declines for 17 major commodities, increases for 4, and no trend for 3 others.[9] These declines in prices of primary commodities have been accompanied by steadily rising prices of products imported by developing countries. Figure 12–1 shows commodity prices varying significantly, with many having spiked in the mid-1970s and early 1980s but otherwise with little trend. When terms of trade data are calculated and separated by region, large differences occur. Asian terms of trade have been relatively stable for many years, while Latin America faced a sharp improvement in the mid-1970s followed by a long decline, and the Middle East depends heavily on oil prices.

Declining terms of trade suggest that developing countries should diversify their economies into manufacturing, as we would expect anyway from development. The question remains whether this should occur through an internal process, shielded from world trade, or through attempts to enter the world market for manufactured goods.

Temporary Protection: The Infant Industry Argument

If trade is a potential engine of growth, but requires a shift from primary commodities to manufactures, it might make sense to temporarily protect local industries from foreign competition. Although economists are suspicious of special-interest pleading, some accept the **infant industry** argument. The argument states that new industries cannot compete internationally in their early stages. Domestic markets are too small to allow firms to reach an efficient scale of production. It could therefore be acceptable to protect the industry temporarily until it matured. (Alexander

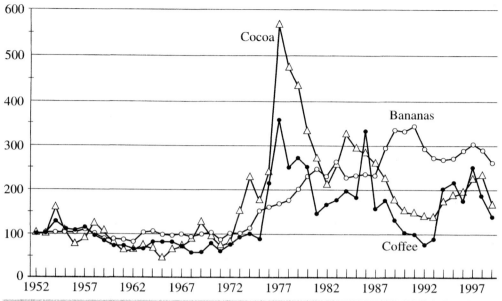

FIGURE 12–1A Commodity Prices (Index: 1952 = 100)

As Figures 12–1a, 12–1b, and 12–1c show, many raw commodity prices share a common history. Despite different degrees of fluctuations, prices showed no general trend during the 1950s and 1960s. There was a general price spike in the early to mid-1970s, followed again by a constant trend, at higher levels, through the end of the 1990s.

Source: IMF/IFS.

FIGURE 12–1B Commodity Prices (Index: 1952 = 100)

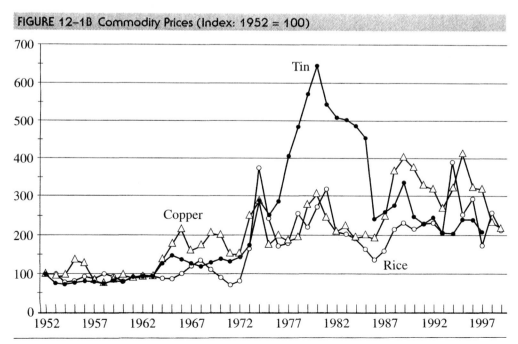

Source: IMF/IFS.

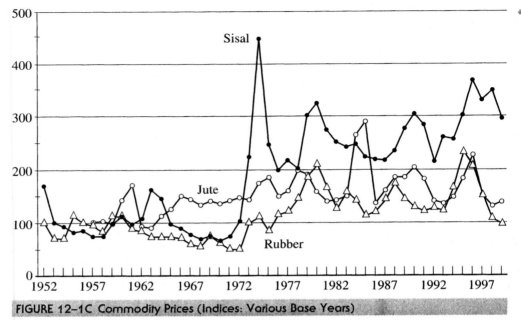

FIGURE 12–1C Commodity Prices (Indices: Various Base Years)

Source: IMF/IFS.

FIGURE 12–1D Regional Terms of Trade (1995 = 100)

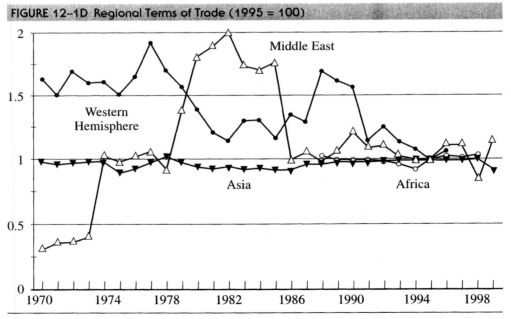

Regional terms of trade have varied considerably, however. Africa and Asia have been flat, while the Middle East and the Western Hemisphere have seen much greater fluctuations.

Source: IMF/IFS.

Hamilton used this argument to justify tariffs in the post-revolutionary United States.) However, protection brings inefficiencies, which are usually politically expedient and difficult to turn around, so more appropriate remedies should be sought.[10]

One argument for infant industry protection is that a new industry initially has high costs and low (or negative) profits, making firms unlikely to receive loans even though economies of scale would eventually bring costs down. Economists argue that if this situation is understood, lending institutions will extend the terms of loans for a period long enough for economies of scale to occur. If capital markets are also poorly developed and less likely to take on such risks, governments should provide better information, or subsidize interest rates or production directly, rather than use the less efficient approach of protection.

What if firms fear losing their investment in training a labor force when trained workers take other jobs? This would impose costs on the firms that provide training, and protection would raise prices of goods to help defray those costs. Economists would prefer that governments fund training, preferably through credits to the firms that provide it, and stay away from protection. Finally, developing countries will at least initially lack the infrastructure required for a domestic company to be competitive in world markets; the answer would be to provide the infrastructure rather than protect the industries.

All these arguments against infant industry protection make economic sense, but the alternatives are often more difficult to accomplish. Virtually all developing-country governments from eighteenth-century Britain to the present have relied heavily on tariffs as a form of revenue because often they are easier to collect than domestic taxes. Alternatives to protection require that governments first collect taxes and then carry out programs, both of which may be difficult, or reduce tax revenues through credits to firms.

In addition, developing countries might protest that what hinders their exports is the control over international markets held by companies in developed countries. This problem has no domestic remedy. Although some developing countries have cracked world markets in goods such as machine tools and computers, it is a very difficult task and frequently has required practices such as export subsidies that the developed countries object to.

Whatever the reason, successfully carrying out an infant industry policy is extremely difficult. Government policy makers have to determine which industries have a true potential for comparative advantage and resist the pleas of special interests. The most efficient means of nurturing an infant industry must be used and the supports removed at an appropriate time. But protection or subsidies may lead to monopoly and inefficiency, thus wasting resources. Protection reduces the incentive for a government to undertake more difficult tasks, and trade barriers are hard to reverse, so protection is hardly risk free.

Even large, middle-income countries may find success difficult to achieve, although some East Asian and Latin American countries have succeeded. One controversial attempt has been Brazil's decision to promote a computer industry. By reserving certain segments of the industry to local firms and restricting imports, Brazil has in fact "raised" an infant industry that, while still not fully competitive on an international level, seems to be closing the gap in this fast-moving industry.[11]

Dynamic Comparative Advantage

Trade need not be stuck in a pattern dictated by existing resource endowments. Development involves changes in economic structure, brought about by investment—itself an activity that creates new factor endowments. While some developing countries have not climbed out of the primary-commodity rut, many have and, in the process, have shown the potential of development strategies that act to *change* a country's comparative advantage. Many Latin American economies, forced to substitute for imports during the 1930s and 1940s by depression and war, developed manufacturing, and East Asian countries promoted exports after the 1960s to join the world markets for sophisticated manufactured goods. Our next step is to look at the debates over strategies for accomplishing this switch.

REDIRECTING THE ENGINE OF GROWTH: IMPORT SUBSTITUTION (IS)

As development proceeds, we expect that a country will begin to produce at least some of the goods that it initially imports. This kind of import substitution is a natural outcome of the development process. Numerous developing countries, however, identifying industrialization with development, have pushed ahead rapidly with measures to promote manufacturing when comparative advantage was not obvious. Government promotion of industrial development by restricting imports is referred to as a strategy of **Import Substitution (IS)**.

Why IS?

Much of the world's development has occurred in countries that have deliberately chosen to promote industries that would substitute for imports. In the second half of the twentieth century, IS has been chosen by a number of developing-country governments on the basis of export pessimism, the presumed superiority of industry to agriculture, and the assumption that developing countries could work backward from the production of consumer goods to producing intermediate products and capital goods and, ultimately, to a vertically integrated economy.

Developing domestic industry would create jobs and linkages to further development. It could help achieve balanced trade by reducing the need for imports and promote technological advance. Industries could begin as infants, using import experience to determine the viability of the market. They might then mature and contribute to export earnings.

Why import so many automobiles if they can be produced at home? Why not learn how to make the components, especially if there are domestic sources of the raw materials that are required? Later, learn to produce the machinery that makes the components and occupies the assembly line. Ultimately, an economy might not only eliminate its dependence on the rich countries for their cars, but also build the capacity to produce machinery of all types: Development happens.

Instruments of IS and Their Costs

How would we go about substituting domestic production for imports? An IS policy would make locally produced goods more accessible than imports by restricting the availability of the foreign products or by making imports more expensive. The most common measures are tariffs and quotas, or quantitative restrictions (QRs).

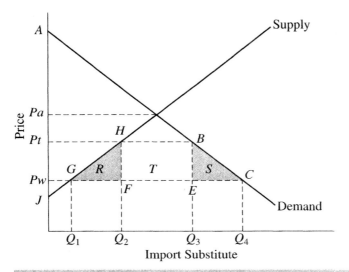

FIGURE 12–2 Effect of a Tariff

Without trade, *Pa* is the domestic price for the import-substitute product. The elimination of barriers lowers the price to *Pw* (world price).

The imposition of the tariff raises the price (*Pt*), with losses to consumers in excess of gains to producers and the government. Consumption falls from Q_4 to Q_3, domestic production rises from Q_1 to Q_2, and imports fall from Q_1Q_4 to Q_2Q_3. Consumer surplus (the value received by those who would be willing to pay more than the market price of the product) falls from *ACPw* to *ABPt*. Domestic producer surplus (the difference between the marginal cost and price for all but the marginal unit of output) rises from *JGPw* to *JHPt*. The government collects the tariff (area *T*), and the net loss is the combined areas *R* and *S*.

Areas *R* and *S* are deadweight loss. Area *R* represents inefficient use of resources allocated to industries not enjoying comparative advantage. Area *S* is a pure loss of utility to consumers who are forced to pay more and receive less.

Tariffs

A **tariff** is a tax on an imported good. It will increase the price of imports to permit higher-cost domestic industry to compete. Figure 12–2 shows a tariff added to the world price of the imported product, resulting in a net loss to the domestic economy.

Quantitative Restrictions

Quantitative restrictions, either **quotas** or outright import bans, are imposed to restrict supply of certain imports. They increase demand for local goods and raise their prices. Government can ration foreign currency holdings to those uses deemed most supportive of its development strategy. Permission to import the allowable amounts may be auctioned off to the highest bidder, allocated by the government according to development priorities, dispensed as a means of political patronage, or simply left to the interplay of bureaucracy and greed. Tariffs, by simply putting a tax on imports, leave allocation of those imports to the market. Appendix 12B compares the tariff and quota.

Effective Protection

Tariffs, while preferable, are a deceptively simple solution. They are easy to impose, usually at the request of domestic firms. But some protected items are inputs to goods intended for export and domestic consumption and raise their prices.

Development Spotlight 12–2 explains the idea of **effective protection**.[12] This shows what happens when a company that is shielded from foreign competition by a tariff has its own costs increased by tariffs on its inputs. If a product uses a lot of imported inputs, and their tariffs are higher than for the finished product, the imported finished good will be cheaper than the protected product: Effective protection will actually be negative. A World Bank study showed rates of effective protection of –85 percent in some Brazilian manufactured goods in 1980 to 1981 and average effective protection of –21 percent in Brazilian agriculture for that period.[13] On the other hand, high effective protection is also troublesome. It promotes assembly of final products

---

DEVELOPMENT SPOTLIGHT 12–2

EFFECTIVE PROTECTION

The effective rate of protection (E) is calculated as:

$$E = \frac{V^* - V}{V}$$

where V^* is value added at tariff-distorted prices and V is value added at world prices. The higher the tariff a firm pays on its imported components, the lower will be its gain from the tariff on its own product. In the Table 12–3 example, a local firm is producing automobiles from imported parts.

If only the automobile is protected, by a 100 percent tariff, domestic value added is $12,000 instead of $2,000, an effective protection rate of 500 percent. In Tariff Scheme B, the tariff on autos is the same as the tariff on parts, and autos remain protected at an effective rate of 100 percent. However, with Tariff Scheme C, where parts have a somewhat higher tariff (125 percent), value added domestically is no more than with no tariffs at all ($2,000), so the gain to manufacturers (hence, the effective protection) is zero. With Scheme D, auto manufacturers pay a much higher tariff on parts than the one that protects them. Effective protection is actually negative: Domestic production is at a disadvantage compared to imports. In general, effective protection is higher as the tariff on the finished good is higher, the nominal tariff on inputs is lower, and the share of imported inputs on finished goods is higher.

TABLE 12–3 Effective Protection (EP)

	Auto	Imported Parts	Value Added	EP Rate
Free Trade Price	$10,000	$ 8,000	$ 2,000	
Tariff Scheme A	100%	0%		
Protected Price	$20,000	$ 8,000	$12,000	500%
Tariff Scheme B	100%	100%		
Protected Price	$20,000	$16,000	$ 4,000	100%
Tariff Scheme C	100%	125%		
Protected Price	$20,000	$18,000	$ 2,000	0%
Tariff Scheme D	100%	150%		
Protected Price	$20,000	$20,000	$ 0	–100%

from imported parts, rather than use of domestic resources. It also promotes rigidity to the extent that local production is dependent on imported inputs.

The point is that if a government engages in deliberate import substitution, it has to be extremely careful not to undo its own objectives by granting every request for tariff protection. High effective protection promotes dependence on imported parts. High tariffs on imported inputs result in negative protection that, by requiring that potential exporters be exceptionally efficient to succeed, is exactly the opposite of what is intended.

The Exchange Rate

The **exchange rate** is the number of units of another country's currency you can buy with one unit of your currency (e.g. 10 pesos per dollar) or, conversely, the number of units of your own currency that foreigners can buy with one unit of their currency (10 cents per peso). Most currency values are determined by markets. For a government engaged in IS, it might seem logical to deliberately keep the value of its currency low in order to keep foreign currencies and goods expensive and protect domestic production. The opposite typically occurs however: IS-oriented governments have kept their currencies priced *above* what would be indicated by world market conditions. Not only does this keep import prices artificially low, but it keeps export prices artificially high, reducing the country's ability to earn foreign exchange through exports. Why would they do this?

Import restrictions increase the prices of imported goods. Higher import prices, by dampening competition, keep domestic prices high and protect local firms with high costs. But a lower-valued currency increases the price of *all* imports, not just those a country wishes to protect. Because such countries are frequently dependent on imports for a wide range of goods, the currency's value is kept high and import prices low.

The lower import prices must be compensated for by *additional* protection on selected goods, further distorting the allocation of resources. The higher world prices of the country's exports discourage those exports, adding to the problems incurred by the initial import restrictions. By itself, the overvaluation causes an external payments deficit that, in many cases, encourages foreign borrowing (see Chapter 14).

Domestic Policy Measures

IS is normally accompanied by other policies that distort price signals and render policy making more difficult. These include price controls, for example on food and public services; factor price distortions (minimum wages, subsidized interest rates); and a set of taxes and subsidies designed to stimulate specific industries.

Problems with IS

It is important to keep in mind that the substitution of domestic production for some foreign goods is a natural result of the development process. And IS, like all intervention strategies, clearly has the potential to accomplish at least some of its objectives, at a cost that may be temporarily acceptable to governments and significant portions of a nation's population. However, IS policies have brought significant problems.

- Emphasis on capital-intensive production can nullify expected gains in employment and increase dependence on imported machinery and parts.
- Protected investment in manufacturing typically takes resources from agriculture.

- Protection increases costs to farmers, worsening the rural–urban terms of trade.
- Overvalued exchange rates reduce exports, particularly of agricultural goods.
- High import prices for industrial inputs and sheltered home markets diminish efficiency and competitiveness.
- The combination of higher imports and lower exports worsens trade balances, encourages foreign borrowing, and can easily lead to debt problems.
- Many countries' domestic markets are too small to support large-scale manufacturing,[14] encouraging monopoly. When income distribution is heavily skewed toward the rich, markets may be smaller still.
- The political nature of import restrictions increases the likelihood of confusion and inefficiency through complexity and rent seeking.

The IS Experience

Historically, IS policies have had some striking results. World depression in the 1930s and economic isolation during World War II led Brazil into IS policies. In 1939, 63 percent of its industrial output was in the food and textile industries, and only 18 percent in intermediate goods such as minerals, metal goods, equipment, and machinery. By 1958, food and textiles accounted for only 44 percent, and intermediate products accounted for 33 percent. South Korea implemented IS policies, especially during the 1950s and 1960s. Between 1960 and 1965, industry's share of GDP increased from 19 percent to 24 percent, and exports of manufactures increased from 13 percent of the total to 61 percent.[15]

Often, however, the results of IS have been disappointing. In those countries that did not move to a more trade-oriented regime, protection became a political tool, with government officials easily succumbing to increasing pressures. Substituting for consumer goods imports shifted imports back to the capital goods sectors: Dependence and inefficiency worsened. Borrowing led to government deficits and foreign debt.

One major review of economic performance in the 1970s identified a number of inappropriate policies including an IS approach in those countries—Ghana, Tanzania, Mexico, Uruguay—with the worst performance.[16] Case 12–1 provides an example. Trade policies were not the only problems in these countries, but IS strategies tend to be accompanied by other policies that have the same objective. Many of these policies involve price distortions: exchange rates, wage rates, interest rates, and prices of imported and domestic goods. A model of Pakistan's economy concludes that the combination of trade, exchange rate, and agricultural price policies over the 1983 to 1987 period reduced wheat production by 24 percent and rice by 52 percent. "Without price interventions—either direct or indirect—farm incomes from . . . five major crops would have been 40 percent higher during the same period."[17]

In Defense of IS

Negative findings do not end the discussion of the IS strategy. Some structuralist and radical critics see the failure of IS as due to its reliance on world and domestic markets, and some harmful domestic policies. They call for more planned development with appropriate policies, especially in favor of agriculture. Such an argument is diffi-

IMPORT SUBSTITUTION IN GHANA

FAST FACTS

On the Map: West Africa

Population: 19 Million

Per Capita GNI and Rank: $400   (166)

Life Expectancy: Male—57   Female—59

Adult Literacy Rate: Male—79%
Female—61%

Political instability has brought frequent changes in trade and other policies in Ghana since independence in 1957. One of the more significant was a shift from export reliance to import substitution in 1961. Average tariffs rose from 17 percent to 25 percent with other taxes added on. Import licensing was begun in 1961. A fair amount of import substitution took place: Import composition switched from over half consumer goods to only 30 percent, with materials and capital goods accounting for almost 65 percent. Manufacturing grew over 10 percent per year between 1962 and 1966.

However, the system of import tariffs and licenses eventually began to hurt the economy. The licensing system was arbitrary and subject to corrupt influences. Tariffs were not coordinated, and effective protection climbed to over 200 percent for some local industries but was often negative for export industries. Some of these had to import materials that exceeded the value of their output.

In addition, the currency was not allowed to depreciate to compensate for inflation, hurting exports other than cocoa, while cocoa exports were hurt by falling world prices. Thus, there was no incentive to invest in diversifying exports. Minimum wages and ceilings on interest rates, together with trade and tax policies, fostered capital-intensive production that was unsustainable. A coup in 1966 resulted in some changes, but overall economic policies resulted in per capita GNP that declined steadily over two decades, investment rates that fell from 20 percent in the 1950s to 5 percent in 1980, and exports declining from 30 percent to 12 percent of GDP in that period.

Ghana moved away from IS in the 1980s, but the earlier policies continued to hurt the economy for many years.

Sources: Michael Roemer, "Ghana, 1950–1980: Missed Opportunities," in Arnold C. Harberger, ed., *World Economic Growth: Case Studies of Developed and Developing Nations* (San Francisco: ICS Press, 1984), pp. 201–226, and Donald Rothchild, ed., *Ghana: The Political Economy of Recovery* (Boulder, CO: Lynne Rienner, 1991).

cult to either verify or refute, except that it seems difficult to avoid continued reliance on world markets and self-interest in creating new policies. Some IS defenders object to the notion that the IS strategy must be tied to balance of payments deficits and foreign borrowing.[18] It may be possible to accept the distortions involved in protectionist trade policies without exacerbating them through overvalued exchange rates, thus keeping a balance on international payments at a lower level of trade. However, governments seldom pursue this course for IS policies.

Henry Bruton offers a more concrete defense of the IS strategy. He focuses on the idea that countries, industries, firms, and people "learn by doing," and suggests that maximum emphasis should be put on "creating an environment in which learning occurs," requiring "strong inducements, to search, to experiment, to test—to learn."[19] IS would require a highly disciplined set of policies. The problem is not with import substitution per se but with certain policies that have historically accompanied it, particularly promoting capital-intensive domestic production, and with the actual policy-making process that often severely distorts the domestic economy. He does not, however, claim that his approach would be any less subject to being hijacked by such policies.

Protection can backfire. Bruton cites India, but India's IS policies had mixed results. IS did reduce dependence on foreign supplies of fertilizer, petroleum, heavy chemicals, iron and steel, and certain types of machinery. However, the structure of protection and associated inefficiencies seriously imperiled the viability of many industries. They encouraged uneconomic diversification that eventually stifled local technological development. Firms that imported technologies closely connected with their current specialization "put more effort into technology choice, absorption and adaptation than others." However, protection often discouraged such activity. A firm that imported a new production technology would receive protection for its product, discouraging competition and innovation, and encouraging others to import yet another new technology in order to carve out their own monopolies.[20]

Still, these policies can be successful for a period of time. A brief history of the IS experience from nineteenth-century Europe to the Latin American and East Asian policies of the late twentieth century, concludes that IS was a necessary beginning stage for many countries.[21] John Waterbury notes that slow world growth and protectionism in the 1950s and early 1960s left many countries with little alternative to start their development. He even concludes that countries that have yet to seriously industrialize may face the same necessity today.

But most early IS countries changed policies once conditions allowed. Continued for too long, import substitution industrialization is a strategy that is fraught with difficulties. If IS proponents are right that the traditional development path is a dead end, the difficulties and high cost of IS would be a legitimate price to pay. But opponents claim that the strategy's assumptions, especially export pessimism, were incorrect. They propose their own trade strategy, to which we now turn.

THE EXPORT-ORIENTATION ALTERNATIVE

The alternative to the IS strategy is to rely on international markets and grow through **Export Orientation (EO)**. At the beginning of the chapter we note the argument that economies advance by exporting those goods for which their productive factors give them a comparative advantage. Most export orientation advocates prefer a neutral environment that is favorable to private activity. They assume that market forces will attract resources to the most profitable opportunities and that, as suggested by economic theory, these would most likely include the export sector. Many EO advocates reject an active government role in promoting exports over other types of economic activity. They tend to reject direct subsidies to export industries or particularly favorable treatment unless this were necessary to counteract other restrictive policies. Active export-promoting policies require a different form of government intervention, albeit one with a more favorable impact on growth than IS.

Claims for the Superiority of EO

EO advocates suggest that a dollar earned from exports is more valuable than a dollar saved through importing. As export industries use more abundant domestic resources, the opportunity cost of those resources is less than that of resources used for import substitution. This use of local resources is likely to be favorable to the agricultural sector and labor in general than would the more capital-intensive IS production. Employment and income distribution would be improved. The world market, being larger than the domestic market, promotes the full use of larger, more efficient plants and provides the competition to induce efforts to improve productivity. Finally, export-oriented policies help attract foreign investment and lending due to natural, not artificial, profitability.

What to Export?

Export, or outward, orientation focuses on comparative advantage, which means, at least initially, exporting primary products and labor-intensive goods. This poses a problem for those countries whose productive structures favor agriculture, as most successful examples of EO have moved into manufactures. The possibility of immiserizing growth is greatest for those countries that still rely on primary commodity exports. In fact, the World Bank now discourages borrowing to increase production of some commodities including coffee, cocoa, and tea for just that reason. One recent study finds that a focus on primary commodities exports frequently provides little stimulus to the rest of the economy. Going the next step to export processed commodities is a more viable strategy but requires a somewhat skilled labor force.[22]

Diversification and development will naturally lead a number of developing countries to exports of manufactured goods. Raymond Vernon's **product cycle theory** suggests that industrial products are developed and first produced in wealthier countries that have skilled labor, but as the products become more standardized and easier to produce (and the original patents expire), production shifts to countries with lower levels of technology. An analysis of export diversification in India showed strong backward linkages for exports of traditional items such as food, textiles, nonmetallic minerals, leather, and rubber.[23]

Countries can promote exports by designating **Export Processing Zones** (**EPZs**—also known as **Free Trade Zones**, or **FTZs**). These may be physical areas or just legally recognized firms that are given special treatment, such as lower taxes or tariffs, rebates of import duties, or even subsidized physical facilities, in exchange for production of manufactured goods for export. They can, in principle, speed up the industrialization process, including training workers, providing backward linkages, and promoting technological change, while earning foreign exchange. In countries with favorable economic conditions, such as South Korea and Taiwan, they have been successful. Elsewhere, gains have been questioned in the light of low wages, poor working conditions, and environmental damage.[24] The high percentage of female employment in these zones has marked them as controversial. They provide work opportunities that may be hard to obtain but often under conditions considered exploitative, such as long hours, little pay, and poor working conditions.[25]

Conditions for Successful Export Promotion

A good summary of the conditions for successful export orientation comes from Anne Krueger's study of the so-called East Asian tigers—Taiwan, South Korea, Singapore, and Hong Kong.[26] These conditions can be divided into two categories relating to the general economic environment and trade-oriented policies.

For the general environment, Krueger suggested a stable macroeconomic and business climate in which inflation is controlled, infrastructure is well developed, labor markets are "free" (no government-mandated wage and employment requirements and, presumably, minimal union power), and the government sustains a clear commitment to its policies so that businesses know that the rules will not be changing frequently. Krueger also frequently stressed the need for human capital development.

For trade policies, she suggested that policies should be clearly export oriented: no quotas or other quantitative restrictions, especially on the imports required by exporting firms, and perhaps some government facilitation of export activities (but no strong actions to create export industries) aimed at a country's evident comparative advantage rather than at industries that might someday be possible exporters.

These conditions spell out a more or less neutral set of policies, counseling domestic economic stability and minimal government intervention, designed to clear the way for economically rational export activities.

The Evidence in Favor of EO

Bela Balassa compared a group of outward-oriented countries (Korea, Singapore, Taiwan) with a more inward-oriented group (Argentina, Brazil, Mexico) and an even more recalcitrant group of Chile, India, and Uruguay. For the period 1960 to 1973, he found that the more outward-oriented countries grew faster, required less capital per unit of output, and generated more employment. Extending his analysis to the period 1973 to 1983, which included two OPEC price shocks, a turbulent period for exchange rates, and major recessions in the West, outward-oriented countries suffered greater initial shocks but recovered to again grow faster, save more, borrow less, have less inflation, and generally perform better on the major macroeconomic variables measured.[27]

Studies have suggested that EO has a more favorable impact on employment than IS. One ambitious study looked at 10 countries over the period 1963 to 1973, measuring a ratio of labor input per unit of value added in exportable goods to the labor input in import-competing goods. For 9 of the 10 countries, the ratio was greater than 1.0, that is, more labor per dollar for export goods than for import-competing goods. The average ratio for the 10 countries was 1.57, and the only country with a ratio less than 1.0 had a value of 0.8.[28] The positive impact of EO on employment is due to both greater labor use in export industries and faster growth of those industries. The gain to labor seems especially to help women; however, most of the employment is low-pay work requiring little education and providing little room for advancement.[29]

Anne Krueger's study compared data on Taiwan, South Korea, Singapore, and Hong Kong to all middle-income countries. Her countries performed better than the average of countries in their income category. She noted that growth rates remained high even during the 1970s when the terms of trade turned against these countries. Despite supposed vulnerability to trade, they withstood the oil price shocks better than others. They even maintained relatively equitable income distribution. But she does introduce a warning that ". . . all four embarked upon their growth and export effort against a background of rapid expansion in international trade. Their success would have been less probable had the international economic environment been less favorable."[30] Still, updating the data continues to show superiority of manufacturing and export for those countries, now firmly established in international trade.

A 1987 World Bank study of 41 countries, divided into strongly and moderately outward oriented and strongly and moderately inward oriented, concluded that the evidence in favor of outward-oriented strategies was "convincing."[31] As the debate continues, both time-series and cross-section studies are being reported showing a correlation between openness and growth. Openness is linked to productivity growth, technology transfer, and investment in human and physical capital.[32]

The evidence was updated in studies covering 1976 to 1985 and 1970 to 1989. In the first, David Dollar used a combination of measures related to the exchange rate, and suggested that had Latin America and Africa followed policies similar to those in Asia, those regions could have grown 1.5 percent and 2.1 percent faster than they did. The second, by Jeffrey Sachs and Andrew Warner, rated the "openness" of trade policies, showing faster growth for most open countries and slower growth for most closed economies. It also suggested that economies that remained closed until at least the mid-1970s were much more likely to suffer from macroeconomic crisis in the 1980s.[33]

Critique of the EO Claims

Not everyone is convinced by the claims of EO advocates.[34] One objection is the one that Krueger herself cites about the hospitality of the world market in the 1960s when the East Asian "tigers" inaugurated their strategy. At the time, world output and trade were expanding rapidly, and trade barriers were falling. Access to international finance was easier than it has become now for many low-income countries, and there was increased activity of multinational corporations toward world sourcing of their products. In addition, relatively few developing countries were making a significant push into manufactured exports. Had a much larger number of them tried, many economists doubt that the world trading system could have absorbed enough new manufactured exports to support them. This conclusion remains open to debate.[35]

Export pessimism has become muted but still has some adherents. Despite evidence that developing countries have increased their penetration of industrialized markets from 1.5 percent to 3.5 percent of manufactured goods consumption between 1970 and 1987, it remains true that most of this improvement came from fewer than 10 developing countries. When growth in the industrialized countries is sluggish, if trade barriers are intensified, the chance for many developing countries to prosper through this route is open to question.[36] Protection in industrialized countries may be low under normal circumstances, but barriers often rise quickly when rich economies are threatened by import surges. Many countries are still too small to sustain export-size industries. Poorer countries remain hindered by lack of access to advanced technology, while declining prices of primary commodities often hurt their traditional industries.

Other difficulties remain for countries such as those in Africa and the Caribbean that are still "specialized" in agricultural production and exports. Since most EO arguments tend to focus on manufactures, they do not clearly address problems of declining terms of trade and price instability for key exports. Would-be manufactures exporters must attain sufficient scale and, in some cases, cope with goods and processes that are protected by copyrights and patents. Subsidizing new exports tends to run afoul of international trade rules.

Some EO advocates suggest that East Asian growth is due to an export orientation promoted by reliance on free markets. But Colin Bradford noted that South Korea gave subsidized credit to exporters and combined import substitution with export promotion. Taiwan managed imports to facilitate exports, gave selected tax benefits to exporters of specific products, and used public enterprises to provide about one-third of fixed investment. Singapore has also aided specific export industries through tax incentives. Of the four countries cited by Krueger, only Hong Kong can be considered a true market-led exporter. Rather than market forces, Bradford concluded that "effective, highly interactive relationships between the public and private sectors characterized by shared goals and commitments" are the real forces behind EO success stories."[37] To the extent that such policies involve export-promoting subsidies, they will be increasingly difficult to implement as developed countries begin to take action against those exports.

There is also some question as to the overall results of EO policies in these countries and its application elsewhere. Among the concerns are whether employment *can* respond significantly in larger countries that have a smaller trade sector (smaller countries tend to trade disproportionately, and many of the success stories are small countries); whether there are diminishing returns to the EO strategy;[38] whether the increased reliance on imported goods, both economic and cultural, is desirable; and whether reliance on foreign technology might inhibit local capacity to innovate.

On the latter point, Bruton's "learning by doing" approach is particularly relevant. He concludes that India's relatively strong protectionist policies, while far from costless, have in the long run given it a much more self-reliant and innovative economy. Korea, which opened before and to a greater extent than Brazil, is better off in terms of its own technical abilities because it relied *less* on foreign firms.[39]

Also, it is clear even from Krueger's conditions that a precondition for this expansion of trade, especially by foreign investors, is a particularly strong government or a national consensus that short-run sacrifices (including restrictions on workers' wages and union activity) is a reasonable price to pay. Lack of consensus will require a heavy-handed government if EO is to succeed. Numerous observers have pointed to the dictatorial nature of the South Korean government as essential in permitting that country to implement the policies responsible for its rapid growth after 1960.[40]

Economists have questioned some of the pro-EO evidence. Studies that acknowledge the *accompaniment* of trade and growth usually are not able to show a *causal* link, indicating to them that another factor may lead to both. One attempt at causal analysis found exports leading to growth in Israel and Mexico but growth leading to exports in Pakistan. Exports and growth were found to cause each other in Colombia and Morocco, while outside causes caused both exports and growth in Brazil and Korea. Another study claims that a structural shift to manufacturing leads to both exports and growth. A study of Colombia, Mexico, and Morocco supports Bruton's emphasis on learning by looking at business firm activity. It concludes that in those countries it was learning that led to exporting, not the other way around as is usually assumed.[41] Figure 12–3 illustrates the problem.

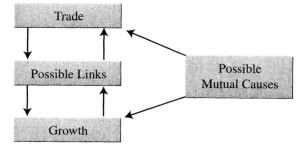

FIGURE 12–3 Trade and Growth

Possible links from trade to growth include learning, increased productivity, efficient resource allocation, attracting foreign investment, and competition from imports.

Possible links from growth to trade include learning, increased investment, and increased efficiency.

Possible mutual causes include structural change.

David Evans questions the generalizations drawn from the case studies and challenges the World Bank study. First, the Bank's criteria for classifying countries are vague. Second, the Bank's own data show that for the 1973 to 1985 period, the record for the moderately inward-oriented countries was *better* than for the moderately outward-oriented countries with respect to the growth of real output, the growth of real GNP per capita, savings ratios, and inflation.[42] Finally, an analysis of various measures of "openness" used to classify outward and inward-oriented economies concludes that there is no correlation among them. If so, their various correlations to economic growth may not mean much.[43]

A review of claims that better trade policy induces more rapid growth raises much the same questions. A critique of the Sachs and Warner study suggested that their results seemed too perfect: It questioned the "closed" classification of any economy that was not "open" for the entire 1970 to 1989 period and the starting date of 1970 as unfairly ignoring the positive economic results of some IS policies in the 1960s. Thus, the case is not at all clear-cut. Even some authors who favor export-oriented strategies have concluded that there are serious questions about the evidence that has been provided for them.[44]

A Limited Consensus

Despite some doubts, the problems of the IS strategy and the success of many developing-country exporters have tipped the scales to EO. However, while those advocating strong inward orientations are in the minority, there is still considerable disagreement as to just what role the government should play, including the possibility of some IS-type policies, in promoting or facilitating exports.

One of the mainstream's more respected analysts, Jagdish Bhagwati,[45] acknowledges that EO regimes are not synonymous with laissez-faire, but claims that most such regimes in practice have been at least stable systems in which governments have not indulged in casual policy changes. He also acknowledges that many countries have started out in an IS phase, then switched to EO: IS may have some advantages in very early stages of development when industrial exports are not feasible, but it should be abandoned as soon as possible. He sees bureaucratic inertia and private privilege as the major obstacles to changes in the regimes that have stayed with IS.

The ease with which countries become export oriented will of course vary. Larger countries with well-developed, or potential, internal markets will tend to develop a wider range of import substitute industries than smaller countries, and it should not be surprising that the more successful exporters of manufactures have had smaller economies with narrower resource bases. Even among the industrialized countries, larger countries rely less on international trade as a percentage of their economic activity than do smaller countries. But this is a natural development and should not be used as an excuse to follow a restrictive approach.

Can Import Substitution and Export Orientation be pursued simultaneously? As a matter of *general* policy, the full set of IS tools would make it impossible to follow the market. But certainly a country can target specific, limited import substitution sectors, perhaps infant industries, while following an overall EO approach. Most countries protect some industries.[46]

Recent modifications to trade theory emphasize the absence of perfect competition. A government may help a domestic company get into international markets by, for example, providing subsidies. The company gets a head start, takes advantage of economies of scale to lower its costs, and becomes established ahead of its competitors. This approach might be difficult to use. But such ideas do open the way for a more balanced consideration of what role governments might play to promote an outward orientation.[47]

GETTING THERE: TRADE POLICY REFORM

Proponents of Import Substitution have some valid objectives and some legitimate problems with Export Orientation claims. However, the typical IS experience is sufficiently dismal that we should now ask how a country moves from IS to a more outward orientation, starting with an entrenched, complex system of trade restrictions and other policies that go along with it.[48]

Objectives and Problems of Trade Policy Reform

The objective of reform is to allow prices to move resources toward their most efficient use in both domestic and international markets. This means producing competitive goods with current factor endowments and those that can be reasonably created through investment, leaving other goods to be purchased from abroad. Therefore, policies that distort prices by discouraging both imports and exports should be removed or modified.

This is relatively simple in theory but very difficult in practice. While protective measures may have been the result of some overall view of how to develop, they are more likely to have been the result of special pleading by domestic interests for their own private benefit. Those who stand to lose this protection will defend their interests, and those attempts will be rationalized by the short-term costs that changing resource allocation always imposes. In addition, trade policy reforms by themselves are not likely to be sufficient; they will probably have to be combined with (and in some cases preceded by) exchange rate devaluation and other policy changes designed to slow down inflation and remove domestic factor market distortions.

The Design of Reform

Some protective measures are worse than others, and some ways of correcting them are better than others. We will mention here some of the principal lessons learned to date.

First, Replace Quotas with Tariffs

Tariffs are more efficient than quotas, but this step is not a simple one: For a government to actually determine the tariff level that will have the restrictive impact of the quota is a more difficult process. But this effort could be crucial. Turkey undertook external reform efforts in 1970 to 1973 and 1980 to 1984. The first effort was half-hearted, but the second time (Case 12–2) was successful and resulted in a major reduction in quotas, along with a more restrictive fiscal policy.[49]

Reducing Tariffs

While developing countries generally rely on tariffs for a higher portion of total revenues than do developed countries, they need not greatly distort economic decisions. They should be reduced as much as possible and their variation reduced: perhaps bringing all tariffs down to the 10 percent to 20 percent level rather than having some very high and some very low with the potential for negative effective protection. Over the last 10 years, a number of Latin American countries, including Chile, Mexico, and Bolivia, have done just that. Tariff reduction may well be an appropriate occasion for reviewing the overall tax system, if necessary to counter lost revenue.[50]

Export Promotion

While trade policy reform focuses on reducing protection against imports, it also seeks to make a country's exports competitive in international markets. So part of a protection-reduction program would be to target imports that are used as inputs in the export industries. Export Processing Zones may be a part of this effort. At the same time, governments are usually advised to resist the temptation to subsidize their exports. Export subsidies are violations of the provisions of the **World Trade Organization (WTO)**, to which most developing countries belong. Also, subsidy programs may become just as much the target of rent-seeking behavior as quotas.

Move Quickly

One political lesson of reform experience is that governments should move quickly to enhance the credibility of their policies, reduce the period of adjustment, and reduce the time available for opponents of the reform to gather strength. Additional policies should encourage the phasing out of noncompetitive firms and industries. Compensatory policies—those that help resolve the legitimate problems caused by adjustment, such as worker training and investment in infrastructure—can help relieve some of the burden while not replacing one set of distortions with another. External assistance, such as World Bank loans, can be crucial during the initial period. The experience of policy reform in Eastern European countries such as Poland shows that the hardship can be considerable and will work against the reforms. Workers and

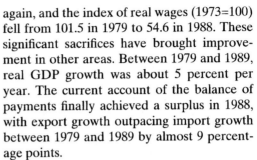

CASE 12–2

PATHS TO TRADE REFORM: TURKEY AND CHINA

FAST FACTS

Turkey on the Map: Southern Europe
Population: 64 Million
Per Capita GNI and Rank: $2,900   (90)
Life Expectancy: Male—67   Female—72
Adult Literacy Rate: Male—93%
Female—76%

China on the Map: Asia
Population: 1.25 Billion
Per Capita GNI and Rank: $780   (142)
Life Expectancy: Male—68   Female—72
Adult Literacy Rate: Male—91%
Female—75%

Turkey and China provide different pictures of trade reform, both of which have gained some success. Turkey's reforms of the early 1980s combined protection-reducing measures with devaluation. Beginning in 1980, quantitative restrictions were drastically cut back. At the same time, the lira was devalued and kept ahead of inflation differentials, thereby providing price incentives for exports. With these reforms in place, tariffs were reduced starting in 1983 to the point where the average rate was around 10 percent. Unfortunately, as tariff rates fell, tariff surcharges and specific levies became more important after 1984.

The trade and devaluation measures were not taken alone. Financial markets, including foreign exchange markets, were liberalized; SOEs' prices were raised; and, at least at first, there was some fiscal restraint. Much of Turkey's external debt was rescheduled at the same time, and external debt rose rapidly, which helped sustain the reform program.

The results have not been entirely satisfactory. The relaxing of fiscal restraint has meant that deficits and inflation began to rise again, and the index of real wages (1973=100) fell from 101.5 in 1979 to 54.6 in 1988. These significant sacrifices have brought improvement in other areas. Between 1979 and 1989, real GDP growth was about 5 percent per year. The current account of the balance of payments finally achieved a surplus in 1988, with export growth outpacing import growth between 1979 and 1989 by almost 9 percentage points.

China took a different approach. Despite low per capita income, it has a very large domestic market and exercises much tighter political control than most countries. These characteristics, and an extensive industrial base, permitted the government to carry out gradual trade reforms that emphasized export promotion with very little reduction in protection.

Beginning in 1978 China moved away from an almost total central control over foreign trade in which 15 government foreign trade corporations (FTCs) handled most transactions. By 1990 there were 5,000 FTCs, with much less central control over trade plans and foreign exchange. Government export subsidies also were removed. These measures were intensified beginning in 1991, and a series of devaluations beginning in 1987 brought the official rate nearly in line with the market. The key result was an increase in the export share in GDP from 4.7 percent in 1978 to 17.1 percent in 1990. As in many cases of economic reform, however, temporary problems have brought a return of some controls.

Reform of the protection system is anticipated soon as China prepares for membership in the World Trade Organization (WTO). Early reforms have provided China with the foreign exchange necessary to increase its imports, particularly for industrial modernization, from 5.2 percent to 14.2 percent of GDP. The next steps should be to revise the tariff and import licensing systems and extend trading authority from the government-owned FTCs to private companies. The Chinese experience underscores the potential for successful reform that does not follow the suggested pattern, as long as the economic and political situation in a country permit.

Sources: For Turkey, see Dani Rodrik, "Premature Liberalization, Incomplete Stabilization: The Ozal Decade in Turkey," in Michael Bruno et al., eds., *Lessons of Economic Stabilization and Its Aftermath* (Cambridge: MIT Press, 1991), pp. 323–358, and Rudiger Dornbusch,

"The Case for Trade Liberalization in Developing Countries," *Journal of Economic Perspectives* 6, no. 1 (winter 1992), pp. 69–85, plus World Bank Operations Evaluation Study, "Trade Policy Reforms Under Adjustment Programs" (Washington: 1992), pp. 36, 68–69. For China, see Peter Harrold, "China's Reform Experience to Date" World Bank's Discussion Paper 180 (1992); Nicholas R. Lardy, *Foreign Trade and Economic Reform in China 1978–1990* (Cambridge: Cambridge University Press, 1992); Kathy Chen, "China Reasserts Control Over Exports, Causing Problems for Foreign Concerns," *Wall Street Journal*, December 14, 1994; Steve Mofson, "China's Second Thoughts on the WTO," *Washington Post National Weekly Edition*, May 7–13, 2001; and Jesse Wong, "China's WTO Bid Is Already Changing the Landscape," *Wall Street Journal*, May 22, 2001.

businesses in import-competing industries will be hurt, and there will be a period in which the trade balance will get worse before it improves. China's reforms have been quite slow because opposition within the state structure has impeded, but not reversed, the direction.

Reform can even hurt overall growth temporarily. A study of numerous reform experiences showed that an initial downturn was common, followed by a modest beneficial impact. In Brazil over the period 1989 to 1996, export industries were slow to respond so that imports grew more quickly than exports. And the share of labor-intensive exports in the total actually fell, while those using natural resources gained a greater share, worsening the distribution of income and dependence on volatile markets.[51]

Cautions: Trade Reform in Overall Reform

It is important for governments to realize that economic reform in one area depends on reform in many areas, and the order in which reform measures are taken may be important. Here it is worth making a general point: Reforms aimed at changing an economy's relations with the outside world have considerable impact on domestic activity, so the ability to sustain external reforms requires a flexible domestic economy. If labor and capital are not able to move relatively quickly to take advantage of changing incentives, this rigidity will quickly be translated into political opposition to trade and exchange rate reforms. Even with a certain degree of flexibility, a country may require foreign funds for a transition period, but these will be wasted and become burdensome if the domestic economy cannot react to changing incentives.

THE INSTITUTIONAL FRAMEWORK OF INTERNATIONAL TRADE

Developing-country trade policies are part of the larger question of the rules that govern international trade. In 1948, 50 governments—mostly of the industrialized countries—established a **General Agreement on Tariffs and Trade (GATT)** to bring structure to the world trading system. Starting with the belief that freer trade would contribute to economic growth, they agreed to reduce trade barriers and created a mechanism for multilateral negotiations to further reduce barriers over time. As more developing countries have joined, there has been conflict between the desire for protection—in developed and developing countries—and the objectives of a freer world trading system. In 1995, the GATT became the World Trade Organization (WTO), which now has 141 members.[52]

From the beginning of the GATT, industrialized countries allowed certain exceptions for themselves in such areas as agriculture and textiles—both important for developing countries. Agricultural subsidies in Europe, the United States, and Japan have been difficult to reduce. Developing countries therefore view as hypocritical the worldwide system of quotas on textiles and apparel and the exhortations that they should develop through "trade, not aid."

The World Trading System and the WTO

WTO rules require that a country provide **Most Favored Nation (MFN) treatment**: A country's trade barriers apply equally to all supplier countries. Quantitative restrictions are supposed to be minimized. Only with special permission, and under unusual circumstances, are trade barriers to be used to resolve balance of payments difficulties. However, a key debate has been the extent to which developing countries should follow the same rules as the industrialized countries.

A **Part IV** was added to the GATT Articles of Agreement in 1965 that permitted "special and differential" treatment for developing countries. For example, when tariff reductions or rules on QRs are negotiated, trading partners are normally expected to make roughly equivalent concessions, but developing countries are not asked for "contributions which are inconsistent with their development, financial and trade needs." Tariffs imposed by countries ordinarily apply to all trading partners, but under preference programs, unilateral tariff reductions are permitted in favor of developing countries. They are given greater leeway in the use of protective measures as a means of correcting balance of payments deficits. However, critics have suggested that since freer trade is beneficial to importing countries, developing countries would receive greater benefits by forgoing special treatment and submitting to the same rules as other countries. In light of the greater acceptance of outward-oriented development policies, and the limited advantages in fact provided by preferences, many suggest a renunciation of Part IV's advantages and a greater integration of developing countries into the international trading system.[53]

If it is true that developing countries hurt themselves through their own trade restrictions, and gain little from preferential treatment, they would gain more by accepting the requirements of WTO membership. A case in point is the Code on Subsidies established in the Tokyo Round of trade negotiations between 1976 and 1979. Because many developing countries did not want to accept the code's restrictions on permissible subsidies, they often did not become parties to it. But the code has the advantage that if one party wants to retaliate against another's subsidies, it must show that the imports resulting from the subsidies have actually caused injury to the importer's industry. But if a country that does not sign the code is found to have unfairly subsidized its exports, the importing country can retaliate (impose tariffs to offset the subsidy) without any proof of injury.

Another advantage of adherence to WTO principles might come in tariff negotiations. To the extent that developing countries are not required to negotiate equivalent compensation for reduced tariffs, the developed countries have an additional incentive to put their energies into negotiating on products that are produced largely among themselves. Thus, in the Uruguay Round of negotiations that created the WTO, signed in 1994, the developed countries again did more to reduce tariffs on each others' goods than on those from developing countries.

The Uruguay Round: Results and Remaining Problems

Economists and governments in the industrialized countries have long encouraged developing countries to move toward freer trade. Developing countries have often countered that the system favors the economically better-off countries. The conclusion of the Uruguay Round has fodder for both sides.

Results

Many of the accomplishments of the Uruguay Round were typically more favorable to the industrialized countries. Tariffs were eliminated or cut, particularly for manufactured goods traded mostly among developed countries. Protection of intellectual property rights was added for the first time, and a framework was established for liberalizing trade in services. Developing countries failed to restrain the use of antidumping duties (tariffs on imports whose prices are below the cost of price in the exporting country). And tougher rules were created against the use of domestic content requirements, by which developing countries enforce minimum levels of local production in the output of foreign firms.

The Uruguay round, however, took steps to reduce subsidies on products that have historically been excluded from normal trade rules, including agriculture and textiles. This step will benefit the many developing countries that export these goods. It was the United States, rather than the developing countries, that exerted the most pressure to achieve these reductions. Developing countries such as Argentina and Thailand that are net food exporters will gain, but net food importers, including many African nations, will be hurt.[54] The **Multifibre Arrangement (MFA)**, by which industrialized countries placed comprehensive quotas on imports of clothing and textiles, is being dismantled over a 10-year period.

The Uruguay Round dispute-settlement agreements may make it easier for developing countries to settle injury claims against other countries. Developing countries could benefit if developed countries reduce their use of measures that permit countries to negotiate informal, discriminatory quotas against imports of particular goods from specific countries, often employed by developed against developing countries.

Increased developing-country participation in the WTO could occur gradually along with the country's own trade liberalization. There are simple measures that could be taken fairly quickly, including notification of all trade restrictions. Some governments might be surprised to find out just what restrictions exist, and this could begin the process of removing all the overlapping restrictions that make many trade regimes inscrutable. In recent years, the process of liberalizing the Mexican economy has brought Mexico into the WTO, and now China and the former socialist countries of Eastern Europe are finding that application for membership makes sense in light of their overall liberalization objectives. China's entry met resistance both from China's own state enterprises, which might be hurt by freer trade, and from the U.S. government.[55]

Remaining Problems

Developing countries remain at some disadvantage within the current trading system.[56] They have not had sufficient political or economic weight over the years to negotiate tariff reductions, so their manufactured exports tend to face higher tariffs than industrialized country exports. Recent additions to the traditional trade agenda—services, intellectual property rights, and measures related to foreign investment—clearly reflect the interests of the industrialized countries.

The complexity of the rules is also a disadvantage because developing-country governments have fewer technical and legal resources to research the impact of trade restrictions and master the fine points of international law. Developed countries with large, diversified economies have more flexibility in switching trade partners in response to a dispute.

The new rules on subsidies restrict those typically given in developing countries to aid specific industries but not those typically given in industrialized countries, such as general funding for research and development. The new rules for agriculture make subsidy reduction slow in the United States, Europe, and Japan but forbid any new subsidies in developing countries. The phaseout of textile quotas started slowly, and developing countries are concerned that their acceleration in the next few years will be delayed by the developed countries. The same rules tend to work to the advantage of the industrialized countries, while they pay little attention to the special treatment for developing countries called for in Part IV.

The Future of the WTO

An attempt to start a new round of trade negotiations came to a crashing halt in Seattle, Washington, in 1999. With the 1994 results yet to be fully implemented, demonstrators raised the issues of labor standards and environmental protection. While these issues are largely the result of pressure from groups in industrialized countries, their impact would be felt most heavily in the developing countries.

Labor standards, for example, have been injected by a combination of humanitarian interests worldwide and portions of the developed-country labor movement. Lower wages are reflections of a country's income level and the relative weakness of labor unions. For other than skilled labor, unions in developing countries have little leverage unless they exert political power. Should trade agreements attempt to enforce better working conditions, limitations on child labor, and acceptance of unions? What should those standards be? How would they be enforced? If the UN's International Labour Organization is not succeeding in these tasks, is restricting trade from noncompliant countries the answer? If developing countries had to enforce higher wages and better working conditions to have their exports allowed into industrialized countries, costs would increase and exports would decline. Meeting the two objectives—higher standards and higher exports—poses significant challenges.

Environmental issues have caused problems for the WTO. Many nonprofit organizations have exerted pressure on governments in the developed countries to push for the right to restrict imports that do not comply with developed-country environmental standards in their use or in their processing. The WTO has generally ruled against such practices as illegal barriers to trade. Developing countries gain from such strict interpretations of the trade rules. While they are well placed to produce natural products, including food, fibers, and fertilizers, developing-country manufacturers need cleaner processing and packaging technology, and access to the information necessary for strict labeling requirements. Cleaner technologies are expensive and often capital- and knowledge-intensive. Without assistance, the result will likely be that, again, the more advanced developing countries will gain the lion's share of such exports.[57]

The Seattle protests had a systemic focus. They called for public access to information about WTO operations, including dispute panels, and the influence of large corporations, through governments, on policy making in the organization. Such concerns will not be easily addressed, but they are now up for discussion.[58]

THE DEVELOPED COUNTRIES AS TRADE PARTNERS

In order for developing countries to grow through exports, they need access to the industrialized countries' markets. The initial incursions of the developing countries into world markets other than for primary commodities tend to be in light manufacturing, with low-cost, labor-intensive methods. However, even in those industries (textiles, shoes), industrialized-country firms may already be efficient and, if not, are frequently protected by tariffs or quotas. Gradually, developing countries have gone into more mature industries such as steel, autos, and semiconductors, taking advantage of natural resources, low wages, relatively modern production processes (often provided by multinational corporations), and often subsidies. Each success, however, tends to be met with resistance from developed countries.[59]

Over the last half century the industrialized countries have made significant progress in reducing import restrictions—particularly tariffs—despite considerable pressure to move in the opposite direction since the late 1970s. Yet along the way, they have maintained, and increased, numerous barriers—mostly nontariff measures including quotas and so-called voluntary restraints—against the products they have encouraged the developing countries to produce.

Protectionist Devices

The United States, the European Union (EU), and Japan all protect certain agricultural products; the EU's Common Agricultural Policy (CAP) is one of the most comprehensive and effective schemes of agricultural protection. Domestic farm prices have been kept above world prices, and output has been protected by a system of tariffs. The result, predictably, has been that huge agricultural surpluses are exported, sometimes below world market prices. This system has raised objections from the United States (which has some agricultural support policies of its own) and from developing countries such as Argentina that are also major producers of temperate-climate crops such as wheat. As a result of the Uruguay Round, agricultural subsidies are being reduced.

For over 30 years, the Multifibre Arrangement has permitted the developed countries to impose quotas against textile and clothing products of the developing countries. The program was initially smaller and intended to be temporary, but until recently product and exporter coverage has expanded as first one, then another developing country has acquired the ability to successfully export such goods.[60] This program is scheduled to be phased out by 2005.

When developed-country industries find themselves subject to strong import competition from low-cost labor in developing countries, even when low productivity offsets labor-cost advantages, their governments are quick to erect supposedly temporary "safeguards" against the imports. U.S. restrictions that impact on those exports cover a wide range of products including, sugar, shoes, and steel. In 1986, the industrialized countries had in place a series of QRs and price decrees on imports that covered 21 percent of the value of their imports from the developing countries, up from 19 percent in 1981 and compared to 16 percent from the other developed countries. Average tariffs on manufactured imports imposed by the United States, EU, and Japan were 4.9 percent, 6.0 percent, and 5.4 percent worldwide, but 8.7 percent, 7.6 percent, and 6.8 percent on developing-country manufactured exports.[61]

Tariff Escalation and the GSP

The pattern of developed-country tariff schedules presents a built-in bias against emerging exporters. This is a pattern of **tariff escalation**, where tariff levels increase as the level of a product's processing increases: Low or zero tariffs are placed on raw materials, and successively higher levels apply to processed materials, components, and final products. While tariff margins are not always large, they still tend to push developing countries toward less-processed goods.

A World Bank report on the impact of developed-country trade policies on the developing countries includes a breakdown of industrialized-country imports according to the level of processing. It shows that for the mid-1980s, nearly three-fourths of the main industrialized-countries' imports from developing countries consisted of Stage 1 goods—those at the lowest level of processing—with another fourth consisting of Stage 2 goods and only 3 percent at Stages 3 and 4.[62] Table 12–4 illustrates tariff escalation in the 1980s and Table 12–5 in the 1990s.

TABLE 12–4 Tariff Escalation by Product (Late 1980s)

Product Categories	Tariff Rates (%) Processing Stage			
	1	2	3	4
Fruit	4.8	12.2	16.6	
Cocoa	2.6	4.3	11.8	
Rubber	2.4	2.9	6.7	
Leather	0.0	4.2	8.5	8.2
Wood	1.8	9.2	4.1	6.6
Tobacco	55.8	81.8		

Source: World Development Report 1987, p. 138.

Tariff escalation provided the rationale for proposals in the late 1960s and early 1970s for exempting North–South trade from the normal pattern of mutual concessions and Most Favored Nation treatment. Part IV of the GATT allowed industrialized countries to introduce **Generalized Systems of Preferences (GSP)** under which manufactured exports from developing countries would be permitted to enter at developed countries at lower tariff rates. They would then be cheaper than similar products imported from other developed countries.

GSP systems have not been as helpful as the developing countries had hoped. They provide lower (often zero) tariff rates for some goods, although there are usually limits to the amount of imports from a particular country that may take advantage of the low tariff. When these imports pose serious competition to domestic production, the products, or sometimes countries, are removed from GSP altogether. The U.S. system provides large tariff reductions, but it exempts numerous products and countries that fail to meet certain political criteria. It also has a formal mechanism whereby products and countries are graduated out of the system under specified conditions: The four East Asian "tigers" were dropped from the eligible list in 1988.

Studies show that such graduation provisions could benefit the poorer countries. The bulk of the GSP benefits have gone to the more advanced of the developing countries, and graduating them (i.e., raising the duty on their exports back to the normal rate) would make the other countries more competitive were they in a position to take advantage of the opportunities. However, the benefits of GSP are minimized when the difference between regular tariff rates and the GSP rate is small, so the progressive reduction of tariffs since the 1980s has eroded the gain from GSP schemes.[63]

An OECD study estimated that between 1976 and 1988 GSP schemes probably increased developing-country exports by 1 percent to 2 percent, and in 1987 only six countries generated about two-thirds of all GSP exports. At the same time, only one-half of exports eligible for GSP treatment actually got the lower duties. The report concluded that at least some developing countries might have done better to participate fully in the tariff reductions and nontariff codes implemented by the GATT negotiations of the late 1970s. The negotiated reductions cannot be taken away, as can

TABLE 12–5 Tariff Escalation by Product Categories (Late 1990s)

All Industrial Products Except Petroleum	*Tariff Rate*
Raw Materials	0.8
Semimanufactures	2.8
Finished Products	6.2
Natural Resource-Based Products Except Petroleum	*Tariff Rate*
Raw Materials	2.0
Semimanufactures	2.0
Finished Products	5.9

Source: World Trade Organization—
⟨www.wto.org/wto/english/thewto_e/whatis_e/eol/e/pdf/urt25.pdf⟩.

GSP treatment, and participation in the codes gives countries rights to challenge other protective measures.[64] On the other hand, the World Bank has estimated that "if the protection in the European Community, Japan, and the United States were halved, developing-country exports could rise by about $50 billion. . . ."[65]

In addition to GSP programs, there are regional preferential trading arrangements for many developing countries. The United States, under its Caribbean Basin Initiative and Enterprise for the Americas Initiative, has since 1983 provided some additional preferential treatment for products from 23 countries in the Caribbean and Central America. A 1991 Andean Trade Preference Act does the same for Bolivia, Colombia, Ecuador, and Peru.

Perhaps the most extensive trade preference system between industrialized and developing countries is provided by the European Union under its **Lomé accords** with 71 developing countries known collectively as the ACP (Asia, Africa, Caribbean, and Pacific) countries. This accord shows the limitations of such preference schemes. Over the period 1980 to 1989, imports of manufactures by EU countries grew 7.7 percent per year from industrial countries; 19.4 percent from the group of Malaysia, Indonesia, the Philippines, and Thailand; 13.5 percent from the group of Hong Kong, South Korea, Singapore, and Taiwan; 12.1 percent from a group of Mediterranean countries that get a separate set of EU preferences; and only 6.6 percent from the ACP countries.[66]

North–South Free Trade: NAFTA

One of the dilemmas of international trade theory is what policy a country should pursue in the absence of a steady progression of the world toward free trade. Groups of countries can gain by forming **free trade areas (FTAs)**, or **customs unions**. Despite concerns that such areas may cement regional blocs that will ultimately stand in the way of free trade, and in spite of the failures of many developing-country attempts at FTAs, the success of the European Community encouraged the formation in 1989 of a U.S.-Canada Free Trade Area, which expanded in 1994 to the **North American Free Trade Agreement (NAFTA)** with the inclusion of Mexico. Although some members of the EU are at lower levels of development than others, NAFTA is the boldest attempt yet to combine developed and developing regions into a single bloc. It phases out most tariffs on trade among the member countries, reduces restrictions on foreign investment, and addresses labor and environmental issues. Through NAFTA, Mexico can insulate itself somewhat from U.S. tariffs and other restrictions.

NAFTA was possible only because Mexico had taken steps since the mid-1980s to liberalize what had been a fairly restrictive foreign trade and investment regime. Mexico joined the GATT in 1986 and began to reduce trade restrictions and revise its internal policies of heavy state intervention. Moreover, for some years Mexico has benefited from provisions in the U.S. tariff laws that permit goods assembled in Mexico from U.S. parts to be reimported into the United States with a tariff on only the extra value added in Mexico, rather than on the entire value of the product.

The NAFTA negotiations raised fears on both sides of the border. Some U.S. citizens were concerned about losing jobs due not only to imports but to companies relocating to take advantage of Mexico's lower wages and less restrictive labor and environmental regulations. Mexican citizens were concerned about the ability of U.S. companies to limit Mexican development through domination of advanced industries.

But the Mexican government saw this agreement as an opportunity to destroy Mexico's inward orientation and improve its economic situation. It was expected to promote manufactured exports, thereby reducing Mexico's reliance on agriculture and oil, and insulate the Mexican economy from U.S. protectionist measures.[67]

Economic theory takes a cautious approach to FTAs. Under the best circumstances, they benefit not only the parties to the agreement but the global economy as well. Trade is created through tariff reduction, resulting in higher production and consumption, lower prices, and greater global efficiency. However, a potential drawback is that they may actually divert trade by having the countries involved shift their trade imports from efficient, low-cost producers outside the area to less efficient producers inside the area, protected by the tariff wall. The trends shown in Figure 12–4 indicate that, while Mexican trade with the United States and Canada has become a larger portion of the total until 1999, its overall trade has increased markedly as well.

NAFTA is by no means a settled issue. While the U.S. government sees net job creation through exports, opponents point to job losses from plant closings and continued environmental problems in northern Mexico. When governments of the Western Hemisphere met in Montreal in April 2001 to discuss an extension of NAFTA to the rest of the hemisphere, protestors took their criticisms to the streets. A proposed Free Trade Agreement of the Americas (FTAA) is being prepared and could be in place by the year 2005.[68]

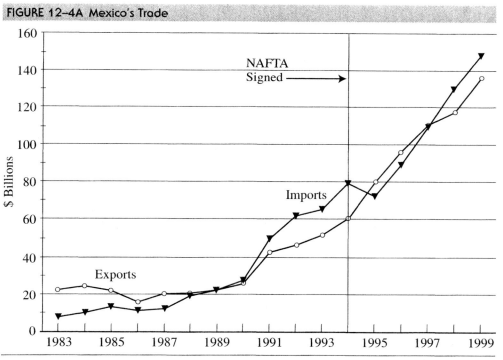

FIGURE 12–4A Mexico's Trade

Source: IMF/DOT.

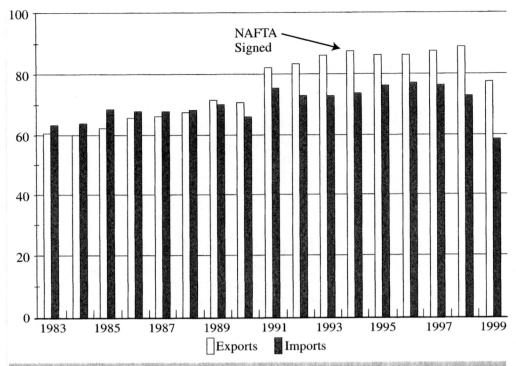

FIGURE 12–4B Mexico's NAFTA Trade (%)

Mexico's trade, particularly imports, has risen rapidly since the signing of NAFTA. However, the share of those imports coming from the United States has fallen after a few years of increase.
Source: IMF/DOT.

DIVERSITY OF CUSTOMERS: THE POTENTIAL FOR SOUTH–SOUTH TRADE

Some economists and government officials have been intrigued by the possibility of a significant expansion of trade among the developing countries. Some export pessimists have hit upon this path as a way to combine their pessimism with the acknowledged benefits of outward-oriented strategies.

Design: The Disappointment and Renewal of Regional Integration

The initial impetus for regional integration among developing countries was Prebisch's logical conclusion that developing countries could not industrialize by taking their place in the existing international division of labor. Instead, if they could form regional trading blocs, they could overcome the small internal markets that might stymie an IS strategy where industrial goods must be produced on a large scale. Greater scale provides more efficient production, and larger markets might also provide needed competition among countries that were more evenly matched. Eventually, dynamic gains from economic growth should add to the benefits.[69]

There were problems, however, with regional integration. From a purely economic perspective, a certain level of industrial development seems to be a precondition for countries with similar resources to gain much from trade. Many of these countries were competitors for export markets, and the protected manufacturing industries faced the same problems of inefficiency. IS was not rendered any less difficult by the somewhat larger markets that were created: The world market is still a better bet, and one study of the failure of African FTA attempts concludes that developing-country FTAs may face better chances if their members pursue outward-oriented strategies rather than IS.[70]

There were political problems as well. While promoting competition might undo the benefits of specialization by duplicating effort, the avoidance of competition would require that governments agree on what industries were to be established where. This frequently proved difficult when countries on the losing end would grow impatient.

Thus, in the 1970s the Andean Pact in South America foundered because of disagreement on the conditions for admittance of foreign investors. For the Central American Common Market, lack of economic complementarity, the small size of the entire region, and continuing political conflicts spelled failure. The East African Common Market fell apart because Kenya, with a more well-developed resource base and more hospitable to private investment than Tanzania, developed more rapidly. Attempts to set up an Economic Community of West African States have failed because of the political and economic dominance of Nigeria. To date, the most successful regional trade arrangement has been the European Community, now expanded to the European Union.[71]

In the developing world, perhaps the most successful regional cooperation scheme is the Association of South East Asian Nations (ASEAN).[72] Its success, however, has been at least partly due to its decision to emphasize areas of cooperation and go more slowly in such potentially troublesome areas such as trade liberalization. More recently, however, with economic liberalization taking place throughout Latin America, a new free trade arrangement, Mercosur, began in 1991, including Argentina, Brazil, Paraguay, and Uruguay (participants in an earlier Latin American Free Trade Association), and old associations such as the Andean Pact and the Central American Common Market are showing new life.[73]

Mercosur has already become controversial. A study of its first few years concluded that at least some of its initial effects were counter to the objectives of free trade. Due to high external tariffs, member countries were increasing internal trade in goods for which they did not have comparative advantage and were therefore becoming less competitive internationally. Objections to this conclusion have highlighted progress in reducing barriers and increasing trade with the outside. The region has enjoyed much greater dynamism in the 1990s, but it is too early to fully evaluate the Mercosur agreement.[74]

By Default: Growing Developing-Country Markets

As the East Asian "tigers" progress, and industrialization proceeds in countries such as Turkey, Brazil, Chile, and Mexico, those countries become larger markets for the next group of developing countries in Central America and Africa. The newly industrializing countries will be producing goods for the United States, Europe, and Japan but will be buying from their former comrades. South–South trade is expanding rapidly. Between 1987 and 1997, lower- and middle-income countries' imports grew at about 11 percent per year: Imports from other low- and middle-income countries grew about 10 percent per year.[75] However, many economists believe that promoting freer trade generally is a better approach than providing specific incentives for south-south trade.[76]

STABILIZATION OF INTERNATIONAL COMMODITY PRICES

A number of developing countries depend on the export of only a few primary commodities for most of their foreign exchange earnings.[77] African countries are particularly affected, whether the product is oil (Nigeria), copper (Zambia), cocoa (Côte d'Ivoire), or coffee (Uganda). In the mid-1980s, 13 African countries relied on only one primary export for three-fourths of their export earnings. Another 11 received over three-fourths of their earnings from only two products. A number of these products are subject to considerable price instability.[78]

Many developing-country governments and some economists have favored international price-stabilization agreements. The typical mechanism is a **commodity stabilization fund** that maintains a **buffer stock** of the commodity. The fund purchases additional quantities for its stock when the world price is low and sells when the world price is high. Such funds have been established for a few commodities but are expensive, subject to misuse, and require the cooperation of producer and consumer countries.

Rubber, sugar, and cocoa have had particularly extreme price instability. Such unpredictable market fluctuations make rational economic calculation extremely difficult for producers. For countries that depend on one or a few commodities for export revenues, economic planning or even macroeconomic policy becomes difficult.[79] Employment from export production is uncertain. Price stability would permit producers to concentrate on efficiency and promote consumer confidence as well. Instability can hinder growth by reducing the ability to save and the incentive to invest.

But there is considerable disagreement with the assumptions behind the argument, as well as with the claim that such schemes can work. Some studies have concluded that commodity prices have not been as unstable as supposed, and even unstable prices do not translate into instability for producer *income*, which is the key variable. Even if the instability exists, buffer stock financing is difficult, because it requires contributions from producers for additional purchases just when prices and incomes are lowest.[80] Further, protection from price declines hides economic signals for producers to diversify out of declining industries. Given the difficulty of forecasting trends, producers might read long-term downward trends as short-term fluctuations, with funds propping up the prices and accumulating large stocks.

Even more troublesome than the theoretical difficulties is the unhappy record of commodity funds, very few of which have been successful. Developing-country governments proposed an Integrated Fund for Commodities (or **Common Fund**), which would oversee individual funds and stabilize their operations. It would finance buffer stocks for individual commodity funds and also help finance research, product improvement, local processing, and other efforts of producer countries. The prospect of such a large international bureaucracy engaged in what some developed-country governments already considered dubious activity was not one easily accepted by the United States. Nonetheless, an agreement to establish the Common Fund was reached in 1980 and ratified in 1988. But most of the individual commodity funds have collapsed, and the Common Fund does not play a major role in commodity markets.[81]

TRADE, DEVELOPMENT, AND THE ENVIRONMENT

The theory of comparative advantage has some disturbing implications for the environment in developing countries. If a poor country has, compared to an industrialized country, relatively clean air and water, should it not specialize in products whose production involves relatively intensive use of those resources? In other words, should it not produce, and export, goods that, all else equal, are relatively pollution intensive? Granted that trade also promotes a more efficient use of a country's resource, meaning fewer units of inputs per unit of output, will this overcome the negative effects of greater production of pollution-intensive goods?[82] Will increasingly strict environmental controls in the developed countries drive their firms to poorer countries with fewer controls and ineffective enforcement?

Early research in this area has reached different conclusions. One study found that developing countries are increasing the "pollution intensity" of their exports. Another found that outward-oriented economies showed declining pollution intensity of production while inward-oriented countries showed an increase in pollution intensity. This would occur presumably due to more capital- and energy-intensive production associated with import substitution and a strong push for industrialization. A third study found the opposite: The pollution intensity of GDP was higher for outward-oriented economies.[83]

More recent studies suggest an optimistic appraisal, parallel to the environmental Kuznets curve analysis (Chapter 5). A multicountry study has confirmed that Japanese and North American growth was accompanied by displacement of dirty industries, such as production of metals and paper, to their trading partners. However, the key causes of higher pollution in Asia and Latin America were not trade related but due to changing demands and, at times, subsidies for energy consumption. While there is shifting of polluting industries to developing-country pollution havens, this tends to be transitory. A study of water pollution in China confirms that trade has increased pollution directly by attracting dirty export industries, but there has been an indirect favorable impact to the extent that trade promotes growth and growth leads to less pollution-intensive production methods.[84]

Optimists suggest that freer trade involves not only more efficient resource allocation, but also increased access to cleaner technologies and higher incomes leading to environmentally conscious populations and governments. Some are careful to add, however, that their assessments require that governments respond to citizen concern with increasingly stringent environmental regulations, vigorously enforced.[85] If governments see a trade-off between environmental protection and growth, they are unlikely to actively enforce whatever laws they might pass.

SUMMARY AND CONCLUSION

Economic growth and development usually require significant trade with the rest of the world. Nevertheless, those who claim that trade is a major engine of growth have been challenged by others who believe modern developing countries gain little from trade because they are trapped in an international division of labor in which they must continue to produce primary products and import industrial goods. This leads to an Import-Substitution strategy. In principle, there may be many sound reasons for developing countries initially to avoid full-scale integration into an existing international trading system, in order to develop a comparative advantage consistent with a different structure of production. In practice, however, the attempts to reduce trade dependence have been very costly. The IS strategy has usually been accompanied by distorting policies that promote inefficiency and hinder growth. Even successful IS strategies have eventually been abandoned.

Export Orientation is favored by those more optimistic about the capacity of the world economy to absorb increasing volumes of manufactured exports from developing countries. But export-oriented development does not guarantee any particular path or pace of development; sound private and public investment in natural, human, and physical capital will be necessary to take best advantage of a country's potential.

The evidence to date is that development is more successful under an outward-oriented strategy, although it is clear that governments are often heavily involved in this strategy, rather than content to let the market do the work. The best advice for such countries is to exchange quantitative restrictions for tariffs and to keep tariffs broad based and as low as possible consistent with the country's revenue needs.

The world trading system, formalized in the WTO, is gradually liberalizing trade. Developing countries have often benefited least from tariff reductions, but special treatment has often reduced the incentive to reform counterproductive trading regimes. Moving into the mainstream is increasingly being chosen by developing countries, although they are still vulnerable participants. Their best bet is most likely to use the system to pressure the industrialized countries to reduce their trade barriers.

Developing countries must ultimately obtain most of their external resources from their own exports. The industrialized countries are their main markets, but those markets are often protected in areas where new export growth needs to occur. Protectionism and tariff escalation are only somewhat offset by preference schemes that ordinarily benefit few countries.

Free trade agreements among developing countries are generally unsuccessful unless the countries are otherwise following policies favorable to development. They have often failed, but ASEAN and Mercosur are examples of regional trade agreements that are succeeding along with rapid economic growth.

Special attempts to structure commodity markets have been unsuccessful and are less likely to promote development than sound economic policies that take advantage of domestic and foreign resources to diversify a country's productive base.

It is not yet clear what impact outward-oriented policies will have on the environment in developing countries. Development will bring the ability to enforce environmental regulations, but the costs may be resisted by governments and businesses.

While a country's exports must ultimately provide most of the foreign exchange needed for imports, virtually every country that has developed has had additional flows of capital from the outside. These typically come in the form of direct foreign investment, gifts, and shorter-term capital flows. The next three chapters examine these flows.

Key Terms

- buffer stock (p. 364)
- commodity stabilization fund (p. 364)
- Common Fund (p. 364)
- comparative advantage (p. 330)
- customs unions (also known as free trade areas) (p. 360)
- effective protection (p. 340)
- Engel's law (p. 333)
- engine of growth (p. 329)
- exchange rate (p. 341)
- Export Orientation (EO) (p. 344)
- export pessimism (p. 331)
- Export Processing Zone (EPZ) (also known as Free Trade Zone) (p. 345)

- factor endowments (p. 331)
- factor intensity (p. 331)
- free trade area (FTA) (p. 360)
- Free Trade Zone (FTZ) (p. 345)
- General Agreement on Tariffs and Trade (GATT) (p. 353)
- Generalized Systems of Preferences (GSP) (p. 359)
- immiserizing growth (p. 333)
- Import Substitution (IS) (p. 338)
- infant industry (p. 334)
- Lomé accords (p. 360)
- Most Favored Nation (MFN) treatment (p. 354)

- Multifibre Arrangement (MFA) (p. 355)
- North American Free Trade Agreement (NAFTA) (p. 360)
- Part IV (of GATT) (p. 354)
- product cycle theory (p. 345)
- protectionism (p. 333)
- quantitative restrictions (p. 339)
- quota (p. 339)
- tariff (p. 339)
- tariff escalation (p. 358)
- terms of trade (net barter, p. 332; income, p. 334)
- vent-for-surplus theory (p. 331)
- World Trade Organization (WTO) (p. 351)

Questions for Review

1. What are the main conclusions of economic theory about the benefits of trade? How would those conclusions extend to the process of economic development?
2. What is the Prebisch objection to accepting trade as the engine of growth, and what sort of evidence would you look for in evaluating that objection?
3. What is the Import Substitution development strategy? How would it be implemented? What difficulties would confront it?
 4. What were some of the problems encountered by Ghana's import-substitution policies?
5. Describe the workings of a tariff and a quota. Which do economists prefer and why?
6. What are some of the arguments in favor of an outward-oriented development strategy? How is it implemented? What are some objections to it?
7. If a country were to shift from an inward to an outward strategy, what steps should it take, and what obstacles would it meet?
 8. How did Turkey and China differ in their approaches to trade reform? Why did Turkey's earlier effort fail?
9. What aspects of world markets are favorable to developing-country exports? What aspects hinder those exports? What policies in the developed countries would help or hinder developing-country exports?
10. State the case for requiring developing countries to play "by the rules" set up by the WTO, particularly Most Favored Nation treatment and low tariffs and other barriers to trade.
11. What are the potential gains and losses from free trade arrangements (customs unions)?

12. What are the benefits and drawbacks to preferential treatment given by industrialized countries to manufactured imports from developing countries?
13. Describe the operations of a commodity stabilization fund. What are the economic objections to such funds?
14. What are the implications of trade theory for the pollution intensity of developing-country trading patterns?

Related Internet Resources

Although all the major multilateral economic organizations devote attention to trade, the primary source of information is the WTO itself, at ⟨www.wto.org⟩. Among the developing-country regional organizations, the most active in the trade area is Mercosur, whose Web site is ⟨www.mercosur.org⟩. The easiest source for official information on NAFTA is the U.S. government's site, ⟨www.mac.doc.gov/nafta⟩. The government has a site devoted to preparations for a possible FTAA, at ⟨www.mac.doc/gov/ftaa2005/⟩, while a separate site also addresses this agreement, at ⟨www.ftaa-alca.org⟩. A number of organizations are actively campaigning to eliminate, change, or reduce the scope of multilateral trade agreements. A central source for these critiques is Public Citizen, at ⟨www.citizen.org/trade/index.cfm⟩. Also see WTO WATCH at ⟨www.wtowatch.org⟩.

Appendix 12A

GENERAL EQUILIBRIUM ANALYSIS OF INTERNATIONAL TRADE

The easiest way to visualize the gains from trade is through the general equilibrium analysis of an economy. It starts by depicting the limits on an economy's production and consumption, then shows how trade can expand the consumption level.

Figure 12A–1 introduces the tools of general equilibrium analysis.

PP is a production possibilities frontier that limits the full-employment output of an economy at any time. Its slope, the Marginal Rate of Technical Transformation, is the ratio of the Marginal Cost of agricultural goods to the Marginal Cost of manufactured goods (*MCa/MCm*): the cost trade-off between the two goods. Points outside are currently unobtainable, while points inside do not fully utilize resources.

CC is an indifference curve for a country, showing a level of utility obtained from consuming different combinations of agricultural and manufactured goods. Its slope, the Marginal Rate of Transformation in consumption, is the ratio of the Marginal Utility of agricultural goods to the Marginal Utility of manufactured goods (*MUa/MUm*). Higher indifference curves indicate greater levels of utility from consumption, hence, greater economic welfare.

The point of tangency of the indifference curve and production possibilities frontier (P_0C_0) marks the highest level of utility the country can obtain from its given production possibilities.

Figure 12A–2 uses this framework to analyze the impact of foreign trade on the economy.

Points P_1 and P_2 on the production possibilities frontier are combinations of agricultural and manufactured goods production. Price ratio lines represent the terms of trade (*Pa/Pm*) between agricultural and manufactured goods. Point C_1 is a combination of those goods that

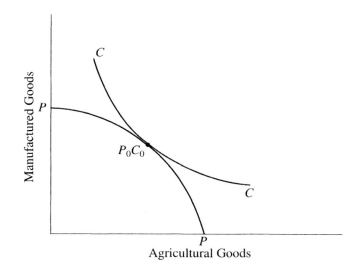

FIGURE 12A–1 General Equilibrium Framework

An economy attains its greatest welfare by producing and consuming where its highest feasible indifference is tangent to its production possibilities frontier.

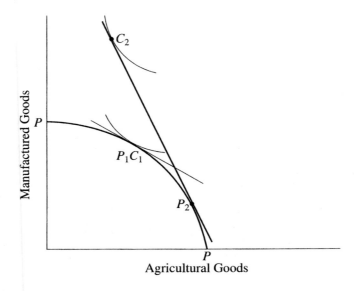

FIGURE 12A–2 Benefits of Trade

The pre-trade equilibrium is point P_1C_1. Trade shifts production to P_2, according to the country's comparative advantage. The new price ratio permits consumption (C_2) at a higher level of utility.

can be consumed before trade. The figure illustrates a small country that cannot affect the international terms of trade.

At P_1C_1 there is no trade (autarky), and the ratio of agricultural to manufactured prices (Pa/Pm) reflects domestic costs only. The opening of trade increases the demand for the export (agricultural) goods and lowers the demand for domestic production of the manufactured (import) goods. At P_2 the economy has moved toward specialization in agricultural

goods. The new price ratio (higher agricultural and lower manufactured prices) is the same for the domestic and world markets. This price ratio permits the country to increase its consumption and well-being to point C_2 (on a higher indifference curve).

If the country restricts its trade, for example, by imposing a tariff on the imported good, the price ratio moves back in the direction of the original line, production and consumption move back toward P_1C_1, and welfare is reduced.

Appendix 12B

IMPACT OF A QUOTA

A quota is an alternative restrictive measure, often used by governments trying to protect their domestic industries. We can illustrate a quota's impact in the same manner as we show a tariff.

Figure 12B–1 shows the protective effect of a quota of *BC* units, equal to the effect of the tariff in Figure 12–2. The same impact on consumption and production occurs, but what would have been the tariff revenue—now called a quota rent—will accrue to the importing firm unless import permits are sold off. If quotas do not go to the most efficient import use, additional loss will occur. The figure also shows that when demand increases, the rigid quota permits domestic firms to raise the price, whereas with a tariff the price would have remained the same.

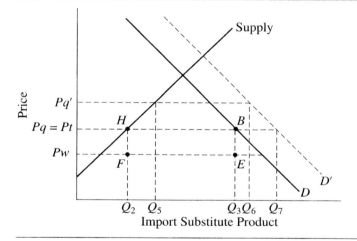

FIGURE 12B–1 Effect of a Quota

A quota (Q_2Q_3 units) can, in principle, be designed to have the same impact as a tariff, provided the quota rights are auctioned off to the highest bidder. The price rises from *Pw* to *Pq* (= *Pt* in Figure 12–2). The former tariff revenue *HBEF* is now received by the importer unless the government charges for the right to import. The extra money received by the importer is a quota rent.

An increase in demand to *D′* with the same quota (now Q_5Q_6) causes a rise in the price to *Pq′* and more inefficient domestic production. With a tariff, the price (*Pt* = *Pq*) would have remained the same and imports would have risen to Q_2Q_7.

Endnotes and Further Readings

1. Ricardo's *Principles of Political Economy and Taxation* (1817) is one of the classic texts in the history of economic thought.

2. Gottfried Haberler, "International Trade and Economic Development," (1959), reprinted by the International Center for Economic Growth (San Francisco, 1988).

3. Hla Myint, "The Gains from International Trade and the Backward Countries," *Review of Economic Studies* 22, no. 58 (1954–1955), and "The 'Classical Theory' of International Trade and the Underdeveloped Countries," *Economic Journal* 68, no. 270 (June 1958) pp. 317–337.

4. Gunnar Myrdal, "Development and Underdevelopment," National Bank of Egypt Fiftieth Anniversary Commemoration Lectures (Cairo, 1956), and *Economic Theory and Underdeveloped Regions* (London: Duckworth Press, 1957).

5. Ragnar Nurkse, "Trade Theory and Development Policy," in H. S. Ellis, ed., *Economic Development for Latin America* (New York: St. Martin's Press, 1961), and "Some International Aspects of the Problem of Economic Development," *American Economic Review* 62, no. 2 (May 1952), pp. 571–583. For a critique of Nurkse, see Irving B. Kravis, "Trade as a Handmaiden of Growth: Similarities Between the Nineteenth and Twentieth Centuries," *Economic Journal* 80 (December 1970), pp. 850–872.

6. Raul Prebisch's key works are *The Economic Development of Latin America and Its Principal Problems* (New York: United Nations, 1950), and "Commercial Policy in Underdeveloped Countries," *American Economic Review* 69, no. 2 (May 1959), pp. 251–273. See also Hans W. Singer, "The Distribution of Gains Between Investing and Borrowing Countries," *American Economic Review* 60, no. 2 (May 1950), pp. 473–485.

7. See Eric D. Larson, Marc H. Ross, and Robert H. Williams, "Beyond the Era of Materials," in *Scientific American* 254, no. 6 (June 1986).

8. See M. June Flanders, "Prebisch on Protectionism: An Evaluation," *Economic Journal* 74, no. 2 (June 1964), pp. 305–326; Stephen R. Lewis's chapter on "Primary Exporting Countries," pp. 1541–1600, and Balassa's chapter on "Outward Orientation," pp. 1645–1690, in H. B. Chenery and T. N. Srinivasan, eds., the *Handbook of Development Economics*, vol. 2 (Amsterdam: Elsevier Science Publishers, 1989). Specific studies include Enzo R. Grilli and Maw Cheng Yang, "Primary Commodity Prices, Manufactured Goods Prices, and the Terms of Trade of Developing Countries: What the Long Run Shows," *World Bank Economic Review* 3, no. 1 (January 1988), pp. 1–47; J. Cuddington and C. Urzua, "Trends and Cycles in the Net Barter Terms of Trade: A New Approach," *Economic Journal* 99, no. 396 (June 1989), pp. 426–442; D. Sapsford, P. Sarkar, and H. W. Singer, "The Prebisch–Singer Terms of Trade Controversy Revisited," *Journal of International Development* 4, no. 3, May–June 1992), pp. 315–332; Carmen Reinhart and Peter Wickham, "Commodity Prices: Cyclical Weakness or Secular Decline?" *International Monetary Fund Staff Papers* 41, no. 2 (June 1994), pp. 175–213; and Javier Leon Raimundo Soto, "Structural Breaks and Long-Run Trends in Commodity Prices," *Journal of International Development* 9, no. 3 (May–June 1997), pp. 347–366.

9. Soto, "Structural Breaks and Long-Run Trends in Commodity Prices."

10. See Robert E. Baldwin, "The Case Against Infant-Industry Tariff Protection," *Journal of Political Economy* 77, no. 3 (May–June 1969), pp. 295–305, and Gerald M. Meier, "Infant Industry," in *The New Palgrave Dictionary of Economics* (London: Macmillan Press, 1987), pp. 828–830.

11. See Hubert Schmitz and Tom Hewitt, "Learning to Raise Infants: A Case-Study in Industrial Policy," in Christopher Colclough and James Manor, eds., *States or Markets? Neoliberalism and the Development Policy Debate* (Oxford: Oxford University Press, 1991), pp. 173–196, and Jaymin Lee, "The Maturation and Growth of Infant Industries: The Case of Korea," *World Development* 25, no. 8 (August 1997), pp. 1271–1281.

12. See W. M. Corden, "The Structure of a Tariff System and the Effective Protection Rate," *Journal of Political Economy* 74, no. 3 (June 1966), pp. 221–237.

13. *World Development Report 1987*, p. 89.

14. See David Morawetz, "Import Substitution, Employment, and Foreign Exchange in Colombia: No Cheers for Petrochemicals," in C. Peter Timmer et al., *The Choice of Technology in Developing Countries: Some Cautionary Tales* (Harvard University: Center for International Affairs, 1975), pp. 95–107; Premachandra Athukoralage, "Import Substitution, Structural Transformation, and Import Dependence—A Case Study of Sri Lanka," *The Developing Economies* 19, no. 2 (June 1981), pp. 119–142; Anne O. Krueger, Maurice Schiff, and Alberto Valdes, "Agricultural Incentives in Developing Countries: Measuring the Effect of Sectoral and Economywide Policies," *World Bank Economic Review* 2, no. 3 (September 1987), pp. 255–271; and Lino Pascal Briguglio, "Small Country Size and Returns to Scale in Manufacturing," *World Development* 26, no. 3 (March 1998), pp. 507–515.

15. Werner Baer, *The Brazilian Economy: Growth and Development*, 3rd ed. (New York: Praeger, 1989), pp. 42, 365, and Byung-Nak Song, *The Rise of the Korean Economy* (New York: Oxford University Press, 1990), pp. 104–109.

16. See Arnold C. Harberger, ed., *World Economic Growth* (San Francisco: Institute for Contemporary Studies, 1984), especially Harberger's "Economic Policy and Economic Growth," pp. 427–468.

17. Paul Dorosh and Alberto Valdes, "Effects of Exchange Rate and Trade Policies on Agriculture in Pakistan," International Food Policy Research Institute, Research Report No. 84 (Washington: December 1990).

18. See Dani Rodrik, "The Limits of Trade Policy Reform in Developing Countries," *Journal of Economic Perspectives* 6, no. 1 (winter 1992), pp. 87–106.

19. Henry Bruton, "Import Substitution," in the *Handbook of Development Economics*, vol. 2, pp. 1601–1644. The quote is on p. 1606. Also see his "A Reconsideration of Import Substitution," *Journal of Economic Literature* 36, no. 2 (June 1998), pp. 903–936.

20. See Mrinal Datta-Chaudhuri, "The Background to the Current Debate on Economic Reform: Oil-Shocks, Recession in World Trade and Adjustment Problems for the Indian Economy," in Ashok Guha, ed., *Economic Liberalization, Industrial Structure and Growth in India* (Delhi: Oxford University Press, 1990), pp. 9–37; Abhijit Sen, "Trade Restrictions and Growth Constraints," in the same volume, pp. 59–73; Raphael Kaplinsky, "India's Industrial Development: An Interpretative Survey," *World Development* 25, no. 5 (May 1997), pp. 681–694; and Ashok V. Desai, "Recent Technology Imports into India: Results of a Survey," *Development and Change* 21, no. 4 (October 1990), pp. 723–749.

21. John Waterbury, "The Long Gestation and Brief Triumph of Import-Substituting Industrialization," *World Development* 27, no. 2 (February 1999), pp. 323–341; Alice Amsden, *Asia's Next Giant: South Korea and Late Industrialization* (New York: Oxford University Press, 1989); and Patrice Franko, *The Puzzle of Latin American Economic Development* (Lanham, MD: Rowman and Littlefield, 1999), chapter 3.

22. Arvind Panagariya and Maurice Schiff, "Commodity Exports and Real Income in Africa: A Preliminary Analysis," in Ajay Chhibber and Stanley Fischer, eds., *Economic Reform in Sub-Saharan Africa* (Washington: World Bank, 1991), pp. 170–181; Augustin Kwasi Fosu, "Primary Exports and Economic Growth in Developing Economies," *The World Economy* 19, no. 4 (July 1996), pp. 465–475; and Trudy Owens and Adrian Wood, "Export-Oriented Industrialization Through Primary Processing?" *World Development* 25, no. 9 (September 1997), pp. 1453–1470.

23. Dhanmanjiri Sathe, "Impact of Diversification of Exports: An Analysis of the Linkages of Indian Exports," *Indian Economic Journal* 42, no. 3 (January–March 1995), pp. 114–130.

24. See Dorsati Madani, "A Review of the Role of Export Processing Zones," World Bank Working Paper 2238 (Washington: 1999).

25. See the *1999 World Survey on the Role of Women in Development* (New York: United Nations, 1999), pp. 9–11.

26. "Trade Policies in Developing Countries," in R. W. Jones, ed., *International Trade: Surveys from the Handbook of International Economics* (Amsterdam, NY: North Holland, 1986).

27. Bela Balassa, "Outward Orientation," pp. 1672–1684. Also, Deepak Lal and Sarath Rajapatirana, "Foreign Trade Regimes and Economic Growth in Developing Countries," *World Bank Research Observer* 2, no. 2 (July 1987), pp. 189–218.

28. Anne O. Krueger et al., *Trade and Employment in Developing Countries*, vol. 3, *Synthesis and Conclusions* (Chicago: University of Chicago Press, 1983), p. 96. Also see Kwan S. Kim and P. Yorasopontaviporn, "International Trade, Employment, and Income: The Case of Thailand," *The Developing Economies* 27, no. 1 (March 1989), pp. 60–74.

29. Lyn Squire, *Employment Policy in Developing Countries* (New York: Oxford University Press/World Bank, 1981), pp. 144–152, and United Nations, *Women in a Changing Global Economy* (New York: United Nations, 1994), pp. 19–23.

30. Anne O. Krueger, "The Experience and Lessons of Asia's Super Exporters," in Vittorio Corbo, Anne O. Krueger, and Fernando Ossa, eds., *Export-Oriented Development Strategies: The Success of Five Newly Industrializing Countries* (Boulder, CO: Westview Press, 1985), p. 210.

31. *World Development Report 1987*, chapter 5. Also, Hadi Salehi Esfahani, "Exports, Imports, and Economic Growth in Semi-Industrialized Economies," *Journal of Development Economics* 31, no. 1 (January 1991), pp. 93–116, and Tain-jy Chen and De-piao Tang, "Comparing Technical Efficiency Between Import-Substitution-Oriented and Export-Oriented Foreign Firms in a Developing Country," *Journal of Development Economics* 26, no. 2 (August 1987), pp. 277–289.

32. Sebastian Edwards, "Openness, Productivity and Growth: What Do We Really Know?" *Economic Journal* 108, no. 447 (March 1998), pp. 383–398; Andrew Levin and Kakshmi K. Raut, "Complementarities Between Exports and Human Capital in Economic Growth: Evidence from the Semi-Industrialized Countries," *Economic Development and Cultural Change* 46, no. 1 (October 1997), pp. 155–174; Christopher A. Pissarides, "Learning by Trading and the Returns to Human Capital in Developing Countries," *World Bank Economic Review* 11, no. 1 (January 1997), pp. 17–32; Hendrik van den Berg and James R. Schmidt, "Foreign Trade and Economic Growth: Time Series Evidence from Latin America," *Journal of International Trade and Economic Development* 3, no. 3 (November 1994), pp. 249–268; and Jeffrey A. Frankel and David Romer, "Does Trade Cause Growth?" *American Economic Review* 89, no. 3 (June 1999), pp. 379–399.

33. David Dollar, "Outward-Oriented Developing Economies Really Do Grow More Rapidly: Evidence from 95 LDCs, 1976–85," *Economic Development and Cultural Change* 40, no. 3 (April 1992), pp. 523–544, and Jeffrey D. Sachs and Andrew Warner, "Economic Reform and the Process of Global Integration," *Brookings Papers on Economic Activity* 1995 (1), pp. 1–95.

34. See Colin Kirkpatrick, "Trade Policy and Industrialization in LDCs," in Norman Gemmell, ed., *Surveys in Development Economics* (New York: Basil Blackwell, 1987), pp. 56–89, and Colin I. Bradford, Jr., "East Asian 'Models': Myths and Lessons," in John P. Lewis and Valeriana Kallab, eds., *Development Strategies Reconsidered* (Washington: Overseas Development Council, 1986), pp. 115–128.

35. Balassa, "Outward Orientation," pp. 1650–1652. See also William R. Cline, "Can The East Asian Experience Be Generalized?" *World Development* 10 (1982), pp. 81–90, and Will Martin, "The Fallacy of Composition and Developing Country Exports of Manufactures," *The World Economy* 16, no. 2 (March 1993), pp. 159–172.

36. See Vasilis Panoutsopoulis, "The Growth of Exports from Developing Countries: Export Pessimism and Reality," in Helen Hughes, ed., *The Dangers of Export Pessimism: Developing Countries and Industrial Markets* (San Francisco: ICS Press, 1992), pp. 9–43, and in the same volume, Jayati Ghosh, "Can World Markets Continue to Absorb Export-Led Strategies of Developing Countries? The Export Pessimist's Case," pp. 115–142.

37. Bradford, "East Asian 'Models': Myths and Lessons," p. 123.

38. See Demetrios Moschos, "Export Expansion, Growth and the Level of Economic Development: An Empirical Analysis," *Journal of Development Economics* 30, no. 1 (January 1989), pp. 93–102, and Inderjit Kohli and Nirvikar Singh, "Exports and Growth: Critical Minimum Effort and Diminishing Returns," *Journal of Development Economics* 30, no. 2 (April 1989), pp. 391–400.

39. Bruton, "Import Substitution," pp. 1619–1633.

40. See L. P. Jones and I. Sakong, *Government, Business and Entrepreneurship in Economic Development: The Korean Case* (Cambridge: Harvard University Press, 1980).

41. Swarma D. Dutt and Dipak Ghosh, "The Export Growth-Economic Growth Nexus: A Causality Analysis," *Journal of Developing Areas* 30, no. 2 (January 1996), pp. 167–192; Behzad Yaghmaian, "An Empirical Investigation of Exports, Development and Growth in Developing Countries: Challenging the Neoclassical Theory of Export-Led Growth," *World Development* 22, no. 12 (December 1994), pp. 1977–1995; and Sofronis K. Clerides, Saul Lach, and James R. Tybout, "Is Learning by Exporting Important? Micro-Dynamic Evidence from Colombia, Mexico and Morroco," *Quarterly Journal of Economics* 113, no. 3 (August 1998), pp. 903–947.

42. David Evans, "Visible and Invisible Hands in Trade Policy Reform," in Colclough and Manor, *States or Markets? Neo-liberalism and the Development Policy Debate*, pp. 48–77.

43. Lant Pritchett, "Measuring Outward Orientation in LDCs: Can It Be Done?" *Journal of Development Economics* 49, no. 2 (June 1996), pp. 307–336.

44. Francisco Rodriguez and Dani Rodrik, "Trade Policy and Economic Growth: A Skeptic's Guide to Cross-National Evidence," National Bureau of Economic Research Working Paper 7081 (Washington: April 1999). Stanley Fischer's critique of Sachs and Warner is his "Comments," *Economic Reform in Sub-Saharan Africa*, p. 103. Also see Oli Havrylyshyn, "Trade Policy and Productivity Gains in Developing Countries: A Survey of the Literature," *World Bank Research Observer* 5, no. 1 (January 1990), pp. 1–24; Dominick Salvatore and Thomas Hatcher, "Inward Oriented and Outward Oriented Trade Statistics," *Journal of Development Studies* 27, no. 3 (April 1991), pp. 7–25; and Sebastian Edwards, "Openness, Trade Liberalization, and Growth in Developing Countries," *Journal of Economic Literature* 31, no. 3 (September 1993), pp. 1358–1393.

45. See Bhagwati's "Rethinking Trade Strategy," in Lewis and Kallab, *Development Strategies Reconsidered*, pp. 91–104.

46. Jaimin Lee, "Comparative Advantage in Manufacturing as a Determinant of Industrialization: The Korean Case," *World Development* 23, no. 7 (July 1995), pp. 1195–1214, and Elio Londero and Simon Teitel, "Industrialization and the Factor Content of Latin American Exports of Manufactures," *Journal of Development Studies* 32, no. 4 (April 1996), pp. 581–601.

47. See Gerald K. Helleiner, "Industrial Organization, Trade and Investment in Developing Countries," in his *The New Global Economy and the Developing Countries* (Hants, U.K.: Edward Elgar, 1990), pp. 210–228, and Rodney E. Falvey, "Intra-Industry Trade Theory and Export-Oriented Strategies," in Helen Hughes, ed., *The Dangers of Export Pessimism* (San Francisco: ICS Press, 1992).

48. See Vinod Thomas, John Nash and Associates, *Best Practices in Trade Policy Reform* (Washington: World Bank, 1991). See also Wendy E. Takacs, "Options for Dismantling Trade Restrictions in Developing Countries," *World Bank Research Observer* 5, no. 1 (January 1990), pp. 25–46; Anne O. Krueger, "Trade Policy and Economic Development: How We Learn," *American Economic Review* 87, no. 1 (March 1997), pp. 1–22; and Judith M. Dean, "The Trade Policy Revolution in Developing Countries," *The World Economy* 32, no. 4 (December 1994), pp. 373–397.

49. Dani Rodrik, "Premature Liberalization, Incomplete Stabilization: The Ozal Decade in Turkey," in Michael Bruno et al., eds., *Lessons of Economic Stabilization and Its Aftermath* (Cambridge: MIT Press, 1991), pp. 323–358; Ameane M. Choksi, Michael Michaely, and Demetris Papageorgiou, "The Design of Successful Trade Liberalization Policies," in Adras Koves and Paul Marer, eds., *Foreign Economic Liberalization: Transformations in Socialist and Market Economies* (Boulder, CO: Westview Press, 1991), pp. 37–56; and Rudiger Dornbusch, "The Case for Trade Liberaliza-

tion in Developing Countries," *Journal of Economic Perspectives* 6, no. 1 (winter 1992), pp. 69–85.

50. See Vittorio Corbo, "Trade Reform and Uniform Import Tariffs: The Chilean Experience," *American Economic Review* 87, no. 2 (May 1997), pp. 73–77, and Pradeep Mitra, "The Coordinated Reform of Tariffs and Indirect Taxes," *World Bank Research Observer* 7, no. 2 (July 1992), pp. 195–220.

51. David Greenway, Wyn Morgan, and Peter Wright, "Trade Reform, Adjustment and Growth: What Does the Evidence Tell Us?" *Economic Journal* 108, no. 450 (September 1998), pp. 1547–1561, and Mauricio Mesquita Moreira and Paulo Guilherme Correa, "A First Look at the Impacts of Trade Liberalization on Brazilian Manufacturing Industry," *World Development* 26, no. 10 (October 1998), pp. 1859–1874.

52. The WTO Web site is ⟨www.wto.org⟩.

53. See OECD, *Integrating of Developing Countries into the International Trading System* (Paris: 1992).

54. Kunibert Raffer, "Helping Southern Net Food Importers after the Uruguay Round: A Proposal," *World Development* 25, no. 11 (November 1997), pp. 1901–1907.

55. Michael M. Phillips, "U.S. Reaches Deal to Clear Admission of China to WTO," *Wall Street Journal*, June 11, 2001, and "China Officially Joins WTO," ⟨www.cnn.com/2001/WORLD/asiapcf/central/11/10/china.WTO/index.html⟩.

56. See particularly Bhagirath Lal Das, *The WTO Agreements: Deficiencies, Imbalances and Required Changes* (London: Zed Books, 1998).

57. See OECD, *Reconciling Trade, Environment and Development Policies* (Paris: 1996).

58. For example, congressional testimony by Lori Wallach at ⟨www.citizen.org/pctrade/gattwto/Seattle%20Ministerial/homepage.htm⟩.

59. See Gerald Helleiner, "The New Industrial Protectionism and the Developing Countries," in his *International Economic Disorder* (Toronto: University of Toronto Press, 1981), and "International Trade Theory and Northern Protectionism Against Southern Manufactures," in Helleiner, ed., *For Good or Evil: Economic Theory and North–South Negotiations* (Toronto: University of Toronto Press, 1982).

60. See Yongzheng Yang, "The Impact of MFA Phasing Out on World Clothing and Textile Markets," *Journal of Development Studies* 30, no. 3 (April 1994), pp. 892–915, and Sri Ram Khanna's *International Trade in Textiles: MFA Quotas and a Developing Exporting Country* (New Delhi: Sage Publications, 1991).

61. *World Development Report 1987*, p. 142, and Amarendra Bhattacharya and Johannes F. Linn, "Trade and Industrial Policies in the Developing Countries of East Asia," World Bank Discussion Paper 27 (Washington: 1988).

62. J. Michael Finger and Patrick A. Messerlin, "The Effects of Industrial Countries' Policies on Developing Countries," World Bank Policy and Research Series No. 3 (Washington: World Bank, 1989), p. 8.

63. See Andre Sapir and Lars Lundberg, "The U.S. Generalized System of Preferences and Its Impacts," in Robert E. Baldwin and Anne O. Krueger, *The Structure and Evolution of Recent U.S. Trade Policy* (Chicago: University of Chicago Press, 1984).

64. OECD, *Integrating of Developing Countries into the International Trading System*, pp. 32–34. See also Drusilla K. Brown, "Trade Preferences for Developing Countries: A Survey of Results," *Journal of Development Studies* 24, no. 3 (April 1988), pp. 335–363.

65. World Bank, *Sustaining Rapid Development in East Asia and the Pacific* (Washington: World Bank, 1993).

66. Gerhard Pohl and Piritta Sorsa, "European Integration and Trade with the Developing World," World Bank Policy and Research Series No. 21 (Washington: 1992), p. 25.

67. See Riordan Roett, ed., *Mexico and the United States: Managing the Relationship* (Boulder, CO: Westview Press, 1988); Sidney Weintraub, *A Marriage of Convenience: Relations Between Mexico and the United States* (New York: Oxford University Press, 1990); Gary Clyde Hufbauer and Jeffrey J. Schott, *NAFTA: An Assessment* (Washington: Institute for International Economics, 1993); Ricardo Grinspun and Maxwell A. Cameron, eds., *The Political Economy of North American Free Trade* (New York: St. Martin's Press, 1993); Richard S. Belous and Jonathan Lemco, eds., *NAFTA as a Model of Development* (Washington: National Planning Association, 1993); and Sidney Weintraub, *NAFTA at Three: A Progress Report* (Washington: Center for Strategic and International Studies, 1997). Numerous Web sites have information and opinions on NAFTA: ⟨www.tcf.org/Publications/Basics/NAFTA/Evaluating_NAFTA.html⟩; the U.S. government's NAFTA Homepage at ⟨www.mac.doc.gov/nafta/⟩; and criticism from Ralph Nader's Public Citizen group at ⟨www.citizen.org/pctrade/nafta/naftapg.html⟩.

68. See ⟨www.mac.doc/gov/ftaa2005/index.htm⟩ and ⟨www.ftaa-alca.org⟩.

69. See ⟨www1.worldbank.org/wbiep/trade/RI_map.htm#south-south⟩.

70. Ali Mansoor and Andras Inotai, "Integration Efforts in Sub-Saharan Africa: Failures, Results and Prospects—A Suggested Strategy for Achieving Efficient Integration," in Chhibber and Fischer, eds., *Economic Reform in Sub-Saharan Africa*, pp. 217–232, and Athanasios Vamvakidis, "Regional Integration and Economic Growth," *World Bank Economic Review* 12, no. 2 (May 1998), pp. 251–270.

71. Web sites include the Andean Pact at ⟨www.comunidadandina.org⟩, the Central American Common Market at ⟨www.cries.org/⟩, and the Economic Community of West African States at ⟨www.ecowas.int⟩.

72. The ASEAN member countries are Indonesia, Malaysia, the Philippines, Singapore, Thailand, and Brunei. See John Wong, "The ASEAN Model of Regional Cooperation," in Seiji Naya et al., eds., *Lessons*

in *Development: A Comparative Study of Asia and Latin America* (San Francisco: International Center for Economic Growth, 1989), pp. 121–142.

73. The Mercosur Web site is ⟨www.mercosur.org⟩.

74. Alexander J. Yeats, "Does Mercosur's Trade Performance Raise Concerns About the Effects of Regional Trade Arrangements?" *World Bank Economic Review* 12, no. 1 (January 1998), pp. 1–28, and Edward L. Hudgins, "Mercosur Gets a 'Not Guilty' on Trade Diversion," *Wall Street Journal*, March 21, 1997. Also see Riordan Roett, ed., *MERCOSUR: Regional Integration, World Markets* (Boulder, CO: Lynne Rienner, 1999).

75. *World Development Indicators 1999.*

76. See Oli Havrylyshyn, "The Direction of Developing Country Trade: Empirical Evidence of Differences Between South–South and South–North Trade," *Journal of Development Economics* 19, no. 3 (December 1985), pp. 255–281, and David Greenaway and Chris Milner, "South–South Trade: Theory, Evidence, and Policy," *World Bank Research Observer* 5, no. 1 (January 1990), pp. 47–68.

77. See Jere R. Behrman, "International Commodity Agreements: An Evaluation of the UNCTAD Integrated Commodity Programme," in William R. Cline, ed., *Policy Alternatives for a New International Economic Order: An Economic Analysis* (New York: Praeger, 1979), pp. 63–156; Marian E. Bond, "An Econometric Study of Primary Commodity Exports from Developing Country Regions to the World," *IMF Staff Papers* 34, no. 2 (June 1987), pp. 191–227; and Stephen R. Lewis, Jr., "Primary Exporting Countries," especially pp. 1551–1552. For the debate over instability of primary products prices, see Alasdair I. MacBean, *Export Instability and Economic Development* (Cambridge: Harvard University Press, 1966); James Love, "Export Instability in Less Developed Countries: Consequences and Causes," *Journal of Development Studies* 25, no. 2 (January 1989), pp. 183–191; Sandwip K. Das and Manoj Pant, "Trade Liberalization, Export Earnings Instability, and Growth," in Ashok Guha ed., *Economic Liberalization, Industrial Structure and Growth in India* (Delhi: Oxford University Press, 1990); and James Love, "Commodity Concentration and Export Earnings Instability: A Shift from Cross-section to Time Series Analysis," *Journal of Development Economics* 24, no. 2 (December 1986), pp. 239–248.

78. See Michael Barratt Brown and Pauline Tiffen, *Short-Changed: Africa and World Trade* (London: Pluto Press, 1992), p. 22.

79. See James Love, "Export Instability in Less Developed Countries: Consequences and Causes," pp. 183–191.

80. See Matthias Lutz, "The Effects of Volatility in the Terms of Trade on Output Growth: New Evidence," *World Development* 22, no. 12 (December 1994), pp. 1959–1975, and David Dawe, "A New Look at the Effects of Export Instability on Investment and Growth," *World Development* 24, no. 12 (December 1996), pp. 1905–1914.

81. Christopher L. Gilbert, "International Commodity Agreements: An Obituary Notice," *World Development* 24, no. 1 (January 1996), pp. 1–19. The Common Fund is alive and well and on the Web at ⟨www.common-fund.org⟩.

82. C. Ford Runge, "Trade, Pollution, and Environmental Protection," in Daniel W. Bromley, ed., *Handbook of Environmental Economics* (Cambridge: Blackwell Publishers, 1995), pp. 353–375.

83. For contrasting findings, see Patrick Low and Alexander Yeats, "Do 'Dirty' Industries Migrate?" in Low, ed., *International Trade and the Environment*, World Bank Discussion Paper No. 159 (Washington: World Bank, 1992), pp. 89–104; Robert Lucas, David Wheeler, and Hemamala Hettige, "Economic Development, Environmental Regulation and the International Migration of Toxic Industrial Pollution: 1960–1988," pp. 67–86 in the same volume; and Michael T. Rock, "Pollution Intensity of GDP and Trade Policy: Can the World Bank Be Wrong?" *World Development* 24, no. 3 (March 1996), pp. 471–479. Also see Irma Adelman, Habib Fetini, and Elise Hardy Golan, "Development Strategies and the Environment," in Partha Dasgupta and Karl-Goran Maler, *The Environment and Emerging Development Issues*, vol. 1 (Oxford: Clarendon Press, 1997), pp. 161–197.

84. The multicountry study is Muthukumara Mani and David Wheeler, "In Search of Pollution Havens: Dirty Industry in the World Economy," in Per G. Fredricksson, ed., *Trade, Global Policy, and the Environment*, World Bank Discussion Paper No. 402 (Washington: World Bank, 1999), pp. 115–128. For China, see Judith M. Dean, "Testing the Impact of Trade Liberalization on the Environment: Theory and Evidence," pp. 55–64 of the same volume.

85. See Juan Carlos Belausteguigoitia and Luis F. Guadarrama, "United States–Mexico Relations: Environmental Issues," in Barry P. Bosworth et al., eds., *Coming Together? Mexico–US Relations* (Washington: Brookings Institution Press, 1997), pp. 91–117.

13

FOREIGN AID AND DIRECT INVESTMENT

If you give a man a fish,
He will live for a day;
Give him a net and
He will live for a lifetime.
—CHINESE PROVERB

The bourgeoisie . . . must nestle everywhere, settle everywhere, establish
connections everywhere . . . [it] has . . . given a cosmopolitan character to
production and consumption in every country. . . .
—KARL MARX (1818–1883)

INTRODUCTION

Financial resources that cannot be obtained from domestic savings and export revenues must be sought from outsiders. Developing countries with significant resources, good management, and private projects with promise can borrow money from commercial banks. They can obtain other resources through foreign investment from companies abroad who see the potential for a profit, and foreign aid, including loans or gifts from other governments or multilateral development banks. Aid is provided on concessional terms, as projects may yield lower returns or might be less efficient than expected due to the development status of the borrower and because the borrowers are poor. Foreign aid is a controversial topic: Many people have criticized aid as a waste of resources that puts undue power in the hands of governments. However, over the last 40 years, foreign aid has had a fair amount of success.

In addition to foreign aid, capital flows into developing countries as direct investment by foreign firms. Investment and other private capital flows are replacing aid as a major source of foreign capital. But investment, like aid, is controversial: Some developing countries have welcomed it, and others have chased it out. While foreign investment can be profitable for both investor and host country, not every investment is a wise one. In this chapter, we discuss the rationales for foreign aid and direct investment.

WHAT IS AID AND HOW IMPORTANT IS IT?

The terms **aid**, foreign aid, and foreign assistance refer to gifts or loans on terms that are more favorable than commercial loans. **Bilateral aid** goes from one government to another, while **multilateral aid** comes from an institution such as the World Bank, which is governed by member countries. Although aid is simply additional resources, the donor and recipient may not have the same objectives for its use.[1]

Development Spotlight 13–1 provides examples of various categories of financial flows. Figure 13–1 shows how much money is involved in foreign aid and how it compares to other sources. Table 13–1 shows how aid receipts relate to output and population in representative countries.

Official Development Assistance (ODA) constituted 40 percent of net external capital received by developing countries in 1970 but fell to only 24 percent in 1980 as bank lending increased. It increased to 42 percent in 1985 and 1990 because several years of debt crisis had severely reduced private investment and lending, which have now resumed. Preliminary figures for 1998 show large outflows of bank funds due to the financial crisis in Asia and elsewhere. While ODA has grown slowly and has fallen in real terms, it still accounts for 3 percent of GDP for low-income countries.

Aid's Concessional Character

The clearest difference between aid and other sources of funds is that aid is provided on **concessional terms**: more favorable than ordinary bank loans. For example, where a commercial loan might carry 10 percent interest, due in payments over a 5-year period starting the year after the loan is made, an aid loan might carry just 4 percent interest or less, and be payable over a 20-year or longer period that starts 5 years (the grace period) after the loan is made. Such terms are based on the borrower's less developed status, and allow the borrower to undertake projects that are considered socially desirable, but have a long-term payout and low private rate of return. Examples include transportation infrastructure, education, and health care.

Every aid package has its own degree of concessionality that can be determined by comparing its repayment terms with prevailing commercial terms. Thus conces-

DEVELOPMENT SPOTLIGHT 13–1

CATEGORIES OF FOREIGN FUNDING

Aid: Grants, or loans on favorable conditions, generally from governments and multilateral organizations to government. These may be used for projects—such as a steel mill, a school, agricultural research, or a dam—or a "program" covering a sector of the economy. ODA is Official Development Assistance.

Foreign Direct Investment (FDI): A foreign company creates a subsidiary to provide goods or services. The foreign company may own all or part of the subsidiary. Such companies may run utilities or banks, grow pineapples or sugar cane, or produce automobiles or athletic shoes.

Bank Lending: Foreign banks lend money to local companies or governments for a variety of purposes, often involving imports of machinery, components, and materials. Domestic firms borrow in foreign currency to pay their suppliers.

Bonds: Foreign individuals and companies buy the bonds of local firms or governments.

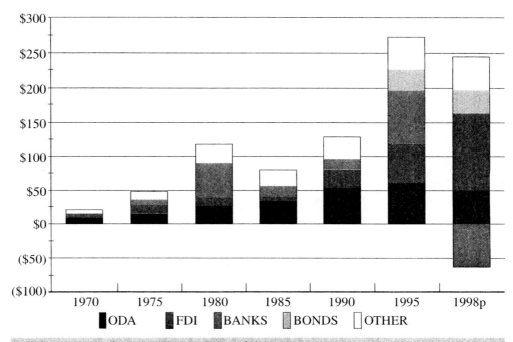

FIGURE 13–1 Net Resource Flows (Current $ Billions)

While financial flows have risen over the last 30 years, official aid has remained constant over the last decade. Direct investment is up, but bank lending shrank during the crises of the 1980s and late 1990s.

Sources: Tony Killick, "Responding to the Aid Crisis," in UNCTAD, *International Monetary and Financial Issues for the 1990s* (New York: United Nations, 1998), p. 21, and OECD, "Financial Flows to Developing Countries in 1998: Rise in Aid; Sharp Fall in Private Flows," OECD news release, Paris, June 10, 1999.

sional aid is said to have some **grant element**, or departure from commercial terms. The grant element is a percentage equivalent to an outright grant were the remainder of the loan on normal commercial terms. The lower the interest rate, the longer the repayment period; and the longer the grace period, the more concessional aid is and the higher the grant element. For example, if a $1 million commercial loan carries 10 percent interest and an aid loan is at 5 percent, this is equivalent to $500,000 at 10 percent and a $500,000 grant: a grant element of 50 percent.

The **Development Assistance Committee (DAC)** of the OECD collects data and oversees aid efforts of member countries. It counts as **Official Development Assistance (ODA)** only contributions with a grant element of 25 percent or more. For bilateral aid in 1994, the average grant element was 62.4 percent, averaging 2.1 percent interest, a 9-year grace period, and maturity of 28 years. In 1996 the grant element of DAC country aid had reached 91.8 percent.[2]

One problem with capital being available on concessional terms is that there may be an incentive to apply it to commercial projects that might not meet normal lending criteria. Aid donors have until recently tended to restrict their lending to public-sector activities in order to prevent recipient governments from undertaking normal commercial ventures with concessional money. For such ventures, recipient governments are expected to approach the private capital markets, domestic or international.

TABLE 13–1 Aid Receipts: Selected Countries

	$ Millions		Percentage of GNI		Dollars Per Capita	
	1985	*1999*	*1985*	*1999*	*1985*	*1999*
Botswana	96	61	13.7	1.1	91	38
Burkina Faso	198	398	18.4	15.5	25	36
Lesotho	94	31	16.5	2.8	61	15
Malawi	113	446	11.0	25.1	16	41
Mauritania	209	219	31.2	23.6	121	84
Senegal	295	534	12.2	11.4	45	58
Tanzania	487	990	7.9	11.3	22	30
Zambia	328	623	15.4	20.8	49	63
China	940	2,324	0.4	0.2	1	2
India	1,470	1,484	0.7	0.3	2	1
Pakistan	801	732	2.2	1.2	8	5
Sri Lanka	484	251	8.2	1.6	31	13
Costa Rica	280	–10	8.0	–0.1	108	–3
El Salvador	345	183	9.4	1.5	72	30
Haiti	153	263	8.0	6.1	26	34
Israel	1,978	906	10.3	0.9	467	148
Jordan	538	430	14.5	5.4	157	91
All Low Income	12,674	22,339	2.1	2.2	5	9
Low-Middle Income	9,827	17,816	2.0	0.7	15	9

Sources: World Development Report 1987, World Development Indicators 2001.

This works only if aid is not **fungible**, that is, capable of being moved to other uses. If aid finances a public-sector project that would have been undertaken anyway, the recipient can then simply use its own funds for the commercial venture, thus frustrating the donor's intent. Some research suggests that unless aid represents more than 15 percent of a recipient's GNP, fungibility on a macro scale results in all aid resources being shifted from investment to consumption, thus frustrating one of the purposes of that aid. An additional type of fungibility may permit a country's finances, freed up by aid money, to be used for military purposes.[3]

The widespread fungibility of aid is indicated by studies showing that a dollar of aid loans results, on average, in government spending of only 63 cents, and if grants and loans are considered, the result is only 33 cents. This means that aid allows governments to tax less than they would have. But even where government spending increases by the full aid dollar, an average of only 29 cents goes for investment in development and the rest for ordinary government expenses.[4]

The Purposes of Aid: Projects and Programs

Starting in the mid-1950s, the characteristic approach of the first 20 years or so was to lend money in the form of **project aid**, from the huge Aswan High Dam in Egypt to a small women's weaving project in Jordan. While recipients usually wanted money that could be used for more general purposes, donors felt that they could and should maintain closer control of how the money was being spent. There were other advantages of this approach for donors: Whatever was built with the aid (a dam, a school, an agricultural research facility) could be easily identified with a specific donor, and donors often direct their aid to projects that require goods sold by the donor's own companies. Finally, project aid was one way of assuring that the recipient's development efforts went in directions approved by the donor.

Today **program aid** is often provided: It supports a wider development purpose and allows the recipient some discretion in how to spend the money. In earlier decades, program aid was often pushed by recipients who were capable of carrying out programs and interested in minimizing donor interference. Since the mid-1970s, at the insistence of some donors such as the World Bank, Structural Adjustment Loans (SALs) have been instituted to counteract policies that have damaged broad sectors of an economy (agriculture, exports, transportation), by allocating money more flexibly within the sector. These loans, examined in more detail in Chapter 14, are monitored by the donor agencies who look for evidence that a specific set of economic reforms is instituted to increase the effectiveness of those loans. The percentage of bilateral aid going to programs doubled from six percent in the mid-1970s to 12 percent in the early 1990s.

The Value of Aid: Tying

Bilateral donors often provide **tied aid**: money is tied to the purchase of inputs from the donor country. For example, a donor might support a textile mill in a developing country but require that the machinery be purchased from its own companies. This reduces the value of aid when the donor's firms are not the most cost-effective source of the needed equipment. If the donor were the most cost-effective source of inputs (and the recipient were not pressured to buy from third countries), the tying would be unnecessary.

The prevalence of tying has varied over time. In 1993, DAC donors tied, in whole or in part, 45 percent of their bilateral aid, which may have reduced the value of the aid by at least 20 percent. By 1999 only 16 percent of bilateral ODA was tied. Food aid and **technical assistance** (foreign experts who come to work with or advise the recipient government) may be fully tied. While donor countries understand the costs, no donor is comfortable giving up the practice while others retain it.[5]

Delivery of Aid: Nongovernmental Organizations

A significant change over the last two decades has been the increased role of **Nongovernmental Organizations (NGOs)** in the delivery of foreign aid. NGOs originating in developed countries range from single-issue organizations to broader institutions that work with or replace official agencies in the delivery of programs. CARE, which started out providing emergency food relief, has become more fully involved with agricultural development, as have organizations such as Oxfam. Planned Parenthood carries out family planning projects. Most denominations of Christian churches have focused on health, education, and community development.

In 1987, northern NGOs raised $3.3 billion for developing countries and channeled $2.2 billion from official aid organizations. A more recent estimate is that from 10 percent to 13 percent of all ODA is channeled through NGOs. The primary advantage of

NGOs is their effectiveness in promoting grassroots participation, and their willingness to tackle environmental and social issues that government aid organizations will not. They have led the way in primary health care, women in development, small-scale credit, and appropriate technology. They have been particularly noted for promoting the development of effective institutions that help poor people help themselves.

The benefits of organizations placed between governments and recipient groups has spurred the creation of thousands of NGOs in developing countries. Development-oriented groups, sometimes referred to as Grassroots Organizations (GROs), include many of the banking and credit groups discussed in Chapter 4, organizations like the Kaira District Dairy Cooperative in India that are focused on one activity and those with more diverse goals, such as the Federaçao de Orgâos para Asistência Sociale e Educacional in Brazil. Some have been particularly effective, but their proliferation may threaten the ability of a smaller number to obtain funds and perform effectively. While many NGOs are able to avoid government bureaucracy, some from the North have grown to the point where they acquire some of the same institutional characteristics and receive more of their funding from official agencies, perhaps threatening their ability to innovate.[6]

HOW MUCH AID SHOULD BE PROVIDED?

Many developing-country governments believe they need as much aid as they can get. However, this approach assumes that all money, for whatever purpose, can and should be spent. To the contrary, there are a number of reasons why more than a certain amount of money might be useless or even counterproductive.

Recipients' Constraints

The availability of money on concessional terms is a temptation to fund commercial projects that may not be profitable under normal circumstances. Every project can be given an estimated rate of return. If a steel mill is expected to yield a 7 percent return, a government cannot borrow from a bank at 10 percent, but aid money may be available at 5 percent. But even if an infrastructure project such as a highway has an expected rate of return of only 4 percent, why not ask for 5 percent aid money and hope for the best? There is ample room for mistakes and corruption, so care must be taken in providing concessional assistance for particular projects.

Moreover, the viability of any single project may well disintegrate if the overall economy is not well managed. Or a project that fits all the criteria of profitability may do so only because the calculations are distorted by monopoly, interest rate ceilings, and import protection. If such policies are remedied, profitability may well disappear. If they are not, the project's social return may be far less than estimated, and the investment may be unwise for the economy.

How much additional money can a country reasonably use at any time? The contribution of an investment to growth and development is likely to be constrained by the lack of complementary factors such as trained labor, skilled administrators, infrastructure, and data-analyzing capacity. These limits collectively are an economy's **absorptive capacity**; its capacity to make efficient use of an amount of capital.

One approach to measuring aid requirements would begin by setting a realistic target growth rate of GDP, then using an incremental capital-output ratio to determine how much investment is necessary. If the economy is not expected to generate sufficient savings and voluntary external resources to permit that amount of investment, the difference would be the amount of aid needed.

Issues for Donors

The other side of the *how much* question is how much aid donors *should* provide. Should donors provide whatever our economic criteria tell us recipients need or want? Developing-country governments have urged donors to provide seven-tenths of 1 percent of their GDP as bilateral economic assistance. While some industrialized countries have accepted that goal for themselves, and the DAC uses it as a guideline, some OECD countries, including the United States, have not accepted any target. Table 13–2 ranks DAC donors by amount of aid provided and the percentage of their respective GDP accounted for by aid. While the United States has been the top provider of bilateral aid in most years, its rank in terms of a percentage of GDP has slipped steadily and currently is last within the OECD at less than .1 percent of GDP.[7]

TABLE 13–2A Ranking of DAC Bilateral Aid Donors by Amount				
	1965	*1975*	*1985*	*1999*
Japan	5	4	5	1
United States	1	1	1	2
France	2	2	2	3
Germany	4	3	4	4
United Kindom	3	5	5	5
Netherlands	9	7	7	6
Italy	10	13	8	7
Denmark	12	11	12	8
Canada	8	6	5	9
Sweden	11	8	9	10

TABLE 13–2B Ranking by Aid as Percentage of GDP				
	1965	*1975*	*1985*	*1999*
Japan	8	13	17	7
United States	3	12	20	22
France	1	5	5	6
Germany	6	10	9	14
United Kindom	5	11	15	18
Netherlands	7	2	2	3
Italy	13	17	18	20
Denmark	12	7	4	1
Canada	9	8	7	12
Sweden	9	1	3	4

Sources: World Development Report 1992 and *World Development Indicators 2001.*

Donors presumably have something to gain from providing aid. While there have been attempts to estimate the economic costs and benefits of aid, political leverage is often more important. Until the end of the Cold War, a good portion of U.S. aid was aimed at winning and keeping support of anti-Communist regimes.[8] The Middle East and the international narcotics trade are now key aid targets.

Development Fads: Changing Economic Rationales for Aid

Donors provide aid presumably in order to foster development. The initial focus of many aid programs was the construction of infrastructure projects such as highways and dams. There has also been support for population control, education, and agricultural research. These kinds of projects reflect the view that certain types of public investment provide the foundation for development and generate positive externalities. Other aid went to manufacturing projects, from steel mills to textile mills.

Regardless of the benefits of individual projects, however, impatience with the overall results of aid began to set in by the early 1970s. Some recipients made little economic progress, and a number of countries were limiting the benefits of their growth to the upper-income groups. In response came a new approach, aimed at satisfying basic human needs (BHN). Aid programs would emphasize areas such as health, primary education, agriculture, and regions of the recipient country where programs could aid the poorest of the poor. If earlier aid and development efforts had failed to trickle down to the poor, the new approach would try to create development from the bottom up.

However, many economists dismissed BHN as misguided egalitarianism and bad economics. The logic of market economics was said to dictate that funds should be placed where the prospective return on investment was greatest, and the income produced in that fashion would, eventually, trickle down. Dissatisfaction with BHN led to an emphasis on establishing and expanding markets, and reversing trends toward a larger government role in developing economies. Privatization ideas still hold considerable power, but donors have come to recognize the need for good governance: governments that are responsive to the people, competent, and relatively free from corruption. For example, the World Bank has several judicial reform projects in countries from Guatemala to Georgia. These projects help courts and judicial systems through personnel training and upgrading equipment.

THE DEBATE OVER AID

Discussion over the *how* of aid has been tame compared to the debate over the why or the whether. A debate exists among those who attack aid from the right, those who attack from the left, and those who both attack and support aid from a middle-of-the-road perspective.

The Rightist Critique

Peter Bauer, a prominent development economist, believes that aid rarely works, is not needed, and has high economic and political costs. It may substitute for capital provided at market terms but encourages governments to undertake prestige projects (such as new capital cities in Nigeria and Tanzania) that do not meet market criteria. And some countries have grown, even rapidly, over periods during which they received no aid.

Political costs include allowing recipient governments to pursue bad policies that benefit public bureaucracies at the expense of the majority of the population and private companies. Food aid to African and Asian nations, Bauer contends, masks the failure of governments to promote agriculture. Civil wars, such as in Ethiopia, have been prolonged by aid from Western governments.

Bauer realizes that aid is a fact of life, so he offers a set of recommendations: First, aid should be provided through grants, not loans, to make the cost transparent and permit lower outlays since repayment would not be required. Second, individual governments should provide aid on a bilateral basis, without international agencies. Donor governments should put clear conditions on their aid: This political control cannot be exercised through agencies such as the World Bank. Third, aid should focus on governments with policies that are most likely to promote the welfare of their people. Next, NGOs should provide humanitarian aid in order to remove government bureaucracies from both the giving and receiving ends. Finally, remove developed-country trade barriers. Bauer firmly believes in "trade, not aid"; the industrialized countries could do more good by making trade easier.[9]

The Leftist Critique

The left end of the political spectrum, including Marxists and *dependistas*, see aid only as furthering the West's goal of the integration of the world capitalist system. They minimize the benefits of aid by pointing to its small size, its ties to donor exports, and its political conditions.

Further, the left sees costs to the recipient countries. They have been under pressure to support the politics of their benefactors, which has often meant political power for anti-Communist dictators such as Marcos in the Philippines. The Socialist government elected in Chile in 1970 was denied World Bank assistance under pressure from the United States. Aid has supported inappropriate technology, pushed development in directions that has minimized competition with Western industries, and cemented the developing countries' dependent status in the international division of labor.[10]

Donors do not deny many of the left's charges. The public statements of American politicians and business executives in favor of foreign aid have always sought to reassure a somewhat skeptical American Congress and public that aid is beneficial to the United States as well as to recipients. Its links to U.S. national security interests, exports, private investment, and an open world trading system have been not secrets but key aspects to the promotion of the program. While U.S. supporters of aid see these as legitimate points, those from the left see them as cynical or sinister.

Development Misconceived: Aid from the Bottom Up

A newer critique of aid claims that even when successful on its own terms, aid does not promote development because it misconstrues development and views the recipient population as targets of, rather than participants in, the process.[11]

This critique is an attack on bureaucracy, both in donor and recipient countries. The Development GAP organization charges that USAID, for example, has ignored legislative mandates to increase the participation of the poor in its programs and remains "structured primarily to satisfy the needs of U.S. security, those of vested economic interests and, ultimately, those of its own bureaucracy."[12] Government institutions in the recipient countries tend to be distant from and even adversarial to the people whose lives are supposed to be improved.[13]

The concept of development embodied in aid programs bothers these critics, who charge that development is just a fancy word for economic growth and that aid programs that merely provide capital, technology, or training ignore the needs of the people to be helped. Grassroots development efforts require that the people be involved in the process from the beginning: not only in the implementation of projects but also in their identification. This claim is supported by a study for the World Bank of 121 rural water supply projects: Those for which participation was a project goal had a 62 percent success rate while others had a 10 percent success rate.[14] One of the key reforms suggested by this approach is the greater use of NGOs, which ideally would be groups of committed private citizens who would consult people on their needs and help them realize those needs in the context of aid programs.

The Defense

Reports by the Pearson Commission (for the World Bank, 1969), the Peterson Task Force (for the U.S. government, 1970), and the Brandt Commission (1980) concluded that foreign aid can be improved but that it is fundamentally sound.[15] It was the Pearson Commission that first suggested the donor aid target of 0.7 percent of GNP.

John P. Lewis and Gerald Meier have written extensively to defend aid. Lewis acknowledges numerous examples of failure and counterproductive use of aid but cites numerous achievements: agricultural research leading to increased food production in Asia; reduced birth rates through family planning programs; institution building—the creation or strengthening of governmental, commercial, educational, and financial institutions; and some quickening of growth rates. We have improved our aid practices through experience, and the cases of growth without aid, noted by Bauer, are by and large the exception rather than the rule.[16]

Meier says aid can be made more valuable to its recipients by breaking the ties to donor exports and specific projects and, in direct contrast to Bauer's view, by removing the political strings attached to bilateral aid through a more multilateral approach.

On the receiving side, Meier suggests a more thorough integration of aid with the country's development program and ensuring that aid is an addition to, not a substitute for, domestic resources. Recipients' domestic policies should be reformed, and aid should be conditioned on performance criteria, such as increased saving ratios, lowered capital-output ratios, reduced external deficits, increased employment, more equal income distributions, and stimulation of private investment. At the same time, we must allow some aid on the basis of need. We should recognize the interaction among aid, private capital, and trade and minimize the debt-service burden by paying attention to sound investment criteria.[17] Cases 13–1 and 13–2 provide examples of unsuccessful and successful aid projects.

Lewis agrees that aid needs to take a more antipoverty approach (similar to BHN) and should target agriculture, human resource development, special needs of women, and grassroots institutions. He believes that traditional aid agencies are necessary for large-scale projects. He also insists that aid programs cannot reject growth-oriented goals and programs, because growth is one of the best ways to reduce poverty. To Lewis, there is no conflict, only complementarity, between centrist and grassroots approaches.[18]

AID PROBLEMS IN CAMEROON AND MALI

FAST FACTS

Cameroon on the Map: West Africa

Population: 15 Million

Per Capita GNI and Rank: 460   (150)

Life Expectancy: Male—50   Female—52

Adult Literacy Rate: Male—81%
Female—69%

Mali on the Map: West Africa

Population: 11 Million

Per Capita GNI and Rank: 240   (193)

Life Expectancy: Male—41   Female—44

Adult Literacy Rate: Male—47%
Female—33%

Aid can fail for many reasons. Projects may be ill-advised from the start because they have little economic merit or because donors want to finance capital exports regardless of the value of the project to the recipient. The funds can be wasted through corruption or inefficiency. But two agricultural projects failed to meet expectations for more technical and economic reasons.

The North Cameroon Seed Multiplication Project, financed by U.S. Agency for International Development, attempted to produce and distribute improved seeds for peanuts, maize, sorghum, and millet on a budget of $1.5 million in 1975. This proved overambitious, and more money was provided in 1982. But poor coordination among agencies and poor management made implementation slow: It was not possible to make seed for the four crops available when needed. The project design used "inappropriately capital-intensive technologies." Selling the seed at 50 percent to 100 percent below market meant the project costs could not be recovered.

The project seems to have put undue emphasis on the production and distribution phases, underfunding research. Thus, the seed was not noticeably higher yielding than locally available varieties.

The Mali Sud Rural Development Project was an attempt to alleviate the distress of some very poor farmers in a reasonably promising region of Africa.

The project, funded by the World Bank's International Development Association (IDA), the UN's International Fund for Agricultural Development (IFAD), and the French and Dutch governments, was designed to provide credit and technical advice to small farmers. However for several years, until criticism brought about some change, the poorest farmers ended up being ineligible for assistance. To qualify, villages had to organize associations (VDA's, or *tons*) as channels for credit. However, the poorest farmers tended to also have less organizational skills and so were less likely to form VDAs. At least 500 of the 3,500 villages, including the poorest, were denied credit.

Technical mistakes were also made in the project design. Villages were encouraged to increase the output of maize, although that crop requires consistent rainfall. Many villages had erratic rainfall and no irrigation, so their maize crops failed. A related IFAD project in Mali encouraged poor farmers to plant peanuts, groundnuts, and cowpeas—crops for which there turned out to be no market.

Sources: For Cameroon, see Bruce F. Johnston, Allan Hoben, and William K. Jaeger, "United States Activities to Promote Agricultural and Rural Development in Sub-Saharan Africa," in Uma Lele, ed., *Aid to African Agriculture: Lessons from Two Decades of Experiences* (Baltimore: Johns Hopkins University Press, 1991), pp. 277–324. For Mali, see John Madeley, *When Aid Is No Help: How Projects Fail, and How They Could Succeed* (London: Intermediate Technology Publications, 1991).

CASE 13–2

SUCCESSFUL AID PROJECTS: THE USUTU PULP COMPANY IN SWAZILAND AND THE MICROHYDRO PROGRAM IN NEPAL

FAST FACTS

Swaziland on the Map: South Africa

Population: 1 Million

Per Capita GNI and Rank: $1,350   (124)

Life Expectancy: 46

Adult Literacy Rate: 79%

Nepal on the Map: South Asia

Population: 23 Million

Per Capita GNI and Rank: $220   (195)

Life Expectancy: Male—58   Female—58

Adult Literacy Rate: Male—58%
Female—23%

The Usutu Pulp Company began as a forestry project to export timber from Swaziland. External funding was received from the British-based Commonwealth Development Corporation (CDC), with local funding from a private company, Courtalds Ltd., and the Swazi government. It was transformed into a pulp mill in 1962 and has been expanded several times since, using both internally generated and external funds.

Economically, it has been extremely successful. By the late 1980s it was "one of the three lowest cost major producers of unbleached Kraft pulp in the world," the country's largest private employer, and accounted for 12 percent of GNP and 20 percent of exports, producing a positive trade balance. In the process, the company has built two complete towns. There is no reliable accounting of the environmental impact, but the land has been upgraded by the afforestation.

There remains some concern that despite a fair amount of employee training, the 100 or so top executives are expatriates. Further, the mill produces only one product and

is vulnerable to temporary declines in demand or ultimately replacement by other products, despite a significant amount of research and upgrading of the product and production process. The international marketing is done by a British company, although the CDC and Courtaulds are part owners.

The microhydro project in Nepal was a joint project between a group of Protestant church organizations and a joint-venture engineering company owned by the governments of Switzerland and Nepal, with additional external funding. It designed, produced, and installed small water-driven turbines to run mills that grind wheat, maize, and rice, improving on traditional technology but taking advantage of the country's significant water resources. The capital costs are somewhat higher than the diesel turbines used locally, but operating costs are much less and do not rely on imported fuel.

The turbines have a number of other advantages. They save significant labor time, largely for women and children; add to other electrification needs; provided a significant net increase in employment in milling, manufacturing of the turbines, and construction; and the project has involved much transfer of technology and skills. The environmental impact of the milling itself seems to be neutral, but the increased electrification has reduced fuelwood consumption at less environmental cost than larger hydro projects. The ownership of the mills is potentially skewed toward the wealthy, but this could be mitigated by cooperative ownership. The project, begun in the 1960s, continued to require some outside assistance for expansion, but most of the project, from design to operation, can be handled locally.

―――――

Sources: Julian Evans and David Wright, "The Usutu Pulp Company—The Development of an Integrated

Forestry Project," pp. 151–171, and Drummond Hilsop, "The Micro-Hydro Programme in Nepal—A Case Study," pp. 74–100, both in Marilyn Carr, ed., *Sustainable Industrial Development* (London: Intermediate Technology Publications, 1988).

The DAC has also evaluated members' aid programs and has published a Development Assistance Manual entitled *DAC Principles for Effective Aid*. It notes the need to strengthen project analysis and implementation; actively involve the target groups at all stages of the project from selection to implementation; increase attention to institution building, technical cooperation, the environment (including population) and involvement of women; reduce donor competition; increase efficiency of procurement; and move toward more democracy and human rights and reduced military spending. Most of the same conclusions were reached in a World Bank study in 1991.[19]

DOES AID WORK? THE ECONOMIC INVESTIGATION

In the face of criticisms, there have been numerous investigations as to whether, in fact, government-to-government aid has worked. These investigations have taken place on both the macro- and micro level and have addressed institutional and technical concerns.

Specific Issues

"Does Aid Work?" has been asked for so long that it seems only fair to have a report with that title.[20] As usual, the answer is "yes, but . . . ." The conclusions of the Cassen report and other studies deserve a review.

Aid's Impact on Savings and Investment

If aid is to contribute to growth, it should add to the amount that a recipient country can save and invest, rather than just substitute for domestic savings. Some early investigations concluded that aid could have a minimal or even negative impact on domestic savings, government tax receipts, and investment. By reducing incentives to save and tax, aid would permit an economy to increase its current consumption above levels it might otherwise have attained, nullifying its intended impact and possibly reducing economic growth.

However, other studies found higher ratios of savings and investment to income after aid. In addition, any negative correlation between aid and savings might be explained in various ways. Aid might have been received *because* savings and tax ratios had fallen, rather than being the reason for the declines. Also, some of the studies had used total aid figures, including food aid that usually is intended for consumption rather than to add to savings. Thus, there is little hard evidence that aid is generally counterproductive to savings and investment.[21]

A recent study by Janine Bowen finds that in poorer countries aid seems to have in fact caused reductions in saving. At middle-income levels, aid seems to have supplemented—not replaced—domestic saving.[22] If the results of this study are supported, it would suggest that at lower incomes, aid can work only if particular efforts are made to ensure its effective use and that governments do not offset its impact through lower taxes or switching investment expenditures to consumption.

Projects and Programs

The Cassen study found that projects "on average do produce satisfactory results in a very large proportion of cases,"[23] despite donor disappointment with large industrial projects that often run at a loss without continued aid. There is much room for improving project sustainability; helping small-scale industry; considering environmental impacts; learning from mistakes; improving coordination among donors; resisting pressure to make loans for bureaucratic purposes; and identifying, appraising, and evaluating projects. Particularly, better management and attention to efficiency of entire sectors would be helpful.

Some program lending has not been effective due to lack of careful identification of objectives and coordination among donors. Donor coordination has received a great deal of attention, yet it is not clear that it has been successful in reducing duplication and conflicts of objectives.

The Cassen report found coordination of efforts, both among donors and between donors and recipients "sadly wanting." Typically, the different donors' activities do not mesh into a coherent program. Duplication leads to waste, such as when 18 brands of water pumps were supplied to Kenya's water system, due to proliferation of donors. All this increases administrative costs and lack of fiscal control. The report recommends that there be a better understanding and sharing of objectives between donor and recipient, and among donors, to maximize the effectiveness of aid.

Aid and Poverty

Projects that are explicitly aimed at reducing poverty, including those that focus on the income potential of the poor rather than on particular sectors or industries, are successful: They yield high rates of return, and there is no necessary trade-off between alleviating poverty and efficient allocation of resources. The Cassen report suggests, therefore, that more aid projects incorporate an explicitly antipoverty element, and insists that recipients must be committed to dealing specifically with poverty. Reduction of poverty must be a commitment of national policy; otherwise aid will be ineffective on its own.

A recent examination of donors' operations concludes, however, that they vary considerably with respect to poverty reduction (PR) goals. Some donors do not even state PR as a goal, while for others such a stated goal is not well defined. In some programs, PR may be subordinated to maximizing the benefit of aid to the donor's own companies, while others construct PR goals without consulting the would-be beneficiaries.[24]

Food Aid

Many developed-country governments provide aid directly in the form of food, either at or below market prices, especially when they have surpluses at home. The Cassen report concludes that food aid generally achieves its objectives, but more attention should be paid to reducing costs through triangular trade that would permit regional products to be sent to some recipients in exchange for donor food to others.

While there have been many failures in this area, the report claims that food can be used successfully under two conditions: it should be part of the assistance provided for already-existing projects, rather than special food-aid projects; and the additional food should not reduce prices to the point where farmers reduce their own production.

To the concern that food aid covers poor agricultural policies, the report replies that some countries have responded to food aid by improving policies, leading to higher output. And while the specific commodities can depress prices in the receiving countries, this has helped India by keeping industrial wages down and encouraging farmers to shift to higher-value crops.[25]

Aid and the Market

In answer to those who have claimed that aid promotes nonmarket approaches to development, this report concludes that "aid is, on balance, a good friend of market forces, and has been so for many years."[26] In this respect, at least, the left-wing critique of aid is on the mark, but their opponents believe that this market orientation is essential.

Aid and Economic Growth

The Cassen report concluded that "... *the majority of aid is successful in terms of its own objectives*. Over a wide range of countries and sectors, aid has made positive and valuable contributions."[27] Case 13–3 summarizes one of the longest-running aid efforts, aid to India.

However, numerous studies have failed to find a correlation across countries between foreign aid and economic growth. These studies all warn that this should not be surprising given (*a*) the relatively small ratio of aid flows to any recipient country's total output and (*b*) the wide variety of other factors involved, most especially the development policies of the recipient country.

Bowen's study, however, has produced an interesting result: Aid is negatively associated with growth at low per capita income levels (below about $1,000 in 1988 prices) but positively associated with growth above that level.[28] One reason, perhaps, is that governments of the poorest countries are unable to make effective use of aid. Perhaps they are poor because their policies stymie growth and nullify aid. More to the point, however, is whether a country's economic policies will support aid's efforts to spur growth and development. This question has been the subject of more intense focus over the last 10 years.

Summarizing the lessons of 11 case studies, Lele and Nabi suggested that aid can work properly only when the recipient country follows sound economic policies (outward orientation, limited government, and maximum competition), and when there is coordination of effort among the recipient and all donors within the context of a clear development strategy.[29]

A major World Bank study[30] supports the notion that government policies are crucial. The conclusion is based in part on research that relates aid's effectiveness to a policy index that includes the budgets surplus or deficit, the inflation rate, and the degree of openness to trade. While this type of index needs to be treated with caution, the resulting estimates support common sense: Where countries have low deficits, low inflation, and are relatively open to trade, aid can increase the growth rate of GDP (by about .5 percent). Where macroeconomic policies are poor, aid may have no impact

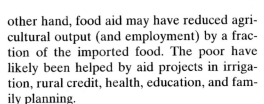

CASE 13–3

THE LONG HISTORY OF AID TO INDIA

FAST FACTS

On the Map: South Asia

Population: 998 Million

Per Capita GNI and Rank: $440   (163)

Life Expectancy: Male—62   Female—64

Adult Literacy Rate: Male—68%
Female—44%

India achieved independence in 1947 with a large population that included many with a high-level Western education. The government set up a planning commission that immediately began to crank out development plans, making the country a likely candidate to receive foreign aid. Although comparable data for the entire period are difficult to come by, total aid receipts between 1971 and 1985 averaged about $1.8 billion annually, of which over half was used to repay aid loans. The proportion of the aid that was tied varied over the years from 13 percent to 53 percent per year. Aid use in different years has provided as much as 39 percent of imports, 11 percent of investment, and 32 percent of government's development spending, although all of these figures are significantly lower now.

Lipton and Toye report that there was no convincing link between aid and growth, aid has generally not closed the country's foreign exchange gap, and increased saving and investment have been largely offset by declining performance in the utilization and productivity of capital. While total aid has been "not obviously relevant" to poverty reduction attempts, aid connected to the Green Revolution has helped poor consumers by keeping food prices down. On the other hand, food aid may have reduced agricultural output (and employment) by a fraction of the imported food. The poor have likely been helped by aid projects in irrigation, rural credit, health, education, and family planning.

Most Indian projects seem to have had reasonable rates of return, even though a study of World Bank projects showed delays and cost overruns to be common. The agricultural sector, beyond food aid and Green Revolution projects, has been aided through programs of education, research, and community development.

Aid seems to have neither caused, nor increased, the Indian government's restrictions on the private sector, and in fact the dialogue between donors and the government may have helped convince India to liberalize its economy beginning in the 1980s. Most funds do go through government hands but often have a positive impact on the private sector through subcontracting and through lowering prices on the metals, steel, chemicals, and petroleum produced by the government. Lipton and Toye conclude that despite some serious shortcomings, aid has been largely successful in India.

Sources: Michael Lipton and John Toye, *Does Aid Work in India?* (London: Routledge, 1990); Uma Lele and Manmohan Agarwal, "Four Decades of Economic Development in India and the Role of External Assistance," in Uma Lele and Ijaz Nabi, *Transitions in Development: The Role of Aid and Commercial Flows* (San Francisco: ICS Press, 1991), pp. 17–42; and Vasant Sukhatme, "Assistance to India," in Anne Krueger, Constantine Michalopoulos, and Vernon Ruttan, *Aid and Development* (Baltimore: Johns Hopkins University Press, 1988), pp. 203–225.

or even make things worse. The authors also note that while bilateral aid does not seem to favor countries with good policies, multilateral aid does.[31]

Conditionality

The deterioration of many African economies and the growing awareness of the importance of good policies for effective aid have ushered in a new stage of **conditionality**, the imposition of specific conditions of policy change in exchange for program assistance. The IMF and the World Bank have taken a much stronger policy advice and conditionality role over the last 15 years with their Structural Adjustment Programs. However, the World Bank study shows that the kind of conditionality usually imposed by aid donors is often ineffective. If the government opposes reform, it will thwart the effectiveness of aid and conditions put on it. While reform is essential, donors should look to broad indicators of success rather than a multitude of specific conditions.[32]

The greater disposition of donors and recipients to discuss outward-oriented policies and greater encouragement to private enterprise has moved the question of conditionality to a more cooperative level for the time being. Developing countries are more willing to listen, up to a point, but as Lipton and Toye suggest in their review of the policy dialogue in India, "conditionality cuts both ways"; when recipients listen and act, the importance of donors following up in terms of amounts or stability of aid flows increases.[33] It is also incumbent upon donors to give sensible, consistent advice.

New areas for potential conditionality, including environmental matters and the participation of women and the poor are arising. The detrimental impact on development of recipient governments' military spending and the broader issues of democratic governance are now explicit concerns.[34] Developing-country complaints about applying human rights standards to developing countries indicate that some recipient governments will resist these other types of conditionality as irrelevant and out of place in aid programs.

MULTILATERAL AID: THE WORLD BANK

The International Bank for Reconstruction and Development, better known as the World Bank, was created after World War II primarily to assist European countries rebuild their economies.[35] Once that task was largely completed, attention shifted to the developing countries. The Bank's stated purposes are to help countries improve their economies so as to "promote private foreign investment," to "promote the long-range balanced growth of international trade . . . by encouraging international investment," and "to conduct its operations with due regard to the effect of international investment on business conditions" in borrowing countries.[36]

The Bank makes long-term loans to countries at interest rates that generally reflect its own cost of borrowing, which is the main source of its funds. Member countries contribute capital in accordance with their economic ability, but a large portion of the contribution is callable, or in reserve, rather than actually held by the Bank. On the basis of these contributions, the Bank then borrows on international capital markets by selling its bonds, for the funds it lends to developing countries. In addition to the Bank proper, members created in 1960 an affiliate, the **International**

Development Association (IDA), which provides credits to low-income countries (per capita GDP below $785 in 1997 prices) for longer periods of time and at zero interest. The Bank group also includes the International Finance Corporation (IFC), which makes loans and buys shares in private companies in developing countries; an arbitration organization called the International Center for the Settlement of Investment Disputes (ICSID); and the **Multilateral Investment Guarantee Agency (MIGA)**.

The Bank is a political institution, although ostensibly its decisions are based on economic variables. Voting on the Bank's Executive Board is based on member contributions. As of June 30, 2000, the United States held 16.50 percent of the votes, followed by Japan with 7.92 percent. Germany, France, and Britain together had 13.38 percent, giving these five countries almost 38 percent of the vote. All other executive directors represent groups of countries, with directors from developed countries accounting for another 29 percent of the votes.[37] It is not difficult to see why developing countries may see the deck stacked against them.

The Bank disburses large sums of money, but its net flows are not always large. As Table 13–3 shows, over the 1990s the Bank loaned over $230 billion, but over the years 1994 to 1999, after accounting for repayments and interest, its net transfers to developing and transition economies were only $1.5 billion. During that period, net transfers were positive to most regions, although not large, but the Bank received over $12 billion more than it spent in the Americas and over $3 billion more than it spent in the Middle East/North Africa region. The Bank has become the world's largest development-oriented research institution, and provides training and employment opportunities to a large number of developing-country professionals.

There are also three regional development banks: the Inter-American Development ment Bank (IDB), the Asian Development Bank (ADB), and the African Development ment Bank (AfDB). Each of these is an independent entity with somewhat different rules and priorities. The United States is a major source of funding and policy advice for the IDB, and both the United States and Japan play important roles in the ADB. The African Bank has less impact and attempts to insulate itself a bit more from donor countries, although, again, the United States plays an important role in its activities. Because the primary source of policy direction is the World Bank itself, we focus on it.

TABLE 13–3 World Bank Lending by Region ($ Billions)

Region	1990–1994 (Average)	1995	1996	1997	1998	1999	1994–1999 (Net)
Sub-Saharan Africa	3.4	2.3	2.7	1.7	2.9	2.1	5.5
East Asia/Pacific	5.1	5.7	5.4	4.9	9.6	9.8	5.4
South Asia	3.2	3.1	2.9	2.0	3.9	2.6	0.8
Europe/Central Asia	3.2	4.5	4.4	5.1	5.2	5.3	5.4
Latin America/Caribbean	5.6	6.1	4.4	4.6	6.0	7.7	–12.2
Mideast/North Africa	1.6	1.0	1.6	0.9	1.0	1.6	–3.4
Total	22.1	22.7	21.4	19.2	28.6	29.1	1.5

Source: World Bank *Annual Report 1999*, various pages.

Lending Activities of the World Bank

Distribution of Bank/IDA lending by sector in 1998 and 1999 is given in Table 13–4. Once the Bank began its development role in earnest, it focused on financing specific projects, usually in infrastructure (particularly roads) and industry. It then shifted emphasis to agriculture and energy. Asia and Latin America have been the key regions for regular Bank loans, with Asia and Africa the main recipients for IDA loans. In principle, the Bank is committed to take into account only the economic merits of a proposed project, and to ignore political and broader economic considerations, but this principle is now routinely and openly violated.

The World Bank's policy emphases reflect larger trends in development assistance. Loans were traditionally made for specific projects. From the 1950s, project criteria were assessed narrowly in terms of rates of return and contributions to a borrower's overall economic growth. However, the Bank's concerns have broadened to consider the impact of a project on overall development, including on the poorer parts of the population. As the Basic Human Needs philosophy found its way into some Bank lending, its sectoral emphasis shifted to include basic services, agricultural and urban development, as well as poverty- and environment-specific projects, while taking greater care to include training and institutional reform and development.[38]

Since 1980 the Bank has devoted a larger share of its lending to broad adjustment loans, either for specific sectors of the economy (Sector Adjustment Loans, or SECALs) or for overall economic reform (Structural Adjustment Loans, or SALs). These program loans provide balance of payments support and funds to help the borrower change economic policies and the institutions required to implement the new

TABLE 13–4 World Bank Lending by Sector ($ Billions)

Sector	*1998*	*1999*
Agriculture	3.1	2.6
Education	3.1	2.0
Electric Power and Other Energy	1.9	0.6
Environment	1.1	1.0
Finance	5.8	6.6
Industry	Negligible	0.7
Mining	1.2	0.3
Multisector	1.3	4.3
Oil and Gas	0.1	Negligible
Population, Health, Nutrition	2.2	1.7
Public Sector Management	1.3	1.1
Social Protection	2.5	3.6
Telecommunications	0.1	0.2
Transportation	3.0	3.0
Urban Development	1.3	0.6
Water Supply and Sanitation	0.5	0.6
Total	28.6	29.0

Source: World Bank *Annual Report 1999*, p. 10.

policies. In 1997 to 1999, commitments for adjustment lending accounted for 27 percent, 39 percent, and 53 percent of total lending.[39] The $15 billion in 1999 included $4 billion in sector loans (the largest was over $750 million for the social security program in Brazil) and $11 billion in structural adjustment loans (including over $2.5 billion to Argentina and $2 billion to South Korea). In the last few years, the Bank has become increasingly active in crisis economies. Of the Bank's $29 billion of lending in 1999, for example, almost $6 billion went to the finance sector, including $5 billion to South Korea to support financial sector reform and the balance of payments generally.[40]

Critiques of the World Bank

As foreign aid in general has been attacked, so naturally has the World Bank. From the right come the claims that the Bank has been throwing money at development, funding dubious projects and programs that permit a government to reduce its own development efforts, and supporting governments that have little regard for their own people and the workings of the market system. In response, the Bank usually documents the favorable rates of return on its projects and the extent to which private activity is promoted by its programs, and examines its program priorities from time to time.

Critical views of the Bank from the left maintain just the opposite: that the Bank lives up to its mandated mission to make conditions comfortable for private foreign investment and for market-oriented development. Bank documents and spokespeople at the very least claim that this is what they are doing, and the left agrees.[41]

As attention to the specific problems of poverty in developing countries has become more prominent, a grassroots critique maintains that the Bank is incapable of alleviating poverty due to its "primary commitment to the international financial community, the pressure upon it to loan money, and its lack of contact with, and methodologies to reach and involve, local populations."[42] The Bank's Structural Adjustment Loans (see Chapter 14) are accused of pushing export-led growth strategies that exclude the poor and harm the environment. The Bank is said to work through institutions in the recipient country that have no contact or sympathy with the poor. Further, the Bank's policies are generally seen as hostage to U.S. government views, because the United States is the largest contributor and voter in the Bank and the Bank's president is, by custom, always an American.*[43] The voting structure, as we have seen, gives the major industrialized countries 56 percent of the votes.

The Bank has come under more intense recent criticism from groups that feel developing countries are ill served by the world's multilateral institutions. The groups cite the environmental impact of some projects and claim that adjustment programs hurt the poor. A critique from the Mobilization for Global Justice singled out a cashew-export project in Mozambique that forced the government to send raw cashews to India, where they are "shelled by hand by children" and close a processing plant in Mozambique, costing 10,000 jobs.[44] A large coal mining project in India put the coal company in charge of resettling thousands of people, with disastrous results. And an antipoverty program for China, intended to resettle 58,000 people to disputed

---

*This arrangement was agreed upon at the 1944 Bretton Woods conference that set up the Bank and the Fund. The Managing Director of the IMF is always a European. The regional development banks are headed by residents of the region, with the president of the Asian bank always being Japanese.

Tibetan land, was scratched when the Chinese government refused to accept conditions recommended by human rights groups.[45]

A more friendly critique echoes some of these issues. Sheldon Annis believes that while the Bank began focusing on poverty in the mid-1970s, it had a number of weaknesses including identifying effective policies, sustaining projects, trying to look at poverty as an issue in isolation from overall economic problems, and effectively reaching the poorest people.[46] He agrees that more loans to poor countries do not necessarily mean that the poorest people are getting the benefits. And he sees Bank policies in the 1980s as receding from a real commitment to fighting poverty.

The Bank's vulnerability to divergent critiques is exemplified in a 1987 steel-sector loan to Mexico. While the Steel Caucus of the U.S. Congress complained that the Bank was helping Mexico produce more steel and thus undermine the U.S. industry, the left complained that the loan was conditioned on Mexico privatizing its steel industry. The Bank argued that the loan would actually reduce Mexico's steel output and make the industry more efficient.

All the critical reviews can draw on numerous specific examples of Bank projects and policy decisions to support their claims. A book-length critique cites Nigerian policies that discriminated against agriculture, prejudice against cash-crop farmers in Tanzania, corruption and incompetence in Paraguay, lack of local institutions in Haiti, and absence of meaningful land tenure for the poor in Brazil as problems leading to failure or inadequate success in various projects. But it also faults the Bank projects for having too many objectives, excessive reliance on expatriates and consequent inadequate training of local citizens, limited involvement of the target population, lack of field testing of agricultural technologies, inadequate feasibility studies, and insufficient attention to social issues, particularly the resettlement of people uprooted by projects such as large-scale irrigation schemes in the Philippines and Brazil.[47]

The Bank has answered its critics by putting a greater emphasis on poverty reduction, environmental and gender concerns, greater participation by poor recipients in project design and operation, and by more attention to project evaluation. Its 1999 "Annual Review of Development Effectiveness" suggests that 70 percent of the projects concluded that year, involving almost 80 percent of its disbursements, had "satisfactory" outcomes—above the norm for the decade but a decline from the previous year. On the other hand, only 40 percent of the projects had a "substantial" impact and about 50 percent were likely to be "sustainable."[48] Clearly, much remains to be done in this area.

The World Bank's Past and Future

The Bank has greatly expanded its role over the years. Its initial focus on development projects often avoided larger economic issues as well as problems of poverty and the environment. But Bank economists were active in developing the Basic Human Needs approach, and the Bank now considers the impact of its lending on the poor. The Bank responded slowly to criticisms of its failure to consider environmental problems and the role of women in development but now incorporates these concerns into its projects. Medium-term adjustment lending is a product of the past 20 years or so, as the Bank has learned that individual projects will fail if the policy environment is not conducive to development. But in these loans, the Bank has had to rediscover the need to address poverty directly.

The Bank now expects to focus on poverty reduction. It is developing a Comprehensive Development Framework approach, focusing on what it calls Poverty Reduction Strategies, and making additional efforts toward debt relief for the Heavily Indebted Poor Countries, starting with Bolivia, Mauritania, Mozambique, Tanzania, and Uganda. Another recent initiative is to intensify focus on worldwide problems, such as the AIDS epidemic, which have consequences beyond a country's borders.[49]

The emphasis on overall development policy is consistent with the Bank's recent concern for the structure and behavior of governments as they attempt to direct the development process. But is the Bank equipped to give political advice? Should it? How much should the Bank have to say about the governance of borrowing countries? Would the Bank be better advised to simply withdraw if its money is not being used effectively?

Anne Krueger, who has worked with the Bank and in 2001 became its chief economist, suggests that the Bank focus its role on traditional economic development issues in the poorest countries where private capital is unlikely to go. She refers to the Bank's current path as a penchant for going after "soft" issues—women, labor standards, health and safety, the environment, and relations with NGOs—and doubts the Bank can do all these things well. She is also concerned that these social issues may not be appropriate for the Bank. Especially in middle-income countries, if governments themselves will not address these questions, why should the Bank get involved? What would be the means and goals of Bank involvement?[50]

WHAT FUTURE FOR AID?

There has been a decline in Western interest in foreign aid during the final decades of the twentieth century. Net ODA from DAC countries declined from $63 billion in 1992 to $56 billion in 1999. What might the future hold?

Aid Fatigue

Conditions in many developing countries indicate that foreign aid is still needed, and history shows that effective aid, with reforms and new emphases, is possible. However, aid fatigue, especially in the United States, seems to be setting in. There are many reasons for it, including the perception that aid has failed to deliver development or votes in the United Nations. Clearly, aid donors and aid recipients must demonstrate that the money is being well used.[51]

But there are other issues as well. Many industrialized economies have had their own difficulties in the last two decades, and some sectors have not adapted well to international competition. This situation is exacerbated by the need for money to rebuild the Eastern European and former Soviet economies. Also, the revival of private capital flows, which go primarily to the better-off countries in Asia and Latin America, may lead to the view that development aid is unnecessary, despite significant need among the poorest economies.[52]

Attitudes in the United States are especially problematic. A DAC report on U.S. policies notes the particularly strong need in the United States for aid to be based on national self-interest and national security: rationales that may be losing their force.[53] But Americans tend to be unaware of what they actually provide. In early 1995, a survey showed that most Americans want to cut aid. When asked what portion of the federal budget would be about right, the median response was 5 percent, when in reality the figure is only 1 percent for total economic and military aid. When asked how much they thought was being spent, the median response was 15 percent. The two-thirds cut desired would still leave the aid budget five times higher than it actually is.[54]

Future Directions for Aid

Faced with budget-cutting desires in some industrialized countries, many traditional aid projects will have a harder time being funded. The World Bank is discussing private funding of infrastructure projects, and many governments are increasing the portion of their aid that flows through NGOs. Aid organizations are also putting aid money into private projects as investments. Still, many old problems call for traditional solutions. The poorest people and the poorest countries can still benefit from publically funded family planning clinics, agricultural research, education, and infrastructure. The need for aid may have narrowed its focus, but it remains strong.

FOREIGN DIRECT INVESTMENT: DEFINITION AND RATIONALE

Long before there was foreign aid there were companies from Western countries investing in the developing world, largely in those areas that were colonies of Europe. This activity is now called **Foreign Direct Investment (FDI)**, and, in most years, it represents the primary means of private capital transfer.

What Is Foreign Direct Investment?

Foreign Direct Investment (FDI) refers to control over an enterprise in a country other than the home country of the individual(s) exercising control. The U.S. government designates as FDI any investment that involves a lower limit on *ownership* of 10 percent, although actual *control* would depend on how the other 90 percent is distributed. While ownership of the foreign investment usually remains in the investing (home) country, the recipient (host) country generally receives some combination of financial capital, technology, physical capital, personnel, and access to brand names and marketing advantages. As Figure 13–1 shows, FDI has become the largest source of external capital to developing countries. As foreign aid has become important only for the poorest countries, FDI has assumed primary significance for the rest.

The Transnational Corporation

FDI used to describe the activity of a company from one country with business overseas. Now many companies operate worldwide integrated operations: Their headquarters are historically located in one place, but their motive is to look for maximum profits globally by undertaking different aspects of their operation in different countries and/or by contracting with smaller firms globally to undertake specific facets of the production process. The home country is no more favored than any other. Many references to Foreign Direct Investment are now references to **Transnational Corporations (TNCs)**.[55]

How Much FDI Is There?

Until the end of World War II, most of the world's foreign investment was found in the less developed portions of the world, primarily in agriculture, extractive industries, and public utilities.[56] Now, most FDI is found in the developed countries, and the emphasis has shifted to manufacturing and finance.

In 1999, there was an estimated stock of $865 billion worth of foreign direct investment in the world. Developing countries received 24 percent of $47 billion in 1980 and only 14 percent of $196 billion in 1989, but renewed interest in Latin America and the opening of China raised the developing-country share to 42 percent of $194 billion in 1993. Financial uncertainty has reduced the share of developing and emerging countries to 26 percent in 1999. Of the flows to developing countries in the 1980s, almost three-fourths went to Latin America and East Asia, especially Brazil, Mexico, China, and Malaysia. In 1999, 81 percent of the developing- and transition-economy flow went to South, Southeast, and East Asia, and Latin America. Two-thirds of the Asian inflow went to China and Hong Kong, and 60 percent of the Latin American inflow went to Brazil and Argentina. Table 13–5 shows the major developing-country recipients of FDI in 1999, together with the ratio of that FDI to their national income and investment in 1998.

Why Do Firms Invest Overseas?

Microeconomic theory suggests that investors look for the most profitable use of their capital. At least initially, foreign returns would have to be relatively high to compensate for the costs of operating in a different environment. Investment often has gone

TABLE 13–5 Major Developing and Emerging Country Recipients of FDI

	$Billions (Flow) 1999	Stock as Percentage of GDP 1998	Flow as Percentage of Total Investment 1998
All Developing Economies	207.6	20.0	11.5
Transition Economies	21.4	12.1	12.9
China	40.4	27.6	12.9
Brazil	31.4	17.1	18.4
Argentina	23.2	13.9	11.0
Hong Kong, China	23.1	65.7	29.6
Mexico	11.2	14.3	11.6
South Korea	10.3	6.1	5.5
Chile	9.2	40.4	25.0
Poland	7.5	15.1	15.8
Thailand	7.0	17.5	25.1
Singapore	6.1	85.8	17.6

Note: Top 10 recipients obtained 74 percent of the total.

Source: United Nations, *World Investment Report 2001.*

to areas where entry was protected in some way; hence, competition was minimal and profits were high.

Traditional Explanations

John Dunning, an authority in this field, explains that firms invest overseas for advantages in ownership, location, and internalization.[57] *Ownership* factors are those specific to the firm that provide unique advantages and so permit it to become established in foreign markets. These could include specific technology, product characteristics, or even greater access to funds. *Location* factors are those that provide the incentive to invest abroad, including access to markets, reduction of foreign competition, and reduction of input and distribution costs. They may also include incentives based on government policy, such as the desire to get around tariff walls or host government incentives to establish in a given location. *Internalization* factors answer the question of why the firm locates overseas rather than make licensing or other arrangements with a local firm. The firm has the security of being able to coordinate all the relevant activities without exposing internal operations and information to the market. Foreign investment may also spread a company's risks and allow it to take advantage of differing laws and regulations. A United Nations study suggests that firms seek the ability to innovate and retain the rights to technology when deciding whether to invest overseas.[58]

Richard Caves's survey of FDI suggests that the weight of these factors varies with the type of business activity. Firms that need to exploit and process certain raw materials have obvious reasons for going to the source.[59] Processing companies also may find **vertical integration**—combining different production stages in a single firm—more efficient than depending on transactions with independent companies. Manufacturing, export-oriented firms may be attracted by low labor costs, especially if labor is a large portion of total costs. Firms that sell mostly in the host market are likely to locate there to take advantage of some intangible asset—a technology, brand name, specialized employees, innovative capacity—that is not easily sold on the market or that they want to retain.

Marxist-Oriented Theories

The usual explanations of overseas investment are generally consistent with the thesis that the capitalist firm is a profit-seeking entity. Marxist-type analyses of capitalism broaden this perspective by placing the firm within a specific *system* of production that drives successful firms to expand, first within and then outside their national boundaries. V. I. Lenin and numerous others called this pattern of expansion **imperialism** and considered it a natural outgrowth of capitalism.

There seems no doubt about the internationalist tendencies of many firms, but most orthodox economists conclude that foreign investment is on balance beneficial to the host country. Others stress the importance of the terms of the investment negotiated between investor and host government. Marxist-oriented thinkers are divided between more traditional Marxist views that the spread of capitalism is a necessary prelude to a more rational global economy and those, especially the *dependencia* school, who believe that the result is pure exploitation of the host country's resources.[60] What is important is the balance between costs and benefits.

Marxist perspectives were brought into modern economic analysis in the writings of Stephen Hymer. He distinguished direct from portfolio investment (stocks and bonds): Direct investment is governed by firms' needs to control proprietary assets, while portfolio investment was governed by more traditional concerns such as relative interest rates.[61]

Alternatives to Traditional FDI

Not all foreign investment takes the traditional form of starting up (or buying out) a company in another country. In an attempt to minimize the risk of such investments, alternatives, or "new forms," have been created.[62]

One of these is licensing. A company will permit a foreign company to use its product, process, and name for a fee (license fee, royalty). This presupposes availability in the host country of most requirements for the product, so that permission from the owner and one or two key inputs (such as the "secret formula" for Coca-Cola) are all that is necessary for a successful operation. This is an inexpensive way of getting the owner's product into another country without making the full-scale investment that would otherwise be required. It also protects the owner against various kinds of risks in the host country. However, insufficient quality control can deter a company from licensing its name to what might be an inferior product.

Two or more companies may create an independent entity—a **joint venture**—to operate in the host country. They share technology, expenses, risk, and profit. This may be by voluntary agreement, or it may be required by a host government as a condition of foreign ownership. Joint ventures may be made up of a foreign private investor and a host government company. This partnership may be formed at the time of investment or may be the result of the foreign company being forced to sell a portion of its interest, as frequently occurred with extractive firms such as petroleum companies. While the partners split the commercial risk, problems arise when their interests conflict.

Finally, a foreign company may undertake to simply manage a local firm, without taking any ownership or providing any other input. This requires a management contract.

WHY A DEBATE OVER FDI?

We would expect that a country lacking in capital would welcome investment from any source. New, foreign capital would increase output and income, provide jobs, provide new technology and thereby improve productivity, provide needed competition for domestic industries, and improve a developing country's access to export markets.

During the 1970s and 1980s however, numerous governments took what seemed an easier path, or an alternative to reduced aid, by borrowing the money on their own and were rewarded with huge foreign debts. Shouldn't developing-country governments prefer investment from a company that could take out only what profits it made to a loan from a bank that would insist on interest payments (at least), regardless of the country's economic condition or foreign exchange situation? Yet, one of the more bitter debates in the economic development literature has been on the role of foreign investment.

Developing countries would seem to pose the greatest risk to foreign investors. Historically, however, this has not always been the case. The relative political strength of the home and host governments, especially when the latter were colonies of the former, frequently made for highly protected environments. When the activities were extractive or agricultural in nature, the easy access to natural resources and relatively inexpensive labor outweighed other problems, especially when a dedicated corps of home-country personnel could make a good living overseeing these operations.

Within a few years of independence, however, resentment against imperialism and dependence led to increasing restrictions on foreign investment, including the ultimate step of **expropriation** and **nationalization**. Expropriations, taking or buying out foreign firms, were often related to anticolonialism, the instability of a particular government, anticapitalist ideologies, and the prominence of foreign firms, especially in sensitive industries. Instances of expropriation increased in the 1960s and surged in the 1970s before declining, partly because fewer foreign firms remained and partly due to the need to attract investment. In fact, many kinds of restrictions on FDI have diminished significantly since the mid-1980s.[63]

HOST COUNTRY CONCERNS ABOUT FDI

The earliest concerns about foreign direct investment raised by host countries led to a number of expropriations in the 1960s and 1970s. These concerns are economic and sociopolitical.

Economic Concerns

The host to foreign capital faces the potential for harm to its economy.[64]

Concentration of Domestic Industry

While new capital, technology, and jobs may be provided, what of the impact on local industry? Foreign firms are often more efficient than smaller local firms and have the resources to attract workers and finance away from those firms. While competition is, in principle, welcome, the result may be the elimination of some or all local firms. Foreign companies, through imports and then production, eliminated many small-scale producers of cigarettes, beer, textiles, and cement in Nigeria. Much large-scale trading in Nigeria was originated by foreign firms, and local competition was preempted by the success of foreign enterprise.[65] There is some evidence that FDI leads to greater industrial concentration, and in fact, industrial concentration is one of the inducements to FDI.[66] A monopoly firm may, especially in an extractive or other natural-resource-based industry, acquire monopsony control over local resources.

TNC Corporate Goals

A transnational corporation's corporate goals may not be consistent with the development goals of the host government. This may occur when an investor uses resources to produce luxury consumer goods rather than more basic products deemed important for development. Or it may occur when the new firm is a local subsidiary that is simply one link in a worldwide chain, where maximizing profits for the global enterprise may mean the subsidiary takes a loss. This could be the case, for example, if the subsidiary in a vertically integrated company provides raw materials or components that must be priced as low as possible so that profits can be recorded in a country with more favorable tax laws. This subsidiary will not be looked upon by the parent as a potentially complete entity: There may be no incentive to advance the skills of local labor, provide new technology, develop a research capacity, or otherwise allow the subsidiary to contribute to the development of the national economy.

Balance of Payments Impact

The balance of payments impact of TNCs in developing countries has also been the subject of considerable debate.[67] Investors want the freedom to **repatriate** (send home) profits and other sums, exchanged into the home country's currency. As a rule, remittances outpace the inflow of investment (more so in developing than in developed countries), at times becoming a burden on the host country's foreign exchange reserves, leading to the charge that the foreign company is bleeding the country. Of course, the total value of the investment to the host country must include the contributions of production, employment, and technology, so remittance of a portion of the profit does not begin to offset the benefits received. Nonetheless, when a developing country faces foreign exchange constraints, a net outflow can be particularly difficult to accept.

Some argue that FDI is better than borrowing abroad because when business is bad profits will not be available for repatriation, whereas loan interest must be paid. It is possible, however, that investors' various remittances—including the desire to withdraw invested capital—will be *higher* when the host country is in trouble and foreign exchange constraints are tightest.

Transfer Pricing

Companies are expected to obey the laws of the host country, but the complexity of large TNCs and the weak administrative capacity of many governments may make effective oversight of the company's activities next to impossible. Even ensuring that the investor faithfully records its transactions for the host country's tax authorities is likely to be difficult, especially if the local subsidiary says that the books are kept at its headquarters. Another issue is the prevalence and impact of **transfer pricing**, whereby the company's internal assignment of prices to transactions between branches in different countries may (*a*) understate prices of raw materials or components exported from the developing country or (*b*) overstate the price of technology and services imported into the developing country, in order to keep the subsidiary's profits and taxes low and to evade foreign exchange restrictions. When the corporate books are unavailable to local authorities, suspicion will be natural. The evidence on transfer pricing is naturally difficult to accumulate, so the prevalence of the practice is impossible to estimate.[68]

Examples include a study of four Colombian industries, where local affiliates paid more than 15 percent over world prices for imports from their parent companies, and a study of Greek affiliates that paid 25 percent or more above world prices to buy chemicals from their parents.[69] The potential seems to increase as TNCs spread their manufacturing activities to take advantage of different locational advantages and falling costs of transport and communications. But abuses of intrafirm pricing practices are more likely when an "intermediate product is specific to the firm [so] there is no exactly equivalent product with whose 'arms-length' price the transfer price can be compared."[70]

Transfer pricing is generally seen as a way of evading the host country's foreign exchange regulations and taxes. The difficulty of monitoring the TNC's financial activities makes all taxation issues more difficult to deal with. Beyond the tax issue, the information to judge whether the company can afford to pay higher wages, is complying with product or environmental standards, or is discriminating against domestic citizens in managerial hiring, is subject to a continuous tug-of-war between local governments and transnational corporations.

Technology and Employment

The nature of and control over the technology used by foreign investors have also been contentious issues.[71] In manufacturing particularly, one of the major benefits of FDI is supposed to be in its greater productivity, largely due to the use of new technology. The technology then becomes a part of the host economy's production—and often export—capability. In fact, it is just this use of modern technology with low-wage labor that disturbs labor unions in industrialized countries: The economic argument that well-paid labor can compete with poorly paid imports depends on the greater productivity of highly paid workers, and the traditional theory of comparative advantage assumes that labor and capital are internationally immobile. Once the technology goes overseas, this foundation of trade theory is nullified.

Some economists have worried that foreign investment brings capital-intensive technology into a labor-intensive environment and thus creates relatively few jobs. Numerous studies of the appropriateness of technology reveal a mixed picture, with foreign firms in some cases using technology *more* suited to the country's factor endowments than do domestic companies. A study of Ghana, for instance, concluded that state-owned companies were the most capital intensive, followed by foreign and local private companies close together. Studies indicate that TNCs are more likely to use appropriate technologies when there is greater competition and when manufacturing costs are a higher proportion of total costs. Preferences for product sophistication, reduction of labor problems, and other nontechnical factors typically skew TNC technology choice toward capital-intensive methods.[72]

Developing countries would presumably benefit if foreign investors ranked employment potential high in their choice of technology. But a study of over 200 TNCs in five countries found that neither companies nor governments made employment a key objective. Companies' technologies appeared to become more capital intensive after they were already established. But the quantity and quality of employment did improve: Foreign investment created employment by way of linkages, and it improved the quality of workers by upgrading the technological capacity of suppliers and educating managers and workers, many of whom later work for local companies.[73]

The well-publicized debate on conditions in factories such as Nike's in Indonesia and Vietnam indicates that conditions are often poor but usually at least as good as local conditions. Still, examples of corporate irresponsibility add fuel to the fire. A 1997 auditing report of Nike operations in Vietnam found employees exposed to cancer-causing chemicals. A 1999 self-study by Reebok found that two Indonesian factories had substandard working conditions, significant health problems, and gender bias.[74]

Recently, attention has been given to the impact of the host government's policies on foreign firms' technology decisions. Some studies have found that the more a government attempts to force backward linkages to, or joint ventures with, local firms,

CASE 13-4

FDI IN MEXICO'S AUTOMOTIVE SECTOR

FAST FACTS

On the Map: North America

Population: 97 Million

Per Capita GNI and Rank: $4,440 (72)

Life Expectancy: Male—69 Female—75

Adult Literacy Rate: Male—93%
Female—89%

Foreign firms have been producing automotive parts and automobiles for the local market in Mexico for many years. In 1972, the government decided to attempt to make this a source of export earnings and issued a decree requiring an increase in foreign auto firms' exports. Beginning in 1977, the government required firms to match imports with exports. U.S. companies, led by Ford, pushed for Mexico to give up its export quest.

In 1979, however, General Motors's desire to cut costs to compete with Japanese firms caused them to start pushing world sourcing. One of their first decisions was to build four engine plants simultaneously in Mexico, which would increase exports twenty-fold. Within a year, Ford, Chrysler, Volkswagen, and Nissan began plans to expand with emphasis on exports. Mexican auto exports increased from $122 million in 1975 to $1.5 billion by 1984, employing 121,000 workers, many high skilled. Wages and benefits were the highest of any private activity in the country.

This activity stimulated investments by foreign and local parts firms, and within five years there were 310 Mexican producers, 110 with annual sales in excess of $1 million. Foreign firms updated manufacturing practices and achieved high-quality production. This progress spread to local firms, which accounted for 6 of the top 10 nonengine parts firms by 1987. The likelihood of a Mexican automotive firm exporting increases with its proximity to TNCs. Mexico is now the largest developing-country auto-sector exporter: $14 billion a year and 354,000 employees in the mid-1990s. Similar results have been achieved in the Brazilian and Thai auto sector and in petrochemicals and electronics in Asia.

Source: Theodore H. Moran, *Foreign Direct Investment and Development* (Washington: Institute for International Economics, 1999), pp. 53–56.

the more reluctant an investor is to bring its advantages—better technology and improved management practices—to the host country. When TNCs are allowed to maintain full ownership, and especially when they face local competition or produce for the export market in technologically challenging industries, they are more likely to improve their practices and to have considerable positive benefits for local firms.[75] This is illustrated by the case of the automotive sector in Mexico (Case 13-4).

These benefits are not guaranteed. When foreign companies retain control of the technology involved, there may be less opportunity for local businesses to develop, leaving the economy dependent on the restricted use of technologies they cannot adapt for their own use. The foreign investment may simply create an enclave of limited prosperity. A study of Latin America showed little difference between foreign and local companies in the initial use of technologies, but foreign companies were less likely to innovate and more likely to rely on external sources for technological change.[76] A study of the electrical and electronics industries in Malaysia showed that the TNCs with stronger local linkages were less likely to bring in new technology. However, hiring local labor for technical and managerial positions was more common for faraway American firms than for Japanese firms. The study concludes that cost is an important factor, so government can encourage local hiring by providing incentives to firms that do so.[77]

Impact on the Environment

One troubling aspect of some foreign technologies is their environmental impact in countries with weak or no regulation. There is little evidence to date that environmental costs are high enough to induce many firms to move to developing countries. However, there has been considerable concern about the impact of lower investment barriers on the environment in Mexico. A 1992 survey of U.S. companies there reported that a fourth of the firms did consider environmental costs to be an incentive to relocate. Also, one-half reported using lower Mexican standards to treat industrial waste.[78] National governments may wish to disregard environmental concerns to attract investment.

NAFTA's critics claim the agreement has intensified pollution of all sorts in northern Mexico due to increased U.S. investment in the maquila industries. From 1993 to 1999, the number of such firms had risen by 37 percent, with no apparent attempt to clean up or reduce pollution. In fact, three U.S. companies are suing the Mexican government for the right to open hazardous waste sites.[79] These problems are typical of other countries' export processing zones. They highlight the trade-offs faced by a government eager for foreign investment. The cost of environmental inspection and cleanup is high, and the potential loss of employment and exports may be exaggerated by a government that is concerned with short-term gains.

One of the more explosive recent issues has been the impact of Shell Oil's operations in Nigeria. The flaring of natural gas close to villages, running pipelines through agricultural land, and the ever-present problems of oil spills have brought worldwide attention to this problem. The Nigerian government has, however, tended to be more concerned about continued oil production than the complaints of local people.[80]

Impact on Growth and Income Distribution

The inflow of capital should contribute to economic growth, but there is no clear evidence as to whether FDI does so.[81] One review of a number of studies concluded that from 1950 to the mid-1970s, TNCs contributed to growth in the short run but reduced it in the long run. Another study found no clear connection: Although it found a correlation between FDI and per capita GNP, this may be because higher GNP attracts more FDI, and it showed no connection with the *growth* of income. More recently, there is some indication that the ability of FDI, like aid, to contribute to growth depends on host government policies. Outward-oriented regimes have tended to show a greater FDI contribution to growth than inward orientation.[82]

One way of contributing to growth and development would be the creation of linkages, especially backward ones. As we have seen, this often depends on host-government policies as well. FDI that occurs in extractive industries often has few linkages; some jobs are created but minerals may be shipped directly to port and overseas without leaving much trace beyond resource depletion. Manufacturing—especially when the host's market is targeted as well as exports—can use more local materials, parts, and workers. Another contribution to the local economy would be to increase saving, but some have contended that FDI actually decreases saving; the additional capital supply would reduce profits and interest rates, thereby reducing the incentive to save. There is no clear evidence on this issue.

An examination of FDI's impact on Thailand's economy concludes that it increased investment, exports, and growth of GDP. The foreign firms did not hurt the ability of local firms to borrow and created important linkages with local firms. However, the net impact on the balance of payments was negative, since the firms imported heavily and repatriated profits.[83]

With respect to income distribution, if TNCs are in high-productivity, high-profit industries, greater inequality could result, but if they use a lot of labor and local resources, they could contribute to greater equality. One study reports that TNCs tend to pay higher wages than local companies and do a lot of employee training, both of which could raise lower-income workers' wages and reduce inequality. Another author finds a direct relationship between FDI and income inequality but stops short of saying whether, or in which direction, there may be causality. Similarly, a better-trained and educated workforce is as likely to attract investment as to be produced by it.[84]

Sociopolitical Concerns

Economic, political, and social concerns are linked. Key among the political concerns is the potential impact of large foreign companies on local politics. The United States prohibits foreign investment in radio and television, domestic airline service, coastal shipping, banking, certain defense-related activities, and mining on public lands. But apart from closing specific industries to foreign investment, the United States has become sensitive to apparently innocent investment from countries perceived to have hostile interests, including some Arab countries in the 1970s and Japan in the 1980s. In the decades immediately following World War II, Europeans and Canadians became increasingly concerned with U.S. dominance of some of their industries. So government officials in developing countries often fear the impact of American and European companies.

Governments recognize that foreign firms, like their own, will lobby for favorable tax treatment and against laws and regulations that increase their costs. Nevertheless, they are more sensitive to foreign lobbying, given that foreign firms may lack access through the more traditional local channels.[85] There is a history of distrust due to the ability of American companies to call upon the power of the U.S. government to intervene to protect business interests. In Latin America, the U.S. government has intervened militarily on a number of occasions over the last century, using the interests of its citizens and businesses as a rationale. The apparent tug-of-war between International Telephone and Telegraph (ITT) and the U.S. Central Intelligence Agency (CIA) over which should help the local military overthrow the Allende government in Chile in 1973 provides a lesson that even in large countries foreign intervention is possible. In 1980, the Nigerian government expropriated what was left of British Petroleum's (BP) joint venture with Shell Oil, claiming that BP had knowingly violated Nigerian government policy by shipping oil to South Africa.

In addition, however, developed and developing countries have complained about the U.S. government's exercise of extraterritoriality, that is, the application of U.S. laws to the activities of overseas subsidiaries of U.S. companies. U.S. companies themselves complain about this kind of interference, whether they are told not to contribute to the building of a natural gas pipeline from Western Europe to the Soviet Union in the 1980s, or when the U.S. Foreign Corrupt Practices Act prevents American companies overseas from offering certain kinds of payments considered normal practice there but defined as bribes in U.S. law.

Finally, there remain the somewhat amorphous problems of the transmission of cultural values among countries, frequently through the vehicle of foreign direct investment. Some Americans worried about the 1990 purchase of the entertainment firm MCA by Japanese investors. It is reasonable, therefore, to expect concerns about American "cultural imperialism" expressed in Canada and France, as well as in developing countries.

Finally, there are concerns that arise from the spread of Western products and conditions of urban life that may undermine traditional products and family relations.[86] The worldwide furor over the promotion of infant formula by Nestlé and its impact on mothers and babies in developing countries is one of the largest controversies of this type. Nestlé spent a lot of money to advertise, even picturing women in white lab coats feeding formula to babies. But not only was formula more expensive, and arguably not as healthful as breast-feeding, but it led to health complications: Water used to mix with formula was often polluted; feeding implements were often dirty, and poor mothers cut down on the amount of the formula to save money.[87] While the increasing access of many people to information about the outside, and the freer movement of people and goods is bound to have similar results, foreign investors provide a concentrated and visible target for these concerns.

TRANSNATIONAL CORPORATIONS' CONCERNS: THE BUSINESS CLIMATE AND GOVERNMENT CONDITIONS

Let us assume that a particular investment makes sense from a microeconomic perspective. What other conditions does the firm consider necessary to establish operations in the country?

What Do Investors Want?

Owners of capital want maximum freedom to profit from their investment. Capital will not go to a country when either (*a*) restrictions on operation are likely to seriously interfere with making or keeping a profit, or (*b*) governments (or their policies) are so unstable that conditions are likely to change drastically or unexpectedly.

Capital owners are concerned about the business climate. This climate is best where taxes are low, regulations are minimal, and the likelihood of major change for the worse is low. Thus, Western companies often operated in Communist countries: If the government appears to be stable and offers the company favorable conditions, a company will take the opportunity. In fact, one of the charges frequently made against TNCs is that they thrive under conditions of oppressive government, and are eager to do business where labor unions are either banned or under government control.[88]

Host Government Responses: Restrictions and Incentives

A foreign company will look first at the potential for profit based on economic conditions, then the general business climate. In addition, however, governments may impose certain restrictions.

Screening

All governments restrict certain kinds of foreign investment. Some governments make known in advance what areas are not open to foreign capital.[89] In addition, some countries maintain agencies that examine all investment proposals and decide which may enter. A pro forma screen with well-recognized restrictions would not be daunting to would-be foreign investors. Such agencies, however, may act within broad guidelines and may in fact be official negotiators who will be discussing the conditions under which firms may enter. Developing-country governments whose advantages make them prime candidates for investment may carry out this activity successfully. For example, Western companies tolerate more restrictions to operate in China, with a large labor and consumer base, than they would in many other countries.

Although many economists would argue against a serious screening effort on the grounds that almost any investment is a good one, there is some evidence that this is not the case. In addition to the concerns we have already outlined, an analysis of benefits and costs of prospective investments may screen out projects that run counter to the government's development objectives. One review suggests that "a sizeable minority" of projects subjected to cost/benefit analysis, "cost the host country more in terms of the opportunity cost of its resources than they earned for it."[90] Another showed that 25 percent to 45 percent of investments were on balance negative, concluding that "in countries with limited domestic markets, barriers to trade, and subsidized inputs, the incidence of economically harmful proposals . . . is likely to be high."[91] These warnings might have been relevant to similar proposals made by domestic companies, although they might not have been scrutinized so closely.

Degree of Foreign Ownership

Governments at times have insisted that local capitalists, or the government itself, hold some minimum share of an investment. This may be a condition of establishment or, as in the case of IBM in India, may come after the company has already begun operations. IBM left, but Western oil companies—essentially stuck in the ground with the oil—have agreed to be partially (and sometimes fully) bought out by governments. Governments may want only a share of the profits, or a large enough share of the company to have a major influence on business decisions. However, a local subsidiary of a multinational corporation may not accede to such demands, and the ultimate restriction on foreign ownership would drive the company out, leaving the government to cope as best it can. Evidence suggests that enforced joint ventures result in *less* host-country benefit, as TNCs are reluctant to supply the latest technology and management practices to local owners.[92]

Limitations on Repatriation of Profits and Other Payments

Foreign exchange constraints in numerous developing countries have led to exchange controls that limit the foreign companies' ability to repatriate their profits and other payments. While some firms will cooperate by reinvesting in the host country as much as possible, TNCs as a rule want control over the internal flow of corporate funds and may leave if they are not allowed such control. The government then faces a dilemma: Lose control over a portion of its scarce foreign exchange, or risk either the departure of the investment or its sale to local concerns that may be less capable and less well established in the international industry. Conflict ensues when the company decides to leave but is not permitted to take its money out.

Trade-Related Performance Requirements

Performance requirements (also referred to as trade-related investment measures, or TRIMs) are restrictions on a company's activities that constrain the investor's foreign trade. On one side are **local content requirements** that specify a minimum percentage of the value added (beyond raw materials) that must come from local resources, thereby setting a ceiling on imports and presumably saving foreign exchange. The results are "decidedly negative."[93] Local content requirements may restrict the size of the firm below a minimum efficient scale and otherwise raise its costs, making it uncompetitive in world markets.

The other side is a minimum export requirement that limits the percentage of the output that can be sold locally, thus increasing foreign exchange income. Minimum export requirements are less offensive because foreign investors are frequently oriented toward exports anyway. In addition, the experience for such requirements has been extremely positive for hosts to export-oriented firms in the automotive, petrochemical, and electronics industries.[94]

Use of the National Labor Force

Perhaps the most important local resource is labor, and governments may want foreign investors to deliver on the claim that they bring jobs, technology, and skills to the host country. They want foreign investors to train local workers for skilled positions, including managerial positions, and to locate some of their Research and Development (R&D) activities in their new home. Employment-related requirements are in fact more widespread than export and import requirements.[95] For semiskilled and skilled labor, the task is often less difficult than TNCs imagine. However, for managerial positions, these conditions are extremely sensitive because they imply much more than a simple shift in the location of activities. Local managers may not have the same loyalty to the company as expatriates brought in to serve the needs of the home office, and transfer of R&D activities runs the risk of a leakage of the company's technology.

Incentives and the Foreign Investment Bargain

In spite of the potential drawbacks, developing countries are eager to attract such firms under acceptable circumstances. But here another problem arises. Aside from extractive firms looking for specific resources, TNCs interested in markets and inexpensive labor may have multiple options, while the host government is stuck in place and may have to bid to attract—and to keep—foreign investment. In a world of diminishing transportation and information costs, the TNC can shop around for the best conditions: lenient taxes, ready infrastructure, and a low-paid and unorganized labor force.

Capital is more internationally mobile than labor. Many companies can look elsewhere when profits in one country fall, but only the most talented and mobile of workers can really maximize their incomes in this way. Thus, wages become a bargaining chip in the struggle for foreign investment. The march of some transnationals from their homes in industrialized countries to progressively lower-wage countries in Asia, for example, from the United States to Japan to South Korea to Malaysia to Vietnam, reinforces the view that investment may be ephemeral and that firms' commitment to a specific location is in inverse proportion to the wages it must pay. Japanese firms have begun to complain that wages are becoming too high in China.[96] Although it is often not easy for a firm to pull up stakes, the threat of withdrawal is always present.

Therefore, a lot of attention has been paid to the bargaining between the developing-country government and TNC over the terms of establishing an investment. Governments that lack specific raw materials may offer tax breaks in the hope that revenue losses will be overshadowed by gains in employment and other areas. But tax incentives alone are not sufficient to attract foreign investment. One review even concludes that TNCs may see extreme tax incentives as a sign that the host lacks more fundamental advantages for investment. Another suggests only that taxes should not be too high (more than about 35 percent).[97]

Similar arguments can be made about export processing zones with minimal or no restrictions on trade, lower taxes, special infrastructure provision, and minimum wage exemptions for the specific purpose of attracting foreign investors to produce for export. These bring in foreign investors through their combination of incentives, although there is much criticism that they provide the host country much less benefit than they should from the incentives provided.[98]

The larger question is the total impact of incentives and the role of bargaining. An OECD study concludes that incentives have a marginal impact because different countries' incentives offset each other. Individual countries gain at the expense of others even though all countries would gain by agreeing not to offer them.[99] The same could be said of incentives offered by cities and states in the United States. There is general agreement that TNCs are attracted primarily by resource advantages, large market size, and a country's stability and business climate. The absence of restrictions is also an incentive.

Finally, the nature of the bargaining process itself is relevant. The advantage in the initial bargain depends on the options available to each side. Developing-country governments start with some distinct disadvantages: They have few experienced negotiators, and TNC assets come as a bundle—if they want one part of that package they must take the whole thing, including elements they may not care about. If the TNC has numerous alternatives, and the developing country wants specific technologies, the host government is in a difficult position, especially as the company may have more information on the country's circumstances than the government will have on the company. Once the investment is established the tables may turn, although not necessarily: Companies can move from country to country easily and may be less susceptible to toughening of terms when their original deal has expired. Natural resource firms are more vulnerable. Any TNC may strengthen its hand by making powerful friends in the host country.[100]

INTERNATIONAL REGULATION: INSURANCE, TREATIES, AND CODES

Developed-country governments are concerned about the actions of developing-country governments against their investors. Governments therefore attempt to insure, and negotiate treaties on behalf of, such investment. Developing countries have tried to promote international rules to regulate foreign investments.

Investment Insurance

The first institutional means toward investment insurance was the creation in 1971 of the U.S. **Overseas Private Investment Corporation (OPIC)**. OPIC is technically a private organization, although its board of directors includes officials of U.S. government agencies along with private businesspeople. Its main business is to provide insurance to American investments in developing countries against political risk, including expropriation, a government's refusal to permit earnings remittance, and losses due to war and other political violence. It might be objected that the existence of such insurance would embolden developing-country governments to take such steps as expropriation or remittance freezes (moral hazard again). But host governments want the investment and sign an agreement that OPIC may review the investments prior to agreeing to provide the insurance. The agreement commits the government to certain standards of behavior, and while breaking the agreement may provide the government with a short-term gain, it is also a signal of untrustworthiness that will discourage future investment. A broader insurance scheme, the Multilateral Investment Guarantee Agency (MIGA), has now been set up by the World Bank.[101]

Bilateral Investment Treaties (BITs)

Many European governments and the United States have negotiated **Bilateral Investment Treaties (BITs)** with developing-country governments. As of the beginning of 1999, almost 1,900 such treaties existed, with almost half concluded between developing countries. The BITs contain the following general provisions.

Nondiscrimination

Host countries are expected to, at a minimum, treat all foreign investors alike (**most favored nation treatment**, or **MFN**) and, at best, to treat all foreign investors the way domestic firms are treated (**national treatment**). This means equal opportunity to establish firms and equal treatment under all laws.

Expropriation

The right of governments to expropriate, or take over, private holdings, under appropriate conditions, is widely accepted. The expropriation must be for a public purpose (not simply for transfer to another private owner), must take place through due process of law, and must be accompanied by "adequate" compensation, usually reflecting a market-related value, which the investor is free to repatriate.

Unrestricted Financial Transfers

Companies should have the right to transfer any and all profits and other payments out of the country without hindrance and, if it desires, to withdraw the investment completely.

Dispute Settlement

Although companies should receive equal treatment under the law of the host country, foreign investors should have access to impartial arbitration in any dispute between the company and the host government. This may involve the International Court of Justice or other suitable international mechanism to arbitrate disputes.

Developing-Country Responses

Developing countries are not hostile to BIT provisions, but they often view the U.S. government's interpretations as rigid compared to more lenient interpretations by many European treaties. The United States promotes national treatment. Developing countries often prefer to treat foreign investors differently from domestic investors and, thus, prefer the MFN approach. Developing countries want recognition—provided by many European BITs—that foreign exchange shortages may require restrictions on remittances, whereas the United States has sometimes insisted that appropriate policies would end those shortages. They are sometimes skeptical about the U.S. stand on appropriate valuation of a firm's assets when compensation for expropriation is in question. And finally, developing countries often exhibit the desire to use their own legal structure to arbitrate investment disputes. In general, the willingness of developing-country governments to accede to the stricter interpretation of BIT provisions is in direct proportion to its perceived need for investment.

Codes of Conduct

For many years, developing countries attempted to negotiate in the United Nations a Code of Conduct for TNCs. Whereas investment treaties spell out the rights of foreign firms, developing-country governments are concerned also with the behavior of those firms. From domestic R&D requirements, to prohibitions against transfer pricing, to requirements to force companies to open their books, host countries want to avoid having their desire for these conditions act as a disadvantage against countries that are willing to forgo such privileges. To date, such attempts have failed because governments of the industrialized countries have been unwilling to permit such an international regime to impose restrictions on private companies.

DEVELOPING-COUNTRY TRANSNATIONAL CORPORATIONS

Economic progress in many developing countries has meant that *their* firms are often large enough to invest overseas. In 1996, two of the world's largest TNCs were Korea's Daewoo Corporation (43rd largest) and Venezuela's Petroleos de Venezuela. The top 50 developing-country TNCs represent those countries plus Mexico, Hong Kong (China), South Africa, Taiwan, Bermuda, China, Argentina, Brazil, Malaysia, Singapore, Panama, the Philippines, India, and Chile. Together, these firms had foreign assets of $104 billion, foreign sales of $338 billion, and over a million and a half foreign employees. Their main activities are classified as "diversified manufacturing," petroleum, and electronics.[102]

These firms are typically from the more advanced developing countries, including China that, despite relatively low per capita GDP, has the world's seventh largest economy. Such activities blur the lines between developing and developed countries. They indicate the extremely rapid progress of some developing countries and the widening gaps among them. In the Korean case, one investigation suggested that domestic labor disputes were one stimulus to foreign investment, reflecting similar charges made in developed countries.[103]

MEETING OF THE MINDS?

Clearly, there are different interests involved in evaluating the role of FDI in developing countries. Firms do not invest unless they believe a profit will be the ultimate outcome, and economic theory suggests that profit-making activity should enrich the society as well as the firm. Negative externalities, such as environmental damage, are no more connected with foreign than domestic ownership.

Nevertheless, the desire of the TNC to subordinate a local subsidiary to its global objectives may not only reduce the gain to the host country but may result in a net loss at a crucial time, for example, during a shortage of foreign exchange. So the question is not whether FDI *can* make a contribution to the local economy, but under what conditions that contribution can be maximized. Attractive countries such as South Korea have shown that by deciding which firms will come in and what they will do, and then providing favorable treatment, they can produce a result in keeping with their own development goals. India, on the other hand, maintained quite restrictive policies and received relatively little benefit.[104]

The current attitude toward FDI in developing countries is positive due to the economic difficulties—including debt problems—faced by many economies. One indication of how foreign investment reacts to the investment climate is the return of FDI to Latin America as countries have opened their economies since the late 1980s, compared to the still-sluggish response of foreign investors to the more uncertain circumstances of the former socialist economies of Eastern Europe.[105] Spurred by more open markets, privatization of former SOEs, and cross-border mergers and acquisitions, flows of FDI into developing countries have grown from an annual average of $29 billion from 1986 to 1991 to $208 billion in 1999. Brazil, with as little as $2 billion in 1994 had $31 billion in 1999. Mexico's inflow grew from $4.4 billion in 1993 to $12 billion in 1999. China had $11 billion in 1992 and $40 billion in 1999. (The 44 poorest countries, however, have not gained at all and had less than $2 billion among them in 1997.) For many, this is an increasingly global economy.

SUMMARY AND CONCLUSION

Developing-country governments, especially in those economies not considered creditworthy in private markets, often receive loans on concessional terms or grants from foreign governments. Such foreign assistance, or aid, has engendered many debates about its targeting, terms, and effectiveness. Aid may be given for specific projects or for more general programs.

How much aid a country needs may depend on economic calculations of resources required to achieve a certain growth rate, to fill a savings or trade gap, or to achieve specific project or program objectives. Assessment of the absorptive capacity is crucial. Donors, on the other hand, have only their own political objectives to satisfy, although an international guideline of 0.7 percent of donor GDP has been proposed. Official Development Assistance, worldwide, is less than $60 billion per year. It represents, in most years, around 40 percent of all foreign capital flows to developing countries, 0.7 percent of recipients' national income (although a higher portion of investment), and about $11 per year per person in the developing world. This amount, even well spent, will not end poverty.

Individual project analysis, however, shows that aid can have a positive impact on people. The case for aid will have to highlight those successes, and show that donors and recipients are able to promote national institutions and policies that raise aid's effectiveness. It will, realistically, also have to show that donors have a stake in successful aid that is at least as important as alternative uses of those funds.

The larger debate over aid often finds critics of the political left, right, and center. All sides charge that aid does not filter down to the poor. Close evaluations of aid programs throughout the world have found many problems but more success than failure. They call for donors and recipients to learn from failures and make aid more responsive to the needs of the poor.

The World Bank has remained largely a project-lending institution, although it has begun sectoral and structural adjustment lending based on market-oriented policy reforms. It has faced and responded to numerous criticisms.

Disappointment with the results of aid, the new needs of former socialist countries, and more active international capital markets have raised concern that development aid will be reduced, hurting the poorest countries.

Developing economies can obtain capital and technology from foreign companies through Foreign Direct Investment (FDI). A Transnational Corporation (TNC) invests overseas for a variety of reasons, including access to markets, raw materials, and cheap labor, or to circumvent import restrictions.

Economists have debated the value of foreign investment, countering the advantages of new capital and technology with concerns about the impact of competition on local firms, foreign control over resources, limited transfer of technology and technical skills, outflow of profits and foreign exchange, and a host of social and political issues. The general conclusion is that FDI can be a positive force if the goals of the host governments and TNCs can be made compatible.

In the competition for foreign capital, however, developing-country governments may have to make concessions that offset the benefits they receive. The ability of firms to move provides many companies with advantages in this competition. When foreign companies consider investing abroad, they look for not only a hospitable business climate but also minimum restrictions on their activities, including right of establishment, protection against expropriation, freedom to repatriate earnings, and neutral arbiters to settle disputes. The interplay of a country's natural advantages, its business climate, and its ability to negotiate will determine its success in attracting foreign investment.

Foreign investment is capable of making a significant contribution to development, but host governments should make sure that their own policies and the activities of TNCs make the most of that potential. The potential contribution is coupled with the potential for problems: To the extent that governments still wish to guide their economic development in specific directions, negotiations will be required to ensure that investment comes in the right areas and with the appropriate contribution to the improvement of the economy's resources, particularly capital and labor.

Key Terms

- absorptive capacity (p. 382)
- aid (p. 378)
- bilateral aid (p. 378)
- Bilateral Investment Treaty (BIT) (p. 413)
- concessional terms (p. 378)
- conditionality (p. 393)
- Development Assistance Committee (DAC) (p. 379)
- expropriation (p. 403)
- Foreign Direct Investment (FDI) (p. 399)
- fungibility (p. 380)
- grant element (p. 379)
- imperialism (p. 401)

- International Development Association (IDA) (pp. 393, 394)
- joint venture (p. 402)
- local content requirements (p. 411)
- most favored nation treatment (MFN) (p. 413)
- multilateral aid (p. 378)
- Multilateral Investment Guarantee Agency (MIGA) (p. 394)
- national treatment (p. 413)
- nationalization (p. 403)
- Nongovernmental Organizations (NGOs) (p. 381)

- Official Development Assistance (ODA) (p. 379)
- Overseas Private Investment Corporation (OPIC) (p. 413)
- performance requirements (p. 411)
- program aid (p. 381)
- project aid (p. 380)
- repatriate (p. 404)
- technical assistance (p. 381)
- tied aid (p. 381)
- transfer pricing (p. 404)
- Transnational Corporation (TNC) (p. 400)
- vertical integration (p. 401)

Questions for Review

1. What are the elements of aid that make it different from normal commercial lending?
2. What criteria ought to be considered in deciding how much aid is appropriate for a given country in a given year?

 3. How do the experiences of Cameroon and Mali illustrate potential problems with aid projects? How do the projects in Swaziland and Nepal illustrate conditions for success?

4. What is the basis of the attacks made on foreign aid by:
   a. Peter Bauer and conservatives generally
   b. Left-wing critics
   c. Proponents of NGOs
5. Summarize key points that arise from studies of aid programs with respect to:
   a. The successes of aid
   b. Lessons to be learned.

 6. How does India's long experience with foreign aid point to the pros and cons of aid?

7. Define Foreign Direct Investment and Transnational Corporation.
8. Why would a company choose to operate overseas rather than just export its products? Why would a company choose a "new form" of foreign investment?
9. What are the benefits that economic theory would claim for foreign direct investment?

 10. How does the Mexican automotive sector demonstrate the potential benefits of FDI?

11. What type of "business climate" is necessary to attract FDI?
12. What are the chief concerns of host countries about the activities of TNCs?

13. What are the chief concerns of TNCs about host countries, and how do the home governments of TNCs try to protect the companies' interests?
14. Weigh the advantages of a TNC and a host country in negotiating the terms of an investment. Under what circumstances is the investor or host government likely to have an advantage?

Related Internet Sites

The multilateral development banks are all online: the World Bank at ⟨www.worldbank.org⟩, the Interamerican Development Bank at ⟨www.iadb.org⟩, the Asian Development Bank at ⟨www.adb.org⟩, and the African Development Bank at ⟨http://Afdb.org⟩. The U.S. Agency for International Development can be accessed at ⟨www.usaid.gov⟩. Links to NGOs recognized by the United Nations can be found at ⟨www.un.org/MoreInfo/ngolink/ngodir.htm⟩ and ⟨www.ngo.org⟩ (the NGO Global Network). The UN has downgraded its home for TNC information. Its Commission for Transnational Corporations has been folded into the UN Conference for Trade and Development and can be accessed at ⟨www.unctad.org⟩.

Endnotes and Further Readings

1. See "Official Development Flows," in *World Development Report 1985* (Washington: World Bank, 1985), pp. 94–109; Anne O. Krueger, "Aid in the Development Process," *World Bank Research Observer* 1, no. 1 (January 1986), pp. 57–78; and Stephen Browne, *Foreign Aid in Practice* (Washington Square, NY: New York University Press, 1990).
2. See the DAC's annual reports, *Development Co-operation*. Data here are from the 1995 report (the grant element data are on p. A49) and the DAC 1998 report on the U.S. program, Development-Cooperation Review Series No. 28 (1998).
3. See Klaus Schmidt-Hebbel, Luis Serven, and Andres Solimano, "Savings and Investment: Paradigms, Puzzles, Policies," *World Bank Research Observer* 11, no. 1 (February 1996), p. 100, and Saadet Deger and Somnath Sen, "Military Expenditure, Aid and Economic Development," *Proceedings of the World Bank Annual Conference on Development Economics, 1991* (Washington: World Bank, 1992), pp. 159–190.
4. World Bank, *Assessing Aid: What Works, What Doesn't, and Why* (New York: Oxford University Press/World Bank, 1998), pp. 64–65. Also see Tashan Geyzioglu, Vinaya Swaroop, and Min Zhu, "A Panel Data Analysis of the Fungibility of Foreign Aid," *World Bank Economic Review* 12, no. 1 (January 1998), pp. 29–58.
5. For 1993, see DAC, *Development Co-operation*, 1995 report, p. A52. For 1999, see *World Development Indicators 2001*, p. 346. The estimate on the reduced value of aid is from Robert Cassen and Associates, *Does Aid Work? Report to an Inter-Governmental Task Force* (Oxford: Oxford University Press, 1986), pp. 285–289. Also see Eduardo Lachica, "U.S., Other OECD Nations Agree to Curb Aid Tied to Donor Countries' Exports," *Wall Street Journal*, November 1, 1991; Catrinus J. Jepma, *The Tying of Aid* (Paris: OECD,

1991); and W. Oliver Morrissey, "The Mixing of Aid and Trade Policies," *The World Economy* 16, no. 1 (January 1993), pp. 69–84.
6. See Aubrey Williams, "A Growing Role for NGOs in Development," *Finance and Development* 27, no. 4 (December 1990), pp. 31–33; John Clark, *Democratizing Development: The Role of Voluntary Organizations* (West Hartford, CT: Kumarian Press, 1991); United Nations Development Program, *Human Development Report 1993* (United Nations/Oxford University Press, 1993), chapter 5; Ian Smillie, *Mastering the Machine: Poverty, Aid and Technology* (Boulder, CO: Westview Press, 1991); Thomas G. Weiss and Leon Gordenker, eds., *NGOs, the UN, & Global Governance* (Boulder, CO: Lynne Rienner, 1996); and Michael Edwards and David Hulme, "Too Close for Comfort? The Impact of Official Aid on Nongovernmental Organizations," *World Development* 24, no. 6 (June 1996), pp. 961–973. Regional perspectives can be found in Sonia Arellano-Lopez and James F. Petras, "Non-Governmental Organizations and Poverty Alleviation in Bolivia," *Development & Change* 25, no. 3 (July 1994), pp. 555–568; Alan Fowler, "Non-Governmental Organizations as Agents of Democratization: An African Perspective," *Journal of International Development* 5, no. 3 (May–June 1993), pp. 325–339; and Mark A. Robinson, "Assessing the Impact of NGO Rural Poverty Alleviation Programmes: Evidence from South India," *Journal of International Development* 4, no. 4 (July–August 1992), pp. 397–417.
7. See J. Mohan Rao, "Ranking Foreign Donors: An Index Combining the Scale and Equity of Aid Giving," *World Development* 25, no. 6 (June 1997), pp. 947–961.
8. See Robert E. Wood, *From Marshall Plan to Debt Crisis* (Berkeley: University of California Press, 1986), p. 76, n. 23.

9. Bauer's many works on this matter include "Foreign Aid, Forever?" *Encounter* (March 1974), pp. 18–25; "Foreign Aid: Rewarding Impoverishment?" with B. S. Yamey, *Commentary* (September 1985), pp. 38–40; and *Equality, The Third World and Economic Delusion* (London: Weidenfield and Nicholson, 1981), especially pp. 87–89. Also, see Peter Bauer and Basil Yamey, "Foreign Aid: What Is at Stake?" *Public Interest*, no. 68 (summer 1982), pp. 53–69, and Nicholas Eberstadt, *Foreign Aid and American Purpose* (Washington: American Enterprise Institute, 1988).

10. See Robert E. Wood, *From Marshall Plan to Debt Crisis*; Teresa Hayter, *Aid as Imperialism* (Baltimore: Penguin Books, 1971); Pierre Jalee, *The Third World in World Economy* (New York: Monthly Review Press, 1969), especially pp. 103–110; Steve Weissman et al., *The Trojan Horse: A Radical Look at Foreign Aid* (San Francisco: Ramparts Press, 1974); and Lynn Richards, "The Context of Foreign Aid: Modern Imperialism," *Review of Radical Political Economics* 9, no. 4 (winter 1977), pp. 43–75.

11. The following material is based on Stephen Hellinger, Douglas Hellinger, and Fred M. O'Regan, *Aid for Just Development* (Boulder, CO: Lynne Rienner, 1988). This "Report on the Future of Foreign Assistance" is an outgrowth of work done by the Development Group for Alternative Policies (Development GAP).

12. *Ibid.*, p. 23.

13. See Robert Klitgaard's *Tropical Gangsters: One Man's Experience with Development and Decadence in Deepest Africa* (New York: Basic Books, 1990), and Timothy Morris, *The Despairing Developer: Diary of an Aid Worker in the Middle East* (London: I. B. Tauris, 1991).

14. Jonathan Isham, Deepa Narayan, and Lance Pritchett, "Does Participation Improve Performance? Establishing Causality with Subjective Data," *World Bank Economic Review* 9, no. 2 (May 1995), pp. 175–200.

15. The Pearson report is *Partners in Development*, formally by the Commission on International Development, Report of the Commission, Lester B. Pearson, Chair (New York: Praeger, 1969). The Peterson report is by the Task Force on International Development, *U.S. Foreign Assistance in the 1970s: A New Approach*, Report to the President (Washington: March 4, 1970). The Brandt Report is *North–South: A Program for Survival*, by the Independent Commission on International Development, a Report of the Commission, Willy Brandt, Chairperson (Cambridge: MIT Press, 1980).

16. John P. Lewis, "Development Promotion: A Time for Regrouping," in Lewis and Valeriana Kallab, eds., *Development Strategies Reconsidered* (New Brunswick, NJ: Transaction Press, 1986).

17. Gerald M. Meier, "Improving the Quality of Aid," in Meier, ed., *Leading Issues in Economic Development* (New York: Oxford University Press, 1964, 1970, 1976, 1984, 1989).

18. See his "Strengthening the Poor: Some Lessons for the International Community," in John P. Lewis and contributors, *Strengthening the Poor: What Have We Learned?* (New Brunswick, NJ: Transaction Press, 1988).

19. The OECD study was published in 1992. The Bank study, originally done in 1991, was summarized in *Strengthening the Effectiveness of Aid: Lessons for Donors* (Washington: World Bank, 1995).

20. Robert Cassen and Associates, *Does Aid Work? Report to an Inter-Governmental Task Force* (Oxford: Oxford University Press, 1986). A less technical edition with some updated references was published by Clarendon Press, 1994.

21. See Ira N. Gang and Haider Ali Khan, "Foreign Aid, Taxes, and Public Investment," *Journal of Development Economics* 34, no. 1–2 (November 1990), pp. 355–369.

22. Janine L. Bowen, *Foreign Aid and Economic Growth: A Theoretical and Empirical Investigation* (Aldershot, U.K.: Ashgate, 1998).

23. Cassen, *Does Aid Work? Report to an Inter-Governmental Task Force*, p. 307.

24. Aidan Cox and John Healey, "Poverty Reduction: A Review of Donor Strategies and Practices," in Raundi Halvorson-Quevedo and Hartmut Schneider, eds., *Waging the Global War on Poverty* (Paris: OECD, 2000), pp. 25–60.

25. Paul J. Isenman and H. W. Singer, "Food Aid: Disincentive Effects and Their Policy Implications," in Vernon W. Ruttan, ed., *Why Food Aid?* (Baltimore: Johns Hopkins University Press, 1993), pp. 99–122.

26. *Ibid.*, p. 322.

27. From the second edition, Cassen, *Does Aid Work? Report to an Inter-Governmental Task Force*, p. 225. Italics in the original.

28. Bowen, *Foreign Aid and Economic Growth: A Theoretical and Empirical Investigation*.

29. Uma Lele and Ijaz Nabi, "Aid, Capital Flows, and Development: A Synthesis," in their *Transitions in Development: The Role of Aid and Commercial Flows* (San Francisco: ICS Press, 1991), pp. 453–474. Also see Constantine Michalopoulos and Vasant Sukhatme, "The Impact of Development Assistance," in Anne Krueger, Constantine Michalopoulos, and Vernon Ruttan, *Aid and Development* (Baltimore: Johns Hopkins University Press, 1988), pp. 111–124.

30. World Bank, *Assessing Aid: What Works, What Doesn't, and Why*.

31. Craig Burnside and David Dollar, "Aid, Policies and Growth," *American Economic Review* 90, no. 4 (September 2000), pp. 847–868.

32. World Bank, *Assessing Aid: What Works, What Doesn't, and Why*. Also see Paul Collier, Patrick Guillaumont, Sylviane Guillamont, and Jan Willem Gunning, "Redesigning Conditionality," *World Development* 25, no. 9 (September 1997), pp. 1399–1407.

33. Lipton and Toye, *Does Aid Work in India?* p. 113.

34. See Joan M. Nelson, *Encouraging Democracy: What Role for Conditioned Aid* (Washington: Overseas Development Council, 1992); John P. Lewis, *Pro-Poor Aid Conditionality* (Washington: Overseas Development Council, 1993); and Mick Moore and Mark Robinson, "Can Foreign Aid Be Used to Promote Good Government in Developing Countries?" *Ethics & International Affairs* 8 (1994), pp. 141–158.

35. The Bank's Web site is ⟨www.worldbank.org⟩.

36. From Article I of the Bank's "Articles of Agreement."

37. World Bank *Annual Report 2000*, pp. 119–120.

38. Warren C. Baum, "The Project Cycle" (Washington: World Bank, 1982), pp. 3–4.

39. World Bank *Annual Report 1999*, p. 97.

40. World Bank *Annual Report 1998*, p. 124.

41. See Teresa Hayter, *Aid as Imperialism*, pp. 46–87; Cheryl Payer, *The World Bank: A Critical Analysis* (New York: Monthly Review Press, 1982); Robert L. Ayres, *Banking on the Poor: The World Bank and World Poverty* (Cambridge: MIT Press, 1983); Richard E. Feinberg, "An Open Letter to the World Bank's New President," and G. K. Helleiner, "Policy-Based Program Lending: A Look at the Bank's New Role," in Feinberg et al., *Between Two Worlds: The World Bank's Next Decade* (New Brunswick, NJ: Transaction Books/Overseas Development Council, 1986), pp. 3–30 and pp. 47–66, respectively.

42. Stephen Hellinger et al., *Aid for Just Development*, pp. 126–127. Also see Roy Culpeper, *Titans or Behemoths?* vol. 5 in the series on multilateral development banks (Boulder, CO: Lynne Rienner and the North–South Institute, 1997), and Joel Millman and Jonathan Friedland, "World Bank Finance Arm Tends to Aid Least Needy," *Wall Street Journal*, September 23, 1997.

43. The authors cite the U.S. government's own admission of its influence in *United States Participation in the Multilateral Development Banks in the 1980s* (Washington: U.S. Government Printing Office, 1982).

44. Bob Naiman, "What's Wrong With the IMF and the World Bank?" ⟨www.a16.org⟩, April 16, 2000.

45. Michael M. Phillips, "Can World Bank Lend Money to Third World Without Hurting Poor?" *Wall Street Journal*, August 14, 2000, and Helene Cooper, "World Bank China-Project Funding Plan Falls Apart in Face of Diverse Opposition," *Wall Street Journal*, July 10, 2000.

46. Sheldon Annis, "The Shifting Grounds of Poverty Lending at the World Bank," in Feinberg et al., *Between Two Worlds: The World Bank's Next Decade*, pp. 87–110.

47. The examples are from Ayres, *Banking on the Poor: The World Bank and World Poverty*.

48. World Bank, "1999 Annual Review of Development Effectiveness: Toward a Comprehensive Development Strategy," (Washington: World Bank, 2000), pp. 36, 38.

49. Communiqué of the World Bank Development Committee, April 17, 2000. ⟨http://wbln0018.worldbank.org/DCS/devcom.nsf/(communiquesm)/⟩.

50. Anne O. Krueger, "Whither the World Bank and the IMF?" *Journal of Economic Literature* 36, no. 4 (December 1998), p. 2009.

51. See the 1993 DAC report, *Development Cooperation: Aid in Transition* (Paris: OECD, 1994).

52. Susan M. Collins, "Capital Flows to Developing Countries: Implications from the Economies in Transition?" *Proceedings of the World Bank Annual Conference on Development Economics 1992*; Robert Lensink and Howard White, "Does the Revival of International Private Capital Flows Mean the End of Aid? An Analysis of Developing Countries' Access to Private Capital," *World Development* 26, no. 7 (July 1998), pp. 1221–1234; and Tony Killick, "Responding to the Aid Crisis," in UNCTAD, *International Monetary and Financial Issues for the 1990s* (New York: United Nations, 1998), pp. 19–44.

53. DAC, *Development Co-operation*, p. 19.

54. See, for example, David Hoffman, "Coming in a Poor Second to 'America First'," *Washington Post Weekly*, December 2–8, 1991; Robert S. Greenberger, "With Cold War Over, Poorer Nations Face Neglect by the Rich," *Wall Street Journal*, May 14, 1992; and Karen De Young, "Who Helps the World? In An Age of Prosperity, the U.S. Foreign Aid Budget is Shrinking," *Washington Post Weekly*, December 13, 1999.

55. See Mark Casson and Robert D. Pearce, "Multinational Enterprises in LDCs," in Norman Gemmell, ed., *Surveys in Development Economics* (Oxford: Basil Blackwell, 1987), pp. 90–134, and Rhys Jenkins, *Transnational Corporations and Uneven Development* (London: Methuen, 1987).

56. The percentage of TNC activity that took place in developing countries has been estimated at 63 percent in 1914, 66 percent in 1938, 32 percent in 1960, and 28 percent in 1978. See Casson and Pearce, "Multinational Enterprises in LDCs," p. 95. According to the UN, this declined to 21 percent in 1990 but has been rising, to 30 percent in 1997. United Nations, *World Investment Report 1998* (New York: United Nations, 1998), p. 5.

57. John H. Dunning, *International Production and the Multinational Enterprise* (London: George Allen and Unwin, 1981).

58. United Nations, *The Determinants of Foreign Direct Investment: A Survey of the Evidence* (New York: United Nations, 1991, p. 54).

59. Richard E. Caves, *Multinational Enterprise and Economic Analysis* (Cambridge: Cambridge University Press, 1982).

60. See Harry Magdoff and Paul Sweezy, "Notes on the Multinational Corporation," in K. T. Fann and Donald C. Hodges, eds., *Readings in U.S. Imperialism* (Boston: Porter Sargent, 1971), pp. 93–116; Ronald E. Müller, "The Multinational Corporation and the Underdevel-

oped World," in Charles K. Wilber, ed., *The Political Economy of Development and Underdevelopment* (New York: Random House, 1973), pp. 124–151; and Richard Newfarmer, "Multinationals and Marketplace Magic in the 1980s," in Charles P. Kindleberger and David B. Audretsch, *The Multinational Corporation in the 1980s* (Cambridge: MIT Press, 1983), pp. 162–197.

61. See Stephen Hymer, *The International Operations of National Firms: A Study of Direct Foreign Investment* (Cambridge: MIT Press, 1976), and a series of papers, *The Multinational Corporation: A Radical Approach* (Cambridge: Cambridge University Press, 1979), especially chapter 6, "The Multinational Corporation and the International Division of Labor," pp. 140–164.

62. This term is attributed to Charles P. Oman. See "New Forms of Investment in Developing Countries," in Theodore H. Moran et al., *Investing in Development: New Roles for Private Capital* (New Brunswick, NJ: Transaction Books, 1986), pp. 131–156.

63. See Charles R. Kennedy, "Relations Between Transnational Corporations and Governments of Host Countries: A Look To the Future," in *Transnational Corporations* 1, no. 1 (February 1992), pp. 67–91, and David Conklin and Donald Lecraw, "Restrictions on Foreign Ownership During 1984–1994: Developments and Alternative Policies," *Transnational Corporations* 6, no. 1 (April 1997), pp. 1–30.

64. See Richard J. Barnet and Ronald E. Müller, *Global Reach: The Power of Multinational Corporations* (New York: Simon and Schuster, 1974).

65. Thomas J. Biersteker, *Distortion or Development? Contending Perspectives on the Multinational Corporation* (Cambridge: MIT Press, 1978), chapter 6.

66. Casson and Pearce, "Multinational Enterprises in LDCs," p. 108; Volker Bornschier and Hanspeter Stamm, "Transnational Corporations," in Alberto Martinelli and Neil J. Smelser, eds., *Economy and Society: Overviews in Economic Sociology* (London: Sage, 1990, p. 218); and Theodore H. Moran, *Foreign Direct Investment and Development* (Washington: Institute for International Economics, 1999), pp. 21–23.

67. See Casson and Pearce, "Multinational Enterprises in LDCs," p. 120, and G. K. Helleiner, "Transnational Corporations and Direct Foreign Investment," in *The Handbook of Development Economics*, vol. 2, H. B. Chenery and S. N. Srinivisan, eds. (Amsterdam: Elsevier Science Publishers, 1989), p. 1456.

68. Helleiner, "Policy-Based Program Lending: A Look at the Bank's New Role," p. 1465.

69. Newfarmer, "Multinationals and Marketplace Magic in the 1980s," p. 181.

70. Casson and Pearce, "Multinational Enterprises in LDCs," p. 119.

71. *Ibid.*, pp. 97–104.

72. James C. W. Ahiakpor, "The Capital Intensity of Foreign, Private Local and State-Owned Firms in a Less Developed Country: Ghana," *Journal of Development*

Economics* 20, no. 1 (January–February 1986), pp. 125–133, and Robert Stobaugh and Louis W. Wells, Jr., "Introduction," to their *Technology Crossing Borders: The Choice, Transfer, and Management of International Technology Flows* (Boston: Harvard Business School Press, 1989), pp. 1–18.

73. International Labour Office, *Technology Choice and Employment Generation by Multinational Enterprises in Developing Countries* (Geneva: ILO, 1984). The conclusions reported are on pp. 71–74.

74. G. Pascal Zachary and Samantha Marshall, "Nike Tries to Quell Exploitation Charges," *Wall Street Journal*, June 25, 1997, and Joseph Pereira, "Reebok Finds Ills at Indonesian Factories," *Wall Street Journal*, October 18, 1999.

75. See Moran, *Foreign Direct Investment and Development*, pp. 41–52; Ari Kokko and Magnus Blomstrom, "Policies to Encourage Inflows of Technology Through Foreign Multinationals," *World Development* 23, no. 3 (March 1995), pp. 459–468; Ari Kokko, Ruben Tansini, and Mario C. Zejan, "Local Technological Capability and Productivity Spillovers from FDI in the Uruguayan Manufacturing Sector," *Journal of Development Studies* 32, no. 4 (April 1996), pp. 602–611; and Ari Kokko "Productivity Spillovers from Competition Between Local Firms and Foreign Affiliates," *Journal of International Development* 8, no. 4 (July–August 1996), pp. 517–530.

76. Loretta Fairchild and Kim Sosin, "Evaluating Differences in Technological Activity Between Transnational and Domestic Firms in Latin America," *Journal of Development Studies* 22, no. 4 (July 1986), pp. 697–708.

77. Nigel Driffield and Abd Halim Mohd Noor, "Foreign Direct Investment and Local Input Linkages in Malaysia," *Transnational Corporations* 8, no. 3 (December 1999), pp. 1–24.

78. Jan Gilbreath and John Benjamin Tonra, "The Environment: Unwelcome Guest at the Free Trade Party," in M. Delal Baer and Sidney Weintraub, *The NAFTA Debate: Grappling with Unconventional Trade Issues* (Boulder, CO: Lynne Rienner, 1994), pp. 53–93. These results are reported on p. 84.

79. ⟨www.citizen.org/pctrade/nafta/reports/5years.htm⟩.

80. See ⟨www.greenpeace.org/~comms/ken/hell.html⟩.

81. See Bornschier and Stamm, "Transnational Corporations," pp. 217–220, and Caves, *Multinational Enterprise and Economic Analysis*, pp. 266–276.

82. V. N. Balesubramanyam, M. Salisu, and David Sapsford, "Foreign Direct Investment and Growth in EP and IS Countries," *Economic Journal* 106, no. 434 (January 1996), pp. 92–105; Luiz R. de Mello, Jr., "Foreign Direct Investment in Developing Countries and Growth: A Selective Survey," *Journal of Development Studies* 34, no. 1 (October 1997), pp. 1–34; and Robert E. Lipsey, "Inward FDI and Economic Growth in Developing Countries," *Transnational Corporations* 9, no. 1 (April 2000), pp. 67–96.

83. Karl Jansen, "The Macroeconomic Effects of Direct Foreign Investment: The Case of Thailand," *World Development* 23, no. 2 (February 1995), pp. 193–210.

84. De Mello, "Foreign Direct Investment in Developing Countries and Growth: A Selective Survey."

85. See Adalberto J. Pinelo, *The Multinational Corporation as a Force in Latin American Politics: A Case Study of the International Petroleum Corporation in Peru* (New York: Praeger, 1973).

86. See, for example, Paul Harrison's *Inside the Third World* (Middlesex, U.K.: Penguin Books, 1982), especially chapter 3, entitled "The Westernization of the World."

87. Newfarmer, "Multinationals and Marketplace Magic in the 1980s," p. 174.

88. See Marcus Brauchli, "Free to Choose: Investors Often Pick Authoritarian over Democratic Countries. Maybe They Shouldn't," *Wall Street Journal*, September 18, 1997. Bret L. Billet disagrees, in *Investment Behavior of Multinational Corporations in Developing Areas* (New Brunswick, NJ: Transactions Publishers, 1991).

89. See Guy Pfeffermann, "Facilitating Foreign Investment," *Finance & Development* 29, no. 1 (March 1992), pp. 46–47.

90. Helleiner, "Policy-Based Program Lending: A Look at the Bank's New Role," p. 1457.

91. Dennis J. Encarnation and Louis T. Wells, Jr., "Evaluating Foreign Investment," in Moran, *Investing in Development: New Roles for Private Capital*, pp. 61–86. The citation is from p. 63.

92. See Thomas J. Biersteker, *Distortion or Development? Contending Perspectives on the Multinational Corporation*, and Moran (1999), pp. 119–126.

93. Moran, *Foreign Direct Investment and Development*, pp. 41–46.

94. *Ibid.*, pp. 49–84.

95. United Nations, *The Impact of Trade-Related Investment Measures on Trade and Development* (New York: United Nations, 1991), p. 15.

96. Masayoshi Kanabayashi, "China's Increasing Costs of Labor Start to Deter Japanese Businesses," *Wall Street Journal*, December 14, 1999, and Dan Biers, "Low-Cost Penang Gives Singapore a Run for Its High-Tech Money," *Wall Street Journal*, December 5, 1994.

97. See Casson and Pearce, "Multinational Enterprises in LDCs," p. 124. Also Vincent Cable and Bisharkha Mukherjee, "Foreign Investment in Low-Income Developing Countries," in Moran, *Investing in Development: New Roles for Private Capital*, pp. 87–112; "U.N. Report Urges Curbs on Incentives Used to Woo Multinational Employers," *Wall Street Journal*, April 14, 1995; and Victor M. Gastanaga, Jeffrey B. Nugent, and Bistra Pashamova, "Host Country Reforms and FDI Inflows: How Much Difference Do They Make?" *World Development* 26, no. 7 (July 1998), pp. 1299–1314.

98. See Casson and Pearce, "Multinational Enterprises in LDCs," pp. 111–112; Sandy Tolan and Jerry Kammer, "Life in the Low-Wage Boomtowns of Mexico," from the *Tucson Weekly*, reprinted in the *Utne Reader* (November–December 1990), pp. 42–50; Helen I. Safa, "Runaway Shops and Female Employment: The Search for Cheap Labor," in *Signs: Journal of Women in Culture and Society* 7, no. 2 (winter 1981), pp. 418–433; and Linda Y. C. Lim, "Women's Work in Export Factories: The Politics of a Cause," in Irene Tinker, ed., *Persistent Inequalities: Women and World Development* (New York: Oxford University Press, 1990), pp. 101–122. The data on EPZ employment come from the *World Investment Report 1994*, p. 190.

99. OECD, *Investing in Developing Countries* (Paris: OECD, 1983), cited in Helleiner, "Policy-Based Program Lending: A Look at the Bank's New Role," p. 1468, and Stephen Guisinger, "Host-Country Policies to Attract and Control Foreign Investment," in Moran, *Investing in Development: New Roles for Private Capital*, pp. 157–172.

100. Casson and Pearce, "Multinational Enterprises in LDCs," pp. 121–123, and Helleiner, "Policy-Based Program Lending: A Look at the Bank's New Role," pp. 1461–1465.

101. See Laura Wallace, "MIGA: Up and Running," in *Finance & Development* 29, no. 1 (March 1992), pp. 48–49.

102. The data come from the UN's *World Investment Report 1998*. See also J. P. Agarwal, "Intra-LDC Foreign Direct Investment: A Comparative Analysis of Third-World Multinationals," *The Developing Economies* 23, no. 3 (September 1985), pp. 236–253; Sanjaya Lall et al., *The New Multinationals: The Spread of Third World Enterprises* (Chichester, U.K.: John Wiley & Sons, 1984); Dana Milbank, "Asian Tigers Are on the Prowl in Europe," *Wall Street Journal*, October 26, 1994; Matt Moffett, "Chilean Firms Blaze Cross-Border Trails," *Wall Street Journal*, November 7, 1994; Louis T. Wells, *Third World Multinationals: The Rise of Foreign Investment from Developing Countries* (Cambridge: MIT Press, 1983); and Daniel Chudnovsky and Andrés López, "A Third Wave of FDI from Developing Countries: Latin American TNCs in the 1990s," *Transnational Corporations* 9, no. 2 (August 2000), pp. 31–74.

103. MoonJong Tcha, "Labor Disputes and Direct Foreign Investment: The Experience of Korea in Transition," *Economic Development and Cultural Change* 46, no. 2 (January 1998), pp. 305–328.

104. See Gerald Helleiner, "Industrial Organization, Trade and Investment in Developing Countries," in his *The New Global Economy and the Developing Countries* (Hants, U.K.: Edward Elgar, 1990), pp. 222–224.

105. See Bernard Wysocki, Jr., "U.S. Business Still Likes Latin America," *Wall Street Journal*, May 12, 1995.

CHAPTER

14 | DEBT AND ADJUSTMENT

If you would know the value of money,
go and try to borrow some;
for he that goes a-borrowing
goes a-sorrowing.
—BENJAMIN FRANKLIN (1706–1790)

INTRODUCTION

Foreign companies and aid donors have little interest in many of the investment opportunities in developing countries. If these potential investments are seen as profitable or necessary for development, foreign borrowing can be an additional source of funds. But it is not that simple. The various motives of borrowers and lenders do not guarantee that debt is incurred sensibly and can be paid back as intended. This chapter first explains why debt is logical for developing countries and the circumstances under which debt may become a problem.

The debt crisis of the 1980s, and the poor performance of many inward-oriented economies that led up to it, ushered in an era of controversy over how governments should adjust their economies in order to better pursue economic development. The World Bank and International Monetary Fund began lending to governments for the broad purpose of restructuring their economies in an outward direction. These structural adjustment programs have been the subject of heated controversy over their appropriateness and effectiveness. We therefore describe the nature of the adjustments that are proposed, particularly when economies are faced with mounting debt payments, and look at the role of the Bank and Fund in dealing with the process.

THE LOGIC OF DEBT

Our first task is to understand why borrowing takes place, then put it in the context of economic development.

The Logic of Developing-Country Debt

A developing country is like a business in its early stages of growth: It needs a period of time to build up productive capacity. Private saving will be either insufficient or unavailable to potential investors. Government's taxing capacity will also be insufficient in the early stages of development. But untapped human and natural resources provide a potential for growth. Foreign capital will normally flow toward that productive capacity, expecting either a return on investment—profit—or repayment of a loan with interest. The United States was a net debtor for the first 150 years of its existence: Much of the imported capital was direct investment, and much was the purchase of corporate and state government bonds.

One important difference between public and private debt is the recourse of creditors if **default** occurs. If a company goes bankrupt and defaults on a loan—that is, declares itself unable to pay—bondholders have legal recourse through seizure and division of the company's remaining assets.

It may be difficult to enforce that claim against a government. The former Soviet Union agreed in the late 1980s to pay Switzerland for some prerevolutionary debts, in exchange for being allowed to use Swiss banks to float loans. Some British bondholders still regularly demand repayment of State of Mississippi bonds that were defaulted on sometime in the nineteenth century. In the Great Depression, thousands of small investors who had been convinced to put their money into the bonds of South American governments lost it all when those governments defaulted. Banks may rely not on evaluation of projects but on a general estimate of the country's capacity to repay and on government guarantees, but may find out later that the lending was for nonproductive purposes and the government does not have the capacity to repay on the agreed terms.

Despite potential problems, however, we assume that factors of production, including capital, will flow to their most productive use unless they are somehow prevented from doing so. As the productivity of a factor is, ceteris paribus, directly related to the scarcity of that factor, the lack of capital in developing countries should translate into anticipated profit, and money will flow. The developing country, if it manages the capital well, will gain through this productivity: Output will increase sufficiently so that the proceeds will permit the loans to be paid off or inspire sufficient confidence that they will be voluntarily rolled over.

Government Debt

National governments, like large corporations, tend to be perpetually in debt. A government not only borrows, but builds up debt over a period of time if its citizens, who buy government bonds, continue to have faith in the stability of the government and its ability to pay off each individual bond. Nevertheless, a government's debt can become excessive, even when it is held largely by its citizens. In addition to the possible inflationary impact of deficits in times of strong demand, a large government debt may raise interest rates and crowd out private borrowing. If government spending is less productive than the private spending would have been, the nation's productivity is adversely affected.

If the debt grows faster than GDP, we have some indication that the economy is being burdened, although there is some range within which this may not be a problem. As the debt grows, a greater portion of the economy's resources—and a greater part of the government budget—becomes tied up in simply paying interest, with no assurance that interest income is used productively. When a large or increasing portion of a government's borrowing comes from sources outside the country and is in foreign currency, rolling over the debt tends increasingly to rely on, and interest payments go to, foreigners. When the government's prospects are not viewed favorably by foreigners, it has a debt problem.

DEBT PROBLEMS IN DEVELOPING COUNTRIES

A full discussion of international debt requires a more detailed account of the macroeconomic situation in which debt arises.

The Macroeconomics of Debt

In macroeconomic terms, a net inflow of foreign capital corresponds to a deficit in the country's **current account** balance: Imports (often combined with debt repayments) exceed exports receipts. The current account is in deficit when private savings and taxes together are not sufficient to pay for business investment and government spending.

Table 14–1 shows the major balance of payments accounts for Tanzania and Mexico in 1999. Both have trade and current account deficits: In both cases the trade deficit is exacerbated by income paid to foreign investors (and partially offset by other transfers). Mexico's deficit is financed by direct investment and other capital flows, so its overall balance is positive. Tanzania is not attractive to investors and, so, does not have enough private capital flows to offset its current account. It does receive some foreign aid (capital transfers), but with errors and omissions factored in, the overall balance is still in deficit. To finance the deficit and build up its foreign exchange reserves, Tanzania had to rely on external ("other") financing (probably from the IMF). Mexico was able to build up its reserves and pay back past external financing.

TABLE 14–1 Balance of Payments—1999

$ Millions	Tanzania	Mexico
Exports of Goods and Services	1,189	148,660
Imports of Goods and Services	−2,287	−156,281
Investment Income	−43	−12,711
Unilateral Transfers	334	6,316
Current Account Balance	−807	−14,016
Net Capital Transfers	323	0
Net Direct Investment	183	11,567
Net Portfolio Investment	0	9,955
Net Other Capital	407	−3,696
Capital/Finance Account Balance	913	17,826
Errors and Omissions	−235	468
Overall Balance	−129	4,278
Foreign Exchange Reserves	−326	−598
Other Financing	456	−3,681

Source: IMF, *International Financial Statistics*, June 2001.

Developing-Country Foreign Debt

For a developing country, foreign debt is in the form of direct borrowing from banks and aid donors. A large portion is likely to be short-term (three months to six months) credits intended to finance particular imports but may be financing consumption rather than productive investment. The country's ability to repay may be in doubt because its currency is not easily convertible into dollars, deutschemärks, and other major currencies; its rate of exchange may be subject to government control; and foreign banks and donors question the economy's ability to generate adequate returns.

Thus, a debt *crisis* is more indicative of an overall economic crisis when the economy is not sufficiently productive to create confidence in continued repayment. It is not the size of the debt that is crucial, but the productivity of capital (compared to the rate of interest) and growth of the economy that are important. If the economy is growing rapidly enough, and in the right direction, it can handle an increasing debt. What is critical is the ability of the economy to pay the **debt service** (interest and principal on the debt), which means the economy must be growing in such a way as to earn sufficient foreign exchange (and tax revenues, in the case of government debt) to pay external creditors. If it is performing adequately, it can easily borrow to roll over old debt.[1]

Who Has Been Hit Hardest?

The World Bank classifies countries as to whether they are severely, moderately, or less indebted. Each category is subdivided into low income and middle income. The designation of "severely indebted" is given to countries that meet three of four criteria: a debt/GNP ratio of 50 percent or more, a debt/export ratio of 275 percent or more, a debt service/export ratio of 30 percent or more, and an interest payment/export ratio of 20 percent or more.

Table 14–2 shows the impact of debt on the Severely Indebted Middle-Income Countries. Between 1980 and 1986, the foreign debt of these countries doubled as a

TABLE 14–2 Debt Indicators: Severely Indebted Middle-Income Countries

	Debt*/GNP	Debt Service[†]/ Exports	Interest/ Exports	Months of Reserves[‡]
1980	32.9	32.6	17.2	4.5
1983	59.5	40.5	27.4	2.9
1986	62.3	39.7	21.9	2.5
1989	52.6	32.7	14.4	5.7
1992	45.5	31.5	12.2	3.3
1996	36.6	36.8	14.9	6.5
1999	46.3	80.7	23.6	5.3

*Debt is total external debt. This refers to "public and publicly guaranteed disbursed long-term debt," that is, debt with maturities of one year or longer owed by governments or owed by private borrowers and guaranteed by their governments.

[†]Debt service is repayments on principal and interest.

[‡]Reserves is foreign exchange reserves. Figure is the number of months' worth of imports that can be paid for with existing reserves. (A developing economy should maintain reserves worth from three months to four months of imports.)

Source: World Bank, *World Debt Tables* and *Global Development Finance*, various years.

TABLE 14–3 Regional Debt Indicators for 2000

	Sub-Saharan Africa	Latin America and Caribbean	East Asia/ Pacific
Debt as Percentage of Exports	180.2	172.6	74.8
Debt as Percentage of GNP	66.1	41.8	32.6
Debt Service as Percentage of Exports	12.8	35.7	10.8
Interest as Percentage of Exports	4.3	11.8	4.0
Reserves: Months of Imports	3.1	3.5	5.2

Source: Global Development Finance 2001.

percentage of GNP. Annual repayments of principal and interest took about two-fifths of export earnings, and foreign exchange reserves fell to only about two and a half months of imports. By 1996 the situation had eased but worsened again through 1999.

In 2000, the severely indebted low-income category included 33 countries, 27 of which were in Sub-Saharan Africa. The middle-income severely indebted category has shrunk. In 1991 it consisted of 15 countries, including the biggest debtors (Brazil, Mexico) among 8 from Latin America. By 2000, there were only 10: Argentina, Bolivia, Bosnia-Herzegovina, Brazil, Bulgaria, Gabon, Guyana, Jordan, Peru, and Syria. While 3 of the world's largest debtors are in Latin America, and others stretch throughout Asia and now include Russia, the problems of indebtedness are worst overall in Africa. While Latin America has received attention for the sheer size of its debt, a regional comparison suggests serious problems in Africa.

Table 14–3 compares regional debt stories for 2000. The countries of Latin America and the Caribbean had the highest average ratio of interest and debt service to exports, indicating significant problems of debt service. The Sub-Saharan African countries, however, had larger debts relative to both GNP and exports. Their debt-service-to-export ratios are lower because more of their debts are on concessional terms. Their reserves were sufficient to pay for barely three months' worth of imports, somewhat less than for Latin America and much less than East Asia.

The situation in Sub-Saharan Africa is both helped and hurt by the fact that most of these countries' debts are from aid. Interest rates are lower, and some governments are more willing and able than are banks to forgive loans. On the other hand, the prominence of aid in capital flows to Africa is a reflection of weaker economies and a lesser ability to borrow from the banks. Finally, while aid-related debts are more easily forgiven, they are not necessarily any easier to renew.[2]

Sources of Debt Problems

Net foreign borrowing, or capital inflow of any sort, is symptomatic of a fundamental imbalance in the international transactions of a country. However, this is a normal part of the development process because industrialization requires a great deal of resources that are available to some extent only from abroad. The country will for a time import at a faster rate than it exports.

What is a sustainable level of debt? There is no simple answer to this. An economy has a sustainable level of debt if it is growing steadily; if its exports are growing rapidly enough to buy needed imports and to handle net short-term capital outflow; and if it has a realistic, stable exchange rate. Government debt is sustainable if debt service remains a small enough portion of its budget that it can pay without having to sacrifice the people's standard of living or growth rate. South Korea, for example, has borrowed heavily and successfully over many years. Trouble starts, however, when the economy does not generate sufficient foreign exchange for repayment over a fairly long period of time or when debts rise unusually rapidly. This may occur for many reasons.

Policy Failures

Policy failures come in many forms: discrimination against agriculture, which reduces output for both domestic consumption and export; inefficient import substitution policies; interest rate levels that discourage saving and encourage wasteful investments; excessive money supply growth, which causes inflation; failure to invest sufficiently in basic infrastructure and efficient institutions; extensive price controls; and wasteful military spending. The more difficult the economic situation becomes, the more governments and private firms try to borrow overseas.

External Shocks

By themselves or in conjunction with poor domestic policy, shocks that arise from outside the country can force a crisis. A year or two of bad weather may hurt agricultural production, causing reduced exports and/or increased imports. Inflation may be imported as a result of unusual events, such as the OPEC price increases or high inflation in developed-country suppliers of inputs. Export prices may collapse as a result of recessions in customer countries or technological replacement of exports. Export proceeds may fall due to protectionism in industrialized economies. Political events such as wars or embargoes may require large expenditure and cut off the normal flow of trade. Even a stroke of good fortune, such as discovery of a natural resource or large inflows of foreign capital can, if handled poorly, cause problems. This paradox is known as Dutch Disease, because it was first noticed after discovery of natural gas in the Netherlands caused such an increase in demand for the guilder that it rose sharply in value, making other Dutch exports extremely expensive.[3]

The Debt Crisis of the 1980s

It will be useful to explore causes of the debt crisis of the 1980s.

External Causes of the Crisis

In 1973 to 1974, when oil and grain prices rose on world markets, the developing countries covered their higher import bills through borrowing, rather than cut development expenditures. They did the same after a brief boom in commodity prices (1976 to 1978) receded and oil prices rose again in 1979. As world inflation rose in the 1970s, interest rates lagged behind, leaving low or negative real rates that encouraged borrowing. One measure shows real interest rates of 3.3 percent in 1976, 2.0 percent in 1977, 1.9 percent in 1978, –1.0 percent in 1979, and –1.3 percent in 1980.*

---

*This is the difference between the average nominal rates on new long-term public debt commitments, as reported in the *World Debt Tables* and changes in the U.S. Wholesale Price Index (WPI). It might be reasonable also to deflate nominal interest rates by a price index of developing-country exports, which would make real interest rates lower in the mid-late 1970s and higher in the early 1980s.

Recessions were frequent in the industrialized countries. Their governments, rather than let oil prices reduce living standards, reacted to recessions with expansionary policies, thus worsening the oil-associated inflation both at home and for developing-country importers of industrial goods. But during those recessionary periods (1973 to 1975, 1978 to 1980), there was both a reduction in demand for developing-country products and a slowdown in developed-country borrowing, leaving banks looking for developing-country outlets for the new reserves being deposited by OPEC countries.[4]

Privatization of Development Lending: Euromarkets

Much of the new lending took the form of credits from large international syndications of banks, operating through the **Euromarkets**, the system whereby one country's currency (e.g. the dollar) is deposited in special accounts in banks operating in another country (e.g. Britain). The wealthier oil-producing countries could not spend all of their new gains, so much of it went into bank accounts in industrialized countries. Bankers in the industrialized countries then began to scour the globe to urge developing countries to borrow, often paying little attention to what the money was used for.[5]

Some developing-country borrowers, especially the middle-income countries, benefited at least in the 1970s. They were able to continue borrowing, and those that were pursuing potentially damaging policies could afford to do so as long as credit was plentiful and cheap. The resulting increase in debt was accompanied by a shift toward a greater portion of the debt from private banks.

Impending Doom: 1979 to 1982

In the early 1980s with the U.S. Federal Reserve looking to slow money growth, real interest rates reversed course: They had been negative in 1979 and 1980, but jumped to a positive rate of 4.7 percent in 1981 and an amazing 10.2 percent in 1982, the year of a major recession in the United States. Between 1982 and 1986, real interest rates continued in the 8 percent to 10 percent range before falling.

Debt grew larger and interest rates on loans increased. Earlier long-maturity loans were starting to come due. With more of the lending offered at variable rates, a borrower's debt burden increased each year even if no new debt were added. And in some countries the increased use of borrowing for consumption (oil, food) precluded the use of new funds for investment, so no revenues were generated for repayment.

The worst worldwide recession since the 1930s brought a further drop in prices of commodities exported by many of the poorest developing countries, stagnation of demand for developing-country manufactures, and increasing protection in the industrialized economies. Borrowers and banks were in trouble, and banks started reducing their lending. When, in August 1982, the Mexican government announced that it could not pay the interest on its debt, the debt crisis spilled onto the world stage.[6]

While the world economy's performance and banking practices contributed to the debt problems, so did the development strategies and policies of the debtor countries. Many countries that followed more outward-oriented strategies and internal discipline were not hurt so much by the world economy. So while debt created havoc in many African and Latin American economies, South Korea, one of the world's top debtors, did not endure a crisis because its policies kept it creditworthy.

Solutions: 1982 to 1989

Throughout most of the 1980s, economists and politicians debated how to address the debt problem. Ideas ranged from writing off the debt to providing more loans to help countries get through a difficult period.

Writing Off the Debt: Thanks, but No Thanks

The idea of requiring banks to forgive some or all of the Third World's debt, on the assumption that it would never be repaid anyway, did not appeal to most bankers or economists. The banks would be required to take large losses, and many of the more developed of the debtor countries believed that forgiveness would bring with it a stigma that would hurt their chances of getting future loans. Besides, not all debtors had severe problems.

What would be the future of international lending should significant write-offs occur? Of course, large defaults have occurred several times in the last two centuries, and the system has always recovered and resumed lending, but banks remain leery of starting a chain reaction.

The Paris Club

Renegotiation and restructuring of official debt (owed by governments to governments) through what was called the Paris Club, moved from being an unusual to a normal step for a number of countries. After an average of 3 restructurings a year in the 1978 to 1982 period, the number rose to more than 16 per year from 1983 to 1989. Most of these were concentrated in the poorest developing countries.

The Private Banks: Continuous Negotiation

Many large banks took a different way out. While cutting back drastically on new lending, they also accepted short-term losses required to set aside reserves against potential default. The nine most affected banks in the United States reduced their exposure as a percentage of their capital, from 228.9 percent in non-OPEC developing countries and 176.5 percent in Latin America in 1982, to 91.1 percent and 83.6 percent, respectively, in 1988.[7]

The Baker Plan

Between 1982 and 1985, the main debate was whether there should be more lending to spur growth and help pay off the debt or actual debt reduction. In 1985, U.S. Treasury Secretary James Baker proposed that new loans be made from the World Bank and commercial banks, while at the same time debtor governments would implement improved policies for economic growth. The Baker Plan proposed additional lending for the 15 largest debtors in exchange for policy reforms that could be growth oriented rather than the demand restraint approach of most IMF programs. The plan failed to attract the adherence of many of the banks, not to mention the countries whose reforms were involved. The banks moved toward lower exposure. Debtors were primarily interested in reducing their debt and were unwilling to undertake politically difficult reforms for small additional amounts.[8]

Debt Reduction

As the decade wore on, the idea of at least some debt reduction gained support. One proponent of debt reduction suggested that "in almost every historical episode of a widespread debt crisis, significant debt reduction has been a part of the resolution."[9] Despite the misgivings of the banks and many developed-country governments, this view became more respectable.

Under the plan, whose final form was suggested by U.S. Treasury Secretary Nicholas Brady in 1989, banks individually could agree to reduce the value of debts by, for example, exchanging new lower-value loans for the old ones, purchasing the debtor government's bonds, or reduced interest payments. New bonds issued by debtor governments to replace old debt have come to be called Brady Bonds.[10]

But what was to stop governments from later claiming they could not pay off the new, smaller debt and calling for another round of negotiations? If the banks were to take the loss involved in a lower market value for their loans, the IMF would have to act as a guarantor of the renegotiated debt levels, ready to pay off if the government endured another crisis, and presumably punish governments that reneged.

Proponents of the plan noted that debtor countries were clearly in trouble and that reducing some debt obligations would strengthen their ability and willingness to meet the rest. Further, the burden of repayment is effectively a tax on economic reform because the benefits of reform are siphoned off by creditors. On the other side, it was argued that countries should be able, with discipline, to pay these debts, so reducing the debt would produce moral hazard by rewarding and encouraging the same policy mistakes that brought on the crisis.

Should the banks be forced to participate? Some argue that no debt reduction scheme could succeed piecemeal because some banks will sit back and let others negotiate debt reductions, and then take advantage of the improved creditworthiness to collect more on their own debt—the free rider problem. If a debt reduction strategy creates benefits beyond those to the banks and countries engaged in it, it has positive externalities, is a public good, and should be enforced by some authority. Opponents argued that there is neither legal nor moral authority to force any bank to participate.

To make debt reduction attractive to the banks, there must be guarantees that the new debt obtained for the old debt will be more secure. If debtor countries are in no better position to guarantee that than before, some international body such as the IMF would have to step in. How good a guarantee could this body give? How much would a guarantee cost? There were no certain answers to these questions.

The World Bank and IMF endorsed the basic approach embodied in this plan but cautioned that negotiations would not be easy and that some additional lending would still be necessary. In the late 1980s, even before the plan had been given a name, bankers reached agreements with 18 countries covering about one-third of their eligible debts of $190 billion. The largest agreements were with Mexico (Case 14–1) and Brazil. After climbing to over $80 billion a year in 1987 and 1988, they averaged only about $30 billion a year from 1989 to 1991 before surging in 1992.[11]

For poor countries, the World Bank's International Development Association (IDA) financed commercial debt reductions amounting to almost $4 billion between 1991 and 1998, at rates ranging from 8 cents to 44 cents on the dollar.[12]

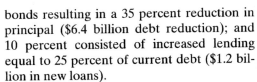

MEXICO AND THE BRADY PLAN

FAST FACTS

On the Map: North America

Population: 97 Million

Per Capita GNI and Rank: $4,440   (72)

Life Expectancy: Male—69   Female—75

Adult Literacy Rate: Male—93%
Female—89%

The first application of the Brady Plan was Mexico. In July 1989, using the Brady Plan approach, banks and the Mexican government began to negotiate terms of a debt restructuring. Mexico offered banks a choice of (*a*) a 35 percent *reduction* in value of current loans through either interest or principal reductions or (*b*) *additional* loans worth 25 percent of the value of current debt. By January 1990, deals were completed for restructuring of $48 billion of bank debt. However, the result was less than the Mexicans had hoped: 49 percent of the renegotiated amount took the form of interest reduction by exchanging loans for Mexican bonds with 6.25 percent interest, saving Mexico about $1.4 billion a year in interest payments; 41 percent was a swap of loans for Mexican

bonds resulting in a 35 percent reduction in principal ($6.4 billion debt reduction); and 10 percent consisted of increased lending equal to 25 percent of current debt ($1.2 billion in new loans).

This agreement was not costless to Mexico. The government had to put up $7 billion in guarantees on the restructured debt, although most of this was to be borrowed: $2 billion from the World Bank, $2 billion from the government of Japan, and $1.7 billion from the IMF. The government believed it had reduced its net payments outflow, but total debt, after falling by some $14 billion between 1987 and 1989, resumed its upward climb. From $95 billion in 1989, the total was up to $125 billion at the time of the country's financial crisis in 1994 and $167 billion in 1999. It will be some time before there is any indication of the plan's contribution to Mexican development.

Sources: Peter Truell, "Mexico, Creditor Banks Complete Pact Covering $48 Billion of Debt," *Wall Street Journal,* January 11, 1990, and Mohamed A. El-Erian, "Mexico's Commercial Bank Financing Package," *Finance & Development* 27, no. 3 (September 1990), pp. 26–27.

Debt–Equity Swaps

Once the idea of trading down the debt was accepted, a number of variations emerged. Many consider equity to be better for a country than debt, because interest on debt is legally binding every year (in principle), whereas equity (again, in principle) requires repatriation of profits only when profits are made. It may also encourage further foreign investment, although foreign investors may also borrow externally. Debt-equity swaps allowed banks to transform a portion of their loans into equity investment. The bank sells its debt, either to local investors or to the central bank, for local currency that is then invested in the debtor country.

But banks are not always eager to become investors. If they want to sell the investment for hard currency, the country may be in no better shape than with the debt. Also, the conditions of exchange may not be acceptable: Banks would presumably make a market-oriented swap, where the debt would be exchanged for equivalently valued equity at market rates, rather than get the full value of their debt. And did the banks want to own these companies?

Debtors may not be happy either. Banks may get preferential rates of exchange to compensate for their losses or below-market prices for their new assets. If conversions are to be less risky, investors must expect more than they would have received from the debt. The swaps cause potentially large additions to the local money supply: The creditor receives domestic currency that remains in circulation when corporate shares are purchased. The equity investment may have taken place anyway; thus, potential foreign exchange inflow is lost. If the debtor has to borrow anew, borrowing costs may be high.

Over the 1984 to 1991 period, almost $42 billion of such swaps took place, including $10 billion each in Chile and Argentina. By the end of 1990, Chile had converted more than two-thirds of its 1985 debt stock into equity, Argentina and the Philippines about one-third each. On the other hand, Brazil (6.9 percent) and Mexico (5.7 percent) slowed down the process after 1988, partly to minimize added inflationary pressures. In a number of these countries, the swaps were part of privatization efforts as private investors obtained all or part of formerly government corporations.[13]

Interesting twists on the swaps idea include the debt-for-nature swap, in which debt is bought by an environmental organization that accepts payment in local currency that is earmarked for the preservation of ecologically at-risk areas, such as rain forests. Another is debt-for-development swaps, in which debt is reduced and the funds used for approved development projects. Between 1987 and mid-1992, almost two-thirds of a billion dollars of debt were converted through these means, the largest being a $33 million Costa Rican debt-for-environment swap sponsored by the government of the Netherlands. Most of these swaps have been for education and health programs.[14] A similar two-thirds of a billion dollars was swapped between 1991 and 1998, although in the last three years of that period, all swaps were made in Mexico and Nigeria.[15]

The Secondhand Debt Market

Some investors buy old debt at a fraction of the original value, in hopes that it will eventually pay off. They may swap it for equity or hope for a capital gain if the country buys the debt back for much below original value but above what the investor paid. Banks that give up their old debt can deduct the losses from profits if they have not already done so. The potential for such transactions is illustrated by the discount that this debt bears on the market, as seen in Table 14–4.

There has been some debate over the *deliberate* establishment of these secondary debt markets as a way of reducing the debt: Will it help or hurt the value of debt not traded? Will it strengthen or weaken the hand of banks that do not sell? Would a government that buys back some of its own debt on such a market "lose" by bidding up the value of its debt? It is clear, however, that they have been established spontaneously as other areas of financial asset trade have expanded over the last two decades, and some smaller banks have used it to wash their hands of developing-country debt. In addition, as might be expected, Brady Bonds are being traded and have done quite well by conventional measures.[16]

TABLE 14-4 Secondhand Debt Market Discount as Percentage of Face Value During 1980s Debt Crisis

	July 1985	*January 1986*	*January 1987*	*January 1988*	*July 1989*
Argentina	60–65	62–66	62–65	30–33	18
Brazil	75–81	75–81	74–77	44–47	32
Chile	65–69	65–69	65–68	60–63	64
Mexico	80–82	69–73	54–57	50–52	44
Peru	45–50	25–30	16–19	2–7	4
Venezuela	81–83	80–82	72–74	55–57	4

Source: Shearson-Lehman Hutton, Salomon Brothers reports.

ADJUSTMENT OF EXTERNAL IMBALANCES

Regardless of the reason for unsustainable debt levels, the result is that a country must reorient parts of its economy. The borrowing country finds that its production capability is not sufficient to both satisfy domestic growth requirements and pay its creditors. While domestic deficits can be financed for a period by foreign capital, if foreign capital owners lose confidence in the economy, capital flows threaten to dry up and the country must find some way to adjust.

Structural Adjustment

Structural adjustment refers to reorienting an economy so as to reduce its external imbalances: More of its production should be available for export while at the same time reducing the imported portion of its consumption. There is considerable controversy over how this should be accomplished. Structural Adjustment Programs (SAPs) sponsored by the IMF and World Bank usually involve several of the following elements:

- Reduction in government spending, especially in those areas not seen as immediately productive, such as social services and consumer subsidies.
- Reduction in credit to (and thus spending by) the government, as well as overall credit limits.
- Tax increases and reform of the tax system.
- Improved management or reductions in the number of State-Owned Enterprises.
- Removal of price controls to make the high cost of protected industries clear.
- Liberalization of factor prices, which generally involves interest rate increases and sometimes minimum wage reductions.
- Devaluation of the currency.
- Trade liberalization.
- Guidelines on foreign credit, so that it does not simply take up where domestic credit leaves off.[17]

Although adjustment lending began in the late 1970s, the program continues to be important. Over half the World Bank's 1999 commitments were to adjustment programs, including 22 Sector Adjustment Loans (SECALs) in 18 countries and 34 Structural Adjustment Loans (SALs) in 28 countries.[18]

Domestic Adjustment Measures

While the disequilibrium in an economy is most apparent in its external accounts, domestic economic policies are often at the root of the problem. In simplest terms, an economy must pay for resources it imports from abroad. Investment requires repatriation of profit, and loans must be paid off. This is not simply money but involves the transfer of real resources abroad because the foreign exchange must be earned by exporting. If an export surplus is to be generated, domestically produced output must be sold overseas rather than being consumed at home: Output must exceed domestic demand, or **absorption**. The essence of domestic adjustment is to reduce the portion of output that goes to satisfy domestic demand and reallocate resources to the production of goods that can be exported for foreign exchange.

Even if a country's problems are in large part caused from the outside, it is likely to have little influence over those events and must rely on its own policies to overcome the effects. When domestic policy is at the root of the problem, the international community is likely to expect market-oriented solutions.

Fiscal Policy

The government will be expected to reduce its expenditures, primarily on subsidies for basic goods such as food and electricity, military spending, salaries of public employees, and on SOEs that account for much of the foreign borrowing in many countries. Unfortunately, many of these targets are politically popular, and their announcement has led to riots in Egypt and elsewhere. In response, many governments often maintain politically visible spending on the military and state enterprises, while reducing spending on infrastructure and public services such as health and education. Such **expenditure-reducing** policies reduce the level of aggregate demand and pressure on domestic resources. To the extent that public expenditure is deemed essential, governments are urged to increase taxes to both pay for the spending and remove a portion of the demand for domestic production and imports. Such policy changes are not easily accomplished, however: The executive and legislative branches may have different views on what the country needs and how much it should heed foreign voices.

Monetary Policy

To the extent that increases in the money supply are meant to feed public spending, reducing the growth of the money supply will also facilitate adjustment to a debt problem. With a fixed exchange rate, however, a successful adjustment policy will move a country toward a trade surplus that will mean an increase in foreign exchange inflow on current account. Much of this will then flow out to pay off debts. If success also brings in foreign private capital, elements of Dutch Disease may arise. The inflow will be converted into domestic currency that, unless sterilized by offsetting reductions, will further increase the domestic money supply. Monetary policy will have to take into account the external sector.

Factor Prices

In addition to fiscal and monetary policy, more micro-oriented policies can contribute to domestic adjustment by realigning the market to eliminate distortions that promote imports and discourage exports. Wages and interest rates influence the products that will be produced and the method of production. Governments should review minimum wage and interest rate ceiling policies if they encourage production in import-using sectors and discourage production in export sectors.

Product Prices

If controls on prices discourage output of export goods or domestically rational import substitutes, or if subsidies encourage imports, price policies can be changed. The usual recommendation, of course, is to move away from government controls toward market determination of prices.

Externally Oriented Adjustment Measures

Since excessive foreign debt shows up clearly as an inability of export receipts to cover both imports and debt service, the external sector must be addressed directly.

Trade Liberalization

Liberalization—reducing barriers to imports—is not an obvious solution to debt problems: Imports rise, worsening the trade deficit. But trade barriers are part of the overall inefficiency of an economy and should be reduced as part of an overall restructuring. As import prices fall, they are likely to improve competitiveness of domestic industries, including export industries, that use imports as inputs. On the other hand, the price-lowering impact of liberalization may be outweighed at first by the other key externally oriented measure: a more realistic exchange rate.

The Real Exchange Rate

Balance of payments deficits are accompanied by two situations: (*a*) some imports have been encouraged, through protection of import-using industries and the availability of foreign lending, while (*b*) exports have been discouraged through internal pricing policies and export taxes. At the same time, the local currency has been generally overvalued in terms of foreign currencies, which keeps unprotected imports cheap and discourages exports.

To understand the full implications of the exchange rate, we have to understand not just the **nominal exchange rate** but the **real exchange rate**. The nominal exchange rate is the price of foreign currency (here the dollar), stated in the domestic currency, for example, five Mexican pesos per U.S. dollar.* Many countries peg, or fix, the value of their currencies to some standard, rather than allow their value to float by the forces of supply and demand. Thus, there is no guarantee that a currency's official value will correspond to the value that would be set by market forces.

As we saw in Chapter 12, governments pursuing Import Substitution policies generally *overvalue* their currencies in this way. Figure 14–1 shows that if the market value of the dollar is 10 pesos, a rate of 5 pesos undervalues the dollar and overvalues the peso. If Mexican citizens can buy a dollar for only 5 pesos, they will buy more dollars than they should, making their imports cheaper and therefore favored over do-

---

*Stating Mexico's exchange rate in pesos per dollar, rather than in dollars per peso, is a matter of convention but an inconvenient one. If Mexico reduces the value of its peso, the dollar price of the peso falls, which makes sense, but it is instead expressed by an increase in the peso price of the dollar. To make matters worse, English grammar prevents anything from being reduced by more than its own value, that is, 100 percent, but expressed as pesos per dollar, the peso was devalued by 130 percent in 1982 and 138 percent in 1986. By 1990, the peso had lost over 11,000 percent of its 1981 value.

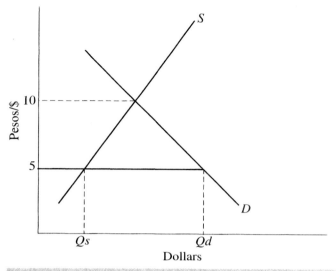

FIGURE 14-1 An Overvalued Exchange Rate

A currency is overvalued when the dollar price foreigners must pay for it exceeds the market value or when each dollar is undervalued. Above, a rate of 5 pesos to the dollar is below the equilibrium, so the dollar is undervalued and the peso is overvalued.

The excess demand for dollars, if satisfied from the government's reserves or foreign borrowing, represents an excess of imports over exports. When foreign exchange reserves are exhausted and creditors withdraw, imports will have to fall back to the level of exports (supply of dollars), or the currency must be devalued.

mestic goods to the detriment of local producers. U.S. citizens would give up more dollars to buy pesos, so Mexico's exports are more expensive and are discouraged. With imports too high and exports too low, the current account will usually be in deficit.

For example, suppose the peso is officially valued at 20 cents (5 pesos/dollar) when the market value is 10 cents (10 pesos/dollar). If Mexico exports a million pounds of tomatoes for 25 million pesos ($5 million) and imports 100 tractors for $10 million (50 million pesos), its trade deficit is 25 million pesos, or $5 million. The government should then devalue (reduce the official value of) the peso. The immediate impact of reaching the market rate will be a higher trade deficit. A million pounds of tomatoes will bring in only $2.5 million (25 million pesos divided by 10), while the tractors will cost 100 million pesos ($10 million times 10) for a deficit of $7.5 million, or 75 million pesos. Over time, however, the cheaper peso should increase exports and the more expensive dollar should decrease imports. If exports rise to 2 million pounds of tomatoes and imports fall to 50 tractors, Mexico's trade will be in balance.

Even if the exchange rate is correct today, that may change quickly. The purchasing power of the peso and the dollar depends on inflation in Mexico and the United States. If Mexico's inflation is higher than in the United States, there is a real appreciation—rise in the inflation-adjusted value—of the peso. In order to keep the real exchange rate stable, a country with relatively high inflation must continuously devalue (or allow to depreciate) the nominal value of its currency.[19] Otherwise, the new

THE REAL EXCHANGE RATE

Exchange rates are not always good guides to the underlying relationship between currencies. Governments may set *nominal* exchange rates to make imports or exports cheaper. To see what is really happening to the ability of an economy to compete internationally, we look at the real exchange rate.

The real exchange rate (*Er*) is an adjustment of the nominal exchange rate to take into account the difference between inflation at home and in trading partners' economies. It is obtained by dividing an index of the nominal exchange rate (*En*) by a ratio of trading partners' inflation (*Pf*) to domestic inflation (*Pd*):

$$Er = \frac{En}{Pf/Pd}$$

The actual number is an index. In the example of Nigeria, 1995 is the base year to index both the nominal exchange rate and the relative inflation rates of the United States and Nigeria.

The nominal value index of Nigeria's naira rose from 3,397 in 1977 to 4,006 in 1980 but then fell to the base of 100 in 1995 and to 24 in 1999. The United States has had consistently lower inflation, so although the nominal naira value was declining, higher inflation in Nigeria meant that the naira was not depreciating *fast enough* to reflect the nominal decline.

The real exchange rate rose in a number of years, most recently from 1993 to 1998 when the naira was kept constant in nominal value despite inflation that rose from 257

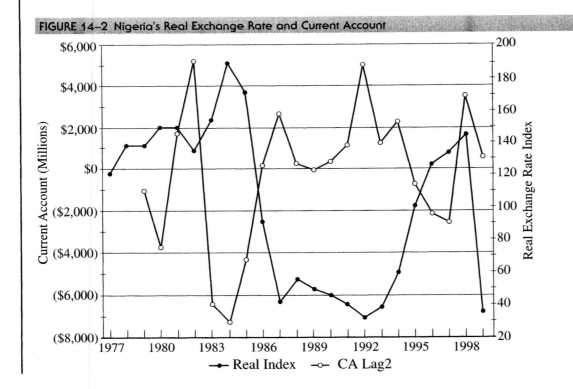

FIGURE 14–2 Nigeria's Real Exchange Rate and Current Account

percent to 975 percent in 1997. Nigeria was forced to devalue dramatically in 1999 after a disastrous current account deficit in 1998. Figure 14–2 shows that if we lag the

current account by two years (a reasonable adjustment period), the real exchange rate has a powerful inverse impact on the current account.

(fixed) exchange rate will again make imports cheaper and exports more expensive than they should be. If the exchange rate is 40 pesos to the dollar and Mexican prices double, the dollar only buys half as much. The peso should fall—to 80 per dollar—to keep the real exchange rate the same. Development Spotlight 14–1 shows how the real rate is determined for Nigerian data and the accompanying impact on the current account.

An overvalued exchange rate encourages borrowing because (*a*) it leads to trade deficits, and (*b*) it permits a given amount of the local currency to be traded for more foreign currency than is warranted by market forces.* It is therefore almost always cited as one of the chief culprits in any debt problem and becomes one of the targets for economic reform.[20]

Problems of Reform: Coordinating Reform Measures

External adjustment measures are aimed at **expenditure switching**, that is, switching resources from producing for domestic demand to producing for export, by achieving a market-determined exchange rate for the local currency. This generally requires currency **depreciation** or **devaluation** and the removal of both internal and external price distortions that focus the economy inward. Removing external distortions means import liberalization and removing disincentives to exports. But the combination of removing import restrictions (making imports cheaper) and devaluation (making imports more expensive and exports more profitable) has to be carefully coordinated to produce the desired result.

Under normal circumstances, this combination should work because, although restricted imports (luxury goods, products competing with domestic production) may increase or decrease, the resulting prices will now more clearly convey market-oriented incentives, previously lost in the maze of distortions. Import-competing industries (including import-substitute target industries) will have to become more efficient to survive as their protection is removed. Luxury goods may still carry restrictions if the government is sufficiently committed to such a policy. But imports that were not restricted previously will now be more expensive, more accurately reflecting their true market value. These will include inputs to import-substitution industries, which will face additional pressure to become more efficient in order to survive.

But devaluation, even accompanied by trade liberalization, is unlikely to be sufficient if domestic policies do not remove market distortions and inflationary tendencies.[21] Opening up the economy to the world market is likely to be much less effective

*One easy way to tell if the official exchange rate is correct is to see how many pesos you can get for your dollars on the street. If you are offered substantially more than the official rate, you know the local currency has been officially overvalued. Be careful though: Such transactions, however common, are illegal in many countries.

if interest rates and wages provide distorted signals to current and prospective investors as to what goods should be produced and how. Expansionary monetary and fiscal policies will exacerbate inflation, constantly bringing the real exchange rate out of equilibrium unless the nominal rate is continually adjusted downward. Free flow of capital will lead to excessive private borrowing. Given an uncertain environment, it will also lead to **capital flight** as investors seek higher returns and less uncertainty outside the country. Although some of this flight is illegal, and therefore hard to measure, one estimate puts its value at $20 million for Mexico alone between 1979 and 1984.[22]

So while there is no easy formula for reform, there is some evidence that market-oriented pricing of domestic resources, along with fiscal and monetary restraint, should accompany or precede trade liberalization. And while an equilibrium real exchange rate is necessary, experience with liberalization in Latin America and Israel suggests that the complete opening up of capital markets should be the last reform attempted.[23]

Problems of Reform: Who Might Get Hurt?

To an even greater extent than simply domestic stabilization policies and trade liberalization, economic adjustment required by full-scale reform will cause injury to some companies and workers. Ideally, market reform and expenditure switching result in the movement of productive factors from one use to another, after which the economy emerges more productive. But even more developed countries do not accomplish these objectives without causing interim damage to businesses whose activities are either wiped out or become much less profitable.[24] First, until production in export industries can respond to the new exchange rate and reduced tariffs on their imported inputs, reducing the trade deficit and using export receipts for debt payments could mean a severe reduction in imports, hurting consumption, investment, and production. This has been such a serious problem that it is referred to as **import compression** or even strangulation; that is, the reduction in imports will reduce standards of living directly (consumption goods), reduce investment and growth (capital goods), and possibly even delay the anticipated increase in exports by depriving export industries of needed inputs.

Next, the lower value of the currency means that those goods still imported are more expensive, worsening inflation (if only temporarily) and putting downward pressure on real wages. If it also stimulates inflationary expectations, the spiral may continue, bringing pressure for even further devaluation.[25] In order to minimize inflation, stabilize real wages, and reduce the need for additional currency devaluations, governments must reduce the money supply, credit, and their own spending, all of which will result in expenditure reduction (loss of jobs, production, and income) long before expenditure can be effectively switched.

Those hardest hit are likely to be the low-productivity, low-wage workers who are either laid off or subjected to reduced wages and who no longer benefit from government subsidies on food and utilities. As compensating measures like unemployment compensation are less well established, there is little cushion for these workers, who likely will become part of the informal sector. Women may be most severely affected.[26] Finally, in some Latin American countries (Brazil, Argentina), the debt crisis of the 1980s was accompanied by the switch from military to elected civilian governments, and although the new democratic governments could not be blamed for the crisis, they still felt the pressure.

Clearly, economic adjustment to reduce high external debt is complex and difficult. The case for World Bank or IMF lending to carry the country over the rough spots is strong. But these Structural Adjustment Programs have been the subject of so much debate over the last 20 years that we should examine the controversy over how they have worked.

THE WORLD BANK, THE IMF, AND ADJUSTMENT

Much of the controversy concerns the World Bank's Structural Adjustment Loans (SALs) and the Structural Adjustment Facility (SAF) programs of the International Monetary Fund. Officials from these institutions say that adjustment and reform are made necessary by the distorting policies that have brought financial imbalance and stagnation to many developing countries. So the question becomes not *will* adjustment take place, but *what kind* of adjustment will take place. And while the studies by these institutions admit that it is difficult to compare what has happened with what might have been, they are encouraged by the showing of higher growth rates after many years of such programs.[27]

For the World Bank, medium-term (three to five years) structural adjustment lending represented a shift from longer-term project lending but was not a major break in terms of its development orientation. For the IMF, however, this was a significant change and might have been motivated in part by the Bank's approach. The IMF has numerous "facilities" available for lending. These facilities are available for countries with temporary financial difficulties, countries that experience externally generated export shortfalls, and countries that are confronted with sudden extreme needs for financing oil imports (since removed). In the mid-1980s, the IMF established a Structural Adjustment Facility (SAF) for low-income countries undertaking significant reform.

Until the SAF was introduced, however, lending was considered temporary. The IMF expected borrowers to be industrialized countries, whose economies could adjust to permanent changes in circumstances, helped by Fund financing where necessary. The Fund's activities were not meant to apply to countries with inflexible economies and long-term adjustment problems. As the developing countries began to experience such problems, many of them saw the Fund as a long-term supplement to normal aid and private capital flows.

Structural Adjustment and Conditionality

However, when SAFs and enhanced SAFs (ESAFs) were begun, developing-country officials were annoyed at the conditions that came with the money. Many governments saw the IMF as an enemy, imposing what they called "austerity" on their economies. The IMF does not see itself as an adversary of the developing countries. An official statement of the Fund says it is not "an agency that can or wishes to force its members to do very much of anything . . . What authority the IMF exercises is narrowly restricted to overseeing policies that impinge directly on how and at what price each member's money is bought and sold." It is recognized that when members borrow from the Fund to overcome financial difficulties there are conditions requiring borrowers to "undertake economic reforms to eliminate these difficulties for their own good and that of the entire membership," but the statement insists that "the membership itself sets down, to the last detail, the policies the IMF follows," and "the IMF acts not on its own but as an intermediary between the will of the majority of the membership and the individual member country."[28]

As in the World Bank, decision making in the IMF is based on a system of weighted voting with the wealthy countries having the majority of the votes. Voting power is based on a country's **quota** or contribution, weighted according to the prominence of an economy in world output and trade: The United States has about 19 percent of the vote. The developing countries have tried to bring the Fund and other international institutions under majority rule, but to do so would undoubtedly cause the wealthier countries to withdraw.

The IMF insists in its financing that, regardless of the cause, if an external imbalance is not temporary the country must undertake policy measures to adjust—that is, to restore a balance between exports and imports to the point that no external funding is required beyond voluntary inflows of private capital. The necessary measures are a condition of the financing; hence, the term **conditionality** of Fund lending.

Conditionality is not mentioned specifically in the original Articles of Agreement, but was approved as a principle in 1952 and reviewed in 1968 and 1979. In the latter year, 12 guidelines were approved that still form the basis for conditionality. The more important of these guidelines (*a*) call for a country's corrective action to be as quick as possible; (*b*) allow the Fund to use certain performance criteria, generally macroeconomic policy instruments, to judge the effectiveness of the country's use of the money (lending can be halted at any time if the country fails to comply); and (*c*) require the Fund to "pay due regard to the domestic social and political objectives of members, to their economic priorities, and to their circumstances. . . ."[29] Case 14–2 summarizes adjustment in Ghana.

The World Bank's View

World Bank officials believe that structural adjustment experiences confirm their analysis of what countries must do to adjust. Its 1992 review concluded that adjusting countries were growing faster than those that do not and that they have done so at least in part through greater focus on exports. The macroeconomic stability provided by adjustment measures is essential for renewed growth. The review suggests that adjusting countries have had falling ratios of investment to GDP, but reasons that this implies a greater efficiency in the use of capital, and has the further benefit of providing rising ratios of consumption to GDP that, at least in the medium term, provide needed political support for adjustment. They find no evidence that adjustment programs are associated with greater poverty.[30]

Conditionality: Attack and Response

Although conditionality accompanies both Bank and IMF programs, the term and surrounding controversy arose first with the Fund. The Fund insists that conditionality is essential and that the country's own situation requires it.[31] The Fund's own resources are limited and must be used as effectively as possible. But its adjustment programs have been attacked on numerous grounds related to their objectives, quite apart from whether they actually work.

STRUCTURAL ADJUSTMENT IN GHANA

FAST FACTS

On the Map: West Africa

Population: 19 Million

Per Capita GNI and Rank: $400   (166)

Life Expectancy: Male—57   Female—59

Adult Literacy Rate: Male—79%
Female—61%

The complexity of adjustment attempts is illustrated by the case of Ghana. So promising were some of the results that the program came to be considered something of a model, but other results were not so admired.

Ghana's economy had been severely damaged, largely through disastrous policies in the 1960s and 1970s. Its primary source of export revenue, cocoa, was devastated by state marketing of the crop, which steadily lowered the price obtained by growers, and by a drastically overvalued currency (cedi). The adjustment program, overseen by the World Bank, engineered a 90 percent real depreciation of the cedi from 1983 to 1987, with a slower but steady decline in the early 1990s. Quantitative restrictions were eliminated, tariffs reduced, corporate and capital gains taxes reduced, government firms privatized, foreign investment encouraged, and incentives created for private investment in infrastructure and export industries.

Inflation fell in the early period through strict control over money and credit creation and large reductions in government's capital spending. Liberalization of product and factor prices began to return domestic markets to economic rationality. A key result of all this was a reversal of the downward trend in cocoa production, due to higher producer prices and some managerial improvement in the Cocoa Marketing Board. Food production also increased. Real wages in the formal sector fell, although per capita consumption expenditures rose slowly from 1984 to 1994 as rural residents and the informal sector have benefited from the reforms. Manufacturing recovered for awhile.

However, the trade and current account deficits have increased as imports, including greater dependence on food imports, have more than matched higher exports. Higher timber exports, without conservation efforts, have accelerated deforestation. Reduction in capital spending has meant the "virtual collapse of health facilities" and damage to educational services as well. There has been little response to investment incentives, and once excess capacity was absorbed, manufacturing firms were unable to compete with imports. The urban population has experienced a significant deterioration in living standards, with higher unemployment. External financing has not lived up to its promises, and declining world prices for cocoa—helped by increased Ghanian production—make continued reliance on that crop quite dangerous. The country continues to be plagued by inefficiency and an unskilled work force. And while the World Bank sometimes touts Ghana as a success based on improvements in macropolicy, one study shows poverty increasing from 29.0 percent to 34.5 percent over the 1985 to 1990 period when performance was rated highly.

Sources: Simon Commander, John Howell, and Wayo Seini, "Ghana: 1983–1987," in Commander, ed., *Structural Adjustment & Agriculture: Theory & Practice in Africa and Latin America* (London: Heinemann/ODI, 1989), pp. 107–126; Walden Bello, *Dark Victory: The United States, Structural Adjustment and Global Poverty* (London: Pluto Press, 1994), pp. 45–50, 61; Lionel Demery and Lyn Squire, "Macroeconomic Adjustment and Poverty in Africa: An Emerging Picture," *World Bank Research Observer* 11, no. 1 (February 1996), pp. 39–60; Sanjaya Lall, "Structural Adjustment and African Industry," *World Development* 23, no. 12 (December 1995), pp. 2019–2031; and Thandika Mkandawire and Charles Soludo, *Our Continent, Our Future* (Trenton: Africa World Press, 1999), pp. 71–72. Also see N. K. Kusi, "Macroeconomic Adjustments, Economic Growth and the Balance of Payments in Ghana 1983–1988," *Journal of International Development* 4, no. 5 (September–October 1992), pp. 541–559.

Does the Fund Impose the Same Conditions on Everyone?

One frequent charge is that the IMF carries a standard set of reforms that it applies indiscriminately to all developing countries regardless of their situation.[32] The IMF denies this and claims that the similarity of policy reforms called for is due to the similarity of conditions facing those countries. Otherwise, the Fund maintains that it does tailor its conditionality to country-specific conditions. The IMF denial was called into question when Asian countries, facing different problems in the 1990s, were initially asked to respond with the same set of reforms.

Does Adjustment Require "Austerity" Programs?

Many developing-country officials have described IMF conditionality as imposing "austerity" measures on their economies: Restrictions on domestic spending reduce output and employment; reductions in subsidies increase prices, as does devaluation. The Fund responds that while painful, the short-run result of these policies would be an improvement in the balance of payments.[33] Critics have suggested that the links between the government policy instruments targeted by the IMF and the objective, a reduction in current account deficits, are so tenuous that the Fund should make the current account itself the target and let the borrowing government best decide how to accomplish it.[34]

Does Import Liberalization Harm the Economy?

Import liberalization may favor luxury goods. While providing discipline to import-competing firms, it makes imports cheaper and in the short run may be contrary to the Fund's objective of bringing the current account into balance. But the harm that is done is generally what economists believe is appropriate: demonstrating the inefficiency of high levels of protection. Luxury imports can still be restricted if a government desires to do so.

Is Devaluation Harmful?

Exchange rate devaluation makes imports more expensive, contributing to inflation, unless counteracted by lower import barriers. On the other hand, the exports that it boosts may be produced by poorer portions of the population. Critics of Fund programs suggest that devaluation should be achieved more slowly and steadily, but the Fund contends that the immediate break with distorted exchange rates is required to achieve adjustment. Slower adjustments have been accepted (in Brazil and Argentina, for example) but reluctantly.[35]

A major study of adjustment programs in Africa suggests that the fears of devaluation-induced inflation have not been realized. A series of exchange rate adjustments in Ghana, amounting to depreciation of more than 1,000 percent over a number of years, shows very little inflation as a result. And while exports in many countries, such as Tanzania, have not responded well, the reason is usually the lack of infrastructure and institutional support for exporters. Still, in Tanzania some traditional manufactured exports, including textiles and wood, paper, and rubber products, did increase.[36] The lack of support for exporters, however, seems to be a common problem. Critics see little export diversification and complain that rapid import liberalization has hurt rising industries.[37]

Do the Programs Target Popular Social Spending?

Reduction of so-called nonproductive government spending tends to hit politically popular programs such as food subsidies and SOEs that employ numerous people. Removal of price controls counters governments' desire to subsidize particular goods, especially those consumed by large numbers of people, and contributes to inflation. Inflation is harsher if wages must also fall. The IMF contends, however, that its conditionality is very broad so that, for example, when reductions in government spending are called for, the Fund stays out of the country's decisions on where to cut. In practice, this does not seem to be the case, but when the Fund does target particular microeconomic measures (wages, prices), it claims that the short-run hardship is overcome eventually by greater efficiency and increased output.

In Ghana, a study of government employment in SOEs and the more traditional government agencies found few problems. Most public-sector employees are relatively well off and were quickly reemployed, usually in the informal sector. Earnings did decline but usually not below the prevailing wage. In general, the authors found that in many African countries, excessive staffing in government agencies had come at the expense of investment and, in some cases, the overall wage level in the public sector. And efficiency of government spending improved with fewer employees: In many countries "a significant proportion of government expenditures produces no useful services."[38]

Does Adjustment Ignore Structural Impediments to Increased Supply and Thereby Stifle Growth?

The Fund's monetarist approach to inflation has downplayed structural causes. Cutting back on imports, credit, and spending will hinder the investment needed for growth. Governments often cut investment first to maintain consumption and popular support. To some extent, this point has been conceded.[39] The IMF agrees that its emphasis on demand management may have been too one-sided and that it is necessary to explicitly take account of problems on the supply side. This involves (*a*) a longer time frame for Fund programs; (*b*) greater acceptance of government spending that will contribute to the development of supply capabilities, that is, infrastructure; (*c*) attention to policies to increase savings for domestic investment; (*d*) increasing the availability of funds for investment; and (*e*) recognizing the need to minimize adjustment costs, including avoiding large shocks to the system. While critics maintain that the Fund ignores growth goals in favor of short-term stabilization measures, the Fund responds that long-term growth will occur only if stabilization is achieved first.[40]

What Are the Global Implications of Country-Specific Programs?

If numerous countries undertake this kind of adjustment simultaneously, there will be a large reduction in their imports, which will hurt the industrialized-country exporters and slow down the world economy. Meanwhile, flooding world markets with similar developing-country exports could drive down prices and reduce the impact on their trade balances. In fact, some African countries have increased the volume of primary exports only to see the value fall due to lower prices.[41] An additional question with respect to the global economy is why the IMF never puts pressure on governments whose policies result in large balance of payments surpluses and contribute to deficits elsewhere.

Do Adjustment Programs Hurt the Poor Disproportionately?

The nature of adjustment may bring greatest hardship on the poorest segments of the population. A UN report suggests that poor women bear the heaviest burden: Women in poor families face the double task of running the household with less income, while also having to take the lowest-paying and least-secure jobs available. A recent World Bank and United Nations conference on similar adjustment problems in Eastern and Central Europe report that women are disproportionately hurt, with greater loss of employment and declining female school attendance.[42]

Both the World Bank and the IMF have responded to criticism of their programs' impact on the poor. The Bank agrees that in many cases the poor often bear the brunt of adjustment programs, but it blames this fact on governments that never focused on the poor in the first place and the nature of the adjustments that must be made for the economy to recover.

In the mid-1980s, a current and a former Bank staffer examined the share of wages in GDP, growth of real per capita purchasing power in the rural sector, the share of urban wages in manufacturing value added, wages as a share of government spending, real wages in construction, the ratio of increases in food prices to all prices, infant and child mortality, immunizations, and the share of government spending that goes to social sectors, including health and education. With a few exceptions, mainly urban wages and spending on education, the study found no discernible difference between those countries that had intensive Bank adjustment programs, those with moderate adjustment programs, and those with none at all. They find no reason to conclude that adjustment programs, per se, have hurt the poorer portions of the population.[43]

More recently, two studies have reached opposite conclusions. One shows that over the 1965 to 1988 period, rural poverty increased in adjusting African countries but fell in nonadjusting countries. Over the 1985 to 1990 period, those countries whose macro policies were considered most improved showed increases in poverty and, in some cases, had worse poverty records than those countries with unsatisfactory macro policies. While Ghana had the most improved macro policy and one of the lowest increases in poverty, Tanzania and Zimbabwe both had better macro policy but relatively large increases in poverty.[44]

The other study looked at specific policy issues and concluded that the poor were hurt less than is believed. Liberalization of foreign trade and exchange regimes have often helped the poor through an increase in labor-intensive exports, while higher import prices have not hurt the poor because they were not likely to have had much access to either rationed foreign exchange or imports at official prices. The poor were less likely to have received the health care services that were cut back, and the same was true to a lesser degree in education. And while spending has been cut relative to historical highs in the early 1980s, they are at about the same percentage of GDP as they were in the mid-1970s. The poor are not hurt much from lower public-sector employment because they never had those jobs. Tax reform has tended to hurt most the middle and upper classes in the formal sector. Higher agricultural exports have not reduced food production.[45]

Similar conclusions are reached in another study: Tony Killick, often critical of the IMF, finds that in urban areas, a wage freeze hurts the working poor but, by making labor more affordable, helps reduce unemployment. For the rural poor, devaluation hurts food-importing areas but helps food exporters. He also accepts the IMF's position that short-term adjustment is necessary to lay the basis for longer-term growth. And he reminds us that a number of East Asian countries, by adjusting on their own initiative, have grown and reduced poverty considerably.[46]

A study of structural reforms in Latin America finds at best no evidence that they have improved income distribution. While the authors believe that reforms should contribute to growth, and growth should reduce inequality, they find poverty higher and distribution less equal in Latin American between 1982 and 1995. Much of the deterioration was due to recession in the 1980s, but subsequent growth does not seem to have helped.[47]

Most observers agree that the Bank and Fund could do more to help the poor in the midst of crisis. They point to the need for infrastructure aimed at serving the needs of rural and urban small-scale workers, more social services (health, education), and direct aid to the poorest groups. Some African countries have established special programs within their adjustment strategies in order to specifically protect the poor.[48]

Now the Bank and the Fund are giving this issue increased attention. The IMF's Enhanced Structural Adjustment Facility has been renamed the Poverty Reduction and Growth Facility. Both organizations say they are helping governments target pro-poor expenditure and identify the negative impact of adjustment programs on the poor. Governments that receive debt relief are expected to have a specific program for reducing poverty. The idea is to construct a **social safety net**, which is a combination of programs such as social security, unemployment compensation, low-cost health care, and the like, which will prevent incomes from falling below some minimum level. Whether these activities actually protect the poor to a significant extent is still a matter of debate. The Bank has highlighted this issue with new pilot programs in Latin America, recognizing that the process of opening economies more fully to global flows of goods, services, and capital will be resisted if the poor are not protected.[49]

Should the Focus Change from Adjustment to Debt Reduction?

Since early in the 1980s debt crisis, there has been debate about the advisability of reducing, if not writing off, the debt of many countries. While this would obviously hurt the lenders, there was also a good case that it would harm the debtors themselves. If debt problems would result in the debts being written off, what would encourage banks to lend again? In fact, many of the middle-income debtors opposed debt relief because they feared it would make future loans more difficult to get.

When it came to the poorest countries, however, the case was stronger. These countries, much of whose debt was owed to official donors, were so poor and so heavily indebted that one could make the case that debt relief was the only way they could ever hope to become viable. One of the most recent arguments in favor of debt reduction moves the question of debt burden from traditional measurements, where debt and debt service is related to foreign exchange earnings from exports, to the burden on government budgets, where governments have either incurred the debt or have assumed responsibility for private-sector debts. Since governments must pay these debts, doing so requires either higher taxes, which could distort and reduce growth incentives to the private sector, or reduced government spending. In many cases, this reduction is hurting infrastructure, education, and health care, all of which are crucial long-term-growth investments.[50]

Government creditors in the Paris Club have been modifying their approach to poor-country debt since 1976. Their initial approach was simply to reschedule, or delay, repayments for debts incurred on commercial terms. Beginning in 1988, rescheduled payments were also given concessional interest rates. In 1991 the degree

CASE 14-3

DEBT RELIEF FOR MOZAMBIQUE

FAST FACTS

On the Map: South Africa

Population: 17 Million

Per Capita GNI and Rank: $220   (195)

Life Expectancy: Male—42   Female—44

Adult Literacy Rate: Male—59%
Female—28%

In April 1998, the World Bank and IMF agreed to a debt reduction for Mozambique amounting to $3 billion over time. While not eliminating Mozambique's debt, this is a significant sum: The net present value (NPV) of the relief was $1.4 billion, about 70 percent of the country's GDP. The bulk of the reduction came from the World Bank, but the IMF and a number of bilateral creditors have joined. Debt was reduced by this and other programs from $5.6 billion to $1.1 billion in present value terms. The Bank noted that Mozambique has been rewarded for good performance. Inflation has been significantly reduced, and over three-fourths of 1,200 SOEs have been privatized.

In the subsequent two years additional relief has been provided, so that by early 2000 the total amount was $4.3 billion. Se-

vere flooding that year prompted an acceleration of the program.

In order for the full amounts to be provided, the government was to implement certain measures "in the areas of social development, public sector reform, and legal and regulatory framework," along with maintaining "a stable macroeconomic environment."

Economic policy requirements may be controversial. In fact, the World Bank and the IMF have disagreed in one area important to the country: The Bank has lent money for a sugar mill, whose success seems to depend on tariffs on foreign sugar. The IMF, in the meanwhile, is pushing Mozambique to eliminate those tariffs and leave what the Fund believes is an inadvisable industry for that country.

Sources: "Debt Relief Package of Nearly US$3 Billion Approved for Mozambique," World Bank Press Release (April 7, 1998); "Mozambique Qualifies for an Additional US$600 Million in Debt Relief," World Bank Press Release No. 2000/297/S; and Michael M. Phillips, "Mozambique Faces Sugar-Industry Debate," *Wall Street Journal*, June 20, 2000. The main Web sites for the Highly Indebted Poor Country initiative are ⟨www.worldbank.org/hipc/⟩ and ⟨www.imf.org/external/np/hipc/index.asp⟩.

of concessionality was increased, and beginning in 1995, reductions in the actual value of debt were permitted.[51]

In 1996, the Bank and the Fund created their Heavily Indebted Poor Country (HIPC) Initiative. For low-income countries with a debt/export ratio of 150 percent or more, the Bank and the Fund, together with bilateral donors, will provide money to pay off some of the debt. Recipients are supposed to ask commercial creditors to participate as well. In return, recipients agree to "sustained implementation of integrated poverty reduction and economic reform programs." Between 1996 and late 2000, 13 countries qualified for debt relief totaling $23 billion. The World Bank estimates its own claims on about 33 countries will be reduced by $12 billion.[52] Case 14–3 summarizes how the program is working in Mozambique. Additional debt relief, promised by the industrial countries in 1999, has bogged down because the United States has not agreed to pay its share.[53]

Do Structural Adjustment Programs Work?

Economists do not always agree on how to tell whether programs have worked, due to the large number of variables that have an impact on a country's performance. They disagree even on how to measure success. Comparing adjusting with nonadjusting countries must account for all the other differences between these two groups. Comparing before and after for adjusting countries also assumes that adjustment is the only change. There are disagreements on just what constitutes adjustment and when an adjustment program may have actually begun.

International Monetary Fund studies in the 1980s gave support to their programs, while critics expressed doubts.[54] The 1993 study mentioned earlier claims some success with its SAF and ESAF loans: On the average, GDP growth and exports have increased, inflation and debt ratios are down. On the other hand, neither savings nor investment has responded well. Even the successes were modest. However, a critic notes that even those countries that experience some recovery rarely have positive growth rates of per capita income.[55] The study suggests that results were worse where governments failed to carry out reforms or where external events hurt the country's terms of trade. Two years later, an IMF study of its Stand-By programs (similar in nature to Structural Adjustment but usually for shorter periods and for countries in better shape) came to similar conclusions and lamented the fact that additional outside resources, needed to help countries sustain early progress, were disappointing.[56]

Tony Killick challenged the 1993 study, objecting to its methods and not finding any connection between the country programs and resulting policy changes. He concluded that the Fund had not shown any proof that their programs had been responsible for what success had been achieved. The primary author of the study objected to his conclusions but admitted there was no good way to isolate the impact of the Fund programs on the country results.[57]

African countries have been frequent critics of adjustment programs. A recent study again questions the effectiveness of the programs on that continent and the World Bank's claims of modest success.[58] The authors see little sustainable progress. While the Bank does agree that successes have not been large, it blames African governments for failure to properly implement the programs. The study notes that the Bank often blames external forces for the failure of its programs, while being skeptical of African claims that external forces have hurt their economies. Critics say the Bank is constantly shifting rationales and case studies to support claims of success. For example, Ghana has at times been cited as a success story, and at other times it has been dropped from the list.

The study concludes that the World Bank adjustment model—getting prices right, macro stabilization, and reducing government's role—is bound to be ineffective in promoting growth in Africa. Small private sectors, active parallel markets that make official prices irrelevant, and competitive world markets for traditional exports call for a different approach. This would include emphasizing education and technology acquisition, helping to improve public-sector performance, and support for export diversification. More investment is needed to promote domestic production. And governments must be strengthened to fulfill such essential roles as providing information, training, and financial support to new companies. The adjustment model may achieve stabilization but rarely succeeds in promoting growth.

The IMF and World Bank have increasingly defended their record through political economy arguments that link the success or failure of their programs to the willingness of recipient governments to "own" the necessary reforms. A recent Bank research paper suggests that the outcome of adjustment lending can be predicted 75 percent of the time by a few such political economy variables. It concludes that the Bank should consider making fewer loans, concentrating on those countries where governments are committed to reform.[59]

SUMMARY AND CONCLUSION

Debt is a normal part of economic life and, in fact, makes good sense for developing countries. Problems arise when any combination of bad luck and bad policies results in a debt that grows faster than a country's ability to repay. This is the story of many developing countries in the 1980s.

A true foreign debt problem arises when a country is consistently unable to earn enough from exports and voluntary capital inflows to finance the imports and debt service to increase or sustain its standard of living. External shocks or domestic policy choices can result in foreign debt that is unsustainable: Export proceeds cannot grow rapidly enough to convince creditors that timely repayment is possible. When policy failures are to blame, adjustment of the economy is essential to restore creditworthiness. Fiscal and monetary policies must be tightened, product and factor markets must be freer. The real exchange rate must be flexible enough to accurately reflect the currency's international buying power. If government has a large collection of SOEs, privatization will be called for. These measures are often difficult to implement, and formerly protected groups of society will be hurt.

Both the World Bank and the International Monetary Fund have been active in lending to countries in need of adjustment. These programs have had mixed results but at their best have been disappointing. The Bank and the Fund believe their basic approach of promoting short-term stabilization through market liberalization and fiscal discipline will lay the groundwork for future growth. While many Latin American countries have emerged from the debt crisis of the 1980s with more market-oriented economies, many African countries have not yet created the market mechanisms that are essential for sustained growth. Critics are pushing the Bank and the Fund to emphasize growth-oriented policies, provide debt relief for the poorest countries, help governments create the institutional mechanisms to support the activities of the private sector in diversifying domestic production and exports, and pay more attention to protecting the poor from adverse consequences of these programs.

Key Terms

- absorption (p. 435)
- capital flight (p. 440)
- conditionality (p. 442)
- current account (p. 425)
- debt service (p. 426)
- default (p. 424)
- depreciation (p. 439)
- devaluation (p. 439)
- Euromarket (p. 429)
- expenditure reducing (p. 435)
- expenditure switching (p. 439)
- import compression (p. 440)
- nominal exchange rate (p. 436)
- quota (p. 442)
- real exchange rate (p. 436)
- social safety net (p. 447)
- structural adjustment (p. 434)

Questions for Review

1. Explain why debt is a normal part of economic development.
2. When would we consider debt sustainable? excessive?
3. What are the macroeconomic indicators of external debt?
4. From a macroeconomic perspective, what steps must be taken to reduce debt?
5. How did Mexico's experience under the Brady Plan illustrate the international approach to debt problems in the late 1980s?
6. Describe macro and micro policies that would achieve the objectives of structural adjustment. What are expenditure-reducing and expenditure-switching policies?
7. What is the real exchange rate? In what ways may a country's currency become overvalued?
8. If a country is exporting 100,000 tons of food priced at 30 conga per ton and importing two tractors at $40,000 each, what is the value of its trade balance at the rate of 50 congas per dollar? If the conga is devalued to a level of 100 per dollar, what is the immediate impact on the trade balance? If the devaluation ultimately increases food exports to 150,000 tons and reduces imports to one tractor, what is the change in the trade balance?
9. How might structural adjustment programs have an adverse impact on the poor? How might the poor benefit?
10. How has Ghana's experience illustrated the problems of achieving structural adjustment?
11. What are the possible conflicts between short-term stabilization (or "austerity"), as addressed in typical IMF programs, and the goal of longer-term growth?
12. How does the current debt relief program for Mozambique illustrate evolving attitudes toward the debt problems of the poorest countries?

Related Internet Resources

 The issue of debt and structural adjustment has increased the public profiles of the World Bank and the International Monetary Fund. Their Web sites are ⟨www.worldbank.org⟩ and ⟨www.imf.org⟩. Their Heavily Indebted Poor Country Initiative is described at ⟨www.worldbank.org/hipc⟩.

Endnotes and Further Readings

1. See Richard N. Cooper and Jeffrey D. Sachs, "Borrowing Abroad: The Debtor's Perspective," in Gordon W. Smith and John T. Cuddington, eds., *International Debt and the Developing Countries*, World Bank Symposium (Washington, 1985).
2. See Tim Carrington, "Debt Crisis in the Developing Countries Appears to Be Forgotten but Not Gone," *Wall Street Journal*, October 17, 1994.
3. See W. M. Corden, "Booming Sector and Dutch Disease Economics: Survey and Consolidation," *Oxford Economic Papers* NS 36, no. 3 (November 1984), pp. 359–380, and John J. Struthers, "Nigerian Oil and Exchange Rates: Indicators of 'Dutch Disease,'" *Development and Change* 21, no. 2 (April 1990), pp. 309–341.
4. See the report of the United Nations Centre on Transnational Corporations, *Transnational Banks and the International Debt Crisis* (New York: United Nations, 1991).

5. See Samuel C. Gwynne, "Adventures in the Loan Trade," *Harper's*, no. 267 (September 1983), pp. 22–26, and Jeffrey A. Friedan, *Banking on the World: The Politics of American International Finance* (New York: Harper and Row, 1987).
6. See Sudarshan Gooptu, *Debt Reduction and Development—The Case of Mexico* (Westport, CT: Praeger, 1993).
7. Seamus O'Cleireacain, *Third World Debt and International Public Policy* (New York: Praeger, 1990), p. 190.
8. See Ishrat Husain, "Recent Experience with the Debt Strategy," *Finance & Development* 26, no. 3 (September 1989), pp. 12–15.
9. Jeffrey Sachs, "Strengthening IMF Programs in Highly Indebted Countries," in Catherine Gwin, Richard E. Feinberg et al., *The International Monetary Fund in a Multipolar World: Pulling Together* (New Brunswick,

NJ: Transaction Books/Overseas Development Council, 1989), p. 105.

10. The key proponents of debt relief were Benjamin J. Cohen, "Developing-Country Debt: A Middle Way," Essays in International Finance No. 173 (Princeton, NJ: Princeton University, May 1989); Peter B. Kenen, especially "Organizing Debt Relief: The Need for a New Institution," *Journal of Economic Perspectives* 4, no. 1 (winter 1990), pp. 7–18; and Jeffrey Sachs, especially "New Approaches to the Latin American Debt Crisis," Essays in International Finance No. 174 (Princeton, NJ: Princeton University, July 1989), and "A Strategy for Efficient Debt Reduction," *Journal of Economic Perspectives* 4, no. 1 (winter 1990), pp. 19–29. Critics included Jeremy Bulow and Kenneth Rogoff, in "The Buyback Boondoggle," *Brookings Papers on Economic Activity* (1988) (2), pp. 675–698, and "Cleaning Up Third World Debt Without Getting Taken to the Cleaners," *Journal of Economic Perspectives* 4, no. 1 (winter 1990), pp. 31–42.

11. Restructuring amounts are reported in the International Monetary Fund's "Private Market Financing for Developing Countries," published annually. Also see William Cline's *International Debt Reexamined* (Washington: Institute for International Economics, 1994), pp. 235–236.

12. World Bank, *Global Development Finance 1999*, p. 115.

13. See Stephany Griffith-Jones, "Conversion of Official Bilateral Debt: The Opportunities and the Issues," in the *Proceedings of the World Bank Annual Conference on Development Economics, 1992* (Washington: 1993), pp. 383–401; the IMF's 1992 survey of "Private Market Financing for Developing Countries," p. 15; and United Nations, *Debt-Equity Swaps and Development* (New York: United Nations, 1993).

14. See IMF, "Private Market Financing for Developing Countries," pp. 17 and 60.

15. World Bank, *Global Development Finance 1999*, p. 116.

16. Thomas T. Vogel, Jr., "From Dog to Darling: Developing-Nation Debt, Rehabilitated with Help from New Investment Devices, Becomes a Hot Commodity," *Wall Street Journal*, September 24, 1993, and Thomas T. Vogel, Jr., Laura Jereski, and Craig Torres, "Hedge Funds Buying Emerging-Market Debt," *Wall Street Journal*, January 12, 1995.

17. See Kendall W. Stiles, *Negotiating Debt: The IMF Lending Process* (Boulder, CO: Westview Press, 1991), and Anne O. Krueger, "Whither the World Bank and the IMF?" *Journal of Economic Literature* 36, no. 4 (December 1998), p. 1993.

18. World Bank *Annual Report 1999*, p. 98.

19. The general consensus of the economic literature is that rates should be flexible but managed by governments to prevent undue fluctuations. See Bijan B. Aghevli, Mohsin S. Khan, and Peter J. Montiel, "Exchange Rate Policy in Developing Countries: Some Analytical Issues," IMF Occasional Paper No. 78 (Washington, March 1991).

20. See, for example, Dhaneshwar Ghura and Thomas J. Grinnes, "The Real Exchange Rate and Macroeconomic Performance in Sub-Saharan Africa," *Journal of Development Economics* 42, no. 1 (October 1993), pp. 155–174.

21. See Steven B. Kamin, "Devaluation, External Balance, and Macroeconomic Performance: A Look at the Numbers," Princeton Studies in International Finance No. 62 (Princeton, NJ: Princeton University, August 1988).

22. See Mohsin S. Khan and Nadeem ul Haque, "Capital Flight from Developing Countries," *Finance & Development* 24, no. 1 (March 1987), pp. 2–5, and Sebastian Edwards, *Crisis and Reform in Latin America* (New York: Oxford University Press/World Bank, 1995), p. 23.

23. Michael Bruno, "Opening Up: Liberalization with Stabilization," in Rudiger Dornbusch and F. Leslie C. H. Helmers, eds., *The Open Economy: Tools for Policymakers in Developing Countries* (New York: Oxford University Press, 1988), pp. 223–248. See also Jeffrey D. Sachs, "Conditionality, Debt Relief, and the Developing Country Debt Crisis," in Sachs, ed., *Developing Country Debt and the World Economy* (Chicago: University of Chicago Press, 1989), pp. 275–284.

24. Robert Devlin, "Options for Tackling the External Debt Problem," in *CEPAL Review* 37 (April 1989), reprinted in Charles K. Wilber and Kenneth P. Jameson, eds., *The Political Economy of Development and Underdevelopment*, 5th ed. (New York: McGraw-Hill, 1992), pp. 210–233. Also see *The Poverty of Nations: A Guide to the Debt Crisis from Argentina to Zaire*, by Elmar Altvater et al., ed. (London: Zed Books, 1991).

25. See Peter Montiel, "Empirical Analysis of High-Inflation Episodes in Argentina, Brazil, and Israel," IMF *Staff Papers* 36, no. 3 (September 1989, p. 547).

26. See Lourdes Beneria and Shelley Feldman, eds., *Unequal Burden: Economic Crisis, Persistent Poverty, and Women's Work* (Boulder, CO: Westview Press, 1992), and a review of that book, "Women's Unequal Burden: Economic Restructuring Hits Women Hardest," by Rose Batt, in *Dollars and Sense*, no. 177 (June 1992), pp. 12–13. Also see George Ann Potter, *Dialogue on Debt: Alternative Analyses and Solutions* (Washington: Center of Concern, 1988).

27. See "Adjustment Lending: An Evaluation of Ten Years of Experience," World Bank Policy and Research Series No. 1 (Washington: World Bank 1988); "Adjustment Lending: Policies for Sustainable Growth," Policy and Research Series No. 14 (Washington: World Bank, 1990); Paul Mosley, Jane Harrigan, and John Toye, eds., *Aid and Power: The World Bank and Policy-Based Lending*, 2 vols. (London: Routledge, 1991); Vinod Thomas et al., eds., *Restructuring Economies in Distress: Policy Reform and the World Bank* (Oxford: Oxford University Press, 1991); and World Bank, *Adjustment in Africa: Reforms, Results, and the Road Ahead* (New York: World Bank/Oxford University Press, 1994).

28. David D. Driscoll, "What Is the International Monetary Fund?" (Washington: IMF, 1991), pp. 1, 6.

29. See "The International Monetary Fund: Its Evolution, Organization, and Activities," IMF Pamphlet Series, no. 37, 4th ed. (Washington: IMF, 1984), pp. 34–42. The quotation appears on p. 39.

30. See Vittorio Corbo, Stanley Fischer, and Steven Webb, eds., *Adjustment Lending Revisited: Policies to Restore Growth*, a World Bank Symposium (Washington: 1992), especially Corbo and Fischer, "Adjustment Programs and Bank Support: Rationale and Main Results," pp. 7–18, and Webb and Karim Shariff, "Designing and Implementing Adjustment Programs," pp. 69–92. But see critical comments by Bacha (pp. 19–20) and Helleiner (pp. 94–95).

31. See Tatjana Chahoud, "The Changing Roles of the IMF and the World Bank," in Atvater et al., *The Poverty of Nations: A Guide to the Debt Crisis from Argentina to Zaire*, pp. 29–38; Manuel Guitian, "Economic Management and International Monetary Fund Conditionality," in Tony Killick, ed., *Adjustment and Financing in the Developing World: The Role of the International Monetary Fund* (Washington: IMF/Overseas Development Institute, 1982), pp. 73–104; Tony Killick and Mary Sutton, "An Overview," in the same collection, pp. 1–47; Cheryl Payer, *The Debt Trap: The International Monetary Fund and the Third World* (New York: Monthly Review Press, 1974); E. Walter Robichek, "The IMF's Conditionality Re-Examined," in Joaquin Muns, ed., *Adjustment, Conditionality, and International Financing* (Washington: IMF, 1984), pp. 67–75; John Spraos, "IMF Conditionality: Ineffectual, Inefficient, Mistargeted" (Princeton, NJ: Essays in International Finance, no. 166, December 1986); John Williamson, "The Economics of IMF Conditionality," in Gerald K. Helleiner, ed., *For Good or Evil: Economic Theory and North–South Negotiations* (Toronto: University of Toronto Press, 1982), pp. 121–134; John Williamson, ed., *IMF Conditionality* (Washington: International Institute of Economics, 1983); Tony Killick, *The Quest for Economic Stabilization: The IMF and the Third World* (London: Heinemann Educational Books, 1984); a discussion by Killick and the editor of *Finance & Development*, "The IMF's Role in Developing Countries," *Finance & Development* 21, no. 3, pp. 21–26; and "Ten Common Misconceptions About the IMF" (Washington: IMF, 1988).

32. See Gerald K. Helleiner, ed., *Africa and the International Monetary Fund* (Washington: IMF, 1986), and Bade Onimode, ed., *The IMF, the World Bank, and the African Debt*, 2 vols. (London: Zed Books, 1989).

33. See IMF, "Does the Fund Impose Austerity?" (Washington: IMF, June 1984).

34. See Spraos, "IMF Conditionality: Ineffectual, Inefficient, Mistargeted."

35. See Thomas Kamm, "After a Devaluation, Two African Nations Fare Very Differently," *Wall Street Journal*, May 10, 1995.

36. David E. Sahn, Paul A. Dorosh, and Stephen D. Younger, *Structural Adjustment Reconsidered: Economic Policy in Africa* (Cambridge: Cambridge University Press, 1997), pp. 57–63.

37. Thandika Mkandawire and Charles C. Soludo, *Our Continent, Our Future*, p. 62.

38. Sahn et al., *Structural Adjustment Reconsidered: Economic Policy in Africa*, pp. 152–177.

39. See Norman Hicks, "Expenditure Reductions in High-Debt Countries," *Finance & Development* 26, no. 1 (March 1989), pp. 35–37.

40. The Fund's review is Susan Schadler et al., "Economic Adjustment in Low-Income Countries: Experience Under the Enhanced Structural Adjustment Facility," IMF Occasional Paper No. 106 (Washington: IMF, September 1993). Criticisms are in Tony Killick, "Can the IMF Help Low-Income Countries? Experience with Its Structural Adjustment Facilities," *The World Economy* 18, no. 4 (July 1995), pp. 603–616, and Jeffrey Sachs, "External Debt, Structural Adjustment and Economic Growth," in *International Monetary and Financial Issues for the 1990s* (New York: United Nations, 1998), pp. 45–56. Schadler responds to Killick in her "Reply," pp. 617–626.

41. Mkandawire and Soludo, *Our Continent, Our Future*, p. 62.

42. United Nations, *1999 World Survey on the Role of Women in Development* (New York: United Nations, 1999), p. 54, and "Social Cost of Transition Greater for Women," World Bank News Release 2001/204/ECA (January 19, 2001).

43. Anne Maasland and Jacques van der Gaag, "World Bank-Supported Adjustment Programs and Living Conditions," and "Comment" by Jere R. Behrman, in Vittorio Corbo, Stanley Fischer, and Steven B. Webb, eds., *Adjustment Lending Revisited: Policies to Restore Growth* (Washington: World Bank, 1992), pp. 40–67. Also see Yukon Huang and Peter Nicholas, "The Social Costs of Adjustment," *Finance & Development* 24, no. 2 (June 1987), pp. 22–24; Tony Addison and Lionel Demery, "Alleviating Poverty Under Structural Adjustment," *Finance & Development* 24, no. 4 (December 1987), pp. 41–43; and Helena Ribe and Soniya Carvalho, "Adjustment and the Poor," *Finance & Development* 27, no. 3 (September 1990), pp. 15–17.

44. Mkandawire and Soludo, *Our Continent, Our Future*.

45. Sahn et al., *Structural Adjustment Reconsidered: Economic Policy in Africa*.

46. Tony Killick, "Structural Adjustment and Poverty Alleviation: An Interpretative Survey," *Development and Change* 26, no. 2 (April 1995), pp. 305–332.

47. Eduardo Lora and Juan Luis Londoño, "Structural Reforms and Equity," in Nancy Birdsall, Carol Graham, and Richard Sabot, eds., *Beyond Trade-Offs: Market Reform and Equitable Growth in Latin America* (Washington: International Development Bank/Brookings Institution Press, 1998), pp. 63–90.

48. See John Toye, "Can the World Bank Resolve the Crisis of Developing Countries?" *Journal of International Development* 1, no. 2 (April 1989), pp. 261–272; Jane Harrigan and Paul Mosley, "Evaluating the Impact of World Bank Structural Adjustment Lending: 1980–87," *Journal of Development Studies* 27, no. 3 (April 1991), pp. 63–94; Paul Mosley and John Weeks, "Adjustment in Africa," a review of the Bank's own report with that title, in *Development Policy Review* 12, no. 3 (September 1994), pp. 319–327; Irma Adelman and J. Edward Taylor, "Is Adjustment with a Human Face Possible? The Case of Mexico," *Journal of Development Studies* 26, no. 3 (April 1990), pp. 387–407; Vali Jamal, "Getting the Crisis Right: Missing Perspectives on Africa," *International Labour Review* 127, no. 6 (1988), pp. 655–678; Peter Heller et al., "The Implications of Fund-Supported Adjustment Programs for Poverty: Experiences in Selected Countries," IMF Occasional Paper No. 58 (Washington: May 1988); Sanjeev Gupta and Karim Nashashibi, "Poverty Concerns in Fund-Supported Programs," *Finance & Development* 27, no. 2 (September 1990), pp. 12–14; and World Bank, "Economic Reforms and the Poor: Social Action Programs and Social Funds in Sub-Saharan Africa," in the "Findings" of the African Technical Department, no. 12 (Washington: February 1994).

49. See World Bank, *From Safety Net to Springboard* (Washington: World Bank, 2001).

50. Sachs, *International Monetary and Financial Issues for the 1990s.*

51. See Robert Powell, "Debt Relief for Poor Countries," *Finance & Development* 37, no. 4 (December 2000), pp. 42–45.

52. See ⟨www.worldbank.org/hipc/about/hipcbr/hipcbr.htm⟩, and ⟨www.worldbank.org/hipc/progress-to-date/May99v3/may99v3.htm⟩.

53. Michael M. Phillips, "G-7's Debt-Relief Proposal Is in Jeopardy," *Wall Street Journal*, July 10, 2000.

54. See Donal J. Donovan, "Macroeconomic Performance and Adjustment Under Fund-Supported Programs: The Experience of the Seventies," IMF *Staff Papers* 29, no. 2 (June 1982), pp. 171–203; Mohsin S. Kahn and Malcolm D. Knight, "Fund-Supported Adjustment Programs for Economic Growth," IMF Occasional Paper No. 41 (Washington: IMF, November 1985); Mohsin S. Khan, "The Macroeconomic Effects of Fund-Supported Adjustment Programs," IMF *Staff Papers* 37, no. 2 (June 1990), pp. 195–231; Spraos, "IMF Conditionality: Ineffectual, Inefficient, Mistargeted"; Killick, *The Quest for Economic Stabilization: The IMF and the Third World*; and Jeffrey D. Sachs, "Strengthening IMF Programs in Highly Indebted Countries," pp. 101–122.

55. Sachs, *International Monetary and Financial Issues for the 1990s.*

56. Susan Schadler et al., "IMF Conditionality: Experience Under Stand-By and Extended Arrangements, Part I: Key Issues and Findings," IMF Occasional Paper No. 128 (Washington: IMF, September 1995).

57. Killick, "Can the IMF Help Low-Income Countries? Experience with Its Structural Adjustment Facilities," and Schadler, "Reply" [to Killick], *The World Economy* 18, no. 4 (July 1995), pp. 617–626.

58. Mkandawire and Soludo, *Our Continent, Our Future.*

59. David Dollar and Jakob Svensson, "What Explains the Success or Failure of Structural Adjustment Programs?" World Bank Policy Research Working Paper No. 1938 (Washington: World Bank, June 1998).

15

GLOBAL CAPITAL MARKETS AND THE EAST ASIAN DEVELOPMENT MODEL

The only cause of depression is prosperity.
—CLEMENT JUGLAR (1819–1905)

INTRODUCTION

Some of the more successful developing countries are the East Asian economies. A northern tier of Taiwan, South Korea, Singapore, and Hong Kong have been recognized since the 1970s as among the early stars. A southern tier of Malaysia, Thailand, and Indonesia have also been doing well since the 1980s. Together with Japan these eight are referred to by the World Bank as the High Performing Asian Economies. The northern tier countries have per capita incomes comparable to European economies, and South Korea has joined the Western industrial economies in the Organization for Economic Cooperation and Development (OECD).

But just when the East Asian development model was gaining widespread acceptability, many of these countries experienced a severe economic crisis that began in 1997 and is not yet resolved. In this chapter we explain the nature of the East Asian model of development. We then tackle the key elements of the currency crisis of 1997 to 1998 and discuss its consequences for the East Asian economies.

THE EAST ASIAN "MIRACLE"

Many of the East Asian economies have performed significantly better than most of the world for 30 years or so. Table 15–1 provides comparative regional growth-rate data, made even more compelling by the fact that the four "tigers"—South Korea, Taiwan, Singapore, and Hong Kong (China)—are not among the East Asian group since 1980 because they are now considered "high-income" economies. In addition, low- and middle-income countries in the region had seen the number of people in poverty drop in half, from 717 million in 1975 to 346 million in 1995, from 58 percent to 21 percent of the population.[1] How have they achieved their success?

TABLE 15-1 Annual Growth Rates of GDP and Population (%)

Region	1970–1980 GDP	1970–1980 Population	1980–1999 1980–1990 GDP	1980–1999 1990–1999 GDP	1980–1999 1980–1999 Population
East Asia/Pacific	6.6	1.9	8.0	7.5	1.4
Europe/Central Asia	NA	NA	NA	–2.3	0.6
Latin America/Caribbean	5.5	2.4	1.7	3.4	1.8
Mideast/North Africa	5.2	2.9	2.0	3.0	2.7
South Asia	3.5	2.4	5.6	5.6	2.0
Sub-Saharan Africa	4.0	2.8	1.7	2.2	2.8
High Income	3.1	0.7	3.4	2.3	0.7

NA = Not Available.

Source: World Development Report 1993, World Development Indicators 2001. Regional data exclude countries in the region considered to be in the high-income category in the latest reporting year, including Israel, South Korea, Singapore, and the Hong Kong province of China. Taiwan is not included in the data nor are countries with populations under 1 million.

Basic Outline of East Asian Policies

A key element of this model is that government and the private sector have worked together in a number of ways. Especially in the four "tigers," government has invested heavily in human capital. This provided an increasingly skilled workforce for the private sector that, until the last decade, had little worries about struggling with unions. In South Korea and Taiwan, land reform promoted efficient small and medium-sized plots that promoted agricultural productivity. Government then worked with, even guided, the private sector to areas of both domestic need and foreign markets. This guidance included permitting, often encouraging, a certain amount of industrial concentration, so that firms could achieve the economy of scale necessary to be competitive in world markets. This was most noticeable in Korea where, in the mid-1990s, the top 30 industrial *chaebol* (conglomerates) produced over half of the nation's output, and the top 5 produced about one-third of output.[2]

Favored firms were given special benefits: at different times tax breaks, subsidies, rebates of import duties, and access to bank credit at relatively low interest rates. Government officials were in constant consultation with firms, often providing what has been called guidance. In exchange for such guidance, firms were often given export targets: If targets were not met, benefits were not continued. Firms were encouraged to compete with each other, even to the point of engaging in sportlike contests to see who could export more.[3]

Aside from these activities, collectively referred to as **industrial policy**, macroeconomic policies were also generally favorable to development. Government-controlled financial institutions discouraged consumption on credit and encouraged personal savings despite low interest rates. Budgets were often in balance or deficits were not large, so that while growth was pursued inflation was kept low. Governments nevertheless spent on infrastructure to help industrial development and make basic services accessible to large portions of the population, reducing poverty rates to the lowest in the developing world.[4]

By the 1980s, high-growth performance began to spread to the southern tier of Thailand, Malaysia, and Indonesia. While some similar policies were used, there were some differences. These countries stayed with import-substitution a bit longer but were able to build up labor-intensive industry behind protectionist policies on the strength of commodity-based exports, including rice, rubber, and oil. They benefited from the relocation of successful firms from Japan and the "tigers" as wages increased in the northern tier. In the case of Malaysia, special efforts were made to ensure that local ethnic groups were enabled to succeed in the face of a strong presence of overseas Chinese.[5]

Too Much of a Good Thing?

Yet some of these same economies experienced a meltdown of sorts in the late 1990s. Were there inherent limits to the early growth policies? Did the close association of governments and business firms lead to mutual self-delusion about the nature of their course? Did government control over banking and credit provide too-easy access to capital, leading to overexpansion and lack of prudent financial regulation? Or did the liberalization of international capital markets in the 1990s break down the Asian model? These are the key questions of this chapter.

GLOBAL CAPITAL MARKETS

As the world economy becomes increasingly integrated, the easiest factor of production to move around is the financial form of capital. Money—whether as currency, bank accounts, short-term financial instruments, loans, bonds, and investment funds—can be sent from one part of the world to another almost instantaneously. Much of the current debate over **globalization** seems to be a reaction to increasing capital flows on top of the increasing importance of trade in the world economy.[6]

Changing Forms of Capital Flows

Until recently, bank lending to developing-country governments and private firms accounted for roughly two-thirds of private capital going to developing countries. Improvements in communications technology, deregulation, and development of developing-country financial markets, and the growth of institutional investing, have increased the flow of short-term capital such as portfolio investing in stock and bond markets. Bank lending has been reduced to about one-third, with Foreign Direct Investment (FDI) almost another third.[7]

Tables 15–2, 15–3, and 15–4 show changes in financial flows to developing countries over the 1990s and changes in their external debt. Private debt was starting to flow again in the 1990s following the debt crisis of the previous decade, but its expansion in the middle of the decade was especially rapid. Short-term debt began its decline in 1996, with the most significant changes occurring in the East Asian countries that experienced crises beginning the following year.

FDI has been less sharply affected, slowing down only somewhat in 1998, and has changed composition from largely extractive to manufacturing and services. Countries that once nationalized foreign companies now welcome them. NAFTA permits such

TABLE 15–2   Net Long-Term Capital Flows to Developing Countries ($ Billions)

	1990	1993	1996	1997	1998	1999	2000*
Total Net Flows	100.8	220.4	311.2	342.6	334.1	264.5	295.8
Official Flows	56.9	53.6	31.9	42.8	54.6	45.3	38.6
Private Flows							
Private Debt							
Banks	3.2	3.4	33.7	45.2	50.0	–24.6	0.7
Bonds	1.2	36.6	62.5	49.0	40.9	25.4	30.3
Other	11.4	9.2	2.4	2.7	–3.0	–1.6	0.3
Portfolio Equity	3.7	51.0	49.2	30.2	15.6	34.5	47.9
Direct Investment	24.5	66.6	131.5	172.6	176.8	185.4	178.0

Private Flows to East Asian Crisis Countries[†]	1990		1996	1997	1998*		
Private Debt	17.9		32.9	–44.5	–44.5		
Portfolio	0.3		20.0	12.6	–6.5		
Direct Investment	6.0		9.5	12.1	4.9		

*Figures are preliminary.

[†]Indonesia, South Korea, Malaysia, Philippines, Thailand.

Sources: International Monetary Fund, *International Capital Markets: Developments, Prospects, and Key Policy Issues* (September 1999), pp. 52–53, and World Bank, *Global Development Finance 2001*, p. 36.

investment. However, many developing countries still want to restrict entry into banking, which is crucial for directing credit.

Bank lending has a checkered history. As the size of loans sought by developing-country governments and companies increased, consortia of developed-country banks were created to facilitate this lending. With small banks taking pieces of the larger consortia, the entire U.S. banking system suffered the shocks associated with the

TABLE 15–3   Developing Country External Debt by Maturity ($ Billions)

	1991	1993	1995	1997	1998	2000
Developing Countries						
Total Debt	1,245	1,461	1,689	1,813	1,922	2,528
Long Term	1,077	1,218	1,368	1,416	1,504	2,061
Short Term	168	243	321	397	418	446
Percentage Short Term	13.5	16.7	19.0	21.9	21.7	18.5
East Asia/Pacific						
Total Debt	367	455	561	640	655	651
Long Term	320	389	466	529	557	526
Short Term	47	67	96	110	98	135
Percentage Short Term	12.8	14.7	17.1	17.2	15.0	20.4

Sources: International Monetary Fund, *World Economic Outlook* (May 1999) and World Bank, *Global Development Financing 2001*.

TABLE 15–4 Short-Term Debt Flows ($ Billions)

	1990	*1995*	*1997*	*1998*	*1999*	*2000*
All Developing Countries	16.7	61.1	21.1	4.9	–18.3	3.5
East Asia and Pacific	9.0	43.1	2.7	–6.1	–13.4	–3.1
Latin America/Caribbean	9.1	5.6	10.3	0.9	–7.0	6.1
Middle East/North Africa	1.8	–0.6	–1.5	0.4	0.4	–1.2
South Asia	1.5	2.1	–2.1	1.4	0.2	–1.3
Sub-Saharan Africa	2.3	2.8	3.3	1.5	2.2	–2.2
Europe/Central Asia	–7.1	8.2	8.4	6.9	–0.8	5.2

Source: World Bank, *Global Development Finance 2001.*

Latin American debt crisis in the 1980s. Bank lending to developing countries plummeted in the middle of the 1980s, only to recover in the early and mid-1990s. The breakdown between long- and short-term debt shows that shorter-term flows were becoming increasingly popular in the mid-1990s but, especially in Asia, have been cut back after 1996.

As developing countries, especially in East Asia and Latin America, acquired significant private sectors, they also began to develop stock markets. These stock markets took off, although often without a sound basis, and small to medium-sized investors in industrialized countries began putting some of their savings in funds that were invested in emerging market securities. So investment companies from the United States and Europe took part in the stocks and bonds issued by companies in developing countries.

Economic Theory and Capital Market Liberalization

Many economists support, at least in principle, unhindered capital flows and agree that it is in the long-term interest of developing countries to liberalize, or open up, their capital markets.[8] They cite the efficiency advantages of competitive markets: Unrestricted capital flows should direct savings to the most productive investments, and competition among funds providers will make the financial system more efficient and lower costs to borrowers. In addition, the development of new financial instruments provides new ways for firms to manage their own risk. From a macroeconomic standpoint, free flow of resources permits greater investment and growth, while competition for funds should require governments to be disciplined in their own spending.

There are some important objections to these conclusions, and some evidence suggests that these benefits have not been achieved.[9] One reason why liberalization may encounter difficulties is that an important requirement for competitive markets, perfect information, is less likely to exist in developing-country capital markets. If investors in developed countries have little accurate information about opportunities in developed countries, they are more likely to put money into risky investments when conditions *seem* good and more likely to take it out when conditions *seem* bad. This leads to **herding** behavior, where a move by a few investors triggers a stampede of many others, and contributes to volatility and uncertainty in returns.[10] Herding behavior is a crucial element in explaining the East Asian crisis of the 1990s.

CAPITAL INFLOWS AND ECONOMIC DEVELOPMENT

In order to better understand the crises associated with capital flows, three important questions must be answered. What causes these flows, especially rapid flows of short-term capital into developing countries? What impact do these surges have on the receiving economy? What happens if they suddenly turn to outflows?

Causes of Capital Inflows

Like population migrations, we can think of capital inflows as responding to push and pull factors, where push factors are largely due to conditions outside the receiving economy and pull factors are due largely to internal conditions. This distinction is somewhat artificial in that capital flows generally respond to perceived differences in rates of return at home and abroad. However, it may matter if the initial change in circumstances took place in the sending or receiving country. In the light of controversy over the IMF's role in the Asian crisis, discussed later in the chapter, it is interesting that one of the early general investigations of these causes was done by the IMF staff.[11]

External Factors

One economy's capital inflows is another's capital outflows. Capital leaves one country because profit opportunities are depleted (markets saturated, or lower income reduces demand); returns fall (lower interest rates); or asset values become threatened (through inflation or political upheaval). Market saturation is not likely for many goods simultaneously. Inflation or upheaval may characterize a region, such as Latin America in the 1980s, but this kind of capital flight typically heads toward the industrialized countries. However, sluggish economies and lower interest rates did characterize much of the industrialized world in the early 1990s, and have been implicated in the capital flows to Latin America and Asia.[12]

Internal Factors

Internal factors may be real or monetary. Real factors refer to strong economies that promise high profits and attract capital to take advantage of them. Some of the capital inflow will be FDI, to participate in the real economy, but there will also be additional bank lending and foreign participation in domestic stock markets. The distinction is important, because FDI will be relatively permanent, while lending, especially if short term, and stock purchases are relatively easy to reverse when domestic conditions deteriorate. Table 15–5 shows the rapid increase in stock market size over the 1990 to 2000 period. The East Asia and Pacific regions were already important in 1990, but over the next eight years the value of stocks more than doubled and increased by a third as a percentage of GDP. The annual value of trades rose almost threefold over the decade, as did the number of domestic companies listed.

Monetary factors usually refer to higher interest rates in the recipient country, which create the differential between returns in home and host country. Since developing countries have a tendency, when departing from market interest rates, to enforce below-equilibrium rates, higher rates are most likely to occur when the government is attempting monetary stringency to fight inflation or when rates fall in industrialized economies.

TABLE 15–5 World Stock Markets

	CAPITALIZATION				*Traded Value as Percentage GDP*		*Number Domestic Companies Listed*	
	$ Billions		*Percentage GDP*					
	1990	*2000*	*1990*	*1999*	*1990*	*1999*	*1990*	*2000*
Low Income	55	268	9.8	31.7	4.7	19.6	3,446	8,332
Low-Middle Income	58	752	5.9	31.0	NA	22.8	1,833	11,420
Upper-Middle Income	372	1,408	27.3	49.8	8.5	37.2	3,081	5,119
High Income	8,915	33,603	55.3	138.7	31.8	120.9	17,064	24,741
Low and Middle								
East Asia/Pacific	197	955	21.3	52.4	13.2	68.1	1,443	3,754
Europe, Central Asia	19	265	2.1	24.6	NA	11.2	110	8,968
Latin America, Caribbean	78	585	7.7	29.7	2.1	7.3	1,748	1,938
Middle East/North Africa	5	152	27.8	33.9	1.5	7.3	817	1,874
South Asia	43	194	10.8	34.0	5.6	25.2	3,231	7,199
Sub-Saharan Africa*	143	276	52.0	121.0	3.8	32.3	1,011	1,138

NA = Not Available.

*Primarily Republic of South Africa.

Sources: World Bank, *World Development Indicators 2000* and *2001.*

Consequences of Capital Inflows

Capital inflows are generally welcomed by developing countries. They increase the amount of resources available for investment and growth, filling a gap created by a shortfall of domestic saving even if, as in East Asia, domestic saving is already large. Problems arise, however, if their magnitude and form seriously disrupt the economy.

Large inflows create two problems. First, unless the central bank offsets them by reducing the domestic money supply, they will be inflationary. To fight inflation, the banks raise interest rates further, thereby creating even greater incentive for short-term inflows. Second, because the inflow of foreign exchange increases the demand for the domestic currency, that currency will appreciate, reducing the competitiveness of exports and pushing the trade balance toward deficit. But even keeping the exchange rate stable in the face of inflation will cause a real appreciation. When inflows are large, a Dutch Disease effect is produced.

Either way, the result is likely to be a trade deficit. Deficits may well be sustainable because they are being voluntarily paid for by the capital inflow, but if that inflow reverses suddenly, the country will be left with a serious balance of payments crisis and downward pressure on its currency.

The possibility of reversal is connected to the composition of the capital flows. The kind of surges that many countries have experienced in the last decade often take the form of short-term or volatile investment flows, including stock purchase and short- and medium-term lending from banks in industrial countries to banks, other financial institutions, and other corporations in developing countries. Participation in stock markets is obviously reversible at a moment's notice. Bank lending presents different problems.

Bank lending is often based on a significant interest rate differential between the two countries. In order to attract capital, developing countries may keep interest rates high. This makes borrowing more difficult for domestic firms, but gives local banks and finance companies an incentive to borrow overseas at low rates and lend the money at home. If international capital markets worked perfectly, those differentials would be narrowed quickly, but market imperfections and barriers usually prevent this from happening.

Short-term borrowing may be transformed into long-term lending. For instance, a bank in Thailand may borrow short term from a Japanese bank and lend long term to a Thai real estate company. If the original loan is not renewed from Japan, the Thai bank may not be able to recover the funds from its borrower. This example presents an additional problem: The real estate company may have little opportunity to earn foreign exchange, so even repayment to the bank in the Thai currency (the baht) does not guarantee that the Thai bank can repay the Japanese yen it has borrowed.

These problems could have been a warning to Asian countries. A UN report, reviewing a number of similar crises, concludes that "there is no known case in any country, developed or developing, where a large increase in liquidity in the banking sector has not led to an overextension of lending, a decline in the quality of assets and increased laxity in risk assessment."[13] It will therefore be instructive to look at some of these previous incidences.

CAPITAL MARKET CRISES IN LATIN AMERICA

In the last 30 years, two market crises in Latin America have foreshadowed the Asian problems of the 1990s.

The Chilean Crisis

After a military coup in 1973, the Chilean government liberalized capital account transactions.[14] Attracted by the policy turnaround in a historically stable and profitable economy, foreign capital of all kinds began to make its way back to Chile. Chilean banks, many of which had been denationalized and deregulated in 1974, were able to borrow at relatively low rates from banks in the industrialized countries when capital controls were removed in 1979. This money was lent to Chilean firms at higher rates.

Capital flows surged in 1981, putting upward pressure on the exchange rate. Tight monetary policy kept real domestic interest rates above 30 percent. At such a level, ordinary business loans are too expensive: Foreign capital and lack of bank supervision and regulation resulted in adverse selection. Only businesses with highly risky projects were willing to pay the high interest rates, and they were more likely to fail. With high debt came defaults and bank insolvencies. Despite government announcements that banks would not be bailed out, everyone assumed it would happen, so banks were not careful with their loans. The Chilean government ended up renationalizing many banks in order to restore order but reprivatized them later.

One of the lessons of this crisis was the importance of a strong, well-enforced regulatory regime for banks to ensure sufficient capital requirements and conditions on lending. Another lesson was the importance of stable macroeconomic conditions and well-developed institutions prior to complete liberalization of capital account transactions.

The Mexican Crisis of 1994 to 1995

In Mexico, economic liberalization and economic growth starting in the late 1980s, together with the promise of an imminent free trade agreement with the United States and Canada (NAFTA), induced new investment flows. But rapid growth of money and short-term government debt helped finance a current account deficit of 7 percent of GDP in 1994, far above a safe level of 3 percent to 4 percent. Domestic saving faltered as foreign capital financed a consumption spending spree, and productivity growth slowed.[15]

Deregulation of the financial sector permitted banks to lend too much with too little guarantee of returns. The banking system was being reprivatized, after nationalizations in 1982, with little supervision and a dearth of trained personnel. Used to lending to low-risk government projects, the new private banks were not prepared to cope with their new freedom and access to huge capital inflows. Their financing grew at 25 percent per year between 1989 and 1994, leaping from 13 percent of GDP in 1988 to over 50 percent in 1994.[16] Long-term foreign liabilities surged from $97 billion at the end of 1993 to $197 billion at the end of 1994 and $278 billion a year later. The ratio of nonperforming loans in bank portfolios doubled to 9 percent in two years.[17]

Inflation caused a real appreciation of the peso, nominally **pegged**, or fixed in value relative to the dollar, exacerbating the trade deficit. The crunch came when, after flight from the peso throughout 1994, the Mexican government devalued by 15 percent in December: The dollar was worth 3.6 pesos in the last quarter of 1994 and 6 pesos in the first quarter of 1995, then rose again from 6.2 in the third quarter to 7.4 in the fourth. However, rather than being seen as a sign that the government was attempting to rectify the problem, the devaluation was taken as a signal of more to come, and asset holders of all types started abandoning the country. This had severe political ramifications, as some accused the Mexican and U.S. governments of conspiring to hold the peso constant through 1994 to assure passage of NAFTA. As investors withdrew their money, the Mexican government had to borrow heavily from the United States and the IMF to keep from depleting its foreign exchange reserves completely. The IMF committed up to $18 billion—its largest program up to that time—although $10 billion was in reserve if other commitments did not come through. The U.S. government committed $20 billion and other sources $13 billion.

After the United States and the IMF had stepped in, a series of economic reforms was initiated, including tax and spending steps to reduce the fiscal deficit; increased prices for SOE output; allowing the peso to respond more flexibly to market pressures; and more stringent banking regulation, including permitting bankruptcies and sales to Mexican and foreign private interests. Responding to pressure about the impact of its programs on the poor and to considerable political instability in Mexico, the reductions in government spending excluded social spending, which was allowed to increase.[18]

Mexico was not the end. Investors who respond to general ideas more than specific information may be prone to lump similarly seeming possibilities together.

Given the broad sweep of the 1980s debt crisis, it was not too far-fetched to believe that the collapse of Mexican asset values presaged a similar collapse in other Latin American markets. The so-called Tequila Effect spread the problems. Brazil, for example, had to raise interest rates to keep capital in while it was escaping Mexico. Argentina was less fortunate but used the crisis as an incentive to strengthen its banking system.[19]

Again, lessons were drawn from this episode. Fiscal and trade deficits, and pegged exchange rates, will ultimately cause problems. A properly regulated banking sector is crucial to any policy of financial deregulation and capital account liberalization. These lessons were not fully absorbed, however, and came back to haunt Asian countries in 1997.

THE EAST ASIAN CRISIS

The crisis that took hold in East Asia in 1997 was all the more surprising because of the phenomenal performance of those economies, some extending over more than three decades. So in addition to the immediate aspects of the crisis, a deeper question arose as to the staying power of the East Asian model of development.

Causes of the Crisis

It may be useful to divide the causes of the Asian crisis into internal and external.

Internal Considerations

Most of the East Asian economies had been growing rapidly for a number of years. This growth had been based not on protected markets but on export-oriented development strategies. Production was largely in labor-intensive industries, although in Northeast Asian countries such as South Korea, that early stage of development had passed into more capital-intensive areas including steel, shipbuilding, autos, and petrochemicals. Savings and investment ratios were high, real interest rates were positive and moderate, and government budgets were largely in balance: The key features of macro stability long considered essential for development were in place. In addition, governments had spent wisely on education and health services.

Tables 15–6 through 15–9 show the performance of four important Asian economies in the years preceding the crisis. Table 15–6 shows the growth rates in those countries hit hardest by the crisis. From 1992 to 1996, growth rates of real GDP were above 5 percent. Tables 15–7 and 15–8 show the high savings and investment ratios that had driven that growth. Ratios of savings to GDP were above 30 percent, and except for one year in Indonesia, gross capital formation (investment) exceeded 30 percent of GDP. For Thailand and Malaysia, investment ratios were typically closer to 40 percent. Stable macroeconomic conditions were ensured partly by sound fiscal policy, as shown in Table 15–9.

However, there were problems at the micro level, which proved much more important. One was the close relationship between companies and governments. Some countries, such as Indonesia, had a large number of SOEs, but even where this was not the case, such as in Korea, years of guided development meant that government and corporate officials cooperated in making strategic corporate decisions, with

TABLE 15–6 Real GDP Growth Rates (%)

Year	Indonesia	South Korea	Malaysia	Thailand
1992	6.5	5.1	7.8	8.1
1993	6.5	5.8	8.3	8.4
1994	7.5	8.6	9.2	8.9
1995	8.2	8.9	9.5	8.8
1996	8.0	7.1	8.6	5.5

Source: IMF, *International Financial Statistics.*

TABLE 15–7 Savings as Percentage of GDP

Year	Indonesia	South Korea	Malaysia	Thailand
1992	38.2	35.2	35.5	35.3
1993	32.5	35.4	36.7	35.4
1994	32.2	35.7	38.8	36.0
1995	30.6	36.8	39.5	36.7
1996	30.2	35.5	42.6	35.4

Source: IMF, *International Financial Statistics.*

TABLE 15–8 Gross Capital Formation as Percentage of GDP

Year	Indonesia	South Korea	Malaysia	Thailand
1992	35.8	36.6	33.5	40.0
1993	29.5	35.1	37.8	39.9
1994	31.1	36.1	40.4	40.3
1995	31.9	37.0	43.5	41.6
1996	30.8	38.4	41.5	41.7

Source: IMF, *International Financial Statistics.*

TABLE 15–9 Budget Surplus (Deficit) as Percentage of GDP

Year	Indonesia	South Korea	Malaysia	Thailand
1992	(0.4)	(0.5)	(0.8)	2.8
1993	0.6	0.6	0.2	2.1
1994	0.9	0.3	2.3	1.9
1995	2.2	0.3	0.9	2.9
1996	1.1	0.5	0.7	2.3

Source: IMF, *International Financial Statistics.*

government officials rewarding, and being rewarded by, favored companies. These relationships are widely credited with fostering rapid economic growth for 30 years and had been dubbed "shared growth."

Most economists would say that this cooperation had gone too far. What was "shared growth" in good times now was attacked as "crony capitalism." The Indonesian situation was particularly egregious, with government officials blatantly promoting and profiting from specific firms. South Korea's situation was less personal. Still, the close association of government officials with the *chaebols* led to a feeling that these groups would not be allowed to fail. Many had "carried out a series of ill-fated investments" approved by government in a struggle for market share, heedless of expected rates of return,[20] so the large investment ratios in Table 15–8 were unsustainable.

The system began to crack in early 1997 when Hanbo Steel, the 14th largest *chaebol*, filed for bankruptcy protection. Three more of the top 30, including number 8 Kia, filed during the first half of the year. Similar problems were evident in Thailand.[21]

Part of the rewards handed out by government included easy credit. In fact, the close relationship among governments, banks, and nonbank corporations was one of the key features of poor corporate governance. Credit was available on easy terms for favored firms, overcapacity was tolerated, and debts allowed to pile up.[22] The worst case of financial system failure was in Thailand, where government had for years been bailing out banks and finance companies.[23] In Korea, bank lending increased 34 percent between the end of 1994 and the end of 1996. When this was stopped, nonbank financial institutions (insurance companies, investment trust companies, and development banks) filled the void.[24] Even by the end of 1996, the top 30 *chaebols* had debt/equity ratios of over 500 percent, while the return on capital was below its cost for most of them.[25] These debts came back to haunt the economies when the financial crunch hit.

Importantly, the easy credit was actually promoted by financial liberalization. Liberalization was supposed to mean putting the financial sector on a more market-oriented footing, including more entry (and competition) into the sector, less control over interest rates, and freeing up of international capital flows—primarily inward. This is a key point of contention in arguments over the cause of the crisis, because proponents of the Asian model in the realm of financial-sector control claim that liberalization is the one new element introduced into economies that previously had little history of financial crisis.

In an effort to handle the inflow of money, Thailand had created a Bangkok International Banking Facility (BIBF) as a major regional financial center, but it produced only debt overload. Three of the hardest-hit countries—Thailand, Indonesia, and South Korea—had high ratios of (*a*) short-term debt to foreign reserves, (*b*) short-term debt to total debt, and (*c*) money supply to foreign reserves in mid-1997.[26] Much of the money intended to be channeled by BIBF to lower-income countries went instead into the Thai financial sector. In Thailand, Malaysia, and the Philippines, real estate investment received between 25 percent and 40 percent of the funds.[27]

Advocates of liberalization, however, suggest that, as in the case of Chile, freeing financial markets and opening a country up to capital movements must be accompanied by appropriate banking supervision and prudential regulation to guard against improper lending practices. And it is true that in most Asian countries this kind of regulation and supervision was either nonexistent or extremely weak. There was little reliable information about the viability of borrowing firms, no concern for the riskiness of loans, and inadequate requirements for holding capital reserves against nonperforming loans. In Thailand, for example, only 40 percent of industrial firms had provided audited financial statements to their banks.[28] The upshot was that while investment rates were high, much investment was of particularly poor quality (high ICOR), and adverse selection meant that the riskiest investments were favored at high interest rates.

Internally, then, the development policies that had succeeded for over 30 years were running into problems. In addition, however, financial liberalization encouraged large capital inflows and ill-advised lending.

External Factors

Factors beyond the immediate control of the countries themselves played an important role in the financial crisis. As Table 15–10 shows, most of the seriously affected countries were not suffering from significant current account deficits. Thailand, where the crisis began, was the exception. It had a 1996 deficit of 8 percent on current account and 11 percent on goods and services. But other countries' deficits were either much smaller or were considered sustainable because they were financed by the capital inflows generated over the previous decade or more.

These current deficits arose from private-sector debt. Comparing the two sets of ratios in Tables 15–7 and 15–8, in most countries for most years, investment exceeded savings. So with government budgets fairly well balanced, the current account deficits reflected very high investment with money borrowed largely by the private sector and considered safer than loans to governments.

The rapid growth of regional exports had begun to slow in 1996. Part of the slowdown was on the demand side: overall reductions in demand from Japan, which was undergoing a crisis of its own, and product-oriented slowdowns in key exports: steel, autos, and electronics. Semiconductor prices had fallen by 90 percent in the previous few years. Part of the slowdown was a supply problem: expansion of capacity in the same sectors by a number of Asian countries. Regional competition had been intensifying over the decade, with some production shifting to ever-lower-cost sites in China and Vietnam.[29] So less capital-intensive production (textiles, garments, shoes) was hurt first in Thailand, Malaysia, and Indonesia but followed by

TABLE 15–10 Trade Surplus (Deficit) as Percentage of GDP

Year	Indonesia	South Korea	Malaysia	Thailand
1992	1.6	(1.5)	1.3	(4.7)
1993	1.3	0.1	(2.1)	(4.5)
1994	0.8	(1.3)	(1.6)	(5.1)
1995	(0.7)	(1.6)	(3.8)	(13.9)
1996	(1.1)	(4.3)	1.4	(11.3)

Source: IMF, *International Financial Statistics.*

autos, steel, and chemicals in Thailand and South Korea. And the Asian economies were highly interdependent in that American and Japanese multinationals had so integrated operations throughout the region, that a problem in one country affected others.

To these factors can be added the stimuli to capital flows, which were now easier with financial liberalization. In addition to FDI, banks and investment firms in Japan, the United States, and Europe began funneling large amounts of funds into East Asian banks and finance companies, directly and through stock market purchases. While part of the impetus was the growth of the region, another was relatively low interest rates, especially in the United States and Japan. Money-market interest rates in Thailand, which had averaged about 10 percent in 1995 to 1996, rose to 19 percent in the third quarter of 1997 and, after a brief drop, back up to almost 21 percent in the first quarter of 1998. "In the mid-1990s, an investor could borrow in yen at a near 0 interest rate and invest in Bangkok skyscrapers, whose expected annual return was 20 percent."[30] Other risky uses of funds included luxury residential building and stock market speculation. So the investment booms that caused the current account deficits were composed of a lot of risky ventures with little foreign exchange-earning capacity.

An additional problem was the nature of exchange rates in East Asian countries. As Table 15–11 shows, these rates had been relatively stable, partly due to sound economic performance and partly due to government policies of pegging their rates, either to combinations of their trading partners' currencies or to the dollar. The history of stability meant that foreign borrowing was not **hedged**—insured against a depreciation of the local currency. See Development Spotlight 15–1 for an example of hedging. In early 1995, Asian economies whose currencies were pegged to the dollar began to suffer the effects of the dollar's appreciation against the yen, putting their exports at a competitive disadvantage vis-à-vis Japan. As Table 15–11 shows, only South Korea had permitted its currency to depreciate, about 10 percent against the dollar, in 1996.

The result of these conditions was a buildup of borrowing for risky investments. Money was often borrowed from abroad short term and lent out at home for longer term. When the original short-term money fell through it was not easily recoverable from those who had borrowed long term, especially on risky investments whose values were plummeting when the capital withdrawal began. In addition, to the extent that domestic assets retained their value, this was in local currency, not dollars or yen.

TABLE 15–11 Exchange Rates (Units of Domestic Currency per Dollar at Year's End)

Year	Rupiah (Indonesia)	Won (South Korea)	Ringgit (Malaysia)	Baht (Thailand)	Yen (Japan)
1992	2,062	788.4	2.61	25.5	124.75
1993	2,110	808.1	2.70	25.5	111.85
1994	2,200	788.7	2.56	25.1	99.74
1995	2,308	774.7	2.54	25.2	102.83
1996	2,383	844.2	2.53	25.6	116.00

Source: IMF, *International Financial Statistics.*

TO HEDGE OR NOT TO HEDGE?

Hedging is a form of insurance on a foreign exchange transaction. If a Thai business borrows 1 million Japanese yen, to be repaid in six months, it does not want to take a chance that the Thai baht will depreciate, requiring more baht to be paid to get the yen in six months. To hedge, it acquires a million-yen asset now to make the exchange even in six months. When currency values are stable, or when the baht is expected to rise in value (exchanging for more yen in six months), hedging seems unnecessary.

The baht had been pegged to the dollar, and the dollar's rise increased the baht's value from 3.36 yen in the second quarter of 1995 to 4.62 yen in the second quarter of 1997. Hedging did not seem necessary. Thus, Thai borrowers were unprepared for the sudden drop in the baht, to 3.58 yen in the third quarter of 1997 and 3.05 yen in the fourth quarter. Losses piled up as the short-term yen loans became due.

When currency values began to plummet, those earlier unhedged yen borrowings had to be repaid with severe losses. Case 15–1 describes the crucial conditions leading to the crisis in three key countries: Thailand, Indonesia, and the Republic of Korea.

The Crisis and Its Spread

First signs of the crisis occurred in Thailand, where capital controls and suspension of a few finance companies were insufficient assurance for the foreign exchange markets.

- After weeks of trying to control capital outflows and using reserves to keep the baht stable, the Bank of Thailand devalued the currency by 20 percent on July 2.
- On July 11, the Philippines and Indonesia widened the trading range for their currencies.
- Malaysia quit supporting its ringgit on July 14.
- On July 28, Thailand requested IMF assistance.
- On August 14, Indonesia floated its rupiah.
- Thailand signed an IMF program on August 20, which eventually reached a commitment of $17 billion.
- Malaysia imposed controls on stock trading on August 27.
- Indonesia went to the IMF on October 8 and signed a $23 billion agreement on October 31.
- Malaysia took "voluntary" austerity measures on October 17.
- A crash on the Hong Kong stock market was followed by huge losses in U.S., Brazilian, Argentine, and Mexican markets on October 27.
- On November 17, Korea abandoned its peg of the won and four days later asked for IMF assistance, which came within two weeks. That program eventually reached a colossal $57 billion. The crisis quickly took its toll on the real economies of the region.

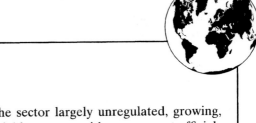

CASE 15–1

BACKGROUND TO CRISIS IN THAILAND, INDONESIA, AND KOREA

FAST FACTS

Thailand on the Map: Southeast Asia

Population: 60 Million

Per Capita GNI and Rank: $2,010   (103)

Life Expectancy: Male—67   Female—71

Adult Literacy Rate: Male—97%
Female—93%

Indonesia on the Map: Southeast Asia

Population: 207 Million

Per Capita GNI and Rank: $4,600   (150)

Life Expectancy: Male—64   Female—68

Adult Literacy Rate: Male—91%
Female—81%

South Korea on the Map: East Asia

Population: 47 Million

Per Capita GNI and Rank: $8,490   (54)

Life Expectancy: Male—69   Female—77

Adult Literacy Rate: Male—99%
Female—96%

The first step of the East Asian economic crisis occurred in Thailand. The current account deficit was 8 percent of GDP in 1996. The creation of the Bangkok International Banking Facility created a frenzy of foreign borrowing, increasing external debt from 34 percent of GDP in 1990 to 51 percent in 1996. More than one-third of this debt had short-term maturities, one year or less, and by 1995 the total of those short-term debts equaled the country's foreign exchange reserves. A large portion of the money was lent to the real estate sector, so that property values in Bangkok were higher than those in San Francisco. A recession then began in 1996 that burst the real estate bubble.

Thailand had undertaken significant financial liberalization in the early 1990s, leaving the sector largely unregulated, growing, and highly corrupt, with government officials heavily involved in ownership of banks and lending companies. The 1996 recession was instigated by an export slump, followed by collapse in asset values in both real estate and the stock market. The export slump, in turn, had been brought about by slowing demand and an increase in the value of the baht, following the dollar. The government resisted pressure to devalue the baht in 1996, supported by private interests with unhedged dollar borrowing. At the same time, tighter monetary policy raised interest rates and invited further money inflow. But continuing pressure finally led to the devaluation on July 2, 1997.

In Indonesia, financial liberalization had begun in the early 1980s. It had the desired effects of stimulating the financial sector: Financial deepening improved and more private financial institutions entered the sector. But regulation was weak, and private lenders were no better than their government counterparts in making prudent loans. Bad debts began piling up due to poor decisions and corruption, but failing banks were allowed to stay in business.

When the Thai crisis erupted, Indonesia had been experiencing rapid economic growth. The current account was in deficit by 4 percent of GDP in 1996, the highest of the decade, but this was considered sustainable because net capital inflows had provided an overall surplus in every year of the decade and, except for 1994, direct investment had exceeded portfolio investment. Inflation had been less than 10 percent per year, and in most years the government budget had seen modest surpluses. While short-term debt had become a larger portion of the total external debt (from 16 percent in 1990 to 25 percent in 1996), the total external debt had actually fallen as a percentage of exports.

Indonesian monetary policy had been tightening somewhat to contain the domestic influence of the capital inflows. When the Thai baht was devalued, there was further tightening to strengthen the rupiah. Restrictions on lending for real estate were increased. However, the nervousness of foreign investors was heightened by political crisis in Indonesia and the appearance of difficulties in South Korea. Central bank intervention to support the rupiah was unable to prevent the eventual collapse of the currency.

Unlike Thailand and Indonesia, Korea was one of the early group of "Newly Industrializing Countries" that was astonishing the world with its growth record since the 1960s. As the crisis was unfolding to the south, the Korean economy was expected to be spared, despite a somewhat overvalued currency and a current account deficit about 3 percent of GNP. Foreign borrowing had been funneled largely into the manufacturing sector for export, and Korea's fiscal house was in order. Steps toward financial liberalization in the previous decades had earned the country a place in the Organization for Economic Cooperation and Development (OECD).

The banking sector was not in unusually bad shape. Nonperforming loans were less than 7 percent of the total, nearly the same as they had been for several years. Foreign debt had been growing rapidly, but had then begun to level off and was well below what the World Bank considers dangerous relative to GNP. The debt was increasingly short term, accounting for almost 60 percent in 1996, although that too was leveling off.

However, under both the earlier regime of directed credits and the somewhat more liberal banking regime of the 1990s, connections among the government, the banks, and the major industrial conglomerates, or *chaebols*, were extremely close. Collapse of the Hanbo steel company in January and problems for the Kia automobile company caused considerable concern just as Thailand, Malaysia, Indonesia, and the Philippines were watching their currencies plunge. These countries competed with Korea in some export markets, and some Korean financial institutions had invested in their countries.

While some have blamed Korea's financial problems on the basic policy of state direction of credit and investment, others have suggested that the financial liberalization had in fact weakened that system, with its proliferation of financial institutions and greater foreign borrowing, unprotected by supervision and prudential regulation. The government had also begun to keep the currency, the won, more rigidly pegged than before and to become less interested in the informal coordination of major industrial projects than it had been, with growing excess capacity in many industries and vulnerability to downturns.

Sources: From Jomo K. S., ed., *Tigers in Trouble: Financial Governance, Liberalisation and Crisis in East Asia* (New York: Zed Books, 1998); Laurids S. Lauridsen, "Thailand: Causes, Conduct, Consequences," pp. 137–161; Manuel F. Montes and Muhammad Ali Abdusalamov, "Indonesia: Reaping the Market," pp. 162–180; and Chang Ha-Joon, "South Korea: The Misunderstood Crisis," pp. 222–231.

Figure 15–1 shows what happened to currency values. It shows exchange rate movements by quarter from 1996 through the first quarter of 2001, relative to the average rate in 1996. At their low points, the Korean won and the Thai baht lost nearly half their original value against the dollar, and the Indonesian rupiah lost over 80 percent of its previous value.

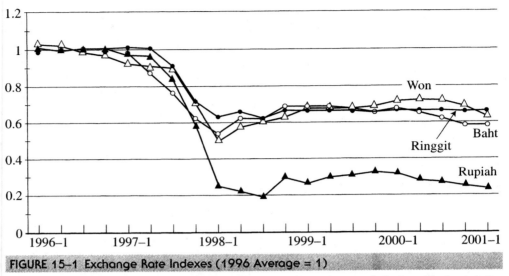

FIGURE 15–1 Exchange Rate Indexes (1996 Average = 1)

The currencies of Indonesia, South Korea, Malaysia, and Thailand were relatively stable through the mid-1990s. When the crisis hit, all four, particularly Indonesia's rupiah, fell dramatically. While all have stabilized, they remain well below their earlier levels.

Source: IMF, *International Financial Statistics.*

Another financial indicator was the plunge in stock markets of the affected countries. While stock exchanges in emerging markets throughout the world suffered in the last half of 1997 (down 22 percent in Brazil, 16 percent in South Africa), East Asia was hardest hit. The Korean stock index fell 51 percent, those of Indonesia and Malaysia fell 45 percent, and Thailand's fell 34 percent. There was some subsequent recovery, but by the end of 1998 Malaysia's index was off 48 percent, Indonesia's 43 percent, Thailand's 37 percent, and Korea's 27 percent from June 1997.[31]

One of the worrisome aspects of this crisis was the rapidity with which it spread. As with the 1980s in Latin America, countries throughout the region had similar problems, but this does not explain why so many would undergo crises within a period of five or six months, or what became known as **contagion**. Most analyses have implicated the herding behavior of investors: Funds had surged into the region in just a few years' time, but given the lack of reliable information on the target investments, it seems reasonable that the individuals involved in these markets knew little about where their money was going. Good news brought money in and, even more rapidly, bad news took money out.[32] Some money continued to come into the region, but the decline was significant. Tables 15–2, 15–3, and 15–4 show negative long-term flows in 1997 and 1998 for these four countries and the Philippines. For the East Asia/Pacific region as a whole, average monthly capital-market financing was $8.4 billion in the first half of 1997, $6.7 billion in the second half, and about $2.5 billion in 1998.[33]

This is not to say that investors were irrational in removing their money. Many of the region's assets were overpriced, although most of the economies were fundamentally sound. But such asset market bubbles have historically been followed by asset market collapses. Once the process begins, it is likely that investors will overreact, and the market declines will be more drastic than are ultimately warranted. Such a process is self-fulfilling and usually affects not just asset markets but the real economy, creating even worse expectations. The only question is where the bottom is and how long it will take before asset values, and the real economy, can recover.

In this case the crash went beyond Asia, due in part to the collapse of East Asian demand for the imports of other countries. There were already some weaknesses in the Brazilian and, especially, the Russian economies, and the holdings by Korean banks of both Brazilian and Russian bonds sent the financial panic to those markets as well.[34]

Policy Response: The IMF Again

As we have seen, countries enduring an economic crisis must change their policies in an attempt to repair the damage and prevent recurrences. Policy changes are frequently harmful to some domestic interests and can be better tolerated if there is external funding to cushion the shock. For the kinds of problems we are considering here, the IMF is the most likely source of external funding.

Country Responses and the IMF

The policy responses to the crisis were debated by the IMF and its critics.[35]

Financial Sector Restructuring   Regardless of differences in opinion about the East Asian model, everyone agreed that the immediate problem was in the financial sector. But agreement seemed to end there. Those who fingered liberalization as the culprit suggested a return to more government control over the sector, anywhere from merely higher reserve requirements for short-term inflows to a return to government as the principal agent for allocating financial flows. Proponents of liberalization—the IMF among them—pointed to the need for sound supervision and prudential regulation and the discipline of the market to force failing banks to fold or be bought out.

On November 1, in response to IMF pressure, the Indonesian government closed 16 insolvent banks. In December, Korea suspended 9 banks and Thailand closed 56 finance companies that had earlier been suspended. Indonesia's financial restructuring was comprehensive: Institutions holding 18 percent of the nation's assets were closed; the state took over private institutions holding 20 percent; and 7 of the largest institutions, with 54 percent of all assets, were merged into 4. Similar restructurings covered 55 percent of financial assets in Korea and 49 percent in Thailand.[36]

Closing failed banks is supposed to boost confidence in the rest of the banks, and it was a key element in the Fund's attempts to reestablish confidence in national banking systems. Clearly, in the long run, insolvent banks make the financial system unworkable. Some critics have maintained, however, that the closings made things worse by increasing distrust in remaining banks, causing a run on deposits that endangered those that were still sound, which in fact happened in Indonesia.[37] There is also concern that restructuring the banking sector will be used as a way for industrialized countries to get their own banks into the picture by opening up FDI in that sector.[38]

Monetary Policy   Further, in order to address the economic conditions brought on by bankruptcies and general slowdown, the usual questions of macro policy were raised. Ordinarily, recessions call for expansionary fiscal and monetary policies, especially if current accounts are in rough balance and inflation is minimal or, in this case, caused by higher import prices stemming from devaluation. The Fund had other priorities: A typical reaction to falling currencies is to raise interest rates to reverse the capital outflow, and that is what the IMF prescribed.

But high interest rates contract the economy and exacerbate firms' debts to the point of more bankruptcies.[39] The percentage of business firms unable to pay their current debt obligations in Indonesia rose from 13 in 1995 to 58 in 1998; from 9 percent to 34 percent in Korea, from 3 percent to 34 percent in Malaysia, and from 7 percent to 30 percent in Thailand.[40] In Malaysia, bankruptcies increased from 50 per month in 1996 to over 350 per month in 1998.[41]

If capital flight was to some extent irrational, or based on herd behavior, higher interest rates might be beside the point. One review suggests that Indonesia and Thailand, which accepted the high-interest-rate medicine, fared worse than Malaysia, which did not.[42] The former chief economist at the World Bank contends that financial crises are more likely to be associated with high interest rates than depreciating currencies.[43] But the IMF believes high interest rates are necessary to reassure markets, after which they can safely fall, as occurred in Thailand.[44] Of course, opponents of financial liberalization are not sure that a fresh inflow of short-term capital, prone to leave at a moment's notice, is what was called for.

The Fund maintains that there were no good alternatives. Its 1999 study admits that the extent of the downward pressure on exchange rates was unanticipated and that monetary tightening did hurt the economy in Thailand and Korea, although not in Indonesia. On the other hand, firms that had heavy foreign debts were subject to severe damage from exchange rate depreciation, so higher interest rates made sense as an attempt to minimize that damage.[45]

Fiscal Policy   Fiscal policy too was an area of disagreement. In Latin America in the 1980s, fiscal tightening was necessary. Budget deficits, and the money needed to finance them, were one source of the demand for imports that were well in excess of exports. One step removed, deficits were also feeding the inflation that caused real exchange rate appreciation and further exacerbated the trade deficits. But in many Asian countries, current account deficits were small enough and inflation had not been a problem. Budgets were already in balance. Why tighten fiscal policy?

The IMF wanted even smaller current account deficits and was concerned about the impact of imported inflation on the governments' ability to finance reform in their financial sectors. But as its own study admits, the recessions resulting from capital flight and fiscal stringency were far deeper than anticipated. Another critic points out that, unlike Mexico where in 1995 the U.S. import demand helped recovery, there was now no similar pull because the regional economic power, Japan, was itself in bad shape and unable to draw exports from the damaged economies.[46] The original IMF fiscal targets in the November Indonesia program were relaxed in January and June of 1998. The Thai program in August was modified in February and again in May.

Role of Foreign Lenders   Another strong criticism of the IMF approach has been its failure to acknowledge in a meaningful way that there are two sides to every loan: While Asian financial institutions borrowed at low interest rates from Western banks, those banks should take responsibility for their failure to monitor their lending efforts. The same argument had been made in the 1980s, and many banks eventually suffered losses on their Latin American lending. If bank supervision was inadequate in borrowing countries, perhaps it was also inadequate in lending countries. The private organizations such as Moody's and Standard and Poor that issue ratings of the security of government bonds clearly failed to foresee the Asian crash, downgrading those ratings only after the crisis hit.[47]

This implies that IMF programs should parcel out the damage to borrowers and lenders alike. In the IMF program for Korea, the government took over the liabilities of the failing banks, thereby ensuring that creditors would get repaid at higher interest rates, although not necessarily on time. The IMF says this was an essential, but temporary, step to prevent financial collapse. Others have argued that some losses on both sides would have been acceptable, or that more rescheduling should have taken place, to encourage more careful lending in the future.[48]

Capital Controls: Can They Help?

While almost all governments have shown a willingness to allow capital to flow into and out of their economies, arguments remain over a key issue. Should governments have some controls over the flow of capital, especially short-term capital, to reduce the problems of unregulated inflow and the chances of uncontrolled outflow in emergencies?

The economic mainstream has little doubt: An IMF staff study was summarized for the public in a pamphlet that concludes that controls are generally unwise because "it is not financial liberalization that is at the root of the problem but rather weak management in the financial sector and inadequate prudential supervision and regulation, whose consequences are magnified by liberalization."[49] What is needed is more accurate information to lenders about their targets; specifically, international banks need to be "more accurate in assessing the riskiness of their interbank lending, in particular their loans in emerging markets."[50] Aside from these micro-level considerations, sound fiscal policies should reduce the emergence of deficits requiring large foreign borrowing, and monetary policies should be ready to raise interest rates as needed to discourage needless panic-led sales of local currency. Banking systems need to be well run before opening up wide to foreign capital flows. Another author concludes that historically capital controls have not worked: They "are easily circumvented, encourage corruption and, in most historical episodes, have not helped the economic adjustment process."[51] The IMF notes that Thailand attempted capital controls in May of 1997 and they did not work.[52] By then the situation was too far out of hand.

But the Malaysian government disagreed and on September 1, 1998, went against the grain. Having stayed away from the IMF during the crisis, it proceeded to impose some controls on capital movement: Overseas trading in Malaysian securities was banned, foreign investment in Malaysian securities could not be taken out for a year, nonresident currency transactions were banned, among other things. In February, the ban on removal of short-term investments was replaced with a graduated tax: 30 percent on profits taken out before a year, 10 percent otherwise.

The IMF has taken a cautious stance toward what they casually term such "nonstandard" responses to currency crises.[53] It notes that Malaysia was subject to unusual circumstances: Short-term corporate debt was extremely high—178 percent of GDP at the end of 1997 compared to 145 percent in Thailand and 76 percent for Indonesia—so corporate vulnerability to the standard high-interest-rate recommendation was considerable. Malaysia therefore hoped to use controls to permit looser monetary (and fiscal) policies. In fact, from the first quarter of 1997 to the period of highest interest rates, Malaysian rates increased only about 3 percentage points, as opposed to 9 in Thailand, 12 in Korea, and 62 in Indonesia. And the IMF also admits that controls did not appear to be harmful: Malaysia successfully floated a $1 billion international bond issue in May of 1999, showing considerable investor confidence in the country. The economy is recovering and the authorities were able to fix the rate of the ringgit above its previous low point.

The IMF is not, however, ready to admit that controls are therefore good in an emergency or even that the Malaysian policy has worked. It says that controls were carried out after much capital had already left; that Malaysia is also strengthening discipline in its financial sector; that other currencies in the region are rising. And besides, Malaysia's recovery could conceivably have been stronger without the controls. The jury, according to the IMF, is still out.

The IMF as World Economist

After the protests against the WTO in November 1999 (Chapter 12), the scene shifted to the IMF and World Bank in Washington in April 2000 (Chapter 13) and again in Prague in September. The Asian crisis has become one of the focal points for this debate. A major figure in the attack on the IMF has been Joseph Stiglitz, who was the chief economist at the World Bank from 1996 until November 1999.[54]

Stiglitz does not stop at criticizing the IMF for identifying the wrong problem (crony capitalism rather than excessively rapid financial liberalization) and posing the wrong solution (austerity). He returns to the 1980s critique that the Fund ignores country-specific issues in favor of an ideological fervor for free markets at any cost, and he adds from his experience on the front lines that IMF leaders are impervious to even the most reasoned arguments and willing to change course only after their policies have had disastrous results.[55] The battle continues.

Cleaning Up After the Storm

Case 15–2 summarizes some of the key aspects of the financial crisis in Thailand. Although the worst seems to be over, this is most noticeable in the financial sector, where some stock prices and exchange rates have begun to recover. As Figure 15–2 shows using IMF data, however, the inflation-adjusted GDP of Indonesia and Thailand have sustained substantial damage. In 1999, their output was still below 1995 levels.

Inflation resulting from currency depreciation raised the prices of food and medicine at the same time that unemployment was increasing rapidly, creating a class of what is being called the "newly poor" while inflicting greater hardship on those already poor.[56] Although good data are scarce, the hard-won gains against poverty in the region have certainly been reversed. The poverty rate in Indonesia rose from 11.3 percent in 1996 to 20.3 percent in 1998, according to the World Bank. Devaluation increased the price of imported components, adding to bankruptcies and lost jobs.

Again, indications are that women are being hit hardest. They are fired first to protect male jobs and are also concentrated in small export firms. Devaluation should eventually help exports, but many require imported components that have become much more expensive. Even where safety nets exist, as in Korea, many women are not eligible. The UN reports women and children being hurt most by malnutrition, girls being hit first by cuts in health care and education, and an increase in the number of daughters being sold into prostitution in some countries.[57]

CRISIS AND THE IMF IN THAILAND

FAST FACTS

On the Map: Southeast Asia

Population: 60 Million

Per Capita GNI and Rank: $2,010   (103)

Life Expectancy: Male—67   Female—71

Adult Literacy Rate: Male—97%
Female—93%

The first currency to fall, and the first IMF program to be introduced, was in Thailand. On August 20, 1997, less than six weeks after the baht was devalued, the IMF approved a program that called for almost $17 billion in assistance from a combination of the IMF, World Bank, and governments of several countries including Japan and China but not the United States. The main elements of the program included restructuring of the financial sector, fiscal stringency (a small budget surplus), and control over domestic credit in order to raise interest rates. The fiscal and monetary adjustments were made, but progress toward financial restructuring was held back by what the IMF called "delays in the implementation of . . . reforms, political uncertainty, and initial difficulties in communicating key aspects of the program."

Within two months the IMF realized that deterioration of the economy was "more pronounced than anticipated." Still, its first reaction was to tighten macro policy "to help stabilize the exchange market situation." While the baht turned around in early 1998, GDP was falling. So fiscal policy was permitted to become expansionary, including greater spending on social safety net items such as unemployment compensation, although monetary policy was to stay tight to maintain the turnaround in the baht. The result was "stronger-than-expected foreign ex-

change reserves, but a deepening recession." Interest rates were then permitted to fall.

A year following the devaluation, exports remained stalled but imports had undergone a "sharp compression" due to the recession. The financial sector restructuring was, in the Fund's words, "complicated by growing difficulties in the corporate sector," meaning that the recession had so greatly hurt the economy that the banks could not be established on a sound footing. While financial restructuring was not all the IMF expected, 56 finance companies were shut down in the first year. The government nationalized four banks as a prelude to selling them to foreign investors. The Fund responded by calling for even more corporate restructuring, plus increased privatization and foreign ownership, and also spending on measures to help cushion poverty.

Meanwhile, sales of Thai companies to foreign investors have increased. Banking and finance, retail trade, automobiles, and cement now have a more noticeable foreign presence. But as late as May 1999, less than 20 percent of bad loans had been "restructured," which means that by far the majority are still in trouble.

GDP was stagnant in 1999, but the current account had a $12 billion surplus. Thailand used only $14 billion of the $17 billion allocated but has not drawn on it since June 1999. Thailand has switched to a flexible exchange rate. In early 2000 the Fund declared the program a success, and GDP grew by more than 6 percent that year. In addition to recovery, the banking system has been provided with additional government funds while "an enhanced prudential framework" is being put into place. The Fund said it was concerned about the "continuing high level of nonperforming loans," which could become a problem if not taken care of.

Sources: Timothy Lane and Marianne Schulze-Ghattas, "Overview" in Lane et al., "IMF-Supported Programs in Indonesia, Korea, and Thailand: A Preliminary Assessment," Occasional Paper No. 178 (Washington: International Monetary Fund, 1999), pp. 1–8; Laurids S. Lauridsen, "Thailand: Causes, Conduct, Consequences," in Jomo K. S., *Tigers in Trouble: Financial Governance, Liberalisation and Crisis in East Asia* (New York: Zed Books, 1998), pp. 137–161; Jon E. Hilsenrath and Pichayaporn Utumporn, "Asian Turmoil Forced Restructuring in Thailand," *Wall Street Journal*, July 2, 1999; and IMF, "IMF Concludes Article IV Consultation with Thailand," Public Information Notice 00/5 (February 10, 2000), at ⟨www.imf.org/external/np/sec/pn/2000/PN0005.htm⟩.

Recovery and Its Discontents

Recent data from the Asian Development Bank indicate that all four countries increased GDP in 1999, although in Indonesia the increase of 0.2 percent left per capita GDP lower.[58] Amid indications of modest recoveries in Asia and Latin America, there are concerns that some of the underlying causes are unresolved. Currency values have rebounded, yet restructuring has ground to a halt in Thailand and Korea, leading to some concern that lessons will not be learned.[59] Some are worried that nationalizations meant to hasten restructuring are instead becoming a new round of government interventionism, and government spending is increasing to maintain some social stability in the crisis. Estimates of the cost to governments of bailing out the banks

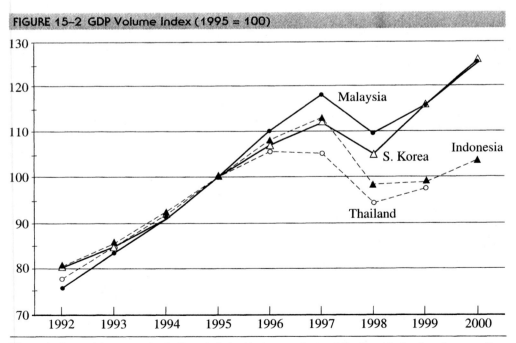

FIGURE 15–2 GDP Volume Index (1995 = 100)

The main four crisis economies in East Asia had been growing rapidly through the decade preceding the crisis. Starting in 1997 for Indonesia, and 1998 for the others, real GDP fell precipitously before resuming growth.

Source: IMF, *International Financial Statistics.*

are $164 billion—60 percent of GDP—in Korea, $51 billion—45 percent of GDP—in Thailand, and $37 billion—50 percent of GDP—in Indonesia.[60]

The downturn in the United States and global economies in 2000 to 2001 has removed a key element of the Asian recovery—the demand for exports—and currency values are falling again. In Indonesia, the recovery is slow and corporate debt is still high. In South Korea, healthy growth at the macro level may be undermined by inflation (including oil prices) and resistance to restructuring by the *chaebols*, as indicated by failed attempts to find buyers for Daewoo Motors and Hanbo Iron and Steel.[61]

THE EAST ASIAN CRISIS AND THE EAST ASIAN MODEL

This brings us back to the question we asked at the beginning of the chapter. Did the Asian model fail because of international financial markets? Had it gone too far? Or, perhaps, is it now just taking a new turn?

How Has Government Direction Been Implicated?

While government direction has in many cases proven successful, it has spawned the inevitable conflict of interest between those pushing individual sectors and the overall national strategy. In South Korea, at least, output is highly concentrated in a small number of firms, and the relationship between government officials and corporate officials has gotten too cozy, as frequently occurs with government regulation. Thus, governments have too easily funded excess capacity, failed to force failing firms into bankruptcy, and failed to effectively oversee financial institutions. Government officials have taken advantage of their positions to profit from the economic activity they are supposed to be guiding.

It is this dimension of the model that has been particularly vulnerable to the liberalization of financial markets and international capital flows during the 1990s. South Korea began the liberalization process early in order to gain acceptance into the OECD. Government officials still, however, allowed credit to be given to firms in the steel, auto, and petrochemical industries that were already suffering from global excess capacity. Thai officials had financial ties to much of the speculative activity in real estate that benefited from foreign lending. And members of the ruling Suharto family in Indonesia were tied to many of the manufacturing and financial corporations that were being threatened with closure.

On the other hand, small to medium-sized economies like those in East Asia are not likely to have room for too many firms of a size needed to compete in world markets. And if there are few firms in some of these industries, some government monitoring and regulation might be essential. The open question is how to strike the balance between the market and regulatory oversight.

Did Financial Liberalization Fit the Model?

The role of financial liberalization has been crucial in the crisis. But rather than an indication of the model's failure, some claim that it was in fact a departure from the model that was working reasonably well on its own. Macro stability, emphasis on agriculture, education and exports, and mildly positive interest rates got the Asian economies where they were. The question is then whether some of these economies had matured to the point where they should have become more market oriented. Some answer that question by noting that the crisis has wrecked two of the less interventionist economies—Thailand and Indonesia—while leaving relatively un-scathed two of the best examples of the model, Taiwan and Singapore.[62] Nor has China, still a highly state-oriented economy with closed capital markets, been affected.

Globalization of Financial Markets: How Far?

Is the free flow of capital throughout the world a viable concept? While almost no one suggests that countries return to highly restricted capital markets, the skeptics suggest there is room for significantly more caution among countries than implied by the IMF push toward a barrier-free world. In a major broadside against all-out liberalization, in which many of the supposed benefits are denied, John Eatwell still supports the general trend while suggesting countries take some steps to reduce the volatility that has come with large, sudden short-term inflows. Jagdish Bhagwati, one of the world's most vocal proponents of free trade, says there are circumstances in which countries should be cautious because financial markets are subject to panics and self-justifying speculation that can hurt even countries with sound economic fundamentals. Even the IMF, before the recent crisis but after Mexico's problems, suggested that "during times of surges in inflows, a country might consider measures to influence the level and characteristics of capital inflows," including borrowing restrictions and taxes on short-term foreign bor-rowing.[63] Others have suggested very high reserve requirements on such inflows.

Lessons from the Crisis

Economists and public officials will continue to debate how well the Asian model per-forms and how far financial liberalization can go. However, most agree on three key lessons. One is the necessity of strong prudential regulation and supervision of finan-cial institutions.[64] This is not something that can be left until later. It must accompany (if not precede) deregulation. Second, the nature of capital inflows is important. The short- vs. long-term impact of the volatility of flows and their susceptibility to sudden reversals are crucial considerations. Whether stricter banking regulations will suffice, or whether high reserve requirements or taxes on short-term capital flows are useful, will be determined only through trial and error. Third, what happens to the money when it enters a country is important. Even more than normal domestic lending, the viability of projects financed with foreign lending and its ability to generate foreign exchange for repayment must be closely watched.

The question of exchange rates is still open. Arguments over fixed or flexible or bands (ranges) of flexibility around a pegged rate come into play here. Complete flexi-bility leaves currency markets vulnerable to the same destabilizing flows that trig-gered the Asian crisis. The cost of pegging, in addition to being tied to somebody else's economic fundamentals, was clear in the lack of hedging or insurance against rate changes. When crisis comes, even bands have to be abandoned.[65]

SUMMARY AND CONCLUSION

The growth of international trade and financial transactions is pushing us toward a more global economy. As liberalization of international capital markets and national financial sectors has proceeded, developing countries are having to cope with unregu-lated surges of capital into and out of their economies.

Crises in Chile in the early 1980s and Mexico in the mid-1990s have warned us about the need for sound supervision and regulation of financial sectors, and the problems of borrowing abroad for risky investments at home. The Asian crisis of 1997 shows that these lessons have not been well learned.

Asian countries borrowed short term in foreign currencies and lent long term at home, often in speculative ventures with no foreign exchange potential. When their markets collapsed, contagion caused a broad crisis.

The IMF solutions of financial sector restructuring and fiscal and monetary tightening may have gone too far or even been counterproductive in the short term, although the Fund contends they were ultimately the right set of policies. Asian economies are recovering, but preventing a recurrence will depend on what lessons are learned and what long-term solutions are accepted. It is not clear whether the East Asian development model is partly to blame or whether financial liberalization to such an extent was incompatible with that model.

Key Terms

- contagion (p. 472)
- globalization (p. 457)
- hedging (p. 468)
- herding (p. 459)
- industrial policy (p. 456)
- pegging (p. 463)

Questions for Review

1. How did the liberalization of capital markets change the nature of capital flows to developing countries during the 1990s?
2. What is herding behavior, and how did it contribute to the financial crisis in Asia?
3. What are some of the aspects of the East Asian model of development? What role did they play in the crisis?
 4. Why, in spite of generally good macroeconomic performance through 1996, did South Korea, Indonesia, and Thailand face a crisis in 1997?
5. In the following areas, what was the IMF approach to the crisis, and what were some of the objections:
   a. Liberalization of financial markets
   b. Monetary policy
   c. Fiscal policy
   d. Capital controls
 6. What conditions did the IMF require of Thailand in order to provide its rescue package? What policy failures were these conditions meant to address?
7. What is "prudential regulation" of financial sectors, and how does it differ from government "intervention" in financial markets discussed throughout the book?

Related Internet Resources

 Visit the IMF Web site at ⟨www.imf.org⟩ for references to its policies during the height of the Asian financial crisis. The Asian Development Bank keeps track of the progress of those economies most directly affected at ⟨http://aric.adb.org/⟩. For an outside commentary on the crisis, see Nouriel Roubini's Web site at the Stern School of New York University, ⟨www.stern.nyu.edu/~nroubini/asia/AsiaHomepage.html⟩.

Endnotes and Further Readings

1. World Bank, *East Asia: The Road to Recovery* (Washington: World Bank, 1998).
2. Hak K. Pyo, "The Financial Crisis in South Korea: Anatomy and Policy Imperatives," in Karl D. Jackson, ed., *Asian Contagion: The Causes and Consequences of a Financial Crisis* (Boulder, CO: Westview Press, 1999), p. 159.
3. See Joseph Stiglitz, "Some Lessons from the East Asian Miracle," *World Bank Research Observer* 11, no. 2 (August 1996), pp. 151–178.
4. See World Bank, *East Asia: The Road to Recovery*, and Kevin Watkins, *Economic Growth with Equity: Lessons from East Asia* (Oxford: Oxfam, 1998), chapter 7.
5. See Jomo K. S. et al., *Southeast Asia's Misunderstood Miracle: Industrial Policy and Economic Development in Thailand, Malaysia, and Indonesia* (Boulder, CO: Westview Press, 1997), especially pp. 154–156.
6. See Benjamin R. Barber, *Jihad vs. McWorld* (New York: Times Books, 1995); Michael Veseth, *Selling Globalization: The Myth of the Global Economy* (Boulder, CO: Lynne Rienner, 1998); Thomas L. Friedman, *The Lexus and the Olive Tree* (New York: Garrar, Straus and Giroux, 1999); and a symposium on "Globalization in Perspective," in the *Journal of Economic Perspectives* 12, no. 4 (fall 1998), pp. 3–72.
7. Barry Eichengreen and Michael Mussa et al., "Capital Account Liberalization: Theoretical and Practical Aspects," Occasional Paper No. 172 (Washington: International Monetary Fund, 1998), pp. 5–7.
8. See John Eatwell, "International Liberalization: The Impact on World Development," ODS Discussion Paper No. 12 (New York: United Nations, 1997), p. 11, and John Williamson and Molly Mahar, "A Survey of Financial Liberalization," Essays in International Finance No. 211 (Princeton, NJ: Princeton University, November 1998).
9. John Eatwell, "International Liberalization: The Impact on World Development," pp. 13–24.
10. Eichengreen and Mussa, "Capital Account Liberalization: Theoretical and Practical Aspects," pp. 12–14.
11. Susan Schadler et al., "Recent Experiences with Surges in Capital Inflows," Occasional Paper No. 108 (Washington: International Monetary Fund, 1993).
12. See Guillermo A. Calvo, Leonardo Leiderman, and Carmen M. Reinhart, "Capital Inflows and Real Exchange Rate Appreciation in Latin America: The Role of External Factors," *International Monetary Fund Staff Papers* 40, no. 1 (March 1993), pp. 108–151; Roberto Steiner, "Capital Inflows in Latin America: Causes, Consequences, and Policy Options," in International Monetary Fund, *Policies for Growth: The Latin American Experience* (Washington: IMF, 1995), pp. 81–104; and Morris Goldstein, *The Asian Financial Crisis: Causes, Cures, and Systemic Implications* (Washington: Institute for International Economics, 1998), especially p. 13.
13. United Nations Conference on Trade and Development, *Trade and Development Report, 1998* (New York and Geneva: United Nations, 1998), p. 57.
14. This experience is discussed in Chapter 5. For a brief summary, see Annex I to Chapter III of Part One in the 1998 UNCTAD, *Trade and Development Report*.
15. See Sebastian Edwards, *Crisis and Reform in Latin America* (New York: Oxford University Press/World Bank, 1995); Guillermo A. Calvo and Enrique G. Mendoza, "Petty Crime and Cruel Punishment: Lessons from the Mexican Debacle," *American Economic Review* 86, no. 2 (May 1996), pp. 170–175; Jonathon Sapsford, Craig Torres, and David Wessel, "Ailing Asian Countries Might Hunt for Cures in a Surprising Place," *Wall Street Journal*, December 9, 1997; and J. A. Kregel, "East Asia Is Not Mexico: The Difference Between Balance of Payments Crisis and Debt Deflation," in Jomo K. S., ed., *Tigers in Trouble: Financial Governance, Liberalisation and Crisis in East Asia* (London: Zed Books, 1998), pp. 44–62.
16. Guillermo Ortiz Martinez, "What Lessons Does the Mexican Crisis Hold for Recovery in Asia?" *Finance & Development* 35, no. 2 (June 1998); also on the Web at ⟨www.imf.org/external/pubs/ft/fandd/1998/06/ortiz.htm⟩.
17. Jose De Luna-Martinez, "Management and Resolution of Banking Crises: Lessons from the Republic of Korea and Mexico," World Bank Discussion Paper No. 413 (Washington: World Bank, 2000).
18. "IMF Approves US$17.8 Billion Stand-By Credit for Mexico" (February 1, 1995), ⟨www.imf.org/external/np/sec/pr/1995/PR9510.HTM⟩, and "IMF Welcomes New Mexican Economic Measures" (March 10, 1995), ⟨www.imf.org/external/np/sec/nb/1995/NB9508.HTM⟩.
19. See Gustavo H. B. Franco, "The Real Plan and the Exchange Rate," Essays in International Finance, No. 217 (Princeton, NJ: Princeton University, April 2000), and Maurisio Carrizosa, Danny Leipziger, and Hemant Shah, "The Tequila Effect and Argentina's Banking Reform," *Finance & Development* 33, no. 1 (March 1996), pp. 22–25.
20. Pyo, "The Financial Crisis in South Korea: Anatomy and Policy Imperatives," pp. 159–160.
21. See Giancarlo Corsetti, Paolo Pesenti, and Nouriel Roubini, "What Caused the Asian Currency and Financial Crisis? Part II," at ⟨www.stern.nyu.edu/~nroubini/asia/AsiaHomepage.htm⟩, p. 7, and David Dollar and Marcy Hallward-Driemeier, "Crisis, Adjustment, and Reform in Thailand's Industrial Firms," *World Bank Research Observer* 15, no. 1 (February 2000), pp. 1–22.
22. C. P. Chandrasekhar and Jayati Ghosh, "Hubris, Hysteria, Hope: The Political Economy of Crisis and Response in Southeast Asia," in Jomo K. S., *Tigers in Trouble: Financial Governance, Liberalisation and Crisis in East Asia*, pp. 63–84.

23. See Corsetti et al., "What Caused the Asian Currency and Financial Crisis?" pp. 4–6, and Richard F. Doner and Ansil Ramsay, "Thailand: From Economic Miracle to Economic Crisis," in Karl D. Jackson, ed., *Asian Contagion: The Causes and Consequences of a Financial Crisis*, pp. 171–208.

24. See De Luna-Martinez, "Management and Resolution of Banking Crisis: Lessons from the Republic of Korea and Mexico," p. 5.

25. Vinod Thomas et al., *The Quality of Growth* (New York: World Bank/Oxford University Press, 2000), pp. 118–119.

26. Goldstein, *The Asian Financial Crisis: Causes, Cures, and Systemic Implications*, p. 11.

27. UNCTAD, *Trade and Development Report*, p. 63, and "Golfonomics: Asia in the Rough," *The Economist* (December 20, 1997), pp. 85–87.

28. Dollar and Hallward-Driemeier, "Crisis Adjustment and Reform in Thailand's Industrial Firms."

29. Pyo, *The Financial Crisis in South Korea: Anatomy and Policy Imperatives*, p. 156.

30. World Bank, *East Asia: The Road to Recovery* (Washington: World Bank, 1998), p. 9.

31. Data are from the World Bank's *Global Development Finance 1999* (Washington: World Bank, 1999), p. 33.

32. See Taimur Baig and Ilan Goldfajn, "Financial Market Contagion in the Asian Crisis," IMF *Staff Papers* 46, no. 2 (June 1999), pp. 167–195, and Lawrence H. Summers, "International Financial Crises: Causes, Prevention, and Cures," *American Economic Review* 90, no. 2 (May 2000), pp. 1–16.

33. World Bank, *Global Development Finance 1999*, p. 28.

34. Goldstein, "The Asian Financial Crisis: Causes, Cures and Systemic Implications," p. 18; Bob Davis, Jonathan Friedland, and Matt Moffett, "As Currency Crisis Spreads, Need of a Cure Grows More Pressing," *Wall Street Journal*, August 24, 1998; and Anthony Faiola, "Brazil's Ills Spread Like a 'Samba' Fever," *Washington Post National Weekly Edition*, February 8, 1999.

35. See Timothy Lane et al., "IMF-Supported Programs in Indonesia, Korea, and Thailand: A Preliminary Assessment," Occasional Paper No. 178 (Washington: IMF, 1999).

36. World Bank, *Global Economic Prospects 2000*, p. 85.

37. Kregel, "East Asia Is Not Mexico: The Difference Between Balance of Payments Crisis and Debt Deflation," p. 59.

38. *The Economist*, "New Illness, Same Old Medicine" (December 13, 1997), and Sara Webb, "Asian Banks Are Being Snapped Up as Foreign Firms Seek Attractive Deals," *Wall Street Journal*, June 9, 1999.

39. UNCTAD, *Trade and Development Report*, p. 70, and G. Pierre Goad and Darren McDermott, "IMF's Dose of High Rates Hurts Asia, Economists Say," *Wall Street Journal*, June 18, 1998.

40. World Bank, *Global Economic Prospects 2000*, p. 77.

41. Accessed at ⟨www.worldbank.org/prospects/gep2000/slideshow/tsld017.htm⟩.

42. Yilmaz Akyuz, "The East Asian Financial Crisis: Back to the Future," in Jomo K. S., *Tigers in Trouble: Financial Governance, Liberalisation and Crises in East Asia*, pp. 33–43.

43. Joseph E. Stiglitz, "Knowledge for Development: Economic Science, Economic Policy, and Economic Advice," in Boris Pleskovic and Joseph E. Stiglitz, eds., *Annual World Bank Conference on Development Economics 1998* (Washington: World Bank, 1999), pp. 9–58. This comment appears on p. 26.

44. Bob Davis and David Wessel, "World Bank, IMF at Odds Over Asian Austerity," *Wall Street Journal*, January 8, 1998.

45. Atish Ghosh and Steven Phillips, "Monetary and Exchange Rate Policies," in Lane et al., "IMF-Supported Programs in Indonesia, Korea, and Thailand: A Preliminary Assessment," pp. 35–55.

46. Paul Krugman, "Saving Asia: It's Time to Get Radical," *Fortune* 138, no. 5 (September 7, 1998), pp. 74–81, and "The Confidence Game: How Washington Worsened Asia's Crash," *Revista de Economia Politica* 19, no. 1 (January–March 1999), pp. 205–208.

47. Joseph Stiglitz, "What Caused Asia's Crash? Bad Private-Sector Decisions," *Wall Street Journal*, February 4, 1998, and *The Economist*, "Risks Beyond Measure" (December 13, 1997), pp. 68–71.

48. Lane et al., "IMF-Supported Programs in Indonesia, Korea, and Thailand: A Preliminary Assessment," pp. 69–70; David Wessel, "Korean Bailout Raises Tough Questions," *Wall Street Journal*, December 26, 1997; and Goldstein, *The Asian Financial Crisis: Causes, Cures, and Systemic Implications*, p. 39.

49. Barry Eichengreen and Michael Mussa et al., "Liberalizing Capital Movements: Some Analytical Issues," Economic Issues No. 17 (Washington: IMF, 1999), p. 8. The pamphlet is largely a condensation of Occasional Paper 172.

50. *Ibid.*, p. 9.

51. Sebastian Edwards, "How Effective Are Capital Controls?" *Journal of Economic Perspectives* 13, no. 4 (fall 1999), p. 82.

52. Eduardo Lachica, "Asian Capital Controls Were No Panacea," *Wall Street Journal*, January 12, 2000.

53. IMF, *International Capital Markets: Developments, Prospects, and Key Policy Issues* (Washington: September 1999). The section on Malaysian controls is on pp. 98–101.

54. See Stiglitz, "Knowledge for Development: Economic Science, Economic Policy, and Economic Advice," and "What Caused Asia's Crash? Bad Private-Sector Decisions." Also see Marcus Walter and Paul Hofheinz, "Prague's Subdued Protests Score Points," *Wall Street Journal*, September 25, 2000.

55. "The Insider: What I Learned at the World Economic Crisis," *The New Republic*, April 17, 2000. This may

be accessed at ⟨www.thenewrepublic.com/041700/stiglitz041700.html⟩.

56. World Bank, *East Asia: The Road to Recovery*, chapter 5, and Kevin Watkins, *Economic Growth with Equity: Lessons from East Asia* (Oxford: Oxfam, 1998), chapter 7.

57. United Nations, *1999 World Survey on the Role of Women in Development: Globalization, Gender and Work* (New York: United Nations, 1999).

58. See the Asian Development Bank's "Asia Recovery Report 2000, May Update, at ⟨http://aric.adb.org/external/arr2000/arr_may.htm#menu⟩.

59. Darren McDermott, "For Asia, Recovery Carries a Peril," *Wall Street Journal*, October 22, 1998; Robert Frank, "Asian Firms May Be Forgoing Reform Too Soon Amid Climbing Stocks and Signs of a Recovery," *Wall Street Journal*, April 28, 1999; and Michael Schuman, "Korea's Fast Recovery Suggests That Reform Isn't the Only Answer," *Wall Street Journal*, May 14, 1999.

60. Michael Schuman, "Asian Governments Bid Adieu to Invisible Hand," *Wall Street Journal*, August 24, 1998, and McDermott, "For Asia, Recovery Carries a Peril."

61. See Robert Frank, "Suddenly, Southeast Asia's Recovery Looks Dubious," *Wall Street Journal*, June 13, 2000; Erik Guyot, "Asian Currencies Falter on Export Worries," *Wall Street Journal*, November 27, 2000; Jeremy Wagstaff, "World Bank Is Worried About Indonesia,"

Wall Street Journal, October 16, 2000; Jay Solomon, "Jakarta Says Loan Misuse May Cost $16 Billion," *Wall Street Journal*, August 5, 2000; and Michael Schuman, "Big Korean Firms Sicker Than Thought," *Wall Street Journal*, August 2, 2000, and "Will Half-Finished Reforms Jeopardize South Korea's Rebound?" *Wall Street Journal*, October 12, 2000.

62. UNCTAD, *Trade and Development Report*, p. 75.

63. Eatwell, "International Liberalization: The Impact on World Development," and his "Rejoinder" in Isabelle Grunberg, ed., "Perspectives on International Financial Liberalization," ODS Discussion Paper No. 15 (New York: United Nations, 1998), pp. 60–68; Jagdish Bhagwati, "Yes to Free Trade, Maybe to Capital Controls," *Wall Street Journal*, November 16, 1998; and David Wessel, "IMF Urges Developing Nations to Study Controls on Inflows of Foreign Capital," *Wall Street Journal*, August 22, 1995.

64. See, for example, Joseph E. Stiglitz and Amar Bhattacharya, "The Underpinnings of a Stable and Equitable Global Financial System: From Old Debates to New Paradigm," *Annual World Bank Conference on Development Economics 1999* (Washington: World Bank, 1999), pp. 91–130.

65. See John Williamson, *The Crawling Band as an Exchange Rate Regime: Lessons from Chile, Colombia and Israel* (Washington: Institute for International Economics, 1996).

CHAPTER

16

LESSONS LEARNED AND OPEN QUESTIONS

Relevance in economics depends on its being integrally tied up with the fundamentals of institutional history.
—FRANK H. KNIGHT (1885–1972)

The rate of growth at a given time is . . . rooted in past economic, social, and technological developments rather than determined fully by the coefficients of our equations.
—MICHAEL KALECKI (1899–1970)

INTRODUCTION

We have surveyed the economic problems faced by developing countries and the kinds of policies that governments have used to solve them. The record of development is mixed. On the discouraging side, income levels in some countries have stagnated or declined. In 1990, more than a billion people had standards of living below those existing in Western Europe and the United States 200 years earlier.[1]

On the other hand, from 1960 to 1990 the developing countries, on average, nearly doubled their income levels, and some have quintupled their incomes. Overall developing-country growth has been positive even during the 1980s when many African and Latin American countries slid back, because Asian countries, including China and India, continued to grow. Tables 16–1 and 16–2 show that, along with higher levels of output, social indicators have shown significant improvement: Between 1960 and 1999, infant mortality rates have been cut more than in half, from 149 to 59 per thousand; life expectancy has increased from 46 to 64. From 1970 to 1999, the crude birth rate of the developing world has fallen from 38 to 24 per thousand, faster than the death rate's drop from 13 to 9; adult illiteracy has fallen from 54 percent to 18 percent for males and 32 percent for females.

It is useful now to pose the following question: Why do developing countries deserve their own course? Why not just a general course in economic policy or public policy?

We will approach the question from two perspectives. The first is that of the discipline of development economics, asking what people who have called themselves

TABLE 16–1 Average Annual Growth of GDP per Capita

	1980–1990	*1990–1999*
All Developing Countries	3.5	3.5
Low-Income Countries	4.7	3.2
Middle-Income Countries	3.3	3.5
High-Income Countries	3.4	2.3

Source: World Development Indicators 2001.

TABLE 16–2 Progress in Social Indicators

Indicator	*1960*	*1999*
Infant Mortality Rate (per 1,000)	149	59
Life Expectancy	46	64
	1970	*1999*
Crude Birth Rate (per 1,000)	38	24
Crude Death Rate	13	9
Adult Illiteracy (%): Overall	54	
Male		18
Female		32

Sources: World Development Report 1982 and World Development Indicators 2001.

development economists thought they were doing and how well they may have done it. Second, we cover a debate that has been simmering for years and is now boiling over: Why have some countries apparently made the transition from poor societies to modern economies while others have not, looking specifically at what can and should be learned from the experience of the rapidly growing economies of East Asia.

DEVELOPMENT ECONOMICS

In the opening chapter we introduced a distinction between *economic development* and *development economics*: The question for the latter is not what is involved in the process of development, but what is the nature of the discipline that studies this process and how well have we done in that study.[2]

We define development economics as the branch of economics that studies the process of growth and structural change in those countries whose economic structure does not match that of the more industrialized countries; where economies are less completely absorbed in market relations, and where, therefore, the usual economic principles must be rethought as they are applied. This definition is broad but useful because it allows us to investigate all aspects of economic change in a large number of countries that differ from others in their structure and position along a continuum from premarket to market relations.

Development Economics as a Distinct Topic

Should development economics be a separate topic? Much of this debate has revolved around some form of the argument made by Albert O. Hirschman (of "unbalanced growth" fame) that early development economists believed they should downplay the neoclassical, competitive market in analyzing developing countries. They felt there had to be a different type of analysis for countries where large-scale rural unemployment and **fragmented markets** hinder the process of industrialization. More recently, development economists have considered market failure and to what extent government should substitute for markets or help create markets. Development historians Irma Adelman and Cynthia Taft Morris agree that the rigidities that hinder transfer of resources among sectors was the key problem that early development economists thought required solutions.[3] These early writers accepted the idea that international trade and aid could eventually mobilize the resources necessary to make the transition, but meanwhile, developing economies had to make special efforts to overcome the lack of effective market mechanisms. The implication was that a far greater government role was required for successful development in the late twentieth century.

The initial challenge to this position came less from the neoclassically oriented economists themselves than from a group that Hirschman and others have loosely called neo-Marxists. Neo-Marxists considered development economics to be too *accepting* of mainstream economic constructs and unrealistically wedded to international cooperation within a capitalist system. Their focus on inequality, both within countries and internationally, pointed to a major problem that neither neoclassical nor development economics had successfully understood or addressed.

As Hirschman saw it in 1981, development economists became discouraged by having no easy answers for either the successes or failures of different developing economies. More than economics was important, but without the ability to make a leap outside the discipline, some development economists withdrew into fairly technical issues, and others expanded into broader questions surrounding income distribution and basic human needs.

The argument that developed and developing economies should be approached somewhat differently was continued by W. Arthur Lewis, whose article on the surplus-labor economy has been described as "perhaps the single most influential article in the history of the economics of development."[4] Lewis rejected the argument that a lack of functioning markets, creating a divergence of prices from marginal social costs and imposing structural constraints on growth, requires a separate development economics. However, he believed that in economies not fully integrated into the market, production and exchange are carried out within the bounds of cultural assumptions that diverge from the usual economic ones of profit and utility maximization. Governments then play a large role in such economies, but they tend not to be representative, nor do they function efficiently.

This means that fertile ground remains for development economics. We are still unable to explain why some countries are better than others at raising savings-income ratios or how entrepreneurship develops. A greater historical emphasis is necessary to understand how developing-country institutions affect economic incentives. To evaluate success and failure, Lewis called for incorporating the insights of political science and social psychology, and for possibly giving up the idea of finding a single unifying theory of economic development that fits all places and times. We have to learn how a society "learns, chooses new directions, creates new loyalties, faces up to costly tasks, and so on. . . ."[5]

Progress in the Discipline

Development economists believe they have arrived at some worthwhile answers to some crucial questions about the development process. How well have they done?

Growth and Development

Development economics has been unable to completely disentangle growth and development. Perhaps the easiest distinction is the one made in Chapter 1: Growth is simply more production, an outward shift in the Production Possibilities Frontier, while development involves a change in the structure of production or changing the shape of the frontier. While the two are different, most economists insist that development will not occur without growth. Development economics originally looked for simplistic answers to such basic questions as how to increase investment (e.g., the Big Push) and how to best allocate investment (e.g., maximize linkages). They assumed the existence of untapped resources in developing countries (labor, for Lewis, capital and entrepreneurship for Hirschman) and searched for ways to put these resources into motion.[6]

When confronting the requirements for economic growth, Lewis started at a basic level. Given a certain level of resources, "the fundamental requirements of growth are water and internal peace."[7] Each country has its own optimal rate and path of growth, which change over time. A crucial problem in Lewis's view is that in some countries the struggle for political gain has taken precedence over the struggle for economic progress. So the operation of political systems becomes a critical issue.

At a higher level of specificity, we believe that growth requires the ability to mobilize saving and to use it for productive investment. For the most part, high savings and investment rates are present in countries that have achieved high growth rates. Although high savings-to-GDP ratios are somewhat associated with growth, this may be deceiving because saving is partly the result of growth and may be supplemented by outside resources. Still, saving is a crucial requirement for growth, so we study why some countries have been able to save much more than others.

We are probably better off suggesting that from a macro perspective, high investment-to-GDP ratios accompany and help cause growth,[8] and note that the proper allocation and productivity of capital are crucial questions. So development economics has shifted from a more aggregate emphasis (Harrod-Domar and Big Push approaches) to a greater appreciation of the sources of improved productivity. High investment rates in the Soviet Union, Brazil, and elsewhere have sometimes had disappointing results: We need to invest efficiently, thereby reducing the ICOR at the micro level. By some estimates, 20 percent to 30 percent of developing economies' growth can be attributed to more efficient allocation of resources.[9] This permits lower ICORs: more output with less investment. Reallocation along with better human capital and improvements (imported or homegrown) in technology contribute to increases in **Total Factor Productivity (TFP)**, the portion of increased output that is due to more productive resources rather than an increase in the amount of labor and capital applied to production. Nevertheless, there are still a number of questions about how to develop policies for attracting investment and for allocating investable resources in an economy with significant market fragmentation. The increasing attention to the environmental impact of investment projects widens the analysis of costs and benefits, both for the present across national and regional economies and for the future.

Development and Income Distribution

Jagdish Bhagwati maintains that despite allegations of growth fixation, early development economists believed that growth combined with land redistribution and human capital investment would reduce poverty: Most were concerned with poverty from the beginning.[10] Some followed Simon Kuznets in believing that there was a natural course of inequality: worsening in the early stages of development but improving thereafter. Newer studies show no evidence for such a natural course, so the implications of income and wealth distribution now have a more important status in the explanation of a country's ability to develop.

It is clear that growth does not always trickle down from the rich. Rapid growth for two decades worsened Chile's Gini coefficient, from 0.46 to 0.58,[11] while the Indian province of Kerala has taken great strides in reducing inequality without achieving a very enviable growth record. It ranks first among India's 15 states in human development but tenth in per capita output.[12] On the other hand, "a more equitable distribution of assets at the start of the growth process will generally imply that the new incomes will, in turn, be distributed better...."[13] This is more easily said than done. For example, land reform as a way of creating greater equality of assets has proved difficult to accomplish.

Population

Although population growth remains problematic in some areas, particularly Africa, economists advise integrating family planning with investments in human capital. There is some culturally based opposition to birth control, but pragmatic action, such as in Bangladesh and Indonesia, has often overcome this difficulty. Development helps reduce population growth rates.

In the 1950s some feared that spending on health and education was in the nature of consumption and therefore competed with physical capital investment. We now accept investment in both physical and human capital as complementary and necessary.

Agriculture

Many economists and politicians interested in development made the mistake of underestimating the role of agriculture and the need for policies to ensure that farmers would have incentives to produce more and to produce more efficiently. The emphasis in the 1950s and 1960s on industrialization was misplaced. While industrialization remains a significant goal of the development process in most countries, it must have a strong agricultural base if it is not to be undercut by the need to import food.

The pessimism of some early development economists that developing-country farmers (and workers generally) were irrational—would not respond to price incentives as we might expect—proved incorrect. While there is much research left to be done on the workings of rural markets for land and labor, household consumption, and producer risk, we now focus on understanding how market responses are conditioned by institutions that are often unfamiliar to outsiders. Inequality matters here too, because equitable land distribution improves farmers' incentives and productivity.

Technology

Economists have always believed, without being able to formally show, that technology change is a key ingredient to growth and development. While early models addressed changes in the quantity of capital and labor as generators of growth, tests usually showed large unexplained residuals that economists attributed to technological change, embodied in new capital equipment. The Solow growth model treated technology as an exogenous factor, while recent growth models have brought technology into the picture as a kind of factor of production, one that is noted for bringing increasing returns. Technological change can be fostered directly through government activity or subsidies, or indirectly by encouraging firms to import or adapt newer technologies and by providing appropriate training. The Green Revolution is generally recognized as an outstanding example of how technology can be developed and incentives provided to foster its adaptation. Incentives to create and/or adapt new technologies are now recognized as a key element in the growth equation.

Attention shifted in the 1970s to appropriate, or intermediate technology (IT), to make better use of an economy's resources. Some claim that, despite its benefits, IT has been disappointing so far because manufacturing processes remain fairly rigid. Governments frequently refuse to fund IT projects if output does not seem to be as great for the same spending as for a modern technology[14] or when anything less than the most modern equipment is seen as indicating an economy's second-class status. Certainly, those countries that have emphasized exports have searched for technologies that would be internationally competitive, even if they were not precisely "appropriate" for the country's resource base. Nevertheless, a significant amount of technological adaptation has taken place.

Market and Government

Development economics' original focus on government action to overcome market failure was extremely useful for understanding the limitations of the market mechanism, especially externalities. It also stressed the problem of fragmented markets and in so doing highlighted the importance of creating the institutions, including property rights, contract law, and banks, that would allow markets to function effectively.

The fact that a number of governments' attempts to forcefully direct the development process were unsuccessful and even detrimental to growth and development spurred a counterrevolution that emphasized the likelihood of government failure.[15] Earlier faith in the ability of governments to plan development in any formal and precise way has given way to an appreciation of specific interventions that governments can make in certain areas associated with human capital investments, legal and social infrastructure, incentives for acquisition of technology and learning, and its responsibilities for maintaining fiscal discipline and systems of taxes that minimize market distortions. Most development economists now have a healthy respect for the productive force of the private sector—formal and informal—and a sense that most prices should be determined by market forces to the degree that those forces imply reasonable competition.

Many sense, however, that this counterrevolution has gone a bit far. Opening the World Bank's Annual Conference on Development Economics in 1993, I. G. Patel cautioned, for example, that government borrowing for capital projects makes sense even if the result is a budget deficit; that some subsidies for the poor should be allowable and it may be cost-effective to make them generally available if mainly the poor benefit; and that financial markets are sensitive enough in every country to warrant some government intervention over and above simple prudential regulation.[16]

Problems such as risk and inadequate information cause market imperfections that call for government action. Bankers and other financial market agents may not be interested in funding new industries that require untried technologies. In such cases, in spite of numerous problems of directed credit, government or government-directed finance can make economic sense.[17]

The debate between neoclassical economists and development economists has often been biased against government. For example, the debate on whether development strategy should be outward or inward oriented (discussed in the next section) opposed markets to governments: Because inward-oriented strategies were all accompanied by strong government intervention, it was often assumed that outward, or export-oriented, strategies were therefore examples of market principles at work; whereas, in fact, governments are actively involved in outward-oriented strategies. The fact that such government policies tended to work with, rather than against, market forces is crucial, but it does not negate the strong government role.

Outward vs. Inward Orientation

After long debate among development (and other) economists, it appears that much of the export pessimism associated with Raul Prebisch and others was unfounded. Terms of trade have deteriorated for many developing countries, but this is a serious problem mainly for those specializing in a relatively small number of primary products. Those countries that have succeeded have been exporters of manufactures, although there is disagreement about whether there would be room for many more countries to succeed on that basis simultaneously. Chinese competition in the 1990s has certainly given other East Asian countries something to think about.

On the other hand, successful exporting countries usually began with important barriers to foreign goods and investment. They eventually shifted to policies that promoted exports, but they were strengthened by their initial protectionism. Therefore, the question of outward vs. inward is often a matter of degree and timing rather than a pure strategy.

While some countries have grown at acceptable rates with long periods of bias against imports, the temptation to persist with such a strategy is greater for larger countries (India, Brazil, China), and all have suffered from considerable inefficiency associated with large-scale government intervention and protection from foreign competition. The debate has now shifted to whether the neoclassical emphasis on markets is correct in calling for a neutral export *facilitation* strategy or whether the experience of the successful countries may in fact call for a more interventionist export *push* strategy.

Contributions to Economics

Development economists have tackled some issues that are applicable to all economies but had not received detailed study. These include policy analysis, planning models, cost-benefit analysis, reform of tax systems and trade restrictions, and price reform to remove market distortions. Much of this research has formed the basis of more general economic knowledge.[18]

NEW FRONTIERS: GOVERNANCE AND INSTITUTIONS

In the late 1980s, two experienced development economists suggested that development economics should move on to a better understanding of how policy is determined.[19] If the development path is paved with appropriate government policies, and if we can separate the successes from the failures on this basis, the next step is to find out what accounts for the ability or inability of governments to adopt the appropriate policies. Now political economy is in fashion.[20]

At least three questions are important here. One is the nature of specific government mechanisms that enable good policies to be introduced and sustained. A second has to do with the contributions of institutions of government itself to development. The third is whether democratic regimes are better than authoritarian regimes for promoting development.

Mechanisms of Government: The Developmental State

Beginning in the 1990s, economists and others have applied statistical techniques—at times using dubious data—to see if institutions matter to economic growth (if not development) in any provable way. Given the difficulties of measuring institutions, the results can be questioned, but this aside, the answer appears to be "yes."[21] One of those institutions is effective government, where effectiveness means the ability to implement policies and mechanisms that provide incentives for growth and development to take place. These include market mechanisms, land reform, education and training, stimulus to technological innovation, macroeconomic stability, and a capable and honest bureaucracy.

The concept of the "developmental state" has been created to identify specific government mechanisms.[22] This is a government that has sufficient authority and credibility to apply specific policies to favor firms and industries that are deemed important for development.

Government must first be able to reward successful firms with tax breaks, subsidies, infrastructure investment, and other benefits. What separates the successful state from one that is simply a mechanism for dispensing favors is the ability to decide who gets these favors on the basis of national strategy rather than on the personal gains of government officials (unless the two coincide). And it will withdraw those favors from firms that do not accomplish their agreed goals. There is, of course, no magic formula for creating such government mechanisms, although a previous history of shared values seems to be a good start. And, unless the whole system—including monetary and tax authorities—is perceived as legitimate and responsible, even these mechanisms might not work.[23] The debate over "crony capitalism" in East Asia illustrates the difficulty of maintaining a successful developmental state over long periods.

A closely related question is how a government can implement reforms for an economy that needs them. We have already noted, in the areas of tax and trade reform, that questions of the speed and sequence of reforms are crucial. In addition, however, is the credibility of the government. A government with broad credibility and support can afford to go more slowly, especially if it begins with those elements of reform that have broad benefits. Otherwise, a more leisurely pace could give more time for opposition and result in derailment of the reforms.[24]

Political economy furthers this discussion by asking about the circumstances under which politicians will support policy change, especially if such change might be politically unpopular, how institutions affect these choices, and how new institutions are created.[25] One approach emphasizes politicians' self-interest: Will they aim for the next election, or are there forces that push them to support policies with long-term benefits even if they are costly in the short run? Another draws on the disciplines of sociology and political science to look at the influence of institutions and groups on policy decision making. These questions are in their infancy.

The Contribution of Institutions

The success of some developmental states is being increasingly attributed to more fundamental aspects of society: the basic institutions of civil society and the trust of the population. We have discussed the need for secure property rights, and security implies the honest, competent, and reliable administration of justice. Such an institutional structure is difficult to quantify, but we can tell when it is absent.

A recent review of the growing literature on institutions and development finds problems of defining and measuring institutions, not to mention finding a correlation with economic growth. But there are some commonalities and interesting findings. It appears so far that efficient and honest government bureaucracies, combined with secure property rights, may be able to permit greater investment that, allocated efficiently, can improve economic growth.[26] Although a far cry from what used to be considered development project work, there is now increasing attention to these matters. Harvard Law School is coordinating a review of property registration systems in five Central American countries. The World Bank, in one of its new policy directions, has provided funding for Judicial Reform Projects in Ecuador, Peru (later canceled), Guatemala, and Georgia over the 1996 to 1999 period.[27]

As we might expect, competent institutions, and the public's trust in them, take a long time to grow. There is now a fashionable emphasis on the buildup of **social capital**, the informal networks of trust that people create in their neighborhoods and communities, and eventually extend to larger political entities.[28] In most countries, the period in which that trust can build up is measured in decades if not centuries. In those countries that have been independent only for 40 years, only the most stable societies with historical continuity from the preindependence period would be likely to have succeeded at this stage. Where countries had little political history before independence and where civil strife has been significant, as in many parts of Africa, these institutions are not functioning well and sometimes break down completely.

While quantification is premature, it is easy to understand why the attempts of newly independent national governments, even when led by the heros of independence, may be unsuccessful. In spite of the presumed benefits of having governments create, and temporarily substitute for, absent markets, it is clear that bigger often means worse: "Clearly it is important initially to match the state's role to its capabilities,"[29] and those capabilities have often been quite minimal.

Democracy and Civil Liberties

At least since the early 1960s, when Robert Heilbroner painted a picture of development requiring wrenching social change, many economists and others have believed that successful development would require at least temporary authoritarian rule. Much of the economic progress in South Korea and Taiwan, not to mention Chile after 1973, took place under various forms of repressive government. On the other hand, dictatorships in North Korea and Albania, as well as more benign one-party rule in some African countries, produced little in the way of economic advance. The extent of economic freedoms in successful developers varied from virtually none in China to directed development in South Korea to virtually laissez-faire in Hong Kong and Chile, always with the proviso that labor organization was not tolerated.

What about political freedom, that is, democratic governance and civil liberties? Democracy was accused of inviting corruption, labor unrest, and giving in to consumption rather than imposing a discipline permitting savings.[30] The new interest in governance has sent some economists looking for statistical relationships between economic growth and democracy, using various measures relating to elections and civil liberties.

One 1995 study concluded that economic growth was normally accompanied by economic freedom (individual property rights) and democracy. A 1998 study suggests that "democratic" regimes have faster GDP growth.[31] In explaining some of the results, other studies have linked political variables to economic factors. One found that civil liberties in African countries increased the responsiveness of workers to economic incentives, allowing migration to areas of higher wages. Another found that economic reforms meant to stabilize inflationary situations were carried out more effectively under democratic regimes because crisis helped create a consensus that supported reform measures. A third concluded that civil liberties are more likely to encourage education, thus furthering the accumulation of human capital.[32]

A lot of clarification is necessary on such issues. Yet evidence so far suggests that democracy and civil liberties can contribute to development. It may be that a particular level of social and economic progress is necessary before democratic institutions can take hold, but it may also be that most nations have already reached that point.

DEVELOPMENT POLICY: PROGRESS AND QUESTIONS

A large and increasing amount of the literature in development economics is directly relevant to policy. Debates about theory are often also debates about policy: what may or may not contribute to successful development. The progress—or lack thereof—of various countries is continually charted (with data of varying reliability, of course).

Progress and Stagnation

We started the chapter with an overview of the progress of developing countries as a group. But the variation among countries is perhaps even more striking than the overall record. Table 15–1 provided the rates of growth of per capita income over the period 1970 to 1999. In the 1970s, while the high-income countries suffered periods of stagflation associated at least in part with oil price increases, many developing countries borrowed their way into continued growth. Only a lower population growth rate leaves the high-income performance comparable, but this is expected for mature economies. Of more significance is the variation among developing-country groups, with the East Asia/Pacific region clearly outpacing the others, and South Asia and Sub-Saharan Africa at the bottom but still with positive per capita growth rates.

The story of the 1980s and 1990s is more of a contrast. The East Asia/Pacific region *improved* its performance, as did South Asia, while performance in other regions deteriorated, including negative per capita growth in Sub-Saharan Africa and many countries of the Middle East, North Africa, Latin America, and the Caribbean. It is apparent that a country such as South Korea can come from being extremely poor to nearly a world-class economy in less than two generations, while others have made little if any progress. We have noted a number of the causes of growth suggested by economists: high investment ratios and government policies in the areas of trade, technology, and human capital. All of this can be applied to the current debate over the East Asian "miracle."

East Asia: Model or Miracle?

Economists are not prone to speak in terms of "miracles." But the East Asian development model before the financial crisis of the late 1990s produced economic growth rates that, when compared with other developing countries and the industrialized countries, seemed miraculous. Once it became clear that this was not the result of free market approaches but of government working actively with the market, the search was on to determine what policies were responsible.

In the meantime, however, the nature of the "miracle" itself came under review. The traditional sources of growth are the accumulation and use of productive factors and increased productivity of those factors. One source of greater productivity was observable in the reallocation of resources to export industries. Another, closely associated with this, was the switch from lower to higher productivity industries. Resources devoted to semiconductors give a higher value of output than those devoted to textiles.

Such changes would help these economies increase Total Factor Productivity.[33] However, the focus on productivity improvements has been strongly challenged by recent studies that have attempted to separate out, statistically, the sources of East Asian growth. The first, by Alwyn Young in 1995,[34] concluded that the main sources of growth in Taiwan, South Korea, Singapore and Hong Kong were increased supplies of labor and capital, improving the quality of labor through education, and shifting labor from agriculture to manufacturing. TFP growth outside of agriculture was good but nothing "miraculous" (Table 16–3). A 1996 article by Susan Collins and Barry Bosworth extended a similar analysis to the southern tier of Indonesia, Malaysia, the Philippines, and Thailand, and came to the same conclusions. Recent commentary, while acknowledging that Young's data are "quite controversial," agrees with the conclusions.[35]

So what? The fact of East Asia's growth remains. Does it matter what the sources are? If our objective is to learn *how* countries grow and develop, it does. To know how policy affects growth, we should understand the path from policy to economic causes to economic effects. If productivity is the link, the prospects for the

TABLE 16–3 Total Factor Productivity Growth

Country	Period	TFP Growth
Taiwan	1966–1990	2.6
Hong Kong	1966–1991	2.3
South Korea	1966–1990	1.7
Singapore	1966–1990	0.2
Brazil	1950–1985	1.6
Chile	1940–1985	6.8
Mexico	1940–1985	1.2
West Germany	1960–1989	1.6
Japan	1960–1989	2.0
United States	1960–1989	0.4

Source: Alwyn Young, "The Tyranny of Numbers: Confronting the Statistical Realities of the East Asian Growth Experience," *Quarterly Journal of Economics* 110, no. 3 (August 1995), pp. 641–680.

future depend on tapping the sources of productivity—resource allocation, learning, technology, and so forth—and these may have continuing potential. But if the link is the accumulation of productive resources, different policies are relevant and the strategy may well run into diminishing returns sooner rather than later.

The World Bank's Explanation

While among the general public the World Bank is often considered a supporter of government-oriented development, the orientation of its lending has in fact been, for at least the last 20 years, biased toward reliance on the market. It has accepted specific government roles that are common worldwide—building physical infrastructure, investing in health and education—but it has persistently put the private sector squarely in the center of development strategy.

Yet, when it comes to analyzing the success of many East Asian economies, the accumulated evidence has convinced almost everyone of the crucial role played by governments in actively fostering and directing outward strategies. The Bank's initial reluctance to officially recognize this situation eventually annoyed one of its key contributors, the government of Japan, whose own economic success was often considered to be a model for East Asia, most noticeably South Korea and Taiwan. Japan had to put up its own money—over $1 million—to have World Bank staff do a study of the "East Asian Miracle." That study, published in 1993 under the title *The East Asian Miracle: Economic Growth and Public Policy*, proved extremely controversial.[36]

Development Spotlight 16–1 lists the countries that the Bank has lumped together as the High-Performing Asian Economies (HPAEs), together with their rates of growth of per capita GDP over a quarter of a century. The newly industrializing economies of Indonesia, Malaysia, and Thailand have become high-performing economies only over the last 15 years or so, while the four "tigers" have experienced success over the last 35 years. The Bank study noted that high rates of output growth were combined with slowing population growth; a dynamic agricultural sector (except

DEVELOPMENT SPOTLIGHT 16–1

HIGH-PERFORMING ASIAN ECONOMIES

Category	Country	*Growth Rate 1960–1985 Per Capita GDP (%)*
Longtime High Income	Japan	3.0
The "Four Tigers"	Hong Kong	3.4
	South Korea	3.2
	Singapore	3.3
	Taiwan	3.6
Newly Industrializing	Indonesia	3.5
	Malaysia	1.6
	Thailand	1.5

for Hong Kong and Singapore) becoming a smaller portion of economic activity; and, equally as impressive, greater equality of income.

What policies accounted for such performance? The study distinguished between two types of government policies. The foundation consists of legal structures conducive to private activity, government investment in education and health, and stable macroeconomic performance (i.e., low inflation) and is not controversial. But the Bank included some government intervention, its first official admission that some departure from market strategies can work under specific circumstances. The interventions used by East Asian governments were (a) promotion of specific industries, (b) "mild" financial repression (i.e. somewhat below-market, but still positive real interest rates) combined with some government allocation of credit, and (c) export push policies. The Bank accepted, with limitations, financial repression and export push policies.

Financial Repression and Allocation of Credit

The World Bank now admits that in the East Asian case some departure from strict market-oriented credit allocation was beneficial. The argument had been made by Joseph Stiglitz and Alice Amsden that subsidized, or below-market, interest rates (or deliberately getting the interest rate "wrong") could at times put credit to more socially productive purposes.[37] The Bank study, citing early policy in Korea and Taiwan and more current policies in Malaysia, agreed that some subsidization of interest rates, combined with either government lending or government requirements for private lending, "appear to have improved credit allocation, especially during the early stages of rapid growth."[38]

The study warned that such a course is becoming increasingly difficult in the more highly integrated world capital market: Any significant, sustained undercutting of interest rates will lead to capital outflows. As it turned out, financial liberalization led to quite the opposite: a surge of capital inflows, precipitating the crisis in 1997. And, as we have seen, a disciplined approach to monitoring the boundary between internal and external capital markets has had some success in Malaysia.

Export Push

With respect to export-promotion policies, the Bank now goes beyond the neutral policies championed earlier to lend some credence to the more activist attempts to promote exports. The study suggests that governments provided special incentives to exporters or potential exporters, such as tariff rebates on their inputs, some protection of their products, and subsidized credit but within well-defined guidelines. The guidelines required that export targets be met: Firms had to meet international competition through adaptation of efficient technology, continuous product improvement, and successful marketing. If a firm failed to meet targets, incentives were withdrawn.

The Bank and others have warned that the ability of developing countries to continue these policies successfully is in doubt because they have become increasingly unacceptable to the industrialized countries. Through new requirements in the WTO and requirements of adjustment programs through the IMF and the Bank itself, industrialized countries are less willing to tolerate subsidies, dumping, patent pirating, and performance requirements on foreign investors.[39]

The World Bank's Warnings

The study insisted that these policies could work only to the extent that they took place in a "market-friendly" environment with a stable macroeconomy, a legal system conducive to the workings of the private sector, the dominance of private investment decisions, and openness to foreign investment and technology. They required a competent, independent civil service that could hold private companies to strict performance standards in exchange for government assistance, and could halt programs that did not work or became too expensive but nevertheless was willing to work constructively with the private sector. But while the Bank admits reluctantly that a government-directed development could work for awhile in a few places, it insists that these were exceptional cases and the usual noninterventionist (i.e., neoclassical) policy conclusions remain valid. More recently, a Bank-sponsored study maintains that industrial policy in Korea and Japan may have increased growth rates by a maximum of one percentage point under the best of circumstances[40]—hardly the type of vindication the Japanese government sought for its million dollars.

Criticisms of the Bank's Analysis

The Bank's study immediately came under fire for the tentativeness of its conclusions about the role of the government and for ignoring crucial elements of the East Asian experience. All agree that stable macroeconomic conditions, flexible markets, and a dynamic private sector were, and should continue to be, crucial to successful development. Rather, the critics have suggested that the Bank has consistently underplayed the role of the state and overstated the difficulties of reproducing what happened in these countries.

The Role of Equity

The Bank study notes with approval that the HPAEs have achieved greater equality of income while growing rapidly. The problem to some, however, is that the Bank views this greater equality largely as a *result* of the particular type of growth achieved and does not acknowledge it as an important *cause*. Stephan Haggard, a political scientist, notes that much of the current state of income distribution existed before the growth "miracle" began, due to either lack of a strong landholding or commercial class or to vigorous government action to redistribute landholdings.[41] Dani Rodrik, in an article whose title portrays the battle between the World Bank and East Asia as "King Kong vs. Godzilla," notes the early equality in both income and landholdings as well as initially high levels of education. Running his own statistical tests, he suggests that equality and education are associated with high growth: Without them, the growth performance would have been quite ordinary. The significance of seeing a more equal distribution of income as result instead of cause is clear: If it is a result, we need merely grow in the right direction to achieve it. If it is a cause, some government intervention would likely be necessary to bring it about first, in order to achieve high growth.[42]

Industrial Policy

Of the three sorts of policies the Bank study identifies as having been given credit for East Asian growth, it clearly rejects one of them: policies to promote specific industries, or industrial policy. It concludes that there is no evidence that government policies such as South Korea's promotion of heavy and chemical industries (HCI) changed the sectoral distribution of output beyond what the market mechanism would have achieved alone, or that they improved Total Factor Productivity. But Robert Wade, whose earlier work on Taiwan has been an important reference on policies in the region, rejects the standards set and the methods used by the World Bank to reach its conclusions. He also says the Bank's claim that the Korean textile industry expanded more rapidly than HCI despite lack of government promotion is actually incorrect: Textiles received considerable promotional efforts.[43]

Rodrik pointed out a logical flaw in the Bank's rejection of governments' promotion of specific industries: It accepts as successful, in varying degrees, the *instruments* of industrial policy (financial repression, special treatment for exports), without recognizing that the *targets* of those instruments were precisely the specific industries that the Bank claims were not helped. If the instruments are considered useful, they must have achieved their goals.

Wade contends that the Bank's objections involve a misunderstanding of what industrial policy means in East Asia. In academic and policy discussions in the West, industrial policy has been popularly associated with government attempts to *predict* high-tech industry "winners" and then promote them through protective devices and subsidies. East Asian practice, however, has been to look for industries that policy makers *want* to play a key role in development, on the basis of their current and potential linkages, and then to use trade, investment, and technology policies to promote those industries. The targeted industries have not been speculative high-tech ventures but rather "postadolescent or midtech industries" whose development is economically and technically feasible.[44] This is all very reminiscent of "unbalanced growth."

The Validity of Export Push as a Strategy

The World Bank report has continued the debate we discussed in Chapter 12: It maintains that exports are one of the keys to development, and recommends policies that will spur exports without causing retaliation. These policies call for freer trade for exporting firms, financial and support services for small- and medium-sized exporters, attracting export-oriented foreign investors, and improving the infrastructure that serves exporters. But others still challenge these conditions. Of the two indicators used by the Bank to associate growth with open economies, Rodrik suggests that one confuses cause and effect while the other one is meaningless. He claims that a thorough review of the evidence still does not substantiate the link between openness and growth.[45]

One examination of this link suggests that the chain of causation runs from growth to exports, not from exports to growth.[46] Whereas the policy of neutral export *promotion* counts on world demand to be hospitable to developing-country exports and pull development along an open path, export *push* is a supply-driven attempt to increase market share, accomplished by investments that create scale economies and incorporate technological advance. In this view, what governments in East Asia have been doing is fostering the kind of development that will lead to exports rather than fostering exports that lead to development.

Governance in East Asia

The emphasis on sound policies, and especially policies that require government intervention, brings us back to the issue of governance: the relationship between economic development and government institutions.[47] The Bank study is fairly clear about this relationship in East Asia: Its leaders "tended to be either authoritarian or paternalistic" but were "willing to grant a voice and genuine authority to a technocratic elite and key leaders of the private sector."[48] While this is far from Heilbroner's vision of a modernizing elite ruthlessly uprooting old traditions, and much different from what are sometimes referred to as "predatory" governments, it nevertheless runs in sharp contrast to recent attempts to link foreign aid to more democratic political performance.[49]

Shared Growth

Crucial to the Bank's acceptance of authoritarian government is its concept of *shared growth*. Shared growth includes first, consultation with and support of business leaders, and second, policies such as land reform, public services, and price incentives to bring people into the market.[50] The first provides benefits directly to the elite and only then to workers, while the second is intended to provide benefits directly to the poor. In return, government leaders and civil servants should be insulated as much as possible from politics and rent seeking. They are then able to set the terms of assistance provided to businesses and extract strict standards of performance for that assistance. The government has the freedom to adjust or cancel policies that do not seem to be working or that threaten fiscal imbalance. One of the reasons that the Bank is pessimistic about the ability of additional countries to follow the East Asian path is pessimism about the ability of other countries to develop the strong government institutions needed to carry out the necessary policies.

Objections to Shared Growth

A number of objections have been raised specifically to the Bank's view of authoritarian government's role in East Asia. The Bank study ignores the question of how governments in those countries were able to push through the policies that are being given credit for growth. Colin Bradford notes that in East Asia after World War II and the Korean War, the need for national security provided a foundation for strong governments, and they were assisted by value systems (such as Confucian be-liefs) that put a greater stress on communal effort than individual success. Haggard documents the point that policy changes were usually preceded by a national crisis: for the Nationalist Chinese government that fled to Taiwan after the Communist vic-tory on the mainland, the postwar regime in a newly divided Korea, and in Indonesia after the overthrow of the Sukarno regime in 1966.[51]

Is the policy support mechanism—government direction but consultation with business—sustainable? Haggard sees greater vulnerability because the initial balance of strength was favorable to governments that were facing weak constituencies: Gov-ernments could pursue programs favorable to specific groups without fear of reprisal from weak and uncoordinated opposition. Will this be as easy in a democracy?[52] Rodrik adds that such consultation has usually consisted of very detailed, complex sets of understandings and that this is at odds with most prescriptions for bureaucratic success that call for simplicity, predictability, and arm's-length transactions.[53]

Haggard also points to a somewhat darker view of authoritarian government than that which pervades the Bank's relatively rosy picture. The Bank is willing to excuse a bit of authoritarianism, at least partly on the grounds that it consults with private busi-ness. He argues that such mechanisms are precisely how modern authoritarian gov-ernments maintain their hold, to the detriment of labor and populist groups. And while he agrees with the Bank that East Asian governments did not deliberately hold down wages, labor organization was suppressed so that labor markets could remain flexible (as the Bank admits) and also in order to attract foreign investment (which the Bank ignores). Labor was kept out of the political arena, and unions were either fragmented or controlled, so even if they could organize they were not allowed to en-gage in real collective bargaining, nor could they strike. The Bank apparently ac-cepted uncritically the view of East Asian governments that labor had to be con-trolled because of its radical tendencies. At no time did it ask if there might not have been some way of incorporating labor into the consultative mechanisms.[54]

The Future of Competent Regimes

While authoritarian regimes are now being democratized in South Korea and Tai-wan, the issues remain relevant in other parts of East Asia and in other parts of the world contemplating the East Asian path. As we have already noted, the Bank study takes a dim view of the prospects for reproducing the East Asian "miracle" elsewhere: The conditions under which the state was able to lead development are not likely to be found elsewhere. But to others, the better approach is to foster those conditions. Haggard would prefer to focus on how to create strong, competent states rather than to say other countries cannot do it. Other countries are now moving in the direction of greater stability in macroeconomic policies: Why not believe they can be successful in allocative policies as well?[55]

The End of the Miracle?

Some of the old doubts about export-led growth are beginning to reemerge as the East Asian countries face recovery from the financial crisis of the later 1990s. Be-cause they all sought the same export markets, troubles in one country led to com-petitive devaluations. We may soon be able to test the thesis that this strategy is lim-ited by the growth of world markets when "too many" countries export. East Asian countries, and their would-be imitators, may now have to pay more attention to internal markets.[56]

It should also be noted that much growth in East Asia has been environmentally destructive. Whether we examine the pollution consequences of industrialization in Taiwan or the rapid exploitation of forest resources in Indonesia, Malaysia, and Thailand, the region's heedlessness of the natural consequences of development will require serious realignment in the twenty-first century.

Will the growing emphasis on democracy make it more difficult for strong states to form, let alone implement, East Asia-type policies? Haggard points to reforming democratic governments in Poland, Argentina, and Bolivia as positive examples. If recent studies showing a link between democracy and growth can be counted on, the best approach now would be to focus on the creation of stable institutions within a democratic setting. The precise mechanisms used by East Asian governments need not be reproduced exactly elsewhere. Historically, countries have established their own institutions and mechanisms, and have succeeded under a variety of circumstances.[57] Nevertheless, there are clearly risks that fragile democracies will not be strong enough for some time to put into place and enforce the kinds of policies that have had a positive impact on development in the more authoritarian East Asian states.

Policy Battleground in Latin America

Latin America has been the focal point of much of the policy debate in economic development, especially with respect to trade strategy, state regulation, and inflation. And while the line between market and state guidance is debated in East Asia, the benefits of liberalizing overregulated economies have been illustrated in Latin America.

A contrast between Chile and Argentina is instructive. Figure 16–1(a–e) shows some comparisons since 1974, which was the beginning of significant restructuring of the Chilean economy. Although Chilean policy has had numerous setbacks, and has heightened inequality, its performance with respect to GDP growth and inflation was superior to Argentina's until about 1990, which saw the beginning of reforms there. Chile began much earlier in liberalizing trade and capital flows, privatizing large state-owned enterprises and maintaining tight control over fiscal and monetary policies. Argentina, in the meantime, avoided market-oriented policies longer and relied on more heterodox anti-inflationary policies.[58]

Much remains in dispute about the Chilean case, largely due to the military overthrow of the Allende government in 1973 and the repressive nature of the Chilean military regime. Chile returned to democratic rule in 1990, compared to Argentina's return in 1983. An article favorable to Chile refers to the results of its first-phase reforms (1974 to 1976) as "impressive," citing among other accomplishments the reduction of employment and wages—hardly a selling point to working people. The longer-term impact of Chile's privatizations on income distribution and poverty is also of considerable concern.[59] Unfortunately, Argentina's attempt to ameliorate the impact of economic adjustment on workers resulted in longer-term harm, which emphasizes the need for a political system that can mobilize popular support for temporarily difficult economic reform.

From a development standpoint, the lessons are clear. Many Latin American countries went too far toward state regulation of the economy. Import-substitution

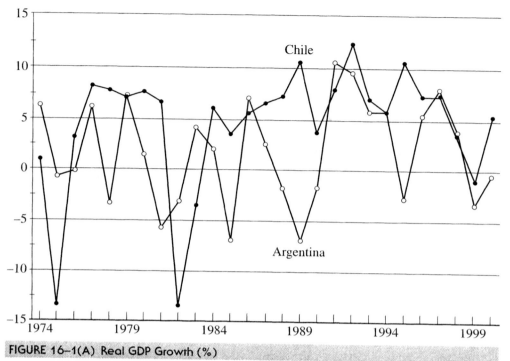

FIGURE 16–1(A) Real GDP Growth (%)

Source: IMF/IFS.

FIGURE 16–1(B) Government Surplus/Deficit (% GDP)

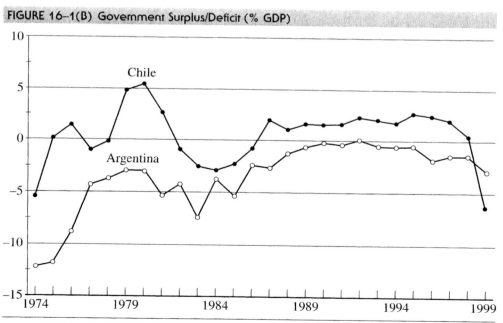

Source: IMF/IFS.

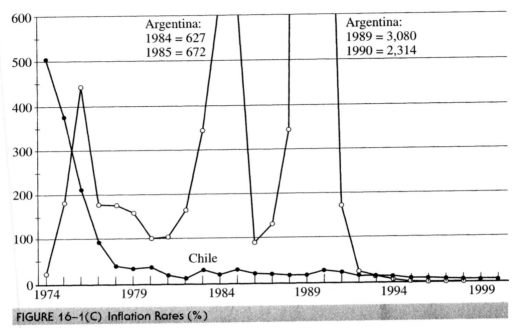

FIGURE 16-1(C) Inflation Rates (%)

Source: IMF/IFS.

FIGURE 16-1(D) Merchandise Trade Balance (Millions)

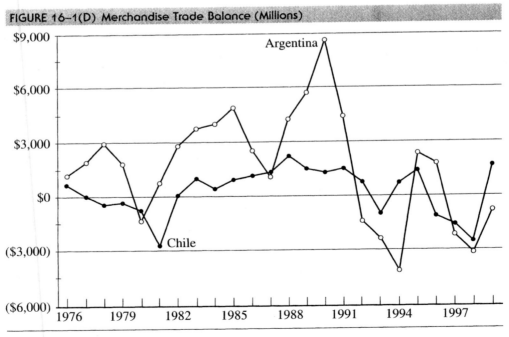

Source: IMF/IFS.

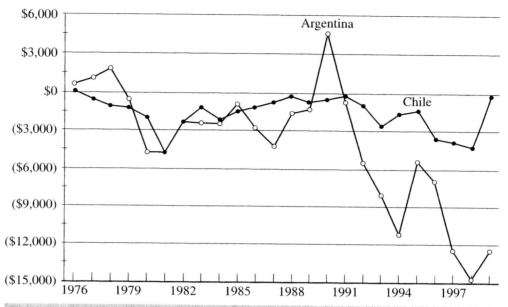

FIGURE 16–1(E) Current Account (Millions)

Chile has sustained better macroeconomic performance than Argentina over the last few decades. GDP has usually grown faster and, until recently, inflation was markedly lower. The government has usually maintained a budget surplus, although in the last 10 years Argentina's deficits have been small. Argentina's merchandise trade has often shown greater surpluses than Chile's, but Argentina's current account deteriorated seriously during the 1990s, due to large services imports and outflows of investment income.

Source: IMF/IFS.

policies to a large extent delayed, rather than hastened, the development of efficient domestic industry. Excessive government spending, financed by money creation, was counterproductive of macroeconomic stability, even though some impressive growth statistics were turned in by Brazil and other countries for a number of years. While East Asian countries have justified interventionist government that works with the market as a development strategy, many Latin American countries showed just how damaging state intervention could be when it worked too much against the market for too long.[60]

Latin America has a sharply lower percentage of saving to GDP than in East Asia. A recent study shows that private savings in Latin America has been hurt by slow growth, less financial deepening, and government contributions to social security programs, as well as by a high age-dependency ratio. Government savings are also low, due partly to low growth, political instability, and reliance on foreign capital. Government policies are truly crucial to successful development.[61]

The revival of many large Latin American economies in the 1990s is an example of what greater emphasis on the market can bring. How far down the new economic progress will trickle and how stable the new economies will remain are still open questions, however.[62]

Whither Africa?

Governance is part of the broader relationship between the economy and other institutions of society that raises the question of whether the East Asian experience is reproducible outside the region.

By just about every measure economists have, African countries are on average doing worse than those in other regions. And while AIDS has devastated some African economies in recent years, the problems preceded the epidemic. In 1990, for example, Africa enrolled only two-thirds of its primary school-age children, compared to 80 percent for Asia in 1965. Half of African adults had not achieved basic literacy in 1990, while only a third of Asians were illiterate in 1965.[63] One reason economists commonly give is that African governments stayed too long with the model of import-substitution and state enterprise that other regions were abandoning. But why were they not as effective, and why did they hold on for so long?

In his provocatively titled article, "Why Is Africa Eating Asia's Dust?" journalist Keith Richburg noted that many Asian and African countries achieved independence at roughly the same time and had had somewhat similar experiences with colonialism.[64] Although starting out slightly ahead and without a legacy of slavery, Asian peoples had ethnic rivalries, small fragmented markets, official corruption, authoritarian governments, and the misfortune of serving as proxies in the U.S.-Soviet rivalry. Yet, as Table 15–1 shows, economic policies have produced growth in East Asia but not in Africa, while changes in economic structure and income distribution are also more favorable in East Asia.

Although better use of market institutions is one part of Richburg's response, the main thrust of his conclusion is that African leaders, in attempting to follow the public policy prescriptions popular in Europe, ignored indigenous cultural experience. Asians, on the other hand, held on to their cultural heritage, including traditions that rewarded education, hard work, acceptance of social hierarchy, and sacrifice of some individual gain to the goal of a larger community. And while Richburg does not attempt to show that Africans' cultural heritage was in fact the same as that of Asians, nor indicate how an indigenous African development approach might have worked, he has focused attention on the possibility that development economists have missed something crucial in their analyses.

The evolving literature on institutions feeds into this strain of thought. If the African continent was more ethnically and politically fragmented—a situation that was reinforced by colonial administration—national governments that took control after independence were no guarantee of true cultural unity or social capital. Political power was barely sufficient to temporarily maintain national economies in countries such as Nigeria, Congo (Zaire), Liberia, Ghana, and Rwanda, and only somewhat more effective in Kenya, Tanzania, Zimbabwe, and others. Following the pattern of Yugoslavia, which split up after the death of its national hero, Tito, about 50 years after becoming a nation, many African countries were unable to develop national institutions to survive local differences.

Some African commentators have objected to the antigovernment tones they hear emanating from the World Bank and the IMF. They argue that governments do not need to be taken out of the picture, but instead need strengthening to do the work of market creation and support in a way that will earn the trust of the population.[65] Creation of social capital will be even more imperative in the wake of the AIDS epidemic, which has undone gains in health and economic development in general. And while social capital consists largely of networks among private individuals and groups, these can be counterproductive without a stable legal framework, which only an effective government can provide.

FINAL QUESTIONS

Clearly, economics captures only part of the development question. Yet economic analysis may still be brought to bear on institutional questions. Much of the more innovative research in development economics has to do with the economic basis of rural village life, until recently treated as an obstruction to development that awaited the more thorough penetration of the market.[66] In recognition of the enduring nature of some indigenous institutions, and in response to the attacks on development economics from anthropologists who have examined these institutions more closely, economists have investigated issues of household work and consumption choice, informal credit, and land-using arrangements. Polly Hill's 1986 book, *Development Economics on Trial: The Anthropological Case for a Prosecution*, makes the case that development economists have ignored the cultural basis of economic activity in developing countries and have therefore failed to understand why peasants act as they do and how the process of change should be conceived.[67]

A final set of issues that must be mentioned, even if we can provide no clear answers, has to do with whether a focus on economic welfare is sufficient or even fully appropriate. Surveys across countries and across time fail to prove that greater economic well-being makes people feel happier. Critics of advanced industrial societies point to what they believe is the disintegration of culture and community, as well as to growing individual insecurity, both physical and emotional. And nagging doubts remain about the ability of the planet to sustain the level of consumption achieved in the United States if it is to be afforded to the other 6 billion people.

CONCLUSION: WHAT DO WE KNOW? WHAT DON'T WE KNOW?

How well have development economics and economic development responded to real problems that affect billions of people? A lot of good and bad has been accomplished, much has been learned and unlearned, and much has been left undone.

What Do We Know?

After about 50 years of discussion and experimentation, some things are clear.

Markets and Property Rights

The contemporary discipline of economics studies the allocation of scarce resources and accepts that markets are the most efficient means of accomplishing this. All successful, large-scale economic development efforts have been based on the formation of markets and creating institutions that help markets work. On the local level, effective regulation of common property resources is possible, but these usually operate within a larger framework of market-based allocation. Markets work best when property rights are well established and regulation is kept to the level necessary for orderly economic activity that protects the rights of all participants. When property rights are in doubt, people must be cautious and will neither take risks nor invest in the long term. When regulation is excessive, resources are wasted in rent-seeking behavior.

Human Capital

True development requires (and some would say can be measured by) a healthy and well-educated population. A recent study of successful developers notes among the common elements of success a concerted effort *in advance* to invest in health and education, with education necessary to make the most effective use of investments in health.[68] Improved conditions of health and education, along with the opportunities provided by development and the availability of contraceptives, are usually enough to permit population growth to slow as income levels grow.

Financial Institutions and the Poor

While the experiments in Kerala show that human development can occur without rapid economic growth, the experience of most economies is that without growth, structural change is less likely and investments in human capital are unlikely to be maintained. Growth requires investment, and investment requires saving. Effective financial institutions are therefore necessary. And for growth to spread out to the majority of the population, financial institutions must allow the poor to participate in economic change. The achievements of the Grameen Bank in Bangladesh have excited development economists, bankers, and small entrepreneurs around the globe, and sparked attempts to apply similar principles in numerous countries.

Agriculture

The agricultural sector is the beginning of most development, and the perils of ignoring or exploiting that sector are among the most solid lessons of economic development. Just as population growth tends to slow along *with* development, so does the importance of the agricultural sector diminish only if it is allowed to play a crucial role in the early stages. Attempts to tax, control, and regulate agriculture beyond a minimal level will push farmers away from the market and slow the rest of the economy.

Technology and Industrialization

Technological innovation and the ability to innovate internally are crucial to an economy finding the type of industrialization most suited to its current and evolving resources. Governments can help support learning, research and development, and can avoid incentives that lead to overemphasis on capital use in a labor-rich economy.

Sustainability

We are just beginning to understand that development must ultimately be environmentally sustainable. What we know so far is both that private decisions may ignore negative externalities and that government decisions can foster them. Action is required in both cases, although the tools for adequately internalizing externalities are still being developed.

International Aspects

Although the bulk of an economy's resources must be generated internally, significant marginal improvements can come from interaction with the rest of the world. Thus, in a general sense, growth and development are associated with that interaction, although the degree to which a successful economy is open to foreign goods and capital may vary. We know that concerted efforts to protect a wide spectrum of domestic activity from foreign competition will have large costs, resulting in inefficient domestic firms and high foreign debt. We know that spurring domestic competition with foreign firms in world markets can have large rewards for developing countries. Foreign capital may be an important part of that process, although not every transnational corporation that wants to set up shop is doing the developing economy a favor.

The Role of Government

To the extent that development economists of the 1950s saw the government as the logical mechanism for resource accumulation and allocation, this view has been replaced by one emphasizing that government policy should strive to create the foundation for well-functioning markets. Thus, market forces should be the primary guide to resource allocation as long as reasonably competitive markets can be established. If there is market failure, governments in both developed and developing countries will always play an important role in economic decision making.

Governments can engage in productive activity, but these should be the exception. Governments already have enough to do. In addition to the areas we have mentioned, governments everywhere are responsible for maintaining stability at the macroeconomic level. Efficient tax systems that do not discourage economic activity and a disciplined approach to government credit creation and spending can help maintain reasonable price stability while promoting employment. And, as governments everywhere determine how their economies interact with the rest of the world, they must draw crucial lines between encouraging international competitiveness and exposing weak productive and financial structures to volatile world markets for goods and capital.

These things are not easily accomplished, and stable political institutions are essential. Economic theory cannot shine much light here, especially if the accumulation of social capital is the key variable. But the record of a number of countries shows that when effective political institutions interact with markets, economic development can be achieved.

What We Have to Learn

There is an old saying that if we knew what we did not know, we would know everything. But knowing the questions is different from having the answers. So there are some areas where there is still much to be learned. These include knowing just how to implement the things we know, including the following:

- How can stable government institutions be created? Most economies do not have blueprints for this, and those that have had blueprints have not been able to follow them. What are the many connections between democracy and economic development, and how is any one society to foster those connections?
- How do national values and culture affect development efforts: How is social capital created?
- How much inequality is good (or bad) for growth and development? The historical record is not clear, and the mechanisms are still subject to conjecture.
- What is the best way to count up the costs of externalities, and what is the best way to account for these in development projects?

- How well do experiments translate from one economy to another? What adjustments in the Grameen Bank model, for example, need to be made for the idea to work in Uganda and Nicaragua, or must other models be created?
- How fast should economic reform measures be implemented, and what determines when and how these reforms can be successful? As with experiments and models of other sorts, this question must be answered in different ways in different places. Some economists were sure that "shock treatment," or immediate reform, was the best way to transform the socialist Eastern European economies into capitalist ones. But while Poland and the Czech Republic were ready to accept shocks and move on in a couple of years, the institutions that permitted this did not exist in Russia. If sudden political change provides a window for reform and may call for rapid implementation, established governments such as in China will not stand for this. In fact, China has illustrated the possibility that slow, lumbering reform may be possible and permit a continually, rapidly growing economy.
- How open should capital markets be? Jagdish Bhagwati, an ardent advocate of free trade, says financial liberalization "is something like fire. It's damn useful to have it, but at the same time, you can burn down your wretched house."[69] Can an economy get the benefits of foreign capital without allowing its sudden shifts to overwhelm it? Should foreign investors be treated differently because they are more likely to follow the herd when times are hard?
- What is the optimal mix—for any given economy—between the government and the private sector? Even a preference for markets leaves us with an unending set of questions regarding this or that economic activity. What are the criteria for when government intervention is permitted and how far that intervention may go?

Where Do We Go from Here?

As there are trends in our thinking about development and development policy, there are periods of optimism and pessimism about the entire development effort. In the 1950s and 1960s, as many developing countries were emerging from their status as colonies and others were rejoicing in the growing number of what were called Third World countries, optimism ran high. The world economy had emerged from a world war with a set of institutions and a stated commitment to promote development. Governments in developing countries felt that with independence, the tools of planning, and foreign aid, the way would be open for their success.

The next two decades turned optimism into doubt, frustration, and confrontation. Extreme fluctuations in commodity prices hurt developing countries' exports (coffee, cocoa, tin, rubber, oil) and increased the prices of their imports (grain, oil, and manufactures in which energy prices played an important role). Recession in the West likewise hurt their exports. These problems and the fallout from inward-oriented policies resulted in mounting debt that set back development efforts in many countries of Africa and Latin America. The doubt and frustration led to confrontation with the developed countries.

The nineties were different again. On the one hand were major reversals in development policies that brought markets to increasing importance and improved economic performance in many Latin American countries. East Asian countries performed well until the end of the decade, and the fallout from that crisis is still being debated. At the other extreme has been the continued problems in Africa: In many countries the withdrawal from formal economic activity during the 1980s and devastation from AIDS have combined with the inability of government institutions to carry out effective programs of reform. In Africa there are many fundamental questions that remain to be answered. And newly asked is a problem that development economists easily recognize: How do the formerly state-run economies of Central and Eastern Europe begin to reverse the roles of state and market so that the state supports the market rather than suppresses it?

There are at least two reasons for optimism. First of all, for most development economists the range of options has been narrowed: There is no longer a serious interest in comprehensive government planning. The question for the government is how to promote markets, help them to work efficiently, and curb their excesses, rather than how to effectively replace them. While this leaves huge open questions, the debate often uses common terminology. During the debate over how to deal with the East Asian crisis of the last decade, those who were concerned with the excesses of global capital markets did not propose closing off economies or having a world body come up with a set of rules. They asked what prudent measures a government could take to reduce the volatility of capital flows, and when the restrictions imposed by Malaysia did not cause foreign capital to flee, a battle for civility had been won.

Second, we have many positive examples to study for clues: Brazil has tamed inflation and Bolivia has implemented credible tax reform. In Bangladesh, credit has been extended to millions of poor women and voluntary population control measures have been accepted by an overwhelmingly Moslem population. Population growth rates are declining in most countries. Increasingly sophisticated environmental analysis and social awareness have raised a cautionary flag against huge dam projects. After many years of denial and neglect, the government of Uganda has begun to reform the economy and to actively involve citizens in the fight against AIDS.

So while there is a long way to go, we are far ahead of where we started, and the search for better answers goes on.

Key Terms

- fragmented markets (p. 487)
- social capital (p. 493)
- Total Factor Productivity (TFP) (p. 488)

Questions for Review

1. Define Development Economics. How, aside from subject matter, does this course differ from other economics courses you have taken?
2. How would you assess the degree of progress made by development economists in understanding the key issues of the discipline?
3. What roles for government are generally accepted among development economists?
4. What departures from market-oriented policies are accepted by the World Bank's analysis of the East Asian experience? What aspects of that experience are rejected by the study as a guide for other developing countries?

5. What criticisms of the Bank's study do you find compelling or interesting?
6. What question are we asking about economic development when we focus on governance and institutions?

Endnotes and Further Readings

1. Vinod Thomas, "Lessons from Economic Development," *Finance & Development* 28, no. 3 (September 1991), pp. 6–9.
2. See John Toye, *Dilemmas of Development: Reflections on the Counterrevolution in Development Economics*, 2nd ed. (Cambridge: Blackwell Press, 1993), and Deepak Lal, *The Poverty of "Development Economics"* (Cambridge: Harvard University Press, 1985).
3. See Albert O. Hirschman, "The Rise and Decline of Development Economics," in his *Essays in Trespassing: Economics to Politics and Beyond* (Cambridge: Cambridge University Press, 1981), pp. 1–24. For criticisms, see Amitava Krishna Dutt, "Two Issues in the State of Development Economics," in Dutt and Kenneth P. Jameson, eds., *New Directions in Development Economics* (Hants, U.K.: Edward Elgar, 1992), pp. 1–34. The Adelman/Morris article is "Development History and Its Implications for Development Theory," *World Development* 25, no. 6 (June 1997), pp. 831–840.
4. Nicholas Stern, "The Economics of Development: A Survey," *Economic Journal* 99, no. 397 (September 1989), p. 624.
5. See W. Arthur Lewis, "The State of Development Theory," *American Economic Review* 74, no. 2 (May 1984), pp. 1–10. The quote is on p. 9. Adelman and Morris come to similar conclusions.
6. Jagdish Bhagwati, "Development Economics: What Have We Learnt? in Jagdish N. Bhagwati, *Wealth and Poverty: Essays in Development Economics*, vol. 1, Gene Grossman, ed. (Cambridge: MIT Press, 1985), pp. 14–15.
7. W. Arthur Lewis, "Reflections on Development" in Gustav Ranis and T. Paul Schultz, eds., *The State of Development Economics* (Oxford: Basil Blackwell, 1988), pp. 13–23. The quote is on p. 15.
8. See Amartya Sen, "Development: Which Way Now?" *Economic Journal* 93 (December 1983), pp. 745–762, and Stern, "The Economics of Development: A Survey," p. 612.
9. See Bhagwati, "Development Economics: What Have We Learnt?" p. 22, and Stern, "The Economics of Development: A Survey," p. 627.
10. Bhagwati, "Development Economics: What Have We Learnt?" pp. 14–18. Also see T. N. Srinivasan, "Human Development: A New Paradigm or Reinvention of the Wheel?" *American Economic Review* 84, no. 2 (May 1994), pp. 238–243.
11. Dani Rodrik, *The New Global Economy and Developing Countries: Making Openness Work*, Policy Essay No. 24 (Washington: Overseas Development Council, 1999).
12. Govindan Parayil, "The 'Kerala Model' of Development: Development and Sustainability in the Third World," *Third World Quarterly* 17, no. 5 (December 1996), pp. 941–957.
13. Bhagwati, "Development Economics: What Have We Learnt?" pp. 24–26. Also, see Nancy Birdsall and Juan Luis Londoño, "Asset Inequality Matters: An Assessment of the World Bank's Approach to Poverty Reduction," *American Economic Review* 87, no. 2 (May 1997), pp. 32–37.
14. W. Arthur Lewis, in Ranis and Schultz, *The State of Development Economics*, pp. 17–18.
15. See Stern, "The Economics of Development: A Survey," p. 615.
16. I. G. Patel, "Limits of the Current Consensus on Development," *World Bank Annual Conference on Development Economics 1993* (Washington: World Bank, 1994), pp. 9–18.
17. See Joseph Stiglitz, "Alternative Tactics and Strategies for Economic Development," in Amitavakrishna Dutt and Kenneth P. Jameson, *New Directions in Development Economics*, pp. 57–80.
18. Stern, "The Economics of Development: A Survey," pp. 597–598.
19. Gustav Ranis and John C. H. Fei, "Development Economics: What Next?" in Gustav Ranis and T. Paul Schultz, *The State of Development Economics* (Oxford: Basil Blackwell, 1988), pp. 100–136.
20. See Alberto Alesina and Roberto Perotti, "The Political Economy of Growth: A Critical Survey of the Recent Literature," *World Bank Economic Review* 8, no. 3 (September 1994), pp. 351–371; Edgardo Boeninger, "Governance and Development: Issues and Constraints," *World Bank Annual Conference on Development Economics 1991* (Washington: World Bank, 1992), pp. 267–287; Ronald Findlay, "The New Political Economy: Its Explanatory Power for LDCs," *Economics and Politics* 2, no. 2 (July 1990), pp. 193–221; Anne O. Krueger, *Political Economy of Policy Reform in Developing Countries* (Cambridge: MIT Press, 1993); and Denis-Constant Martin, "The Cultural Dimensions of Governance," *World Bank Annual Conference on Development Economics 1991*, pp. 325–341.
21. See particularly Mancur Olson, "Big Bills Left on the Sidewalk: Why Some Nations Are Rich, and Others Poor," *Journal of Economic Perspectives* 10, no. 2 (spring 1996), pp. 3–24; Robert E. Hall and Charles I. Jones, "Levels of Economic Activity Across Countries," *American Economic Review* 87, no. 2 (May 1997), pp. 173–177; and Alberto Alesina, "The Political

Economy of High and Low Growth," *Annual World Bank Conference on Development Economics 1997*, Boris Bleskovic and Joseph E. Stiglitz, eds. (Washington: World Bank, 1998), pp. 3–24.

22. See Richard Grabowski, "The Developmental State: Where Does It Come From?" *World Development* 22, no. 3 (March 1994), pp. 413–422, and Meredith Woo-Cumings, ed., *The Developmental State* (Ithaca, NY: Cornell University Press, 1999).

23. See Vinod Thomas and Jisoon Lee, "The Payoffs from Economic Reforms," in Nancy Birdsall and Frederick Jasperson, eds., *Pathways to Growth: Comparing East Asia and Latin America* (Washington: Inter-American Development Bank, 1997), pp. 283–299, and Mary Shirley's "Commentary," pp. 300–304.

24. Thomas and Lee, "The Payoffs from Economic Reforms," and Oliver Morrissey, "Politics and Economic Policy Reform: Trade Liberalization in Sub-Saharan Africa," *Journal of International Development* 7, no. 4 (July–August 1995), pp. 599–618.

25. See Merilee S. Grindle, "In Quest of the Political: The Political Economy of Development Policymaking," in Gerald M. Meier and Joseph E. Stiglitz, eds., *Frontiers of Development Economics: The Future in Perspective* (Washington: World Bank/Oxford University Press, 2001), pp. 345–380, and Stephen Haggard, *The Political Economy of the Asian Financial Crisis* (Washington: Institute for International Economics, 2000).

26. Janine Aron, "Growth and Institutions: A Review of the Evidence," *World Bank Research Observer* 15, no. 1 (February 2000), pp. 99–135. Also see Carol Graham and Moisés Naím, "The Political Economy of Institutional Reform in Latin America," in Nancy Birdsall, Carol Graham, and Richard H. Sabot, eds., *Beyond Trade-Offs: Market Reform and Equitable Growth in Latin America* (Washington: Inter-American Development Bank, 1998), pp. 321–362.

27. See ⟨http://cyber.law.harvard.edu/prs/report.html⟩ and ⟨www1.worldbank.org/publicsector/legal/major_projects.htm⟩.

28. See Jane Jacobs, *The Death and Life of Great American Cities* (New York: Random House, 1961); Robert Putnam, *Making Democracy Work: Civic Traditions in Modern Italy* (Princeton, NJ: Princeton University Press, 1994); Partha Dasgupta and Ismail Serageldin, *Social Capital: A Multifaceted Perspective* (Washington: World Bank, 2000); and Michael Woolcock and Deepa Narayan, "Social Capital: Implications for Development Theory, Research, and Policy," *World Bank Research Observer* 15, no. 2 (August 2000), pp. 225–249.

29. Aron, "Growth and Institutions: A Review of the Evidence," p. 129.

30. See Michael Nelson and Ram D. Singh, "Democracy, Economic Freedom, Fiscal Policy, and Growth in LDCs: A Fresh Look," *Economic Development and Cultural Change* 46, no. 4 (July 1998), pp. 677–696.

31. Arthur A. Goldsmith, "Democracy, Property Rights and Economic Growth," *Journal of Development Studies* 32, no. 2 (December 1995), pp. 157–174, and Nelson and Singh, "Democracy, Economic Freedom, Fiscal Policy, and Growth in LDCs: A Fresh Look." Also see Adam Przeworski and Fernando Limongi, "Political Regimes and Economic Growth," *Journal of Economic Perspectives* 7, no. 3 (summer 1993), pp. 51–70, and Stephan Haggard, "Democracy and Economic Development: A Comparative Perspective," in *Democratic Institutions* 1 (1992), pp. 49–62.

32. Andrew P. Barkley and John McMillan, "Political Freedom and the Response to Economic Incentives: Labor Migration in Africa, 1972–87," *Journal of Development Economics* 45, no. 2 (December 1994), pp. 393–406; Richard Ball and Gordon Rausser, "Governance Structure and the Durability of Economic Reforms: Evidence from Inflation Stabilizations," *World Development* 23, no. 6 (June 1995), pp. 897–912; and John W. Dawson, "Institutions, Investment, and Growth: New Cross-Country and Panel Data Evidence," *Economic Inquiry* 36, no. 4 (October 1998), pp. 603–619. Also see 1998 Nobel Laureate Amartya Sen, *Development and Freedom* (New York: Alfred A. Knopf, 1999).

33. See Vinod Thomas and Yan Wang, "Distortions, Interventions, and Productivity Growth: Is East Asia Different?" *Economic Development and Cultural Change* 44, no. 2 (January 1996), pp. 265–288.

34. Alwyn Young, "The Tyranny of Numbers: Confronting the Statistical Realities of the East Asian Growth Experience," *Quarterly Journal of Economics* 110, no. 3 (August 1995), pp. 641–680.

35. See Susan Collins and Barry Bosworth, "Economic Growth in East Asia: Accumulation versus Assimilation," *Brookings Papers on Economic Activity* 2 (1996), pp. 135–191, and Nicholas Crafts, "East Asian Growth Before and After the Crisis," *IMF Staff Papers* 46, no. 2 (June 1999), pp. 139–166.

36. World Bank, *The East Asian Miracle: Economic Growth and Public Policy* (New York: Oxford University Press, 1993). The April 1994 issue of *World Development* 22, no. 4, devotes a special section to the report.

37. Stiglitz "Alternative Tactics and Strategies for Economic Development," in Dutt and Jameson; Alice H. Amsden, *Asia's Next Giant: South Korea and Late Industrialization* (New York: Oxford University Press, 1989); and Alice H. Amsden and Takashi Hikino, "Staying Behind, Stumbling Back, Sneaking Up, Soaring Ahead: Late Industrialization in Historical Perspective," in William J. Baumol, Richard R. Nelson, and Edward N. Wolff, eds., *Convergence of Productivity: Cross-Country Studies and Historical Evidence* (New York: Oxford University Press, 1994), pp. 285–315.

38. World Bank, *The East Asian Miracle: Economic Growth and Public Policy*, p. 20.

39. Stephan Haggard, "Politics and Institutions in the World Bank's East Asia," in Albert Fishlow et al., *Miracle or*

Design? Lessons from the East Asian Experience (Washington: Overseas Development Council, 1994), pp. 106–108.

40. Howard Pack, "Industrial Policy: Growth Elixir or Poison?" *World Bank Research Observer* 15, no. 1 (February 2000), pp. 47–67.

41. Haggard, "Politics and Institutions in the World Bank's East Asia," pp. 85–87.

42. Dani Rodrick, "King Kong Meets Godzilla: The World Bank and *The East Asian Miracle*," in Fishlow et al., *Miracle or Design? Lessons from the East Asian Experience*, pp. 13–53. Also see Nancy Birdsall, David Ross, and Richard Sabot, "Inequality and Growth Reconsidered: Lessons from East Asia," *World Bank Economic Review* 9, no. 3 (September 1995), pp. 477–508.

43. Robert Wade, "Selective Industrial Policies in East Asia: Is *The East Asian Miracle* Right?" in Fishlow et al., *Miracle or Design? Lessons from the East Asian Experience*, pp. 55–79, and *Governing the Market: Economic Theory and the Role of the Government in East Asian Industrialization* (Princeton, NJ: Princeton University Press, 1990).

44. Wade, "Selective Industrial Policies in East Asia: Is *The East Asian Miracle* Right?" pp. 70–73. Hikino and Amsden, "Staying Behind, Stumbling Back, Sneaking Up, Soaring Ahead: Late Industrialization in Historical Perspective," p. 291. Also see Joseph Stiglitz, "Some Lessons from the East Asian Miracle," *World Bank Research Observer* 11, no. 2 (August 1996), pp. 151–178.

45. World Bank, *The East Asian Miracle: Economic Growth and Public Policy*, p. 25, and Rodrik, "King Kong Meets Godzilla: The World Bank and the East Asian Miracle," pp. 35–39.

46. Colin I. Bradford, Jr., *From Trade-Driven Growth to Growth-Driven Trade: Reappraising the East Asian Development Experience* (Paris: OECD, 1994).

47. See Jeffrey Henderson and Richard P. Appelbaum, "Situating the State in the East Asian Development Process," in Appelbaum and Henderson, eds., *States and Development in the Asian Pacific Rim* (Newbury Park, CA: Sage Publications, 1992), pp. 1–26, and Keun Lee and Hong Yong Lee, "States, Markets and Economic Development in East Asian Capitalism and Socialism," *Development Policy Review* 10, no. 2 (June 1992), pp. 107–130.

48. World Bank, *The East Asian Miracle: Economic Growth and Public Policy*, p. 13. Also see Rhys Jenkins, "The Political Economy of Industrialization: A Comparison of Latin American and East Asian Newly Industrializing Countries," *Development and Change* 22, no. 3 (July 1991), pp. 497–517.

49. See Joan M. Nelson with Stephanie J. Eglinton, *Encouraging Democracy: What Role for Conditioned Aid?* (Washington: Overseas Development Council, 1992).

50. See Jose Edgardo Campos and Hilton L. Root, *The Key to the Asian Miracle: Making Shared Growth Credible* (Washington: Brookings, 1996).

51. Bradford, *From Trade-Driven Growth to Growth-Driven Trade: Reappraising the East Asian Development Experience*, pp. 25–27, and Haggard, "Politics and Institutions in the World Bank's East Asia," pp. 87–89.

52. *Ibid.*, pp. 91–93.

53. Rodrik, "King Kong Meets Godzilla: The World Bank and the East Asian Miracle," p. 44.

54. Haggard, "Politics and Institutions in the World Bank's East Asia," pp. 98–194. However, see Gary S. Fields, "Changing Labor Market Conditions and Economic Development in Hong Kong, the Republic of Korea, Singapore, and Taiwan, China," *World Bank Economic Review* 8, no. 3 (September 1994), pp. 395–414.

55. Haggard, "Politics and Institutions in the World Bank's East Asia," p. 98, and Albert Fishlow and Catherine Gwin, "Lessons from the East Asian Experience," in Fishlow et al., *Miracle or Design? Lessons from the East Asian Experience*, p. 8.

56. Walter Russell Mead, "East Asia Needs a New Growth Strategy," *Wall Street Journal*, April 17, 1997.

57. Adelman and Morris, "Development History and Its Implications for Development Theory."

58. See Adolfo Canitrot and Silva Junco, "Macroeconomic Conditions and Trade Liberalization in Argentina, Brazil, Chile and Uruguay: A Comparative Study," and "Macroeconomic Conditions and Trade Liberalization: The Case of Argentina," in Canitrot and Junco, eds., *Macroeconomic Conditions and Trade Liberalization* (Washington: Inter-American Development Bank, 1993), pp. 1–30 and pp. 31–80, respectively; and Patricio Meller, "Trade Opening of the Chilean Economy: Policy Lessons," pp. 123–158.

59. See Sebastian and Alejandra Cox Edwards, *Monetarism and Liberalization: The Chilean Experiment* (Chicago: University of Chicago Press, 1991), and Alejandro Foxley, *Latin American Experiments in Neo-Conservative Economics* (Berkeley: University of California Press, 1983).

60. See Rhys Jenkins, "The Political Economy of Industrialization: A Comparison of Latin American and East Asian Newly Industrializing Countries," *Development and Change* 22, no. 3 (July 1991), pp. 497–517; Seiji Naya et al., eds., *Lessons in Development: A Comparative Study of Asia and Latin America* (San Francisco: International Center for Economic Growth, 1989); Gary Gereffi and Donald L. Wyman, *Manufacturing Miracles: Paths of Industrialization in Latin America and East Asia* (Princeton, NJ: Princeton University Press, 1990); and Birdsall and Jasperson, *Pathways to Growth: Comparing East Asia and Latin America*.

61. See Sebastian Edwards, "Why Are Latin America's Savings Rates So Low?" in Birdsall and Jasperson, *Pathways to Growth: Comparing East Asia and Latin America*, pp. 131–158; and Inter-American Development Bank, *Economic and Social Progress in Latin America: 1992 Report* (Washington: Inter-American Development Bank, 1992).

62. See *Wall Street Journal* articles: Thomas T. Vogel, Jr., "In Latin American Economy, Fiesta-or-Famine-Cycle May Be a Thing of the Past," July 31, 1997; Jonathan Friedland, "South America Reaps a Harvest of Reforms," August 14, 1997; and Jonathan Friedland and Craig Torres, "Latin America Now Benefits from Lessons of '94," October 29, 1997. Also see *The Economist*, "The Backlash in Latin America," November 30, 1996, and the Inter-American Development Bank, "Progress and Poverty: Latin America's Dilemma of the 1990s," in *Latin American Policies* (Third Quarter 1997).

63. See Thandika Mkandawire and Charles C. Soludo, *Our Continent Our Future: African Perspectives on Structural Adjustment* (Trenton, NJ: African World Press, 1999), p. 5.

64. Keith Richburg, *Washington Post National Weekly Edition*, July 20–26, 1992. Also see the articles in David L. Lindauer and Michael Roemer, eds., *Asia and Africa: Legacies and Opportunities in Development* (San Francisco: ICS Press, 1994).

65. Mkandawire and Soludo, *Our Continent Our Future: African Perspectives on Structural Adjustments*, 1998.

66. See Inderjit Singh, Lyn Square, and John Strauss, "A Survey of Agricultural Household Models: Recent Findings and Policy Implications," *World Bank Economic Review* 1, no. 1 (January 1986), pp. 149–179, and Justin Yifu Lin and Jeffrey B. Nugent, "Institutions and Economic Development," in Jere Behrman and T. N. Srinivasan, eds., *Handbook of Development Economics* 3A (Amsterdam: Elsevier, 1995), pp. 2301–2370.

67. Polly Hill, *Development Economics on Trial: The Anthropological Case for a Prosecution* (Cambridge: Cambridge University Press, 1986).

68. Santosh Mehrotra, "Social Development in High-Achieving Countries: Common Elements and Diversities," in Santosh Mehrotra and Richard Jolly, eds., *Development with a Human Face: Experiences in Social Achievement and Economic Growth* (Oxford: Oxford University Press, 2000).

69. Quoted in Peter Stein, "The Backlash: In Asia, Victims of Capitalism Are Questioning the Devotion to Free Markets," *Wall Street Journal*, September 27, 1999.

Glossary

absorption Domestic demand for a nation's output.

absorptive capacity The capacity of an economy to effectively use additional capital, determined by cooperating factors such as labor, management skill and economic organization.

adverse selection The perverse impact of incentives that encourage less qualified individuals and firms to obtain access to resources. In health insurance, the tendency for those with above-average risk to seek insurance while those with below-average risk tend to avoid it. In banking, the tendency for high interest rates to attract riskier borrowers.

agricultural extension See **extension (agricultural)**.

agricultural productivity Yield, usually measured in tons, per worker or per unit of land (hectare or acre).

aid Grants or concessional loans usually intended to foster the development of the recipient country.

appropriate technology Technology requiring factor proportions that correspond to existing relative factor scarcity.

arable land Land that is suitable for cultivation.

balanced growth Industrialization strategy that emphasizes the need to develop a wide range of industries. Similar to the **big push**, although with less emphasis on direct government activity.

Basic Human Needs (BHN) An approach to development suggesting that government policy should aim to directly improve the health and educational status of the poorest parts of the population rather than relying on faster economic growth to provide these needs indirectly.

big push Industrialization strategy that calls for an intensive, government-financed attempt to develop a wide range of industries simultaneously.

bilateral aid Aid provided from one government to another.

Bilateral Investment Treaty (BIT) A treaty between two governments that guides the host government's treatment of investments from the home country.

biodiversity Variety of animal and plant species maintained in an ecological system.

border price The internationally traded price of an imported product, sometimes used as an acceptable approximation of a **shadow price**.

bottleneck A specific shortage that prevents the effective use of other resources.

brain drain The migration of educated, skilled labor from developing to developed countries.

buffer stock Stockpile of some commodity owned by a commodity stabilization fund to protect against large price fluctuations.

capital A factor of production, which takes the form of machinery and factories, that increases workers' ability to produce goods and services. **Capital stock** is the dollar value of the economy's physical capital. (See **investment**.)

capital flight Departure of financial assets from a country, usually in abnormally large amounts, due to fear that the country's economic circumstances will significantly reduce the value of those assets.

capital intensive Describes a production process that, relative to another, uses a larger amount of capital per worker.

cash crops Crops grown primarily for market rather than for home use. Often refers to crops grown for export markets, especially crops that are not staple foods. Coffee, tea, and cocoa are examples.

center In dependency theory, the location of the rich countries whose firms direct the development process in the poor countries.

central bank Government bank that is charged with control of a nation's money supply and usually supervision of the commercial banking system.

classical economics Economic thought from roughly 1770 to 1870, which developed the framework of market capitalism and the scientific study of production and distribution.

collective farm Farm owned by the state on which peasant farmers are brought together (usually forcibly) to work as a single unit. Originated in modern times by Stalin in the Soviet Union, they have reemerged in some developing countries. If farmers together own the farm, the term **cooperative farm** is used, although the distinction can often blur in reality.

commodity stabilization fund A fund set up to finance buffer stocks of commodities, the purpose of which is to smooth out fluctuations in the prices of those commodities.

Common Fund Short name for the **Integrated Fund for Commodities**, a fund set up to finance a number of individual commodity stabilization funds.

common property resource Any resource, often land or water, that is owned in common by a group, with individuals in the group having certain rights to use the property.

comparative advantage The basis for exchange among individuals, firms, or countries in that resources will be used more efficiently if economic actors tend to concentrate their energies in those areas in which they are capable of producing relatively more cheaply.

complementarity Of industries. Industries that provide inputs or markets for others.

concessional terms Lending terms, offered by governments, that are easier than those that would be offered by commercial lenders.

conditionality Practice of aid donors and multilateral lenders, such as the World Bank and the IMF, imposing conditions in exchange for aid. Usually involves conditions for project performance or for broader policy objectives considered necessary for effective use of aid.

contagion The spreading of economic crisis from one country to another.

controls Government rules imposed on economic activity, usually by requiring specific actions or restrictions (see **standards**).

convergence The idea that poor countries should grow more rapidly than rich ones, allowing their incomes to "converge," or come together. However, the neoclassical model, which predicts convergence, suggests that poor countries will move more quickly toward their own "steady states," which may be far lower than similar "states" in rich countries.

corruption Any of a number of activities in which officials abuse their position by requiring an additional consideration in return for providing a product or service.

cost-benefit analysis A method of evaluating an investment project by comparing the **discounted** value of its accumulated costs and benefits.

crude birth rate The number of births per 1,000 people.

crude death rate The number of deaths per 1,000 people.

current account Section of a country's balance of payments that records financial flows resulting from trade in currently produced goods, services, and assets, including exports, imports, investment income, and transfers such as gifts and remittances.

customs union An arrangement among countries to reduce barriers to trade among them while maintaining higher barriers against imports from other countries. Also see **free trade area**.

debt service Repayments of principal and payments of interest on a debt.

default Declaration (sometimes implied) that a debtor is no longer able to service debts and does not intend to try.

deficit Of government budget. Expenditure in excess of tax revenues.

deforestation Complete removal of forest resources from an area of land.

degradation Deterioration of the productive capacity of land.

demographic transition Period of time during which a society's death and birth rates fall. The initial period of high birth and death rates is followed first by a decline in death rates and rapid population growth until birth rates fall and growth slows down.

dependency ratio Also known as age dependency ratio. The ratio of people of nonworking age to the working age population.

dependency theory A theory of development proposing that firms from the rich countries (**center**) control the direction of development in the poor countries (**periphery**) and underdevelop them by making the poor countries dependent on the rich.

dependent variable In a **model**, the dependent variable is the one whose value is determined by the specified relationship and the value of independent variables, provided through assumption or investigation.

depreciation Of a currency. Decline in a currency's value (in terms of other currencies) due to normal market forces. An increase in value is an appreciation.

desertification Overuse of land to such an extent that it becomes completely exhausted for agricultural purposes.

devaluation Of a currency. Decline in a currency's value (in terms of other currencies), due to a deliberate decision by government, from one legal rate to a lower one. An increase in value is a revaluation.

development Increase in the output of goods and services per capita, accompanied by changes in economic structure and distribution of income.

Development Assistance Committee (DAC) Committee of the OECD (Organization for Economic Cooperation and Development), which studies aid and makes recommendations for its effective use.

Development Bank A special financial institution, usually financed by governments, that provides loans for development projects, often on preferential terms.

diminishing returns The declining marginal product when a unit of the variable factor of production, such as labor, is added to the fixed factor of production, such as land.

direct tax Tax levied on personal or corporate income.

discount rate A measurement of the opportunity cost of capital, used to discount, or reduce, future values (usually costs and benefits) to present values.

disguised unemployment Labor that is employed but whose marginal product is less than the wage. Also known as **underemployment**.

dual economy An economy in which two sectors have very different structures (e.g., labor intensive and capital intensive) and act more or less independently.

ecodevelopment Development projects that are designed explicitly to incorporate elements that help, or prevent deterioration of, the environment.

economic growth Increase in the production of goods and services, usually measured as a percentage increase in the total or per capita gross national income.

effective protection Measure of protection afforded to an industry or activity that accounts not only for explicit barriers to final goods imports but also for the impact of barriers to the protected activity's inputs.

endogenous Arising from within. With respect to economic models, endogenous factors are those that are put within the relationship treated by the model.

Engel's Law Tendency for people to consume different goods in different proportions as income increases. Increases in income bring less than proportionate increases in necessities but greater than proportionate increases in non-necessities. See also **income elasticity of demand**.

engine of growth The singling out of a particular factor, such as trade or technology, that is capable of propelling a country into an era of economic growth.

environmental accounting Modification of national income accounting to include the environmental impact of economic activities, usually resulting in a reduction of the measured level of national income.

environmental Kuznets curve An inverted U curve that shows environmental deterioration as income levels rise up to a point and improvement thereafter.

Euromarket Also known as Eurocurrency market. Term given initially to the market for dollar assets in European financial institutions. It now refers more broadly to the offshore markets of all major currencies.

exchange rate Rate at which a country's currency is bought and sold, relative to other currencies. The actual money rate is the **nominal rate**. (See also **real exchange rate**.) Nominal rates can be **flexible (floating)**, that is, determined in currency markets, or **fixed** by government decision.

exogenous Arising externally. With respect to economic models, exogenous factors are those whose value is given outside the model rather than determined inside it.

expenditure reducing A policy that reduces government spending and increases taxes.

expenditure switching Attempts through various policy means to reorient domestic production from domestic goods to export goods.

Export Orientation (EO) A strategy that relies on exports to drive the economy and earn the foreign exchange to buy needed import goods.

export pessimism Concern that the demand for developing-country exports will not be sustained for a significant period of time.

Export Processing Zone (EPZ) Geographically or economically segregated area of an economy in which normal trade restrictions are relaxed or removed in order to promote exports. Same as **Free Trade Zone (FTZ)**.

expropriation The forcible taking of private property by a government. See also **nationalization**.

extended family Family structure marked by incorporation of many relatives outside the "nuclear family" of parents and children.

extension (agricultural) Services provided by governments to farmers, usually including advice on all aspects of agriculture and research into new techniques.

external economies Gains to a firm from others' activities that increase the availability of its inputs or lower its costs.

externality Benefit or cost of production or consumption that accrues to those other than the producer or consumer. **Positive externalities** occur when firms or individuals other than the producer or consumer obtain benefits and the producer/consumer is unable to obtain a payment. **Negative externalities** occur when individuals or firms other than the producer or consumer bear costs which cannot be charged to the producer/consumer. See also **free rider** and **market failure**.

factor endowments Set of resources available to an economy for the production of goods and services.

factor intensity Measure of the degree to which a product requires a relatively high proportion of one factor of production compared to other factors. Goods may be relatively land, labor, or capital intensive.

factor mobility The ability of the owners of factors of production to move them from one use to another.

factors of production Resources used by businesses in the production of goods and services: usually land, labor, and capital.

feminization of poverty The idea that poverty is disproportionately present in households headed by females.

fertility Birth rate expressed as a number of children born per year per 1,000 females of childbearing age.

financial deepening A process of increasing the proportion of an economy's transactions that is conducted by means of money and other financial instruments.

financial liberalization Process of removing controls over the financial system, moving it toward greater use of market incentives.

financial repression Reducing the proportion of an economy's transactions that is conducted by means of money and other financial instruments.

fiscal policy Government's taxation and spending policy, which affects both resource allocation and macroeconomic stability.

food crops (staples) Crops grown primarily for widespread consumption. In the development context, the term often refers to crops (staples) in wide demand as basic foodstuffs, grown for domestic use rather than for export. Examples would be corn (maize), beans, cassava, and millet.

food security A population's food needs are intended to be met only partly by domestic production, with the rest deliberately imported with the proceeds from other goods that are exported.

forced saving The use of inflation to reallocate resources from consumption to saving.

Foreign Direct Investment (FDI) Investment in a country by a foreign firm, which takes the form of as much ownership of a company as is necessary to guarantee practical control over its activities.

formal sector Portion of the economy in which activities are carried out in compliance with normal laws and regulations.

fragmented markets Situation in which small markets operate in isolation, restricting the advantages of specialization and division of labor provided by larger markets.

free rider Individual or firm that benefits from another's economic activity without having to pay for that benefit.

free trade area An agreement among countries to permit free trade among them while maintaining barriers against other countries.

Free Trade Zone (FTZ) See **Export Processing Zone (EPZ)**.

fungibility Characteristic of resources that permits their being switched to uses other than their intended use.

General Agreement on Tariffs and Trade (GATT) International organization that set out the rules for conducting international trade and provided a forum for negotiating reductions in trade barriers. Superceded in 1995 by the **World Trade Organization (WTO)**.

Generalized System of Preferences (GSP) System in which a more developed country grants lower tariffs to less developed countries than to other advanced countries.

gestation period Time between the initiation of an investment and its ability to generate revenues.

Gini coefficient A measurement of the distribution of income. A lower coefficient indicates more equally distributed income.

global warming Gradual increase in the temperature of the earth's atmosphere. The extent, nature, and causes of global warming are matters of considerable debate.

globalization A popular, if vague, term referring to the increasing interdependence of economies as measured primarily by increased trade and financial flows. In its broadest sense, it is sometimes referred to as a potential homogenizing of the world's cultures through the impact of Western, market-oriented values.

government failure Inability of a government to allocate resources efficiently as a substitute for the market.

grant element Measure of the concessionality of aid. By comparing commercial terms to actual terms, a concessional loan can be considered as partly on commercial terms and partly a grant.

Green Revolution Summary expression for the successful international effort to develop higher-yielding varieties of seeds, and to promote their use together with improved inputs and techniques needed to take advantage of them.

Gross Domestic Product (GDP) The market value of final goods and services produced in a year by factors of production located within a single country. The single most widely used indication of the level of output. A similar measure is the Gross National Product (GNP).

Gross National Income (GNI) The market value of final goods and services produced in a year by the factors of production owned by residents of a country. Same as Gross National Product (GNP).

Harrod–Domar growth model An early growth model in which the rate of economic growth is determined by the **Marginal Propensity to Save (MPS)** and the **Incremental Capital-Output Ratio (ICOR)**.

heavy industry Production of capital-intensive goods, generally capital and consumer durable goods.

hedging Action taken by a buyer or seller of an asset to protect against unfavorable price changes. A borrower of a foreign currency would purchase insurance against its appreciation (the home currency's depreciation) between the time of borrowing and the time of repayment.

herding Behavior of investors who, lacking independent information on the soundness of their assets, simply follow what 'the market' is doing.

heterodox policies Combination of reduced spending and money supply with wage/price controls and other unusual methods to reduce inflation.

horizontal equity Equal tax treatment of given income levels, regardless of the source of the income.

human capital The income-earning potential of a person derived from education and training.

Human Development Index (HDI) An index composed in equal parts of measurements of economic well-being (per capita income), physical well-being (life expectancy), and educational well-being (literacy rates and average years of schooling). It is intended to give a more complete reading of development than can be obtained by simply comparing output per person.

immiserizing growth Possibility that growth fueled by exports of some products will distort the exporting economy to the extent that its citizens are worse off than before.

imperialism As an economic term, the extension of control by developed-country firms over economic activity in developing countries.

import compression Reduction of imports, usually in the context of an adjustment policy that reduces income and thus the ability to import.

Import Substitution (IS) A strategy promoting development by deliberately fostering numerous industries that would replace imported goods. Some import substitution occurs naturally during development, but an explicit strategy attempts to speed up the process by imposing import restrictions in those industries in which substitution is desired.

incentive goods Consumer goods available for farmers to buy, which give them the incentive to produce and sell in formal markets.

incidence of tax The ultimate burden of a tax, as opposed to the firm or individual who actually pays it.

income distribution The pattern of distribution of income in an economy, usually represented by finding what percentage of the economy's income is received by specified portions of the population, often divided into fifths.

income elasticity of demand Ratio of a percentage change in the quantity demanded of a product changes to percentage change in consumer income. **Engel's Law** says that necessities, such as basic foodstuffs, have low elasticities (less than one) and luxuries have high elasticities (greater than one) because as income grows consumer expenditure shifts from the former to the latter.

Incremental Capital-Output Ratio (ICOR) Ratio of a change in capital stock to the resulting change in output.

independent variable In an economic model, a variable whose numerical value helps determine the value of a dependent variable.

indexation Tying some payment (wages, taxes, social security, interest rates) to the change in a price level.

indirect tax Tax on spending rather than income.

indivisibilities Characteristic of some investments, especially capital-intensive sectors, that prevent their use below a certain minimum level.

indivisibility With respect to public goods, the inability to provide discrete amounts of a good or service to individuals because it cannot be divided; for example, national defense, clean air.

induced innovation model A model of agricultural development that focuses on innovation designed to address resource scarcity.

industrial policy A combination of measures taken by governments to promote particular industries, often with the objective of increasing the country's share of world markets.

inertial (explanation of) inflation Some portion of inflation is due to the contest among different sectors to prevent their own incomes from being reduced by inflationary forces. (Also see **neostructuralist**.)

infant industry Term given to a new industry that a government wishes to protect from international competition, presumably because the economy has a potential comparative advantage that will materialize in a relatively short period.

inferior good A good or service that is relatively inexpensive and of poor quality, consumed by poor people but replaced in peoples' budgets when income rises.

inflation An increase in the general price level.

informal sector Activities carried out by individuals and companies that operate outside the usual laws and regulations that apply to other activities. Informal businesses may be illegal or simply not registered with the government.

infrastructure Facilities, such as transportation, communications, and power networks, that provide the basis for productive activity.

innovation Improvements in production technology or improved products that prove commercially viable.

input–output table Table that describes the relationships among sectors of an economy by showing the extent to which one industry requires inputs from, and delivers output to, other sectors. As a more formal mathematical technique, input–output analysis uses linear programming techniques to help planners determine how the economy runs as an integrated whole.

International Comparison Project (ICP) An attempt, under United Nations auspices, to more accurately compare income levels among countries by looking at the purchasing power of incomes, rather than just translating income levels in domestic currencies into dollars via exchange rates.

International Development Association (IDA) Part of the World Bank group. It provides the most lenient terms for loans to developing countries.

inverted U Also known as the Kuznets Curve. The idea, suggested initially by Simon Kuznets, that income distribution might change with development according to a regular pattern: becoming less equal in early stages but then becoming more equal again.

investment Purchase or production of capital goods by firms. A process by which an economy puts resources into those goods that will increase its productive capacity. (See **capital**.)

joint venture Company formed by at least two separate companies, of which at least one is domestic and at least one is foreign.

labor force participation rate Proportion of the available adult population that is either employed or actively seeking employment.

labor intensive A method of producing output that relies on relatively large numbers of workers per unit of capital.

land reform Changes in the legal rights to land. Large holdings may be broken up for distribution to small holders, or small holdings may be amalgamated into larger holdings.

land tenure Conditions under which land is legally used, such as ownership or rental. See also **sharecropping** and **tenancy**.

leading sectors Sectors of the economy that, at any time, are the most dynamic in contributing to economic growth and development.

Lewis labor surplus model An early model of development, which proposed that development in a modern, urban sector could proceed using labor that was unnecessary in the more traditional, rural sector.

light industry Production of labor-intensive goods, generally nondurable consumer goods.

Linkages Connections between industries. **Backward linkages** exist when one industry needs others to provide its inputs. **Forward linkages** exist when one industry needs others to purchase its output.

local content requirement Legal requirement that a company obtain a minimum percentage of its materials, components, and/or labor from domestic sources as a condition for establishment.

Lomé accords Agreements between the European Union (E.U.) and numerous developing countries that provide for special tariff treatment and other benefits.

Lorenz curve A curve that graphically displays **income distribution** data. It compares the percentage of national income earned by successive fifths of the population.

maquiladora Industry created for the purpose of importing materials and components, processing them, and reexporting goods, usually in response to favorable tariff treatment. Originally applied to industries along the Mexico–U.S. border.

marginal product The addition to total output achieved by adding one unit of a variable factor of production to the fixed factors.

Marginal Propensity to Consume (MPC), Save (MPS) The proportion of any change in income that is consumed or saved.

Marginal Rate of Technical Substitution (MRTS) Ratio of the marginal productivity of capital to marginal product of labor, indicating the rate at which one factor can be exchanged for another in a production process and maintain the same level of output.

marginal social benefit/cost The complete marginal benefit or cost of a project that accounts for external benefits or costs in addition to those commonly calculated by a private investor.

marginal utility Addition to the utility (satisfaction) of the consumer from the consumption of one more unit of a good in a given period of time.

market distortion Any artificial price different from the equilibrium level. Often set by law or regulation but may be the result of monopoly power.

market economy Allocation of scarce resources and economic activity by a price mechanism, implying relatively free choice of activity by individuals.

market failure Lack of a market, or inability of the market for a specific good/service to accurately reflect the full cost and benefit of the relevant economic activity.

market imperfection Flaw in the market, such as monopoly, high costs of factor mobility, or lack of a trustworthy legal infrastructure, that hinders the efficiency of markets as a mechanism for allocating resources.

marketing board Government body that buys crops from farmers for resale, often abroad. The original objective was to use the profits for financing development projects.

microfinance Usually refers to very small loans made to small businesses, which are often unable to obtain loans from large financial intermediaries.

model An abstract representation, usually either in graphical or mathematical form, of all or part of an economic system, that permits a focus on key variables in order to understand how the system operates.

monetarist (explanation of) inflation Inflation is due largely or entirely to excessive increases in the supply of money.

monetary policy Government's adjustment of the supply of money and interest rates to achieve macroeconomic stabilization.

monetization Process of increasing the proportion of economic activities carried out with money as opposed to barter.

monocropping Planting large areas with a single crop.

monopsony Market for a factor of production, characterized by a single buyer. Any market in which buyers are not perfect competitors can be said to contain some monopsony element.

Montreal Protocol International agreement under which governments have agreed to specific actions to reduce economic activities that result in depletion of atmospheric ozone.

moral hazard The risk that insurance against an event will reduce attempts to prevent the occurrence of that event.

mortality Death rate, expressed as a number of deaths per year per 1,000 people.

Most Favored Nation (MFN) treatment In the investment context, equal treatment of all foreign investors, regardless of their nationality. In trade, the granting to each supplier country the same trading terms (tariffs, etc.) given to the importer's primary supplier (the most favored nation).

Multifibre Agreement (MFA) A multilateral system of quotas, placed on textiles and apparel, imposed by developed countries on developing countries. A special exception was made under the GATT rules to permit such a system, which would otherwise have been illegal.

multilateral aid Aid provided by international organizations such as the World Bank.

Multilateral Investment Guarantee Agency (MIGA) An agency of the World Bank that insures foreign investors against noncommercial risks.

national treatment Conditions for the operation of foreign investors are the same as conditions for domestic companies.

nationalization The forcible taking of a private company by government, in order to make it a government-owned company. See also **expropriation**.

natural capital Natural resource base of the planet; water, air, and land, including the mineral and forest resources of the land.

natural monopoly Market conditions in which high fixed costs make it inefficient for more than one firm to serve the market.

neostructuralist View of inflation that adds inertial elements to the **structuralist** view.

neoclassical economics Economic thought generated about 1870 and leading to modern microeconomics. Permits graphical and mathematical formalization of a pure market system and analysis of economic issues of the individual consumer and producer.

neoclassical growth model A model of economic growth proposed by Robert Solow in which labor and capital contribute to growth and an economy eventually reaches a steady state where growth stops.

neoliberal A view of economic policy suggesting that governments should limit themselves to helping create efficient markets and keep any market intervention to a minimum.

net present value (NPV) Value of a series of annual benefits of an investment project minus the annual costs, all discounted by the opportunity cost of capital to reflect current (present) values of those future returns.

new growth theory An extension of the **neoclassical growth theory** in which technological change is treated within the model and which focuses on the need for countries to improve their ability to learn and innovate as the key to growth.

Newly Industrializing Countries (NICs) The term given to a set of developing countries that industrialized rapidly in the 1970s and 1980s. These were located primarily in East Asia (Taiwan, South Korea) and South America (including Argentina and Brazil).

nominal exchange rate The actual rate of exchange between two currencies.

nominal income Income as measured at current prices.

nonexclusion With respect to public goods, the inability to prevent an individual from using a good, for example, city streets.

Nongovernmental Organizations (NGOs) Private organizations that provide or administer aid funds.

nonrenewable resources Resources (petroleum, minerals) that are fixed in supply and therefore exhausted by their use.

nonrivalrous consumption When consumption by one person does not prevent consumption by another. A broadcast television signal and a concert in a public park are examples.

North American Free Trade Agreement (NAFTA) Free trade agreement among the United States, Canada, and Mexico.

Official Development Assistance (ODA) Portion of all government-to-government loans that are considered by the DAC to be sufficiently concessional and directed toward economic development aims to be considered foreign aid.

orthodox policy Use of traditional monetary and fiscal tools to reduce inflation.

Overseas Private Investment Corporation (OPIC) U.S. corporation that insures U.S. investors abroad against losses due to actions of the host government.

Part IV (of GATT) Provisions added to permit more advantageous treatment of developing-country exports.

pegging Of exchange rates. Government sets the value of its currency in terms of another currency or currencies, rather than allowing the value to be determined by market forces.

pension fund A fund established by a firm, government, labor union, or other organization to provide retirement pensions.

per capita income The value of income produced per person.

performance requirements Legal requirements imposed on foreign investors, such as minimum local materials content, minimum percentage of personnel hired domestically, minimum export requirements, and so forth.

periphery In **dependency theory**, the poor countries, whose development direction is determined by the activities of firms from the rich countries, or **center**.

Physical Quality of Life Index (PQLI) An attempt to measure the quality of life without resort to measures of production or income. The index was a composite of measurements of infant mortality, life expectancy, and basic literacy.

planned economy An economy in which government performs the function of allocating resources more typically performed by markets.

positive externalities Benefits from economic activity that accrue to entities other than the consumer and may be impossible for the producer to capture in the market price.

poverty In general terms, a very low standard of living. **Absolute poverty** is considered to be a standard of living consistent with only the minimum physical needs in terms of food, clothing, and shelter. Relative poverty refers to a standard of living that is low compared to others in a community, even if that exceeds the absolute minimum.

price ceiling Legally imposed upper limit on a market price.

primary products Goods emanating directly from the earth; includes agriculture (plus forestry and fisheries) and mineral production.

privatization The process of shifting ownership or management of a company or activity from government to private hands.

product cycle theory Idea that production of many goods naturally proceeds from the country of origin, usually an industrialized country, to less developed countries as the production process becomes more routine and technology more accessible.

production function A mathematical relationship between inputs and output.

productivity A measurement of the output per unit of a factor of production employed.

program aid Aid that is provided to permit a government to undertake a broad set of activities in a sector of the economy.

progressivity Of tax structure. Degree to which a tax system takes a greater percentage share of higher incomes. If all income levels pay the same percentage tax, the system is proportional. If higher incomes pay a higher percentage, the system is progressive. If higher incomes pay a lower percentage, the system is regressive.

project aid Aid that is provided to fund a specific project, such as a road, health care facility, or steel mill.

protectionism Policy of protecting large portions of domestic industry from foreign competition by tariffs, quantitative restrictions, and other means.

public good Good or service characterized by indivisibility of consumption and inability to exclude nonpaying individuals from the market.

Purchasing Power Parity (PPP) The concept that rates of exchange among national currencies should reflect the relative ability of currency holders to buy comparable values of goods. If a dollar is worth 10 pesos, then a dollar and 10 pesos should purchase the same goods. Because of distortions in exchange markets, PPP is being used in the **ICP** to attempt a more accurate measure of comparative income levels among countries than would ordinarily come from translating domestic-currency incomes into a common currency.

push/pull Contrasting explanations of migration, usually in the context of rural-to-urban migration. Push emphasizes deteriorating conditions that push people to leave their home areas. Pull emphasizes the opportunities—real or perceived—in a new location.

Quantitative Restriction (QR) Numerical limitation on the import of a particular product. (Also known as a quota.)

quota Share of the capital of the IMF or World Bank contributed by each member country.

Certain borrowing facilities from the IMF are permitted as a specific percentage of a country's quota. In trade, same as a QR.

real exchange rate Index that measures the nominal rate adjusted for relative inflation in the countries whose currencies are being compared. A currency can be nominally unchanged, but if the country's inflation rate is high relative to others, the currency will still see a real appreciation.

real income Income measured at constant prices by deflating nominal income figures by a suitable price index.

real interest rate Nominal interest rate adjusted to remove the impact of inflation.

regulation Government interference in the operations of a market by some action, such as restricting price movements or setting conditions of operation for a market or activity.

remittances Money sent to the home country by people or companies abroad.

renewable resources Natural resources that are capable of being replenished, in part or whole, by "natural" means including forests, fish, and other animal populations. Renewable resources *may* be exhausted if used beyond the point where they can be naturally regenerated. Some resources, such as forests, take a longer time to regenerate and are sometimes referred to as *conditionally* renewable resources.

rent seeking Activity of an economic entity attempting to capture monopoly profits (rents); frequently a private actor attempting to capture rents created by government regulation.

repatriation Sending profits and other payments by a foreign investor back to the home country.

returns to scale Also known as economies of scale. The degree to which addition of all factors of production permits output to increase. For example, doubling of all resources may result in less than proportional output increases (diminishing returns to scale), proportional increases (constant returns to scale), or more than proportional increases (increasing returns to scale).

rural–urban migration Movement of people from rural areas to cities.

screening Use of a minimum education level as a convenient way to eliminate presumably unfit individuals in a hiring process.

sectoral terms of trade Relative prices of the output of one sector compared to another; for exam-

ple, the terms of trade between agriculture (*Pa*) and industry (*Pi*) is expressed as *Pa/Pi*.

seigniorage Gain to a government achieved by reducing the value of money through inflation. Sometimes measured as simply the increased supply of money provided to the government.

shadow economy Also known as second economy. Economic activities that are not officially recorded and therefore not counted in GDP statistics.

shadow price A hypothetical price that would prevail in the absence of externalities and market distortions. Frequently applied to factor prices, such as wage and interest rates.

shadow wage See **shadow price**.

sharecropping Tenure arrangement under which a farmer produces on someone else's land and pays a portion of the crop to the owner of the land.

social capital Informal networks of trust and confidence among members of a community that permit the effective, secure functioning of the community's day-to-day activities.

social overhead capital The stock of facilities, such as the transportation and communications network, that provides the groundwork for the activities of individual firms.

social productivity An assessment of the productivity of an investment that includes costs and benefits to society that are external to the costs and revenues of the firm.

social safety net Groups of programs intended to provide a minimum level of income. These may include Social Security programs, unemployment compensation, funds for employment-creating projects, free health care, and others.

standards Criteria (in this context, set by government) that must be met by individuals or firms in their economic activities.

state-owned enterprise (SOE) Corporation owned and operated by a government.

structural adjustment Process by which an economy reorients its policies from inward to outward. The reorientation usually involves a shift away from government intervention and toward a greater role for the private sector, and away from protected production for the domestic economy to export-oriented production.

structural change Change in the kinds of activities that predominate in an economy; usually a movement from a predominantly agricultural economy to major reliance on manufacturing, and often then to greater share of services.

structuralist (explanation of) inflation Inflation occurs because different sectors cannot expand supply quickly enough to meet rapidly growing and shifting demand.

subsistence agriculture Agricultural production engaged in by those who produce little more than their immediate needs.

subsistence sector Sector of an economy in which activities are undertaken largely for the consumption of the individuals involved, as opposed to being marketed to others.

sustainable development Development path that maintains the value of total capital resources, including both natural and artificially produced capital.

targeting Means of pinpointing appropriate beneficiaries of government programs.

tariff Tax on an imported product.

tariff escalation Schedule of tariffs that rise with the stage of production encountered: Raw materials would have no tariff, components a higher tariff, and finished products the highest tariff.

technical assistance Aid that takes the form of experts to advise the recipient government or firm.

tenancy Tenure arrangement under which a farmer produces on someone else's land and pays a fixed rent.

terms of trade Relationship between the prices or incomes of exports and imports. The **net barter** terms of trade is a ratio of export prices to import prices. The **income** terms of trade is a ratio of export income (price times quantity) to import prices.

tied aid Aid that must be used to purchase goods or services from the country whose government has provided the aid.

top/bottom ratio The ratio of the percentage of income received by the wealthiest 20 percent of the population to the percentage received by the poorest 20 percent.

Total Factor Productivity (TFP) Portion of an increase in output due to increases in the productivity of the inputs (capital and labor) rather than due to increases in the volume of inputs.

traditional society Society in which an individual's economic role is determined by inheritance or social mechanism other than market-driven choice.

transfer pricing Artificial prices used by TNCs for internal transactions.

Transnational Corporation (TNC) Corporation that operates in more than one country and, by implication, has no specific national loyalty. (Also known as multinational corporation or multinational enterprise.)

unbalanced growth Industrialization strategy calling for government to promote certain sectors that will induce private activity to take advantage of those sectors.

unemployment rate Percentage of the labor force that is unemployed.

urban bias Tendency for governments to favor cities over rural areas in their development policies.

urbanization Increasing percentage of the population living in cities.

Value Added Tax (VAT) Tax that is imposed on production by assessing each stage in the production process on the value added to the product at that stage. An increasingly popular form of indirect tax.

vent-for-surplus theory Idea that exports simply represent the shipping overseas of production that cannot be consumed domestically.

vertical integration Aspect of corporate structure whereby a company operates at different levels of the production process.

vicious cycle A situation where low productivity limits any possible economic surplus so that saving and investment are not possible and productivity remains low.

World Bank The largest of several multilateral organizations devoted to lending money for economic development purposes. It also conducts considerable research on development issues.

World Trade Organization (WTO) International organization that sets rules for the conduct of international trade and provides a forum for negotiations and disputes over trade. Superceded in 1995 the **General Agreement on Tariffs and Trade (GATT)** formed in 1948.

Index